# Turkey's Modernization

**Published and Forthcoming by New Academia Publishing**

GOD, GREED, AND GENOCIDE: The Holocaust through the Centuries, by Arthur Grenke.

NATIONALISM, HISTORIOGRAPHY AND THE (RE)CONSTRUCTION OF THE PAST, edited by Claire Norton

AN ARCHITECT OF DEMOCRACY: Buildig a Mosaic of Peace, by James Robert Huntley.

SHAKESPEARE'S THEATER OF LIKENESS, by R. Allen Shoaf.

HERETICAL EMPIRICISM, by Pier Paolo Pasolini. Eds., trs., Ben Lawton and Louise K.Barnett.

ON THE ROAD TO BAGHDAD, OR TRAVELING BICULTURALISM: Theorizing a Bicultural Approach to Contemporary World Fiction, Edited by Gönül Pultar.

LIVING NOVELS: A JOURNEY THROUGH TWENTIETH-CENTURY FICTION, by Sascha Talmor

**Russian History and Culture Series**

RUSSIAN FUTURISM: A HISTORY, by Vladimir Markov. With an Introduction by Ronald Vroon.

WORDS IN REVOLUTION: Russian Futurist Manifestoes 1912-1928. Eds., trs., Anna Lawton and Herbert Eagle.

THE INNER ADVERSARY: Struggle Against Philistinism as the Moral Mission of the Russian Intelligentsia, by Timo Vihavainen.

IMAGING RUSSIA 2000: FILM AND FACTS, Anna Lawton (CHOICE Outstanding Academic Title 2005)

BEFORE THE FALL: SOVIET CINEMA IN THE GORBACHEV YEARS, Anna Lawton

RED ATTACK, WHITE RESISTANCE: Civil War in South Russia 1918, by Peter Kenez.

RED ADVANCE, WHITE DEFEAT: Civil War in South Russia 1919-1920, by Peter Kenez.

ASPECTS OF BALKAN CULTURE, Jelena Milojković-Djurić

SLAVIC THINKERS OR THE CREATION OF POLITIES, Josette Baers

**SCARITH Books (fiction)**

ON THE WAY TO RED SQUARE, by Julieta Almeida Rodrigues.

THE DA VINCI BARCODE, by Judith P. Shoaf

**VELLUM Books (non fiction)**

A RED SOX FAN'S DIARY OF THE 2004 SEASON, by Derek Catsam

# Turkey's Modernization
## Refugees from Nazism and Atatürk's Vision

**Arnold Reisman**

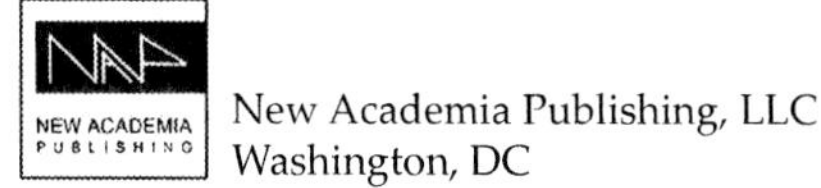


New Academia Publishing, LLC
Washington, DC

New Academia Publishing, 2006



Printed in the United States of America

Library of Congress Control Number: 2006928369
ISBN 0-9777908-8-6 paperback (alk. paper)

New Academia Publishing, LLC
P.O. Box 27420, Washington, DC 20038-7420
www.newacademia.com - info@newacademia.com

To Ellen who stands by me.

# Praise for *Turkey's Modernization*

"In the story of the Righteous, there are many little-known aspects. One of these is the willingness of the Turkish Government of Mustafa Kemal Atatürk and Ismet Inönü to take in German and Austrian Jews, and to use the talents of these victims of race prejudice and persecution to the benefit of the Turkish Republic in its academic, scientific, and medical endeavours[sic]. This book gives a detailed and revealing account of how this was done and who were its beneficiaries. It thereby adds to our knowledge of an important aspect of the Holocaust, and of the behaviour[sic] of Nation States in the modern world of woe and grief."
*- Sir Martin Gilbert, Winston Churchill's official biographer and a leading historian of the modern world. His book The Holocaust: The Jewish Tragedy (published in the United States as The Holocaust: A History of the Jews of Europe During the Second World War) is a classic work on the subject.*

"This book should be on the 'must-read' list of books about World War II and the years preceding it. At first glance, the book is about a limited subject: the contribution of scientist refugees from countries under Nazi rule to the modernization of Turkish academic institutions. Yet, the author presents the personal stories within a global perspective that makes the book much more important than its main subject.... The book documents how the Turkish government welcomed these scientists while the United States had its doors closed to most refugees, even to these world-class professors.... The concluding chapter of the book presents a comparative analysis of the scientific and technological development of Turkey. . . . Arnold Reisman has done a great service in documenting history and providing us with plenty of lessons for the future."
*- Dr. Israel Hanukoglu, Former Science Adviser to the Prime Minister of Israel. Currently Professor and Chairman of the Department of Molecular Biology, College of Judea and Samaria, Ariel, Israel.*

"Arnold Reisman's scholarly and painstaking research is a very important contribution to the history of relations between Germany and Turkey during WWII, and to Holocaust studies as well. It also provides contributions to the history of science and higher education, and a case study to national development.
*- Rifat N.Bali, Independent scholar, and author of several books on Turkish Jewry. The most recent is Bali, R. (2005) The 'varlik vergisi' affair: A study of its legacy. Istanbul, Turkey.*

"It brings back so much of the past. All those names I remember, all those people we used to know.... Little is known about how these "cream of the crop" professors transformed Turkey's higher education. So the appearance of your book is very timely."
- *Elizabeth [Reichenbach] Austin. Sacramento, CA.*

"I believe I can speak for my late husband Hans Güterbock and his University of Chicago colleague Benno Landsberger, and say that they would have been pleased at the recognition of their contributions and those of other similarly situated German, Austrian, and Czech émigrés who, during the darkest years of the 20th century, created and developed the modern university system that now exists in Turkey."
- *Frances Güterbock, Chicago, IL.*

"I am sure your book will be a source of rarely known information for those who want to know more about each of the very famous people you are mentioning. It is also of interest for those who want to learn more about the Diaspora of the Jewish people before and after the holocaust."
- *Miriam [Hellmann] Schmidt, Ramat Hasharon, Israel.*

"This history is not well known in the English-speaking world. Reisman's book, therefore, is a significant and welcome addition to the existing literature on the subject, rich in documentation, memoirs and oral histories that provide precious first hand accounts of a dangerous and difficult period."
- *Dr. Lâle Aka Burk , Senior Lecturer in Chemistry, Smith College, Northampton, Massachusetts, and author of "An Open Door: German Refugee Professors in Turkey" in Peter I. Rose, ed., The Dispossessed-An Anatomy of Exile.*

"German-Jewish refugee scientists in Turkey is a fascinating topic and I have seen little good research about it, which makes it doubly appealing. The subject of this book is of enormous interest."
- *Noah Efron, Chair Graduate Program in Science, Technology & Society Committee on Interdisciplinary Studies, Bar Ilan University, Ramat Gan, Israel.*

"This book involves five major topics: science, history, politics, economics, and the arts. It is the earliest comprehensive essay in the English language, on the German émigrés who, while taking refuge in Turkey after 1933, contributed to the modernization of its higher education, to implementation of research activities, and social reforms. Most of these scholars left Turkey as WWII came to a close, to carry their scientific activities in the US and other countries. Arnold Reisman's work, based on a large array

of sources makes their history known to a public with a wide variety of interests.
*- Prof. Dr. Feza Günergun, Chair for History of Science, Faculty of Letters, Istanbul University, Beyazit-Istanbul, Turkey.*

"As I am working on German-Jewish interwar migration, it is most relevant and innovative, apart from its importance to the history of science development and transfer."
*- Hagit Lavsky, the Samuel L. and Perry Haber Chair in Post- Holocaust Studies at the Avraham Harman Institute of Contemporary Jewry at The Hebrew University of Jerusalem. A leading expert on the Jewish experience during and prior to the Holocaust, Prof. Lavsky is a Matthew Family Fellow at the Center for Advanced Holocaust Studies within the U.S. Holocaust Memorial Museum. She is the author of five books including Before Catastrophe: The Distinctive Path of German Zionism, 1918-1932, which won the esteemed Arnold Wiznitzer Prize for best book of the year in the field of Jewish history.*

"Turkey's Modernization" is uniquely well researched and it describes a chapter of history not well known to the public. It illustrates in rare form and with great accuracy the significant contributions that the Jewish German, Austrian, and Czechoslovakian scientists; exiled by the Nazis made on emerging Turkey under the leadership of Ataturk's vision. From a "Zeitzeuge" survivor my gratitude to Arnold Reisman for his tremendous work and for bringing this chapter of history to the public."
*- Robert R. Weiss, Organizer of some of the down the Danube, through the Bosphorus and on to Palestine refugee transports during the midst of WWII and author of Joshko's Children.*

"Many thanks for sending me the chapters that included information about my mother and v. Mises. I am truly impressed by all the work you did in pursuit of the topic."
*Magda (Geiringer-von Mises) Tisza. Chestnut Hill, MA.*

# Contents

# Illustrations

# Foreword

As a sophomore at UCLA, I remember juniors and seniors excitedly discussing "the German professor's" philosophy lectures. I couldn't wait till I could take his course as an elective outside of my engineering major. Sadly for me, he died just before the semester I was to take his class. Little did I know then that over half a century later, I would be learning about *Hans Reichenbach's* life, talking via long distance to his 96-year-old widow, Maria, and his daughter, Elizabeth. As a first-year graduate student I was unaware that *Richard von Mises, William Prager,* and *Arthur von Hippel,* authors of seminal texts I was reading, would appear in the course of my research for a book manuscript on their forced exile years.

While moving away from mathematical dynamics of fluid flow and the highly experimental materials science and beginning to read for my dissertation in the fast-emerging field of Operations Research, I quickly learned about America's pioneers in the science of management—the time studies of Frederick W. Taylor and the motions studies by Frank and Lillian Gilbreth (*Cheaper by the Dozen*, 1948). I was also impressed to learn that the modern American (as well as urban Turkish) home kitchen was designed to conserve limb motion and body movement. It was not until doing research for this book that I learned who had first converted these efficiency ideas into kitchen-design blueprints. In the 1920s *Margarete Schütte-Lihotzky,* an Austrian architect, integrated this concept into large multi-dwelling complexes that had been built in Austria and Germany for working-class families. I also learned that there was an anti-Nazi underground in Austria and that *Schütte-Lihotzky,* (and a fellow Austrian architect) left Turkey to join this movement. I did not understand that each time my doctoral advisor would invite me to have lunch at the UCLA Faculty Club, I would be sitting in the same room as the great Turkologist, *Andreas Tietze*, the superb sinologist/sociologist, *Wolfram Eberhard*, and the renowned theatrical producer and opera director, *Carl Ebert*.

Long after my student days, I listened to *Paul Hindemith's* music being performed by the Cleveland Orchestra. By the time the children of my children had reached young adulthood, I had spent many a Saturday morning at the Atatürk Arts Complex in the Taksim Square of Istanbul where the music was always good, as was the company of my Turkish friends, and the ticket price always low thanks to municipal subsidies. I have only recently learned that the original concert hall was designed by *Clemens Holzmeister* in collaboration with the very same *Carl Ebert* whose theatrical and operatic productions I had so enjoyed in Los Angeles back in the 1950s (Fig. 1).

In the late 1950s, I did not reflect on the possibility that the optical, solar, and radio telescopes I was helping design would be used over the coming decades by astronomers who, like me, had been lucky to escape from the Nazis. Nor could I have known in the early 1940s that, in Istanbul, only one night's voyage away across the Black Sea from Feodossiya, there were young displaced persons like me. But, unlike me, they were living fairly normal, happy lives surrounded by family, and each was receiving a good education. They were under the protection of the "barbarian" Turks while I was in Feodossiya and elsewhere often just trying to be on the "right side" of the battle between armies of the "proletariat" Russians and those of the "civilized" Germans. It was the Germans that I feared most.

I was keenly listening to the news coming in from Europe when the Soviet Union cut off ground traffic in an attempt to starve the Allies out of Berlin during the first stand-off of the Cold War (1948), but I did not make the connection that Berlin's mayor at that time was *Ernst Reuter*, whose life had been saved by a Turkish invitation to help set up their universities and city planning organizations.

As an amateur sculptor, I enjoyed seeing a *Rudolf Belling* sculpture every time I went to give guest lectures at the Maçka campus of Istanbul Technical University. The older I become, the more X-rayed, CTed, and MRIed I get. So when that happens, I think of physicist, *Friedrich Dessauer*, an early X-ray researcher, and *Carl Weissglass*, his engineer. I also think of radiologist *Max Sgalitzer*, a victim of excessive exposure over a lifetime of pioneering this wonderful diagnostic medium, and his Istanbul wingmates, *Walter Reininger*, the engineer and inventor of an early dosimeter, and *Margarethe Reininger*, an early radiological nurse, one of a husband-and-wife team.

As I researched material for this book, I came to the conclusion that *Erica Bruck's* research publications and laboratory manuals/standards have influenced the heath care I received in California, Wisconsin, and Ohio. The same is true for my children and grandchildren who are scattered around the globe. Also, with age, many more of my friends have to fight off cancer, a dreadful disease indeed. Each time the word comes up, I think that if a cure is ever found, zoologist *Curt Kosswig* will have played a role in that outcome.

Ignorant as I am of immunology, I cannot help but wonder whether the work in this field by immunologist *Felix Haurowitz* influenced the use of Bacillus Calmette-Guerin vaccine (BCG), an anti-tubercular agent, widely used to prevent reoccurrence of bladder cancer. As I followed the controversy surrounding the Smithsonian National Air and Space Museum's exhibit entitled "The Crossroads: The End of World War II, the Atomic Bomb and the Cold War" and the uproar in 1995 regarding the refurbishment of the warrior plane *Enola Gay,* all to mark the 50th anniversary of the end of the war, I had no idea the museum's director at the time was *Dr. Martin Harwit,* the son of *Felix Haurowitz.* And to my great, although pleasant, surprise, while in the final stages of getting the manuscript ready for the publisher, one of its guest copy editors, Jean Hull Herman who spent sixteen years as editor-in-chief of *MÖBIUS The Poetry Magazine* was shocked to learn that *Erich Auerbach,* one of her literary idols, wrote his classic account of the genesis of the novel, *Mimesis,* while in Turkey.

Being interested in the history of science, I was delighted to read in Albert Einstein's own words that astronomer *E. Finlay Freundlich* "was the first among fellow-scientists who has taken pains to put the [relativity] theory to the test." But I was shocked to read Albert Einstein's letter of May 2 1936, saying, "he was told explicitly that they did not want to hire Jews at Princeton [University]." On the other hand, as a survivor of the Holocaust I was delighted to learn that an invitation from the Turkish government extracted dentistry professor *Alfred Kantorowicz* from nine months of concentration camp incarceration, that ENT specialist *Karl Hellmann* was able to yank his brother Bruno out of *Buchenwald* and bring him to safety in Turkey, and that pediatrician *Albert Eckstein* was influential in persuading ministers of Turkey's government to let European Jews go through Turkey, thus saving over 20,000 Jews from extermination, including a train load of 233 souls that came out of *Bergen-Belsen* in July of 1944.

It is sad but true that when I contacted professionals teaching Holocaust history at the local schools, and colleges, as well as some of the rabbis who had recently presented sermons on the subject, none had any knowledge whatsoever of Turkey's role in saving so many intellectuals. Of the larger issue of Turkey and the Holocaust, they either had fragmentary knowledge (such as the sinking of the refugee ship *Struma* in the Black Sea with great loss of life), were grossly misinformed, negatively predisposed (particularly in the *Struma* incident), or all of the above.

Likewise, each time I run into a Turkish intellectual, academic, or practicing physician, engineer, musician, artist, or lawyer, I can't help but think about how profoundly their educations were influenced by their "German" professors.

But above all, I think of the men and women whose stories of forced but life-saving exile are the very essence of this book. And each time I read of a scientific or technological development affecting all of us, I can't help but consider possible linkages back to the work of the émigrés in Turkey, their progeny, their students, and the ensuing generations of all of the above.

***Sleep in peace! Turkish medicine is grateful to you.***

So reads *Alfred Erich Frank's* gravestone at a cemetery overlooking the Bosphorus. It was erected by the Medical Faculty of Istanbul University.

The work of these émigrés and their advancements, as well as the work they each inspired in their students and colleagues worldwide, boggles the imagination. Had that been lost, a large range of disciplines would have certainly been impacted, some irreparably.

*Figure 1*
Model of original Atatürk Concert Hall and Exhibition Center, Taksim Square, Istanbul.

# Acknowledgments

Many individuals have been involved in this project. Starting with a few old friends, the outreach expanded across countries and continents. The author is especially grateful to an old and dear friend, Aysu Oral, for her knowledge of Turkish history, language, and culture, which greatly contributed to finding, abstracting, and translating much text from Turkish language documents; to another old and dear friend, Eva Sands, who translated German archival documents, including the hand-written ones such as the early Albert Einstein letters. Thanks also to a group who provided many insights because they were there at the time, were not too young to understand events nor too old to recall and retell their stories. Among these are Eugen Merzbacher, distinguished quantum-physics Professor Emeritus, University of North Carolina; Martin Harwit, distinguished astrophysics Professor Emeritus, Cornell University; Matthias Neumark of Charlottesville, Virginia, and Andrew Schwartz of Acton, Massachusetts, both retired businessmen; the Hellmann sisters, Frances Gutterbok of Chicago, Illinois, and Miriam Schmidt of Hod Hasharon, Israel; Klaus Eckstein, a retired schoolteacher in Cambridge, UK; Talma Yasur, Kibbutz Gan Shmuel and Ury Osry, Kibbutz Rosh Hanikra, both in Israel; and Serena Woolrich of Washington, D.C., Director, Allgenerations Network. Special thanks goes to my old and dear friends, Rita and Marek Glazer of Tel Aviv, Israel, for researching archival information and contacting Holocaust survivors for personal experiences that are relevant. Also greatly appreciated are graduate students Ismail Capar and Emel Aktas who found some of the Turkish material during the early stages of this project.

Clearly, a number of scholars, archivists, and institutions have provided much of the information contained in this book. Among these are Anthony Tedeschi and Becky Cape, Head of Reference and Public Services, The Lilly Library, Indiana University; Samira Teuteberg, AHRB Resource Officer, Centre for German-Jewish Studies, University of Sussex;

Dr Norman H. Reid, Head of Special Collections and J. J. O'Connor and E. F. Robertson, Department of Mathematics and Statistics, University of St. Andrews Library, Scotland; to Andrea B. Goldstein, Reference Archivist, Harvard; Elaine Engst, University Archivist, Cornell University; Barbara L. Krieger, Archivist, Dartmouth College; Tim Pyatt, Duke University Archivist; Nancy H. Watkins, Emory University Archives; Holly Snyder, University Archivist, Brown University; Viola Voss, Archivist at the Leo Baeck Institute of New York; Ralph Jaeckel and staff of the von Grunebaum Center for Near East Studies at UCLA; Chris Petersen, curator of the Ava Helen and Linus Pauling Papers, Valley Library, Oregon State University; Stephen Feinstein, Historian, University of Minnesota; Rainer Marutzky, Braunschweig Institute for Wood Research; Dr. Klaus Kallmann, New York Natural History Museum (Ret); Prof. Dr. Johannes Horst Schröder, Institut fur Biologie, Munich (Ret); Michael Stolleis, Professor für Öffentliches Recht, Neuere Rechtsgeschichte und Kirchenrecht in Frankfurt am Main, and Direktor of the Max-Planck-Institut für Europäische Rechtsgeschichte; Margaret Rich, Archivist, and Daniel J. Linke, University Archivist and Curator of Public Policy Papers, Seeley G. Mudd Manuscript Library, Princeton University; Marcia Tucker, Historical Studies-Social Science Library, Institute for Advanced Study, Princeton; Professor Ken Rosek, Assistant Director, Rockefeller Foundation Archive Center; and Paul G. Anderson, Archivist, Becker Medical Library, Washington University in St. Louis. Thanks also to Patrick M. Quinn, University Archivist, Northwestern University; Julia Gardner, Reference/Instruction Librarian, Special Collections Research Center, University of Chicago Library; Howard Falksohn, Wiener Library, London; Virginia G. Saha, Director, Cleveland Health Sciences Library; Nejat Akar, MD, Professor of Pediatric Molecular Genetics, Faculty of Medicine, Ankara University; Professor Arin Namal, Istanbul University's Medical Faculty, Department of Medical Ethics and Medical History; Kyna Hamill, Tisch Library Archives, and Amy E. Lavertu, Information Services Librarians Hirsh Health Sciences Library at Tufts University; James Stimpert, Archivist, Johns Hopkins University; Mark Lloyd, Director, University Archives and Records Center, University of Pennsylvania; Ginger Cain and Nancy Watkins, Emory University Archivists. Thanks to Historian Tuvia Friling of Ben Gurion University, Beer Sheva, Israel, an expert on Jewish issues in the Balkans and Turkey during the period of concern in this book, and to his able Research Assistant Hadas Blum; Daniel Rooney, Archivist, National [US] Archives and Records Administration (NARA); Amy Schmidt, Archivist, NARA Modern Military Records Division; Patrick Kerwin, Manuscript Division, Library of Congress; Mary Osielski, Grenander, Department of Special Collections &Archives, University at Albany, New York; Shaul Ferrero, archivist, Yad Vashem, Jerusalem; Severin Hochberg, Historian, United States Holocaust Memorial Museum, Washington DC; and especially to Ron Coleman, Reference Librarian of that very same museum who went way beyond the call of duty in providing references and did so very quickly.

Lastly, I would like to thank a number of people for the editorial assistance they provided at various manuscript preparation stages. Thanks to my dear friend, Yair Weinstock, who provided a number of suggestions to improve what I would call the manuscript's architecture, and Janine Beck, at Queensland University of Technology, Australia, who took time out from her own PhD research on Holocaust survivors to read the manuscript and make many substantive and useful suggestions. And, to the World Wide Web which opened up possibilities without which this book would have never passed the idea stage.

# Introduction

Distinguished Professor of Political Science as well as Sociology, Dankwart A. Rüstow, of Princeton and the City University of New York, wrote in the prestigious journal *Foreign Affairs* back in 1979:

> No nation that has maintained close relations with the United States for the last generation is so little understood by well-informed Americans as is Turkey. Even West Europeans, from their closer vantage point, are rarely better informed. In part, this lack of understanding may be due simply to limited contact. There is in the United States no sizable Turkish-American community, hence, no ready Turkish constituency in American public opinion. In western Europe, Turks are present in large numbers but as guest workers living with their families, apart and unassimilated in the more crowded parts of the cities, and eager to save enough of their wages for the ultimate return home to Turkey.[1]

Not much has changed in this respect in spite of Turkey's bid for EU membership and the ensuing dangling of Turkey by "old Europe's" leaders. When Dankwart Rüstow penned the above lines, his knowledge in this area did not derive strictly from academic research or readings. The son of sociology professor Alexander Rüstow, who was kicked out by the Nazis from his position at Berlin's *Handelshochschule* in 1933, Dankwart Rüstow received his undergraduate education in Turkey.

This is the tale of individuals caught at the cross roads of history and in the line of its fire. While their native lands were discarding them, their lives were saved because an alien country was discarding a societal culture inherited from the Ottoman Empire. Turkey had recognized the need to modernize its society while Germany and Austria were regressing into Fascism. As Nazis came to power, these émigré professors and professionals who were notable in their own fields, but were mostly Jewish and were opposed to Nazism, left an indelible mark on Turkey on their way to their ultimate destinations in the west and to what is now the State of Israel.

No other act served republican Turkey's founding fathers' vision of modernizing and westernizing Turkish society more than the development of the country's universities.[2] Without a doubt the total impact on Turkey's higher education was much greater than the sum of the émigré professors' individual contributions. No other policy served that country's educational reforms more than those invitations that had been extended to Nazi-persecuted German, Austrian, and later German-speaking Czech intelligentsia. No other country had a national policy to salvage so much discarded intellectual capital from elsewhere, in order to facilitate the achievement of its own goals and objectives.

This arrangement served the Nazis' aim of making their universities, professions, and their arts *Judenrein* or cleansed of Jewish influence before the activation of death camps and, at the same time, benefiting the Turks. Germany also saw this "benefit" as an exploitable chit on issues of Turkey's neutrality during wartime.[3] Thus, the national self-serving policies of two disparate governments served humanity's ends during the darkest years of the 20th century.

As fortuitous as the timeliness of the émigrés' arrivals had been for Turkey, so had been their voluntary, and in some cases, forced, departures. Unfortunately for all, Atatürk died in 1938 before his vision and the blueprint for its creation and implementation had been completely set down for his successors. And, by the late 1940s, the critical mass of trained Turkish cadres, essential for sustained takeoff, had finally been developed[4] and over three hundred émigré families moved on. It must now be noted that like Turkey, the United States, directly or indirectly, was also a major beneficiary of the Nazi-dictated exodus of intellectuals, starting about 1933. However, there were many missed cues. Information received from many sources including America's own ambassadors was not acted upon. President Franklin Delano Roosevelt was disinterested. Bureaucratic impediments on the part of the US government were everywhere, so was widespread anti-Semitism, sexism, age discrimination, and the financial woes of America's research and/or private universities. Yet, had Albert Einstein not fled Germany in December 1932, a month before the Nazis came to power, the *Manhattan Project* would not have been initiated when it was, the atomic bomb would not have been produced when it was, and Japan would not have surrendered when it did.

Hungarian-born Leo Szilard left Germany in 1933 and Enrico Fermi left Italy in 1939, both to escape persecution. The impact that these men, together with Hungarian émigrés like Edward Teller and Theodore von Karman (who anticipated Nazi persecution), made on American science and technological development cannot be overstated. By contrast, Germany in 2005 was not even close to regaining the stature in the scientific world it held prior to 1933.

Moreover, "[t]he triumphant rise of American economics after 1940 was enormously accelerated by the importation of scholars from Hitlerian Europe."[5] Likewise, Germany's current community of expatriate Turks is overwhelmingly comprised of laborers[6] and their families while in America Turkish expatriates are predominantly professionals.

America's society continues to reap some of the fruits of Turkey's efforts to modernize its system of higher education via the second or perhaps the third generation of those trained by the émigré professors. Moreover, American science, humanities, and arts have benefited even more directly from the wisdom and fortitude of successive Turkish administrations during the trying years preceding and during World War II, an unexpected and unforeseen consequence of that policy or practice. Though some of the émigré professors adapted to the host culture, learned its language, stayed on, and continued to make contributions into the 60s, others re-emigrated in the 30s and 40s as soon as their contracts elapsed and other opportunities opened.

Immediately after the war, the United States allowed entry to refugees from Nazism much more readily than it did in the 30s and during wartime. Hence, for differing reasons, re-emigration started at the war's onset and peaked within a few years of the war's end. Almost all who came to the United States continued their work, making significant contributions at America's institutions. At least 188 persons, i.e., the professionals and their immediate families, are known to have reached America's shores.[7]

## *Machtergreifung!* The Nazi Takeover of Germany

The year was 1933. The date was January 30. Hitler came to power. The *Gesetz zur Wiederherstellung des Berufsbeamtentums* or the Reestablishment of the Civil Service Law was passed a few weeks later. The end! The capstone had been placed over one of the world's wonderfully productive wellsprings of science, technology, and culture. All this happened in the German-speaking part of Europe. On the whole, Europe has never recovered from Germany's devastations. The new civil service rules were designed to enable speedy dismissal of professors with Jewish lineage and others considered politically suspect from all positions in German universities and institutes.[8] Austria followed in Germany's boot-steps after the March 9 1938 *Anschluss,* the annexation of Austria by Germany although the writings on the walls were writ large long before that. Similarly, in the

Sudetenland portion of Czechoslovakia after the September 29 1938 talks ended with the "Munich Agreement," a "meeting of the minds" between Adolf Hitler, British Prime Minister Neville Chamberlain, French Premier Édouard Daladier, and Italian Dictator Benito Mussolini. Hidden in the Agreement's bottom line was *Raus!* Out with the Jews and the new Order's non-believers from German-speaking Europe.

Soon gone and dispersed was the "Berlin Group." The *Gesellschaft für empirische Philosophie* or the Berlin Society for Empirical Philosophy was comprised of some of the world's leading philosophers and scientists who gathered round Hans Reichenbach in the late 1920s. Its informal membership included the great mathematician, aerodynamicist, engineer and positivist philosopher Richard von Mises, the Prague theoretical physicist Philipp Frank, mathematicians David Hilbert, Kurt Grelling, and Walter Dubislav, mathematician-philosopher Carl Hempel, and the scientist's scientist Albert Einstein listened on its sidelines. The Society's members were particularly active in analyzing contemporary physics, especially the theory of relativity and the development of the frequency interpretation of probability. After the rise of Nazism, several of these great minds emigrated from Germany. Reichenbach moved to Turkey in 1933 and to the United States in 1938, Hempel to Belgium in 1934 and to the United States in 1939, but Kurt Grelling was killed in a concentration camp. The "Berlin Group" was *kaput!*

The "Vienna Circle" which also started as a cooperative discussion group in 1922 and later renamed *Verein Ernst Mach,* or the Ernst Mach Association, collapsed as well. The Circle encompassed Austria's most prominent philosophers, scientists, and mathematicians. They were scientifically or mathematically oriented philosophers, and philosophically gifted scientists and mathematicians. Included were Richard von Mises, applied mathematician-physicist Philip Frank, logician-mathematician H. Hahn, mathematician Kurt Reidemeister, and the Circle's magnet, ethicist Moritz Schlick who had paved the way for much that became the crux of Logical Positivism in his *Allgemeine Erkenntnislehre* or "General Theory of Knowledge." Others included psychologist- sociologist-economist Otto Neurath, philosopher-mathematician Rudolf Carnap who gave us *The Logical Syntax of Language,* as well as other important works in modern logic including the foundations of mathematics, concept-formation in physics, and a logical systematization of the concepts of empirical knowledge in general.

Gone was the Circle that met regularly in Vienna to investigate scientific language and scientific methodology. The Circle-spawned philosophical movement has been called variously logical positivism, logical empiricism, scientific empiricism, neopositivism, and the unity of science movement. It gave us the philosophical ideas of logical positivism, unified science, a scientific world-view, epistemology, and philosophy of science, necessary propositions, the principle of verification, consistent empiricism and so on.[9] The great philosopher of science, *Karl R. Popper*, although he never attended the Circle's meetings, was influential in the reception and criticism of their doctrines. In their heyday, there was a close connection between the *Berlin Group* and the *Vienna Circle*. Together they organized several congresses on epistemology and philosophy of science. Some of the Circle members attended meetings in Berlin, notably Otto Neurath and Rudolf Carnap. Interestingly, several "Gestalt" psychologists such as Wolfgang Köhler and Max Wertheimer at times attended the Berlin meetings as well. In fact, there was not just one, but several "Vienna Circles."

The most striking feature of these circles was precisely their points of contact. Almost all of these circles overlapped with other neighboring circles which, in their various cultural formations—including literature, music, architecture, satire, psychoanalysis, and Zionism—pursued similarly radical goals.

> Germany the way it used to be was a [cultural] oasis in the desert.
> —Albert Einstein, July 1934. Letter to Alfred Kerr, Einstein Archive 50-687[10]

Dispersed were the thinkers whose works were translated in unified science—as The Vienna Circle monograph series originally edited by Otto Neurath. Fortunately, many were able to emigrate to the United States where they taught in several universities. Some went to the UK. Schlick, who remained in Austria, was killed at the University of Vienna in 1936 by a student with Nazi sympathies.

Also dispersed were many of the major contributors to the arts, such as renowned composer *Paul Hindemith*, conductor *Ernst Praetorius*, famous theatrical producer *Carl Ebert*, and *Rudolph Belling*, professor of sculpture at the Fine Arts Academy in Berlin. Originally, all had sped to Turkey to escape the Nazis, as did some Austrian intellectuals just before and after the Anschluss. Among these were *Margarete Schütte-Lihotzky*, the first, and surely the most famous, Austrian female architect, and *Andreas Tietze*, a world-renowned Turkologist. Turkey was also a destination for *Leopold Levy*, a French Jew and academic painter, and for a number of Czech scientists and physicians.

Germany! In physics alone, Germany yielded Nobel laureates the likes of Wilhelm Conrad Röntgen (1901); Philipp Lenard (1905); Ferdinand Braun (1909); Wilhelm Wien (1911); Max Laue (1914); Max Planck (1918); Johannes Stark (1919); Albert Einstein (1921); James Franck (1925); Gustav

Hertz (1925); and Werner Heisenberg (1932). In addition to these, there were many others including Hermann von Helmholtz and Gustav Robert Kirchhoff, names enshrined in our modern college textbooks. Germany! In the city of Göttingen were such luminaries as Enrico Fermi, Walther Boothe, Otto Hahn, Werner Heisenberg, Max von Laue, and a galaxy of other Nobel laureates and laureates-to-be. In earlier days, Göttingen used to be an intellectual feast. Göttingen's University and its various institutes were "Nazified" soon after the start of 1933.

Post-Nazi Germany would never again claim so many Nobel-stature physicists in its midst. The same is true for Austria (Fig. 2).

## Emergence of Turkey as a Republic

Germany's loss proved to be a gain for the new Republic of Turkey. German-speaking Europe's grievous developments followed the creation of the Turkish Republic by no more than one decade, ten years after the end of Turkey's prolonged War of Independence. The Ottoman Empire's rule was abolished and in July 1923, the *Lausanne Treaty of Peace* with Great Britain, France, Greece, Italy, Turkey, and others was signed. In mid-October, Ankara became the capital of the new Turkish State. On October 29, the Republic was proclaimed. These developments were followed in short order by radical social and economic reforms championed by modern Turkey's founder and its first president, *Kemal Atatürk*. He was a career military officer turned revolutionary and statesman.

Mustafa Kemal Atatürk was born in 1881 in the Ottoman city called Salonica. Starting with the traditional religious education, then a military high school education, he graduated from Istanbul's War Academy in 1905. Upon graduation, he was commissioned Staff Captain. In 1915, the Dardanelles campaign was launched by Winston Churchill to aid Russia in order to draw some Turkish troops away from the Caucasus where Russia was being pushed back. In those battles, Colonel Atatürk became a national hero by winning successive victories and repelling all invaders. Promoted to general in 1916 when only 35, he went on to liberate two major provinces of eastern Turkey that year. During the next two years, he served as commander of several Ottoman armies in Palestine, Aleppo, and elsewhere. He achieved another major victory by stopping Allied advances at Aleppo.

On May 19 1919, Atatürk landed in the Black Sea port of *Samsun* to start the Turkish War of Independence. In defiance of the Sultan's government, he and his "Young Turks" rallied a liberation army in Anatolia and convened the *Congress of Erzurum* and *Sivas* which established the basis for the new national effort under his leadership. On April 23 1920, the Grand National Assembly was inaugurated and Atatürk was elected President. Fighting on many fronts, he led Turkey's forces to victory. Following the Turkish triumph in the two major battles at Inönü in western Turkey, the Grand National Assembly conferred on him the title of Commander-in-Chief with the rank of Marshal. At the end of August 1922, the Turkish armies won their ultimate victory. Within a few weeks, the armistice was signed. The Republic of Turkey had a social visionary at its head, a man who had plans for great changes for his country.

However, for its system of higher education, the Republic of Turkey inherited around three to four hundred Ottoman vintage (Islamic) *madrasas*,[11] the *Dar-ül Fünun* ("house of knowledge" in Arabic), a fledgling state university teaching some western sciences based on the French university model and using Turkish and French professors. It also had three military academies.[12] As one of their first acts, the Young Turks abolished all the madrasas. That left the country three military academies and the *Dar-ül Fünun* as a system of higher education. To be sure, toward the end of the 19th century, due to the urgency of wars, the military academies were upgraded to include instruction in western science taught for the most part in French by expatriate French military officers, the empire's *lingua franca*. One such academy became a civil engineering school in 1909 and early in the Republican era it evolved into the *Istanbul Technical University*.

Secularization was one of the Republic's (and Atatürk's) missions from the outset. This principle was later enshrined in Turkey's constitution. A number of major reforms had to take place to meet the goals of government policies of modernization and even westernization or Europeanization throughout Turkish society. With breakneck speed, Atatürk forced a "revolution from above" on to his people. The reforms included, secular governance, abolition of the traditional headwear (the fez and the veil), the replacement of Arabic script with Roman characters, enforcement of monogamy, opening three western-mode state universities, creating an industrial (as opposed to agricultural) infrastructure, and the introduction of a civil code structured according to European standards (no caliph). (Fig. 3)

All of these visions have indeed been implemented and they survive to this very day. The abolition of the head scarves, however, is being challenged on university campuses. They are worn widely on the streets of Istanbul today.

Even though most were career military officers, the leadership of Turkey's new government was aware that the *madrasa*-based system of civilian higher education, which had served an empire for centuries, was woefully behind the education provided by western knowledge-seeking universities. Although training of civil administrators to serve the empire was a mission for some of the madrasas, the system and its components needed to be redesigned if not replaced.[13] Consequently, the *Dar-ül Fünun* was transformed into the University of Istanbul and, as was mentioned earlier, Istanbul Technical University was created out of a former military academy.[14]

On the other hand, it was Atatürk himself who said that Ankara University was founded from the ground up, "for those principles that describe a modern society, science, and enlightenment. "Borrowing comments made in a different context by John Staudenmaier, SJ,[15] this "value-laden embrace" of modern universities by Mustafa Kemal Atatürk, Turkey's most revered personage, initiated a "design stage" of the country's system of higher education. Beholden to his "leadership qualities and position" the "enduring nature of government policy" was institutionalized simultaneously with the "enduring nature of cultural values." The three universities were to be fashioned on the prevailing German university model.[16] However, personnel to do all this were not to be found in this new country.

The passage of Germany's "Civil Service Law" forced departure by its intellectuals having (or thought to have) Jewish heritage. Realizing that the worst was yet to come, many looked for ways of leaving their beloved *heimat*, or motherland. Most did not have the option of going to the States or Great Britain, given the restrictive immigration laws in place in those countries at the time. All were keenly aware of the lack of university job opportunities due to America's emergence from economic depression and widespread anti-Semitism in university hiring.

Among those first fired from their jobs was Hungarian-born Frankfurt pathologist, Dr. Philipp Schwarz. He quickly fled with his family to Switzerland. Schwarz's father-in-law was Professor Sinai Tschulok, a natural scientist, who had taken refuge in Switzerland after the 1905 Russian Revolution. He was a good friend of Albert Malche, professor of pedagogy who was called on to visit Turkey in 1932 and prepare a report on the Turkish educational reform. Malche was in touch with Tschulok. The persecution of some scientists had already begun in Germany. It seems Albert Malche saw the double opportunity and got in touch with Schwarz. The actions of this man were of tremendous importance to many of his colleagues: in March 1933, Schwarz established the *Notgemeinschaft Deutscher Wissenschaftler im Ausland,* The Emergency Assistance Organization for German Scientists, to help Jewish and other persecuted German scholars secure employment in countries prepared to receive such refugees.[17] (Fig. 4).

Predisposed to German science and culture because of longstanding ties between the two countries and recognizing the opportunity that presented itself, Turkey invited Philipp Schwarz[18] to Ankara for meetings with representatives of the government. Schwarz had brought with him a list of names from the *Notgemeinschaft*, and provided these names to his Turkish counterparts.[19] Their mission was to select individuals with the highest academic credentials in disciplines and professions most needed in Turkey. Minister of education *Resit Galip* arrived with a complete list of professorships at the University of Istanbul.[20] In his memoirs, Fritz Neumark, one of the émigré professors who went to Turkey, describes the day when Schwarz sat down with his Turkish counterparts as "the day of the German-Turk miracle." In nine hours of negotiations, it was possible to put together a complete list of names for the professorships of the new Istanbul University—and all were members of the *Notgemeinschaft!* At the end of the day, an overjoyed Schwarz was able to telegraph Zurich from Ankara: "Not three, but thirty!" However, "it was clear from the beginning that the German professors were meant to stay only until their Turkish pupils, i.e., their assistants and lecturers, could take over these positions. Therefore, five-year contracts became the rule. Courses were to be taught as soon as possible in Turkish, using textbooks which had been translated into Turkish as well."[21]

Although the 1933 appointments were negotiated directly by the *Notgemeinschaft* with the Turkish government they later all had to be pre-approved by the Nazi government, even though that very government forced the dismissal from their posts of all candidates. Its objective was to secure chits from Turkey. However, the Nazis' disinformation on the "Turkish project" implied that it was part of "Kultur propaganda abroad."[22]

Following the precedent set by Sultan Bayazid II in 1492,[23] and which became again a matter of government policy from 1933 through WWII, Turkey extended invitations to those it selected. It provided safe-haven to intellectuals and professionals fleeing Austria, Germany, Czechoslovakia, and France. All could bring their immediate families; many were even allowed to bring assistants and their families. Even if some could have received a US or UK visa, they chose the certainty of having an academic position within their expertise in Turkey against the possibility of being unemployed or underemployed in the West. Rudolf Nissen, a surgeon, switched his itinerary while en route to the US upon receipt of a telegram with a job offer in Turkey. Albert Einstein, on the other hand, was allegedly taking the Turkish option until a job offer from the Princeton Institute came at the last minute.[24]

Altogether, approximately 300 academicians and 50 technicians and supporting staff went to Turkey. Including family members, this meant more than 1000 persons.[25] Most thrived in Turkey. Most were given university positions as Ordinarius[26] professors and as professors both in Istanbul and Ankara.[27] Some received appointments at the Academy of Fine

Arts. These refugees included leading professors, research scientists, physicians, dentists, attorneys, architects, urban planners, engineers, artists, librarians, conservationists, and laboratory workers as well as hundreds of lesser-status professionals.[28] At the outset, Turkey's government attempted to give the émigrés every possible facility to carry out their work. Great sums were spent on equipment for laboratories and for hospitals. Appropriations were made for operating the physical plants.[29]

The impact of these émigré professors[30] is immeasurable. They totally transformed Turkey's higher education in the sciences, professions, humanities, and the arts. They also re-engineered its public health, library, legal, engineering, and administrative practices. The multi-faceted legacy to present Turkish society is everywhere. However, many counteractive forces were in place and active.

Turkey was teeming with Nazi sympathizers and nationalists. Because of Turkey's neutrality, some of the émigrés were actually able to leave during the course of the war. Some secured good positions at American universities. Such was the case with *Richard von Mises* joining Harvard and *Arthur von Hippel,* MIT. In the years following the war's end and having accomplished their mandate, most of the other émigrés came to the United States. They made major contributions to American science, engineering, and culture. The Albert Einstein archives yield one indication of the caliber of the people involved: Einstein maintained a personal correspondence with at least sixteen of the émigrés to Turkey.[31]

It should be noted that during the period starting with the Nazis gaining formal power on January 30 1933 and Germany's surrender on May 8 1945, the Republic of Turkey had two presidents. Kemal Atatürk served until his death November 10 1938. He was immediately succeeded by *Ismet Inönü* who served in that capacity until May 22 1950. Additionally, this period spanned over four prime ministers, five foreign ministers, six interior ministers, and five education ministers. Obviously, the policy of providing safe haven to these intellectuals was not dependent on the largesse of any one individual. It was indeed institutionalized. But at various points in time in this period, neutral Turkey was under relentless pressure by the German Reich (as high up as Hitler himself) that the Jewish professors[32] "be returned to Germany for punishment along with all Jewish Turks."[33]

Not to be overlooked or underestimated is the fact that Turkey was still healing its wounds from World War I—a war in which it was soundly defeated. Its economic, industrial, transportation, and agricultural infrastructures were destroyed. The war's trauma and the poverty, hunger, and epidemics that followed took their toll. Of its 25 million population, close to two million, died in that war. Also, three sides of Turkey's borders abutted the vast Muslim world. Its own population predominantly Muslim, Turkey had a natural affinity for its neighbors. Some of these neighbors, however, harbored large and overtly pro-Nazi elements. In Turkey itself, factions opposing the government and its policies made political capital of the difficult memories. They did this preying on fears, real and imagined, to keep Turkey from getting entangled in yet another war. Other motives for other groups abounded. Germany's Nazis and their in-country agents fed the fear that any Turkish policy appearing to contradict their own would be interpreted as a violation of neutrality and a pretext for war. Lastly, Turkey was caught between the Nazi hammer and the Soviet anvil at a time when the West was ambivalent to the plight of Europe's Jews.[34]

In retrospect, no other nation had the kind of bold policies to compare with Turkey's explicit plan to invite, save, and allow to flourish and conserve for future generations so much intellectual capital during the darkest years of the twentieth century. The consequences of that brave decision are like the ripples from a pebble tossed into still water. However, these have gained a momentum of their own. They can be seen worldwide to this very day and will be seen in perpetuity. Yet this bit of history is dimly lit[35] and largely unknown. Therefore, this book has been written to see that the future generations "do not live alienated from their ancestry and in ignorance of the events that have given shape to their present."[36]

Unfortunately, Atatürk's death came much too early for all concerned, especially Turkey itself. A number of his visionary programs were not fully developed by his successors. Some were curtailed for economic reasons; some were allowed to be sabotaged by petty functionaries.

In his memoir, Fritz Neumark, one of the émigré economists, observed that "although in the years following 1933 the number of German-speaking refugees in other countries, especially in the United States, far exceeded those in Turkey, in no other place was the relative significance of German refugees as great as it was in Turkey, and nowhere else did their work leave as permanent an impact."[37] On the other hand, "the image of Turkey in present-day Germany is determined by the so called 'Gastarbeiter,' literally guest workers, but actually foreign laborers, and "mainly negative," while in Turkey "Germany is regarded as a country in which people who, for political and religious reasons are being persecuted."[38]

### Turkish hospitality

The tradition of Turkish hospitality—especially to the persecuted—is not widely known in the Eurocentric West. Arguably, the first to avail themselves of refuge in Turkish lands were Jews persecuted in Christian Europe. The first recorded migrations to Ottoman Turkey were in 1376 from Hungary and 1394 from France when they were expelled by Charles VI. Later, after Sultan Mehmet the Conqueror took Constantinople and the Jews there experienced life under Turkish rule, Rabbi Isaac Zarfati wrote to his co-religionists in Europe calling on them to escape Christian persecution by coming to live in the domain of the Sultans. The largest number came in 1492. These were Jews who had lived in Spain for centuries under Moslem rule but were expelled by King Ferdinand as part of the Spanish Inquisition. The Russian Revolution of 1917 sent a flood of refugees to Turkey. And Turkey, although still at war, took in these refugees even though they came from countries that formerly had been enemies. In 1929, Leon Trotsky, the Soviet revolutionary who had a falling out with Stalin, himself was granted refuge on one of the Princes' Islands before departing for Mexico where he was assassinated.

In summation, Turkey's educational reforms were served well by her invitations to Nazi-persecuted intelligentsia. Development of the country's universities likewise enhanced Atatürk's vision of modernizing and westernizing Turkish society. The results were astounding and are felt to this very day. Albeit unintended, the preservation of so much intellectual capital for current and future generations was a gift beyond measure to the world at large.

By comparison, the United States and Europe failed in their duties or promises to promote liberty and preserve lives. "All attempts to liberalize the US quota system of immigration failed, even during the emergencies of the war and the Holocaust period. Many [German and Austrian scholars] could have been saved if the U.S. government and public had understood the seriousness of the Jewish plight of the Holocaust period, and had acted on that understanding."[39]

Here is the text of a remarkably important letter from Robert Skinner, American Ambassador, Istanbul, on November 10 1933, sent to the American Secretary of State, Cordell Hull, winner of the Nobel Peace Prize in 1945 (Fig. 5 and 6)[40]:

> Sir:
> The far-reaching effect of the expulsion from Germany under the Hitler regime cannot be actually measured as yet, but it may take on the importance of the expulsion of the Huguenots from France several centuries ago, and at all events, is likely to turn out advantageously for countries like Turkey which are endeavoring to make intellectual progress along western lines. According to my information, 35 newly employed foreign professors have been

taken into the University of Istanbul, of whom 30 are understood to have arrived and all of whom, with the exception of one Austrian and one Swiss, are German Jews who were either expelled or who left Germany on account of the recent political troubles. All of these professors were recommended to Professor Malche, who is at the head of the university reform movement here, by a certain Professor Schwarz, the Secretary of an organization with its seat in Zurich, and which endeavors to find employment for German intellectuals who were obliged to leave that country for political and racial reasons. Professor Schwarz, himself now figures among the professors employed by the Istanbul University.

At Ankara two German Jews have been employed recently, one a professor of chemistry in the Ministry of Agriculture, who is now teaching in one of the Institutes of Agriculture which opened during recent national festivities. One is a photographer employed by the Department of Museums under the Ministry of Public Instruction. There are also four German doctors of medicine, engaged to work with the Ministry of Public Hygiene in the newly inaugurated hospital at Ankara, whose duties according to the contracts, begin in the hospital at the end of the year.

Respectfully yours,
Robert P. Skinner
American Ambassador.

This letter speaks for itself. However, it was followed on the very same day with, "In regard to the difficulties of the Jews in Germany and the engagement of German Jewish professors in this country, I now enclose as of possible interest in this connection a list of the names of foreign professors appointed to the University of Istanbul, all of them, I imagine being of the Jewish race, as indeed the names themselves sufficiently indicate."[41]

German-speaking Europe's Age of Enlightenment dwindled into the darkness of war. The world suffered the loss of its own humanistic ideals, and there came in the darkness an age unparalleled in its barbarisms.[42] The German-Jewish symbiosis which has spawned such irrevocably monumental cultural and scientific achievements, came to a crashing and irreparable end.

I cannot understand the passive response of the whole civilized world to this modern barbarism. Doesn't the world see that Hitler is aiming for war?
—Albert Einstein, October 1, 1933; quoted by a reporter for *Bunte Welt* (Vienna) in Pais, Einstein Lived Here, p. 194.

*Figure 2*
May 10. berlin Book burning.

*Figure 3*
Beyazit Portal to Istanbul University, circa 1933.

*Figure 4*
Dr. Philipp Schwarz

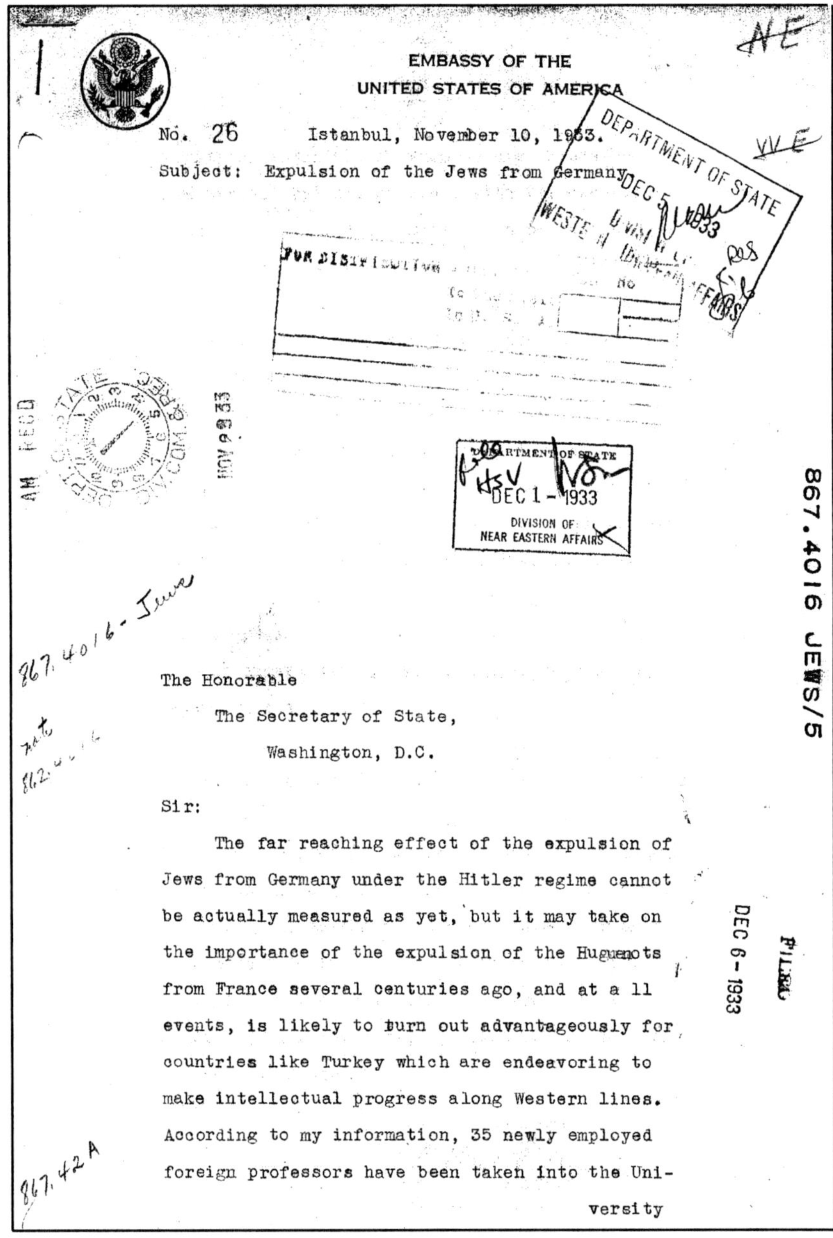

EMBASSY OF THE
UNITED STATES OF AMERICA

No. 26 Istanbul, November 10, 1933.

Subject: Expulsion of the Jews from Germany

The Honorable
The Secretary of State,
Washington, D.C.

Sir:

The far reaching effect of the expulsion of Jews from Germany under the Hitler regime cannot be actually measured as yet, but it may take on the importance of the expulsion of the Huguenots from France several centuries ago, and at all events, is likely to turn out advantageously for countries like Turkey which are endeavoring to make intellectual progress along Western lines. According to my information, 35 newly employed foreign professors have been taken into the University



*Figure 5*
Letter to the U.S. Secretary of State from American Ambassador in Istanbul, on November 10, 1933.

-2-

versity of Istanbul, of whom 30 are understood to have arrived and all of whom, with the exception of one Austrian and one Swiss, are German Jews who were either expelled or who left Germany on account of the recent political troubles. All of these professors were recommended to Professor Malche, who is at the head of the university reform movement here, by a certain Professor Schwartz, the Secretary of an organization with its seat in Zurich, a nd which endeavors to find employment for German intellectuals who were obliged to leave that country for political or racial reasons. Professor Schwartz, himself, now figures among the professors employed by the Istanbul University.

At Ankara two German Jews have been employed recently, one a professor of chemistry in the Ministry of Agriculture, who is now teaching in one of the Institutes of Agriculture which was opened during the recent national festivities. One is a photographer employed by the Department of Museums under the Ministry of Public Instruction. There are also four German doctors of medicine, engaged to work with the Ministry of Public Hygiene in the newly inaugurated hospital at Ankara, whose duties, according to the contracts, begin in the hospital at the end of the year.

*Figure 6*
Letter continued

# 1
# Atatürk's "Üniversite Reformu"

"In its essence, the affair that we call or understand as the Atatürk Üniversite Reformu was not a mere university reform, but the ultimate apex of the Atatürk cultural movement started in the years 1925 to 1926."[1]

> Before the early part of the nineteenth century, the Ottoman state never accepted responsibility for the basic education of its citizens or subjects. Hence, no formal system of public education then existed. The state trained some of its military and bureaucratic officials; the clergy instructed some of its own future members; but the education of non-official, non-clerical subjects was not conceived as a public responsibility. The process of 'modernization' in education involved the gradual and grudging acceptance of this responsibility by the Ottoman state.[2]

Until the 17th century, the Ottoman Empire was one of the most powerful countries in the world. Then it dramatically lost status as well as power because it did not keep up with, or better, Europe's scientific and technological gains, especially during the 18th century. Development of the Empire's army was the top priority. To achieve this goal, many French officers were brought in to aid the Ottoman modernization. For a long time, the Empire continued to benefit from importing officers, experts, and scientists, mostly from Europe and mostly for its army.[3] Officers from Europe were used in its new military schools. In 1735, a new artillery school was established by Sultan Mahmud I, and Alexander Comte de Bonneval from France was named administrator. Some forty years later, in 1773, under Ottoman Sultan Mustafa III, the *Muhendishane-i Bahr-i Humayun*, the Royal School of Naval Engineering, was established to educate chart masters and shipbuilders.

During the Royal School's formative years, it was supervised by Baron de Tott, a French expatriate military officer. Furthermore, in 1795 bearing the same name *Muhendishane-i Berr-i Humayun*, the Royal School of Military Engineering, was established to educate technical support personnel. In addition to Baron de Tott, many others were brought in from foreign countries to modernize the army and to teach at those schools. Among these were Englishman Kampell Mustafa, a convert to Islam, a Frenchman named Le Roi et du Reste (naval engineering), Major Lafitte Clavet and a Captain Monier (military and civil engineering), Francois Petolin (cannon testing), Captain Saint-Remy (artillery), and an officer named Tondul (astronomy).[4]

According to Sisman,[5] over a century after the Ottomans westernized education of their military officer corps and following the Reform Edict of 1856, individual students were sent to Europe and to France, in particular, for further education while "a school known as the *Mekteb-i Sultani* opened in Paris." At the same time, secondary schools providing a "modern" education were being created within the Empire. Of these, the most important was the *Galatasaray Mekteb-i Sultanisi,* later known as *Galatasaray Lycee.*[6] In many studies, "this school, has been described as the first window opened on to the West."

Additionally Turkish secondary education was affected by the telegraph. In 1861, the *Funu-i Telgrafiye Mektebi* (School of Telegraphic Science) was established. It offered a two-year program for technical education in all aspects of telegraphy.[7] Later, *Galatasaray,* a high school for the poor and orphans, launched courses in telegraphy. Between 1869 and 1923, a number of vocational "Technical Schools" were opened. Among these were a School of Finance (1876), a Civil Medical School (1877), School of Law (1878), School of Commerce (1882), a Civil Veterinary School (1889), a School for Vaccinators (1894), the Finance Officials School (1910), the Tax Collectors School (1911), and a Railroad Officials School opened in (1915).[8] None of these was considered to be of university caliber except for the Dar-ül Fünun. The Dar-ül Fünun, built by the Swiss architect Gaspare Fossati in 1854, became the first Ottoman University via a 1919 ordinance.

The Dar-ül Fünun went through three major reforms. In its transformation from a major *madrasa,* it became a secular university circa 1900; in 1915, its second reform, German academics were brought by the Ottoman Government to upgrade several academic disciplines. Among those invited was *Fritz Arndt* and two other German chemists. This trio helped to establish the first chemistry department in Turkey. Its curriculum was based on the prevailing German model. However, because the Dar-ül fünun was an Ottoman University, many of its other curricula continued to have a Moslem orientation. Dar-ül Fünun's third reform took place in 1933 and created the basis for this book.

It all began in 1924. Atatürk, now firmly in power, obliterated the existing system of religious education. The *madrasas* and all other religious schools maintained by the religious establishment were taken over by the now-secularized Ministry of Education. For centuries, these schools had been responsible for maintaining traditionalism. This was antithetic to the new regime. Consequently, the State under Atatürk assumed the responsibility of educating its citizens at all levels. In 1924, the government launched a process of expanding and improving the existing structure of secular public schools.

On July 31 1933, the *Dar-ül Fünun* was officially closed by government decree, as a means of canceling all existing good-for-life faculty contracts.[9] The very next day, the Istanbul University was opened using *Dar-ül Fünun*'s physical plant, a small fraction of the original faculty, and more than thirty world-renowned émigré German professors.

Each professor signed some variation of a formal contract similar to the one given to and signed by pediatrician Albert Eckstein:

> The Ministry of Health and Social Assistance has appointed Prof. Eckstein as the Director of the Pediatrics Service of the Ankara Nümune Hospital. He should consecrate all his activities to the medical and scientific requirements of the clinical services and the laboratory work attached to his specialty. He is expected to develop the knowledge of the doctors and the assistants and to contribute to the education of the students when necessary. He is also bound to report his thoughts about the scientific matters pertaining to his specialty as requested by the Ministry and to publish articles prepared according to the usual practices of the scientific circles.
>
> The duration of this contract is 5 years.
>
> This contract may be renewed for 3-5 years on the wishes of both parties.
>
> The salary is 750 Turkish liras[10] net after all taxes and fees are deducted.
>
> Prof. Eckstein may take out with him all the savings from his salary when he leaves Turkey with the permission of the public office he works for.
>
> He will be paid 250 Turkish liras for himself, his wife and his children aged over 10 years and 125 Turkish liras for each child aged less than 10 as relocation expenses.
>
> He will be granted six weeks paid leave every year. He can travel wherever he wishes but will not be paid travel expenses for these trips.
>
> He will be compensated according to the same rules for civil

> servants of high grade whenever he is asked to travel by the government.
>
> This contract may only be annulled by the consent of both parties due to inevitable causes. Full salary is paid for the first three months in case of sickness. After three years of service, the total amount corresponding up to 6-months salary will be paid for each year. Dr. Eckstein accepts to submit a medical report on his health prepared by an official doctor. In case of death, an amount of 1000 Turkish liras as well as six months' salary will be paid to his widowed wife or to his children in the absence of a wife.
>
> Prof. Eckstein cannot practice medicine privately outside the Ankara Nümune Hospital, nor can he open an office. In exceptional cases, if he is invited for consultation by Turkish doctors and his opinion is requested on the case under consultation, he may accept the invitation and submit his opinion on the case, provided it does not take the form of private medical practice.
>
> Prof. Eckstein does not have the right to demand any compensation whatsoever in return for the medical and surgical care he provides for the non-paying and paying patients admitted to the hospital or examined in the polyclinic.
>
> This contract enters in force the day it is signed by both parties. His salary will begin to be paid when he starts working in Ankara.

Contracts were signed every year. Most of the senior faculty were given the title Ordinarius Professor or "Ord. Prof." for short. It corresponds to the German *Auserordentlicher* (extraordinary) professor. In America, there is no fully equivalent title. The closest might be Distinguished or Chaired professor except the latter usually carries an endowment from some individual's, family's, company's, or foundation's financing, generally good for the professor's lifetime. The latter was not at all the case with the Ordinarius appointments in Turkey. In fact, all contracts albeit renewable were for fixed terms and did not include pension rights.

In 1933, distinguished American mathematician, professor Richard Courant and Nobel Laureate in Physics James Franck were asked by the American Rockefeller Foundation to assess the state of Istanbul University. On October 25, Courant filed their joint report. Courant and Franck noted that they had found "a decided wish [among the officials] to create a promising scientific center in Istanbul, which should contribute to the development of higher education in Turkey. The earnest wish to reconstruct [to change] existing conditions was repeatedly expressed in conversations with the Minister, other officials and private individuals as well as in the press."[11]

At the same time, the Americans were shocked at prevailing conditions, writing that the state "of the so-called university organizations in Istanbul is so miserable that for the present there can be no question for the next few years of a university life modeled on European lines, especially since the [available] Turkish material in students and assistants probably is not yet sufficiently trained for a true cultivation of the sciences."

One particular barrier to progress they saw was that "between students and foreign professors considerable difficulty would exist at the beginning owing to language." There were some areas—they noted geography and chemistry—in which the starting point would be better because European professors had made previous progress (during Dar-ül Fünun's 1915 reform), and they found the clinics also promising. But, "in the field of physics and mathematics, there are, however, almost no practical preparations. They [the Turks] lack institutes, equipment, apparatus, and library. The acquisition of all these things will require much organizing power on the part of the professors in question." Courant goes on to say:

> We had the impression that out of a certain ignorance the Turks underestimate these problems and are of the opinion that merely adding a line-up of recognized scholars, would be sufficient to start up a real university. Although by doing so we somewhat offended their prestige requirement, we advised them to recruit primarily younger workers for mathematics and the natural sciences and occasionally bring in older scientists like Frank [sic] for a limited time as guests and liaisons with European science.

History shows that the Turks did not follow the above advice. The overall assessment by Courant and Franck however was optimistic:

> Our whole impression is that if general conditions remain as they are in Turkey, a promising career for science can spring up in Turkey, that the enterprise promises to be profitable to the country, and that in our fields after a certain preparatory period, scientific research will also be possible.[12]

Moreover, on December 8 1933, Arnold Knapp, M.D. of New York wrote to Dr. Alan Gregg of the Rockefeller Foundation: "Prof. *Joseph Igersheimer*, of Frankfort, Germany, is now taking charge of the Eye Clinic at the University of Istanbul. He writes me that conditions are very primitive there, and all opportunities for doing research work are very meager, principally on account of lack of funds.... The Professor is one of the eminent younger ophthalmologists of Germany.... He was one of three men selected to report on tuberculous eye diseases at the International Ophthalmological Congress, in Madrid."[13]

## Les nouveaux professeurs de l'Université

Les professeurs invités d'Europe pour enseigner à l'Université commencent à arriver à Istanbul. Le professeur Hirshin qui enseignera le commerce maritime à la faculté de droit est arrivé avant-hier à l'Université où il a eu des entretiens avec le doyen et ses autres collègues.

Il a déclaré qu'il habiterait dans un milieu Turc afin d'apprendre notre langue dans un délai de 3 ans, et qu'il considérerait la Turquie comme sa propre patrie.

Tous les professeurs étrangers seront à leur poste jusqu'au 25 octobre.

New professors of the University:

New professors invited from Europe to teach at the University have started to arrive in Istanbul. Professor Hirsch who will teach Trade Law at the Law Faculty arrived the day before at the university where he had talks with the dean and his colleagues. He stated that he will reside in a Turkish milieu in Istanbul so that he can learn Turkish within three years and that he considered Turkey as his own country. All the foreign professors will be at their posts by 25th of October. *Le Journal d'Orient, October 20 1933*.

Just a couple of decades after the Ottoman Empire had taken its last breath, the general exodus had so depleted Germany's premier higher-learning institutions of professors that the University of Istanbul was rightfully considered and sincerely called "the best German University in the world."[14] According to Onur Öymen, a 2003 Member of Turkey's Parliament, the Turkish government's contracts with the émigré professors set salaries "well exceeding" those of the Turkish professors. Öymen pointed out that "the purpose of the Turkish government was to upgrade the academic level of Istanbul University to that of western European universities."[15]

By October 19 1933, *Dr. R. A. Lambert*, Associate Director of Rockefeller Foundation's European Office, wrote to his friend Dr. Lorrin Sheppard, the resident Director of Istanbul's American Hospital, in disbelief: "I got the impression from some of the recent visitors that the new developments represented a more sweeping change than I understood to be the case. I share your hope that the splendid effort the Turks are making in the field of education will have the fullest success."[16] Almost incredibly, courses began on November 5 1933 as reported in various media including Istanbul's French language, newspaper, *Le Journal d'Orient*.

Just ten years later, sufficiently impressed with the undergraduate education provided by Istanbul University, Harvard's Medical School admitted Lahut Uzman, one of Istanbul's undergraduates, to study medicine.[17] Eugen Merzbacher, also a 1943 graduate from the University of Istanbul, was admitted to Harvard's school of graduate studies where he earned an M.A. and a Ph.D. in physics.[18] Moreover, on arrival in the United States before, during, and shortly after WWII, several engineering graduates of Istanbul Technical University, which had also been significantly upgraded by émigré professors, had their educational credentials recognized by the *New York State Registration Board for Civil and Professional Engineers* for purposes of licensing.[19]

It was not only undergraduate degrees from Istanbul University that were being recognized by top-notch American universities. Elizabeth S. [Sgalitzer] Ettinghausen, a 1943 Ph.D. recipient in history of art and archaeology from Istanbul University, received Post-doctoral fellowships from Harvard University (1943-45) for research in Byzantine churches of Istanbul. Princeton later awarded her a post-doctoral degree as well.[20] At the same time, [Turkish] graduates of émigré-founded Ankara State Conservatory came to be recognized by playing to critical audiences worldwide. They included violinists such as Ayla Erduran (Suisse Romande Orchestra, Warsaw Philharmonic, Paris Conservatory, and Moscow Conservatory, and others) and Suna Kan (London Symphony, the Los Angeles Philharmonic, Bamberg Symphony, Residentie Orchestra (Holland), Moscow Symphony, and French National Radio Symphony {ORTF} among others).

With less world acclaim, but nonetheless filling a great need, the early graduates of Ankara University's medical school became Turkey's most revered practitioners and professors. One of these is retired Professor *Behçet Tahsin Kamay*. In discussing *Albert Eckstein*, one of his own mentors, émigré pediatrics professor Kamay said:

> He reached the remotest corners of Anatolia [Asia Minor part of Turkey] and he walked over every inch of the land. He visited the villages and went among the villagers; he knocked on their doors and became their guest. He was a doctor of the people and a Turkophile; in every place he visited, he ate the peasants' food, drank their buttermilk, and learned their health and social problems.... He had the courage to tell of both the diseases [he encountered] and the treatments [prescribed] to his students, the university circles, and state [provincial] and government officials through his writings, lectures, and conferences.[21]

Similarly, Dr. Mustaffer Sertabiboglu, recalled: "I am one of the first graduates of the Ankara Medical Faculty. My diploma has the number 68 on it. I am one of those who was nourished by the wisdom of [Albert] Eckstein." Sertabiboglu was referring to émigré pediatrican *Albert Eckstein* who introduced modern public-health and pediatrics practices to Turkey. He continued by pointing out one element of Eckstein's success: "[He] considered Turkey as his second home and was able to lecture without translators by learning Turkish in a short time."[22]

Professors Behçet Tahsin Kamay and Mustaffer Sertabiboglu both referred to Albert Eckstein as their *hoca*—an affectionate old Turkish term for the "Teacher" with a capital "T."

The distribution of the European professors was not equal among the four Faculties, or what we call colleges or schools. The vast majority of émigré professors were in medicine and the Faculty devoted to mathematics and natural science. There were fewer émigrés in the Faculties of law and the arts. But academics of great renown were to be found in all of these administrative units. Dr. Lambert, who was sent from Paris to Turkey, entered the following observation in his diary of February 18 1934.

> The state of the science departments is much like that of medicine, namely, activity and disorder, inevitable in the task of hasty reorganization. We find [physics] Prof. von Hippel trying to teach, through an interpreter, a group of interested students; he looks happy. Freundlich, [astronomy] on the contrary, looks worried and raises immediately the question of RF [Rockefeller Foundation] aid for an observatory.
>
> I have a short talk with [surgery] Prof. Rud[olf]. Nissen while he is scrubbing up for an operation. He is a young, energetic man who, like Schwarz, has jumped into the work immediately. There is, I am told, considerable criticism, of the new clinicians by the displaced Turks, but, as S. [Schwarz] points out, it is remarkable

that the native professors should have accepted the situation as gracefully as they have.[23]

Fewer of the academics found their way to Ankara than to Istanbul. This was due mainly to the infrastructure of the University of Ankara at the time. The university was still in the planning stages and mainly existed on paper. It was still mostly undeveloped land. Only a few institutes and scientific organizations were functioning. The disciplinary borderlines were not as clearly defined in Ankara as they were in Istanbul. Unlike those who came to the University of Istanbul under *Notgemeinschaft's* auspices, most of the scientists, architects, and artists who went to Ankara were invited through the official German and Austrian legations.

The largest share of émigrés in Ankara was to be found in the State school of music and the next largest was in the Faculty of Arts and the medical institutes. From a merely external point of view, achievements of the emigrants in Ankara can best be measured by the impressive buildings designed by Clemens Holzmeister and his colleagues and by the reputation of the state's orchestra and school of opera founded by Paul Hindemith and his colleagues.[24]

This all happened because in 1931 Atatürk had commissioned a study of the concept of creating a completely modern system of higher education modeled on West European universities. The *Rapport sur l'universite´ d'Istanbul* by Swiss educationalist Albert Malche was submitted in 1932. And, in the next year, an internal Rockefeller Foundation memorandum states: "The new developments in Turkey should be followed closely and sympathetically. The transplantation of so many eminent German scholars in Istanbul cannot but have far-reaching repercussions. The present transformation of Turkey offers so many problems of economic, social and political significance as to provide a fruitful field of research."[25]

Two years later, the Rockefeller Foundation sent Dr. R. A. Lambert back to Istanbul for a first-hand assessment of the situation. In Lambert's diary, an entry dated Friday, February 16 1934, recognizes that "[T]here is no doubt that Mustapha Kemal [Atatürk] and his Ministers of Hygiene and Education are determined to have in Istanbul, in the shortest possible time, a first class University with a Med. School that will command the respect of the West. Ankara is also to have a university, with later on a Med. Faculty. Agricultural institutes, including veterinary medicine, have already been established there."[26]

Thus, in scarcely more than a decade, Turkey was well on its way to having upgraded and modernized all the major basic and practical sciences, and to having made its distinctive mark in western classical music.

Appendix 1 of this book shows the *history* and *mission* statements as posted on the web by the original three Turkish universities in their own words. Each of the three contemporary statements independently attests to the national pride in the legacy that was left behind by the émigré professors. Each independently attests to the social groupings created by that legacy, and recognizes the effect that these groupings continue to have on Turkish higher education and on society at large.

Through Atatürk's "leadership qualities and position," a government policy was institutionalized and simultaneously so was the "enduring nature of cultural values."[27] To appreciate the achievements praised in the contemporary statements that are cited above, it is necessary to go back to the 1933-1934 academic year when the exiled professors from Germany[28] first served as directors in eight of the twelve basic science institutes as well as heading six of the seventeen clinics in the Faculty of Medicine. And the conditions were far from ideal. According to reports submitted in the fall of 1933 by Professor Philipp Schwarz, the new Director of the Institute of Pathology, the entire Faculty of Medicine experienced scarcities of equipment and buildings. There were only thirty extremely old microscopes for all seven basic science disciplines. The clinics were in bad shape, neglected, and under-equipped.[29] In order to overcome difficulties, the émigré professors used every bit of ingenuity God had given them. They went to the local bazaars and had merchants find for them pieces and parts of equipment from sources unknown. They pleaded for institutional donations from abroad, and the Rockefeller Foundation responded. Harvard and Yale sent back-issues of their journals for library research. The "Germans" overcame most if not all obstacles, including the ones put in their way by Turks they had dispossessed, or somehow offended, and who were not about to let this transition be easy.

In order to facilitate the Ottomans' descendants' progress in modern science and medicine, and to satisfy terms of their contracts, the émigré professors were obligated to write Turkish language textbooks in their respective subjects. To do so often required invention of new words and new alphaneumeric symbols and acronyms. The words had to reflect Turkish roots. The symbols would follow. However, they needed to reflect all that was inherited over centuries in the Arabic alphabet. For the German-speaking émigrés who knew no Turkish, this was a daunting task indeed. With Turkish colleagues as wingmates, many of the émigrés stood up to the challenge. Many textbooks resulted and were published.

Some seventy years later, retired professor and chair of Istanbul University's Chemical Engineering Department, Professor *İsmet Gürgey*, took issue with a speech that was published in the 200th issue of *Çağdaş Türk Dili Dergisi* (*The Journal of Contemporary Turkish Language*) celebrating the Turkish Language Reform's 72nd anniversary. The speaker was distinguished Professor *Tahsin Yücel*. Yücel, according to Gürgey, had ignored the major contributions made to Turkish sciences by the émigré, Professor *Fritz Arndt*.[30]

Significantly, Gürgey claimed that Yücel's article ignored the important contributions Arndt and other scientists had made to development of the Turkish language and its scientific nomenclature. Listed at the end of Yücel's speech, Gürgey says, "are the names of scientists, writers, and poets who have contributed to the purification and development of our language." Gürgey takes especial umbrage with Yücel's list of scientists and writers "who have contributed to the purification and development of our language." He claimed that the names were drawn from somewhat limited circles, all but ignoring these pioneers, Turkish and European, from the 30s. Gürgey writes, "I asked myself whether the improvement of Turkish within the passage of time was only due to efforts of the *Turkish Language Association*, the *Language Society*, the linguists and the poets." "[S]hould not others such as Prof. Dr. Oktay Sinanoğlu, Prof. Dr. Enver Altınlı, *Ord. Prof. Fritz Arndt* of indisputable reputation in the sciences, and proponents of Turkish, have been mentioned?" Gürgey stressed that these scientists must be acknowledged for having recognized and for believing "that Turkish was adequate to communicate in all fields of science." He paid special tribute to "Ord. Prof. Dr. Fritz Arndt[31] [who] should not only be included among such scientists,... but also perhaps cited as the foremost of all."[32]

Gürgey was Arndt's student during the 1954-1955 academic year, the close of Arndt's career in Turkey. He provides a dramatic picture of Arndt's teaching. During Gürgey's time, Arndt "used to give his lectures in an amphitheatre-shaped classroom which was later named for him. Attendance at lectures was not obligatory and attendance was not taken; however, the classroom used to fill up to the brim."[33] It is widely acclaimed by those who knew him that by the mid-1950s Arndt's lectures were free of linguistic faults except intonation. In conversation his language was joyful, lively, humorous, and to the point. His written language had a structure which continuously took into account cause-outcome relationships. Arndt wrote in short sentences, free of ornamentation. They flowed meaningfully and were easy to understand. He did not shy away from creating words when necessary.

It is widely believed that Arndt invented the following Turkish words: *çözücü*, for solvent, *çözelti* for solution, *çözünme* for dissolution, *çözünen* for solute, *tartı* for atomic weight, *değerlik* for valance, *anıklamak* for to prepare, *seyreltik* for dilute, and *çökelti* for precipitate, among others. Professor İsmet Gürgey recollects Arndt's favorite play on words as a demonstration of the Master Teacher's mastery of the Turkish language: "*Elemente elaman diyen elemandan el'aman!*" Arndt admonished "any student who says 'elaman' instead of 'element' will find himself immediately out of the classroom!" He was indeed famous for this play on three words which sound the same but have different meanings, namely: *element* = element, but *elaman* = personnel, and *el'aman* = save me, or sick and tired of. The sentence may thus be translated as: "Sick and tired of the person who calls an element 'a person.'"

Beyond any doubt, Fritz Arndt made major contributions to chemistry worldwide. His work on diazoketons resulted in what is still known as the *Arndt-Eistert* reaction that made possible the creation of larger acids from their smaller homologues. He made major contributions to Turkish chemistry, and as has been shown, he also contributed to the development of scientific terminology in the Turkish language.

More broadly, the dynamism of the original three universities came from recognition by the Republic's founding fathers of a need to educate future Turkish leaders in the ways of a "modern society" in "science," and in the various dimensions of "enlightenment" as actually stated by Atatürk himself. This dynamism was accelerated by fallout from the sad political events taking place in lands northwest of Turkey. The result was a ferment of intellectual activity, spurred on by Turkey's invitation of a select group of German, Austrian, and Czech academicians who were as indicated literally being discarded by their home institutions and ousted from their native countries. This ingathering created a developmental momentum in Turkey that continued generations after all of the foreigners had passed from the scene.

This momentum or diffusion process spawned many other state-supported as well as privately endowed universities within Turkey.[34] In addition to the state universities whose development was sketched above, there was the venerable Robert College. It was the first Anglo-American institution in Turkey, and was founded in Istanbul in 1863 as a typical liberal arts college by American missionary and philanthropist Cyrus Hamlin. Engineering departments were added in 1912. Subsequently, the Robert College organization included a secondary school for boys and another one for girls. Among its graduates are leaders of Turkey's academic, professional, and administrative cadres. Significantly, several sons and daughters of the émigré professors received their undergraduate degrees from Robert College. There are currently no fewer than 72 universities in Turkey.

Among these are at least six created by family groupings and endowed from personal wealth accumulated while creating national wealth within Turkey's process of modernization and industrialization. These include Istanbul's Koç and Sabanci universities. Ankara's Bilkent University (the oldest and most renowned) was established in 1983 with funding from private foundations controlled by *Ihsan Doğramaci,* MD. Doğramaci, a co-signer of the World Health Organization's constitution (New York, July 1946), graduated from Istanbul University's medical school in 1938.[35] Thus, he is a direct product of a curriculum that, as will be shown, was greatly influenced and at the time, largely taught by the émigré professors. Among his many career honors is the fact that he served as President of the International Pediatric Association (1968-1977).[36]

The other three universities endowed by businessmen, are *Kadir Has Üniversitesi, İzzet Baysal Üniversitesi,* and *Istanbul Bilgi Üniversitesi.* An e-mail message from Prof. Dr. Orhan N. Ulutin, "honorary member of the Turkish Academy of Science. and student of émigré professor *Erich Frank,*"[37] states:

> We now have 72 universities in Turkey. But we still look back to our golden age with German professors; *Frank, Winterstein, Schwarz, Cosswig, Heilbronn, Hirsch,* and the rest. (emphasis added)

Yes, these developments have indeed integrated western higher education into the fabric of a large and important segment of Turkish society while making its universities an integral part of higher education worldwide.

# 2
# The Émigrés

With Turkish visas in hand, obtaining first-class passage by train, ship, or both, was no problem whatsoever. And those who insisted on bringing their house servants were given permission to do so. Most had their libraries and furniture shipped to Turkey; several brought their assistants and had their laboratory and/or clinical equipment sent as well. For the Nazis, whose strategic forecasts contemplated long-term payoff, such an invitation from the Turkish government had a special significance, the release of an individual (*Dr. Kantorowicz*) from a concentration camp and expelling him and his family to Istanbul is but one example. There were others. Once in Turkey, these German families for the most part chose to reside in the same neighborhoods, often in the same buildings. The community of German-speaking émigrés was socially very close-knit both in Istanbul and in Ankara.

Almost uniformly, the children of émigrés attended the same few private schools in Turkey. Invariably, these were either German or English schools. As the German schools became more and more politicized by the Nazis, the émigrés removed their children and placed them in the English schools. Regardless, all children were well schooled, as their lifelong careers demonstrated. Few of the youngsters had any social interactions with their Turkish counterparts other than those from minority families, e.g., Armenians or Greeks. A number of the Ankara families had sons and daughters studying in Istanbul. When the schools were in session, these youngsters lived in the homes of the Istanbul-based émigré families.

There was much interaction of the newcomers with the larger community of German expatriates. Some of the ex-pats were outright Nazis, while others were vehement opponents of the new regime back home. Most of the émigrés were Jewish or part-Jewish, or they had Jewish spouses. Some were full-blooded Aryans. *These labels, however, refer to the Nazi definition of who was or was not an Aryan. They had nothing to do with whether or not any aspect of the Jewish religion* was practiced in the home. No matter what their ancestry, the lion's share of the émigrés were agnostic or nonbelievers.

It is fair to say that the between-the-wars generation of Jewish intellectuals in both Germany and Austria did not particularly identify with their religious roots. They were very much assimilated socially and culturally. With but one known exception, the *Freundlichs*, none observed any of the Jewish holidays. Many had their children baptized as Christians and some converted to one or another denomination of Christianity. Some émigrés were very proud of being decorated WWI veterans. They were Austrians or they were Germans! They did not look at themselves as Jews. They were all social reformers of one kind or another, regardless of profession or scientific discipline. Some were, or became, Communists. Almost all were Socialists at some time. Some flip-flopped between the two schools of thought.

There were spies and informers among the émigrés and these lived a double life for the spying. Some émigrés were blackmailed by embassy staffers who knew of relatives still alive and in Germany, and some did it for pay. Still others did it in hopes of professional advancement. But one thing all Germans in Turkey had in common: they were constantly secretly monitored and had reports sent to Berlin. Dr. Herbert Scurla, a senior executive officer in Germany's Ministry of Science and Education, was, on at least two occasions in 1938-39, sent to Istanbul and Ankara by the Reich. His mission was to assess the activities of the émigré professors, verify the monitoring being done, and accuracy of reports provided him and others by the German legation.

Because Turkey was, for the majority of the time, officially neutral in the years preceding and during WWII, some of the émigrés acted as communication conduits between those in Nazified lands and their relatives in the free world. They were also used as a pipeline to let the free world know what was happening inside Germany. Such was the case with at least one Nobelist, Max von Lau: though a non-Nazi who stayed in Germany, Lau forwarded to a colleague in Istanbul his [Lau's] personal correspondence with another Nobel laureate (Johannes Stark), a devout Nazi ideologue and self-appointed reformer of Germany's science.

Most of the émigrés were adamantly anti-Zionist, i.e., they did not believe in the need for a Jewish State. However, at least one (*Dr. Eckstein*) is known to have helped persuade senior Turkish ministers on behalf of the *Yishuv*,[1] to let a number of *kinder* (children's) transports go by rail through Turkey and on to safety in Palestine. With some significant pauses, such transports continued into 1944.

The émigrés made every effort to improve their lot, maintain what safety they could for themselves and their families, and still reach out across the seas to America. However, circumstances in the world around them were forever changing, and most of the time for the worst. Until the cold winter of 1942-1943, when the Red [Soviet] Army reversed Germany's fortunes at Stalingrad, the émigrés' only other emotional relief came when it became apparent that the German, Hungarian, and Romanian, armies[2] would move on Stalingrad and the Caspian oil fields via Russia's steppes rather than making Turkey their stepping-stone. From the early 1930s, some of the émigrés attempted to get America to recognize the true nature of Nazism and act accordingly. Yet, as will be shown they were rebuffed in this by members of the American Jewish establishment. Unfortunately, until it was too late, some of the more prominent Jews were so assimilated within America's greater social establishment that they did not want to rock the boat by bringing attention to the plight of Jews in Europe, and thereby the attention of memory to their own "Jewishness." On the other hand, some non-Jewish scientific communities jumped into the fray without any hesitation on behalf of their embattled science colleagues. A number of American research universities recognized a triple opportunity being presented: that of acquiring world-class talent; acquiring outside funding that would otherwise not be available to them; and being altruistic in the process.

After Atatürk's death in 1938 a combination of social, political, and economic factors began to gnaw away at the welcome the émigrés had enjoyed. This was manifested in many different ways. Some were destructive and troubling, some had elements of a tragicomedy, and many were of the type that mediocrities in administrative positions invoke worldwide to force a senior even luminary academic out. By spring of 1941, the Nazis troops had come within a stone's throw of Turkey's northern and western land borders and were but a few hours sail along the Black Sea shores from most of its northern provinces; moreover, the Soviet hammer threatening to strike the western and southern Black Sea coast was visibly there. Turkey learned from Poland's experience not to depend on France or England to come to its defense. The German legation was doing whatever it could to make the émigrés' lives miserable. However, these developments did not stop the consular officials, from Ambassador von Pappen down, in using the Jewish physicians' services when in need.

No matter what was happening around them, the émigrés tried to live as normal a life as possible. They organized publication of a scientific journal that accepted papers from all disciplines. On weekends and holidays, the families, with kids in tow, went on outings to the countryside. The education of their children was paramount. Some students received college degrees and all education was transferable to other countries. All those contacted by the author continue to have good memories of growing up in Turkey. Regardless of their circumstances and hardships, it seems the émigré parents were careful not to inflict their personal traumas on their cherished children. These young people lived a very privileged life compared to their Turkish hosts. To put it mildly, the "Germans" had much better lives than did at least 99% of their Turkish cohorts (Fig. 7).

Klaus Eckstein, a son of pediatrician Albert Eckstein contributed the following essay regarding his childhood in Ankara, 1935–1945:

> Before I start to recount my memories, I must state as a preamble that, if there should ever be such a thing as a "normal childhood," mine was certainly not such. As a German "émigré," I as a foreign body within the Turkish community, could, of course, not have any contact with the German children from the *Corps Diplomatique*, and even among the children of the Allied diplomats, I was a foreign body—and foreign bodies cause irritation. Thus my experiences, the impressions that I still have from that time, are specifically my own, and cannot be simply transferred to other children.
>
> When I arrived in Ankara in December 1935, with my brothers and my mother, I was about three and a half years old. Of course, I have but few memories from that time. We had a children's maid/cook, Hungarian, I believe, who could speak German and who particularly loved me and wanted to demonstrate this fact constantly by kissing me. Sadly, I did not have the corresponding inclination and, on one occasion, hit out with a wooden brick, causing her to lose a gold tooth—and she left. I think we already had our Turkish manservant, *Mehmet*, at that time, who remained with us for many years. Shortly after came *Minna* who had been cook for my parents in Germany for many years and before that for my [maternal] grandfather Schlossmann. She returned to Germany in 1938 and was replaced by a Swiss woman, Fraulein Krug. As became apparent some time later, Krug was a spy for the NS [Nazis] who reported on every visit and every event in our household. She left very suddenly when my parents found out this fact. She used to take me along when, in the afternoons, she used to visit the *Blockwart* (the local Nazi person in charge) to give her daily report, but, of course, I had no knowledge of why she went there or what went on. At that time, I already knew how to read and write, and I collected stamps. The *Blockwart* once gave me some, but [her reports] were not of any particular interest or value. In 1938, while *Minna* was still with us, my mother's aunt came from Germany to visit us and brought me a schoolboy's leather satchel. It was my mother's duty to make clear to her that she could not travel back to

Germany, but had to go on to her daughter in England. In order to celebrate her arrival, we planned to eat a turkey; these birds were regularly herded through the streets in Ankara—even the most important ones, such as the *Ismet Pasha Caddesi* (now *Mithat Pasha Caddesi*), and one then picked out a bird from that flock, which was, it was to be hoped, not too tough; however these birds still had a fine taste, even if, in comparison to the ones commercially available nowadays, they were rather small. Our bird had been bought in a few days before, but sadly it died of a natural death before *Mehmet* could slaughter it. I cannot remember whether we did finally eat it.

Summer in Ankara was always very hot. Often, we would go to the swimming pool in *Orman Ciftlik*. In later years, when I was perhaps 11, I was allowed to take the bus to *Bahcelievler* (at that time, a smart suburb quite a ways out of town) by myself or with *Muzzafer*, the son of the cleaning lady of my teacher Mrs. *Kudret,* and from there walk across the fields to the swimming pool. The path passed through the steppe and, on the way, we might see a tortoise and plenty of insects, but practically no animals or people. At the weekend, we almost always went for a walk—often to friends who had their summer house in *Kücük Esat*. The way was rather long and went through the steppe; only few houses, almost all of them old half-timbered houses of the Armenian style, i.e., with each succeeding floor projecting above the lower one, standing by the way, but there were, in May, lovely flowers, such as dog roses, and many kinds of insects to be seen. The professor for entomology had encouraged us to collect insects for him in glass jars with a cork bung, and with cotton wool-soaked in prussic acid inside to kill the insects, so that he could determine the many kinds and numbers of insects living there. In winter (that must have been after 1941), as we now no longer lived in the *Coruh Sokak,* but in the *Karanfil Sokak*), I could get with my sleigh to a road in less than 5 minutes that was fairly steep, and, like all roads, free of traffic, and ideal for tobogganing. On Sundays, we would go skiing on the *Dikmen* hills, or, if the snow was not deep enough there, to the *Elma Dag*. I suppose the Turks at that time found these weekend activities somewhat bizarre.

We usually spent the summer in Istanbul, sometimes with Turkish friends in *Ciftehavuzlar*, once in a boarding house in *Suadiye*, and once on *Heybeli Ada*, later on (1944 and 1945) in *Bebek* with Prof. Kosswig, whose eldest son is about one year older than I. I still remember well the swimming in the *Marmara* and the *Bosphorus*. No doubt we occasionally found some pollution in the water but did not take that very seriously, and no one thought it might endanger our health, nor did it. We would dive for mussels, which were then immediately cooked and eaten. Wherever we were, all around was green and open. If we went from *Suadiye* or *Ciftehavuzlar* into Istanbul, we had to travel by ferry, or by tramway to Kadiköy, and then from there by ferry. From *Bebek*, there went a tram as far as *Eminönü*, or we went by steamer, which crossed to and from on the *Bosphorus* until it finally arrived by the *Galata* Bridge. Both tram and steamer had two classes, and as far as I can remember, we used to travel first class. Second class was always overcrowded.

A further memory is the food. I was something of a glutton and could eat enormous quantities, but if we were invited to a proper Turkish feast, then this did occasionally surpass my capacity. Such a meal would always start with an extensive *Meze* (various starters) and then, perhaps two hours later, the meal proper would begin. I cannot now remember the precise sequence of courses, but there were many of them: rice, *Dolma* (stuffed vegetables), vegetables cooked in oil, chicken, meat, fish, and *Börek* (filo pastry filled with meat and cheese, etc.). Fortunately, desert was usually fruit, and not the very sweet variety of Turkish deserts. I was very fat, much to the chagrin of my mother, who often, unsuccessfully, tried to subject me to a diet. On the other hand, I was the ideal beauty for Turkish mothers who often would ask my father for the secret of how he managed to get me so wonderfully fat, and, I think, would never believe him that he did not at all want me to be so fat, and claimed that he did not know how one could get a normal child to be so.

I received my education mainly from Mrs. *Kudret*, an exceptionally good teacher, a German woman who had married a Turkish engineer after her studies and moved to Ankara with him. From her, I learned enough English to go to a school in England at the age of thirteen, without any major linguistic problems, and to pass English examinations, *inter alia*, in Latin and French, at sixteen, and in the other subjects without much work. At the age of ten, I had been sent to a Turkish primary school, the best in town, with small classes of only sixty-five children. Before that, I had been taught the Turkish language by an outstanding teacher who had no knowledge of any language other than her own nor of any theory of "direct method" teaching, so that I had no difficulties when I joined the school, at least as far as language was concerned. Of course, I was given special treatment, perhaps in part because I was abler than most, or all, in the class, but also because I was not only the only foreigner in the whole school but also the son of a very well-known man. At some point, most of the children had passed under him. Nevertheless, I had a few good friends there. All in all, my fellow pupils did not resent that I was given special treatment.

The following year, I went to the Middle School where again I had some good friends, but I did not so much like the teaching there. What finally and definitively spoiled it [school] for me was the teaching of history. We had to write an essay on the siege of Vienna (1529). At that time, I was very ambitious and wanted to write the best essay in the class, so I did not only use the Turkish school textbook as source material, but also the very comprehensive German *History of the World* by Otto Jaeger, which contained at least four times as much on this subject as the Turkish school book. Thus, my extensive essay contained four times as much from the German source as from the Turkish and was much longer and more detailed. But, as I did not appreciate at the time, the German material provided the aspect opposite to the Turkish, and thus I also wrote four times as much on the German point of view. My Turkish teacher was not amused by this and I was given the mark "0." The best mark would have been a "10." From that day onwards, I refused to have anything to do with history until 1982 when I had to mug up on local English history for an English language course for German children. But I did learn from this experience how careful a teacher has to be if a pupil puts forward an idea that is counter to the one held or supported by the teacher.

If I now look back on my time in Turkey, I see a time when I was very happy, free, and free from danger. I still go to Turkey frequently and see there still that children are loved and that they know that they have the right to be loved, and not, as is so often the case here [the UK], that any expression of love is immediately considered suspect. Friendship and love are still virtues there, and I look back on my time in Turkey with gratitude.

The year was 1937. Astronomer *E. Finlay Freundlich* had become thoroughly frustrated while trying to build Turkey's first astronomical observatory in an administrative culture he did not understand, nor appreciate. So, he pulled up stakes early and left Turkey with his family. Unfortunately for Freundlich, the only academic opening available at that time was in Prague, Czechoslovakia. Luckily, he was able to re-emigrate to Scotland before the Nazis entered Prague. There was a great exodus from Turkey around 1939 when many of the contracts had expired and were not to be renewed, mostly for economic reasons. An exodus again happened in 1949, this time of those whose contracts had been twice renewed by the Turks. Most of this group ended up in the U.S. The break-up of the homes established with such pain in Turkey scattered these survivors throughout both continents straddling the Bosphorus and across the seas to America, but even this did not stop their work and contributions to knowledge. Some of the more elderly did go back to Germany to recoup pension rights; others went on to what then was Palestine. At all times, most sought a visa and a quality job offer from the U.S. or the UK. It is true that until long after the end of WWII, many of the more prestigious American universities would not have Jews on their faculty, much less in the administrative structure; women and older academics among them had additional strikes against them. Some universities would take in the superstars even if Jewish, but only if some benefactor outside the university would pay their salaries and any overhead costs that might be required.

Other than the *Cedars of Lebanon* and *Mount Sinai* hospitals created by and for large Jewish communities in New York City, Chicago, and Cleveland, most of the larger hospitals would not allow Jewish doctors privileges of practice. Contrary to popular belief, these Jewish hospitals had not been established to serve the special dietary needs of observant Jewish patients but rather were established to give Jewish doctors a place to practice. The émigrés were not ignorant of all this.

Some of the émigrés, visa in hand but no job elsewhere, stayed on their jobs in Turkey but sent their sons and daughters to continue their educations in the U.S. Most of these children of émigrés went on to become major contributors to America's science, medicine, law, engineering, the arts, and some entered the world of business.

No matter where the émigrés landed on re-emigration, the U.S., UK, Germany, or Israel, all continued to be productive members of society and many continued to make major contributions. Quite a few were at all times in personal correspondence with one or more of over a dozen Nobel laureates. According to Albert Einstein's hand-written correspondence, one of the émigrés, E. Finlay Freundlich, was the first to show that the relativity theory was borne out by empirical observations.

More then half a century later, all of the dirty tricks played on individual émigrés by their local administrators in Turkey have been mostly forgotten by both sides. The only memories of such unpleasantries are to be found in archival documents, correspondence, and some memoirs. Of these memoirs, the most poignant were penned not by the émigrés themselves and not by their offspring. They were written some sixty years later by former students who had risen to the pinnacle of Turkish academe, and professions.

All that aside, in retrospect, Turkey can justly take pride in what it has done for humanity and be equally prideful about what these individuals as a group have done for her. Another interesting fallout is described in a German government *Cultural Relations* website:

> More than *80*[3] *renowned German scientists and artists took refuge* in Turkey from Nazi persecution in the 1930s and 1940s. *They helped to establish, and worked in, Turkish institutions and universities.* Among them were the Berlin Opera director *Carl Ebert* and the composer *Paul Hindemith,* legal scholars such as *Andreas Schwarz* and *Ernst Hirsch,* philosophers and orientalists such as *Ernst von Aster* and *Hellmut Ritter,* natural scientists and physicians like *Friedrich Dessauer* and *Rudolf Nissen,* and the economists *Alexander Rüstow* and *Wilhelm Röpke.* Close ties developed amongst various universities in the two countries as a result and these persist today. The German Academic Exchange Service awards various scholarships in Turkey. Professors and students teach and study in both countries. Scholars and artists were not the only ones to find a safe haven in Turkey: later to become Berlin's governing mayor, *Ernst Reuter* worked as an expert for administration and transport in Ankara and Istanbul.[4] (emphasis added)

On one issue there is no disagreement between any of the myriad of contentious factions within and outside Turkey: the German-speaking émigrés completely reformed, even created, Turkey's now-excellent higher education system. The results of Atatürk's gamble had paid off handsomely. At the time the émigrés departed, Turkey had three major institutions of higher learning, a full-service arts academy, a symphony orchestra, an opera company, and a system of libraries and librarianship, all functioning at the level of western standards while staffed by native Turkish intellectuals, professionals, and artists. To boot, most of the classical works of western literature had been translated into Turkish and are still made available to the 1.7 million Turkish teenagers who now take the university entrance examination every year.

*Figure 7*
Outside of Ankara. A typical Sunday excursion. This one combined the *Reuter, Merzbacher, Eckstein,* and *Gerngross* families.

# 3
# The Builders

## Modernization of Architecture and City Planning

Greater Istanbul is full of old mosques, palaces, military quarters, *hamams* (communal bath houses), and former *madrasas*. These are well-preserved examples of Ottoman architecture. One can find similar landmarks throughout the Middle East and other outlying districts of the old empire. In the eyes of Turkey's reformists, however, architecture would provide a very visible symbol of Turkey's modernization, second only to creating a new alphabet. Moving Turkey's central government from Istanbul to Ankara, the country's rural interior was a political message of major proportions. Its implementation, and the visual development of Ankara from ground up as a major city, was another matter. Since the statement needed to be articulated in modern or western design, Ottoman-Turkish architects were not considered for the job (Fig. 8 and 9).

Among the many professors and/or professionals invited was a group of leading architects. In 1938, together with her architect husband, *Margarete Schütte-Lihotzky* was called to Istanbul to teach at the Academy of Fine Arts, and to reunite with exiled German architect Bruno Taut. Schütte-Lihotzky was brought in because she epitomized several of the goals and objectives of the Republic's fathers. That she was a female was of significance and an important signal sent by the Young Turks in government, who were mostly career army officers. She was the first and, to this day, the most famous, Austrian female architect. She represented the *Neuen Bauens,* New Constructions. Between the World Wars, Schütte-Lihotzky planned and built the New Frankfurt for the *Wein Siedlerbewegung,* or Vienna Building Society. Significantly, she had already completely planned and designed cities new from ground up. Magnitogorsk, a major industrial center in the Soviet Union's Ural region of Siberia, was one of them (Fig. 10).

Schütte-Lihotzky was among the foremost social architects practicing in Europe before World War II. She specialized in designing housing for the working class. Her designs reduced the labor involved in "house labor" of working wives. Her kitchens became the prototype for those in any modern home or apartment worldwide. Just as significantly, in terms of Turkey's new ideology, she had designed motion-saving kitchens for the home, which she based on Frederick W. Taylor's time efficiency studies and the motion-efficiency studies of Frank and Lillian Gilbreth. "Schütte-Lihotzky designed the famed Frankfurt kitchen which was functional, inexpensive, and could be mass-produced. Beginning in 1927, the Frankfurt City Council installed 10,000 of her prefabricated kitchens in working-class apartments. Before her innovative design, kitchens were mostly planned for households with servants." She learned about the Taylor system, a scientific approach to understanding the necessity of accurately measuring the time required for each task performed in a given job in order to better organize work and redesign the workplace so as to increase efficiency. During the 1920s, Taylorism was transforming the industrial workplace in the United States. According to architectural writer Billie Ann Lopez, around 1922, Schütte-Lihotzky "read an essay called "How Can Appropriate Housing Construction Reduce the Work of Housewives" in the Breslau journal *The Silesian Home*. Schütte-Lihotzky immediately understood that by connecting design to function in the kitchen, there would be a positive impact for the working woman, providing her with more time for her family and for herself."[1] Using a stopwatch, Schütte-Lihotzky timed each task required within the kitchen from preparing a meal to cleaning up afterward. She then proceeded to design her trend-setting kitchen, one that became famous worldwide (Fig. 11, 12, 13).

Schütte-Lihotzky also designed kindergarten pavilions using Maria Montessori's ideas. (Montessori was the first woman in Italy to qualify as a physician and founder of the Montessori Method of education.) In each of these settings, Schütte-Lihotzky can be credited as being the first to introduce the women's perspective into architectural design. Arguably, the role model she provided can be credited for the fact that currently more than a third of practicing architects in Turkey are women![2]

*Herbert Eichholzer,* another Austrian architect, was Schütte-Lihotzky's colleague in Istanbul. While performing his contractual duties for Ankara's government, he was also busy organizing Communist anti Nazi resistance at home. In 1939, Schütte-Lihotzky joined the Austrian Communist Party (KPÖ). In December 1940, she and Eichholzer returned to Vienna to secretly contact and aid the Austrian Communist resistance movement. She was arrested by the Gestapo on January 22 1941 managed to survive the war and continued to practice architecture.

In 1946, Schütte-Lihotzky returned to Vienna, but during the Cold War, her Communist Party membership stood in the way of her winning many architectural assignments. Late in life, in 1980, she received the City of Vienna Architecture Award for her lifetime contributions, and, in 1988, she was offered the *Austrian Medal of Science and Art* but declined it because of the alleged Nazi affiliations of Kurt Waldheim, Austria's president at the time. She celebrated her 100th birthday in 1997, dancing a short waltz with Vienna's mayor and remarking, "I would have enjoyed it, for a change, to design a house for a rich man."

In her memoirs, Schütte-Lihotzky tells about the years she spent in the "Resistance," her fellow prisoners and fellow fighters, and their efforts and courage in an uncompromising solidarity which actually saved her life. Her comrade, Herbert Eicholzer, was also arrested in 1941, but he was executed in 1943 by the Gestapo. Schütte-Lihotzky escaped this fate.[3]

Schütte-Lihotzky's legacy can be found in each and every Turkish kitchen, be it in a modest apartment building flat or in a large villa. When preparing the meal or washing and putting away the dishes, one needs not to walk more than two or at most three steps front to back or side to side.

However, because her tenure in Turkey had been relatively short, Margarete Schütte-Lihotzky's imprint on Turkish architecture was in some respects not as significant as that of fellow Austrian *Clemens Holzmeister* (Fig. 14). In February 1938, Holzmeister was commissioned by Atatürk to build the Republic's Parliament building. At the time, Hitler's troops were about to enter Austria. Because Holzmeister supported the Austrian government and fought for Austria's independence against the Nazis, he was officially expelled from his Vienna and Dusseldorf posts. Holzmeister served as Administrator of Vienna's Fine Arts Academy's Architectural Section before 1938. He designed many still-functioning government buildings. From 1940 to 1954, he was Architectural Section Director at Istanbul Technical University. He designed many Turkish government buildings in Ankara, including the Grand National Assembly (1938), the ministries of Agriculture (1934), War (1931), Interior(1932), and that of the Turkish General Staff (1930) (Fig. 15).

Between 1938 and 1954, Holzmeister lived and worked in Istanbul and Ankara. He retired in 1954 and returned to Austria and served in his prior capacity at the Viennese academy up to 1957.[4]

At Istanbul Technical University, he educated many of Turkey's architects. Holzmeister never lost contact with Turkey. His last visit to Ankara, in 1978, was as a consultant on the enlargement of the Grand National Assembly complex. During his career, Holzmeister planned 700 projects in Austria, Italy, Germany, and Turkey. One of the most outstanding was the Salzburg Theatre Building.

Clemens Holzmeister, the master builder and leader of the band of émigré architects, had this to say about the modernist architects' experience in Turkey:

> It is solely thanks to the fact that my eleven projects were completed without the slightest cause for complaint or reproach that I increasingly gained the government's confidence—until as the crowning achievement of my career Atatürk commissioned me to plan his private palace. The great father and founder of the New Turkey resided at that time in a modest old house in the upper part of the city.

According to Holzmeister, in the first project meeting the basic issue discussed was chiefly about whether the new palace should be built on the site of the old house or alternatively next to it on a newly acquired location. When asked for his opinion, Holzmeister replied "that this old house represented a significant part of the history of the New Turkey and thereby clearly won Atatürk's heart." During the design and construction phase of the Presidential Palace (Fig. 16), Holzmeister "had the opportunity to meet this outstanding personality, this man of frightening severity and the voice of a 'Basserman/bass singer.' 'For him [Atatürk], the respect for the professional expert counted above everything and, if one had gained this respect through decent work, everything else was easy.' Cheerful and proud-hearted, we did everything possible to accomplish this project, on which last but not least a large number of excellent Viennese craftsmen were employed."[5] (Fig. 17).

Among these "craftsmen" was *Martin Wagner* who, after being discharged from his position with the City of Berlin, came to Turkey in 1934 after a short stint at Harvard on the recommendation of Walter Gropius. He stayed until 1938 and worked as an architect. *Gustaf Oelsner* was another émigré architect "who in addition to teaching architecture and city planning played an important role in actuating Turkey's municipal planning programs."[6]

*Alfred Schücking*, a mechanical engineer, was the expert in heating and ventilation on the team. Born in 1886, a non-Jewish Austrian, he was employed without a fixed contract in the Turkish construction industry starting in 1937. Previous to that, he had worked as an assistant to Professor Taut. He was not, however, one of the university lecturers.

*Bruno Taut* (Fig. 18), too, was a member of this small and exclusive club of architects. He was responsible for the design of several public buildings in Ankara and served as Professor of Architecture at both the Istanbul Technical University and the Istanbul Academy of Fine Arts. Among others projects, he designed a building to house the Faculty of *Languages, History, and Geography*, and was the architect who built the Ankara *Atatürk Lycee,* the *Trabzon Lycee,* as well as the *Cebeci Secondary School.* Born in Königsberg, Germany, in 1880, he trained in Königsberg, and the Berlin Charlottenburge. Taut opened his own office in Berlin in 1910 where he maintained a busy practice until the advent of World War I. During that war, he published Pacifist polemical works, some of which came out as *Alpin Architectur* (Alpine Architecture), showing the Alps redesigned as a gigantic task of construction, the antithesis of destructive war.[7]

In the late 1920s, Taut gained recognition as a leader of architecture's "New Objective" school. He produced his book *Modern Architecture* in 1930. Following World War I, Germany experienced a critical housing shortage; at the same time, a Socialist ideology prevailed. Consequently various co-op housing societies and associations, public housing associations, and trade union housing groups were formed to build economical housing for the working classes in Berlin. *Gehag* (a public utility homes, savings and construction company) was one of the largest such associations. It was "founded in 1919 to build housing for its members. Committed to a progressive program of modern housing, *Gehag* sought collaboration with modern architects and, in 1924, Bruno Taut was appointed chief architect."[8] Taut was instrumental in developing the *Großsiedlungen* (large residential community) concept for "building large garden city-type housing complexes. He had had some experience designing a similar garden city development in Magdeburg in 1912-15." In *Hufeisen* alone, there are over 1000 two- to four-bedroom flats equally divided between three-story row houses and three-story point access slabs. Not one of the thousand is isolated, enclosed, or denied quick access and egress. Balconies opening to the opposite side dominate the garden facades. The small openings at the top floor—a normal feature of housing of this period, light an attic space that was used for washing and storage.[9]

Taut emphasized glass and color in architecture even though color had been neglected by both architects and architectural historians. "Taut is unique among his European modernist contemporaries in his devotion to color." A lifelong painter, "he applied lively, clashing colors to his first major commission, the 1912 *Falkenberg* housing estate in Berlin, which became known as 'Paint Box Estates.' The 1914 Glass Pavilion, familiar from black and white reproduction, was also brightly colored."[10] Taut's contribution to the 1927 *Weissenhofsiedlung* housing exhibition in Stuttgart differed greatly from the pure-white Mies van der Rohe, Le Corbusier, and Walter Gropius entries. "Taut's house Number 19 was painted up in primary colors. Mies hated it."[11] (Fig. 18)[12].

Taut used color for environmental, energy saving, aesthetic, and spatial effect. His approach to design was based on a belief that architecture included more than a strictly functional role, but could change and enhance the quality of life. To quote Winfried Brenne who rediscovered the colors of Taut's Berlin apartments:

> Taut always used colour to enhance architecture and give it an extra dimension. He knew that colour developed plastic effect and conferred a specific character on urban space, which helped settle it into the surrounding landscape. In everything, he strove to use colour to broaden the notion of function in architecture, in view of creating form to produce a harmonious building enhanced by a human and artistic dimension.[13]

And, to give Taut himself the last word on the subject:

> Before the war, I was denounced as a glass architect. In Magdeburg they called me the apostle of colour. The one is only a consequence of the other; for delight in light is the same as delight in colour.[14]

The *Glasspavillion* building (Fig. 19) was designed especially for the *Werkbund* Exhibition held in Cologne in 1914. Its "polygonal dome-like roof constructed of a space frame with diamond-shaped glass panels employed glass of various forms colours, and water cascades as well. It caused something of a sensation, and is his most celebrated work."[15] After WWI ended, Taut became the leading light of the avant-garde and exercised influence through various writings, and cultural and professional, organizations. However, after becoming Director of Building and Planning in 1921 for Marburg, a city that was the administrative center for all of Prussia and hosted a world famous university, Taut's Expressionist and utopian tendencies withered.[16]

Taut left Germany for the USSR in 1932 and came back in February 1933 to a very hostile political environment. He first fled to Switzerland then moved to Takasaki, Japan, where he produced three influential books on Japanese culture and architecture, and did furniture and interior design work. Offered a job as Professor of Architecture at Istanbul Technical University, Taut moved to Turkey in 1936, wrote at least one more book, and designed buildings in Ankara. Of all architects foreign and domestic, Bruno Taut was given a most esteemed commission. He was chosen to design Atatürk's catafalque. That turned out to be Taut's last creation. He died prematurely shortly thereafter and is buried in Istanbul's Martyr's cemetery. Unfortunately, much of Taut's written work was never translated into English.

These architects are all gone, but their edifices remain for us to see. In retrospect, it appears that the Turkish reforms, at least as far as architecture is concerned, were not at all unlike the contemporaneous Nazi reforms. Though certainly nowhere near as brutal, both eliminated a high level of cultural development. Turkey's architecture, like Germany's science, has never recovered its respective qualitative, distinctive stylistic edge. *Yıldız* Technical University's Architecture Professor, Ugur Tanyeli, provides a recent review and assessment of the above developments in Turkey:

> What took place in architecture and design seems to be very different from what transpired in other branches of science. In social sciences, those who came to Turkey were scholars and academicians. But almost none of those who came in the field of architecture had undergone the standard academic stages. Or a significant majority did not. A large number of these individuals came to the Academy of Fine Arts, the only school of architecture in Turkey at that period. They were real architects and designers and the reasons for their arrival were not similar to the ones of the other scholars and academicians. Anyway, nobody thought of them in the context of the university reform. They were seen as people who would implement the new architectural program of the state. The new architectural program of the state was not deeper than a quite simple, even crudely defined, idea that "in modern Turkey, there must be modern architecture." Looking from an architectural perspective, it looks as if they [the State] brought in anybody they could find. There is no evidence that they proceeded according to certain preferences or according to the basic qualities of the people they brought in. That is, when they took in a specialist on China, he was a real Chinese specialist. But some of the architects who came were ordinary ones without any significance though some were universally acclaimed ones. It seems the method of action was to bring in whoever was available at the time. We even know that most of the time the bureaucrats were not even aware of the basic architectural tendencies of the people brought in. For example, there is a little brochure that was published by the Academy dated 1936 which includes a short explanation of the department of architecture. It says, "We have found an architect named Bruno Taut outside the country. With his arrival shortly, we will have a new instructor who will fight against the ugly cubic buildings which have invaded the provincial centers and the countryside in the name of modern architecture." A comment so wrong and so devoid of understanding Taut's qualities must be very rare

> indeed. Taut himself was a very determined Modernist. While the administration claimed that Taut was invited to fight against Modernism. This is such a comical and ignorant choice. And why did Taut really come? Very simple. Taut was both a Communist and a Jew and he was out of his country at the time. He was living in Japan and the Japanese did not create opportunities for him to stay there. Taut was obliged to accept Turkey's invitation since he had nowhere else to go. And thus one of the principal actors of the world architectural scene arrived in Turkey by coincidence. However, Turkey was not aware of this. As we said before, the administration was expecting someone who would fight against Modernism. Many came to Turkey. Some were insignificant; some were people who should have been refused according to the ideological preferences of the period. It is interesting that many communists arrived among the architects. As an example, Margarete Schütte-Lihotzky came, a committed communist. After she went back to her country, she joined the Austrian underground and we know that she fought actively against the Nazis for many years. Margerete Schütte-Lihotzky was one of the first women architects and active communist leaders in Austria. It is interesting to note that she could teach without a problem at the Academy and could produce Primary School Programs for the Ministry of Education. She is a designer of note, even if not as important as Taut.[17]

Unlike their counterparts in the sciences, economics, medicine, and law, all senior members of the architectural team came to Turkey from Austria and returned to Austria with the exception of Bruno Taut. He was born in East Prussia and is buried in Istanbul. In retrospect, they did greatly impact the life of Turkey's urban dwellers for the better. As for the esthetics of the country's institutional buildings which they had introduced, that is a matter of taste (Fig. 20[18] and 21).

*Figure 8*
Blue Mosque (Sultanahmet Camii), Istanbul, Turkey. Built between 1609 and 1616 by Mehmet Aga, the imperial architect, for Sultan Ahmet I.

*Figure 9*
Within the Blue Mosque.

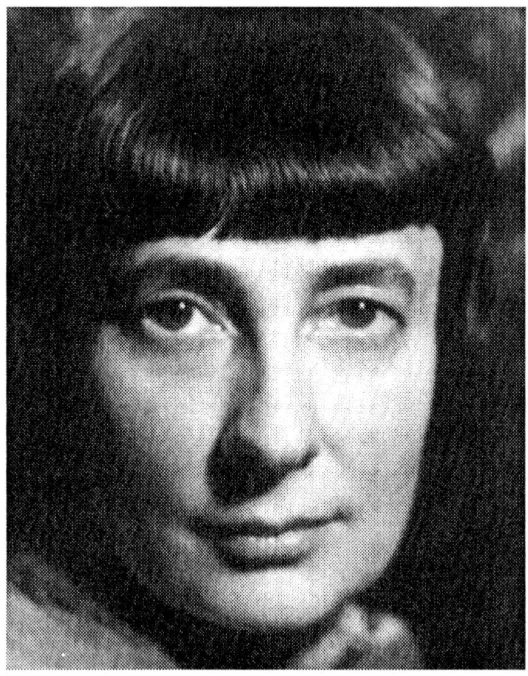

*Figure 10*
Margarete Schütte-Lihotzky.

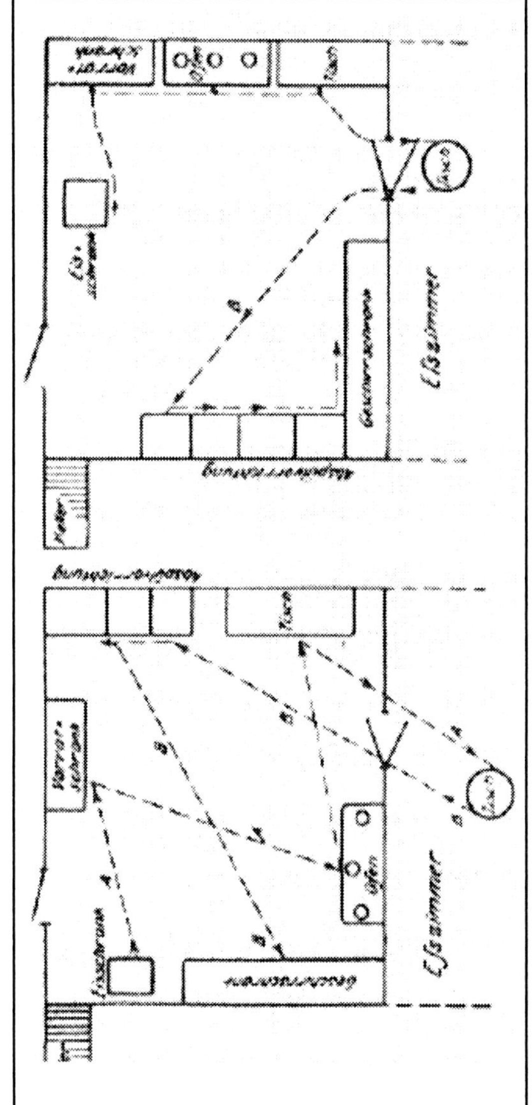

*Figure 11*
According to Schütte-Lihotzky, badly located kitchen cabinetry on the left and design with efficiently located cabinetry on the right.

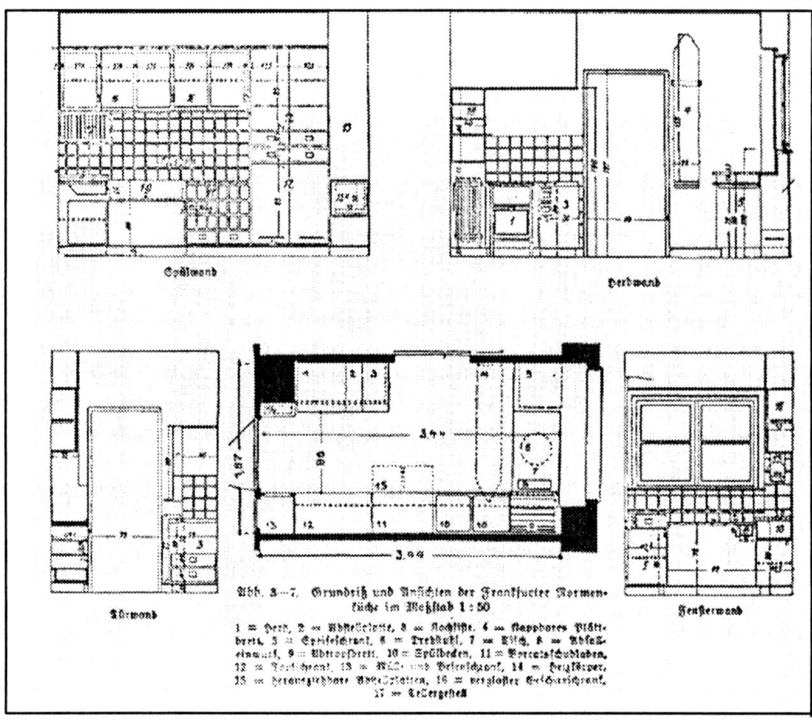


*Figure 12*
Schütte-Lihotzky's Frankfurt Kitchen: Plan and elevations.

*Figure 13*
Schütte-Lihotzky's Frankfurt Kitchen: Isometric.

*Figure 14*
Clemens Holzmeister.

*Figure 15*
Headquarters of Turkish Armed Forces General Staff, Ankara.

*Figure 16*
Presidential Residence. Atatürk personally invited Holzmeister to design Turkey's first Presidential residence.

*Figure 17*
The Central Bank, Ankara.

*Figure 18*
Bruno Taut.

*Figure 19*
Taut's *Glasspavillion*, Cologne.

*Figure 20*
Fountain of Sultan Abdülhamid I.

*Figure 21*
Entrance to the Dolmabahce Palace. The Palace was built between 1842 and 1853 on land reclaimed from the sea by Sultan Abdulmecid and designed by Nikogos Balyan, an Armenian architect and member of a three-generation dynasty designing monuments for the Ottomans.

# 4
# The Preservers

## Contributions to Turkey's Archeology

While architecture creates new edifices for a society, archeology attempts to preserve the remnants of cultures past. And while the Ottoman Empire could have rightfully boasted of having had excellent architects, such is not quite the case with archeologists. Yes, the Ottoman *Dar-ül Fünun* was familiar with archeology. Over the years, its faculty did teach archeology courses. However the Imperial Museum, now known as Istanbul's Museum of Archeology, founded by the artist and museum director *Osman Hamdi* and opened to public on June 13 1891 was more informed in this respect than the *Dar-ül Fünun*. Archeology was practiced there. Surely Turkey's republican fathers did not want to live in the past. They found much of their more recent cultural legacy ideologically repugnant. Nevertheless, they were convinced that all history needs to be discovered, preserved, and studied (Fig. 22).

Consequently, among the invitees, there were those whose mission would be to develop capabilities to do all this. Clearly, archeology as we know it today was a necessary discipline, but it was not sufficient for accomplishing the mission. This had been dealt with by including among the invitees many broad-gauged scientists who had demonstrated an ability to work both within and across traditional disciplines. The most senior of these were Assyriologist, *Benno Landsberger*[1] and Hittitologist *Hans Güterbock*. Many years later, Güterbock wrote that "Landsberger could keep his position in Leipzig because he fought in the front lines for Germany in WWI. Nevertheless in 1935 he was relieved of duties for 'racial' reasons."[2] Silesian native Benno Landsberger, born in *Friedek*, Czechoslovakia on April 21 1890, was the son of manufacturer Leopold Landsberger and his wife Hedwig (Hitschmann). He attended the local Gymnasium and, in 1908, entered the University of Leipzig to study Assyriology with Heinrich Zimmern and Arabic with August Fischer. He was drafted at the outbreak of WWI. Wounded on the Eastern front, he earned the Golden *Verdienstkreuz* while fighting in the Ukraine and was discharged in 1918. Landsberger went on to lay the foundations for the study of modern Assyriology, and, with his linguistic capabilities, he succeeded in freeing Assyriology from its dependence on the Arab and Hebrew languages. He attempted to characterize Mesopotamian culture on the basis of language, laws, literature, and economic and social culture rather than depending on the Bible. His genius found expression not only in his linguistic works but also in his penetrating and original analyses of critical questions of Mesopotamian history and chronology. His work in comparative semantics and lexicography hold special significance for Semitic history as well.

Although Landsberger passed away in 1968, decades before the emergence of the *World Wide Web*, his name pulls up dozens of references in this relatively new medium, and they appear in several languages. Even the Czech Moravians in America take pride in one of their own, Benno Landsberger.[3] Many websites discuss his work in Turkey. Landsberger started working in the *Language, History, and Geography* Faculty in Ankara. The Faculty had just been created and this scholar, forty-five at the time, played an active role in its establishment. In 1948, he was invited to teach at the Oriental Institute of the University of Chicago. He taught there until 1955 but continued his scholarly work after retirement. He passed away in Chicago April 26 1968. Hans Güterbock wrote the following of his teacher turned colleague: "Landsberger was a rare breed of scholar and he was the foremost representative of his branch. He had left a lasting impression on his students in Ankara. He concentrated all his energy to his students, to the point of neglecting his own studies; in return, they always maintained their gratitude and attachment to him."[4]

*Hans Güterbock* was born May 27 1908, in Berlin. Because his father served as secretary of the *Deutsche Orient Gesellschaft*, young Hans became interested in the languages and cultures of the ancient Near East. At first, he studied Hittitology, which was then an emerging discipline. The deciphering of Hittite records, written in cuneiform script, and the establishment of its place among the Indo-European language family were barely twenty years old at the time. Linguistic training and archaeological skills were essential for mastering the subject. Güterbock grew with the field and made important contributions to understanding this civilization born in Anatolia. He learned the ancient Near Eastern languages, including Sumerian and the Semitic Akkadian (which also used the cuneiform system of writing), on his own. Later, he studied Sumerian and Babylonian cuneiform texts with Benno Landsberger and Hittite with Johannes Friedrich in Leipzig. He received his Ph.D. from Leipzig University in the momentous year 1933. Güterbock was an archaeologist, philologist, and historian. Such a combination of disciplines in a single individual is rare in today's academic community. Current scholars find his greatest influence in the philological area, but he considered himself, and was proud to be, an archaeologist. An archaeologist of the old school, one who was well-versed in reading the inscriptions and tablets that archaeologists uncovered, he was his own epigrapher and was gifted with such keen eyesight that even his teacher, Benno Landsberger, made use of it when a particularly difficult-to-read photo of a tablet needed deciphering. This threefold combination was put to the task of "resurrecting the Hittites," as he himself described his career in the retrospective essay in *Civilizations of the Ancient Near East.*

In addition to studying the Hittite cuneifom texts, he made seminal contributions to the decipherment of the Indo-European dialect related to Hittite, known today as the Luwian language. Luwian was written in a unique hieroglyphic script on stone monuments as well as on seals. These seals, edited and interpreted by Güterbock in the two volumes of *Siegel aus Boghazkoy*, furnished the key to many a "Hittite" hieroglyph. Güterbock recognized early on the threads that connected the Hittite culture to the culture of other early Indo-European groups. With his edition of the myth of *Kumarbi*,[5] he laid the foundations for the comparison of Hurrian mythology with early Greek myths, especially as they are found in the works of Hesiod. Today, classicists take the Eastern influence on Greece for granted.

Güterbock "organized and led major archeological excavations in Anatolia before and during World War II"[6] and trained the first generation of Turkish Hittitologists and archaeologists. He followed Landsberger to Turkey in 1936. Having spent several seasons over there, Güterbock knew Turkey well. He worked with German excavation teams as epigrapher and archaeologist both. To the very end of his life, he was proud of this double career. His spoken and written Turkish were excellent. He was particularly proud of having written the guide to the Hittite Museum (now the Museum of Anatolian Civilizations) in both German and Turkish. After his Turkish contract was not renewed, Güterbock spent a year as guest lecturer at the Karolina University in Uppsala, Sweden, and followed Landsberger to Chicago. In Chicago, he was asked to teach courses in the history of the ancient Near East, a task he performed dutifully even though the field was not his primary interest. However, by doing this, he did exercise an important influence on young scholars.

During the latter part of his lifetime, Hans Gustav Güterbock received many honors. Among these was the Tiffany and Margaret Blake Distinguished Service Professor at the University of Chicago award in 1959. He served as president of the American Oriental Society in 1962 and of the American Research Institute in Turkey from 1968 to 1977. He was elected to membership in the Bavarian Academy of Sciences, the American Academy of Arts and Sciences, and the American Philosophical Society, and was a corresponding fellow of the British Academy. In 1996, he became the second person to receive the American Oriental Society Medal of Merit in recognition of his lifetime contributions to the field of Hittitology. Established in 1985, the award was designed to be given infrequently and only for work of particularly outstanding quality. Hans Gustav Güterbock died on March 29 2000.

In 2002, a book was published titled *Recent Developments in Hittite Archaeology and History: Papers in Memory of Hans G. Güterbock*. The book was edited by University of Chicago professors K. Aslihan Yener and Harry A. Hoffner. The reviews it received speak for themselves. Two are below:

> (T)he volume is a valuable overview in English of the state of the field and is therefore essential reading for specialists in Anatolian studies and related fields."
> —Billie Jean Collins, Emory University, in *Religious Studies Review* 30/1 January 2004

> This book collects presentations delivered in 1997 at the Hittite sessions of the American Oriental Society meeting in Miami. It is dedicated to the memory of Hans Gustav Güterbock, whose recent death is a great loss to science. He will be remembered not only for his work but also for his human qualities and his generosity."
> —Stefano de Martino, University of Trieste, *JAOS* 123.4, 2003

In addition, the émigré "archeology" team in Turkey included *Walter Kranz*, classical philology, and *Fritz Kraus*, Assyriologist and student of *Benno Landsberger* at the Universität Leipzig, who worked in Turkey from 1937 to 1950 as expert preservationist in the Istanbul Archeological Museum and professor at the University. His Austrian citizenship was revoked by the *Generalkonsulat* in 1942. In 1954, Kraus accepted an invitation from Holland's University of Leiden.

According to contemporary Assyriologist/historian Bertrand Lafont, the Istanbul Archaeological Museum is quantitatively much richer than the Louvre in cuneiform tablets dating to the third millennium. The beginnings of the cuneiform tablets collection in Istanbul go back to the creation of the Ottoman Imperial Museum and to the implementation of the Turkish Law on Antiquities of 1883 that claimed for this Museum all the antiquities discovered on the territory of the Ottoman Empire. The first cuneiform tablets reached the Museum in 1890.[7]

It is noteworthy that since the end of the First World War and the subsequent creation of the Turkish Republic, these tablet collections in Istanbul did not increase in numbers. First attempts to classify the tablets took place before 1920. But it was only with the arrival of Fritz Kraus in 1937 that a real inventory and classification work could begin on the museum collections. Kraus dedicated ten years of his life to this job before going to Leiden. He stayed in Istanbul at the same time that Landsberger was teaching in Ankara.

On the whole, according to Kraus himself, "the number of cuneiform tablets in the Istanbul collection, deriving from 12 different sites, comprises 75,000 exemplars. Of that number, 40,000 tablets and fragments come from the single site of Tello. But we must admit that most of these Tello tablets are today in a fragmentary state, some indeed very small. The reason for this is that theses documents, notably the great number of Tello's large multiple-column tablets seem to have suffered substantially from the attempts of conservators in the 1930s to preserve them through baking."

War-time military service at times influences future career choices. While serving the German Army in Istanbul and on the Iraq and Palestine fronts during World War I, *Helmut Ritter*,[8] became interested in studying the Orient. Born in *Hessich-Lichtenau*, Germany, in 1892, Ritter became Professor of Oriental Languages in 1919 at the University of Hamburg. He was a member of that faculty until 1926 when he decided to go to Turkey to buy books for the German Oriental Society. While there, he founded the *German Archaeological Institute* in Istanbul and served as its Director, and founded the *International Oriental Society* and published its journal *Oriens*. In 1935, he became Professor of Arabic, Turkish, and Persian Philology at the University of Istanbul. He stayed in those posts until 1948 when he returned to Germany as professor of Eastern Languages at the University of Frankfurt. After retirement from Frankfurt, he returned to Turkey to continue his research at Istanbul University's Institute of Oriental Studies.[9] Staying in Turkey while the Nazis reigned in his native land saved his life not only because he was Jewish but also because he was openly homosexual.[10]

The numismatic expert at the Istanbul Archeological Museum between 1935 and 1940, *Clemens Bosch*, was forced out from his position at *Halle/Saale* University's Archeological Institute because his wife was not Aryan. So he came to Turkey with wife and five children where he remained until death in 1955. From 1940 to 1955, he was Professor of Ancient History at the University of Istanbul.

The years 1947 and 1948 were bad years for those émigré scholars who studied the ancients but who were not museum-connected. No matter how senior they were in the academic community worldwide and regardless of how much they contributed to building Turkish institutions and curricula, most did not get their contracts renewed.

The July 17 1948, edition of *ULUS*, a Turkish newspaper, carried an article titled "Our Universities." The article said:

> The budget for our students has been enlarged. This has been achieved by cutting down on the expenses of foreign professors. The tenure of these professors has been terminated in order to confirm our entrenchment:
> Prof. Landsberger: Sumerian studies
> Prof. Güterbock: Hittitology
> Prof. Eberhard: Sinology
> Prof. Halasi-Kuhn: Hungarian studies
> Prof. Ruben: Hindology
> Lecturer: Eckman

Except for *Halasi-Kuhn,* who returned to Hungary, and Lecturer *Eckman,* ultimately the rest found a good home in the West and continued to flourish. The worthiness of these men's achievements to society is clearly visible and justifiably appreciated.

### Introducing Library Science, Librarianship, and Document Preservation

The work of the archivist and the librarian is just as important as that of the archeologist. However, librarians are not accorded the respect or the salaries they deserve. This very book could not have passed the idea stage were it not for a score or more of archivists and librarians spread over three continents. More globally, for many excellent reasons, a modern society's need for such experts was not neglected by those representing Ankara in Basel, Switzerland, in 1933. *Philipp Schwarz* did collect a team of expert librarians, archivists, document preservators, and bookbinders. All these conservators of knowledge and wisdom that had been gathered by generations past and present were ready and willing to oblige. The opportunity presented them was literally a gift of life. They knew it all too well.

"The German librarians…contributed greatly to the organization of a modern European university system in Turkey," according to German library scientist Hildegard Müller, writing in the highly regarded University of Texas Press journal, *Libraries & Culture*. "From a mere quantitative point of view, this emigration to Turkey certainly does not rank first, but seen from a qualitative point of view, that is, the importance it had for their country of adoption, it is surely the case that it was of primary importance."[11]

Among the senior members of the library contingent was *Walter Gottschalk.* He was born in 1891 in Aachen and studied orientalism, philosophy, history, and the history of art in Wurzburg and Berlin. He was granted a Ph.D. in 1914. In 1916, Gottschalk was drafted to serve Germany in WWI. His postings were in Turkey, Syria, and Palestine. At war's end in 1919, he joined the staff of the Prussian State Library in Berlin as senior librarian for language and history of the Middle East. Gottschalk made significant contributions in establishing that library's Oriental Department. Specifically, he organized the department's reference library and a precise catalogue. His work was acknowledged by a major promotion in 1923. However, in 1935, he was dismissed because of Jewish origins and forced into retirement. He managed to find work in the field of science and give lectures such as introduction to Arabic.

By February 1939, he had to leave Germany altogether and he went to Belgium to stay with relatives. While in Belgium, Gottschalk served as a personal go-between for Albert Einstein himself, primarily for the purpose of funneling small monthly stipends from America to Einstein's relatives who were left behind in Nazi Germany. These days we might call it money laundering. Then, in May 1940, the Germans occupied Belgium and Gottschalk started once again to look for escape alternatives. In 1941, he came to Turkey where he was asked to work for Istanbul University as an expert on library matters. Connected with this was the supervision of all the libraries in the various university institutes. He also "played a prominent part in the development of the Turkish library system...."[12]

From approximately 1949 onward, Gottschalk held a chair of Library Science at Istanbul University. Gottschalk lived in Istanbul until his retirement in 1954. He then returned to Germany and settled in Frankfurt. After Gottschalk's departure, the chair in Library Science at Istanbul University was awarded to his assistant, Dr. *Rudolf Juchhoff*[13] who held it until 1968 and was succeeded by Meral Alpay, a Turkish native and an assistant to Dr. Juchhoff.

The senior librarians who emigrated to Turkey were joined by junior colleagues, bookbinders, and restorers. In particular, these skilled and well-trained refugees constructed corresponding bookbinding and restoration departments, and it is to their credit that many Turkish scholars and pupils would be trained. In so doing, the émigrés helped to conserve cultural riches accumulated throughout the Ottoman period and some preceding it. Their efforts made such documents and artifacts accessible for all future generations. Also among the German-speaking librarians brought to Turkey was an Austrian, Dr. *Joseph Stummvoll*. Unlike Gottschalk, Stummvoll worked as librarian at the newly founded *Yuksek Ziraat Enstitusu*, (University for Agriculture and Veterinary Science) in Ankara. While there, he contributed a number of articles on library systems and conducted many training courses for Turkish librarians outside of Istanbul, Turkey's most developed and cosmopolitan city then and now.

Dr. *Max Pfannenstiel was* born in Alsace in 1902. After his studies in geology and mineralogy, he worked at the University library in Freiburg and from 1930 to 1932 at the Bavarian State Library in Munich, where he sat for his qualifying examinations. In January 1933, he returned to the University library in Freiburg and, in August of that same year, he was deemed "non-Aryan." Although the director of his library, Josef Rest, interceded with the Ministry of Education, pointing out that Pfannenstiel was only part-Jewish (his grandfather on his mother's side was a Jew), he was nevertheless dismissed on October 12 1933. Unemployed, he looked for work that would present some scientific attributes. From January 1934 to March 1935, he worked in a medical bookshop. Following that, he received a small grant from the "Society of German Natural Scientists and Doctors" to concentrate on various estates. Finally, in February 1935, he managed to obtain a Rockefeller Scholarship and a modest librarian position with the League of Nations in Geneva. While there, he built up that Library's medical department.[14]

As it turns out, on January 19 1938, the Turkish Minister of Science and Education wrote to his colleague in *Baden* that the Director of Libraries position at the University of Agriculture and Veterinary Science in Ankara was vacant. Through the German embassy, the Minister had heard that Pfannenstiel was interested in that position. The embassy, however, advised that, "it is not in the interest of Germany, for political-cultural reasons, that Dr. Pfannenstiel be given this job in Ankara." Germany's official position on the matter notwithstanding, on April 15 1938, Pfannenstiel became Library Director at the University of Agriculture and Veterinary Science in Ankara. It did not take long for him to start researching Turkey's geological formations and writing articles on the subject.

From 1940, Pfannenstiel worked for *Türk Tarih Kurumu*, the Turkish Historical Society, where he catalogued Atatürk's library that was bequeathed to the Society.[15] Pfannenstiel's contract with the Turkish government ended in August of 1941 and, due to political and wartime pressures, was not renewed. Pfannenstiel never gave up his contacts with Freiburg University's Library and unlike his fellow émigrés, at all times he looked for a way to return to a German library, under a loophole in the civil service law.

On June 16 1939, he had actually applied through the German embassy in Ankara. Josef Rest, Freiburg's Library Director, unconditionally supported his former staff member's return. Other former colleagues reacted similarly except for one; at the time and in Germany "highly esteemed" Herr Dr. Professor *Julius Ludwig Wilser* the sitting Director of Heidelberg University's Geological-Palaeontologic Institute. He can be quoted as writing the following about Dr. Max Pfannenstiel his former University of Freiburg colleague.

> *A Jew remains a Jew!*
> *And further, he was part of a decidedly Jewish set in Freiburg, which had had a hostile attitude toward National Socialism. Even if Dr. Pfannenstiel tried to change himself inwardly and outwardly, he remains by blood a half-Jew and does not belong to a community whose aim it is to fulfill the mission set for us by the Fuhrer. German civil servants are brothers-in-arms of Adolf Hitler!*[16]

This is just one example of what happened at Heidelberg, until then among the world's premiere universities. In a matter of months, if not weeks, following passage of the Civil Service Law in 1933, it, too, had been Nazified, and taken over by the likes of *Ludwig Wilser*. Sadly, Heidelberg was not the only previously great German university to become so politicized, nor was Herr Dr. Professor Julius Ludwig Wilser the only academic who jumped on the Nazi's bandwagon and beat their drums. As will be shown some Nobel laureates acted no differently than did Wilser.

> The conduct of German intellectuals—seen as a group—was no better than that of the mob.
> —Albert Einstein, January 28, 1949. Letter to Otto Hahn, Einstein Archive 12-072.

Pfannenstiel returned to Germany and, using the law's loophole, he again became a German civil servant. Pfannenstiel worked in the Erlangen University library until 1947 at which time he was offered a geology chair in Freiburg, and, in 1954, became chancellor of that university. In 1976, he died in Freiburg.[17]

Adding to the above contributions, "In 1935, *Helmut Ritter,* Oriental scholar, at the University of Istanbul set up a 'library expertise' in his function as president of a reform commission."[18] So there is no question that the German-speaking professors advanced libraries and librarianship in Turkey. They achieved this through donating their own books, arranging for book and document donations from American and British universities, through public lectures, in-residence workshops, expansion of old and creation of new institutes, publication of modern style manuals, and launching of scientific journals. These are some of the prerequisites for teaching and doing scientific work.

These émigré senior librarians, their junior colleagues, and the restoration experts, created several facilities for document restoration and bookbinding in both Istanbul and Ankara. Not only did these men and women do their jobs well, but they also taught the next generation and generously shared their skills and their knowledge.

### Translating the Classics of Western Literature into Turkish and Introducing Philology

In the early 1930s, *Georg Rohde* and *Hasan-Ali Yücel*, the Turkish Minister of Education, organized a monumental program for translating the major works of classical (Greek and Roman) and general European literature into the Turkish language. Between 1940 and 1950, no fewer than 76 literary works were translated from German as part of this program, 180 from French, 46 from English, 64 from Russian, and 13 from Italian. Moreover, 28 major works were translated from Latin, 76 from Ancient Greek, and 23 from Persian and Arabic.[19] They were published by the Turkish Ministry of Education[20] and remain in print to this very day.

> There was no philology; in this country, we kept going on to Osman Hamdi all the time. (Osman Hamdi, founder of the Imperial Museum, also a painter, etc.) He knew neither Semitic languages, nor Greek, nor did he know epigraphy. These are very important subjects that were first looked at in the 1930s. Today, Turkey is a country that has a say in the areas of Assyriology and Sumerology. Some Turkish specialisits, those of our generation and even younger, are pioneer Hittitologists. All this was not possible before 1933. That someone would be able to sit down and read Assyrian texts in this country, this was impossible. Then of course, another important development was the initiation of classical philology. Rohde came and started Latin and Greek.[21] In addition to translating the classics, Rohde and his students also published a number of Latin texts for use at the secondary school level.

Georg Rohde was born in Berlin in 1899. He had been appointed Privat Dozent at Marburg University in 1931 where he taught classic philology. Relieved of duties because his wife was Jewish, he came to Turkey in 1935 and was appointed Professor of Philology of Ancient Languages at Ankara University. In that capacity, he taught the famous Turkish archaeologist and author, *Ekrem Akurgal*, in addition to training a generation of philologists[22] before leaving for West Germany in 1949 (Fig. 23).[23]

> *Erich Auerbach's* "work is a strikingly successful combination of philology, stylistics, history of ideas, and sociology, of meticulous learning and artistic taste, of historical imagination, and awareness of our own age."[24]

German philologist, educator, critic, and literary historian Erich Auerbach was born in Berlin into an upper-middle class Jewish family in 1892. He studied at the universities of Berlin, Freiburg, and Munich. In 1913, Auerbach received a Doctor of Law degree from the University of Heidelberg. During the First World War, he served in Germany's army. After the war, Auerbach changed disciplines and received a Ph.D. in Romance philology from the University of Greifswald in 1921. Between 1923 and 1929, he was librarian at the Prussian State Library in Berlin, and, in 1929, he went on to become professor of Romance philology at the University of Marburg.

In Marburg, Auerbach gained recognition with his work, *Dante: Poet of the Secular World* (1929). Dismissed in 1935, he went to Istanbul where he taught at Istanbul University until 1947. During his years in Turkey, Auerbach wrote his famous work, *Mimesis*, which was first published in German in 1946 and seven years later in English. It represents an account of the genesis of the novel. Since its appearance, *Mimesis* has been among the most widely read scholarly works on literary history and criticism. The famous Harvard scholar Edward Said provides the following interpretation on the genesis of *Mimesis*:

> The book owed its existence to the very fact of Oriental, non-Occidental exile and homelessness. And if this is so, then *Mimesis* itself is not, as it has so frequently been taken to be, only a massive reaffirmation of the western cultural tradition, but also a work built upon a critically important alienation from it, a work whose conditions and circumstances of existence are not immediately derived from the culture it describes with such extraordinary insight and brilliance but built rather on an agonizing distance from it.[25]

Regarding the limited European studies collections of Istanbul libraries at the time and not having access to all the literature he needed, Auerbach quipped, "On the other hand, it is quite possible that the book owes its existence to just this lack of a rich and specialized library. If it had been possible for me to acquaint myself with all the work that has been done on so many subjects, I might never have reached the point of writing."[26]

Two smaller studies dating from this period appeared in Finland's *Neuphilologische Mitteilungen* journal. In 1947, Auerbach moved to the United States. He taught at Pennsylvania State University and was a member of the Institute for Advanced Study at Princeton before being appointed Professor of Romance philology at Yale University in 1950. Auerbach died in Wallingford, Connecticut, on October 13 1957, but his writings are still being taught worldwide to all those who seek a well-rounded education.[27]

## Making Turkology an Academic Discipline in Turkey

*Andreas Tietze,* world-renowned Turkologist, was born in Vienna on April 26 1914. The son of prominent art historians Hans Tietze and Erica Conrad-Tietze, he studied history and languages at the University of Vienna starting 1932 and received his doctorate in 1937 - for Austria, a year of note. A diary (*Unsere* und *Die Zweite Anatolienreise)* kept by one of his companions concerning two trips that Tietze made to Anatolia between 1936 and 1937 with *Robert Anhegger,* remains one of perhaps just two firsthand accounts by foreign visitors of life as lived in the countryside outside of Istanbul and Ankara in those early days of the Turkish Republic. A photocopy of Tietze's diary now resides in the archives of the *International Institute of Social History* in Amsterdam.

At the time of Austria's Anschluss, Tietze moved to Istanbul. There he was a Lecturer in German from 1938 to 1952 and a Lecturer in English from 1953 to 1958. In addition to his teaching, he was the editor of a series of 16 titles, *Istanbuler Schriften,* that included his first reader for foreign students of Turkish, *Türkisches Lesebuch für Auslaender* (Istanbul, 1943), written jointly with *Sura Lisiev.* Tietze was also active in the field of folklore as co-editor and contributing translator on the orientalist, *Helmut Ritter's* monumental three-volume study of Turkey's shadow puppet theater, *Karagöz: Türkische Schattenspiele* (Hanover, 1924-53). It was during this time that he became deeply involved in lexicography. He prepared a Turkish-German dictionary (*Türkçe-Almanca Sözlügü*) with Ritter, and, from 1946 to 1958, he directed the American Board Publication Office project involving the revision of the original *Redhouse English-Turkish Dictionary* of 1861 and the companion *Redhouse Turkish-English Dictionary* of 1890. Both works, now further updated, remain indispensable to students of Turkish and vice versa of Turks studying English.

With the scholars Henry and Renée Kahane, Tietze also co-authored an etymological dictionary of Turkish nautical terms of Italian and Greek origin, *The Lingua Franca in the Levant* (University of Illinois Press, 1958).

This work aimed to demonstrate the linguistic-cultural unity of the Mediterranean area. In 1958, he came to UCLA and is considered "one of the founders of Turkic studies in the United States." "Professor Tietze was best known for his contributions to Turkish lexicography, his work on Turkish riddles and Turkish *Karagöz* (Blackeye) plays, his editions and translations of Ottoman works, and his founding and editorship of an annual bibliography covering all aspects of Turkish and Ottoman life. He was also a translator of modern fiction, from German to Turkish, Turkish to German, and Azerbaijani to Turkish"[28]

While at UCLA, Professor Tietze authored numerous scholarly articles and continued his research on folklore. Comparing the oldest collection of Turkish riddles, those found in a section of the 14th-century document known as the *Codex Cumanicus,* (a Latin guide to the Cuman tongue) with related riddles from other Turkic sources, he described a new vision of this early codex in *The Koman Riddles and Turkic Folklore* (University of California Press, 1966). With the folklorist *Ilhan Basgöz,* he compiled *Bilmece: A Corpus of Turkish Riddles,* a large collection of the genre based on the efforts of several leading scholars (University of California Press, 1973). With his colleague, *Avedis K. Sanjian,* Professor of Armenian, he edited *Eremya Chelebi Kömürjian's Armeno-Turkish Poem "The Jewish Bride"* (Budapest, 1981), a 17th-century work significant for its revelations about the Turkish spoken in Istanbul in the second half of that century and about the relations between the different religious communities in the turbulent period following the appearance of the self-styled Jewish Messiah, *Sabbatai Sevi.*

Throughout his tenure at UCLA, Professor Tietze was instrumental in building up the Turkish and Ottoman books and manuscripts collections at the Young Research Library. By making it one of the largest repositories of such works in the United States, Tietze enabled America's young scholars to learn about Turkey's cultural heritage.[29]

Professor of Roman and Comparative Philology at Cologne University *Leo Spitzer* was released in 1933 for the usual and customary reasons. During that year, he was offered the position of Professor of Roman Languages and Literatures at Istanbul University. There he was first to introduce courses on philology and to establish the university's School of Foreign Languages. When he re-emigrated to the US in 1936 with a job at Baltimore's prestigious Johns Hopkins University, his institution-building work was taken on by *Erich Auerbach.*

Recently retired Turkish professor *Aykut Kazancıgil,* a physician and translator of several books into Turkish, including the one on émigré professors by Horst Widman, wrote the following about *Wolfram Eberhard*: He "had about 689 publications. I collected all of these and included them in my new book *Chinese Symbols*. For example, he liked *Halit Ziya*

[Uşaklıgil, A Turkish author of fiction] a lot. He published the Journal of Sociology in Germany. He even made *Sait Faik* [Abasıyanık, writer of very modern stories] a known name in America. Yes, these men created a scientific whirlwind in Turkey. It can be asked what is our gain from them. Under no conditions will I say that it was negative. We benefited from them as much as we were able to."[30] However, Eberhard's contract was not renewed in 1948. He joined the University of California and shifted from sinology to sociology. "The change was not as drastic as it appears, for Eberhard had always been interested in the sociological aspects of Chinese culture. As a sinologist he stressed cultural factors, and as a sociologist he drew examples from Chinese societies."[31]

Thus, well over four centuries after the Jews exiled from Spain introduced the first printing press to the Ottoman Empire,[32] Jewish refugees from fascism were instrumental in introducing philology, making Turkology an Academic Discipline in Turkey, and having a large body of western thought translated into Turkish and printed using the newly created Turkish alphabet. However, the translations program flew in the face of the prevailing Turkish nationalist fervor. Consequently, 1941 to date, every edition of every translated book published by the Education Ministry has in its Foreword *Hasan-Ali Yücel's* argument that "the wealthier a nation's library of translations is, the higher its status among the nations of the civilized world." [33]

## Introducing Botany and Zoology as Research Disciplines and as Conservation Professions

While working in West Anatolia, zoologist *Curt Kosswig* discovered an area at the edge of Lake *Manyas* that is now known as *Kuş Cenneti* (Birds' Heaven). It is a nesting location of major importance for migratory birds. He also discovered the area in *Birecik* where the *Kelaynak* (bald ibis) birds nest. These finds are widely considered to be of worldwide importance. Subsequent work by Kosswig and his wife, Leonore, was instrumental in having Lake Manyas declared a national and international nature preserve. The "Birds' Heaven" is one of the most important worldwide natural reserves for migratory birds and for wildfowl.[35] Additionally, through the efforts of Professor Kosswig, the Institute of Hydrobiology at *Baltalimanı*, a part of the Faculty of Science, was established in 1950 (Fig. 24 and 25).

The émigré botanists and zoologists proved to be as much conservators of Nature's treasures as they were scientists trying to understand her secrets. In 1935, *Andre Neville* together with Botanist Prof. Dr. *Alfred Heilbronn* and Prof. Dr. *Leo Brauner* established Turkey's first Zoology Museum. It was initially located on the same floor as the zoology department within the Faculty of Science building. Some birdcages and singing birds were brought from the *Yildiz* Palace in Istanbul. Others were obtained as gifts from France and Germany.[36]

While practicing preservation of Nature's treasures, Professor Curt Kosswig also made significant contributions to medical science. If a cure for cancer is ever found, one of Kosswig's discoveries will have played a role. Justus Liebig is on record in the *Genetisches Institut* that "modern cancerology is based on the oncogene concept. This is rather new. The idea of the oncogene, however, is old, and can be traced back to two sources, namely to 'cancer families,' reported in 1866 by P. Broka, and to 'virus–induced' neoplasia, detected by P. Rous in 1911." Liebig goes on to say that to the best of his knowledge "a gene which is the first reported oncogene by definition was detected in the little ornamental Mexican fish Xiphophorus by Myron Gordon, *Curt Kosswig,* and Georg Haussler in 1928 when they observed the terrible hereditary melanomas *that we are now coming to understand and compare with other kinds of neoplasms in Xiphophorus and in mammals, including humans.* Although the Xiphophorus model was always modest in its claims, it has—sometimes too early in its history—contributed many facts to the present concept of neoplasia."[37] (emphasis added)

During Kosswig's sojourn in Turkey, he was widely considered to be the leading, if not the only, scientific authority for zoology in the country and he greatly enlarged the collections of its Zoological Museum. But Kosswig's contributions ranged beyond zoology and conservation. An educator, he proved to be a skilled administrator and institution builder, and, as a man of conviction, he acted as a cross-regional diplomat on behalf of science. He served in Turkey between 1937 and 1954.

His scientific achievements were broad and deep. While researching the various cancer indicators found in a given species of fish, he created a taxonomic approach to zoology and encouraged its use and expanded applications. A geneticist and zoologist, his most important scientific contributions are in mechanisms of sex determination, carcinogenesis, regressive and constructive evolution, the genetics of domestic animals, faunal history, zoogeography, and the rarely mentioned field of *systematics.* Kosswig's ideas and concepts as well as the results of his research are indeed of crucial importance to *biological systematics.* As part of his tribute to Kosswig, German Professor Wolfgang Villwock pointed out that "scientific answers to questions posed in the specialized disciplines" of zoogeography and faunal history, require a "comprehensive and detailed analysis of faunal diversity based on a reliable phylogenetic taxonomic system."[38]

In 1932, Kosswig took the "Extraordinariat" for Zoology at the Technical University of Braunschweig and a year later was appointed director of the Natural History Museum in that city. After 1933, he refused to dismiss Jewish employees and to sever relations with scientists and friends forced to emigrate. Eventually, he himself felt threatened and had to flee Braunschweig. Kosswig emigrated to Turkey in 1937. Shortly after being appointed Professor of Zoology in the fall of 1937, he mastered the Turkish language and lectured future biologists and medical doctors on the foundations of natural science. He published several textbooks in Turkish for both university and high school students. One of these books went through five revised and upgraded editions. He founded the magazine "*Bioloji*" aimed at the general public. Besides enlarging the Institute of Zoology, in 1950, Kosswig established the Institute of Hydrobiology that became a center for fisheries research. Eventually a seagoing research vessel was acquired as well. Perhaps the best example of his scientific drive and his diplomatic skill was his success, in spite of strong (political) tensions after the second World War, to forge cooperation and to extend research on the zoogeography of Anatolia to the entire Near East. Kosswig received the "Distinguished Service Medal" from the Federal Government of Germany and a similar medal in 1981 from the Government of Turkey on the occasion of Atatürk's 100th birthday

During the course of a 2001 Istanbul aquaculture development workshop, *Isik Oray*, a Turkish native, and *Harald Rosenthal*, a German, reminisced about their graduate studies at Hamburg University and instructors they had had in common. It dawned on them that the 20th anniversary of their beloved Professor Kosswig's death was but a few months away. The idea to honor him was born there and then. The occasion envisaged should stress "the achievements of this outstanding science teacher and internationally widely recognized scientist jointly with his former Turkish and German students."[39] A quick, albeit informal, opinion survey of Turkish colleagues who were also former Kosswig students about organizing a joint Memorial Symposium to be held in Turkey was well received. Back in Germany, Rosenthal presented a proposal to *Wolfgang Villwock,*[40] Kosswig's student in Hamburg, to serve as co-chair of the Symposium along with Isik Oray. Villwock accepted. The Symposium was to serve the entire zoological science community in Turkey as well as attract former Kosswig students from throughout the world albeit predominantly from Germany and Austria. Because of logistical problems, however, it was decided to celebrate the 100$^{th}$ anniversary of Kosswig's birthday—in Istanbul during October 2003. Cosponsors of the event were the Hamburg Zoological Museum and Institute,[41] University of Hamburg, and the University of Istanbul. "In October 2003, more than twenty German colleagues, and students," as well as several of Kosswig's "quasi-scientific grandchildren" traveled to Istanbul to jointly celebrate this special event with their Turkish counterparts.[42]

The symposium proceedings were published in 2004 by the *Hamburg Zoological Museum and Institute.* In addition to having twenty refereed scientific papers, there are also three testimonial and/or biographical contributions. There is a three-page foreword by Villwock in German. He also has a shorter version in English. There is the official Memorial speech by Professor Fischer-Appelt. Some part of his speech deals with the general scientific and cultural climate in Turkey before 1933. And there is a paper by Professor *Michael Dzwillo* on "The relevance of Curt Kosswig's scientific achievements to systematic zoology." Written in English, it shows that while in Turkey, Kosswig did a great deal of work on zoogeography of cyprinodontid fishes (killifishes, pupfishes, and toothcarps) of Anatolia.

Kosswig, while in Turkey, also expanded his fields of scientific inquiry to include the faunal history and biogeography of Anatolia and the Middle East. He particularly focused on species of freshwater fish in an area of overlapping bio-geographical regions. Kosswig's studies of cyprinodontids of Anatolia turned out to be especially valuable because they yielded results the relevance of which extended far beyond regional faunal problems. Based on these investigations into cyprinodontids, Kosswig initiated a substantial research program into the faunal history and biogeography of the entire Middle East. Understandably, a project of this scale was beyond the capacities of a single group to tackle. Only international cooperation with competent experts promised to disentangle the complexities of the zoogeography and faunal history of the Middle East. At this point, Kosswig skillfully demonstrated his talents for encouraging specialists of important taxa to contribute to the investigation of the local fauna that is characterized by elements of different faunal regions.

Thanks to his academic reputation and his diplomatic talents, Kosswig, in 1951, managed to organize a UNESCO-funded international symposium on zoogeography of the Middle East at University of Istanbul's hydro-biological institute (UNESCO 1954) which had only recently been founded by him. Even in those days of high political tension, Kosswig succeeded in initiating fruitful cooperation and stimulating exchange of ideas between zoologists from Turkey, Israel, Egypt, Iraq, and Lebanon as well as from Italy and England. In the years and decades following this symposium, Kosswig collected comprehensive zoological material of many different taxa and, together with precise data on the exact localities of collection, passed it on to specialists and museums of natural history for systematic research.

In 1950, Kosswig described some new *Teleost* species. It is also worth noting that he supported researchers from different countries while collecting and working in Turkey. Many general species and subspecies were named after Kosswig, thus demonstrating the degree to which his contributions were appreciated by zoologists in the field of systematics. Among these are: Kosswigius Verhoeff, 1941 Isopoda, Kosswigichthys Sozer, 1942 Cyprinodontidae, Kosswigia Jeannel, 1947 Coleoptera, Kosswigibilis Chamberlin, 1952 Chilopoda, and Kosswigianella Wagner, 1962.

Curt Kosswig felt especially attached to Turkey. In a short time, he learned the language very well. And he returned to live in Turkey at retirement after fifteen years as Hamburg University's Ordinarius professor following the war.[43] Fortunately, for Turkey's *Üniversite Reformu* and the intellectual ferment it created, Kosswig was accompanied in his work by other life scientists.

Botanist *Gustav Gassner,* one of the pioneers of wood science, was professor of botany at the Braunschweig Technical *Hochschule* (today Technical University). In 1932, elected its rector, he became involved in a conflict between the *Hochschule* and Braunschweig's provincial administration that, starting 1930/1931, was already in Nazi Party hands. This was about two years before Hitler's seizure of power in January 1933. In March of 1932, the local Nazi government dismissed Gassner[44] from rectorship and imprisoned him for 11 days. On September 30 1933, this was followed with dismissal as professor of botany.[45] Between 1934 and 1939, Gassner served as one of the émigré professors at Ankara University and as director of plant preservation in the government's agriculture department. He was an acknowledged expert and scientist. His book, *Microscopic Examinations of Plant Food* was republished in 1989.[46]

Gassner's return to Germany in 1939 had been facilitated by a Gestapo clearance. As a matter of significance to be explored later, after returning, he published a scientific paper. His scientific collaborator and coauthor during the midst of the war was *Dr. Friedrich (Fritz) Christiansen-Weniger* a German agricultural scientist who worked in Ankara for roughly seven years. After much deliberation, Germany's embassy in Ankara cleared his return as well. Christiansen-Weniger left Turkey in 1940 to take up a research and consulting position in Nazi-occupied Poland.

Gustav Gassner was also a close friend and colleague of zoologist Curt Kosswig.[47] Soon after émigré zoologist *Andre Neville's* death of typhus on April 1 1937, Prof. Dr. Curt Kosswig was appointed Professor of Zoology in the fall of 1937. Although not particularly happy with Germany's political climate, Kosswig was not among those who had to leave or die. There is reason to suspect that Kosswig[48] heard about the position having been opened or was offered this position while still in Braunschweig. Was Gassner instrumental? Although there is no definitive answer to that question, circumstantial archival evidence suggests such to be the case (Fig. 26).

*Alfred Heilbron* founded modern botanics in Turkey.[49]

Professor Heilbron was born in Furth, Bavaria, in 1885. Starting as a Dozent at the University of Münster in 1912, he was promoted to Professor of Botany in 1919. Between 1919 and 1933, he also served as Director of the Münster *Farmabotanik* Institute. With wife and three children, Heilbronn came to Turkey in the first wave of German émigré professors.

Professor Heilbron was forced to take refuge in Switzerland with his colleagues *Leo Brauner* and *Andre Neville*. These valuable scientists came to Istanbul in October 1933 on Atatürk's personal invitation. They started to give courses in botany and zoology in the Biology Institute as the school was then called. From the first day he started lecturing in Istanbul, Heilbron hoped to establish a botanical garden under University auspices. The construction of the Institute building was started in 1934 on the campus of the Istanbul Girls High School that belonged to the Istanbul *Müftülüğü* (Directorate of Religious Affairs) and Heilbron was assigned the job to found its botanical garden. He was supported in this effort by German garden specialists *Leo Brauner* and *Walter Stephan*.

Founded in 1973, and starting with a Faculty of Agriculture, the *Cukurova* University in Adana, Turkey, maintains a website discussing all aspects of plant science. Referring to the above émigrés, the site states, "these three men and their entourage worked in such a systematic and disciplined manner that the botanical garden was ready to be opened in the spring of 1936. Another great attainment of these three is the first seed catalogue of the botanical garden published in 1935." The site goes on to point out that "this first seed catalogue of the Istanbul University Plant Garden (*Hortus Botanicus Istanbuensis: Index Seminum*), simple yet very valuable, includes an introduction by *A. Heilbron, L. Brauner*, and Garden Specialist *W. Stephan* describing the objectives of the garden. The first attempt to set up a botanical garden in Turkey was in about 1949 with the establishment of an Arboretum in Bahçeköy near Istanbul with the support of the University of Istanbul Faculty of Forestry." However, the site laments the fact that "in spite of the rich biodiversity and high number of species both in flora and fauna in Turkey, the number of botanical gardens are [still] quite few."[50]

Botanist *Ludwig Schnee* who was born in 1908 was also part of the life-science team in Turkey between 1933 and 1938 after being discharged from the *Universität Köln*. Both he and his wife worked in the Institut for Pharmabotaniks and Genetics at the University of Istanbul. They left Turkey for Venezuela in 1938.

On arrival at the University of Istanbul in 1933, after being discharged as Professor of Botany from *Jena* University, Leo Brauner became professor of Botany and first Director of the Botanical Physiology Institute.

In addition to inviting those who needed a safe haven from the Nazis during the prewar period, Turkey also invited German-Jewish scholars who were settled elsewhere. *Frederick Simon Bodenheimer* was brought in from the Hebrew University of Jerusalem. "While serving as visiting professor and founder of the department of agricultural entomology at the University of Ankara, he [Bodenheimer] wrote four textbooks that were translated and published in the Turkish language: two on entomology, one in zoology, and one in beekeeping, plus a surprise bonus in the form of a fifth book in Hebrew on Turkish folk art."[51] Bodenheimer brought to Turkey his experience of writing modern scientific textbooks in an ancient language.

In an article that appeared in the *Annual Review of Entomology*, after noting that the Hebrew language was revived as a spoken language for everyday secular usage only at the beginning of the twentieth century, Professor Isaac Harpaz points out that "it was desperately lacking modern scientific terminology, let alone suitable updated textbooks for higher education." Harpaz continues by stating that, "Bodenheimer had to compile such textbooks in zoology, entomology, and the history of biology first in German and later in English, while others had to help translate the manuscripts to Hebrew. However, all these enormous obstacles were overcome by enthusiastic efforts of both students and teachers.

Recalling that only a few years had passed since Turkey converted its alphabet from Arabic, many symbols and scientific terms having Turkish roots needed to be invented. This was certainly the case in all discussions involving chemistry and biochemistry. Thus Bodenheimer's experience in what was then Palestine was invaluable to these efforts. Having completed his work in Turkey, Bodenheimer returned to his beloved Hebrew University of Jerusalem and continued to make major contributions to knowledge and to educating new cadres. "Of the forty M.Sc. and Ph.D. theses that were carried out under his supervision during 1934-1959, the majority were on subjects with significant practical implications for crop protection, public heath, animal husbandry, and apiculture."[52]

The following extract from an obituary to a first-generation émigré professor's trained Turkish scientist speaks to the enduring national pride in the legacy these life science professors left behind:

> Prof. Dr. Muhtar BASOGLU, the first Turkish scientific herpetologist, was born in 1913 at Odemis near Izmir. In 1932, he enrolled, and, in 1936, he graduated from the Natural Sciences Section of Istanbul University's Science Faculty, where, he was appointed as Assistant in 1941 after completing his military service. There, based on his thesis "Sur le métabolisme de la

corde nerveuse du ver de terre," Basoglu was promoted to Doctor of Zoology.... He was guided by the German Professor Curt Kosswig, who, at that time, was teaching at Istanbul University. In 1946, Basoglu translated Bodenheimer's Introduction to the knowledge of Amphibia and Reptilia of Turkey (1944), into Turkish. Thereafter Basoglu became an engaged herpetologist, and his publication "Experiments on the composition of the alveolar air in Testudo graeca and Clemmys rivulata" helped him become associate professor.... During all these years his research work was devoted to herpetology, and, together with six doctors of zoology, raised by Basoglu himself, he founded and organized the first "Turkish Herpetological Centre" at Ege University. This Institute has brought together a large and comprehensive herpetological collection of more than 20,000 specimens, including material of every taxon of amphibians and reptiles living in Turkey. Since then, one of the above mentioned six doctors was appointed to the Istanbul University (now retired), the other five have become full professors, one of which is now at the 9 Eylül University, the remaining four are still with the Biology Department of the Science Faculty, Ege University.... During his last 20 years, Professor Dr. Muhtar Basoglu and his team studied the herpetofauna of Turkey, and, summing up the results of these concentrated efforts, he published three books.... Thus the untimely death of Professor Dr. Muhtar Basoglu on February 21st, 1981 ended the career of an outstanding herpetologist and distinguished teacher, whose lifelong ideal was to raise and form a group of zoologists, willing and able to efficiently carry out scientific work in the "Turkish Herpetological Centre" that he himself founded.[53] (emphasis added).

According to its most recent posting on the Web, this is what the University of Istanbul has to say about the legacy left behind by the long-gone émigrés:[54]

The Department of Biology at Istanbul University teaches joint courses in biology, for a three-year period after which, in their fourth year, the students select, according to their fields of interest, one of the seven proposed package programs and take their first steps towards specialization. Research on the subjects such as flora-fauna systematic, morphology, ecology, cytology, histology, physiology, microbiology, radiobiology, hydrobiology, molecular biology, genetics, and biochemistry is undertaken in well-equipped laboratories, with facilities like the latest appliances and electron microscopes. Some of the work is done through international cooperation and some through projects sponsored by national institutions. The department has a Botanical Garden and an Herbarium, a Zoology Museum and a Hydrobiology Museum used for research purposes.

*Figure 22*
Istanbul Archeological Museum.

*Figure 23*
Georg Rohde (1899-1960).

*Figure 24*
Manyas Lake.

*Figure 25*
Bald ibis.

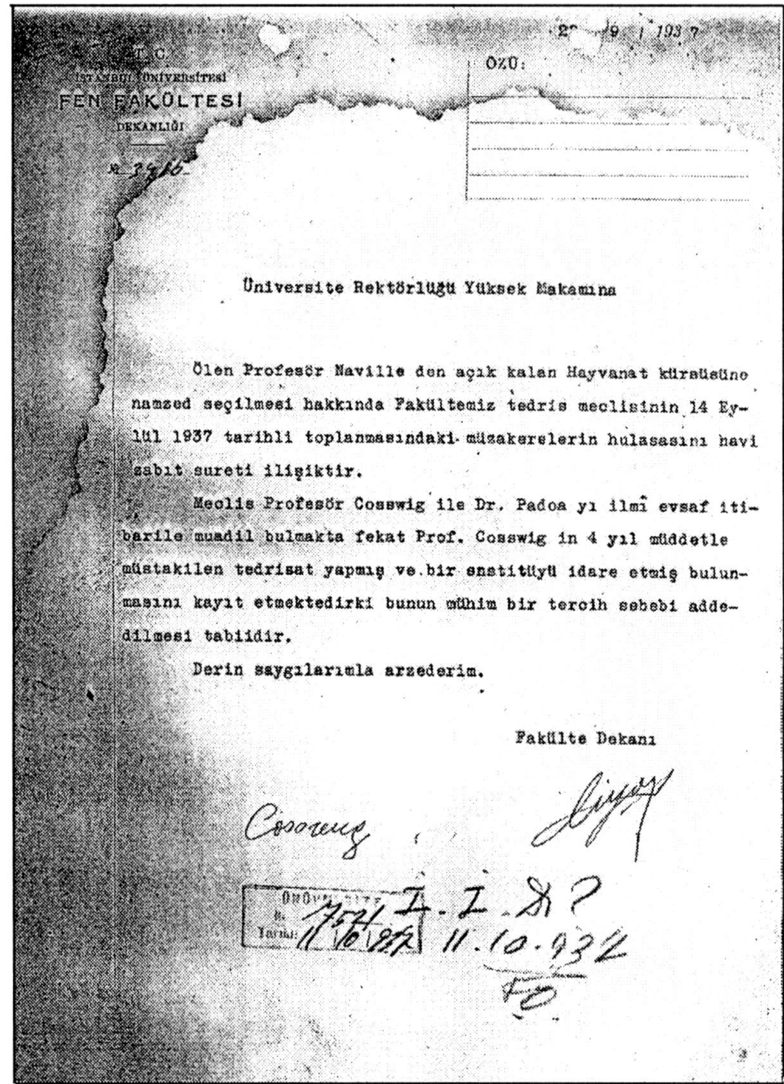

T.C.
İSTANBUL ÜNİVERSİTESİ
FEN FAKÜLTESİ
DEKANLIĞI

27/9/1937

Üniversite Rektörlüğü Yüksek Makamına

Ölen Profesör Naville den açık kalan Hayvanat kürsüsüne namzed seçilmesi hakkında Fakültemiz tedris meclisinin 14 Eylül 1937 tarihli toplanmasındaki müzakerelerin hulasasını havi zabıt sureti ilişiktir.

Meclis Profesör Cosswig ile Dr. Padoa yı ilmî evsaf itibarile muadil bulmakta fekat Prof. Cosswig in 4 yıl müddetle müstakilen tedrisat yapmış ve bir enstitüyü idare etmiş bulunmasını kayıt etmektedirki bunun mühim bir tercih sebebi addedilmesi tabiidir.

Derin saygılarımla arzederim.

Fakülte Dekanı

Figure 26
September 14 1937. Letter from Faculty of Medicine Dean to the university's Rector calling a faculty committee meeting to choose Professor Neville's replacement. Kosswig is recommended.

# 5
# The Creators

## Creating Conservatories, Symphony Orchestras, Arts Academies, and Introducing Opera in Turkey

The author of this book, a trained and formerly practicing engineer, has at times rhetorically asked the question, "Do composers, orchestra conductors, and theatrical directors exhibit more creativity than do engineers?" Even at cocktail parties, that question was always answered with a resounding, "Of course!" What about comparing the orchestra conductor using someone else's arranged score, or the theater director using a well-scripted play, against the engineer who starts a new technology or designs a class of new products? Most would still say yes. However, in the case of *Paul Hindemith,* there is little controversy. He proved himself to be not only a well-trained and gifted technician, but also a creative man of genius. "This multi-talented musician, who could play virtually every instrument in an orchestra, was best known as a violinist and a composer."[1]

Born near Frankfurt on November 16 1895, Paul Hindemith studied with the world-renowned Felix Mendelssohn in Frankfurt from 1908 to 1917 to be a violinist and composer. "He made his mark early with his chamber music and expressionist operas. But then he turned to neo-classicism in his *Kammermusik No.1,* the first of seven such works that imitated the Baroque concerto while using an expanded tonal harmony and distinctively modern elements, notably jazz. Each uses a different mixed chamber orchestra, suited to music of linear counterpoint and, in, the fast movements, strongly pulsed rhythm."[2]

Early in his career, Hindemith was *concertmeister* for the Frankfurt Opera orchestra between1915 and 1923, with a break for army service. Starting in 1921, he played the viola in the *Amar-Hindemith Quartet.* He did that until 1929. Hindemith wrote most of his chamber music between 1917 and 1924. This included four of his six quartets plus numerous sonatas. He, as part of his administrative work for the *Donaueschingen* Festival (1923-1930), promoted chamber music. Throughout this time, he also prolifically composed in other genres, including lieder (Das *Marienleben*, to Rainer Maria Rilke poems), music for newly invented mechanical instruments, music for schoolchildren and amateurs, and an opera ("*Cardillac*," a fantasy melodrama in neo-classical forms).

In addition, beginning in 1927, he taught at the Berlin *Musikhochschule*. His interest in so many branches of music according to The *Grove Concise Dictionary of Music* "sprang from a sense of ethical responsibility that inevitably became more acute with the rise of the Nazis." In the early 1930s, he moved "from chamber ensembles back into the more public domain—the symphony orchestra, and at the same time his music became harmonically smoother and less intensely contrapuntal."[3]

Then in the opera, *Mathis der Maler* (preceded by a symphony of orchestral excerpts), he dramatized the dilemma of the artist in society, eventually opposing Brechtian engagement and insisting on a greater responsibility to art. Nevertheless, his music fell under official disapproval, and, in 1938, he left for Switzerland.[4]

By 1933, Hindemith's works were branded "culturally Bolshevist" in Germany. On December 6 1934, during a speech at the Berlin Sports Palace, Germany's Minister of Propaganda, *Joseph Goebbels* publicly denounced Hindemith as an "atonal noisemaker." Coming from the infamous Goebbels and announced in such a public venue, Hindemith should perhaps have been pleased. Few performers received that kind of free worldwide publicity. Considering the source and the venue, the intended bad publicity was indeed good publicity outside the Nazi world.

In 1935, he was commissioned by the Turkish government to reorganize that country's system of musical education. And, more specifically, he was given the task of preparing material for the "Universal and Turkish Polyphonic Music Education Programme" for all music-related institutions in Turkey, a feat which he accomplished to universal acclaim.[5]

Paul Hindemith did not stay in Turkey as long as many of the other émigrés. Regardless, he greatly influenced the developments of Turkish musical life. The *Ankara State Conservatory* owes much to his efforts at launching it. In fact, Hindemith was regarded to be a "real master" by young Turkish musicians and he is appreciated and greatly respected.

According to the government's official 2004 website posting titled *The Republic of Turkey, Ministry of Culture—Opera in Turkey,* the famous composer Paul Hindemith and theater director *Karl Ebert* were invited to Ankara from Germany during the 1935-36 academic year. Based on a report of their "joint studies, state conservatory classes began to be held at the *Musiki Muallim Mektebi*" in the 1935-36 academic term. In addition, all aspects of musical education also included theatre and opera instruction. Even though "Paul Hindemith declined to accept a permanent post, [he] visited Ankara to inspect the music school and report on its activities."[6] *Karl Ebert*, however, stayed on in Ankara and directed the State Conservatory theater school and opera studio for nine years.

At the outset, Karl Ebert's classes at the Ankara State Conservatory opera studio used standard western works with Turkish text. Such was the case with Mozart's one-act opera *Bastien et Bastienne* that was staged by students and accompanied by the *Presidential Symphony Orchestra*. All indications are that the performance "attracted the attention of the press of the time."[7] Given the positive reviews, "librettos in Turkish were experimented with, and in 1940, for the first time in Turkey, the second act of Puccini's *Madame Butterfly* was performed in Turkish by the opera studio." In May of 1941, this was followed by the second act of Puccini's *Tosca*. Again, the "performances were a great success, and this was reflected in the press. That success was the result of three years of hard work."[8]

By a May 16 1940 act of Parliament, the State Conservatory's classes initiated at the *Musiki Muallim Mektebi* were officially turned into the State Conservatory consisting of music, opera, ballet, and theatre. "As the years passed, Atatürk's dream came true. The State Conservatory trained talented composers, musicians, soloists, and ballet dancers."[9] Moreover, each year between 1937 and 1957, the Ankara State Conservatory sent out teams of musicologists into the countryside to compile traditional folk melodies. Some may consider this a sideshow for publicity, some would think it a "routine objective" while others would consider such preservation to be a major mission of a national conservatory of music in a developing country. "Some 10,000 melodies were compiled and many were recorded on wax records. They are now preserved in the archives of the Ankara State Conservatory at *Hacettepe* University."[10]

Mustafa Kemal Atatürk, Turkey's first president, Ismet Inönü, her second president, and Hasan Ali Yücel, a Minister of Culture and Education, were patrons of the Turkish national opera. Paul Hindemith founded the State Conservatory in 1935, and Karl Ebert set up departments of opera and theatre in the Conservatory as well as founding a "practice theatre" where opera and drama students could appear in public performance. As indicated, the first opera performed was Mozart's *Bastien et Bastienne*. The second acts only of Puccini's *Madama Butterfly* and *Tosca* were performed in 1940 and 1941 respectively, with Beethoven's *Fidelio* and *Madama Butterfly* in full the following year. Subsequent opera productions included Smetana's *The Bartered Bride* (1943), Mozart's *The Marriage of Figaro* (1944), Puccini's *La Bohème* (1945), Verdi's *Masked Ball* (1947), and Bizet's *Carmen* (1948). The Exhibition Hall in Ankara was converted into a theatre and opera building in 1947-48. Known as the *Buyuk Tiyatro* or Great Theatre, it opened on April 2 1948 with a performance of Ahmet Adnan Saygun's opera, *Kerem*. The Ankara State Opera and Ballet commenced activities in 1949 following the enactment of a special law. Two of Atatürk's great dreams were thus realized. Today, operas are produced regularly in five of Turkey's cities.[11]

Thus, Hindemith helped the Turkish government reorganize musical education, assisted in the creation of the Turkish State Conservatory in Ankara, and served as a founding member of its faculty. Among that faculty was Carl Ebert. Ebert founded and directed Ankara Academy's theatrical department and between 1941 and 1947, founded and directed the Turkish State School of Opera and Drama, and directed the Turkish State Theater. Between 1936 and 1947, he had served as official adviser on theatrical affairs to the Turkish Ministry of Education. Later, he spent eight years (1948-1956) in Los Angeles as professor and head of the opera department at UCLA, as director of the Guild Opera Company, and became a United States citizen before returning to Germany in 1956.[12]

Another émigré, Dr. *Ernst Praetorius* was about to become Director of the Berlin Philharmonic when the Nazis expelled him because he was Jewish. Forced out of his position as *Generalmusikdirektor* (Music Director) of the *Deutschen Nationaltheaters* (German National Theater) in 1933, he drove taxis in Berlin for two years, after which he came to Ankara where he worked until his death in 1946 (Fig. 27).

A 1996 editorial in the *Turkish Daily News*, Turkey's English language daily had an editorial on Dr. Ernst Praetorius: "in 1935, upon the recommendation of Paul Hindemith...renowned German conductor Dr. Ernst Praetorius was appointed as conductor of the [Turkish Presidency's Symphonic Orchestra] CSO." The editorial concluded with "Praetorius, a great orchestra pedagogue, helped the CSO achieve technical international standards.... The CSO not only introduced Turkish classical music to the world at large but also to the Turkish public, through concerts all over the country." [13]

Over the years, the émigrés trained local talent and staged performances of many operas written by the leading western composers and involving Turkish performers (Fig. 28, 29, 30, and 31).

As well as directors, Turkey invited a number of German musicians. Among these were Austrian flutist *Friedrich Schönfeld*, who spent the years from 1940 to 1947 performing and teaching at the Ankara Conservatory; Viennese pianist *Walter Schlösinger* who was with the Conservatory between 1938 and 1946; and Berlin violinist, *Wolfgang Schocken*, who came to Ankara in 1933 but left a year later for Palestine. Among the renowned violinists was *Gilbert Back*, who arrived from Vienna in 1937 and left for the USA in 1946, and *Heinrich Jacoby*, who came in 1933 from Frankfurt, stayed a year, and left for Palestine in 1934.

At least another twenty-five accomplished musicians were part of the cultural arts contingent. The invited performers also included a number of opera singers. Among these were *Max Klein* and his wife, *Steffi Klein*. Both stayed from 1938 to 1949 when they left for the USA.

*Licco Amar* was by far the most renowned émigré violinist. *Fritz Neumark*, an economist by profession and a classical musician by avocation, and a fellow émigré, recalls that Amar was a "true-to-style"musician best demonstrated when he played solo the sonatas of Bach. "He had an extensive repertoire, and he was a supporter and popularizer of modern music as shown by his active participation in the '*Donaueschìng* Music Days.'At the same time, he was an excellent teacher. [Turkish] violinists who were his students, such as *Ayla Erduran* and *Suna Kan*, became recognized on the world music scene. Amar was professor of violin first in Istanbul and later at the Ankara Music Conservatory."[14]

Born in Hungary, Amar taught in Frankfurt for many years before 1933. He had come to Turkey from Berlin via France in 1934, stayed until 1957, and then left for Germany. Licco Amar had a long association with Hindemith. On August 1 1922, they performed the debut of the *3 Streichquartet op. 16* as part of the subsequently named "Amar Quartet" in Donaueschingen. The Amar Quartet and the Association for Music were founded in Frankfurt in 1922 and Hindemith had an active concert schedule with it until 1929. The memory of that quartet lives on in many ways. Among these are:

> The *Amar Quartet*, based in Zurich, was founded in 1987 by the sisters Anna Brunner, violin, and Maja Weber, violoncello, and plays with Igor Keller, violin, and Hannes Bärtschi, viola. Upon the occasion of Paul Hindemith's 100th birthday in 1995, the Hindemith Institute in Frankfurt awarded the ensemble the historic name *Amar Quartet*. (Fig. 32).[15]

Born in 1890, *Eduard K. Zuckmayer* composed and taught at progressive schools in Germany. Dismissed from the national music association as a "mixed breed," he accepted Paul Hindemith's invitation to teach at the conservatory and the state music school in Ankara in 1936. Between 1938 and 1970, Zuckmeyer was Director of Music at the Teacher Training Institute in Ankara. When Turkey finally severed diplomatic relations with Germany on August 2 1944 and ordered all German citizens to leave within 10 days, Zuckmeyer was denied repatriation to Germany, significantly once again on this "mixed breed" label. As a result, he ended up being one of the "good" Germans who had been interned in *Kirşehir* along with the "bad" Germans for the last few months of the war in Europe.

He and his family lived on support provided by the International Red Cross (IRRC) and donations from his non-interned (fully Jewish) émigré colleagues. While there, he organized a chorus by and for fellow detainees. A free man in 1946, he became a teacher of music theory and choir director at Ankara's Conservatory. Previously unable to marry his significant other, Gisela Jokisch, because he was denied a declaration certifying that he was worthy of marriage as he was a "mixed breed," he finally married Gisela in 1947 and adopted her daughter, Michaela. Though mother and daughter returned to Germany in 1950, Zuckmayer stayed in Ankara and died there in 1972.

Recollections by University of North Carolina distinguished Quantum Physics Professor Emeritus, Eugen Merzbacher provide a more personal touch to Zuckmayer's story.[16]

> Eduard Zuckmayer, simply called "Zuck" by his many friends, was one of the most influential among the German émigrés' "creative contingent." He was a music educator, pianist, composer, and choral director. We became close friends when my family met him on a sea voyage from Venice to Istanbul in the summer of 1936 (Fig. 33).
>
> Zuckmayer was an enormously gifted man. In Germany, he was a music teacher in several of the Weimar Republic's famous Waldschulheime or progressive boarding schools, and had been recommended to the Turkish Ministry of Education by Hindemith as a person who could modernize the system of music education and music teacher training. In short order, he became a leading figure in this field, first in the Müzik Konservatuvarı in Ankara-Cebeci, and then for many years in the school teacher-training program at the Gazi Enstitüsü, also near Ankara. He is warmly remembered by innumerable students who became outstanding musicians and music teachers, often in remote areas of Anatolia. And he was one of the few émigrés who did not leave Turkey after the War, and eventually died in Ankara. He was half-Jewish through his mother. Theirs was a talented family, coming from the wine country on the Rhine, near Mainz.
>
> Zuck's brother, Carl, was a famous writer, mostly of enormously successful plays during the twenties and later. Among his biggest hits were "Der Fröhliche Weinberg" and "Der Hauptmann von Köpenick" which brought him wide acclaim and a small fortune in the pre-Nazi era. He ended up in Vermont during the War and then retired to Switzerland. I do not think he ever visited his brother in Turkey, although I am not sure. German literary artists

were, understandably, never a good match with Turkish culture. On the other hand, music, which was deemed so important as a target of westernization by Kemal Atatürk, was an altogether different matter. Bela Bartok came briefly from Hungary, to participate in Turkey's efforts to modernize its musical culture. He used the opportunity to travel to the hinterlands and record some of the wonderful indigenous Turkish folk music, in which Zuckmayer also became intensely interested, as a teacher, composer, and choral director. I heard Bartok play the piano in a concert in Ankara—a very special memory.

Personally, Zuck was a close friend of my family. He often played the piano (my parents had managed to bring one of our two German grand pianos with them) in our house, and I was allowed to serve as his page-turner. J. S. Bach was his specialty, but he knew the entire classical piano repertoire extremely well, and I remember him performing a Brahms piano concerto with the excellent Philharmonic Orchestra, under the direction of Praetorius, at one of the weekly Saturday afternoon concerts in Cebeci.

Zuckmayer was not Jewish enough to escape internment[17] in Kirşehir during the War, but I believe that he was released relatively early and allowed to return to his teaching position in Ankara. He spoke and wrote Turkish almost like a native and became more embedded in the Turkish culture than almost any other of his compatriots. His contribution to Turkish education was also perhaps more lasting than almost any of the other members of this remarkable group of people.[18] (Fig. 34).

Eduard Zuckmayer is but one of a myriad of examples of the damage done by the Nazis to a creative and fine human being for the sin of having a Jewish grand-parent. But Zuck was one of the lucky ones. Zuck lived out his life and did it with music.

According to Neumark, "what is now called 'Turkish music' is not identical to the music of Turks at all. It should be qualified as Arabic music with respect to form and content. In reality, the Turkish music is very interesting and particular to itself, especially its modern works: this music resembles modern western music in many respects. This fact should explain why followers of European-based 'musica viva' such as Hindemith and Amar have gotten on so well so quickly with their Turkish colleagues and students."[19]

However, there is more. The Republic's founding fathers, the Young Turks, laid the foundation for bringing western music to a traditional Moslem society and have seen to it that such music became part of modern

Turkey's culture and society. All of the republic's founding fathers lived to see Turkey's western music infrastructure in place and enjoyed many a performance by the sons and daughters of their own country. The same was true for opera and ballet perfomances.

## Music and Islam

Three-quarters of a century later, the President of Iran's theocracy banned such music by edict. In response to that act, *Daniel Pipes*, a political and social columnist specializing in Islam wrote in a December 15, 2005, web-based column,[20] that "western music symbolizes the whole of western culture; and therefore mastery of western music serves as a proxy for mastery of western, i.e., modern, culture as a whole." In a 1998 column, Pipes wrote, "fully reaping the benefits of western creativity requires an immersion into the western culture that produced it. Modernity does not exist by itself, but is inextricably attached to its makers."[21]

He went on to say, "western music proves this point with special clarity, precisely because it is so irrelevant to modernization. Playing the Kreuzer Sonata by Ludvig van Beethoven adds nothing to one's GDP [gross domestic product]; enjoying an operetta does not enhance one's [military] force projection. And yet, to be fully modern means mastering western music. Competence at western music, in fact, closely parallels a country's wealth and power, as the experiences of two civilizations, Muslim and Japanese, show. Muslim reluctance to accept western music foreshadows a general difficulty with modernity; Japanese mastery of every style from classical to jazz help explain everything from a strong yen to institutional stability."

So, by not limiting their *üniversite reformu* to the sciences and to medicine, and by including western philology, music, the performing, and visual arts among their other societal changes, the "Young Turks" preempted the kind of 20$^{th}$ century developments that have taken place decades later not just in Iran but in Afghanistan as well.

## The Visual Arts

Turkey's founding fathers recognized the fact that some architects are good artists and that some sculptors could play a role in educating architects. Hence, there were a number of cross-disciplinary academic appointments between the visual arts and architecture (Fig. 35).

*Rudolph Belling* studied at the Berlin Academy of Fine Arts between 1911 and 1912. In 1918, he helped found the *November Group* and followed western trends of *Cubism* and *Futurism* until 1920. His works display the influence of contrasting massed fullness and empty space seen in Alexander Archipenko's sculpture.[22] In 1937, Belling became Head of the Sculpture Studio at the Academy of Fine Arts in Istanbul. He continued in this position until 1954. He also gave classes in modeling at the Istanbul Technical University (ITU) from 1949 to 1966.

Among Belling's works are two large statues that are very prominently displayed in Turkey. The *Ismet Inönü* Monument stands in the garden of Ankara University's Faculty of Agriculture, and, an equestrian statue of Inönü originally designed to be erected at *Taksim* Square in Istanbul was not placed there for fear that it might divert attention from the Monument to the Republic by the Italian sculptor Pietro Canonica which stands at the very center of *Taksim* square, the very epicenter of Istanbul's European side. In 1982, the Belling statue was placed in front of Inönü's house at Istanbul's *Maçka* Park.

At the outset of the 20th century, Rudolf Belling's name was "something like a battle cry." The designer of the "Dreiklang" (triad), he "evoked frequent and hefty discussions" according to Belling's daughter, Elisabeth Weber-Belling, who manages his estate. Belling's work evoked "thoughts of the famous Italian sculptor Benvenuto Cellini (1500-1570),"[23] whose philosophy was that a sculpture should show several good views, perhaps as many as "seven, or eleven, or even forty." Belling's "theories of space and form convinced even critics like Carl Einstein (Albert's nephew) and Paul Westheim, and influenced generations of sculptors after him. It is just this point which isn't evident enough today." However, after 1933 Belling could no longer work in his homeland. His works were declared, "degenerate, many of them were melted down or smashed." The Nazis allowed sculpture in terms of two-dimensional bas relief of well-muscled farming blondes.

Because his political opinions were out of line with the Nazis, Belling's membership in the Berlin *Akademie der Künste* was terminated by the Academy's President on advice of non other than the Third Reich's Minister of Education and Arts himself. Rudolf Belling spent eight months in New York City during 1935 when he exhibited his most important works from the "Modern Classic Period" at the Weyhe Gallery and lectured on modern sculpture and on his own theories. Although "America offered him a marvelous possibility"[24] to live his life there, he felt compelled to return to Germany because his nine-year-old son was in danger as Belling's first wife had been Jewish. "Fortunately, he succeeded in saving his son and once more he was lucky to emigrate, 1937, this time to Istanbul." Two years later, "he managed to fly his son out illegally from Berlin to Turkey."[25]

In 1956, Belling was called back by the Academy in West Berlin and his works that survived by storage in New York were returned with the help of Germany's Foreign Office. At age eighty, he decided to return to Germany and lived in *Krailling*, near Munich. Rudolph Belling died in Munich in June 1966, highly decorated by the post-Nazi German government. Among other awards bestowed on him was the *Federal Cross of Merit with a Star*.[26]

Due to Moslem religious prohibitions against displaying the human figure, republican Turkey had no significant sculpture heritage. Hence, Belling's influence on Turkish sculpture was enormous. This is especially true of sculpture as a public art form. In the course of his academic teaching, Belling greatly influenced many Turkish sculptors. Among these were Kamil Sonad, Sadi Calık, Huseyin Gezer, Ilhan Koman, Hakki Atamulu, Yavuz Gorey, and Ali Teoman Germaner. That said, except for relatively recent installations at Istanbul's commercial banks, public outdoor sculpture in Turkey is still almost entirely limited to monuments memorializing the Republic's founding founders and other national heroes. However, public galleries in the major cities are showing retrospective exhibitions of smaller pieces by Turkish sculptors who have attained international acclaim and these masters are now teaching sculpture at art academies and in universities.

Although Turkey is an overwhelmingly Moslem country, it has never witnessed the kind of desecrations of other religions' sculptures dating to antiquity that we have seen in Afghanistan vis-à-vis those soaring statues of Buddha that had been hewn into an Afghanistani barren valley's towering sandstone cliffs. Those ancient monuments escaped damage during the ten-year Soviet invasion and Afghanistan's civil war in the 1990s. But they were demolished sometime in 2001 by the Moslem Taliban regime, because the "Buddhas violated Islamic bans on human images and idolatry."[27]

As cash-strapped as modern Turkey may have been over the decades, both state and the private-sector banks did, and continue to, play a significant role in promoting various art forms. In the *Beyoğlu* section of Istanbul alone, on any given day one can view not one but a half dozen excellent national and international art exhibitions in as many galleries owned and operated by individual banks. These exhibitions (which are frequently rotated so that all the collections can be seen) are assembled by professional curators and are offered to the public free of charge. Many of the banks have their own private collections made up of historic and contemporary works. And, in 2004, Turkey opened its first museum of modern art. It is privately funded by Bulent Eczacibasi, Turkey's sixth-richest man, according to *Forbes* magazine,[28] and the key owner of the *Eczacibasi Holding* company, which started out distributing pharmaceuticals and is currently one of the handful of Turkish oligarchic family groupings.[29]

On January 16 2000, in its "Istanbul Gallery and City Listings," the *Turkish Daily News* announced that "Turgut Atalay's painting exhibition can be seen until Feb. 2 at *Doku Art Gallery* at *Avukat Sureyya Agaoglu Sok, No: 4/2, Tesvikiye. One* of the leading names among Turkish realist painters, Atalay has worked with such prominent artists as Nazmi Ziya, Ibrahim Calli, *Leopold Levy,* and *Rudolph Belling*. Atalay won the Academy Arts Award in 1964 and has more than 2,000 works in museums and special collections in Turkey and abroad." (emphasis added)

*Leopold Levy,* a French Jew and academic painter, was invited to head the Academy of Fine Arts in Istanbul. As its Director until the end of 1949, he was instrumental in developing the Turkish school of modern painting.[30] (Fig.36)

## Art and Dictatorships

Hellmut Lehmann-Haupt who came to the United States in 1929 and served as Curator of the Department of Rare Books at Columbia University from 1930 to 1937 and later as a Monuments, Fine Arts, and Archives official with the U.S. Occupation Army in Germany, claims that "all of the fine arts are important to totalitarian regimes." The relationship between art and totalitarian politics is discussed in his book *Art under a Dictatorship.*[31] Accordingly, "most of us who live in a democratic country have understood the art policies of Nazi Germany...mainly as a form of especially rigid censorship or of extremely thorough propaganda. That is only part of the story.... What we must realize is the central role assigned to the arts by the modern dictator. He always sees it as a vital part of the very nerve center of the social organism. He has a healthy respect for it."

The Nazis asked and demanded that art and the vast system supporting the arts (commissions, curatorial policies, teaching, and art education) serve the State. The government understood how the visual arts could serve as a display of Germany's power and authority.[32]

*Figure 27*
Ernst Praetorius.

*Figure 28*
President's Philharmonic Orchestra in Ankara, 1996.

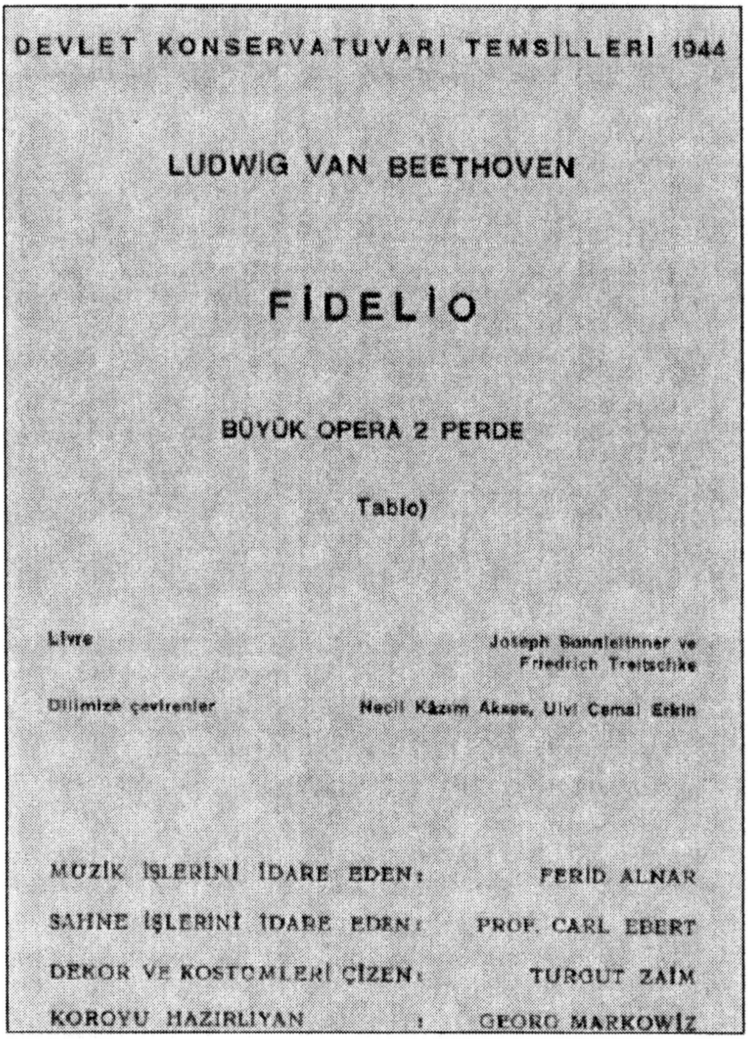

DEVLET KONSERVATUVARI TEMSİLLERİ 1944

LUDWİG VAN BEETHOVEN

FİDELİO

BÜYÜK OPERA 2 PERDE

Tablo)

Livre — Joseph Sonnleithner ve Friedrich Treitschke

Dilimize çevirenler — Necil Kâzım Akses, Ulvi Cemal Erkin

MUZİK İŞLERİNİ İDARE EDEN: FERİD ALNAR

SAHNE İŞLERİNİ İDARE EDEN: PROF. CARL EBERT

DEKOR VE KOSTÜMLERİ ÇİZEN: TURGUT ZAİM

KOROYU HAZIRLIYAN : GEORG MARKOWİZ

*Figure 29*
1944 playbill from a Carl Ebert-directed opera.

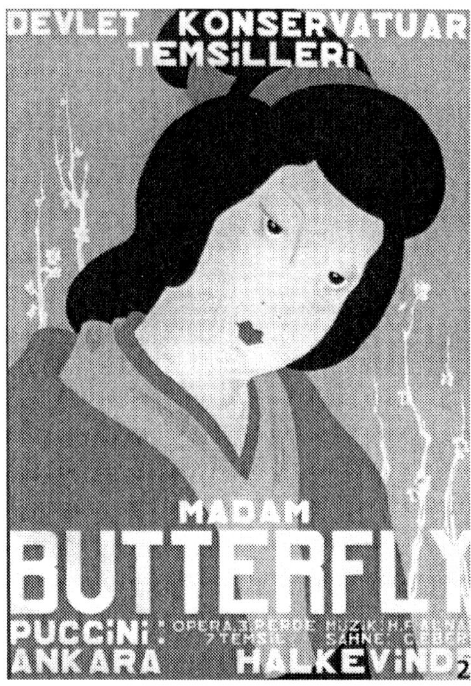


*Figure 30*
A Carl Ebert Production of *Madame Butterfly*, Ankara, 1942.

*Figure 31*
Presidency's Symphonic Orchestra (CSO).

*Figure 32*
Amar Quartet.

*Figure 33*
Eduard Zuckmayer.

*Figure 34*
Zuckmayer's Turkish translation of a German folk song, "True friendship shall not waver."

*Figure 35*
Painting in watercolors by Architect C. Holzmeister. Chapel of St. Barbara in Göreme, Turkey.

*Figure 36*
Village de Poivres. Leopold Levy, courtesy Fine Arts Museum of San Francisco.

# 6
# The Social Reformers

## Introducing Business Economics and Management as University Disciplines

> While up until the 19th century the Ottomans had been willing to borrow only strictly technical elements, beginning in the 19th century, they began to adopt western forms in administration, law, and even social customs.[1]

All the émigrés were considered to be "reformers" while still in their native Germany or Austria, because the Nazis wanted a tightly controlled, tightly organized state. Turkey, on the other hand, was eager to accommodate such "reformers" and their reformations and improvements since Kemal Atatürk was dedicated to modernizing his country's ways. No matter what their field of study, those intellectuals who came to Turkey had "change" or reformation on their mind!

Upon arrival, the German émigrés found a setting that was ripe for social reforms. Indeed, at the end of the nineteenth century, Turkish society had been rent into two parts: the "ruling elite" and the peasant masses.[2] The economy was basically agrarian, and, although free-enterprise, it was feudal and tightly overseen by Ankara. There was no middle class. This was not at all like many other 20th century societies. However, following the Industrial Revolution, the class boundaries of many countries, especially in the West, changed. The usual ticket of change was money. The difference in the Ottoman Empire was that "the passe partout for entry into the governing class was education as manifested in a minimal literary competence. In general, few doors of opportunity were closed to the Muslim youth, of whatever origin, who could speak and write properly; no talents of any sort ordinarily availed the youth who could not."[3]

There was no caste system as in India, nor classes according to lineage as in the UK. The Ottomans' system offered the educated person universally open, upward mobility without a ceiling. However, "the Ottoman guilds continued to dominate the social and economic life in the Ottoman towns as late as the second half of the 19th century.... Those who saw cultural change as an inseparable part of the general transformation of society and who believed that complete modernization would only be achieved with the development of a particular (i.e., western) kind of social structure, took the leadership only during the Republican period under Atatürk."[4] This included the level of equality for women in Turkey's professional cadres that was already coming in Europe to the West, and in the Soviet Union to the East, but hardly so in its nearby Islamic countries nor in the far distant United States of America.

Starting in 1933, "business economics" and other aspects of management education (the *Betribwirtschaftslehre*) were introduced into the undergraduate university curriculum and doctoral programs of the *Faculty of Economics and Political Science* and, by 1950, these developments resulted in Turkey's first undergraduate degree in "Business Administration."[5]

Istanbul University's Economics Faculty officially opened its doors on December 14 1936. According to *Fritz Neumark*, "during the first years, *Wilhelm Röpke, Alexander Rüstow, Gerhard Kessler,* and *Alfred Isaac* were among my closest friends. We lived in *Kadıköy* which still resembled a village and is located on the Asian side of the city. It was attractive in its own way and from where, the magical view of the European parts of the city could be seen. *Rüstow,* Isaac, and later *Dobretsberger*, three of the four refugee Economics Professors, also lived on the same street in *Kadıköy* the whole time. This facilitated our personal and scientific relations."[6]

In those days, Istanbul sported two communities or colonies of expatriate German-speaking intellectuals. Both colonies were on the very shores of the Bosphorus. *Kadıköy* on its Asian side is somewhat diagonically to the south-east across the waterway from *Bebek* on its European side. Municipally operated ferries provided the transportation of choice between the two communities. The two magnificent suspension bridges that currently connect the continents had not yet been constructed (Fig. 37).

*Ernst Reuter* was by far the most illustrious among the social reformers who came to Turkey. "[He] was the only politician of significance who escaped to Turkey. He symbolized a peerless combination of politician, university lecturer, and experienced administrator."[7] While in Ankara, Ernst Reuter worked as a taxation specialist at the Economics Ministry first in Ankara and later in Istanbul. He was made Professor of Social Sciences in recognition of the courses he gave at the *Ankara Superior School of Administrative Sciences*. According to Professor *Philipp Schwarz*: "When Reuter was celebrating his 50th anniversary in 1939, he was considered to be among the greatest personalities of the Turkish cultural life."[8] His fields of teaching covered city planning and environmental management for which he drew from his past experiences in politics. Many of his students later held important positions such as city mayors, government officials, and general directors. They initiated modern city planning. Reuter also worked as technical advisor to the government. He contributed to the establishment of the *Institute of Environment Arrangement and City Building* at the Faculty of Political Sciences in Ankara. His 350-page book, *Social Science: Introduction to City Planning,* was published in 1940. Among other issues covered, the book included subjects such as the planning of public spaces and legislation for public administration.[9] Reuter greatly benefited from the urban planning experience that architect *Margarete Schütte-Lihotzky* brought to Turkey from her native Austria. Her planning of entire cities that the emerging and expanding Soviet Union wanted to create in its Siberian wastelands was obviously relevant to creating Ankara out of Turkey's steppes. It was also of interest to Reuter as a social planner. These projects integrated industrialization with livable space and easily accessible close-to-nature open areas for the workers. In other words, it was planned development following socialism's ideology. The city of Milwaukee, Wisconsin, with its main streets radiating out from the original city center to allow workers easy outlet to the countryside for rest and relaxation was laid out based on similar thinking at the beginning of the 20th century.

Reuter also worked for the Turkish Ministry of Transportation. Being the socialist and reformer that he was, Reuter quickly recognized Turkey's lack of good, low-cost, and easily available transportation for working people to use, to commute and to move about in its cities with ease and convenience. He perceived this need both as a social obligation on the part of government and as a means of urban and economic development.

While at the Ministry of Transportation, Reuter modernized the little of public (mostly municipal bus transportation) that existed in Istanbul and Ankara. This included specification of and mix of rolling stock to be acquired, rails to be placed, vehicle routing and scheduling, personnel assignment, and job descriptions as well as ticket pricing funding it all. Reuter is credited as being the architect of Turkey's modern urban public transportation system. In today's Istanbul, one can find modern, although still limited, rail-based mass transportation and various types of bus systems with ease of connection to a large fleet of ferries plying along and between the coasts of Europe and Asia along the Bosphorus, the Golden Horn, and the Sea of Marmara. While to a westerner the price of tickets is almost negligible, it is very reasonable to a Turk.

Toward the end of World War I in 1916, German draftee Ernst Reuter found himself badly wounded and interned in a Russian POW camp. This was his first but not his last internment. While he was in that camp, Russia had its 1918 Bolshevik revolution, and POW Reuter was persuaded to its cause. During the first Soviet years, Reuter rose in the Communist party ranks to become a Commissar in the *Volga German Autonomous Workers' Commune* near *Saratov*, Russia starting 1918. Viewed in its historical context, that was not an unreasonable transition in ideology from being a member of Germany's Social Democratic Party which Reuter had first joined in 1912.

After Reuter's first return to the *heimat* [motherland] in December of 1918, following the Russian revolution, he was appointed the Communist Party Secretary for Berlin and was a member of the *KPD* (German Communist Party) until 1922 when he rejoined the Social Democrats. Déjà vu! In 1926, Reuter was elected to Berlin's city assembly, served as mayor of Magdeburg (1931), and entered the Reichstag (federal lower house) the next year. Between 1922 and 1926, he served as Editor of the Party's two official organs, the *Vorwarts* [Forwards] and the *Freiheit* [Freedom], and, between 1926 and 1931 he was also in charge of Berlin's traffic control, public transport system, and the toll-ticket pricing for all bus and rail lines.

Arrested by the Nazis, Reuter spent two years in an early version concentration camp. He escaped this, his second internment, via Holland to England in 1935. During that same year, he came to Ankara with wife Hanna and young son, Edzard. Technically, Reuter was part of the economics group as he was not quite an architect nor a designer but more of an urban planner. Some years after the Reuters arrived in Turkey, he was swimming at the *Orman Çiftliği* "experımental" farm and recreational area near Ankara, with his colleague, *Kudret Erkönen*, who noticed scars on Reuter's back. When asked if they were from a war injury, Reuter replied, "No, they're from the concentration camp."[10]

An anti-Nazi to the core, Reuter was the leader of Turkey's German and Austrian expatriates who were similarly disposed. Then came August 2 1944 and Turkey, seeing the handwriting on the wall, broke off diplomatic relations with Germany and proceeded to round up all those still bearing valid German passports and interned them all in one of three camps. No distinction was made between Nazis and anti-Nazis. The Reuter family survived this internment with the help of the ICRC (International Red Cross) and contributions from other German émigrés who had had their passports revoked earlier by Germany and Austria for being Jewish. These were declared *Haymatloz* (stateless, in Turkish) and they were allowed to continue doing what they had come to do.

A non-Jewish socialist for most of his adult life, but a Communist for several years (1918-1921), Reuter came to Turkey in 1935 and stayed a full decade. With his family intact, he returned from Ankara to his native land in 1946. Soon after, he became the first mayor of post-World War II Berlin. Reuter was in office during the city's 1948-1949 blockade by Russian army tanks and the Americans' 324 days airlift of food, coal, blankets, soap, and other supplies to Berlin's population. A few readers may still remember his inspirational radio addresses during that blockade. His leadership within, and America's determination from without, prevailed. The blockade was broken. The Soviets failed to annex all of Berlin (Fig. 38).

Reuters' son Edzard received much of his education while in Turkey. He speaks the language fluently and publicly expresses his fond memories of growing up in that country. He rose through the ranks of the Daimler Benz Corporation to become its CEO from 1987 to 1995.

While his fellow émigré and colleague former *Bolshevik*, Ernst Reuter, was presiding as mayor of devastated and Soviet-encircled Berlin, market economy and individual freedom advocate Wilhelm Röpke "was a key intellectual architect of postwar prosperity in Europe."[11]

*Wilhelm Röpke* was a genuine Renaissance man—"though in the tradition of Erasmus rather than Machiavelli."[12] He "combined profound knowledge of several intellectual disciplines with a genuine confidence that people can indeed know the truth." For his relentless pursuit of truth, "Röpke paid a heavy price, including, at times, outright persecution from ideologues of the Left and the Right."[13]

Röpke was more than just an economist. During some of the darkest decades of the twentieth century, he sounded more like an Old Testament prophet warning of the dangers from a loss of our moral compass.[14]

Born on October 10 1899 in Hanover, Germany, Röpke was the son of a physician and was brought up in the classical and Protestant Christian tradition. Serving in the German army during World War I, he was shocked by the sheer brutality of war. The experience had a profound effect on his life. He became, in his words, "a fervent hater of war, of brutal and stupid national pride, of the greed for domination and of every collective outrage against ethics." A drive to understand the causes and crisis of World War I led Röpke to pursue the study of economics and sociology. He studied economics at the University of Marburg, receiving the Dr.rer.pol in 1921 and the Habilitation in 1922. In time, Röpke became a scathing critic of the welfare state on both economic and ethical grounds.[15]

Röpke was, without a doubt, the most famous of the German-speaking economists who took refuge in Turkey. He resembled so strongly the Siegfried figure imagined by the Nazis as the ideal type that some people could not understand why someone like him would not "go along" with the regime. They overlooked the fact that he was determined not to make any concessions to Hitler and his theories after this dictator came to power. He was one of the classic liberals and he was certain that the illusion of the "Third Reich" would disappear after a period, short or long, and that later he, Röpke, would be placed again in an important position in and for Germany. Even the passing of time after the euphoria of the 1934 Röhm coup[16] did not turn his optimism into disappointment. Moreover, Röpke never aimed to really settle in Turkey even for the medium-range period.[17]

Following the political victories of the Nazis in 1933, Röpke's uncompromising opposition to fascism earned him the honor of being one of the first professors to be forced into "early retirement" for having denounced Hitler's new regime by delivering a lecture describing National Socialism as a "mass revolt against reason, freedom, and humanity, and against the written and unwritten millennial rules that enable a highly differentiated human community to exist without degrading individuals into slaves of the state."[18]

For a number of years, Röpke had fought the National Socialists, even spending his modest professor's salary to print anti-Nazi election leaflets that he handed out at the polls himself warning Germans not to return their country to "primeval darkness." That speech in Frankfurt was the last straw. At least in Nazi Germany, Röpke's budding career had come to a screeching halt. "Röpke also spoke out against the Nazi dismissal of Jewish professors and students from German universities.... The Nazis denounced him as an 'enemy of the people.' ....After an angry exchange with two SS men sent to 'reason' with him, Röpke decided to leave Germany and accept exile rather than live under National Socialism."[19] "He left Germany one step ahead of the Gestapo, and made his way to Istanbul."[20]

After the war's end, to restore the broadest possible understanding of freedom, Röpke, along with *Ludwig von Mises* and *Friedrich A. Hayek,* called an international meeting of historians, philosophers, economists, and journalists who shared his concern over the steady erosion of liberty, and, in 1947, this group formed the *Mont Pelerin Society.* Through the Society, Röpke was able to meet with and influence the thinking of Ludwig Erhard, the economic minister and Chancellor of West Germany. Erhard later revealed that during World War II he was able to illegally obtain Röpke's books, which he "devoured like the desert [does] the life-giving water." The product of Röpke's influence on Erhard was tagged the post-World War II "German Economic Miracle," although Röpke pointed out that the economic success experienced by West Germany was not a miracle at all: it was the result of adopting correct social and legal institutions fostering the market economy.[21]

As indicated, Röpke had a "disciple in Ludwig Erhard (1897-1977) who had secretly educated himself in free-market economics during the war by reading Ropke's prohibited books."[22] In the war-devastated West Germany of 1948, most of the expert opinions, most of the Allied Occupation officials, and a majority of West Germans were calling for a planned economy. However, Ludwig Erhard was not convinced and in this regard indeed rejected the prevailing and popular wisdom. By issuing a new, sound currency—the *Deutschmark*—and by abolishing wage and price controls which had survived the fall of the Third Reich, "his administration halted a disastrous postwar inflation and stagnation. This launched West Germany's polity as a federal, free-market democracy. It sparked a rebirth of that shattered nation which astonished the world--and inspired similar reforms in Italy, France, and other countries."[23]

Starting June 21 1948 when the new *Deutschmark* appeared, "unemployment rose, spawning political discontent, but Erhard persevered, stoutly supported by Röpke's newspaper writings, and soon Germany was prospering." This "was a great personal vindication for Röpke. Even more, Röpke and his allies had made West Germany immune to communism"[24] an outcome of major significance during the early years of the Cold War.

Backtracking in time a bit, "the four years Röpke spent on the Bosphorus were productive ones, full of fellowship with other German exiles."[25] However, during the 1930s, Turkey was certainly not ready for Röpke's anti-etatist positions and free-market economics. But, then, neither were most of the "developed" countries in those years. Though Röpke's professional stature as an economist was very much appreciated by Turkey's establishment and by his Turkish students, his economic philosophy was at least a full half-century ahead of being acceptable. This was especially so to modern Turkey's founding fathers, the "Young Turks." Turkey was on the march toward economic development. Heavy industrialization was its roadmap. Because, at the time, there was still no wealthy upper class in position to create major manufacturing enterprises in Turkey, only the State was able to accomplish it. Röpke clashed with the country's dominant ideology…and Röpke lost.

He left in 1937 for the Institute of International Studies in Geneva, Switzerland, but his imprint on a generation of Turkish economists, politicians, and managers was indelible. His writings were being read in Turkey much after his return to the West. However, it was not much after the Thatcher revolution (Margaret Thatcher, prime minister of Great Britain) in the 1980s that the World Bank literally forced Turkey to begin a process of privatization. This process began with the large state-owned commercial banks.[26] Fast-forwarding even more in time, on November 8 2005, the EU granted Turkey market economy status.

One could argue that Germany's national election of 2005 was all about how much more of Röpkenism the country should adopt. Alternately stated, how much more should Germany revert to the Röpkenist policies credited for to its post WWII miraculous economic recovery. According to John Leicester, AP's Paris Bureau Chief:

> In the wake of Sunday's [August 18 2005] election, arguments over the way forward for ailing continental Europe seem more unresolved than ever. Should Germany, France, and Italy embrace Anglo-Saxon-style reforms, cutting *costly welfare programs and freeing up labor markets*?
>
> Moreover, British Prime Minister Tony Blair says the European Union must streamline its bureaucracy, embrace globalization, spend more on science, technology, and research, and *less on propping up farmers in France* if it hopes to compete against growing powers like China.[27] (emphasis added)

While in Turkey, "Röpke had maintained international relations with many countries but mainly with Switzerland, England, and the United States. And he was very happy when he finally could go to Geneva from Istanbul in 1937. In his yearning for the climate of Central Europe and its lifestyle, he would, in his special manner, curse Istanbul's 'perpetually blue sky' from time to time."[28]

Röpke's intellectual evolution owed much to the political philosopher cum economist *Alexander Rüstow*. In turn, Rüstow singles out Röpke as one of the major catalysts for writing while in Istanbul, his own *magnum opus* with the rather nondescript title, *Taking Bearings on the Present*.[29] According to Dr. John Attarian of the *Mackinac Center for Public Policy*, a non-profit free-market research and educational organization located in Midland, Michigan:

> Laissez-faire economists argued that a natural harmony of interests would enable egotistical economic action to serve the common good. Rüstow traced this viewpoint to deism and beyond it to a mystical pre-Socratic Greek belief in a harmonious universe. This belief prevented development of a strong system of social institutions such as the family and the rule of law that actually support free markets. Moreover, Rüstow pointed out, in capitalism's early years there existed an abundance of ethical capital from a previous Christian society that greatly enhanced the beneficial effects of the free market. Having absorbed Rüstow's arguments, Röpke developed a growing respect for religion, traditions, and institutions intermediate between the individual and the state.[30]

Born in Wiesbaden, Germany, in 1885, economist and sociologist *Alexander Rüstow*, served as legal expert in Germany's Ministry of the Economy. In that capacity, he prepared the first German Cartel (monopoly or anti-trust) law. Afterwards, he became the administrative director of the German Machine Manufacturing Association (*Verein deutscher Maschinenbauanstalten*) and Dozent at the Berlin Commercial Institute (Berliner *Handelshochschule*). When his efforts to form a coalition government to keep Hitler out of power failed, he left for Turkey. A classicist by training and a Socialist by calling, Rüstow was a political activist, cultural sociologist, economist, and philosopher. Rüstow taught economics, economic geography, and philosophy at the University of Istanbul between 1933 and 1949.[31] He was also active in the anti-Nazi movement of the German refugees in Istanbul and acted as liaison between the OSS (Office of Strategic Services, an American wartime intelligence agency) and the German resistance. Rüstow's many areas of scholarly expertise are considered the forerunner of the interdisciplinary field of cultural studies.[32] Fellow economist Fritz Neumark,[33] one of Rüstow's colleagues in Turkey, remembers him well (Fig. 39).

> Although he [Rüstow] led a sort of "ivory tower" existence in Istanbul, he was extremely grateful to the country where he stayed from 1933 until 1949. The reason was clear: His life there had provided for him the necessary material means and the leisure to to be able to write his great three-volume work titled Taking Bearings on the Present which was published in Switzerland a short while after the war ended. This monumental work exhibits the amazing breadth of Rüstow's knowledge, the effort he made to ensure accuracy in description, the lucidity and incisiveness of the socio-economic analyses and frequent evidence of the existence of an imaginative force not only by its text but also by detailed footnotes. It is not necessary to accept all its results in their detail in order to appreciate this accomplisment. I consider *Taking Bearings on the Present* as one of the most valuable works in German written by exiled social scientists. Above all, in my opinion, this statement is especially valid for the critical chapters in the second volume.[34]

Rüstow experienced World War I firsthand as a German army lieutenant. Witnessing the rise of Hitler, he was not a detached academic. In the foreword to his *Taking Bearings on the Present* book, Rüstow makes his position clear:

> I affirm freedom and reject domination, I affirm humaneness and reject barbarism, I affirm peace and reject violence. These pairs of opposites are the great poles between which the drama of human history is enacted.[35]

In 1950, Alexander Rüstow returned to Germany and taught at Heidelberg University until retirement in 1953. According to a group blog maintained by Grinder and Hagel:

> *Taking Bearings on the Present* remains today one of the most powerful statements of historical sociology in the classical liberal tradition. Although the full original work has never been translated from the German, Princeton University Press published in 1980 a one-volume edited translation of Rüstow's work under the much more compelling title of *Freedom and Domination.*
>
> This is a book with extraordinarily rich insights from a classical liberal perspective—one that could shape promising research agendas for many younger scholars—yet it remains largely neglected in the social science disciplines. As a catalyst for research, Rüstow's book could also help to address two of the key weaknesses of the current classical liberal movement—its relative lack of depth in history or sociology.[36]

Citing Rüstow's own letters, Kathrin Meier-Rust comments in her biography of Alexander Rüstow that:

> While Rüstow's earlier circle of friends found itself almost entirely in the USA—most of them taught at least for a time at the New School for Social Research in New York—he himself spent 16 years in exile in Istanbul "in relative isolation in the lovely workroom with the semicircular windows in Kadiköy . . . beyond the entrance to the Sea of Marmara." The climate and the language, the foreign environment and mentality were a problem and, basically, always remained alien to him—none of the emigrants succeeded "in really putting down roots" and there could be no question of "any productive integration into the situation of the country."[37]

Meier-Rust also notes that as a result of inflation during the war years, the emigrants came into serious financial distress, since salary adjustments came late and were unsatisfactory: "We emigrants are now in the position of a poorly paid assistant at the time we were hired; we have used up our reserves and are selling off our furniture, books, etc." Rüstow wrote in 1944. It was not until 1946 that the situation was ameliorated through salary increases that at least "assured a minimum living wage," and Rüstow's contract was extended to 1950.[38]

Although he felt "politically and humanly isolated," Rüstow stayed in Turkey for sixteen years, during which he was quite productive in spite of the lack of library holdings he needed for his research and writing. It was with the most bitter irony that Rüstow understandably responded to critical objections to his patchy source readings: "Why don't I read *Calvinum ipsum*? Because it isn't available in *Roma nova quae est Constantinapolis* and the university library understandably refuses to acquire these 40 volumes simply for my sake."[39]

This comment is not much different from Erich Auerbach's, epilogue to his broadly conceived literary study, *Mimesis,* produced in Istanbul (1942-1945), where he stated that the book was created precisely due to the lack of a large specialized library.[40]

Kathrin Meier-Rust rationalizes [Rüstow's] comments with the possibility that "the difficult scientific conditions with which the German emigrants were confronted...have promoted the tendency toward historical synthesis, comprehensive scope, and preference for the history of ideas in [their] social scientific and historical writings."[41]

Alexander Rüstow's experience in drafting Germany's first monopoly, or anti-trust laws, may well have been the reason why he was kept in splendid isolation while in Turkey. Ankara may have felt a need to know what not to do. During those years, the country was busily growing three or four oligarchs into a position of being able to take over the country's industrialization. And that they did.

In the year of the *Anschluss*, when *Wilhelm Röpke* left Istanbul for an academic position in Geneva, *Josef Dobretsberger* was both a professor and Rector in Graz, Austria, in those days a famous university. Dobretsberger also served as Austria's minister for social matters in what is known as "Schuschnigg's Cabinet," Austria's last pre-Nazi government. Suddenly, Dobretsberger disappeared. There was no news in the papers about his immediate fate and nothing other than the fact that he had been fired from his job as Rektor. Fritz Neumark and his Istanbul colleagues worried about Dobretsberger's status because he had been a member of a fairly leftist party. So Neumark sent a letter to Dobretsberger's residence asking him rather diplomatically whether he could recommend someone to take over Röpke's position. Dobretsberger's wife Carla brought this letter to her husband's prison cell, where he had landed in the interim. Carla then sent an answer by telegram indicating Dobretsberger's own interest in such a position. Subsequently, he was able to escape from Austria in a rather adventuresome and complicated way. An Austrian official who had known him personally permitted him to leave jail and "go home."

However, a few days after his "disappearance," the Gestapo appeared at the apartment to re-arrest him. Meanwhile, Dobretsberger and his family, carrying no luggage, traveled to Switzerland. He had contacts with various Swiss officials going back to his days as a minister in the Austrian government. The president of the Swiss National Bank, a Mr. Bachmann, was instrumental in getting Dobretsberger a ninety-day permit to stay in Switzerland. After completing his negotiations with the Turkish ministry of Education, according to his colleague, Fritz Neumark:

> Dobretsberger was able to reach Istanbul in September 1938 through adventerous routes. This new colleague became one of our best friends in a short time and this friendship endured until his death. A short time before I returned to Frankfurt, he also went back to his country. We saw each other often in Graz and in Vienna. The reason why Dobretsberger left Turkey after about three years—although he adapted easily right away and won great respect from his colleagues and students—was due to the fact that he felt threathened by Franz von Pappen, who had performed his duty in Vienna so brilliantly with respect to Hitler and then sent to Ankara as the German ambassador. Dobretsberger had started feeling insecure especially during the time when the war seemed to develop in favor of Hitler. He conducted anti-Nazi propaganda work first in Palestine, then in Cairo. After the war ended, he went often to Cairo which he loved so much as visiting professor.[42]

On arrival in Istanbul, he occupied the Professorial Chair for Political Economy. Some Nazis thought they were sending Dobretsberger there to spy on the other émigrés. And some documentation does attest to that effect, but the very same document also indicates that he might have had second thoughts.[43] In a personal communication, Fritz Neumark's son Matthias, who knew the Dobretsbergers while in Istanbul and knew them well, has unequivocally quashed any possibility of Dobretsberger being a spy. Did Dobretsberger deceive the Nazis? Most likely so. After the war, Dobretsberger returned to Vienna where he became publisher of a communist-leaning newspaper. In 1949, Dobretsberger co-founded and served as federal representative of Austria's Democratic Union, which united with the Austrian Communist Party and the left-wing Socialists to become the "People's Opposition" in 1953. However, he was unable to get back into politics, his first love, in any major way.[44]

*Gerard Kessler* " . . . trained hundreds of Turkish students in labor economics at Istanbul University and, with some of his students, helped *found the first Turkish labor unions*."[45] Born in East Prussia in 1883, Kessler was

Professor of Economics and Sociology at Leipzig between 1927 and 1933. An active anti-Nazi, Kessler was moving around Germany to hide from the Nazis. In the spring of 1933, he suddenly surfaced in Frankfurt where he was hiding using false documents. (Fig. 40).

Even though he was invited there, Kessler was physically assaulted in Leipzig; his home was partially destroyed and he no longer had any guarantee of security. There was a political reason for this persecution. In the last free election campaign of the Weimar Republic, he had worked for his party the German State Party, comparable to Free Democratic Party (F.D.P.) of today, and of course against Hitler. He immediately lost his professorship.[46]

When the Turkish government asked for Kessler, Hitler's men found him and sent him and his family to Istanbul, where he established a program in Sociology and Social Politics at the University of Istanbul and became its Director.[47] His wife, Dorothea, and daughters, Gerhild (b. 1915), and Adelheid (b. 1926), deserted him secretly during the middle of a night and, with help of the German Consulate officials, returned to Nazi Germany in 1939.[48] His sons, Gottfried (b. 1921), and Hans (b. 1918), stayed with him in Istanbul until some time in the early 1940s. Both sons came to the United States. Kessler himself continued on in Istanbul until 1951 when he returned to Germany and taught at the University of Göttingen.

> Kessler was succesful in gathering determined young people around himself both in Germany and in Turkey, and training many of them into bold economic and social politicians. He could be kind as well as obstinate in many ways and one had to get to know him closely in order to get along with him. For those who were able to do this, he could be a loyal and true fatherly companion. His comprehension and tolerant manner in helping many students, including foreigners, was compatible with his humanistic and Christian thinking and his belief that one should love his close friends.
>
> As an example of many whom he helped, I should like to mention here the Indonesian youth, Alfiya Yusuf Hilmi, who was finacially supported by Kessler during the war period as his stipend from home was cut. Later Hilmi completed his doctorate with Kessler with a thesis on petroleum problems (I was an examiner). It was a happy surprise for me to meet Hilmi and his Turkish wife years later in Bonn as the ambassador of his country which had won its independence in the meantime.[49] *Umberto Ricci* was a self-educated Italian agricultural economist who gradually

moved towards more theoretical issues. He succeeded a professor Pantaleoni at the University of Rome in 1924. However, a series of articles criticizing Fascist policies led Mussolini to deprive Ricci of his chair in Rome as far back as 1928. He subsequently took up a position at Cairo where he stayed until 1940 when Italy entered the war.

> After Dobretsberger's departure from Istanbul, another position opened up for an ordinarious professor. This time it was Mussolini who helped us find a wonderful person of course without knowing it; Umberto Ricci...had attracted Il Duce's hate as a representative of the classical liberal school which was totally opposite the corporate state viewpoint.... I knew him from a meeting in Geneva although little. Ricci was a visiting professor in the *Institut de Hautes Etudes Internationales* where I had gone at the invitation of William Rappard to give a series of lectures in 1933.
>
> Having accepted our invitation right away, Ricci was able to reach Istanbul with his wife in 1942, in spite of the war fully raging. In reality, Ricci was not among the "German-speaking refugees." However, he felt very close to our circle due to both external circumstances and morally.

Umberto Ricci was the exact opposite of Kessler, a theoretician above all. In Turkey, he published an excellent book about "value theory" which was later translated into French. He was a person who had achieved a true Latin courtesy and sincerity, intelligent and humorous in conversations, and a fiery patriot as well as an undefeatable enemy of fascism.[50] Ricci returned to Rome after the war's end. His endowed chair was restored to him (Fig. 41).

Another member of the *Betribwirtschaftslehre* contingent was agricultural economist and management expert *Fritz Baade.* However, unlike most of the rest, his base of operations was in Ankara. He, too, was not only a teacher and researcher but also a reformer. Prior to his arrival, the Turks had no standards for fruit conservation. Although methods of drying and other means of preserving fruit for use in the wintertime were passed on from generation to generation in Anatolia, creating exportable products was another matter. Farmers did things in their own traditional way with traditions differing between region, and locality.

To help Turkey expand its exports, Baade introduced standardization of raisins and the drying of apricots and other fruit as required by importers in western countries. Baade organized Turkish food processors and taught them how to make their final products uniform, be properly packaged in order to have the greatest shelf life, remain at highest quality and therefore be sought after by the more sophisticated purchasers, and fetch the highest price. These were indeed major contributions to Turkey's agrarian economy.

Baade is also the founder of a spa at *Kirşehir*, where he happened to be interned as an "enemy alien" by the Turks toward the waning months of WWII. There he discovered an ancient spring with healing waters that had been capped since antiquity. He excavated it and as part of a spa it has flourished ever since. His other contribution to Turkey's economy was the founding of a crafts industry out of the remains (sinters) left by chalky sea waters. Carved Meerschaum pipes especially are very much appreciated by smoking connoisseurs. Small carvings are sold as souvenirs.

Prior to coming to Turkey, Fritz Baade was a member of the Reichstag and was the agricultural policy spokesman for the SPD's parliamentary group. In January 1932, when Germany's unemployment level swelled to 6 million, Baade's position toward the real economy can be summed up by the fact that he considered it absurd that "people should starve in front of over-filled granaries." For Baade, that spoke for the necessity to adopt an "active economic policy."' He was instrumental in introducing The *Woytinsky-Tarnow-Baade* plan to fight the economic depression in Germany.[51] Baade came to Turkey in 1934 and stayed until 1946. He served as advisor to the Agriculture Ministry and as professor at the Ankara School of Agriculture. After a two-year sojourn in the United States, he returned to (West) Germany in 1948.

Previously mentioned *Fritz Neumark*[52] served as government advisor on the introduction of the first income tax in Turkey. He was also the architect of Turkey's 1950 Tax Reform. As can be seen from his statement to the 1945 graduating class translated and reprinted below, unlike Röpke, Fritz Neumark was definitely a proponent of etatism in economic development. That ideology made his professional consulting services very much desired by Ankara's government ministries. However, Neumark's son, Matthias, apparently rebelled against his father's economic philosophy. After obtaining a bachelor's degree in Turkey, he came to the United States where he received an MBA from the Harvard Business School and served America's business firms in various managerial capacities.

Matthias provides the following oral history:

> My father was born on July 20 1900 in Hanover, Germany. His father, Jacob Neumark, owned a piece-goods store and was married to Antonia Mengers, the daughter of a leather-tanning master. Both parents were children of Jewish families, and both leaned toward the liberal bent of Judaism. According to my

father's recollection, my grandfather was referred to as a "killer-Zionist" [diehard] by Hanover's conservative Jewish community. My father and his sister studied music. She became proficient at the piano and he enjoyed playing the violin (Fig. 42).

The family enjoyed a comfortable, middle-class lifestyle. From the ripe old age of six and a half, my father attended a so-called Realgymnasium. Completion of this type of school and passing the Abitur, a rigorous final examination, was required for university admission. Prior to the gymnasium, students had to have three years of preliminary school to learn basic skills such as reading, writing, and arithmetic.

Those born in 1900 were the last to be drafted for service in the Prussian army. After completing basic training, my father was sent for special training as a truck driver. One or two weeks before being sent to the front, a revolution took place (November 9 1918) and my father had to serve four more months as a private first class.

My grandfather wanted my father to go on to the university. Initially, he wanted to study literature and attended the University of Jena. While there, he became interested in economics, primarily because one of the professors of economics there, Gerhard Kessler, was an exciting lecturer. Later they became colleagues in Istanbul. As was common, and still is, in Germany, after three semesters in Jena, my father transferred to the University of Munich. After one semester there, he transferred back to Jena and matriculated with a thesis titled "The Concept and the Nature of Inflation." The dissertation was given a „summa cum laude" grade as was the oral exam that followed. Subsequently, he moved to Hamburg with the idea of studying law.

Germany's inflation started in 1921. By 1923, it assumed monumental proportions. This put an end to study years, and Fritz Neumark moved to Berlin to pursue gainful employment and a new career. After some initial difficulties, he landed a low-level job in the ministry of finance, Germany's Treasury. While in Berlin, he also met his future wife, Erica Sievers, the daughter of a Hamburg businessman.

Neumark returned to the Academe at the urging of his mentor Wilhelm Gerloff. He started as an Assistant Professor and was promoted to Associate Professor in 1927. He and my mother were married in 1925, and they spent the years prior to the immigration to Turkey in Frankfurt as a young academic couple. I was born in 1927, my sister in 1931. Subsequent milestones are listed by years.

> In September 1933, the family emigrated to Turkey. Neumark was Professor of Economics at the University of Istanbul until 1951 and served as a senior Economics Advisor to the Turkish Government. Following the war, he renewed contacts in the international economics community and served as Consultant to the Allies on planning the reconstruction of Germany's higher education system. My father had very positive feelings towards Turkey and mastered its language. However, he sensed a strong need to teach again in his homeland. He needed to teach a new generation of Germans.
>
> In 1951, my father accepted an invitation to return to the University of Frankfurt as professor for public finance in its Department of Economics. My mother was not in favor of the return, even though she was the „Aryan" member of the marriage, but she and my sister moved to Frankfurt with him.
>
> Neumark continued to teach in Frankfurt. He was quite successful in his field. His colleagues twice elected him to the post of University Rektor [President] and he became very active internationally. He served the German government as a member of the advisory Boards of both the Economics Ministry and the Finance Ministry. He retired in 1971 but continued to serve on the Finance Ministry's advisory board until his death in 1991. Perhaps one of the highlights of this period was a 1986 invitation to accompany the president of the German Federal Republic, Richard von Weizsaecker, to Istanbul for the installation of a memorial tablet dedicated to the German professors who had taught at the University of Istanbul.[53]

Neumark's neighbor in Kadıköy, was economics professor *Alfred Isaak.* Born in Cologne in 1988, Isaak became professor at Nuremberg's *Handelshochschule* in 1928 where he served until 1934. Being "retired" from that institution he found his way to Istanbul University in 1937. There he taught business management as Professor in the Faculty of Economics. He learned sufficient Turkish to be able to lecture within two years of arrival in the country. Without a doubt, that was appreciated by the students. The Isaacs loved social events, especially the musical ones. His wife was a peerless piano teacher and he a joyous flutist.[54]

While in Turkey, Isaak advised the Ankara government on the mission for and organization of its Ministry of Labor. In that capacity, he played a major role in formulating Turkey's laws on social insurance and therefore social welfare.[55] Among other things, he was first to introduce to Turkey what was then the new educational discipline of managerial economics,[56] the theory of how administrators of public agencies and managers of industrial and commercial enterprises should make choices among competing investment alternatives. Isaak also trained hundreds of Turkish economists and financial experts.

The Class of 1944-1945 yearbook or *The Album of the Economics Faculty of Istanbul* contains a series of "Letters to Graduates" by some of the above professors. Ord. Prof. Dr. Fritz Neumark wrote:

> *To the Graduates of our Faculty for the Academic Year of 1944-1945*
> Economics is in the process of gaining increasing importance almost everywhere. While traditional methods were applied in the past for economic activities, today effort is made to find rational and perfect methods as much as possible. Moreover, intervention of the state in economic life is accepted to be useful and even necessary vs. the "liberalism" which was popular in the last century. As a result, public institutions in many states control, direct, and manage close to almost half of the national income.
>
> Our republic is also a proponent of the principle of etatism with respect to economic policy. There is no doubt that the clear successes seen in the fields of industry, agriculture, and cultivation could not have been realized without the planned and strong action (entrepreneurship) and support of the government. We should also point out that all measures related to economics cannot be ascribed only to economic actors. They also have to do with factors outside economics such as social policy, etc. However, even in such cases, it is the duty of economists to follow the principle of rationality as much as possible so that things get done.
>
> Under the present conditions we have briefly described, it is clear that it will not be correct just to emphasize "legality" during the formation of public servants. Therefore, increasing importance is attached to economics education in Turkey as well as in many other countries. An open expression of this importance is the establishment of an independent Economics Faculty. Being a part of a scientific institution such as the university, the Economics Faculty of course is naturally occupied above all with science. At the same time, the importance of our Faculty with respect to practical life should not be disregarded. In reality, the realization of great institutions and works envisaged in the fields of agriculture, industry, or finance largely depends on the presence of individuals who know the mechanism of economic life as well as the effects of and reactions to the measures of economic policy. Even if these individuals work as free and private entrepreneurs instead of government officials, it is certain that they will contribute to the

economic development of our country. It is clear that our Faculty, which is relatively young, cannot produce all the expected results at once. However, the belief is strong that the objective set will be realized in a progressively more perfect fashion. The increasing knowledge and abilities of our graduates from year to year give rise to expectations. This observation gives great happiness to the Faculty's teachers.

It is my heartfelt wish that the dear students graduating this year will help develop the economic life of our country greatly in the near future by using and increasing the knowledge they have gained during their higher education.

Ord. Professor of Management Economics Alfred Isaac wrote:

*Theory and Practice*

It is important to know and understand the difference between theory and practice for every student of the economics faculty and economics graduate. However, this difference is not always understood very well by everybody. It is popularly believed that theory is foreign to practice and even is its enemy.

In reality, theory strives to understand and explain the events and relationships that happen in practical life. On the other hand, we are faced with the events explained in theory under various fashions in practice.

Not only the general populace, but also those who work in the field of economics cannot understand the differences and the relationships between theory and practice in many instances. On one hand, past and present students of economics believe that after this education, practical applications will pose no difficulty. In reality, similar to other professions (such as medicine and law) economic life also requires practical knowledge. Therefore, those who have just completed their education should not insist on wanting to accede to important administrative positions right away.

On the other hand, those in practical life are of the opinion that their precious experiences are more valuable than education and theory. This belief also is not correct. Although experience is of great value in life, there exists a host of information that cannot be gained by experience. A typical example for this is the problem of inflation, since measures necessitated by inflation with regard to accounting are only learnt through theoretical investigation.

Therefore, theory and practice are complementary to each other. This truth must be known by all young people.

Ord. Prof. Dr. Alexander Rüstow wrote:

> *The Position of the Economics Faculty with Respect to Current Problems*
> The Second World War is finally over. Some economic, social and political problems have surfaced in Turkey similar to the whole world with demobilization and the passage from a war economy to peace economy.
>
> In this period of passage, it is more important to arrive at a total consensus about the new state of affairs than the problems of technical organization that will arise from adapting to this new state of things. The solution to these serious and vital problems is closely connected to all the disciplines taught in our Faculty. Therefore, it is evident that, at this time, practical life cannot be isolated from the studies of the Economics Faculty.

Armed with the latest knowledge, the graduates had very productive careers in all sectors of Turkey's society. Fortunately, Hikmet Küney, a member of the class of 1944-1945, allowed the recording of an oral history. Here are some excerpts:

> Hikmet was the son of a leather craftsman with two shops. He was born in Izmir in 1923. Because of the Great (worldwide) Depression, business became bad in Izmir and the family moved to Istanbul in 1929. Hikmet's father found work as an upholsterer at a Ford motor cars assembly plant. Daily wage was 9 liras 75 kuruş (9.75 liras). Workers who knew English were paid 12 liras per day. Both were good wages for those times. Mother kept the money in a belt around her waist. The Depression struck again and the plant closed. The elder Küney opened a shop at the rear of what is now the French Consulate near Taksim square—one of Istanbul's major landmarks. Hikmet attended what was then called a Second Primary School. Afterwards, he attended the Istanbul Boys' Lycée and enrolled at the Economics Faculty of Istanbul University in 1941. The family bought a house behind the Sultan Ahmet Mosque (the Blue Mosque) when Hikmet was at the university (Fig.43).
>
> His courses were taught mostly by Neumark, Isaac, Kessler, and Rüstow. In the beginning, the lectures were translated into Turkish by assistants. By the time Küney was ready to graduate, all his professors had learned Turkish except for Kessler. Hikmet thinks this was because he was German and not Jewish. Hikmet

suggested that Kessler did not have his family in Istanbul.[57] Küney liked all of his professors but admired Neumark most of all. He was the first to lecture in Turkish. Soon after arrival, he spoke the language perfectly. After graduation, Hikmet could not find work for two whole years. All hirings were frozen, so he served the obligatory military service. In 1949, he took and passed the required examinations to be employed as "Inspector" in *Iş Bank*, one of Turkey's major state-owned banks. Only ten people were recruited in that year. In his capacity as inspector, he toured different branches of the bank for a few years, then was given an administrative position at headquarters in Ankara as Chief Inspector. From there he was promoted to Director of Accounting and later a senior vice-president. While heading Accounting, he was responsible for bringing "automation" to the bank. Working with Remington, Inc., an American company, many bank activities were computerized under his supervision. The work performed for generations by clerks wearing green eye shades and elbow pads while sitting on high stools with pen and ink was automated. He served on the board of directors of several companies in which the bank held shares. Hikmet married in 1956 and has two children. His son, Murat, is a civil engineer and his daughter, Zeynep, is a computer expert. Both are graduates of METU (Middle East Technical Univesity), one of the best state universities in Turkey. He retired in 1983 at 60, as is customary at *Iş Bank*.

## Introducing Western Civil, Commercial and Labor Law to the Land of the Ottomans

On arrival in Turkey, the émigrés became subject to a code of laws that commingled Islamic, Ottoman, and some western components that were introduced at the turn of the century. These legal structures and procedures clearly affected the way prospective jurists were being trained. Starting in 1933, both began a major process of transformation, so much so that the 2004 Istanbul University Faculty of Law website proudly declares:

> Until other universities established their Faculties of Law, ours was the first to train young jurists. After the University Reform of 1933 and, with the contribution of academics fleeing the Nazi regime, the principles of contemporary legal education originated and were developed at this institution. Many prominent and

> well-known figures, famous academics such as Prof. Andreas Schwarz, Prof. Ernst E. Hirsch, Prof. Sıddık Sami Onar, many judges, politicians, lawyers, writers, and journalists feature in the annals of the faculty. The academic staff of our faculty is proud of this heritage and aims to retain and promote the tradition of high quality education.[58] (emphasis added)

Born in Budapest in 1892, *Andreas Bertalan Schwarz*, after dismissal from a Law professorship at the University of Freiburg in 1933, became Professor of Roman and Civil Law at Istanbul University and remained in Istanbul until death. Andreas Schwarz "made important contributions to the adoption of western law in Turkey during the 1930s as well as training a whole generation of Turkish legal scholars at the Law Faculty of Istanbul University."[59] He was married to Ruth who had been born into a Jewish family in Budapest, Hungary. She converted to Catholicism during her own studies in Germany.

According to Fritz Neumark, Andreas Bertholan Schwarz

> ...was one of the most impressive and scientifically invaluable persons among us. He had a particular self-respect that was commensurate with his abilities. He influenced his colleagues in a permanent fashion, if not his students at first. Even his deep assimilation of the notion of law did not prevent his acting in a manner based on the hypothesis that a university professor could naturally have social privileges sometimes, a true hypothesis according to the traditions in Turkey. This can be described better by this example. As did many other German refugees, Schwarz lived in Bebek, one of the most beautiful areas of Istanbul. During the war, on a day when certain streets were closed for several hours due to military maneuvers, thinking that such an interdiction would not be valid for him, he went out of his home in his bathing suit to cross the 20-30 meters which separated his house from the Bosphorus for his daily morning swim. He got arrested by the police immediately and taken to the nearest police station to be interrogated. After it was understood that he is not a "normal" citizen or a spy but a respectable professor in Istanbul University, he survived the interrogation in spite of his interesting costume.[60]

Classics professor Charles B. Welles, writing on Yale University stationery on October 18 1940, tells that Schwarz "has been a prolific writer in a little-practiced field of ancient studies which has an important sociological character. I should very much like to see him in America, both because of my personal regard for him and because of my interest in his work."[61]

Another jurist, *Ernst E. Hirsch* came to Turkey in 1933 after dismissal from the University of Frankfurt am Main and declining an offer from Amsterdam University. This choice saved him much sorrow in later years. Between 1933 and 1943, he taught Commercial Law in Istanbul. During 1943, he moved to the University of Ankara, where he taught commercial and maritime law, legal philosophy, and legal sociology while advising the Ministry of Justice. Hirsch played a significant role in modernizing (westernizing) Turkey's *Commercial Code.* In 1943, he was granted Turkish citizenship and stayed in the country until a 1952 return to West Berlin (Fig. 44).

At the Seminar on "Culture as a Weapon, Academicians in Exile" in Berlin on July 19 2003, a member of the Turkish Parliament, Mr. Onur Öymen, said:[62]

> One of the most interesting books on the immigration of the Jews from Nazi Germany to Turkey was written by Prof. Ernst Hirsch. Hirsch says that *Ermachtigungsgesetz* adopted on March 24 1933 enabled Nazi party to start first discrimination and oppression of the Jews. On April 1 1933, the Nazis made, an appeal for the boycotting of Jewish merchants, lawyers, doctors etc. He believes that the German people have not reacted with enough strength to the terrorization of the Jews. Hirsh believes that the Nazi party's boycott against Jewish firms and institutions was more shameful than the *Kristallnacht* of November 9 1938. Soon after the Nazi boycott Professor Hirsch, who was until then serving as a judge in a Hessen Court, was forced to resign along with other judges or civil servants of Jewish origin. Professor Hirsch tried to teach in French universities. But under the political conditions prevailing at that time in France, his friends were not able to manage a teaching post in Paris. The only option available was a possibility to teach in Amsterdam University, but only as an Assistant Professor.

Sabanci University professor Behlul Üsdiken, a contemporary historian of economics, accounting, and management education, recognized that:

> Perhaps the most significant change was the conversion in 1936 of the Institute of National Economy and Society within the Faculty

of Law in the University of Istanbul into a separate Faculty of Economics. "A year later, a chair in 'Business Economics' was established in this faculty to be filled by a German professor...Alfred Isaak. This was an opportunity ....of remedying faculty shortages after the conversion from the Ottoman institution to a university and an additional means of educating a new generation of scholars."[63]

Moreover:

These institutional developments and the accompanying activities [were]...taking place in the context of an economically backward country that had generated a relatively limited industrial base in which larger and more significant enterprises were under the control of the state. So was the "industrial relations" system, within which strikes or lockouts were banned (until 1947), as was the founding of labour unions, the state acting as the arbitrator in the case of industrial dispute. Education for business was confined to two schools of commerce patterned after French models.[64]

It can be rightfully said that the émigré professors were the first to introduce management, public administration, business economics, accounting, and western law as university level curricula in Turkey. They also wrote the needed textbooks. Some of the German professors like Hirsch received Turkish citizenship as an expression of gratitude by the Turkish government. Honorary doctoral degrees were later bestowed upon several others.

The 2004 Istanbul University website proudly declares:

The Faculty of Economics of the University of Istanbul is the oldest in its field in Turkey. Among the academic staff of the faculty, which was founded in 1936, there were world-famous figures such as Ord. Prof. *Umberto Ricci*, Ord. Prof. *Josef Dobretsberger*, Ord. Prof. *Wilhelm Röpke*, Ord. Prof. *Fritz Neumark*, Ord. Prof. *Alexander Rüstow*, Ord. Prof. *Alfred Issac*, and Ord. Prof. *Gerhard Kessler*. These academics greatly contributed in the founding of the faculty.[65]

It is fair to say that Turkey's economic policies for many decades were in line with economist Neumark's teachings. Starting in the 1990s, these policies became more and more Röpkenist in orientation. Although there were no Marxists in its midst, the *Economics* contingent was obviously diverse in orientation yet quite respectful of the differing economic views represented. The transformation in government policy from etatism to a doctrine of free enterprise has found favor with the World Bank, the International Monetary Fund, and its major trading partner, the European Union (EU). In fact, the EU has made such transformation one of several preconditions that had to be satisfied before any consideration would be given to Turkey's bid for membership in the organization.

In the legal sphere, however, the émigrés' legacy has fallen short of expectations, and developments in the field receive mixed reviews. Leaving implementation issues aside, Turkey's *Commercial Code* as originally modified by the émigrés is to this day in harmony with its counterparts in western countries. However, over the decades, her civil and criminal laws were seriously affected by many real and some imagined threats. Externally, Turkey always felt threatened by its Greek neighbors. As the result of the breakup of the Ottoman Empire, and by a multinational treaty imposed on them and never fully accepted by the Turks, several Greek islands are visible to the naked eye off the Turkish coasts. The flare-up over Cyprus and its long legacy is yet another part of that story.

Although good trading partners, the political powder kegs of bordering Iraq and Syria have always given Turkey cause for concern. In recent years, so have the Islamic theocracies of neighboring Iran and Afghanistan. And the Soviet block, which until the 1980s included the neighboring Balkan countries' machinations in the Middle East while Turkey was a partner in NATO, has kept Turkey at bay for many decades.

After the Soviet Union's breakup, most of the Central Asian countries have had good relations with Turkey. This is especially the case with Azerbaijan. However, the Azeris (who are Moslem with a language that is understandable to an average Turk) have not as yet fully resolved their border issues with Armenia, a Christian people with a large diaspora. Armenia, especially the "overseas" Armenian contingent, wants to put closure to events that took place during the First World War and during Turkey's War of Independence which followed. Between 1915 and 1923, 1.5 million out of a total 2.5 million Armenians in the Ottoman Empire have perished under circumstances that are still in dispute. The Armenians are adamant that it was genocide. The Turks' counter-claim is that the deaths were attributable to war and hunger. And the dispute to this very day is not always civil. This brings us to the situation within Turkey itself.

Internally, it has not heretofore been easy to keep the Republic as secular as intended by its founding fathers. Nor is it now. Turkey's military establishment, which was always religiously dedicated to being anti-religious, has assumed the responsibility of maintaining the country secular and democratic. Odd as this may seem to us westerners, coups to restore the government back to that path have in fact taken place. The army has never allowed Turkey to lean too much either to a theocracy like in neighboring Iran or Afghanistan nor communist as in neighboring Rumania, Bulgaria, and the Soviet Union in years past, even if such leanings reflected ballot-box results. This seeming oxymoron is a direct legacy of the "Young Turks'" vision and understanding of the country's people.

Additionally, one cannot overlook the Kurdish minority's desire for independence. Some 30,000 casualties among ethnic Kurds and Turkish military have been counted as of the time of this writing. Sadly, the counting continues. During the 1990s, several respected staunchly Republican intellectuals had been assassinated in cold blood. Although the crimes had never been solved, both Iran and Saudi Arabia were suspected of thus meddling in Turkey's body politic. These and similarly situated scenarios have maintained a national paranoia of non-trivial proportions. Consequently, over the decades since the émigrés helped to rewrite its laws, Ankara enacted legislation and condoned practices on the part of its military and police forces that would have been considered undemocratic by the émigré legal scholars and had, in fact, been deemed antithetical to its own set of values by the EU. However, with radical Islam knocking on its very doors these values may well assume a state of reconsideration by the European Union itself.

*Figure 37*
Ernst Reuter.

*Figure 38*
Ernst Reuter surrounded by some of his students in Ankara.

*Figure 39*
Alexander Rüstow, 1945.

*Figure 40*
Gerard Kessler.

*Figure 41*
Umberto Ricci.

*Figure 42*
Fritz Neumark, 1945.

*Figure 43*
Hikmet Küney, 1945.

*Figure 44*
Ernst E. Hirsch.

# 7
# The Healers

## Re-engineering Medicine, Dentistry, and Public Health

> Most influential of all the physicians in Ottoman service were members of the Hamon (Amon) family. The [Hamon] family dynasty originated with Joseph Hamon born in Granada about 1450 who emigrated to Istanbul during the reign of Mehmed II and served as physician to Sultan Bayezid II and Selim I.[1]

According to Ottoman historian Stanford Shaw, the Hamon family was expelled from Spain during the Spanish Inquisition for being Jewish. Although the reader might have a picture of a quaint medieval hysteria, the Spanish Inquisition went on for three hundred years, lasting well into the 1800s.

By contemporary western standards circa 1930s, the Ottomans' medical legacy left much to be desired. Much of the medical "practice" was not based on current science; some was not based on science at all. Infant mortality was known to be high and longevity short. However, epidemiologic "data" were rudimentary and mostly based on anecdotal information. There were questions on public health issues, to wit concern for local water quality standards. In the countryside, and most of Turkey was just that, all food distribution, preparation, and consumption, was "traditional." The practices may not have changed for hundreds of years. Same for the "knowledge of dietary requirements."

In an agrarian society where meat was scarce or predominantly consumed by the upper class, protein was rare unless one lived on a seacoast. There were too few doctors and too few clinics for the rural population. Those who attempted a practice in general did not have access to the latest technology as in radiology and surgery. It was obvious that Turkey desperately needed medical schools based on western medicine. She needed major infusions of western medical technology and know-how in its use.

Her doctors needed to be brought up to date in medical methods.

It was with this as a scenario back in 1933 that Philipp Schwarz and in Basel began seeking candidates with impeccable credentials for the medical positions needed. All evidence shows that they did their job well and quickly. The medical contingent was by far the largest among the group. A survey of all academic Personnel Department files identified no fewer than seventy-six unduplicated "exile" names who worked in the Istanbul University Faculty of Medicine between the years of 1933 and 1950.[2] There were others at Ankara University's medical school, as well as at various government agencies.[3]

An excerpt from a February 3 2005 article by Dr. *Coskum Özdemir* that appeared in the *Cumhuriyet* Republican Turkey's oldest newspaper (established at Atatürk's request during the War of Independence) and influential in social democrat circles as a defender of Atatürk's reforms:

> My relations with İstanbul University are almost 59 years old. I entered the University of Istanbul as a medical student in 1946. That year, a law was decreed recognizing the autonomy of the universities. We were able to listen to interesting lectures given by world famous scientists gained as the result of the 1933 reform and German fascism. I always respectfully remember the pleasure and the love of science instilled in me by scientists such as Professor of pathology Schwarz, the colourful Professor of zoology, Kosswig, physiology Professor Winterstein, and internal diseases Professor Franklin.
>
> Our [native] Turkish professors were also among the famous people of the country. However, why some of them were so hard and cruel vis-à-vis the students is a thing which has occupied my thoughts a lot.

Professor Özdemir is a prominent Turkish intellectual who chairs the Turkish Association for Muscular Diseases, and is a staunch defender of Atatürk's reforms.

### Public Health

It may well have been a coincidence, but recognizing that Turkey had just come out of a series of wars which took place immediately on the heels of World War I, chances are that it was not a random happening: among the medical staff selected by the Schwarz organization were at least three who had established expertise in treating syphilis. These were *Dr. Alfred Marchionini,* who assessed its effects as a dermatological problem, *Dr. Albert Eckstein,* who considered its impact on children, and *Dr. Joseph*

*Igersheimer,* who had already published a book on syphilis and the eye. The émigré team included several additional individuals concerned with public health. The most admired by the medical students of these was hygienist *Julius Hirsch* who became Professor of Hygiene[4] and Director of the Hygiene Institute at Istanbul University after being released from the Kaiser-Wilhelm-Institut für Biochemie and the University of Berlin in 1933 (Fig. 45).

## Pathology

The organizer of it all, *Dr. Philipp Schwarz,* was born in Werschetz, Hungary, in 1894. He was "the youngest Professor in all of Germany at the time."[5] Schwarz was also a major figure in the reorganization of Istanbul University along modern lines starting in 1933. The Turkish government sought his advice on hiring of additional university teachers and government experts. At his suggestion, mathematician Richard Courant and Nobel laureate physicists James Franck and Max Born visited Turkey as scientific advisers.[6] In 1951, Schwarz returned to his post at Frankfurt University; in 1953, he moved to America where he served as a pathologist at the Warren State Hospital in Pennsylvania and continued his lifelong research on cerebral birth lesions in the newborn.

Although Philipp Schwarz was not labeled a "social reformer," he played a most significant role in organizing emigration of a group of intellectuals who made possible important facets of Turkey's social reforms in all sectors.

Philipp Schwarz was not only trying to save lives, but also build a new institution. While still in Zurich, in behalf of the *Notgemeinschaft* in a letter dated October 6 1933, he wrote to The Rockefeller Foundation's European office: "The Turkish Government is doing everything possible to facilitate our work. Our prestige in Turkey would, however, be greatly enhanced if we were in a position to say that the Rockefeller Foundation is assisting us." This set off a flurry of internal and external Foundation correspondence which culminated in financial support. Though the amounts were not great, the prestige was.[7] As indicated, in early 1934 the Foundation sent an emissary to Istanbul to survey the émigrés' integration and to report on their progress in reforming the university. The emissary was thorough; his diaries for February 17 1934 state: "Schwarz is a confident, dynamic person—the kind of leader the situation requires. He strikes me as being a little over-enthusiastic about the ability of the Turks. He says for example, that the students are not only more serious than German students, but keener; they have not the 'blasé' attitude of the Middle-European. Since very few of them know German and communication must be largely through an interpreter, S' judgment may be premature. (S. is rapidly acquiring Turkish; says his knowledge of Hungarian helps mightily) But all lectures must as yet be delivered through their Turkish assistants most of whom fortunately know German."[8] Time proved R. A. Lambert right.

Economist Fritz Neumark, "one of his oldest friends even during the Frankfurt days,"[9] remembers Schwarz in his memoirs as "the true 'spiritus rector' of the whole Turkish venture."[10]

> With great sorrow, I have to say here that this extraordinary person was treated with distrust and even dislike by both Turks and Germans, something he generally did not deserve; he was not shown the appreciaton he deserved for the great efforts he made for the refugees. (emphasis added)

As quoted in a 1953 biography,[11] Philipp Schwarz said:

> We have been able to remain loyal to the spirit which is the foundation of modern civilization and humane feeling, and to impart that spirit, even in those dark days of history, to thousands of gifted young persons (Fig. 46).

## Dermatology

*Alfred Marchionini* of East Prussia served as Professor of Dermatology in Freiburg. He came to Ankara in March 1938 and stayed until February 1949. He was in Hamburg until October 1950 and later in Munich as Professor of Dermatology where he also served twice as Rector (President of the University). Dermatologist Richard Richter, who was later invited to Ankara, tells of Marchionini's work in Turkey in his "A Letter from Ankara"[12] as follows:

> The department he took over was small and did not fit at all the description of a modern center of research in dermatology. However, the energy of Marchionini and his amiable cooperation with his colleagues in other departments made it possible to expand his clinic and establish an institute which could shoulder a large clinical workload. How Marchionini's influence was felt by a large section of the population is best evidenced by an increase of 24,000 in patients applying to the clinic during one year; this, in a very

> conservative population which was cautious against innovation and even rejected everything new. To succeed thus in the most primitive clinical conditions deserves admiration. As if this would not suffice, advanced scientific research was being conducted, although they did not have their own laboratories and Marchionini opened new horizons in dermatological research with innumerable articles. His work on the climatophysiology and pathology of the skin, his initial descriptions of a diseases' progression, new methods tried in the cure of sub-tropical diseases, will always provide a foundation and new dermatological research will continue to be conducted on this basis. His heritage continues to survive in the hard work of many of his students in Turkey today.[13]

Economist Neumark remembered Marchionini as "a typical Eastern Prussian," one famous as a dermatologist and as a specialist in venereal diseases. After the war, he "organized a German-French Week of interesting conferences and discussions in Munich, the aim of which was scientific sharing as well as rapprochement between German and French scientists."[14]

## Gynecology

*Wilhelm Liepmann* was born in 1878, and, by 1933, he was Director of the *Cecilienhaus* Women's Clinic and Professor of Gynecology at the University of Berlin. He was at risk because his wife, Emma, was Jewish. So, in that fateful year, 1933, they moved on to Turkey where he served as a Faculty of Medicine professor in Istanbul. Liepmann died in 1939. Fritz Neumark recalled that "besides *Rudolf Nissen* and ophthalmologist *Joseph Igersheimer*, gynecologist Wilhelm Liepmann especially became to be loved for his work as professor and clinic director in Istanbul. Liepmann, with his familiar but gentle manner not frequently seen among physicians, was known worldwide among his peers for his efforts while still in Berlin to establish and develop the new branch of *frauenkunde* [gynecology]. After only four years of work, he died in Istanbul. I met him there for the first time. With his quiet and friendly manner, he not only made numerous friends among his colleagues but also made good impressions on his patients"[15] (Fig. 47).

Willhelm Liepmann recognized the need for pregnant women to engage in prenatal physical exercise. In the 1920s, this was quite a revolutionary point of view. Significantly, the record shows that he maintained a personal correspondence with Albert Einstein.

## Internal Medicine

*Alfred Erich Frank* was first to discover the class of anti-diabetic drugs that can be taken orally. He also made important discoveries in the area of thrombocytes. Dr. Frank's personal story is summarized by Professor Emeritus A. Kazancıgil, a noted Turkish scientist, educator, and writer who owes his own education to the émigré professors. Frank "came and settled here; he made his name here, grew old, and did not want to leave. These [German] people were very useful for Turkey in the long run. It is not that internal medicine was not existent in Turkey until then; it did exist. We had first-rate men but [Frank] started a whirlwind of change. Of course, there is also the matter of their deaths for those who stayed on. Many chose Turkish cemeteries"[16] (Fig. 48).

The state funeral given to Frank in 1957 is an open indication of appreciation and love felt for him in Turkey. The Medical Faculty of Istanbul University ordered Dr. Frank's[17] gravestone at Istanbul's Bebek cemetery to be made and to be engraved: "Sleep in peace! Turkish medicine is grateful to you."

*Kurt Steinitz,*[18] a medical doctor and a Ph.D. medical chemist, was born in Breslau, Lower Silesia, or Wroclaw, Poland, and obtained his medical degree from Leipzig in 1931. He left Germany immediately after Hitler came to power, since Jewish physicians were not allowed to work anymore in the non-Jewish hospitals. Steinitz first went to Italy where he did unpaid work in Milan. After a few months, he left for Palestine with a cousin on a tourist visa.

Notwithstanding his immigration status, Steinitz bought a farm in Ramoth Hashavim, a community north of Tel Aviv, where many German immigrants, mostly academics, opened chicken farms. He wanted to learn how to raise chickens and tend bees, there being no jobs for physicians in Palestine at that time. However, in 1934 he returned to Breslau, Germany, in order to marry Elisabeth Bruck.

Steinitz's Breslau's mentor happened to be the above famous internist Alfred Erich Frank who was among the original group of *Notgemeinschaft* invitees to Turkey. Frank was among those given the right to bring with him a competent assistant. Dr. Frank opted for two, each to be paid half of one salary. Kurt Steinitz was one, and Steinitz's sister-in-law, *Dr. Erica Bruck,* was the other. For reasons not stretching one's imagination, both accepted the invitations extended to them. In turn, they tried to bring Erica's mother, *Ada Bruck,* to Turkey but did not succeed. Ada Bruck was one of the six million who perished.[19]

While in Turkey, in addition to continuing his research activities with Drs. Frank and Bruck, Steinitz was active in setting up modern clinical testing laboratories. To facilitate work in the new clinics, he enabled the Internal Diseases Clinic's laboratory in Istanbul to perform most of the needed tests. Steinitz also published numerous articles. Their daughter, Irene, was born in Istanbul at the end of 1936. The family was forced to live a very frugal life on the husband's half-salary. During summer months, they lived in a very old Turkish house on the Asian shore of the Bosphorus and Kurt moonlighted on one of the regular steamboat ferries crisscrossing the Straits. In winter, they lived in the old quarter of Istanbul (Fig. 49).

The most significant service that Steinitz performed for Turkey was establishing the infrastructure for transferring conserved blood. This had never before been done anywhere in that part of the world. Not only was he successful in establishing the means to do so, he also published instructions for performing the procedures. Additionally, in 1942, he published the Turkish textbook book *Clinic Laboratory Procedures.* His colleague, Dr. Alfred Erich Frank, wrote the book's preface, explaining its importance (Fig. 50).

Steinitz's final contract expired on June 1 1943 and he went back to Palestine. There he first went straight to work for *Kupat Holim,* the national health service and insurance agency in the port city of Haifa and at the same time in a small inland farming community called Afula which is located in the Jezreel valley of northern Israel over 30 miles away. In the 1940s, a bus or train ride would have taken at least an hour (the train is long gone). To this day, with no more than 40,000 residents "within Israel, Afula is still known (somewhat rightfully so) as a boring, dusty place in which it is far from desirable to live, whose inhabitants are close-minded, and all dress and act the same."[20]

Between 1945 and 1960, Steinitz was on the staff of the *Rambam,* the major research and teaching government hospital in Haifa. At the same time, he worked for Haifa's *Roschild* Municipal Hospital. Between 1960 and 1966, he directed the chemistry laboratories of *Beilinson* Hospital in Petah Tikva, a prominent research institution. Steinitz died in 1966.

Kurt Steinitz built the first artificial kidney in Israel and continued to publish in the best-refereed journals worldwide. Many of his publications are still available through the services of Pub Med. Unfortunately, Steinitz was never given a university appointment in Israel (Fig. 51).[21]

## Pediatrics and Public Health

*Erica Bruck,*[22] a pediatrician whose life was saved by Turkey in 1934, left Istanbul for the United States in 1939 for a number of reasons. One of these was to make it possible for the growing Steinitz family to have the full Assistant's stipend—she had been living on half. In America, Dr. Bruck enjoyed a brilliant medical career, serving as a pediatrician at the Children's Hospital of Buffalo for fifty years. She published many seminal research articles, such as the "Renal Functions in the Course of the Nephrotic Syndrome in Children" published in the *Journal of Clinical Investigations* in 1954." Another was the paper on the "Perfusion of the Underventilated Compartment of the Lungs in Asthmatic Children," published in the same journal in 1964. During the course of her life in Buffalo New York, she was very active in many causes affecting children worldwide, including the initiative to ban land mines and constant work to assure equitable housing opportunities as in the membership-based nationally recognized civil rights organization called HOME. Her life was saved in 1934 by Professor Frank's ability to invite her out of a Nazi hell and Kurt Steinitz's willingness to share the one-person Assistantship billet at Istanbul University.

It is difficult to contemplate the number of lives Erica Bruck affected during her fifty years at Buffalo's Children's Hospital for fifty years. It is also mind-boggling to consider her impact on the health of children everywhere and forever as the result of her published research, most of which was based on clinical studies. And if that were not enough, as a member of the *National [US] Committee for Clinical Laboratory Standards*, Erica Bruck coauthored at least six procedure manuals on collection of blood for diagnostic purposes, which continue to set the standards in today's medicine.[23]

It is interesting to note that Howard Faden, M.D. and Linda Duffy, Ph.D., from the Department of Pediatrics, *State University of New York*, School of Medicine and Biomedical Sciences and Margot Boeve, from the *Ryksuniversiteit Groningen*, Groningen, of the Netherlands conclude their 1998 article "Otitis media: back to basics" which appeared in the *Pediatric Infectious Disease Journal*[24] with: "We dedicate this article to Dr. Erika Bruck on her ninetieth birthday."

When contacted about the dedication, Howard Faden, M.D. stated, "She was among the most astute faculty we had. A great physician and I use the term 'great' rarely. When others could not figure out the diagnosis, they invariably turned to Erica."[25]

By far the most interesting of all the émigré "healers" in Turkey was pediatrician *Albert Eckstein*. As often is the case, Dr. Erna Schlossmann-Eckstein, also a pediatrician, and the daughter of Weimar Germany's renowned pediatrician Arthur Schlossmann, often operated in the shadows of her husband. Often, but not always! Dr. Erna Schlossmann-Eckstein did accompany her husband and his Turkish assistant on many forays into Turkey's hinterland villages to collect some of the country's first public heath statistics. She was an acknowledged member of the team on these data-collection expeditions.

Albert Eckstein was indeed a social reformer in the field he knew best—pediatrics. He "...made major contributions to the treatment of children's illnesses by creating a series of clinics throughout Turkey."[26] He also redesigned the country's pediatrics curricula. Ordinarius Professor, Albert Eckstein was the architect of modern pediatrics in Turkey. His contributions to Turkey and to helping save other Jewish refugees from the Nazis were so multifaceted and each so significant that they will receive a disproportionate amount of space in this book. This man brought with him the latest knowledge and the latest technology in pediatrics health care delivery to a society in desperate need for such. But he did even more. He used his personal rapport with ministers of state to enable the right of passage through Turkey, for groups of Jews fleeing the Nazis and heading for British-controlled Palestine. Eckstein was remembered and honored in 2005, the sixtieth anniversary of his founding the Pediatric Clinic at Ankara University.

**Drs. Albert and Erna Eckstein[27]**

Noma (*cancrum oris*), a devastating, gangrenous disease found almost exclusively in young malnourished children, was eradicated in Turkey by Dr. Albert Eckstein.[28] (Fig. 52 and 53). He was the first to introduce modern public health concepts and methods to that impoverished land. Eckstein was born on February 9 1891 in Ulm, Germany, and he studied medicine in Freiburg. In World War I, he was awarded the "*Eisernes Kreut* First Class," the German Honor Cross, First Class, for heroism.[29] Following the war, he worked at Freiburg's Physiology Institute. Around 1920, he moved to the University Hospital for Children to work under Carl T. Noeggerath, a very famous pediatrician at the time. In 1923, he became a senior lecturer based on his work, "Influence of natural and artificial light sources on the growth of young rats with simultaneous variation of their living conditions."[30]

Eckstein married Erna Schlossmann, a pediatrician whose father, Arthur Schlossmann, was head of the Children's Hospital at the Academy of Medicine in Dusseldorf. In 1926, Eckstein was promoted to the rank of professor. After Schlossmann's death, Eckstein was appointed chief of the department and had reason to look forward to a brilliant career in the land of his birth.[31] However, on July 1 1935 in his Düsseldorf clinic, Dr. Eckstein received an envolope marked "Personal." It read: "In the name of the Reich, I relieve you of your duties in the service of the Prussian

Government by June 1935 based on the orders dated 12 June 1935. *Adolph Hitler, Hermann Göring.*"[32]

Through the *Notgemeinschaft,* Albert Eckstein received an offer to work at the Ankara Nümune Hospital. He had two more offers, one from England and a tentative one from the United States, however, he and his wife found the offer from Turkey secure and guaranteed. Eckstein's contract was signed on August 1 1935 in Berlin by *Hamdi Arpağ,* Turkey's Ambassador to Germany.[33]

## Ecksteins' First Years in Turkey

Eckstein and family arrived in Ankara during September 1935. The next day he met the Minister of Health and Social Assistance, Dr. *Refik Saydam.*[34] The minister told Eckstein that he had been especially recommended by Professor Schwarz.[35]

During this first meeting, Dr. Eckstein asked the minister what was really expected of him, leaving the official contract aside. Dr. Saydam's answer was, "I would also like you to prepare a report on the subject of Child Health and Diseases in Turkey. This report will determine the child health policy of the ministry for which I am responsible. We believe that it is the principal duty of the State to make sure that our children are healthy and strong and they live under healthy conditions. However, one point that I would like to emphasize is that you do not base this report on German views. A German approach may not be suitable for our country. Therefore visit and examine all of Anatolia, and then come to us with your proposals."[36]

The Ministry of Health and Social Assistance asked Dr. Eckstein and his wife to undertake a trip, accompanied by Eckstein's newly assigned assistant, *Dr. Selahattin Tekand,* during July and August 1937 to investigate children's diseases and mortality in thirteen central and southern Anatolian provinces and villages. Additionally, they were charged with the collection of information about the fertility of women and the number of surviving children.

These studies were the first attempt to collect statistics on the health and demographics of a major segment of Turkey's population.

A column appearing in *ULUS* (Fig. 54) on November 8 1937 by editorial writer *Fali Rifki Alay,* a major national circulation Turkish newspaper, commented:

> Are Turkish Villages as we think they are? Atatürk has declared that agriculture is the backbone of general national development.

Agriculture means the village, and 90% of the Turkish population is employed in it. The Ministry of Health had an investigative village survey conducted by its specialist [Albert] Eckstein and one of our abler doctors, his assistant Dr. Selahattin. The specialists strived to learn the facts by using trustworthy methods in a large geographic area having a total population of 3,000,000. Today, we are publishing this report which is easy to understand by everyone. The Turkish village is still the most significant foundation for the future of Turkey. One should learn about its present state in order to understand what a great force it can be when its cultural, technical, and health requirements are satisfied.

At the end of the trip, Drs. Eckstein wrote:

Thus we visited [a sampling of] 60 the villages having a population of 52,662. To avoid any misunderstanding, here we have to record that each time, the villages were selected with a certain point of view [in order to get a representative sample] and were visited without prior notice. In this way, we were able to visit small villages of just over 100 habitants as well as big ones of about 5000 population; villages poor and rich, on mountains and plains, on fertile and arid land and also those on the high grounds of the Black Sea and the Mediterranean to be able to have an idea about different living conditions. In each village, we had long and close contact with the peasants. We asked and learnt about their customs. We were met with the greatest of trust while we had them tell us their complaints and troubles. We examined each dwelling, each inn inside and out in each village. We examined almost each child and woman or talked with them. Naturally, we also met most of the male population. Since we examined all the sick of all ages, we studied all kinds of diseases in the villages in detail. Moreover, we collected information about cereals, vegetable and fruit cultivation, animal husbandry, and the land lease conditions. Finally, we examined the reading, writing, and arithmetic skills as well as the general knowledge of the children at each opportunity. We think that we are capable to put forward objective opinions on these matters. Since trust in doctors is great and extraordinary in villages, we had no difficulty at all in our investigations. Furthermore, after the last population census, "the concept of statistical investigation" has aroused great interest everywhere. Therefore to collect statistics about female fertility and child mortality statistics was easier than we had previously thought. The peasants were not shy and retiring in the least. They were able to talk freely and give clear answers. The majority of the women knew the number of their dead and surviving children; the numbers they gave were proven to be correct although we verified them in different fashions. During our investigations, we found it was more fitting to ask them about boys and girls separately, even better make them say the names of their children. It is natural that we used all means needed to eliminate mistakes as much as possible. In order to reduce probable errors to a degree, we grouped the women according to ages 18-24, 25-29, 30-34, etc. In this way, small mistakes made in reporting ages did not influence the statistical results. [37]

The Ecksteins' report included the following sections: Results Obtained, Fish Consumption, Nutritional Situation, Fight against Trachoma and Diarrhea, Skin Diseases, Fertility of Mothers and Child Mortality, Child Mortality, Villages, and the Poorer Classes in Ankara.

*Maternal fertility and child deaths*

"We have finally reached the most important subjects of our investigations, namely maternal fertility and child mortality. We conducted statistical research on 8,000 women. This corresponds to 1/3 of all the women in the villages we visited."

The results[38] are surprisingly believable. The number of births increased uniformly and steeply until it reached an average of 6.05 births for women aged 40-44. For those over 45, the average number of births was 6.87. This indicates a slight decrease in births in villages during recent years but this cannot be a cause for concern.[39]

*Child Deaths*

Since documentation of infant deaths or deaths by separate age groups does not exist, it is not possible to determine infant mortality or mortality for other age groups except in the regions where malaria eradication was undertaken. It is possible to calculate child mortality indirectly by finding the average number of dead children for each woman. Naturally, the number of deaths for each age group would necessitate separate evidence. For example, if child mortality for women aged 18-24 is 20%, then this rate should be accepted to be higher than the 30% child mortality for women aged 40-44. Since the average age of marriage was formerly 14, the death of "a child" referred to by a woman aged 40-44 necessarily belongs to an adult.[40]

Therefore, child deaths for groups older than 30-34 are in reality below the rates estimated. The rates found for dead and surviving children are strikingly similar for the 13 provinces visited. This is more so for the younger age groups. This would indicate that the results we obtained are correct. In general, the death rates are much lower than thought. For example, for the first group aged 18-24, the general child mortality (not only infant mortality) is around 25%. If the particular climatic conditions are taken into account, this rate is not at all very high. Therefore, the conviction voiced from time to time that mortality in villages being very high is not supported by our findings. At least, it is not true for the provinces and villages we investigated.[41]

This conclusion is also supported by comparing these results with data collected during the last 6 months [prior to the preparation of the report] in the Ankara polyclinic. These statistics are based on 2,811 women. 2,196 of them are from the poorer classes while 614 are from the educated class. Dr. Albert Eckstein then goes on to discuss the general results obtained from visits to villages and from the Ankara polyclinic:

The figure of 3.4 surviving children per woman is accepted to be the international norm. If this number is true, then an increase of population can be expected with certainty. The number of 3.6 surviving children per woman reached for those aged 35-39 is already above this norm. 3.9 surviving children for older groups are also above this figure. Even groups aged 45 and over surpass the norm with an average of 3.7. In the city, this norm of 3.4 is only surpassed with 3.7 by women aged 45 and over. The "educated class" is significantly lower with 2.5 children! This means that a rural population increase is ensured. Since 80% of the Turkish population consists of peasants, if our findings are true for all provinces, then this population increase is also guaranteed for all of Turkey.

The presence of a sound population policy for the countryside is the principal cornerstone for an auspicious development.[42]

Clearly satisfied with the results obtained, the Ministry of Health and Social Assistance asked Eckstein to go on a second investigative trip into the interior provinces of *Isparta, Burdur, Antalya, Denizli, Muğla, Aydın, İzmir, Manisa, Balıkesir, Bursa, Kocaeli,* and *Bolu* during July and August of 1938. He was accompanied again by his pediatrician wife, *Erna,* and the Chief Pediatrics Assistant, *Dr. Selahattin Tekand.* They collected data on the number of households, male and female population, whether there were cases of malaria, enteritis, the kinds of water sources, and whether or not there was a school.

At the time of their travels around Anatolia, the campaign against malaria and eradication of tuberculosis and trachoma had already been started. Eckstein and party noted that they could see the positive effects of this campaign during their visits to the villages.

According to Dr. Selahattin Tekand:

> During the investigative trips in Anatolia, he [Eckstein] got used to the hardest conditions easily; he established immediate rapport with the peasants, joked with them and ate the food which was offered. He never refused to go even to the most difficult places. When we arrived in Afyon, he grabbed his camera and we climbed up the Afyon hill. It was a very steep climb. A peasant boy had difficulty coming down, so we sent help once we came down. He took a lot of photos there.[43]
>
> [Eckstein] took hundreds of photographs during these visits to the villages, which can be seen at the German Archeological Institute of Istanbul. One of his photographs, taken in Bürmük Village, Bolu, a province located in the northwest of Anatolia, was printed on the 10 Turkish Lira banknote that was put into circulation in 1942. This was also important as it was the first time that a photograph of a woman had appeared on a Turkish banknote. Another photograph taken by him was displayed at the Turkish Pavilion of the World Fair that was held in New York in 1939[44] (Fig. 55, 56, 57).

### İhsan Doğramacı and the Ecksteins

During his 1938 travels in Anatolia, a chance meeting between Eckstein and a young doctor in Manisa would turn out to have a profound impact, not only on the young doctor's individual career but also on the future of pediatrics in Turkey. After returning to Turkey from USA in 1947, İhsan Dorğamacı joined the Ankara Faculty. In 1953, he initiated the establishment of the *Hacettepe* Child Institute which became the *Hacettepe* Children's Hospital and, ultimately, the *Hacettepe* University. Several pediatrics clinics were established by young *Hacettepe* faculty all over Anatolia, including the towns of *Erzurum, Kayseri, Samsun,* and *Trabzon.* İhsan Doğramacı is also the founder of *Bilkent* University.[45]

From an oral history provided by Prof. İhsan Doğramacı to Dr. Akar in 1998:

The carriage stopped in front of the Governor's residence. Prof. Eckstein, his wife and Dr. Selahattin Tekand walked to the main entrance by the stairs of the residence. The fatigue of the whole day was evident from their faces. They saw a tall man approach them at the door. They stopped.

The young man introduced himself in a quiet and soft voice: "I am Dr. İhsan Doğramacı, the nephew of Dr. Lütfi Kırdar, our distinguished governor. Welcome to Manisa."

They walked towards the dining hall by following the young doctor. Dr. Lütfi Kırdar met them at the door of the dining room.

During the meal, they talked at length about the wealth of the Turkish cuisine, getting used to Turkish food and the specialties of olive oil dishes. While drinking their coffees, Dr. Eckstein directed a question to the young doctor: "Where did you graduate from?"

"İstanbul University."

"You must be a new graduate."

"Yes."

"Are you thinking of doing a specialty?"

"I have not thought about it. I plan to settle in a town and practice general medicine."

"Come to visit the villages with us tomorrow if you wish. I would be happy if you could help us with our studies. Perhaps being a pediatrician would seem attractive to you. Turkey needs young dynamic pediatricians such as yourself. One third of the babies born die before they reach one year of age. It is possible to decrease these deaths by some simple measures. However, we need educated people to spread these measures across Anatolia."

From a second oral history, provided by Dr. Selahattin Tekand to Dr. Akar, in 1998:

They [the people in the room] suddenly realized that Eckstein was using the first case plural, "we." They were taken aback. Eckstein, who had been working in Anatolia on the health of children for three years, had adopted Turkey's health policy and the idealism of the Turkish Republic as his own. Suddenly, [Dr.] Erna Eckstein felt a warm feeling towards this young man [İhsan Doğramacı]. During this conversation, she felt that her husband liked this young doctor. Otherwise why would he ask him to help with his work? Up to then, he had worked alone and only had Dr. Tekand with him.

## Eckstein and Turkey's Health Care Modernization

During Dr. Eckstein's stay in Turkey (1935-1950), he worked at Ankara's Nümune State Hospital, the largest hospital in the city at the time. In June of 1945, he was appointed Chief of its Pediatric Clinic. *Dr.Bahtiyar Demirağ,* who did his Pediatrics residency in Berlin between 1936 and 1939, was Eckstein's first associated professor. Dr. Demirağ succeeded Eckstein after his departure from Turkey in 1950 and continued in that position for 30 years. *Drs. Selahattin Tekand, İhsan Doğramacı,* and *Sabiha Cura* were his other assistants. These young doctors respectively went on to establish the Children's Hospitals in İzmir, Ankara's *Hacettepe* Children's Hospital and the Aegean University's Pediatrics Department in İzmir.

The Eckstein et al. (1941) book was one of his more important contributions to Turkish pediatrics in general and to child development and metabolism in particular. This book had been distributed to all medical doctors in Anatolia by the Ministry of Health and was used as part of the medical school's curriculum for many years.[46]

In October 1938, Dr. Albert Eckstein organized the first Turkish Pediatrics Congress in Ankara, and published the first two exclusively pediatrics Turkish textbooks. Their titles in Turkish are *Türkiye'de Nüfus Siyaseti* and *Normal Türk Meme Çocukları* (Fig. 58).

As indicated, Dr. Eckstein is credited with bringing science to bear on the treatment of *noma.* It is a *Borrelia* infection (related to the causative agent of Lyme disease) of the oral mucosa appearing in immune-system-compromised and malnourished children.[47] He succeeded in establishing a treatment model using sulfonamide. His article in the *Annales Pediatrici* provides information on this treatment. A 1947 article in the *Medical Journal of the Medical Faculty of Ankara University,* includes the following observations. Between 1936 and 1945, 373 cases were seen. It was observed in all provinces, particularly in East Turkey and among peasants. Most frequently, the disease was seen under four years of age with no gender differences and with a seasonal disposition present. Noma as a childhood disease has been eradicated in Turkey.[48] The cure for this devastation was hygiene, food, and antibiotics. Similar to the eradication of leprosy, its cure and prevention must have seemed like magic to the illiterate poor.

Albert Eckstein's other main research topic was malaria. He was invited to present a paper on "malaria in children" at the Fifth International Pediatrics Conference in New York, on July 14-17 in 1947, but he could not attend. However, the information he had accumulated, leading to his paper dealing with malaria in children [49] had a major impact in preventing and treating the disease in Turkey.

Dr. Eckstein was also a proponent of preventive medicine. The Faculty of Medicine in Ankara certainly followed in this tradition. His observations on breastfeeding of infants on demand[50] are in line with modern pediatric practices which now advocate mother's milk rather than bottle feeding.[51]

Dr. Eckstein dreamed of establishing a children's hospital in Ankara. He was planning for a hospital of 300 beds—50 beds reserved for orthopaedics cases, 50 for tuberculosis, and the rest for other diseases. It is interesting to note that the population of Ankara at the time was only 120,000. This project was first postponed because of World War II. After the war, a sum of two million Turkish lira was reserved for the hospital in the 1948 government budget. However, cancellation of this project resulted in Eckstein's decision to leave Turkey. In a long letter written to the Dean of the Ankara Medical Faculty during November 1948, he expresses his disappointment at the refusal of the budget reserved for this project. He refers to the original report he had submitted to the Ministry of Health in October 1935. The letter is a detailed record of the campaign he had conducted for thirteen years since his arrival in Turkey from the start for the construction of such a hospital and his many proposals and attempts to this end. Finally, he almost beseeches the Dean "to find the resources and the means to establish a university pediatric clinic in accordance with modern hygenic standards and needs seen as a result of the specialty's experience."

In a letter dated September 23 1949, Ord. Prof. Dr. Albert Eckstein writes:[52]

> To the Office of the Dean, Faculty of Medicine: "It is with sorrow that I am letting you know of my decision to accept a professorship in pediatrics at the Faculty of Medicine, Hamburg University, and therefore my inability to extend my present contract which finishes at the end of this year. I cannot stop myself from repeating one last time, before I leave your country, my belief and expectations for the great necessity of a pediatrics clinic to answer the demand in Ankara University. Even while in Hamburg, receiving news of the establishment of such a pediatrics clinic, the necessity of which I have emphasized in numerous reports, will fill me with joy. While I present my thanks to the Ankara University from which I have received great help and support, I consider it my duty to wish it success for the future.

Fittingly, before leaving Turkey, professor Eckstein served on the academic jury for the associate professorship in architecture of Ali Kızıltan at Istanbul Technical University. The subject of the thesis was a project for a children's hospital. Its program is exactly

> the same as that of Eckstein's described in his article published in 1930.[53]

In turn in the introduction of his architectural thesis, *Ali Kızıltan* writes:

> During the preparation of the project, the specifics of different elements and departments by themselves, within the total framework, as well as with respect to the structure and the organization of the hospital were discussed with Prof. Dr. Eckstein and agreed to the final version.[54]

After Eckstein's departure, two of his assistants brought his dreams of a children's hospital in Ankara to fruition. *Dr. Bahtiyar Demirağ* who replaced him at the Medical Faculty laid the foundations for a 150-bed hospital in 1953. This was followed by *Dr. İhsan Doğramacı* with his 300-bed hospital, at the *Hacettepe* Children's Hospital in the late 1950s. It is evident from whom these two distinguished pediatricians took their inspiration.

On December 22 1949, Eckstein received a letter from the student association:

> Most Honorable Ord. Prof. Dr. Eckstein, the Association of Medical Students would like to express their eternal gratitude for the selfless efforts and exemplary affection conferred on us medical students by your distinguished person. Therefore the Association has decided to enter your name, our dear teacher, as the second Honorary Member in the honors list during its meeting on the 22nd of December, 1949, Thursday by unanimous vote. The Association would also like to take this opportunity to wish you a good trip and success in your work while offering their eternal respects. Hayri Kalabalık Head of Medical Students Association of the Ankara University (Akar 2003).

## Albert Eckstein's Final Days in Germany

Once back in Germany, Eckstein had his professorship approved by the Hamburg Hansestadt Senate on March 21 1948. On June 22 of the same year, he was invited to give the 10th Ludwig Aschoff (his former professor) Conference in Freiburg University on "Malaria in Children." He started his lecture with the following words:

I consider it an honorable duty to commemorate in your presence, with sorrow and gratitude, the memory of Ludwig Aschoff, a peerless pathologist of the scientific world and at the same time, a great man. In spite of all that has happened in the past, I also consider it a sign of increasing mutual understanding, that the honor of speaking on this day consecrated to his memory about his moral heritage, life and work was accorded to me, one of the rare Germans who are in responsible positions outside their homeland. In this mutual understanding, we see the hope that the terrible poverty of the past and the present will end and broken ties and destroyed friendly bridges will be once again established with sincere attachments.[55]

And life goes on[56] (Fig. 59).

We could not have chosen a better country than Turkey when we had to leave Germany. From the first day, we were received with cordiality and helpfulness. After our journeys into all the different provinces, the name of Eckstein was known everywhere, for in most villages and small towns, no doctor had ever been before.

When we left Turkey and I asked for a customs officer, the Director of Customs said that he would personally come on Sunday. He asked, "What do you want to take with you?" I had thought of all the silver (gifts) that had been given to Albert, but he was not interested in that and said: "You are going to a poor country. How many kilos of rice, sugar, raisins, tea, and coffee do you want to take?" And when I said that to take coffee out was forbidden, I got the answer: "I should like to know what could be forbidden in this country for an Eckstein!"

Since Schummi[57] had treated the children of Ankara over time, our friendships were incredibly extended. Wherever we went, children came over to kiss Schummi's hand. As we were leaving Ankara, hundreds of Turks came to the station with their babies or children to bid us a last farewell. The newspapers later wrote that it was the greatest farewell ceremony seen in Ankara until then. The train attendants carried the boxes of sweets and flowers to the next compartment. We gave the flowers to the German Hospital in İstanbul and most of the candies to the Kosswigs[58] (Fig.60).

Professor *Dr. Karl Hellmann* was born in Würzburg, Bavaria, on September 8 1892 and died in 1959. He was among the small group of health professionals who went from Turkey to Palestine. Two of his daughters,

Erica and Miriam went to Palestine with him, and the third, Frances (Franciska), married archaeologist, philologist, and historian Hans Güterbock who obtained a prestigious position at the University of Chicago. Hellmann received most of his higher education in his home town, Abitur (1911) in Würzburg, up to and including his Doctor of Medicine in 1920. Between 1912 and 1919, he served in the German army. From 1924 to 1928, Dr. Hellmann was employed in Westphalia's *Münster* University as an ear specialist. In 1928, he became the clinic's acting director. From 1930 to 1935, he was back at the University of Würzburg as professor and head-physician at its Ear, Nose, and Throat (ENT) Clinic. Dismissed in 1935, Professor Hellmann sent his biography and list of publications to the Rector of Istanbul University from *Würzburg*. He came to Istanbul in 1936 via the Orient Express with his wife and three daughters. Hellmann replaced another German, Professor Ruttin, as Director of Istanbul University's ENT Clinic. Ruttin could not get the support he requested for modernizing the clinic, so he left Turkey for Austria. Hellmann managed to have the clinic moved to a building in much better condition, increased the number of patients examined, and devised a technique that enabled laryngectomies to be performed in a much shorter period of time. He was able to bring his relatives (including a brother Bruno who was already in the *Buchenwald*[59] concentration camp) from Europe to Turkey in 1939. Because his contract was not renewed, Hellmann left Turkey for Palestine at the end of summer 1943 (Fig. 61 and 62).[60]

**Ophthalmology** (Fig. 63).[61]

"Over 2000 American ophthalmologists had listened to his lectures."[62] And Joseph Igersheimer did not start lecturing American doctors before his sixtieth birthday. Igersheimer was a Jewish German-born ophthalmologist. He had chosen his career in opthalmology because, as a teenager in the early 1900s, he had contracted tuberculosis. While recuperating at a Swiss sanatorium, he noticed that many fellow tuberculosis patients had an unusual marking, a white area in their eyes. He began examining their eyes and this led to a lifetime fascination with how other diseases affect the eyes.[63]

Igersheimer completed his medical education in Heidelberg, Berlin, Strasbourg and Tübingen, and received his degree in 1904. Between 1905 and 1909, he worked his way up from assistant to an Assistant Professor in Heidelberg. Igersheimer became full Professor in 1914 and "Extraordinary Professor" in 1920. He was the "Head Physician" in Göttingen between 1915 and 1925, before his appointment at the University of Frankfurt.

Starting in 1915, Igersheimer was first in the world to use arsphenamine for the treatment of syphilis of the eye, and was among the first to write articles and books addressing the impact of syphilis on eyesight. In 1919, the Springer Verlag in Berlin published his seminal text, *Syphilis und Auge* (Syphilis and the Eye). Igersheimer was the first to operate for retinal detachment by closing off the holes. He did all this before 1926, at which time he became full professor in Frankfurt-Am-Main. It looked like he had a brilliant future in Germany's highly advanced medicine. Then came January 30 1933.

Igersheimer was Jewish as was his wife, Alice. Realizing that the worst was yet to come, Igersheimer, like many others, looked for ways of leaving his beloved *heimat*. He was looking for a place that would not only offer refuge but an opportunity to practice his love of ophthalmology. He did not have the option of going to a job waiting for him in the West. Like his compatriots, he was keenly aware of the lack of university job opportunities due to widespread discrimination and the worldwide Great Depression. Fortunately for Igersheimer, Schwarz's *Notgemeinschaft* came through.

Igersheimer was in the first party of scientists to arrive in Turkey. On October 15 1933, he took charge of Istanbul University's Institute of Ophthalmology, a section of its Faculty of Medicine. Igersheimer's first contract with the Turkish government covered the period November 15 1933 to November 15 1938. During the second week on the job, Igersheimer delivered his first Istanbul lecture on "Blindness and Its Causes," in German.

The past is prologue. In his new and very foreign environment, while building his practice from a zero base, constructing a modern eye clinic, training medical residents despite a language barrier, writing papers and books in German, giving seminars to dental students and faculty on the relationship between tooth and eye diseases, and introducing cases he found interesting at meetings of the Turkish Medical and the Turkish Ophthalmology Associations, Igersheimer was expected to speak Turkish by 1936, three years after arriving.

### Turkey's Educational Status, the Need for Reform, and Igersheimer

The Turkish university's library did not have a good collection of books on modern ophthalmology nor did the clinic have the requisite tools for him to perform his work properly. For those, and for personal reasons (money), Igersheimer wanted to bring his books and various clinic tools to Turkey. He had left them behind because the cost of approximately 7000 *Reichs Marks* in Turkish customs duties was excessive for him at the time.

The Turks had promised that no customs duty would be applied if the medical goods came within three months of his arrival. However, because of the delay of the shipments' arrival, Igersheimer ended up paying the customs and donating his medical books and tools to the University on condition "that they be used by the students."

On March 3 1934, Igersheimer wrote to the Dean of the Faculty of Medicine: "...I do not have much information regarding the education of our students prior to the university. 40-50% of my students could understand and talk a little bit of French as far as I can figure out. Only 3 students out of 60 know a little German. On the other hand, Latin is a language that Turkish students do not know at all and hence that situation makes understanding of medical terms very difficult for them."[64]

In another letter to the Dean's office, he made his position quite clear "...Current equipment of Istanbul University Eye Clinic is not adequate...." (Fig.64). In the same letter, he pleaded that the government extend a contract to his assistant *Susanne Hofmann* who had worked for him at the University of Frankfurt and who had come to Turkey in order to work with him.[65]

A notice in a monthly medical journal, circa 1934, states: "The operation performed on the eye of Ex-Minister of Finance *Abdülhalik Bey* by Ophthalmology Professor Igersheimer was similar and even more difficult and important than the operation on the other eye performed in Vienna. This operation met with success."[66] On December 10 1935, Igersheimer was asked to go to Ankara. The purpose of that trip was to examine and treat *Tevfik Aras*, Minister of Foreign Affairs.

Reflecting on his years in Turkey, another exile, Prof. Dr. *Rudolf Nissen*, comments about Igersheimer in his book, *Erinnerungen eines Chirurgen*. "To watch this respected, intelligent, impressive person at work was always a pleasure. He was first to establish a personal relationship with the government by operating on the President of Parliament."[67]

Another émigré colleague, economics professor *Fritz Neumark*, commented in his memoir about how he personally benefited from the developments that Igersheimer had ensured: "I owe much to Igersheimer. My son developed a sudden cornea difficulty when the Second World War had just started and Igersheimer was already in Boston. His young Turkish colleague, Prof. Dr. Naci Bengisu, who replaced Igersheimer, examined my son and said that he needed immediate surgery and performed it in a timely manner. This operation was pioneered by a Dutch doctor at the beginning of the 1930s and it was very difficult under the best of circumstances. Igersheimer taught the method to his Turkish colleagues. Thus, he indirectly saved my son from being blind."[68]

According to Neumark,[69] on a visit to Turkey, the *Shah Pahlevi* of Iran complained to Atatürk about an eye problem, whereupon Atatürk recommended one of "his" German specialists. After a thorough examination Igersheimer pointed out that all the Shah needed was a new pair of lenses and proceeded to write their prescription. When Igersheimer returned to the front office after the examination, he found the Shah's *aide-de-camp* who asked that Igersheimer choose the frames. Igersheimer answered that his majesty can choose a frame with the assistance of any optometrist. The aide got down on his knees and pleaded that Igersheimer make the selection as he had forgotten to mention this to Igersheimer at the outset of the examination process and that this was an order from his master. If Igersheimer did not comply with that command—he would have immediately been booted out of his *aide-de-camp* position. At this point, Neumark offers an explanation. "The Shah came from humble circles. Politically astute he went from the rank of sergeant in Iran's army to become the country's head of state. As can be gathered, the Shah still preferred ancient Oriental traditional ways. Igersheimer selected the frames."

Igersheimer's students were well aware of his fame. In their 1935 yearbook, they entered his caricature and affectionate comments[70] (Fig. 65).

## Igersheimer Was First to Perform Keratoplasty in Turkey

Despite inadequate clinical conditions, Igersheimer performed the first "keratoplasty" procedure in Turkey. This fact was discussed by Prof. *Dr. Naci Bengisu.* "Keratoplasty was applied for the first time by Igersheimer via the v. Hippel[71] trepan in the form of autokeraplasty in the University Eye Clinic in the last months of the year 1935."[72] Since the blindness phenomenon due to loss of transparency of the cornea[73] was often encountered in Turkey, keratoplasty was a frequently required operation in the country. However, only a total of thirty-four keratoplasties were performed in the country between the years of 1935 and 1939. Bengisu explained the reasons of not being able to perform many keratoplasties as follows:

> There were many reasons for this sparseness. . . . Patients that had been accepted to the clinic were backing down from the operation and were leaving the clinic when they learned that a piece from a dead eye would be taken. We contended with the corpse washer of our hospital for a while. He was not informing us when there were fresh cadavers. Another obstacle was the freshness of the cadavers. Generally, we were not able to extract from the patients that had just passed away. We had to extract from the cadavers that had passed away five-six hours ago.[74]

## Igersheimer's First Ophthalmology Textbook in Turkey

By contract, Igersheimer was obliged to write a Turkish textbook in his field within three years of arrival. With time to spare, in March of 1936, he published the 228-page textbook, *Eye Diseases,* which was translated by *Dr. Murad Rami Aydın* into Turkish. In the book's preface, Igersheimer noted that the textbook had been designed as a guide to diagnosis and treatment for students and general practitioners. However, he emphasized that no such textbook should ever replace didactic instruction and clinical patient demonstrations. The book discussed most of the prevalent eye problems in Turkey such as "trachoma." A substantial number of the book's pictures were drawn by Jewish émigré *Kläre Krause,* the Faculty's illustrator. The second edition of the book was published in 1942, long after Igersheimer had left for the United States (Fig. 66).

## His Requests Were Being Listened To—Most Not Acted Upon

In Turkey's unfailingly polite culture, an outright "no" is a rarity; the tendency instead is to delay and deflect.[75] It was so back in the 1930s; it is so now. It takes westerners a long time to recognize this. Some never do. For many it is a source of much frustration. On April 14 1935, the Minister of Education wrote the President of the Istanbul University "...Prof. Igersheimer requests to increase the number of beds scattered in three rooms from 24 to 50 by assigning *Gureba* Hospital's empty rooms to his service. Moreover, he complains about not having an operating room, space for his tools, and about having the smallest polyclinic and only two assistants instead of the four that were promised. I kindly request you to take action in order to increase the number of beds as the Professor requested."[76] Sending that request to the Minister of Health instead of petitioning the University Administration was a last resort due to Igersheimer's understandable frustration at unresponsiveness or inaction or both when due protocol was initially followed. Needless to say, his means of dealing with his frustrations did not endear Igersheimer to his administrative superiors.

As in any bureaucracy, an order from the University's President insured that the matter was duly investigated by the Dean. Without letting more than three weeks pass, in his May 2 1935 report, the Dean accepted the fact that "the Eye Clinic's situation was difficult." "The Eye Clinic actually does not have an independent operating room. The operations could only be carried out at the small operating room of the 1st Surgery Clinic and only when it was not occupied. The number of beds being low, space allocated for the polyclinic being very limited really makes education and service difficult." However, the report was not acted on. It ended up collecting dust on someone's shelf. There is no document to be found showing that Istanbul University's administration did much with its own findings in this matter. There is indirect evidence, however. As late as March 30 1938, another exile scientist, *Prof. Dr. Rudolf Nissen*, an eminent surgeon and Director of the University Surgery Clinic, wrote the University's Rector "the worst equipped clinics in the Faculty are mine and the Eye Clinic."[77]

It is true that during his first yearly vacation, January 28 1934 to February 15 1934, Igersheimer went back to Germany because of a family illness. Also, on the invitation of the Ophthalmology Association in Vienna, he attended a conference in Vienna between January 15 1937 and February 3 1937. And a Turkish medical periodical of that period,[78] shows that he had gone to the "Eye Disease Congress held in Cairo with his Assistant Professor *Dr. Naci Bengisu* in December of 1937. For a while at least, the university facilitated some of Igersheimer's personal and professional objectives.

According to Igersheimer's Turkish colleagues, his unique studies and instructive articles took their place in important medical journals of the country. His studies of syphilis revealed the relevance of uveal (of or relating to the uvea of the eye) inflammation, and his dealing with secondary syphilitic side effects while in Turkey have engraved Igersheimer's name in the world's medical literature. On the other hand, documents in the Istanbul University Personnel Department Archives show that during May of 1939, Igersheimer wanted to go to a region having a high incidence of trachoma in the southeast (near Palestine), however, his request for permission was, for reasons unexplained, actually turned down.[79] This happened to have been a surprising departure from Turkey's "unfailingly polite culture" rules.

Also, in the spring of 1939, Igersheimer applied to University Administration for a budget to publish a second book on retina circulation that he wrote with Assistant Professor Dr. Naci Bengisu. By late fall, he still had not received a reply and in this lay a message. Igersheimer began serious preparations for re-emigration, this time to the USA.[80]

At all times in Turkey, the émigrés endured a myriad of stressful pressures. There were worries about loved ones and colleagues left behind, broken families, acculturation to a new society, and, at times, continual efforts to sabotage their work by locals who had real and imagined reasons for doing so, a most important aspect. A fellow émigré Arthur von Hippel offers the following anecdote: "Ophthalmology professor Igersheimer initially found that his waiting room was always empty. At last he discovered that his predecessor had hired a beggar to sit in front of the office entrance to tell approaching prospective patients that they would be made blind. After this obstacle (the beggar) was removed, his hospital flourished and, a few months later, Igersheimer was asked to do a cataract operation on a minister."[81]

This particular cross-cultural tragi-comedy continued, however. The protagonist and his "blindness" claim resurfaced in the media and in a Ministerial inquiry. After realizing that these claims failed his ultimate objective, the Turkish doctor resorted to poison, but to his consternation, Igersheimer survived the attempt.[82]

In his memoirs, Philipp Schwarz explained how some of the passive resistance encountered by the émigrés was overcome. Igersheimer had had a special role in this matter in addition to having survived poisoning. "Hospitals were managed by the Ministry of Health. The foreign professors assigned to them by the Ministry of Education were considered 'uninvited guests.' However, it did not take long for the word to spread in the country that our surgeons *Nissen*, *Liepmann*, and *Igersheimer* were creating miracles. Soon, seriously ill men, women, and children started to camp, so to say, in the hospital court, on the stairs and in the corridors."[83] However successful with the potential patient population, no matter how productive and adored by his students and the senior politicians in Ankara at the same time, the local medical lobby apparently had the University Rector's ear. The Rector needed only to imply his position for the Dean of the Faculty of Medicine to implement it. Igersheimer lost out in these politics. Apropos in the 1950s, Robert Maynard Hutchins, President of the University of Chicago, has said something to the effect that the people who should be in academic administration positions won't take them, and the people who aspire to them should not even be considered. And so it is, things have not changed over time and such practices were not invented in Turkey.

## Igersheimer's Mission Mostly Accomplished

Law Professor *Dr. Ernst Hirsch*, another fellow émigré wrote in his published memoirs that Turks considered some of the German professors of medicine to be "genuine magicians," Many patients wanted a second opinion by or to be examined in the first place by a German professor. Members of the Parliament, ministers, and other senior functionaries were delighted at not having to go to Vienna, Zurich, or Munich for treatment in serious situations any longer.[84] Igersheimer was undoubtedly one of these "genuine magicians."[85] His fame had become a staple of Turkish popular culture. This was manifested in many ways. One of these was a word game involving the "popular professor" in Turkish. "Popular" also means "in the eye," therefore a popular professor meant "in the eye professor."

In an article titled "Dekolman," *Sabahattin Ali*, a very noted Turkish author and one of the realist/socialist story writers, wrote: [86]

> A young man, staying at the home of an uncle, an Ankara doctor, was the story's protagonist. He was doing translations for physicians to earn money. Because of this association, he became aware of a panic in the air. At issue was an eye operation to be done on an important personage, the Parliament's President. Several famous ophthalmologists had come from Istanbul and examined the "Chief." None, however, dared to perform the operation that was indicated. Therefore it was decided to invite the renowned "German" ophthalmology professor. At this point the young man noticed an article about the very retina detachment operation needed to be performed on the Chief. He told his doctor uncle that he can translate this article. However, to avenge the exploitation of his previous labors, he set a hefty fee for this job. Be that as it may, the doctor and his friends accepted the proposal. They then schemed to ask the German ophthalmology professor about the very information they had just gleaned from the article. They did this to flaunt their knowledge. Because the operation was already scheduled and the job assigned to the Jewish-German professor, they had nothing to lose. Comforted by this, they hoped to squeeze the professor into a corner. Igersheimer listened to their questions and sage comments with a smile on his lips. When they finished he replied by saying that he will be doing the procedure they were talking about. He concluded his response by saying: "In fact I have reported everything you just mentioned in the last issue of the weekly medical journal. However, as you know we cannot publish under our own name because we are Jewish."
> The group of conspirators had put themselves into a ridiculous position while trying to get the better of Igersheimer.[87]

On January 5, 1939, Turkey ended all possibilities for family reunifications to the émigré community.[88] It passed a law that curtailed residence rights of foreigners and ceased to allow any more entry permits for any stateless persons. In his September 18 1940 letter to Istanbul University's rector, Josef Igersheimer justifies his not returning to Turkey from the United States where he had gone to lecture on the grounds that this law would prevent his family from ever being reunited over there. At the time,

Igersheimer's daughter was a resident in England and his son Walter was incarcerated by the British in Canada as an enemy alien (Fig. 67).[89]

## Igersheimer in the United States

According to his son, Walter Igersheimer, who was studying in the UK at the time, unbeknownst to his father, his mother had applied for United States visas under the quota system. Her application was successful. In 1939, the Igersheimers went to the States on a lecture tour. While they were in America, the war broke out in Europe. Igersheimer and his wife could not easily leave. Friends in the Boston area encouraged him to stay and open an office. Joseph Igersheimer took all necessary tests and passed each and every one on his first try. With license to practice in hand, he opened an office.[90]

Igersheimer started publishing books as early as 1919, as is shown in Figure 68. By the time he went to Tufts College in Boston, he had no fewer than ten books in print. Figure 69, on the other hand, shows that he started publishing papers in 1904. The page of this exhibit is followed by five others in his Tufts application, all just as fully loaded with references to papers published. He continued to publish during his exile years as well, understandably not at the same rate. In retrospect, perhaps it had been a hard pill to swallow for so eminent a scholar to have to accept the lowly title of Assistant Professorship appointment at Tuft's Medical School, but it was an appointment in his field and it was in the United States and his life would be safe. Once again, he prospered, reaching even greater heights. In time, Tufts College had recognized its "error" and Igersheimer was asked to act as Head of Opthalmology, since the original had been drafted. He did so and, after the war, stayed on at Tuft's as a full Professor.[91] (Fig. 68 and 69).

Sixty-five years after offering an *Assistant Professor* position to a great scholar and eminent practitioner who was also a superb teacher and practitioner but under great duress, Tufts University had the following to say on its website:

> In the 1930s and 1940s, the Departments of Medicine at both Tufts and the New England Medical Center were enhanced by the addition of a number of distinguished physicians who had fled Germany, including Drs. Siegfried Thannhauser, Gerhard Schmidt, Heinrich Brugsch, Joseph Igersheimer, and Alfred Hauptmann. The department was further strengthened by the arrival of Drs. Edwin Astwood, William Dameshek and William Fishman. After

> Dr. Samuel Proger was named professor and chair at the school and physician-in-chief at the New England Medical Center in 1948, he further strengthened the department at Tufts by recruiting a number of outstanding faculty members, among them, Drs. Marshall Kaplan, Jerome Kassirer, Herbert Levine, Seymour Reichlin, Robert Schwarz, William Schwarz, and Louis Weinstein.[93] (emphasis added).

At all times, Igersheimer was thankful to Turkey for what she had provided for him during the time of his greatest need. After becoming well established in America's ophthalmology ranks, Igersheimer continued to make contributions to its Turkish counterpart in various ways. Among these ways was the publishing of articles as is shown in Turkish medical journals (Fig. 70).[92]

Igersheimer's life was saved because Turkey needed his expertise. In turn, he did much for Turkey. According to Igersheimer's son, Walter, a retired Yale University Clinical Professor of Psychiatry, the family had never practiced the Jewish religion. However, Walter tells the story that, in 1917, Joseph Igersheimer was called in to see Germany's Minister of Health. At the meeting, he was offered the position of Chief of Ophthalmology at the University of Rostok, then the world's most renowned ophthalmology research center. Igersheimer was clearly impressed and flattered by the offer. Joseph Ingersheimer did not accept it, as it was conditional on changing his religion.[93]

"This man was a genius and great humanist caught in the web of a mad historical period. One great love that Joseph had was teaching.... [W]ith his modesty, gentleness, and quiet dignity intact, he came to the United States, a man not destroyed by man's inhumanity to man. There is true hope for an eventual world of peace if some are so capable of proving the nobility of man."[94] And in his own words:

> No matter how beastly some human beings are capable of behaving, we must always remember that we must not act like animals.[95]

## Surgery

Since time immemorial, wars were designed and managed for to kill and maim. Those killed are statistics, at best, memories. For the maimed survivors, civilized society is obligated to provide care through the healing process. Among the healers, surgeons are in great demand. Turkey had quite a great need in the aftermath of the many years of its wars, but it did not have enough qualified surgeons to meet it. Many surgeons had to be trained.

One of the invited teaching surgeons was *Dr. Rudolf Nissen* who did pioneering work in thoracic surgery, and the treatment of gastro-oesophageal reflux disease (acid reflux) and hiatal hernia. He performed the first successful pneumonectomy (surgical removal of entire lung) in humans. The *Nissen-Rossetti* type of fundoplication (procedure that alleviates chronic heartburn in people whose condition cannot be controlled by either lifestyle changes or medication) has remained the standard procedure in Europe and the USA.[96] Nissen developed these procedures while still in Germany and imported them to Turkey and later to the US.

> The first modern anesthesia machine had been brought to the Istanbul Medical School by Prof. Rudolf Nissen.[97]

Nissen had trained as a voluntary physician and assistant in pathology at the universities of Breisgau and Freiburg and had planned to take over his father's clinic in Neisse. However, in September 1922, he received a surprising invitation to work with Ernst Ferdinand Sauerbruch (1875-1951) in Munich. This was the beginning of many fruitful years of work. In 1926, he brilliantly defended his doctoral dissertation. The next year, he followed Sauerbruch to the Berlin *Charité,* where he became Sauerbruch's deputy and Professor Extraordinary in 1930.

When the Nazis came to power, he saw that Germany was not the place to stay. On May 29 1933, Nissen married *Ruth Lieselott* and together they left Germany for the United States of America. However, at their stop in Zürich, Nissen received a telegram from the Turkish government with a request that he assume the Chair of Surgery at the University of Istanbul. Nissen switched his itinerary and enjoyed life on the Bosphorus. He organized a clinic based on the Sauerbruch model for his scientific work. He also had the opportunity to go on study journeys, visiting the U.S. and the Soviet Union, and took lively part in several professional conventions in Europe. However, the close friendship and commercial relations between Turkey and Germany in the years preceding the onset of the war in Europe in the late 1930s gave the émigrés and Nissen cause for concern.

When his contract expired in 1938, Nissen emigrated to the United States of America with his family, settling in New York where he opened an ambulatory surgical practice. He had to come to the United States in 1939 for treatment of a lung abscess due to a retained bullet from World

War I. Additionally, he had the opportunity to perform major operations at the Brooklyn Jewish Hospital, and obtained a position as Associate Professor at the Long Island College of Medicine.

In 1948, Nissen visited Germany and met his old friend and mentor, Sauerbruch. In 1951, he accepted the offer of a Professorship in Basel. In his inaugural address, he took the opportunity to speak his mind about the Nazis. He remained in this position until 1967. In 1966, Rudolf Nissen was made a Doctor of Honour of the *Humboldt-Universität zu Berlin*. Additionally, he was presented an honorary professorship from *Hacettepe* University, Ankara in 1973. Nissen was a critical observant clinician, an efficient and popular physician, and a teacher. He worked with discipline and in cooperation with his Turkish colleagues, such as *Ahmed Burhaneddin Toker, Fahri Arel, Derviş Manizade,* and others who went on to become the leading authorities of general thoracic (chest cavity) surgery in Turkey. During his six years of residence and working in Istanbul, he contributed highly to the practice of general and thoracic surgery. Nissen stayed in New York and later in Basel until his death on January 22 1981.[98] (Fig. 71 and 72).

"Nissen left a deep and indelible impression on everybody he met. Similar to all extraordinary people who had exceptional expectations both from himself and his colleagues, he was both much loved and much feared. An indication of how he was loved by the Anatolian people is the name of 'Nissen' given to their children by many village women successfully treated by him."[99]

*Eduard Melchior,* born 1883, was dismissed from his position as professor in Breslau and head of the Division of Surgery at the *Wenzel-Hancke-Krankenhaus* in 1935 because of his ancestry. He stayed and worked in Turkey until 1954. During those decades, he trained several generations of Turkish surgeons. An acclaimed surgeon, he became Professor of Surgery at the *Nümune Hastanesi* hospital in 1936, and from 1946 until 1954 he was a member of the Medical Faculty in Ankara. He retired in 1954 and returned to Germany, settling in Jugenheim. In 1966, he moved to Switzerland. Eduard. Melchior died in 1974 (Fig. 73 and 74).

## Dentistry

As ophtalmologist Igersheimer had been, *Alfred Kantorowicz* was also called upon to help Iran's Shah during his visit in 1934. The Shah Reza Pahlavi had come to observe first-hand Atatürk's reforms with the idea of introducing their equivalents in his own country (Fig. 75).[100]

While the two rulers sat for lunch talking politics, the Shah suddenly commented on the wonderful teeth of the *Gazi* (affectionate for Atatürk), whereupon the Gazi took them out of his mouth. Full of admiration, the Shah exclaimed that he also wanted such teeth. The *Gazi* obligingly said that he had a remarkable professor of dentistry who would make him a set of teeth outshining all others.

> Therefore that night, past midnight, Army trucks with torches (flashlights) suddenly drove up to the house of our dentistry professor and friend, Professor Kantorowicz . . . The soldiers loaded him and his paraphernalia on the truck, drove to his institute, tore the dentistry chair from its concrete moorings, and deposited the whole kit and caboodle in the Palace of *Dolmahbahce*...as the Shah could not be treated at the dental school for fear of an assassination attempt."[101]

The Shah left Istanbul very pleased with the new dentures Kantorowicz had made for him. However, earlier, this very same Kantorowicz had a close call with certain death. To wit, in a letter from Zurich, marked CONFIDENTIAL and dated October 6 1933 to Professor Lauder W. Jones at The Rockefeller Foundation's European office, Professor Philipp Schwarz wrote on behalf of the *Notgemeinschaft*:

> May I further take the liberty in this purely personal letter of submitting to you another delicate matter.
>
> Colleague Kantorowicz, who was appointed professor of dentistry and whose contract had already been signed by the Turkish government is being held in a concentration camp. I hope the Turkish government, in so far as it is able to, will assist us in freeing this worthy colleague. Might it not be possible that you also could use your efforts in behalf of Mr. Kantorowicz and induce the authorities in Germany in a friendly manner to free Mr. Kantorowicz? This idea is, of course, only a suggestion. I do not know whether it is possible for you to exert such an influence.[102]

A pediatric dentistry innovator, Kantorowicz was born in 1880. He received his dental degree in 1900 and his medical degree in 1906. He was Director of the Dental Institute in Bonn, Germany, in which capacity he served for fifteen years. He was an amazing leader with a special interest in pediatric dentistry. He developed preventive dentistry programs and mobile clinics for children in Germany. "His work in making the benefits of dentistry available even to the poorest sections of the population" was highly regarded throughout the dental profession in pre-Nazi Europe.

In 1933, the Nazis took Kantorowicz into "Protective Custody" and kept him for four months at the prison in Bonn. He was transferred to the Gestapo, SA (Storm Troopers), and SS (Protective Squad, *Schutzstaffel*) run *Boergermoor* hard-labor concentration camp for four months, then was transferred to *Lichtenburg*, the concentration camp for prominent socialists, Jews, and intellectuals.

According to a letter[103] signed by philosopher Hans Reichenbach, who had already relocated to UCLA from Istanbul, and theoretical chemist Fritz London who was at Duke University, Kantorowicz was released because of pressure from prominent authorities in Scandinavian countries, after which he came to Turkey. However, with due respect to Professor Reichenbach, because Alfred Kantorowicz was already sought after by the Turkish government - a contract had already been signed - there is reason to believe that it was the Turkish connection that played the more significant role in the Kantorowicz release from Lichtenburg and safe passage to Istanbul.

Kantorowicz worked in Turkey from 1933 until his retirement in 1948. During this period, he was instrumental in modernizing Turkey's dental curricula.[104] When he arrived in Turkey, dental education was a three-year [post-high school] program and the clinical areas were divided into prosthodontics and conservative dentistry and were based primarily on the French educational system. He separated surgery from general dentistry, obtained the transfer of aesthetic surgery of the face (including cleft lip and palate) into the dental curriculum from the medical department, and introduced orthodontics into the curriculum. The curriculum was also lengthened to four years. He published several textbooks for dentists and auxiliary personnel. In 1943, he published a text on modern dental surgery (*Diştababeti Şirürjisi*) translated by *Pertev Ata*.[105]

Kantorowicz was among the outstanding professors and held many patents for his research.[106] As director of dentistry, he tried to create a department similar to its American counterparts. Not only was he one of the best and brightest scientists to live and work in Turkey, Kantorowicz was also a dedicated social reformer for most of his adult life. In 1950, Kantorowicz returned to Germany from Turkey and continued his work on dental research and caries prevention. His "Lectio Aurea" took place on February 17 1962 in the auditorium of the new and as yet unnamed dental institute of the University of Bonn. He was awarded many honorary degrees (*Honoris causa*) including one in medicine June 1955.[107] As a great sportsman, Fritz Neumark recollects that "Kantorowicz was one of the first to "discover" *Uludağ* in Anatolia as a very suitable place for skiing, a sport that was almost unknown in Turkey then. My wife and Rosemarie Heyd-Burkhart were among the pioneers who had the courage to go up this mountain in the winter of 1934-35 under very primitive and exhaustive conditions"[108]

## Summation for "The Healers"

If one were to ask what the most significant and lasting impact on Turkey's health status made by the émigré "healers" as a group was, the answer would surely be that Turkey learned how to practice methods of public health years, if not decades, ahead of when most of the world recognized the need and benefit of same. And, most, if not all, of these healers were social reformers with political agendas of their own to fulfill.

Thus, well over four centuries after an expellee from Spain became the personal physician to the Ottoman court, expellees from Nazism were invited to serve in the establishment of western medical standards within the Turkish Republic.

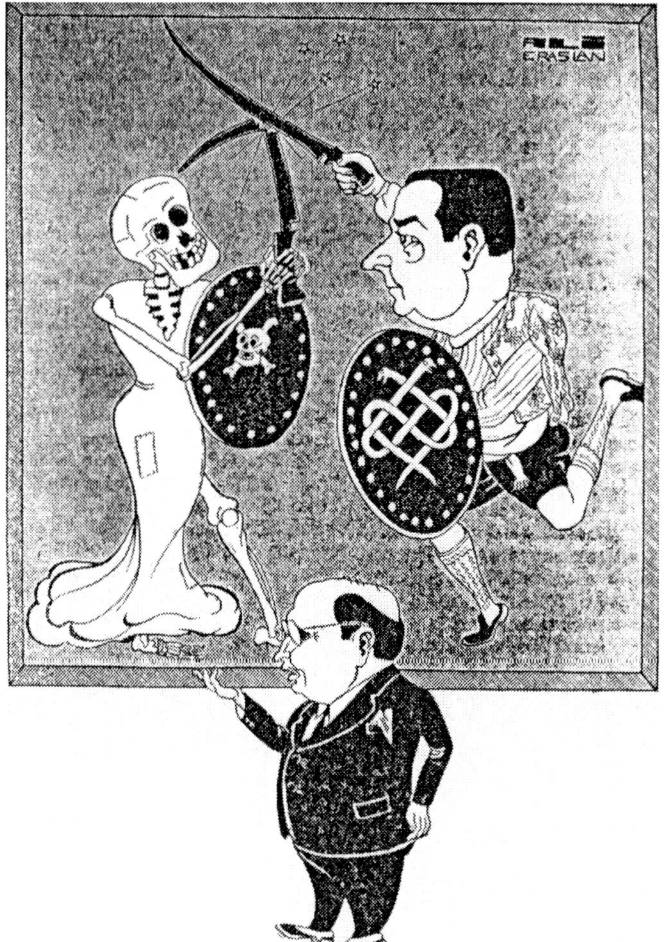
ERASLAN
Hirch — Sağlık böyle korunmalıdır!

*Figure 45*
"Saglik boyle korunmalidir." "Health should be protected like this." A cartoon of Julius Hirsch. Istanbul University's Medical School student New Year's spoof.

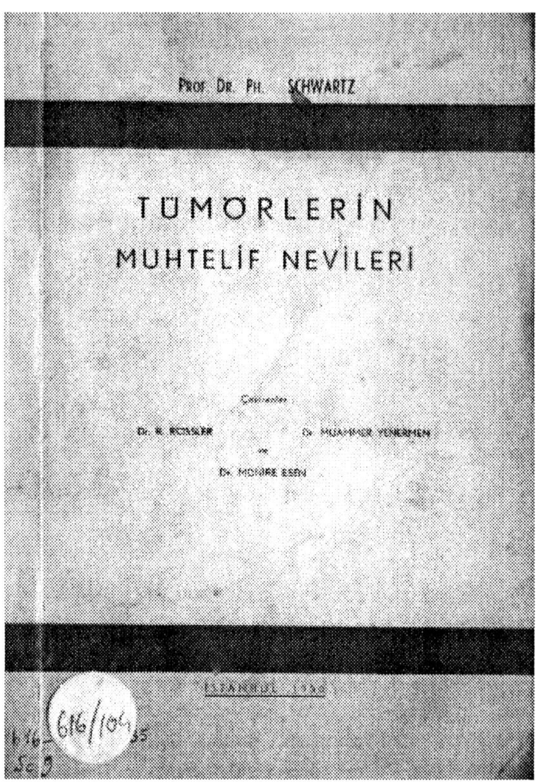


*Figure 46*
*Introduction to Tumor Science* by Philipp Schwarz. 1950 Edition.

*Figure 47*
Wilhelm Liepmann.

*Figure 48*
Dr. Frank's gravestone.

STUDIES ON THE CONDITIONS OF GLUCOSE EXCRETION IN MAN

BY KURT STEINITZ

*(From the Department of Medicine of Istanbul University, Guraba Hospital, Istanbul, Turkey)*

(Received for publication September 29, 1939)

*Figure 49*
Title and byline of a Steinitz paper written in Istanbul and published in America. *Journal of Clinical Investigation,* Vol 19 (2), 1940, (299-305).

*Figure 50*
*Clinic Laboratory Procedures* by Kurt Steinitz with a foreword by Alfred Erich Frank, 1942.

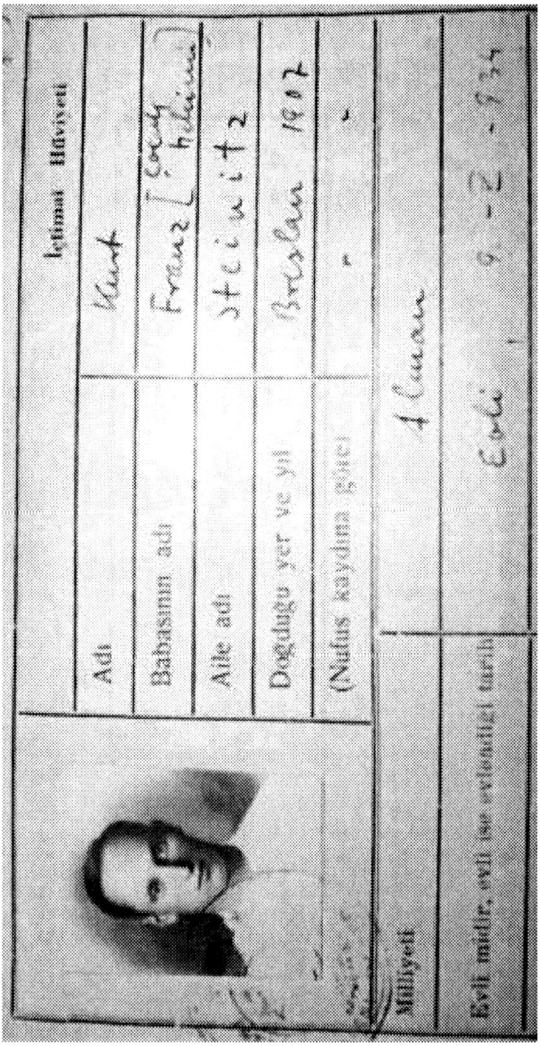

İçtimai Hüviyeti

| | |
|---|---|
| Adı | Kurt |
| Babasının adı | Franz |
| Aile adı | Steinitz |
| Doğduğu yer ve yıl | Breslau 1907 |
| (Nufus kaydına göre) | - - |
| Milliyeti | Alman |
| Evli midir, evli ise evlendiği tarih | Evli 9-2-934 |

*Figure 51*
File copy of Steintz's 1934 Turkish Identity Card.

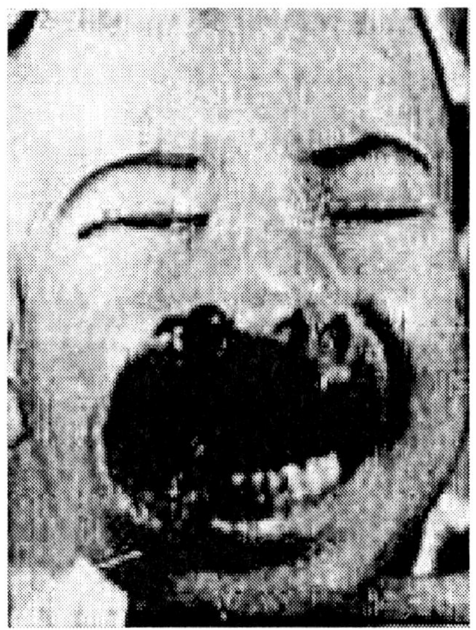

*Figure 52*
A child with Noma

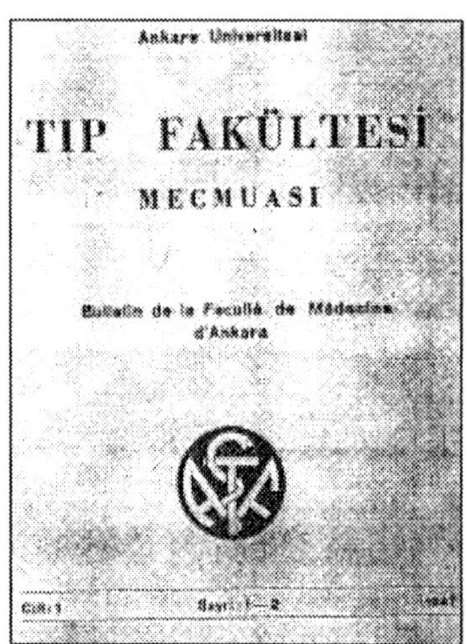


*Figure 53*
1947 Turkish medical journal cover. This issue reports on Eckstein's contribution to the treatment of noma, a childhood disease eradicated in Turkey thanks to Albert Eckstein.

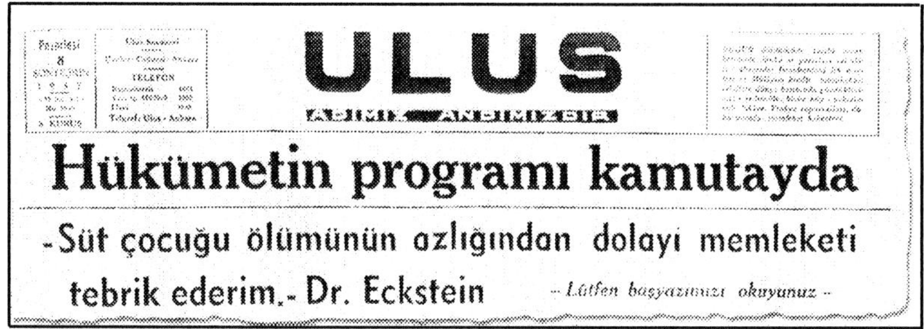

ULUS

# Hükümetin programı kamutayda

-Süt çocuğu ölümünün azlığından dolayı memleketi tebrik ederim.- Dr. Eckstein

- Lütfen başyazımızı okuyunuz -

*Figure 54*
"I congratulate the country for the low death rate of its nursing infants." This is a newspaper article.
—Dr. [Albert] Eckstein.

*Figure 55*
Turkish 10 Lira banknote issued in 1942 using a 1935 Eckstein photo of village women.

*Figure 56*
Photograph taken by Prof. Eckstein in Bürmük Village/Bolu, which was printed on the 10 Turkish Lira banknote in 1942.

*Figure 57*
A photograph that was displayed at the Turkish Pavilion of the World Fair in New York in 1939.

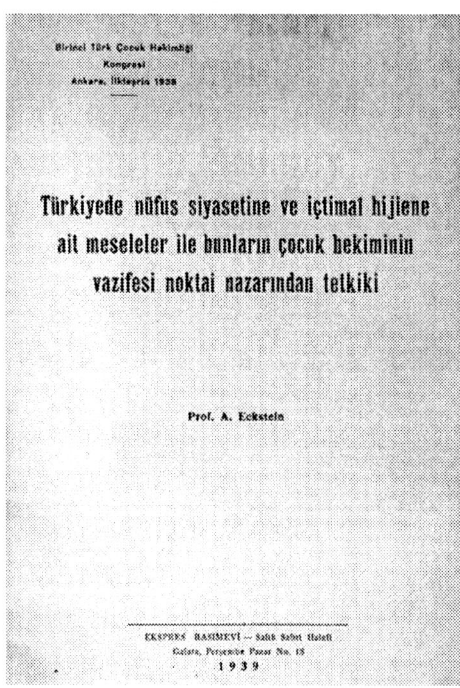

Birinci Türk Çocuk Hekimliği
Kongresi
Ankara, İlkteşrin 1938

Türkiyede nüfus siyasetine ve içtimaî hijiene ait meseleler ile bunların çocuk hekiminin vazifesi noktai nazarından tetkiki

Prof. A. Eckstein

EKSPRES BASIMEVİ — Sahib Sabri Halefi
Galata, Perşembe Pazar No. 18
1939

*Figure 58*
Eckstein's *Problems of Population Policy and Public Health and Their Investigation from the Perspective of the Pediatrician's Duties.* Report presented at the Congress of Turkish Pediatricians in Ankara and published in 1938 by Expres Basimevi in Istanbul.

*Figure 59*
Ord. Prof. Albert Eckstein.

*Figure 60*
Drs. Albert and Erna Eckstein (second row 5th and 6th from their right) and their Turkish co-workers, 1949. A legacy left behind.

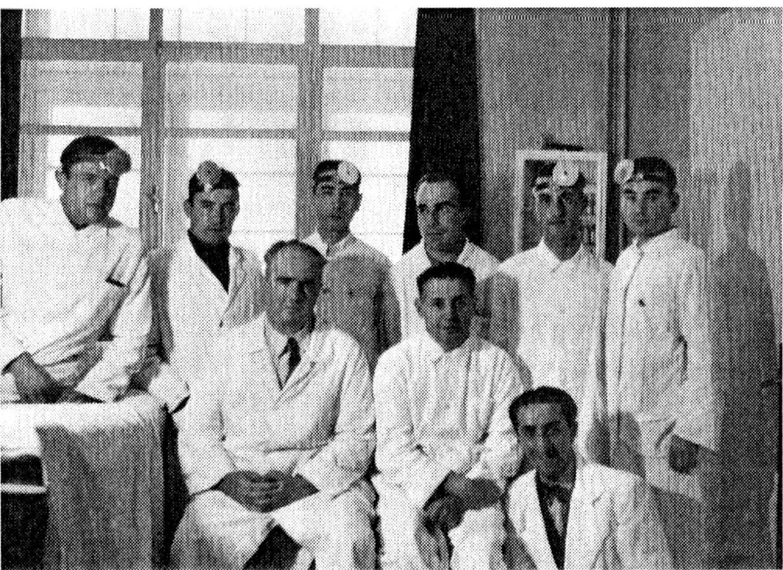

*Figure 61*
"To our beloved teacher." A 1937 photograph of Dr Hellmann and his ENT residents.

*Figure 62*
Dr. Hellmann and his former ENT residents. Some are wearing military uniforms.

*Figure 63*
Joseph Igersheimer.

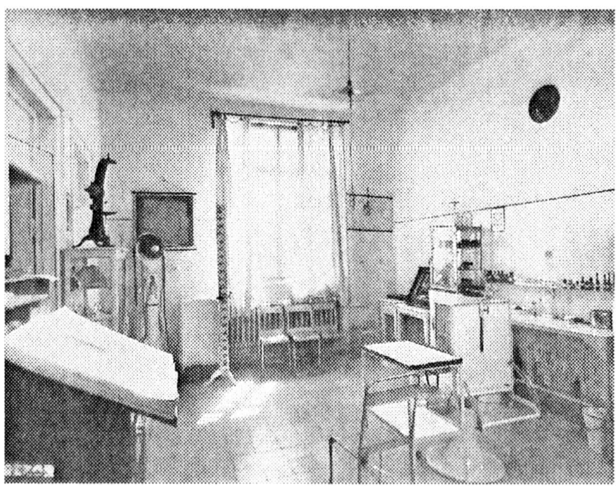

*Figure 64*
Examination room in Igersheimer's Eye Clinic. 1938 Faculty of Medicine Alumni Yearbook.

*Figure 65*
Igersheimer as depicted by his students in their 1935 yearbook.

GÖZ

HASTALIKLARI

Yazan:
Prof. Dr. Josef İgersheimer
İstanbul Üniversitesi Göz Kliniği Ordinaryüsü

Türkçeye çeviren:
Dr. Murad Rami Aydın
Göz Hekimi

TÜRKİYE BASIMEVİ
İSTANBUL
1936

*Figure 66*
Front cover of Igersheimer Turkish textbook *Eye Diseases*, with Dr. Murad Rami Aydın as translator.

*Figure 67*
Igersheimer and some of his post graduate students, residents, and clinical assistants. Faculty of Medicine 1938 Yearbook.

J. Igersheimer, M.D.
636 Beacon St.
Boston, Mass.

A. Monographs and Source-Book Articles.

1919 Syphilis und Auge. Verlag Julius Springer, Berlin.

(Syphilis and the Eye)

1928 Syphilis und Auge. II. Auflage ebendort.

(Syphilis and the Eye-published above)

1930 Syphilis und Auge. Kurzes Handb.d. Ophth. ebendort.

(Syphilis and theEye - published above)

1913 Das Schicksal von Patienten mit Keratitis parenchym. Samml. Zwangl. Anhandlung IX.

(Prognosis of Patients with Keratitis Parenchym.)

1921 Erkrankung der Aderhaut, Netzhaut u.d.Opticus. Diag.u. therap. Irrtum. Verlag Thieme, Leipzig.

(Disease of the Choroid, Retina and OpticalNerve)

1920 Ueber Myopieoperationen. Handb. d. Augenheilk.v. Graef-Saemish

(On Myopia Operations)

1927 Ueber die Beteiligung des Auges bei kong. Lues. Handb.d. Haut u. Geschlechts Krankh. Springer verlag.

(Involvement of the Eye in Congen. Lues )

1927 Das Auge als Experimentalorgan .Handb.d. biol Arbeitsmeth.. Urban u. Schwarzenberg

( The Eye as Experimental Organ )

1930 Tuberkulose d. Auges im Kindesalter. Handb. d . Kindertub. Thieme Leipzig.

( Tuberculosis and theEye in Childhood )

1932 Tuberculose und Auge. Kurz. Handb.d. Ophth. Verlag Springer

( Tuberculosis and the Eye )

*Figure 68*
Page 1 from Dr. Igersheimer's bibliography accompanying his 1939 job application to the medical school at Tufts University.

2.

B. Individual Publications.

1904 Ueber den Blutdrick bei Tuberculosen. Inaug. Disc. Tuebingen
( On the Blood Pressure of Tuberculars )

1906 Ueber die Wirkungen des Strychnins auf das Kalt und Warmblutherz.
Arch.f. exp.Path.u.Pharm. S.73.

( On the Effect of Strychnin on the Heart of Cold and Warmblooded Animals )

1905-06 Ueber die Bactericide Kraft des 60%igen Aethylalkohols.
Centr.Bl. f.Bakt.1905-06 S.414.

( The Bactericital Effect of the 60% Aethyl Alkohol )

1908 Beitrag zur Pathol. Anatomie d. Konjunctival Diphterie. Arch.f. Ophth.
Leipzig. S.162-170.

( Contribution to the Pathol. Anat. of Conjunctival Diphteria.)

Exper.Beitrag zur Wirkung d. Atoxyls a.d. Tierischen Organ.
Arch.f. exp.Pathol.u. Pharmakol.Leipzig. 1908 Supl. Bd.
( Exper. Contribution on the Effect of Atoxyl on th Animal Organ.)

1909 Exper.Studien ueber die Wirkung des Atoxyls a.d. Auge.
Ber. ueb.Vers.d. Ophth. Ges. 1908 Wiesb. 1909 XXXV?42-250

( Exp. Studies on the Effect of Atoxyl on the Eye )

and Rothmann (A) Ueber das Verhalten des Atoxyls im Organismus
Ztschr.f. physiol Chemei Strassburg 1909 S. 256-80

( the Effect of Atoxyl on the Organism)

Ueber die Atoxylvergiftung mit bes. Beruecksichtigung der Wirkung auf das Sehorgan. D.M.W.Leipzig S.142-146.

( The Effect of Atoxyl Poisoning with special reference to the Eye

Ueber die Wirkung d. Atoxyls auf das Auge. Arch f. Opth. Leipzig 379-428

( The Effect of Atoxyl on the Eye )

1910 Zur Morphologie und Pathogenese d. Naphtalinveraenderungen am Auge.
Arch.f.Ophth. Leipzig . (With Ruben )
(Morphology and Pathogenesis of the Changes of the Eye produced by Naphtaline )

Ueber die Beziehung Der Mikuliczschen Krankheit zur Tuberkulose
Arch.f. Ophth. Leipzig .311-66 (with Pollet)

( on the Relationship of the Mikulicz Disease to Tuberculosis .)

*Figure 69*
Page 2 from Dr. Igersheimer's bibliography accompanying his 1939 job application to the medical school at Tufts University.

OTO - NÖRO - OFTALMOLOJİ

Vol. VIII Nisan - Haziran 1953 No. 2

Sahibi : N. BENGİSU Yazı işleri müdürü : N. SEZER

I. Orijinal yazılar

EYE SIGNS IN HEAD INJURIES

by
Prof. Dr. J. IGERSHEIMER (Boston)
and
Dr. G. MALOUF (Beirut, formerly Boston)

The most important ocular sign in head injuries concerns itself with the *pupil.* The pupils may vary in size and have different light reactions. All variations are possible. Very dilated pupils may respond to light normally or sluggishly, or they may not react. On the other hand, very miotic pupils can react well or can be fixed. If one pupil is larger than the other, which happens frequently, the reaction may be good or sluggish on both sides, or one pupil reacts normally. It is generally agreed that very dilated and fixed pupils in an unconscious patient shortly after a head injury is a fatal sign with rare exceptions. *Munro* points out that in severe cases of contusion and laceration of the brain sudden dilatation of the pupils together with sudden increase in pulse rate and temperature occur just prior to death.The prognosis in very marked miosis is not quite as serious. Such pinpoint pupils are probably caused by vascular lesions in the brainstem. Edema and petechiae may be found there *(Brock).* The question as to whether the larger pupil on one side is an indication for the localisation of the brain lesion, especially in sub-and epidural hematoma is much discussed. The opinions in this respect are divided. Looking over the literature and the published statistics we think it is fair to say that the larger pupil is often on the same side

*Figure 70*
OTO ophtalmology. Jozef Igersheimer & G. Malouf, "Eye signs in head injuries."

CERRAHİ
ENDİKASYONLAR

R. NISSEN

*Figure 71*
*Indications in Surgery,* Nissen Textbook, 1938.

*Figure 72*
Professor Rudolph Nissen and some of his surgical residents.

*Figure 73*
Eduard Melchior.

*Figure 74*
Professor Melchior and some of the Turkish surgeons he had trained, 1953.

*Figure 75*
Reza Shah with Kemal Atatürk on his official visit to Turkey in 1934.

# 8 The Scientists

## Building Turkey's First Observatory and Westernizing Its Astronomy

Throughout centuries of Ottoman rule, many of its subjects have studied and written on astronomy.[1] Astronomy was taught in Turkey's three military academies as far back as the first decade of the 19th century. In 1900, astronomy was introduced into the new Faculty of Science at *Dar-ül Fünun* which evolved into Istanbul University. Yet, the Republic of Turkey did not inherit an astronomic observatory of any kind. To remedy this situation, leading astronomy professors were invited to set up an academic department and an observatory. Among these was Professor *Erwin Finlay Freundlich.*

In Albert Einstein's very own words, astronomer E. Finlay Freundlich "was the first among fellow-scientists who had taken pains to put the [relativity] theory to the test."[2] He did it in several different ways; all were observational. Freundlich validated Einstein's theories and thereby showed that Newton's theory of gravity was not fully correct. This made Freundlich a significant partner in shifting the prevailing scientific paradigm, a revolution in science. All this happened in Berlin not much before the city was engulfed in Germany's own political paradigm shift. By 1933, Freundlich found himself in Istanbul launching Turkey's first astronomical laboratory (Fig. 76).[3]

Finlay Freundlich's father was E. Philip Freundlich and his mother was Ellen Elizabeth Finlayson. Philip Freundlich was a German businessman, and his wife was British. Perhaps it is worth explaining that Freundlich only called himself "Finlay" after he came to live in Scotland (that being the Scottish spelling of his name). He was known as Erwin Freundlich for the first fifty years of his life.

Freundlich was one of a family of seven children, five boys and two girls. He attended primary school in his home town of Biebrich, as did his brothers, and then he went to secondary school in the nearby large town of Wiesbaden. In 1903, at eighteen, Freundlich completed his secondary school education and went to work in the Stettin (now Szczecin, Poland) dockyards. At this stage, he aimed to make naval design his career. He entered the *Technische Hochschule* of Charlottenburg to study naval architecture but a health problem, a heart condition, forced him to take a break from his studies.

After recovery, Freundlich decided not to continue in naval architecture and instead entered the University of Göttingen to study mathematics, physics, and astronomy, receiving his doctorate in 1910. His thesis in mathematics specifically concerned the "analytic function theory." Freundlich married Käte Hirschberg in 1913. Since she was Jewish and Freundlich was not, the wedding was a civil one. In the meantime, the Berlin Observatory moved to a new site at *Neubabelsberg* and a house was built for the newly married Freundlichs close to the observatory.

In 1911, Albert Einstein asked Freundlich, a junior member of Germany's emerging group of interdisciplinary scientists and thus Einstein's kindred spirit, to make accurate observations of Mercury's orbit. These were required to observationally validate Einstein's general theory of relativity. He published his findings in a 1913 paper against the wishes and advice of the Berlin Observatory's director who strongly advised Freundlich against backing such a revolutionary idea. Freundlich verified (showed proof) and supported Einstein's statements that Newton's theory of gravitation, so long held as one of the greatest achievements of the human mind, was not quite right. It cannot be overstated how daring this publication by Freundlich had been.

Freundlich further proposed measuring the degree of deflection of a light ray passing close to the sun as this test could even better be used to check the validity of the theory of relativity. The only way to make such measurements was during an eclipse, and Freundlich wanted to be somewhere within the path of totality of the eclipse which would occur in 1914. Such expeditions required large budgets.

Freundlich had the good fortune of being introduced to *Gustav Krupp von Bohlen und Halbach* by a friend. Von Bohlen und Halbach was a German diplomat who had married the heiress Bertha Krupp of the Krupp industrial clan and had taken over the family firm. He was impressed by Freundlich and, as Krupp had considerable funds at his disposal, offered to finance an expedition to Feodosiya, a previously mentioned Crimean peninsula city on the Black Sea. Freundlich's good fortune came to an end, however, when the first World War broke out before the solar eclipse had occurred. His expedition was abandoned. Before he was able to return to Berlin, Freundlich was interned by the Russians.[4]

The University of St Andrews provides biographies of many accomplished astronomers. An entry for Freundlich shows that "he wrote his first book in 1916 following Einstein's publication of the general theory of relativity. Freundlich's book, *Grundlagen der Einsteinschen Gravitationstheorie,* discussed the ways that the general theory of relativity could be tested by astronomical observations. In 1918, Freundlich resigned his post in Berlin to work full time with Einstein."[5]

In 1920, the Einstein tower was added to the Astrophysical Observatory in Potsdam and Freundlich was appointed as observer there in 1921. He was later promoted to Chief Observer and Professor of Astrophysics, a position he held until 1933. Forced to resign from his position in Potsdam, Freundlich emigrated to Turkey. Käte's sister had died early in 1933, and the Freundlichs had become the guardians of his sister-in-law's two young children, Hans and Renate, who, of course, were also Jewish.[6]

Here is what Istanbul University has to say today about its Astronomy and Space Sciences:

> "[The] department currently located on the University Campus at Beyazıt...was set up in 1933 by Prof. *E. F. Freundlich* under the name of Institute of Astronomy, as a branch of the Faculty of Science of Istanbul University. During the years of 1933-34 and 1934-35, the Institute occupied two rooms in the Faculty of Science Building called Zeynep Hanım Konağı. With the building of a small observatory on the Istanbul University Campus at Beyazıt in 1936, technological research on the subject started. An astrograph ordered from Zeiss, Germany, on December 11 1934, arrived in Istanbul via Trieste on September 25 1936, and was placed in the dome of the new building in the fall of 1936. For the year of 1936-37, the Institute of Astronomy started the enrollment of students in its new building.

However, getting the telescope ordered and positioned was administratively frustrating to Freundlich. The telescope's saga is best described in Freundlich's words, typed by his own hand (Fig. 77 and 78).[7]

In addition to building an observatory during his stay in Istanbul confined within a low budget, Freundlich managed to begin a collection of modern astronomy literature for the university by arranging for both Harvard and Yale universities to supply all back issues of their respective astronomy publications and keep the Istanbul library holdings current. This can be seen from the following letter (Fig. 79).

Someone whose signature was illegible, writing on a "21 Avenue Victoria, Bruxelle" letterhead and dated January 19 1937, wrote to Freundlich:

> Finally, I received news from you. I wish you were healthier. I wish you the best recovery. I am sorry that you lost the sight in one eye. I am eager to hear how it went in Prague. When are you moving? How did your talk go and the negotiations about a new observatory? You have a rich life waiting for you which should recompense for the losses you had to suffer.
>
> Our life goes on. You must have heard that Mrs. Einstein passed away.

For reasons that are not completely clear, Freundlich returned to central Europe in 1937 as professor of astronomy at the Charles University of Prague. Perhaps it was the challenge of building yet another observatory but in an administrative atmosphere that was more European and to which he thought he could better relate. Soon, however, Hitler, Chamberlain, Mussolini, and Daladier reached their "understanding" and the Nazis were in power in Czechoslovakia.

In 1939, Freundlich once again managed to escape. This time his destination was Holland. While there, he received an offer from the University of St Andrews in Scotland to set up a Department of Astronomy and to be named to the Napier Professor of Astronomy. He held that post until 1959, despite suffering a heart attack in 1953. During his years in St Andrews, not only did he supervise the work of constructing a thirty-seven-inch Schmidt-Cassegrain telescope, but he also wrote another important text, *Celestial Mechanics,* in 1958.

Freundlich was an outstanding scientist, and wherever his fate took him, he is remembered as an indefatigable institution-builder. But there was yet another equally important side of Finlay Freundlich. In a letter dated January 26 1934, only three months after arrival in Istanbul, he informed his New York City friend Henry Morgenthau: "My wife, two of Käte's cousins, and a six-year-old nephew who lost his mother, are with us." One of these cousins, Lena Goldfield was tubercular. Freundlich arranged to have her placed in a sanatorium run by German doctors in India. As long as she was alive, he paid for all expenses out of his Turkish salary.

The Freundlichs were further unique among the German scientists. They celebrated the Jewish holidays and at times invited children of other émigrés in order to introduce them to Jewish traditions, according to oral histories presented in a later chapter. However, the St Andrews website tells this of Freundlich's professional life:

> ...the closing years of Freundlich's life were marred by incidents arising out of the reluctance of his successor, D W N Stibbs, to grant him open access to the St Andrews observatory in order

> to witness the final stages of the work on the thirty-seven-inch Schmidt-Cassegrain telescope. The tensions that thus arose occasioned, inter alia, the resignation of his highly skilled technician, Robert L. Waland, before the optical components were satisfactorily completed and adjusted, partly explain why that instrument has never yielded the results of which it might otherwise have been capable.[8]

Once again, Freundlich's attempt to build an observatory had come nearly to fruition, but not so close that he could enjoy the rewards. Once again, administrative hassles and professional jealousies in the end had blocked his way. This effort at St Andrews was Freundlich's final such attempt. Eventually Freundlich left for Wiesbaden where he was appointed honorary professor at the University of Mainz. And, for all he has done in behalf of Turkish astronomy during the short period he was there, Freundlich's parting from Istanbul back in 1937 was not at all smooth either. He asked for a leave of absence to go to Prague. His request was denied. He asked to take out 400 Turkish liras from his bank account to bring with him, but he was allowed only 100. So, using the auspices of the Consulate General of the Czech Republic in Istanbul, Freundlich donated the difference to the Czech Red Cross.

## Astronomer Wolfgang Gleisberg

Wolfgang Gleisberg was born in 1903. After being discharged from the University of Breslau in 1933, he went to Istanbul and, as indicated above, headed the department on and off until 1958. After retiring in 1958, he went back to West Germany, where he had accepted a professorship at Frankfurt University. He returned to the University of Ankara as a Guest Professor for the academic year 1965/66.

The Smithsonian/NASA Astrophysics Data System (ADS) shows that Gleisberg authored or coauthored sixty-nine research papers and, starting in 1930, had them published in very respectable scientific journals outside Turkey. Interestingly, his productivity of writing was not slowed down by being in Turkey and or by being an administrator. Between 1933 when he came to Turkey and 1958 when he left, he published no fewer than forty-six of these. His last was delivered at the International Symposium on the Observatories in Islam on September 19-23 1977 and published in 1980. It was titled "Cycle Research at the Observatories in Turkey." He died in 1986 (Fig. 80).

From their days in Istanbul, Eugen Merzbacher recalls that

Wolfgang Gleisberg was a good chess player in addition to being a meticulous—some might say pedantic—astronomer, specializing in celestial mechanics. I was often in the Gleisberg home. The whole family was blond and quite Teutonic. I also recall their daughter Ingrid. Gleisberg went at everything very systematically, including learning Turkish with a vengeance. He was quite fluent, but his pronunciation always betrayed his German origin."[9]

Another fond recollection of Gleisberg came from retired German astronomer *Gerhard Ruben*. By the way, I knew Gleisberg as a teenager. When our family was interned in *Kirşehir* we were asked which books we wanted (we had nearly no literature and were completely isolated). As I was already interested in astronomy, I asked for such books and Gleisberg sent me a book on astronomy which I studied rather thoroughly. After we were released, I spent two weeks during the summer in Istanbul and I visited him and his family and looked at the Andromeda nebula through his telescope. His last years were spent, as far as I remember, in Switzerland. He published a theory on the solar cycle.[10]

## Astronomer Hans Rosenberg Was Another "German" in Istanbul

In 1932, President Robert Hutchins of the University of Chicago appointed Russian astronomer Otto Struve, director of the department of astronomy with the request that he seek out the best men available in the field. As a direct result, the department became highly Europeanized. One of the astronomers brought to Chicago was Ord. Prof. Dr. Hans Rosenberg. However, in 1938, Rosenberg left Chicago to join the astronomy department at the University of Istanbul as Director of its Institutes for Astronomy and the Observatory that had been created by émigré E. Finlay Freundlich who, by then, had left for his ill-advised and short-lived sojourn in Prague. The reasons for Rosenberg's decision to leave Chicago are not clear but will be explored in a later chapter.

The most current Istanbul University Astronomy Department's website states:

> Our department had been established by *Ord. Prof. Dr. Finlay Freundlich, Ord. Prof. Dr Hans Rosenberg, Ord. Prof. Dr. Thomas Royds, Ord. Prof. Dr. Wolfgang Gleisberg*, Prof. Dr. Nüzhet Gökdoğan, Prof. Dr. Edibe Ballı, Prof. Dr. Adnan Kıral, Prof. Dr. Metin Hotinli, Prof. Dr. Tarık Gökmen, Prof. Dr. Kamuran Avcıoğlu, and Prof. Dr. Fatma Esin.

Until 1958, the Astronomy and Space Sciences Department was chaired by a succession of the Émigré professors: Ord. Prof. Dr. E. F. Freundlich (1933-1937), Ord. Prof. Dr. W. Gleisberg (1937-1938), Ord. Prof. Dr. H. Rosenberg (1938-1940), Ord. Prof. Dr. W. Gleisberg (1940-1942), Ord. Prof. Dr. T. Royds (1942-1947), and Ord. Prof. Dr. W. Gleisberg (1948-1958). In 1958, the first native Turk took the helm of the department, Prof. Dr. Nüzhet Gökdoğan, who served in that capacity until 1980. She was succeeded by other fellow countrymen.[11]

Clearly, the Ottoman Officer Corps knew about astronomy. They learned how to make use of it while in the military academies. It was also taught at the *Dar-ül Fünun* even prior to 1933. However, these German Jewish émigrés gave Turkey not just an update and an upgrade on the science being taught. They created for Turkey what this science has always needed most—a capability to observe the heavenly bodies and collect data. The observatory designed by Freundlich is used by Turkish astronomers to this very day. It is also used to train new generations of cadres.

## Reforms and New Programs in Chemistry, Biochemistry, and Biology

When asked how he managed to arrive from Germany, Fritz Arndt is reputed to have answered: "I held on to the last step of the last wagon of the last train on the last day."[12] (Fig. 81).

Arndt's books were among the first in Turkey to apply its new Latin-based alphabet to chemistry. But these contributions were made after Arndt's arrival in "the last wagon of the last train on the last day" which happened to be Arndt's second sojourn in Turkey. Prior to that Arndt had published two texts in Turkish during his first stay there (1915-1918). These of course still used the Arabic alphabet. Arndt first came to that land as part of a group of German academics (including two other chemists) brought to the *Dar-ül Fünun* by the Ottoman Government, to upgrade some of its disciplines. Arndt was a gifted linguist. He started teaching in Turkish after one year. However, he had to leave Turkey in 1918 because of WWI.

Fritz Arndt was born in Hamburg in 1885. He studied chemistry at the universities of Geneva and Freiburg in Breslau and Berlin. He received his doctorate under Howitz at Freiburg.

After a varied academic career in Freiburg, Hamburg, Kiel, Breslau, and Constantinople, he became a professor at Breslau. In 1918 he returned to Breslau from Istanbul where he taught and carried out research until 1933. Forced to leave Germany in 1933, he was briefly at Oxford before returning to Istanbul where, unlike at Oxford, he was awarded a permanent and respectable position. In fact, Arndt was invited back to participate in Atatürk's University Reforms, both because of his knowledge of the language and his past service. On arrival, he took over headship of the Institute he had founded two decades earlier. The Chemistry Institute (*Kimya Enstitüsü*) had been described as a successful model for the University Reforms of 1933.[13] Arndt was among those who remained and served the country the longest. Upon retirement in 1955, he returned to Hamburg.

An organic chemist, Arndt taught both organic and inorganic chemistry while in Istanbul. He also continued his research in organic chemistry. The *Arndt-Eistert* reaction bearing his name involves the synthesis of carboxylic acids. Significantly, he was a pioneer in the field of the newly developing field of physical organic chemistry and contributed to the development of the concept of resonance.[14] He was one of the few non-native speakers invited to serve on the government's official Commission on Terminology (*Terim Komisyonu*) and, in this context, dealt personally with Atatürk, whom he deeply admired.[15]

According to a former student who went on to an illustrious career, retired Turkish chemistry professor Dr. İsmet Gürgey, Arndt "brought the foundations and the principles of contemporary chemistry to Turkey. He became a Turkish citizen during the years of the Second World War."[16]

In chronological order of publication year are some examples of the tangible and long-lasting contributions that Arndt made to science education in Turkey. The full series and list is not shown. Some of these are different editions of the same book.[17] (Fig. 82, 83, 84, 85, 86, 87).

At the end of most of his books, Arndt provided a comparative dictionary of chemical terms and concepts in Turkish, Ottoman Turkish, German, and English.[18] The same Professor Gürgey who, as noted in an earlier chapter, took a colleague to task for not giving physical and life scientists any credit for the evolution of the Turkish language points out that in

> Looking at these small dictionaries, it is possible to see the extent of purification in the language of chemistry, especially when the Ottoman terms and concepts are compared with the Turkish equivalents. These terms and concepts have continued along their path of simplication until today. However, this in no way diminishes what he has achieved. In his books, there is no feeling for an aspiration to use German, English, or Ottoman terminology. Arndt was conscious of the fact that he was the originator of the education and research in the science of chemistry and that he had to be understood as easily as possible.[19]

According to professor Kazancıgil, who chronicled the Arndt family's stay in Turkey, "the first Mrs. Arndt was a Polish Jew. They had three children. One of the sons was serving in the Polish army at the start of World War II."[20] As the Panzer armies attacked Poland on September 1 1939, they found Polish cavalry offering little resistance. So they simply drove on, stopping only briefly at the gates of Warsaw. Fourteen days into the invasion, Warsaw was surrounded. After flattening the city from the air and by artillery, Warsaw was taken on September 27, Poland's mutual defense treaty with France notwithstanding.

Younger Arndt survived only to find himself surrounded and taken prisoner. Upon learning that the new prisoner's father was well-connected with Atatürk himself, the German field officers quickly forwarded the information to headquarters. Sensing an opportunity of gaining additional chits from the neutral Turks, the German information organization in Istanbul passed the information on to Fritz Arndt.

> When young Arndt's father learned of the situation and considered what might happen to a person of German origin caught fighting against the Germans, he was quite upset and feared for his son. So he asked for an appointment with *Refik Saydam*, the prime minister. The meeting took place and was very productive. Saydam agreed to speak to the German ambassador who in turn arranged for the son to be relased and brought to Istanbul. The senior Arndt never forgot this and felt he owed a great debt to Turkey.[21]

Legend has it that when Atatürk died, Arndt went to see the dean of the Faculty and asked about the kind of ceremony he should conduct at the Institute. The dean told Arndt to do as is customary to do in Germany when an important person dies. To which, according to Kazancıgil, Arndt replied, "But in Germany, no one ever has died who was as great as Atatürk."[22]

Turkey has much lore about the Republic's venerated father figure. Whether or not that particular incident actually happened is less consequential than the fact that it is still being retold by very respectable Turkish intellectuals. One thing is certain—Arndt made good on his contractual obligations for the "Great Man" (Atatürk) to actually see come to fruition. In Atatürk's lifetime, not one, but four modern chemistry textbooks using the modern alphabet for text, symbols, and acronyms, were published in Turkish prior to that nation's, and the world's, great loss of November 10, 1938 (Fig. 88 and 89).

Biochemistry professor *Felix Haurowitz*, born in Prague in 1896, obtained his medical degree in 1922 and a doctorate of science in 1923. In

1925, he was appointed Assistant Professor at the German University in Prague. Working with several important biochemists over the next few years, he researched hemoglobin and its derivatives. He began work on his popular "Progress in Biochemistry" series and from 1930 on made immunochemistry his principal area of research. When the Nazi invasion forced Haurowitz to leave Prague in 1939, he took the position of Head of Biological and Medical Chemistry in the Medical School at the University of Istanbul. He devoted himself to teaching, research, and producing a Turkish biochemistry textbook. In 1949, he re-emigrated once again, this time to the United States.

The vast bulk of Haurowitz's trilingual (German, Turkish, and English) correspondence with colleagues starting in the mid-1920s and continuing through the 1960s is archived at the Lilly Library of Indiana University. Much, however, can also be found in the (twice Nobel Laureate) Linus Pauling archives in his native state of Colorado (Fig. 90). This correspondence documents more than his scientific contributions. Both archives were made available for the purposes of this book by Dr. Alice (Haurowitz) Sievert. It shows that while in Turkey, a neutral nation, Haurowitz was used as a conduit for communication between those left behind in Nazi-controlled lands and their relatives in the free world, and it illuminates a human being always concerned with the fate of others. It delineates in Haurowitz's lifelong relationships with former students, the nurturing of more junior colleagues, and the helping hand provided to those in need during the darkest years of the 20th century. He persevered despite his own personal trauma of being dismissed from the institution he contributed so much to for no reason but the fact that he was born Jewish, despite the failure of his many attempts to come to America with his family and despite his nine years in Turkey (Fig. 91). He ultimately succeeded and settled at Indiana University, in tranquil Bloomington.[23]

His Bloomington archives include a half-inch stack of correspondence with Michael Sela, an Israeli immunologist who in the mid-1950s did post-doctorate work at the National Institutes of Health in Bethesda MD. Dr. Sela collaborated with Haurowitz while abroad, in Washington DC, as well as in Bloomington, and became a laureate of many international science prizes. Sela published at least 260 scientific papers, two of which at least he coauthored with Haurowitz. Sela was granted nineteen patents, mostly US, UK and some multi-country.

On October 16 1957 on *National Institute of Health* letterhead, a young Sela wrote to Haurowitz, "I would like to ask you to add to my name on any publication, the remark 'On leave of absence from the Weizmann Institute of Science, Rehovot, Israel.'" Decades later, he was elected to head that venerable institution and served in that capacity for a number of years. And, on August 14 1957, also on NIH letterhead, he wrote, "I would like to thank you once again for the very interesting and stimulating month which I spent in Bloomington."

It is worth noting that the *Journal of Biological Chemistry* published by the American Society for Biochemistry and Molecular Biology, shows that, on April 23 1941, it received for publication a paper by *Felix Haurowitz, Paula Schwerin, and M. Mutahhar Yenson,* all showing as their institutional affiliation the Institute of Biological and Medical Chemistry, Istanbul University. The paper, "Destruction of Hemin and Hemoglobin by the Action of Unsaturated Fatty Acids and Oxygen," appeared in the *J. Biol. Chem.* 1941, 140: 353-359.[24]

In 1953, Haurowitz invited his junior colleague, *Mutahhar Yenson,* to join him for yet another year of close collaboration but this time at the Bloomington laboratories of the University of Indiana (Fig. 92).

The Biographical Memoirs of the (U.S.) National Academy of Sciences describe Haurowitz as a "product of centuries of European intellectual tradition," a member of a group of "learned scholars, dedicated scientists, [and] enlightened human beings" who "were driven by barbaric intolerance to a new land to which they contributed so much. Their impact will be enduring, and Felix Haurowitz was one of the great ones among them."[25] The University of Indiana, his ultimate professional home, has this to say about Felix Haurowitz, one of its greatest adopted sons.

> During his career, he gained widespread recognition for his work on antibodies and received numerous honors which included the Paul Erhlich Gold Medal (West Germany), election to the German Academy of Scientists (Leopoldina), Fellow of the American Academy of Arts and Sciences, and member of the National Academy of Sciences. He was also awarded an honorary MD by the University of Istanbul and an honorary doctorate of science degree by Indiana University.
>
> In 1971, he was honored at the First International Congress of Immunology for "distinguished services to immunology." Of his ten books, he considered the Chemistry and Biology of Proteins, whose second edition was called *Chemistry and Function of Proteins,* to be the most important. Both were reprinted and translated into many languages including Japanese and Russian. He remained active in science up to his death in 1987.[26] (Fig. 91).

From 1930 to 1935, *Friedrich L. Breusch* directed the Chemistry Division at Freiburg University's Pathology Institute. Born in 1903 in Baden, Germany, he fled the Nazis first to Switzerland then to Hungary, and, in 1937, he ended up at Istanbul University. He worked with Haurowitz until 1940 and was appointed Professor and Director of Istanbul University's Second Chemistry Institute, which he founded. He remained in that post until retirement and then moved to Basel, Switzerland, in 1971. Many Turkish chemists have benefited from the education and experience Breusch provided them.

Like Haurowitz, biology professor *Hugo Braun* was born in Prague but in the year 1881. Like Haurowitz, Braun was also fluent in German. Braun, however, attained stature at the University of Frankfurt (1910-1933) His scholarly publications started in 1907. Nevertheless, because Braun's wife was half-Jewish (her father was Jewish, but her mother was not), he was forced to leave Germany in 1933. With his family he went to Turkey and stayed at the University of Istanbul until 1949 at which time he returned to Munich, regained his pension rights and assumed a post there until June 11 1963.

Significantly, of the three "In Memoriam" columns published in the German language, the one penned by an *F. Aub* and published in 1964 makes the Turkish connection only as part of a sentence saying that among Braun's 200 publications there is a "Turkish textbook on microbiology."[27] The one penned by *Georg Hochmann* and published in the same year says simply[28] that in 1949 Hugo Braun was invited back to Munich by a Prof. *Kisskalt*. "He [Braun] was in Istanbul since 1933."[29] However, the tribute penned by *Eyer* (1964) devotes considerable text to Braun's life leading up to and during the Turkish sojourn. Eyer provides a thorough bibliography of Braun's lifetime publications. It shows that by 1930 there are no fewer then ninety-three on record.

A two-year hiatus ends with a publication by I. Springer in Berlin and then others appear in predominantly Turkish outlets with a peppering in Dutch, French, and Swiss publications. As of 1949, Braun had amassed 166 publications. Hence, while in Turkey, Braun contributed over 70 out of a total of 182 works published in the worldwide literature of science.

According to colleague Fritz Neumark, Braun was quite a modest, even shy, person; however, his colleagues valued him greatly because of his scientific talent in spite of his lack of social skills.[30]

*Ernst Wolfgang Caspari* was an important contributor to behavior studies and developmental genetics, working primarily on the mealmoth *Ephestia.* His father directed the Cancer Department at the Institute for Experimental Therapy in Frankfurt from 1920 until he was dismissed under the Nuremberg laws in 1936. Ernst Caspari received his PhD in 1933 but continued his training in *Alfred Kuhn's* laboratory at the University of Göttingen until 1935. Kuhn obtained a research grant from the Rockefeller Foundation, based primarily on "Caspari's findings, and wanted to offer Caspari the opportunity to continue his research."[31]

As a doctoral student and assistant professor at the University of Göttingen, Ernst Caspari was part of Alfred Kuhn's research team investigating the developmental genetics of the mealmoth *Ephestia kuhniella*. In his groundbreaking work on the effects of a pleiotropic gene, Caspari helped establish the basis for sorting out the complex relationship between genes and the temporal and spatial sequence of events in ontogeny, and he contributed to Kuhn's "one gene, one enzyme" hypothesis.[32]

By then, however, the Nazis were in power and there was no way for Kuhn to hire Caspari. Learning through the grapevine about an opening at the University of Istanbul, Caspari sent word back that he was interested. Hugo Braun made an offer in 1935 and Caspari was on his way to Istanbul.

Having already made a number of important contributions to bacteriology involving methods of growing pathogenic bacteria and showing that typhoid bacillus required tryptophan for growth (thus allowing it to be distinguished from the non-tryptophan-requiring paratyphoid bacilli), Braun set out to find a protective vaccine against malaria. Caspari became the project's zoologist. He spent three years as an assistant in microbiology at the University of Istanbul, where his research was restricted to disease transmission by mosquitoes and bedbugs.

While in Istanbul, Caspari met and fell in love with Hermine (Hansi) Abraham, a psychologist who came there in 1935 from Berlin and worked as a "Technical Assistant" at the same university. They were married on August 16 1938. On that very day, Ernst received a telegram from the United States. Assuming that it was yet another congratulatory message, he set it aside for future reading. After their honeymoon, Caspari attended to his "In Box" and happened unto the telegram. It was from the President of Lafayette College in Easton, Pennsylvania, offering him an appointment as a Post-Doctoral Fellow worth $1,000 per year but, most importantly, an opportunity to come to the USA. Because Hansi was still under contract, *Ernst Caspari* went alone to the United States in 1938. Upon expiration of her contract, she rejoined him in 1939.

Caspari served as a professor of biology at *Lafayette College* and *Wesleyan University*. After becoming a naturalized citizen in 1944, Caspari moved to the *University of Rochester* to work with another German refugee, Curt Stern, on projects associated with the genetics program of the *Manhattan Project*. The Rochester group was commissioned to investigate the influence of chronic but low-dose irradiation by gamma rays on the mutation rates of genes in the fruit fly (*Drosophila*). He became the president of the Genetics Society of North America (USA and Canada) and served in that capacity for many years. He was twice a fellow of the Center for Advanced Studies in the Behavioral Sciences at Stanford University (1956-1957 and 1965-1966) working in behavior genetics. He retired in 1975.

A biography published in the scholarly journal *Molecular Genetics of Development* offers an anecdote worth pondering. "One of the saddest events in Caspari's life occurred three years after he came to the United States. In 1941, he obtained a Cuban visa and funds to get his parents out of Germany, but the visa arrived at the American Consulate in Frankfurt two days after his parents had been deported to a concentration camp [Ghetto] in Lodz, Poland. His father served at Lodz as a physician treating the sick until he died of starvation. Years later someone called Caspari's attention to a book written about the Lodz [Ghetto] Caspari was able to obtain the book and found that it included a picture of his father. Caspari's mother was taken from the [Ghetto] in 1942, and he was never able to find when and how she died."[33]

The only picture in the above-mentioned book[34] showing a doctor treating or examining a patient appears without any annotations on page 182.

Because the elder Caspari, who by then must have been in his seventies, is not mentioned in association with his image. Ernst Caspari's photo, circa the 1960s, is reproduced with permission of *Advances in Genetics* for readers to draw their own conclusions (Fig. 93 and 93a).

## Pharmacology

> Ord. Prof. Dr. *Paul Pulewka* was the foundation stone in the establishment of pharmacology and pharmacological controls in our country.[35]

Moreover, during its March 5-7 1996 Congress, held, in Uludağ, Bursa, the Turkish Pharmacological Society placed on the record its recognition that the "founders of pharmacology in Turkey were Prof. Dr. *Akil Muhtar Özden*, Ministry of Health in İstanbul, and Prof. Dr. Paul Pulewka, Ankara University." Many professional conventions have a thematic objective. The theme of that one was "Ord. Prof. Dr. Paul Pulewka: On the 100th Anniversary of His Birth."

Paul Pulewka was born on February 11 1896 in Elbing. He graduated from the Königsberg (Kaliningrad) Prussia Medical Faculty in 1923 and earned doctorates in pharmacology and toxicology from the Pharmacology Institute of the same university in 1927. Pulewka was appointed Docent at Tübingen University in 1929. In May 1933, he was promoted to Professor Extraordinarius of Pharmacology and Toxicology at Tübingen where he lectured on the toxicology of poisonous gases and the protection against them. He was even elected to the university's Senate. However, Behrend Behrens, Paul Pulewka's former assistant whom Pulewka and his wife had once saved from drowning in a sea accident, warned Pulewka that he was in serious danger because of his political beliefs and because his wife was Jewish.

Pulewka resigned, or was released, from his professorship of pharmacy at the University of Tübingen, and with help of an anti-Nazi official in the German foreign ministry, the Pulewkas found their way to Turkey in October 1935. At first, he worked for the Central Hygiene (Public Health) Institute of the Ministry of Health in Ankara. His contract was not renewed in 1940 and he stayed, jobless, in Turkey for almost a year when he was rehired, and, in 1946, Pulewka became Director of the Pharmacy Institute at the University of Ankara. He worked there until 1954, at which time he returned to Germany.

While in Turkey, Paul Pulewka founded the pharmacology departments at the *Refik Saydam* Public Health Institute in Ankara and the Medical Faculty of Ankara University. He also administered the *Materia Medica* Institute and served as a member of the Turkish Codification Commission. The most important characteristic of his pharmacological studies is that they were all directed at local and national problems in Turkey.

The following provides an intriguing example of the way Pulewka identified a local need, analyzed the problem, and suggested a simple and implementable solution. Honey has been a popular Turkish foodstuff since time immemorial. However, honey made by bees from yellow rhododendron plants (*Rhododendron luteum*), commonly called crazy (or mad) honey, was, according to popular belief among the Black Sea Coast peoples, more poisonous than that from purple (*Rhododendron ponticum*) flowers. Hundreds of samples of honey made from *R. luteum* (yellow plant) were sent to the Institute each year to be analyzed to determine the degree of poison contained. Since the amount of andromedotoxin in the honey, the poison in rhododendron, varied greatly, poisoning cases were frequent. Pulewka's experiments performed on the commonly used *Plugge* color reaction test showed that this reaction was caused not only by andromedotoxin but also by substances heretofore thought to be non-poisonous products.

Consequently, Pulewka switched to a test using mice. Pulewka was then able to determine the level of poison in a sample in a few minutes and with a very small margin of error by the "characteristic reflex" test on mice. Experiments further showed that in order to eliminate the poison in the honey by heating, the medium had to be sufficiently acidic. Pulewka therefore recommended that the honey be boiled with some vinegar or citric acid added.[36]

During his twenty years in Turkey, Pulewka did much for pharmacology, pharmacological controls, and for pharmacological curricula in that country. In 1954, he was invited to Tübingen his former university where he built and directed the fist toxicology institute (the Baden Würtemberg Toxicology Institute) in the post-war Federal Republic or West Germany.

There is a very short record stating that after being released from the University of Köln, botanist *Ludwig Schnee* worked at University of Istanbul's *Pharmabotanics and Genetics Institute between* 1933 and 1938, at which time he left for Venezuela.

*Werner Lipschitz,* was born in 1892 in Berlin and passed away in Pearl River, New York, in 1948. He spent the years 1933 to 1939 in Turkey before coming to the United States. Prior to the Nazi takeover, he served as Professor and Director of *Instituts für Pharmazie der Universität Frankfurt am Main.* In Istanbul, he was directing the Biochemistry Institutes (Fig. 94 and 95).

## Physiology is a Must-Have in a Modern Medical School

*Hans Winterstein* was born in Prague in 1879 and died in Munich in 1963. He started his academic career in 1919 as Dozent at the Medical Faculty of Rostock University and, a year later, was promoted to Ordinarius Professor. He later moved on to the University of Breslau and found refuge in Turkey with his English wife and two sons. Winterstein founded and headed the General Physiology program and department at the medical faculty of Istanbul University and became head of its Physiology Institute starting in 1933. In 1956, he retired and returned to West Germany. Winterstein's research into the chemistry of respiration gained international renown as did his "Reaction Theory." (Fig. 96, 97, 98).

As indicated, Dr. R. A. Lambert was sent by the Rockefeller Foundation in 1934, to assess and report on the German émigré professors circumstances in Istanbul. An entry in his diary on February 18 1934 states:

> I have had nearly an hour's talk with Prof. H. Winterstein (Gen. Physiology) for whom MS [Medical Sciences] made a grant at Breslau that was never called for. W. now asks a similar sum (3000RM) to enable him to spend the summer in Cambridge. The proposed research is a study of quantity of blood going to the brain. No satisfactory method of measurement has hitherto been worked out, and W. has a technique which he wants to test. Study would fit into Barcroft's [Sir Joseph Barcroft of the Physiological Laboratory at Cambridge University of] program which is concerned with brain metabolism.

> W. is obviously unhappy here. He is impatient over delay in getting the necessary installation and complains he has not yet an assistant or even a technician. Claims he was promised two Germans for these two positions but the Gov't now refuses them. Says it will be impossible to do any research before Oct.1, and hates to lose the valuable time. I explain that our research aid fund is generally not available for travel expenses; that the Breslau grant was for apparatus and supplies. I agree to put the question before our Committee and to talk to Barcroft, but can give no assurances of help.
>
> I hesitate to tell W. frankly that I think it would be advisable for him to stick to the job here, using his first six months to the fullest in putting the place in order and learning Turkish; his research can wait. W. is the one man of the group who strikes as being a misfit in this atmosphere.

Winterstein evidently was a scientist of note to have received a Rockefeller research grant while still in Germany. However according to Lambert he was initially an unhappy camper but seems to have adjusted. He ended up being very much appreciated by his host country. They gave him citizenship rights in 1941.[37] With the exception of astronomer Wolfgang Gleissberg who stayed from 1933 to 1958 Winterstein had his contract renewed more times than anyone else among the émigrés. Winterstein stayed in Turkey from 1933 to 1956.

## From Roentgenology to Radiology

In the early 1930s, radiology was still in its infancy. Media everywhere were fascinated with its potential for diagnostics and even more so as a cure. *Wilhelm Conrad Röentgen* received his Nobel award in 1901 and *Madame Curie* got her second such prize in 1911. Among the physicists and engineers invited to Turkey several had worked in the emerging field of "roentgenology." They were brought to Istanbul to set up the university's Institute of Radiology and Biophysics. Turkey's founding fathers too were keenly aware of the usefulness for X-rays in medical diagnostics. It was also understood that it would have been folly to simply invite physicians who knew something about the extant X-ray techniques. As a result of scientific developments coming at a fast pace in the West, these techniques each had a short lifespan as it was improved upon. It would have also been folly to bring even the best and the latest equipment to a country without the infrastructure to maintain and to upgrade it.

Quite correctly, it was decided to invite research physicists and experienced engineers along with some knowledgeable doctors and nurses. *Friedrich Dessauer* was the first physicist brought in while *Carl Weissglass, Nikolaus Wolodkewitsch,* and *Kurt Lion* were his engineers. Additionally, *Erich Uhlmann,* a radiologist with a record of scientific publications in radiotherapy going back to 1923, was brought in from Frankfurt University in November 1934. He and Dessauer were the first case of a physicist/physician collaboration in the field of radiotherapy in Turkey. The "Frankfurt" team also included *Grete Lindenbaum,* a nurse who was experienced in radiology. Friedrich Dessauer was the most senior of the "Roentgen machine" pioneers. He had been jailed in Frankfurt for his anti-Nazi beliefs. However at the request of the Turkish government, he was released in 1934 and allowed to join the University of Istanbul faculty[38] where he was given the Chair of the Institute. In 1937, Dessauer left. He went to Fribourg University in Switzerland and became the chair for experimental physics.[39] After Dessauer's departure Uhlmann left for Chicago at the end of summer of that year, and Lindenbaum went to what was then Palestine.

A new "Austrian" team was quickly assembled. *Max Sgalitzer* was the radiologist/physicist and *Walter Reininger* was the engineer. To aid in the team's research and applications, they invited *Margarethe Reininger,* a nurse specializing in roentgenology who happened to be Walter's wife. Significantly, Turkish consular requests based on his excellent credentials helped secure visas for Sgalitzer's arrival in Turkey even after the Anschluss. Sgalitzer, who had authored over 100 scientific publications in leading journals worldwide, came to Turkey on September 17 1938 after having been dismissed from the University of Vienna. He served in Istanbul until September 1943, at which time he came to the US.

While in Turkey, Sgalitzer worked at the University Polyclinic where he raised both the quality of service provided and the number of patients processed. He continued his novel research, mostly in radio diagnostics, and continued to publish internationally. In doing so, he established bridges between the Institute and the worldwide scientific community. His children, whom he had not seen since 1938, were in the States. In 1943, he asked for an unpaid leave from Istanbul University to visit them. Because the administration did not grant the request, Sgalitzer left permanently for the United States.

From telephone book records, as none others could be found, he is known to have spent at least part of a year in Denver (1943). And, from correspondence found in the Haurowitz archives, he is known to have moved on to Seattle. From an "In Memoriam," it is known that he died of radiological poisoning complications in 1973. Unfortunately, not much can be traced in terms of his institutional affiliations while in the USA. His biography prior to coming to the United States however has been well researched, written, and published.[40]

According to his daughter, Dr. Elizabeth S. Ettinghausen,[41] Dr. Sgalitzer served as professor of radiology at the University of Colorado's Medical School in Denver for only eighteen months after arriving in the United States. Upon retirement, he pursued other interests, including traveling.

At the time Sgalitzer was being recruited in Vienna, he was asked to identify an engineer who was highly qualified and experienced in roentgenology and would be willing to join the team in Istanbul. A similar request was also made for an experienced radiology nurse. On April 27 1938, Sgalitzer wrote a letter from Vienna to Istanbul University's Rector that he would look around in Austria and let him know who he found. In an August 31 1938 letter from Prague written in French, Sgalitzer informed the Rector that he found both desired candidates in a husband-and-wife Viennese pair, the *Reiningers, Walter* and *Margarethe,* and both would like to come to Turkey (Fig. 99).

The possibility of going to Turkey and having jobs waiting for them in their respective professions must have come as a gift from heaven for the Reiningers. Austria had already been *Anschlussed* to the German Reich and Reininger had been dismissed from his job at the University of Vienna. In the job application he had sent to Istanbul, Reininger pointed out that he was born in Vienna in 1899 and was a Technical University graduate in electro-technology and mechanical engineering. He had worked for *AEG*, Germany's electrical equipment manufacturer in Berlin, starting in 1923, and, in 1931, he had switched to the Strauss Laboratory in Vienna where one of the inventors of the TSF (flexible medical) tube had worked. There, Reininger developed X-ray radiology-measuring devices including some that were already in use in Turkey such as the *Mecapion.*

Reininger had worked for the University of Vienna where he was responsible for all measurement and calibration of instruments for all university institutes. In collaboration with *Rudolf Pape,* he invented a dosimeter to measure exposure to X-rays and completed a project on the use of radiation on the esophagus. In the application letter, Reininger wrote that this experience gave him skills necessary to use, repair, and calibrate X-ray equipment used for diagnostics and for therapy. Reininger claimed to be capable of teaching and running a State or National research laboratory, if given the opportunity, and had also published papers in various radiological journals. Reininger was fluent in German, English, and French. Since he had been fired from the laboratory job and forced to sell his small manufacturing company, he wrote in his job application, "if the required papers are made available, I could leave immediately. It would be a great honor for me to help you in your national efforts."[42]

On September 2, he sent a follow-up letter to the Rector mentioning his wife's capabilities. Five months and a week after the Anschluss and Austria's officially becoming part of Nazified Europe, Reininger was delighted to sign a four-year contract at the Turkish Embassy in Vienna on September 17 1938. Soon thereafter, the Reiningers with their daughter, Eva-Ruth, arrived in Istanbul and remained on their jobs until 1948 when the family re-emigrated to the United States. During the years they were in Turkey, Walter Reininger, along with physicist/engineer Carl Weissglass, taught many Turkish physicists, engineers, and technicians on all aspects of radiology and kept the university's X-ray equipment in repair and calibrated. During wartime when parts were in short supply, they personally remanufactured many components. A well-trained and capable professional cadre is part of the legacy they left behind.

Margarethe Reininger contributed to this legacy by having trained many Turkish professional nurses in all that they needed to know to facilitate effectiveness and efficiency within medical radiology's operational domains.

In Turkey, the radiology group was very active in conducting experiments to support their theoretical constructs. For instance, Carl Weisglass published several research reports on the "Double-Valve-Rectification System" and on its "Lapping Period in X-ray technology."[43]

## Bringing Applied Mathematics as a University Discipline to Turkey

> Concepts are simply empty when they stop being firmly linked to experiences. They resemble social climbers who are ashamed of their origins and want to deny them.
> —Albert Einstein, letter to Hans Reichenbach, June 30, 1920. Einstein Archives, 20-113.

Is it a coincidence that all three of the mathematicians invited to Turkey were experts in applied mathematics? Probably not! They each approached their subject matter using physical phenomena as springboards. They were more than just provers of abstract theorems. They were problem solvers. Unlike others, they did not have to invent toy examples to show their theories to be applicable. The problems they set themselves were problems drawn from the real world. On the other hand, the Turks extending the invitations were mostly career army officers: officers tend to be pragmatic. There is no doubt the officers, all WWI veterans, had an affinity with people who flew and designed military aircraft.

*Richard von Mises* did both. *Hilda Geiringer* was first his student then became his assistant and scientific collaborator. Later, she became his wife.

*Wilhelm [William] Prager* was also an engineer by training with aircraft design consulting experience. The threesome made Istanbul University's Department of Mathematics the first showpiece of modern undergraduate mathematics education in Turkey. On the staff of any American research university, this trio would have comprised a research group to be envied by all the rest. And not just in 1933, but well into the 1970s.

Richard Edler von Mises was born on April 19 1883 in Lemberg, which was then part of the Austro-Hungarian Monarchy. Later, Lemberg became Lvov in Poland, and in the Soviet Union and, most recently, Lviv of the Ukraine. After attending primary school, von Mises went to the Vienna *Akademische Gymnasium* where he received a classical and humanistic secondary education. From there he moved on to Vienna's *Technische Hochschule* (Technical University) as a student in *Maschinenbau* or Mechanical Engineering. In 1907, he received a doctorate of technical sciences from Vienna and the following year became qualified to lecture on engineering and machine construction.

Upon graduation, von Mises became a lecturer in Brünn, or Brno, in the southeastern Czech Republic and, from 1909 until 1918, served as an *Auserordentlicher Professor* of applied mathematics at Strasburg. It was in Strasburg that von Mises made the first of the decisive advances in plasticity (the theory of permanent deformation of materials) associated with his name. The mechanics of plastically deformable bodies had interested him while still in Brünn and he returned to it from time to time for the rest of his life.

"Von Mises' deepening interest in the poet [Rainer Maria] Rilke[44] and his conversion to Catholicism also date from his days in Strassburg."[45] In 1914, he volunteered to serve in the Austro-Hungarian army as a pilot. Von Mises was indeed a qualified pilot prior to the war. He had given the first university course on powered flight in 1913. Having lectured on the design of aircraft before the war, he put theory into practice by leading a team that constructed a 600-horsepower plane for the Austrian army back in 1915.

At war's end in 1918, von Mises was appointed Lecturer in Mathematics at the University of Frankfurt and, in 1919, he was given a new established chair of hydrodynamics and aerodynamics at the *Technische Hochschule* in Dresden. He soon moved to the University of Berlin as Director of its new Institute of Applied Mathematics where he set up a novel curriculum in applied mathematics with applications to astronomy, geodesy, and technology. By then, von Mises was already interacting and collaborating with Albert Einstein (Fig. 100 and 101).

In this letter, von Mises thanks Einstein for the positive remarks regarding his paper. He tells Einstein of his decision to have it published in the *Physikalische Zeitschrift* (Journal of Physics) and requests Einstein to transmit it to Professor Debya (presumably the editor-in-chief). Von Mises also responds to Einstein's comments on movements of static systems and states that he hopes to clarify his thoughts. Von Mises further mentions that he has recently received a copy of Einstein's 1916 treatise on relativity theory from its Leipzig publisher and thanks Einstein if he was indeed responsible for the book being sent to him (Fig. 102 and 103).

With this letter, von Mises transmits the manuscript of another paper and asks if Einstein, who had just assumed the editorship of the physics section in *Mathematische Annalen*, (Annals of Mathematics) would consider it for publication. If not, he requests that Einstein return it so that he can submit it to the *Physikalische Zeitschrift*.

Perhaps in self-defense against the mathematical establishment's prevailing rigid strictures, von Mises stressed that applied mathematics was every bit as rigorous as pure mathematics, requiring...*a mathematical model of the widest possible generality, where the argument could be made with clarity, elegance, and rigor.*

With von Mises at its helm, the *Berlin Institute of Applied Mathematics* rapidly became a center for research into areas such as probability, statistics, numerical solutions of differential equations, elasticity, plasticity, and aerodynamics. In fact aerodynamic analysis of real world problems required the solution of [partial] differential equations. These could only be solved by numerical methods. The same holds true for problems in plasticity and in elasticity. Thus Von Mises and colleagues had to simultaneously expand knowledge in several fields in order to meaningfully contribute to aircraft design. By 1925, von Mises was actively engaged in the fields of mechanics, probability, and philosophy. While in Berlin, von Mises met Hilda Geiringer, a brilliant mathematician in her own right.

Because of his conversion to Catholicism, von Mises was no longer Jewish, yet he still fell under the non-Aryan definition of the *Act*. However, there was an exemption clause for those non-Aryans who fought in World War I. Von Mises certainly qualified under this clause, and it would have allowed him to keep his chair in Berlin. But, in 1933, he realized, quite correctly, that the exemption clause would not save him for long.[46] An offer of a chair in Turkey was seen by von Mises as a way out of his predicament in Germany, but he tried to ensure that his government pension rights were preserved. On October 12 1933, he wrote to the Ministry explaining that it would benefit Germany if he accepted a post in Turkey and that he should be allowed to retain his pension rights for the twenty-four years of service at Germany's state universities. The response: if he goes he would have to relinquish all rights of salary, pension, and support for his dependents. Von Mises protested in a further letter to the Ministry that he was legally entitled to these rights and that he was not prepared to relinquish them.

At the time, *Theodor Vahlen*, a Nazi, who wanted to take over as the Institute's Director despite his fairly shabby academic abilities, promised that if von Mises would support him to succeed as Director of the Institute, *Vahlen* would ensure that von Mises would not lose his pension rights. To satisfy this arrangement in October 1933, von Mises wrote his letter to support Vahlen as his successor. In the meantime, one of von Mises' students, a fellow by the name *Collatz*, wrote a letter of support to the Ministry, saying in part, "I took my Staatsexamen in November 1933, and Professor von Mises examined me on the day before his departure. The same day, he talked to me for about one hour, giving advice for my further research...."[47] A good try!

Sure enough, Vahlen was appointed Director of the Institute in December of 1933. Almost predictably, while in Istanbul, von Mises received a letter in January 1934 denying him any rights whatsoever. It was something about which von Mises felt extremely aggrieved for his entire life. Many years later in 1953, he wrote to the Ministry still trying to regain his rights and monies. However, von Mises died in Cambridge, Massachusetts, before Germany's post-war government could act on the matter.[48]

Turning the clock back a few years, while in Istanbul, von Mises made frequent trips to Vienna to see his mother who lived until 1937. There he took time out to visit with as many old friends and colleagues as he could, and to refresh memories of days gone by. "In Vienna, a group of men and women, which in von Mises' younger days included the poet P. Altenberg and the architect A. Loos, met often at the 'Kaffeehaus.'" "Later the group meeting in the famous *'Kaffee Central'* consisted primarily of members of the philosophical group known as the "Weiner Kreis" (Vienna Circle).[49] Von Mises' first papers on statistical functions, a book on Rilke, *Bucher Theater, Kunst,* and an essay on Ernst Mach date from this period of time. His major philosophical work, *Kleines Lerbuch des Posivitmus,* which was published in Holland in 1939, evolved at least in part from his association in the Vienna Circle"[50] With the pre-WWI *Junker* spirit and *Prussian* arrogance and militarism gone, in a democratic Germany a land of deep culture enjoying the beginnings of fine political freedom, the group wallowed in their discussions, the breadth of intellectual freedom, their lighthearted camaraderie and the spell of *Unter den Linden.* The music of *Heinrich Mannfred* no doubt added to the Circle's *gemutlichkeit* (good fellowship). Their contemporary, Mannfred's music was very popular in Austria and pre-Nazi Germany. Heinrich Mannfred died in Auschwitz.

With the approach of World War II and after Atatürk's death, von Mises left Turkey for the United States. In 1939, at the invitation of Dean

Harald M. Westergaard, he became a Lecturer in what was to become the Division of Engineering and Applied Physics at Harvard University. Then, in rapid succession, he was promoted to Associate Professor in 1943 and The Gordon-McKay Professor of Aerodynamics and Applied Mathematics in 1946. While at Harvard, von Mises worked on fluid mechanics, aerodynamics, aeronautics, statistics, and probability theory. His studies of aircraft wing theory led him to investigate the physics of air turbulence. As indicated, much of this work required numerical methods for solving partial differential equations, and this led him to develop new techniques in numerical analysis.

Not long before his death, he categorized his own work into eight areas: practical analysis, integral and differential equations, mechanics, hydrodynamics and aerodynamics, constructive geometry, probability calculus, statistics, and philosophy. Five years after von Mises' death, mathematician Hilda Geiringer (von Mises' widow) completed and had published his seminal work in fluid mechanics *The Mathematical Theory of Compressible Fluid Flow* in 1958.[51] His most famous and, at the same time, most controversial, work was in probability theory.[52] During his amazingly diverse and productive career, von Mises was awarded honorary degrees from many universities worldwide. He was elected to the honorific position of *Fellow* by many scientific academies, societies, and institutes. However, when offered an honorary membership from the Communist-dominated East German Academy of Science in 1950, von Mises declined.

To refuse the East German offer was difficult for von Mises, although proffered during the McCarthy era in America, where any link with communism would have been viewed as treason. He sadly declined in a letter written on 15 September 1950:

> I would very gladly accept the nomination in remembrance of my teaching activities in Berlin and thus re-establish the bond which connected me for a long time to the German scientific life. Unfortunately, the present circumstances in Germany as well as those in this country are such that the acceptance of such a distinction could be interpreted as a political demonstration on my part. ...I only relinquish acceptance of this nomination under the pressure of outward circumstances, a nomination which I regard as a great honor in every respect.[53]

In the late 1940s and early 1950s, he served as a civilian advisor to the US Navy and the National Advisory Committee on Aeronautics (NACA), the forerunner of NASA. With over 150 works copyrighted and published in Germany, von Mises died in Boston, Massachusetts (Fig. 104 and 105).

Time spent in Germany during 1932, where he lectured at Göttingen, Berlin, and Hamburg gave Oswald Veblen, the Henry B. Fine Professor of Mathematics at Princeton University, "a first-hand glimpse of the approaching turbulence in Germany." After this experience, Veblen resigned his chaired Professorship at Princeton University in order to organize the *Institute for Advanced Study in Princeton,* an independent institution. He became the first professor at the Institute in 1932.[54] Veblen and his *Institute* colleagues, Albert Einstein and Hermann Weyl, worked tirelessly to help bring and place refugees who came to the United States.

One of these was mathematician *Hilda Geiringer*. Trying to place her at Queens College in Flushing, New York, because Harvard would not even contemplate hiring a woman, Veblen wrote on May 13 1940 that "Mrs. Geiringer was already well known at the time of the Nazi uprising in 1933. She went with a group of mathematicians to Istanbul in 1934."[55] Prior to that, Geiringer had already published (in 1931) what are now referred to as "the fundamental Geiringer equations for plane plastic distortions of solids."[56] A recommendation was made to the Minister of Education in Ankara (which unfortunately remains anonymous because of damage to the archival document), summarizing Hilda Geiringer's contributions to Turkey as well as her tenuous predicament there. Accordingly, "Frau Dr. Geiringer (under contract until 1.30.36) took over most of the mathematical instruction. Without her, a smooth continuation of the teaching program would have been impossible. A prolonging of her contract was of great importance."[57]

Hilda Geiringer's father, Ludwig Geiringer, was born in Hungary. Her mother, Martha Wertheimer, was from Vienna, and Ludwig and Martha had married while he was working in Vienna as a textile manufacturer. While still in high school, Hilda showed great mathematical ability. After receiving her first degree, Geiringer continued her study of mathematics at Vienna. Her Ph.D. was awarded in 1917 for a thesis on the *Fourier Series* in two variables. She spent the following two years as Leon Lichtenstein's assistant editing the *Jahrbuch über die Fortschritte der Mathematik*, a mathematics review journal. In 1921, Geiringer moved to Berlin where she was employed as an assistant to von Mises at the Institute of Applied Mathematics. In this same year, she married *Felix Pollaczek* who, like Geiringer, was born in Vienna into a Jewish family and had studied in Berlin.

Pollaczek obtained his doctorate in 1922 and went on to work for the *Reichspost* (Postal service) in Berlin, applying mathematical methods to telephone connections. Hilda and Felix had a child, *Magda*, in 1922, but their marriage broke up. After the divorce, Geiringer continued working for von Mises and at the same time raised her child. Her mathematical contributions were noticed by Albert Einstein. As will be shown, they corresponded over many years on matters of science and her immigration to the United States.[58]

Although trained as a pure mathematician, Geiringer moved towards applied mathematics to fit in with the work being undertaken at the Institute of Applied Mathematics. Her work at this time was on statistics, probability theory, and also the mathematical theory of plasticity. She submitted a thesis for her *Habilitation* to qualify as an instructor at the University of Berlin, but it was not immediately accepted. According to a website[59] maintained by the School of Mathematics and Statistics at the University of St Andrews, which provides biographies of the world's most accomplished mathematicians, "the controversy surrounding Hilda Geiringer's application for *Habilitation* at the University of Berlin (1925-1927) sheds some light on the struggle of "applied mathematics" for cognitive and institutional independence in a world dominated by pure or abstract mathematicians. The controversy and Geiringer's unpublished reminiscences reveal the decisive influence of Richard von Mises....on both her career and the course of applied mathematics at the University of Berlin. ...The debate over Geiringer's theses for *Habilitation* opens up a new chapter of the history of mathematical statistics."

Geiringer lost her right to teach at the university in December 1933. In fact, she had been proposed for appointment to the position of Extraordinary Professor in 1933 but the proposal had been" put on hold" once the *Civil Service Law* came into effect. Geiringer left Germany and, with *Magda,* she went to Brussels. There she was appointed to the Institute of Mechanics and began to apply mathematics to the theory of vibrations.

In 1934, Geiringer followed von Mises to Istanbul where she had been appointed as Full Professor of Mathematics and continued to research in applied mathematics, statistics, and probability theory. While in Turkey, Geiringer became intrigued with the basic principles of genetics formulated by Augustinian monk Gregor Mendel.[60] Between 1935 and 1939, she was preoccupied with uses for the theory of probability to which she and von Mises had made major, early contributions.

Indisputably, Hilda Geiringer was one of the pioneers of what emerged as the burgeoning disciplines bearing such names as molecular genetics, human genetics, plant genetics, heredity in man, genomics, bioinformatics, biotechnology, biomedical engineering, and genetic engineering, among others. The world has not given sufficient credit to this intelligent woman's pioneering work mainly because it was done in Istanbul and published in Turkish journals.

With her colleagues von Mises and *Wilhelm (William) Prager,* Geiringer taught several cohorts of Turkish natives. Many of these students became the mentors of following years' generations, in fact, of Turkish mathematicians, physicists, statisticians, and actuaries, perhaps later computer experts. Some continued their education in the West. Most of these, however, were lost to Turkey. They stayed at American, German, and Australian universities as faculty members.

Following Atatürk's death Geiringer and her daughter found their way to *Bryn Mawr* (Women's) *College* where she was appointed to a lecturer position. Geiringer had to learn yet another language in order to teach. (She may well have been conversant in English as it related to her field.) She also had to adjust to what she referred to as "the American form of teaching." In addition to her lecturing duties at Bryn Mawr College, Geiringer undertook classified work for the National Research Council, as part of the war effort.

During 1942, she gave an advanced summer course in mechanics (then a very theoretical branch of engineering science) at Brown University, with the aim of raising the American standards of education to the level that had been attained in Germany. She wrote up her outstanding series of lectures on the geometrical foundations of mechanics and, although they were never properly published, these were widely disseminated and used in the United States for many years.

Even though Brown University never offered Geiringer permanent employment, the university takes full birthplace credit for these "mimeographed notes."[61] One has to understand the problems that existed in America. At the time, the United States was trying to integrate many leading German scientists fleeing from their former employers, the Nazis, into American employment. Apparently a Professor Neyman,[62] who himself had emigrated to the United States, wrote a report on Geiringer in April 1940, shortly after she arrived from Turkey. He was very explicit in *his* view of where Geiringer fit into the spectrum of professors of mathematics:

> Whether she is to be considered outstanding in ability or not depends on the standards of comparison. Among the present day mathematicians, there are few whose names will remain in the history of mathematics.... As for the newcomers to this country, I have not the slightest doubt that von Mises is one of the men of such caliber. ...There will perhaps be a dozen or perhaps a score of such persons all over the world. ...And Mrs. Geiringer does not belong in this category. But *it may be reasonable to take another standard, that of a university professor of probability and statistics*, perhaps an author of the now numerous books on statistical methods. *In comparison with many of these people, Mrs. Geiringer is an outstanding person* and I think *it would be in the interests of American science and instruction* to keep her in some university. (emphasis added).

Geiringer and von Mises married in 1943 and, the following year, she left her part-time, low-pay lecturing post at Bryn Mawr College to be nearer to him and because the *Wheaton* (Women's) *College* offered her her first permanent position in the USA. She accepted a post as Professor and Chairman of the Mathematics Department at Wheaton College in Norton, Massachusetts. During the week, she taught at the college, then traveled to Cambridge every weekend to be with von Mises.

For many reasons, this was not a good arrangement. There were only two members of the mathematics faculty at *Wheaton* and Geiringer longed for a situation where she was among mathematicians who were carrying out research. She applied for positions at other New England universities, but these failed due to fairly open discrimination against women. Geiringer had another strike to overcome: she never disassociated herself from her Jewish upbringing. However, she took it all remarkably calmly, believing that if she could do something for future generations of women then she would have achieved something positive. She also never gave up her research while at Wheaton College. In 1953, she wrote, "I have to work scientifically, besides my college work. This is a necessity for me; I never stopped it since my student days, it is the deepest need of my life."[63]

One response to a job application she received was quite typical: "I am sure that our President would not approve of a woman. We have some women on our staff, so it is not merely prejudice against women, yet it is partly that, for we do not want to bring in more if we can get men." For Geiringer, who had been so discriminated against in Germany because she was Jewish, to now be discriminated against because she was a woman must have been difficult to say the least.[64] After a while, all those trying to have her placed in a permanent position were contacting women's schools only. During June of 1939, the 23rd to be exact, Harvard's astronomy professor Harlow Shapley wrote on her behalf to Radcliffe College which operated as Harvard's little sister school. Though it drew instructors and other resources from Harvard, Radcliffe graduates were not granted Harvard degrees until 1963. Even though Geiringer was a better mathematician and a better teacher than Harvard could provide to the women at Radcliffe, Geiringer was never offered a real job by either.

In a March 7 1941 letter, Oswald Veblen, writing in her behalf, stated what is to this very day very much the case when he said: "You know of course that there is more and more demand for knowledge of statistics in several sciences. It is very desirable that when possible the courses in statistics should be given by people who are well grounded mathematically as well as interested in its applications. Teachers who satisfy both of these conditions are by no means common." He concluded that thought with "*Mrs. Geiringer is perhaps the only woman who satisfies both conditions.*" Three days later, Hermann Weyl wrote: "In her field of applied mathematics, and especially in mathematical statistics, she is a first-rate scholar of great experience and accomplishment." He then added, "In my opinion applied mathematics, which forms the bridge from abstract mathematics to the more concrete neighbor sciences, has up to now been unduly neglected in this country; that in the present (wartime) circumstances its importance has increased considerably."[65]

In retrospect, one could make a convincing argument that it was applied mathematics and mathematical statistics that in great measure helped the Allies win supremacy in the air during World War II and made America the technological and economic powerhouse that has catapulted upward the quality of life for at least two generations so far.

Hilda Geiringer took being passed over again and again by America's best rather gracefully. As late as May 28 1943, she wrote to Herman Weyl at the Institute for Higher Studies in Princeton. "I am certainly conscious of the fact that it is hard for a refugee + woman to find something. Nevertheless, I have not quite given up hope. I need not say that a research position would be just as welcome to me as teaching."[66] *"I hope there will be better conditions for the next generations of women,"* she wrote. "In the meantime, one has to go on as well as possible."[67]

In 1953, Richard von Mises died, and, thc following year, Geiringer, although retaining her job at Wheaton College, began to work at Harvard, completing and editing many of von Mises' unfinished works. To do this, however, she had to secure a grant from the Office of Naval Research[68] and it was then that Harvard offered her a temporary position as a Research Fellow in Mathematics. It is interesting to note that even though Hilda Geiringer was never offered a professorial appointment, in its Archives at Harvard University, one can find no fewer then eight boxes bearing the caption "MISES, HILDA VON (Mrs. Richard von Mises, known professionally as Hilda Geiringer ) (Applied Mathematics)" HUG 4574.142. The contents of these boxes involve only professional matters such as her "speeches and variants of published works…a few related letters and two notebooks. Boxes 2 and 3 contain manuscripts relating to published items and have numbers referring to the bibliography in HUG 4574.160."

In 1956, the University of Berlin, perhaps to assuage group guilt, perhaps to add a luminary name to its roster, elected her Professor Emeritus and placed her on full salary. In 1959, she formally retired from Wheaton College and, in the following year, that College honored her with the award of an honorary Doctorate of Science.[69] (Fig. 106 and 107).

The other colleague and collaborator of both von Mises and of Geiringer, first in Germany and then in Turkey, *Dr. William Prager* was recognized by the National [US] Academy of Sciences in many ways, but this particular notation is touching:

> His almost 20 books and many of his 200 papers have appeared or have been translated into several languages. *They have had a tremendous worldwide influence on those not fortunate enough to have direct contact with this truly unusual person* who was always willing and ready to share ideas and credit. Dr. Prager's many *former students and junior colleagues* whom he encouraged so warmly and helped so unselfishly to develop, now *occupy key positions in research and teaching in many countries.*[70] (emphasis added)

Born May 23 1903 in Karlsruhe, Germany, William Prager received his Dipl. Ing. (equivalent of a BS in Engineering) degree from the Institute of Technology in Darmtsadt in 1925 and his Dr. Ing. in the following year. At the age of twenty-six, he was appointed Acting Director of the Institute of Applied Mechanics at the prestigious Göttingen University and three years later was made Professor of Technical Mechanics in Karlsruhe and consultant to the *Fiesler Aircraft* Company in Kassel. Starting in the 1930s, Prager was gaining international recognition as an expert in the fields of vibrations, elasticity and plasticity of materials, and the theory of structures or structural analysis. Much of this was and continues to be of great importace in the design of airfcraft as well as their engines.

As an indication of just how rapid his success had been, his appointment in Karlsruhe made him the youngest professor in all Germany. The fact that the Nazis forced Prager out of his professorship in 1934 is more or less generally known. The fact that he accepted an invitation by the government of Turkey in 1934 because at the time he had no alternatives is less well known. However, the University of St Andrews offers the following bit of mostly unknown history about Prager and about what was in 1934 still possible to do.

Prager did not accept his treatment by the Nazis without protest. "*He fought his dismissal through the German courts and, perhaps surprisingly, won his case. He accepted the back pay which the court awarded him to cover what his salary would have been if he had remained in post.* He was also given permission to return to his professorship in Germany but he declined."[71] (emphasis added)

Although his Turkish contract allowed him four years to learn sufficient Turkish to give lectures in that language, he mastered the language in two years and wrote four mathematical texts in Turkish for his students, including one on descriptive geometry and another on the elementary theory of mechanics.

In Turkey, Prager continued to produce research results of the first quality. He published articles in German, Turkish, French, and English. During part of the period Prager was in Turkey (1934-1939), he managed to publish no fewer than thirteen scientific papers.[72] (Fig. 108).

The outbreak of war in 1939, however, was distressing to Prager, and the German advances by 1940 made him decide that he would be best placed if he could emigrate from Turkey to the United States. This, however, was not easy, even for a scientist with the high international reputation enjoyed by Prager. Prager succeeded, however, because Brown needed him. On arrival at Brown University in 1941, he was a key member of the world-famous group that was brought together at that time to place the engineering science known as *applied mechanics* in the United States at a firm level and an integral part of *mathematics*.

The first issue of the *Quarterly of Applied Mathematics*, which he edited continuously from the time he founded it until 1965, appeared in 1943. A memorial tribute to William Prager (d. 1980) by the (U.S.) National Academy of Engineering, points out that "Brown University recognized his scientific and administrative abilities by designating him as the first Chairman of the Physical Sciences Council and then the L. Herbert Ballou University Professor."[73] The tribute stated that "industrial concerns as well as universities and professional societies valued his advice and counsel." Most significantly, the tribute continued, "The National Academy of Engineering and National Research Council were beneficiaries of his thoughtful input."[74]

For the 25th anniversary celebration on September 7-10 in 1971, Brown University published a commemorative booklet *Applied Mathematics at Brown: A Description and History of the Division of Applied Mathematics at Brown University.* It includes coverage of the 1942 Summer Program to which *Hilda Geiringer* contributed as well. In 1974, William Prager was elected a Corresponding Member of the French Academy of Sciences, the highest honor bestowed by France on a scientist who is not a French citizen. Each year, the Society of Engineering Science, a worldwide professional organization, awards the *William Prager Medal* for the greatest contribution made anywhere in the world to the field known as solid mechanics or the mechanical behavior of solids under stress.

William Prager passed away in 1980. He carried the title University Professor Emeritus of Engineering and Applied Mechanics, Brown University.

**Nanoscience and Nanotechnology[75]Could Have Been Invented in Turkey: A Missed Opportunity**

Much as the mathematicians invited to Turkey were involved with *applied mathematics*, the physicists among them were technology-oriented. Physicist *Arthur von Hippel*[76] was one of the most colorful individuals among all of the émigrés. As he lived to be 105 (1898-2003), he outlived architect *Margarete Schütte-Lihotzky* by two years. Late in life, both managed to write and publish their memoirs. Each of these reads like a tragicomedy at times. Both émigrés left Turkey prematurely, she to fight the Nazis and he because his contract was prematurely terminated for reasons unimaginable and unimagined. Whereas she would have wished to have had at least one opportunity in her long career "to design a kitchen for a rich family," von Hippel, upon getting a major scientific award, commented that such was only possible because "his friends have outlived his enemies."

It is a truism that the few creative academics that there are create waves, and waves unsettle many in the bulk who are not. Some of these become "enemies" for life. It is also a truism that many academics have high and fragile egos. Arthur von Hippel was outspoken—of that there is no doubt! His "enemies" notwithstanding, an obituary in *Physics Today* states:

Arguably, his vision about the importance of interdisciplinary research to materials physics and its success in terms of problem solving and educational impact was important for the creation of the national program of federally sponsored materials research laboratories, first by the US Department Defense (1960-72) and later by NSF [National Science Foundation] (1972 to present) and subsequently by other countries.[77]

A luminary of material physics, Arthur von Hippel was born in Rostock, Germany, on November 19 1898. Upon completion of his doctoral thesis in 1924, von Hippel became an assistant to Max Wein at the Physics Institute in Jena. He married Dagmar Franck, the daughter of Nobelist James Franck. Because Dagmar was Jewish and because of his own outspoken anti-Nazi stand at the university and in the press, von Hippel and his growing family were compelled to leave. Fortunately, he was able to secure a professorship in Turkey in 1934.[78] Arthur von Hippel authored the book *Molecular Science and Molecular Engineering* (1959). He coined the term "molecular engineering" in the late 1950s and suggested the feasibility of constructing nanomolecular devices.[79] (Fig. 109).[80, 81]

Before leaving Germany, von Hippel packed twenty boxes of scientific equipment that he would need to set up a modern physics laboratory from ground up in Turkey. These boxes did arrive in Istanbul in a timely manner. However, it took an additional half-year to get them released by the not technically savvy and bureaucratic Turkish customs officials. With these boxes in hack and pressures to get the laboratory up and running, von Hippel had to resort to what we would refer to as "Yankee ingenuity." (Fig. 110).

> In the meantime, my wonderful master mechanic, Rieger, and I helped ourselves. We had discovered that the bazaar was an inexhaustible supply source of the strangest items. You had only to go to the entrance and ask for the "sword of Alexander the Great" and, in five minutes, someone would appear with the "sword of Alexander the Great." We therefore made a "wish list" and the strangest contraptions appeared—leftovers from old battleships, etc.—which we could rework for our purposes.[82]
>
> I inherited a section of the old Sultan's palace as my future laboratory, and the botanists Heilbronn and Brauner were installed in the former Mohammedan seminary.[83]
>
> My laboratory, thanks to my excellent master mechanic, Rieger, was the first one ready for student instruction in modern experimentation. The self-appointed Dean of the Science Faculty, Professor of Mathematics von Mises came to visit and congratulated on this outstanding success.[84]

Though marrying a Nobel laureate's daughter may not be on a young scientist radar screen, von Hippel's recollections[85] of his early scientific career would make the young ones blind with envy.

> In Opa [James] Franck's Second Physics Institute at Göttingen, scientific life flourished in a last beautiful display. International celebrities like Bohr and Rutherford came for lecture series. I had the privilege of getting to know Rutherford better during such a series and climbing our Johannis church tower with him. When he gave his gala lecture at the University, Opa forgot Rutherford's name when he introduced him. After hedging about with "the man we all know," etc., he at last burst out with, "Damn it! What *is* your name?" and brought the house down. We had a number of Rockefeller fellows in the Institute, including Bob Brode and Sam Allison. Robert Oppenheimer also passed through. But somehow they had been involved in my life when I dreamed and spoke daily of Marianne. Therefore a bridge of understanding had been broken. Bob Brode became famous through a visit to our local apothecary where he wanted to weigh a parcel and inquired, "Haben Sie eine Wiege? Ich will etwas wagen!"—a lovely indirect

suggestion for sexual intercourse, as he discovered to his surprise. This last period in Göttingen was a fruitful one for me scientifically. In a series of experiments, I developed a basic understanding of the electric breakdown in gases and single crystals, discovering the negative sparks in gases, the direction of breakdown in solids, the meaning of Lichtenberg figures, etc. This work led to a deeper understanding of the role of electrons in the onset of breakdown in gases, liquids and solids; the determination of the true electrical strengths of alkali halide crystals and their changes as a result of added impurities; an understanding of the formation of color centers; and the extension of these ideas to thunderstorms and lightning strikes.

On the human side, my studies of crystals brought me into close contact with Professor V. M. Goldschmidt of the University's Institute of Crystallography, a genius and wonderful bachelor. He lived with his father and a number of pet squirrels who visited him through his open windows. They were named after his scientific enemies in his home country, Norway. His father, sporting a mighty beard— very unusual at that time—was an admired spectacle in the swimming pool. In 1932, I gave a lecture at the German university in Prague and was recommended for a professorship. I also gave a lecture in Berlin, which was attended by Einstein, Planck, Haber, Nernst and Gustav Hertz. A few months later, I was back with Opa Franck for discussions about a new Kaiser-Wilhelm Institute for Physics that was to be built for him. On that occasion, we were invited for the evening by Professor Nernst. He was not musical but very inventive and, with the help of a technician, had built the first "electric" piano. Max Planck, in contrast, was very musical. Invited to play the piano, he did so with deep distress and left immediately afterward.[86]

One of the tragicomic stories von-Hippel recollects is:

[T]he crisis in Germany began to approach its climax. The Rector of the University, a Professor of Agriculture and ardent Nazi, called a meeting of all of the faculty and declared the constitution of the University annulled. He asked us to look out the windows where *Reichswehr* and Nazi Storm Troopers were lined up to break any incipient resistance. The First Physics Institute under Professor Pohl joined the Nazis. Our Second Physics Institute resisted but found a traitor in its midst. One of our Ph.D. students turned out to be a Nazi leader who had hidden secret Nazi plans for the

> takeover in his cabinet. Accidentally he had also locked away in the same cabinet a spectrograph I required for my next lecture. I needed the instrument but he was away in Berlin for a last briefing. I therefore had our master mechanic open the cabinet and took the instrument out without looking at the other contents. When the student came back, he feared his secret had been discovered and gave himself away by threatening me with arrest. We asked him to leave the Institute. After playing a big Nazi role for a while, he was killed in World War II.[87]

The worldwide *Materials Research Society* named its "premier award" in the name of Arthur von Hippel. The society recognized him as a pioneer in the study of dielectrics, semiconductors, ferromagnetics, and ferroelectrics and an early advocate of the interdisciplinary approach to materials research. "His example substantially furthered the science of materials."[88] While his colleague William Prager viewed materials from a phenomenological perspective and mathematically modeled their behavior under stress, von Hippel got inside and studied their behavior from a molecular perspective. Arthur von Hippel gave us *nanotechnology.* This term was not even known at the time.

Nanotechnology represents a break-through in 21st-century technology. As televisions, airplanes, and computers revolutionized the world in the 20th century, many scientists predict that nanotechnology will have an even more profound effect during the course of this century. In fact, it is widely considered the driving engine for the next industrial revolution. In the case of Arthur von Hippel, Turkey missed out in letting the goose that laid the golden egg slip through its fingers.

The other physicist cum/engineer, *Kurt Lion,* was in Turkey for only two years beginning the end of August 1935 and leaving exactly two years later. He worked as a biophysicist helping fellow émigré Friedrich Dessauer launch the Institute for Radiology at Istanbul University. When Dessauer went to Switzerland in 1937, Lion went with him. Lion was more of an engineer than the others. He was interested in developing instrumentation needed for scientific and engineering research. Like von Hippel, upon re-emigration in 1941, Lion settled at MIT. Unlike von Hippel, however, he didn't stay long in academe. He had ideas. He wanted his ideas commercialized and he wanted to do it his way. So he started his own company.

While still at MIT, Kurt Lion started Lion Precision in 1958 to provide capacitance-sensing solutions to industry. Over the years, the company provided unique testing solutions for a variety of industrial products. In most cases, these products had a powerful and lasting impact on the industry they served. Among these is a high-performance capacitance sensor to measure precision spindles used in machine tools and hard-disk drives. Lion also produced the "world's first and most popular clear-label sensor, which revolutionized the packaging industry" worldwide and a tester which measures high-speed drill spindles for the medical and printed-circuit board industries to maintain peak production performance.[89]

While still an academic, he wrote the seminal text on *Instrumentation in Scientific Research*. It was published in 1959 by the McGraw-Hill Book Company of New York and has served as the scientists' textbook and handbook for many years. Lion Precision is still in existence, producing sensing devices for laboratories and for manufacturing.

Then there was *Harry Dember* who was born in 1882 and died in 1948. After being summarily discharged from Dresden's Technical University because his wife, Agnes, was Jewish, he arrived at Istanbul University in 1933. Student days' recollections provided by Eugen Merzbacher tell us much about Professor Harry Dember:

> Harry Dember was my teacher at the University of Istanbul, from my first year in 1939 until he left Turkey for the US in 1941. He was an experimental physicist and gave the large two-semester introductory physics course in the so-called PCN curriculum (physics, chemistry, biology), somewhat but not wholly similar to what is a pre-med undergraduate program in this country. His lectures were in the traditional European mode, given in a giant auditorium to about one thousand students. Dember had an assistant whom he brought from Dresden, Thomas Mendelssohn, and they, together with at least one female Turkish sub-assistant, rehearsed the lecture for an hour or two before the 9 AM lecture. The lecture demonstrations were projected on a screen in the manner developed and promoted by the famous physics demonstrators, the experimentalists Pohl (Göttingen) and Paul Scherrer (Zurich). It was a spectacular and flawless performance, three times a week. In addition, Dember presided over the weekly laboratory sections that were compulsory. My experimental skills were minimal, and I was usually nervous when Dember cruised from one experimental station to the next (we worked in pairs) and asked searching questions.
>
> But in the best European tradition I introduced myself to Dember when I arrived In Istanbul in the fall of 1939, and I was frequently invited to their home for dinner. I remember both Dembers as friendly and warm people.
>
> Dember's own physics research area was the same as it had been since his student days, when he got his Ph.D. under

> Hallwachs, who in turn had been a pupil of Heinrich Hertz, the discoverer of the photoelectric effect, in addition to being the first to produce electromagnetic radiation, which made him famous. Hertz observed that a discharge that creates radiation somehow also caused a nearby spark generator to fire, because of ionization due to the radiation. He was too busy with studying the electromagnetic radiation and assigned the investigation of what became known as the photoelectric effect to his student Hallwachs. Eventually, Dember, student of Hallwachs, became an authority on the so-called crystal photoelectric effect, and that's what his student and assistant Mendelssohn worked on diligently in Istanbul, with limited resources. After Dember left, his position as chair of Experimental Physics was filled by a Swiss nuclear physicist named Zuber, but by that time I was no longer taking any experimental courses, concentrating instead on theoretical physics and mathematics, which had a quite strong Turkish faculty. The professor who influenced me far more than Dember was Willy Prager, who moved to Brown University in the middle of my student years.[90]

A previously mentioned anonymous document, most likely drafted by Philipp Schwarz, that was found in the E. Finlay Freundlich archives at St Andrews University was addressed to the "Minister of Education, Ankara, beginning with: "Your Excellency," makes a number of contract renewal recommendations for members of the émigré faculty. Within these, it is pointed out that Professor Dember is teaching classes of 600 to 800 students so it is necessary to provide some relief to him. This way he would also further the education of young assistants who would work with him on the experiments in the planned Praktikum.

Significantly, the document also addresses the need to retain émigré support personnel. In subcategories Technical Helpers and Mechanics among others, it mentions:

> Mr. Rieger, (Contract ends 1.1.36); and Mr. Vallander (Contract ends 1.10.36), who are respectively in charge of the Science Faculty and Institute for Chemistry shops. Glass-blower Witlich, (Contract ends 1.10.36); Miss Lotte Loewe (Contract ends 10.1.36). She is responsible for large amounts of apparatus. The new project of a larger Institute of Chemistry will make her help even more important. Her work was promised for the next five years to the Director of the Institute; Inspector of Gardens and Mr. Stephen (Contract to 1938) is responsible for construction of the new Botanical Gardens.

> These specialists, (all foreigners) are also charged with teaching their methods to local interested workers who will then continue in this work.[91]

## Taking Philosophy out of the Realm of Ottomanist Theology

While many of the émigrés did interdisciplinary work, perhaps the best generalist of them all was *Hans Reichenbach*, the founding member of the *Berlin Circle*. Was he a philosopher? Yes. Mathematician? Yes. Physicist? Yes. Probabilist? Yes. Logician? Yes. Historian? Yes. And more! One thing is sure. He was a generalist and integrator of knowledge coming from many a discipline, a veritable knowledge-synthesizer (Fig. 111).

The Internet Encyclopedia of Philosophy[92] summarizes Hans Reichenbach as follows:

> The major intellectual influences in his own life and thought came from outside philosophy, a fact which was responsible for some of his most outstanding contributions to philosophy. He was an expert in physics and mathematics, and his philosophical contributions centered around and consistently returned to the borderline between science and philosophy; in particular, to the two great theoretical developments in contemporary physics: relativity and quantum mechanics. Philosophy was for him the logical and epistemological reconstruction of scientific knowledge; and to this task he devoted his entire work with remarkable consistency throughout his life.
>
> The first book he published was on *Relativitätstheorie und Erkenntnis a priori* (1920) and to the problem of interpreting and clarifying the logical foundations of relativity, involving the basic concepts of space, time, and causality, he returned in several major works: *Axiomatik der relativistischen Raum-Zeit-Lehre* (1924); *From Copernicus to Einstein* (1927; American edition, 1942); *Philosophie der Raum-Zeit-Lehre* (1928, an English translation published posthumously); *Atom and Cosmos* (1930; translated into four languages); and *Ziele und Wege der heutigen Naturphilosophie* (1931). At the time of his death, he was completing another comprehensive work on the nature of time with special emphasis on thermodynamics, quantum mechanics, and information theory.

When the Reichenbachs left their urbane and sophisticated homeland, they went to Istanbul, which was by most standards considered also a very cosmopolitan city. It is fair to say that in terms of its varied and coexisting cultures it was more advanced then Berlin. It certainly could proudly boast of a longer and richer history. The Istanbul university campus (buildings and grounds) was well established since it had served Turkey's higher education in its various incarnations for over a century. As mentioned with the arrival of Reichenbach and his academic superstar colleagues in 1933, the university became known academically as the "best German university in the world" almost overnight. In its public pronouncements, the University of Istanbul to this day goes out of its way to attribute its current stature to the heritage left behind by the "German" professors.

Reichenbach left Istanbul in 1938 because the fledgling UCLA, still deep in the shadows of its big sister, the Berkeley campus of the University of California, wanted its own superstars. It had just granted its first Ph.D. degree and that was in history. California made Reichenbach an offer he could not refuse, and so he packed up and set out for Pacific Palisades with his wife and two children. There, he had a house built on a firm foundation, a house that still stands and his widow (his second wife), Maria, says she still enjoys.

When Reichenbach arrived on the UCLA campus in 1938, he found no more than a handful of permanent buildings, none more than a decade old. These abutted sweet-smelling experimental citrus orchards run by the California Land Grant University's *Agricultural Extension Division.* Indeed, the orchards were the most established part of the campus. All this was situated in an unused part of a Spanish land-grant ranch[93] with a huge ravine running through it. On the northern perimeter, a winding two-lane road, now called Sunset Boulevard, separated campus lands from the Santa Monica mountain wilderness. The land had been donated to the University of California; so the better sections of the ranch could be parceled and sold for a good price.

Abutting UCLA, Westwood village was a sleepy little town with but one cinema through the 1950s. Los Angeles, an hour's drive away, was hardly more sophisticated and perhaps even less cosmopolitan. If one took Wilshire Blvd., the drive into Los Angeles took one through truck-farming country all the way to the Beverly Hills Country Club. Nowadays, things are a bit different over there: a canyon of high-rises. On the other hand, if Hans Reichenbach were still with us and was asked to revisit Istanbul University's campus and its vicinity, he would find very little to have changed.

So UCLA, like the University of Istanbul, gained much of its early stature due to the presence on its faculty of people like Hans Reichenbach and other "German" exiles, several of whom were saved by Turkey from extinction if they had been left in Nazi hands.

Reichenbach was born on September 26 1891 in Hamburg, Germany, and became a leading philosopher of science, and a proponent of logical positivism (also known as neopositivism, or logical empiricism). He studied physics, mathematics, and philosophy at Berlin, Erlangen, Göttingen, and Munich during the first decade of the 20th century. Among equally prominent philosophers, Reichenbach studied with Nobel laureate physicists Max Planck, Max Born, and Albert Einstein. He received his Ph.D. in philosophy from the University at Erlangen in 1915 and his dissertation on the theory of probability was published in 1916. He attended Einstein's Berlin lectures on the theory of relativity between 1917 and 1920. It was then that Reichenbach chose the theory of relativity as the subject for his own philosophical research. He became a professor at Stuttgart Polytechnic in 1920.

In Turkey, he was given the chairmanship of the Department of Philosophy at the University at Istanbul. While there, Reichenbach changed the philosophy curriculum by introducing interdisciplinary seminars and courses on scientific subjects. Significantly, *The Theory of Probability* was published in 1935 and his *Experience and Prediction* was published in 1938, the very same year that he moved to the United States. Obviously, the stay in Turkey did not adversely impact his productivity or his creativity. Nor did the Turkey sojourn interfere with Reichenbach's long-standing working relationship with Albert Einstein. A letter from Einstein to Reichenbach, circa 1926, demonstrates the mutual respect of that relationship. Einstein begins his letter, writing, "You are totally right, it is wrong to believe that geometrizing is something significant…." The letter ends with "If there is anything else I can do, please write." Their warm interaction on matters both scientific and personal continued until Reichenbach's premature death in 1953. Einstein outlived him by two years (Fig. 112).[94]

In retrospect, it is amazing how wide-ranging the interests of many of these individuals were. They were not solely mathematicians, scientists, or engineers; most of them were all of the above. They all had interdisciplinary interests. In the sciences, some crossed over from mathematics to physics and in physics they crossed over from aerodynamics to elasticity of materials. In mathematics, broadly construed, they were into probability, statistics, and numerical solutions of differential equations. The engineers among them were truly what are now called biomedical engineers, doing biotechnology. They worked side by side with medical doctors. Stateside, such interdisciplinarity was rarely to be found until the late 1950s at the earliest. The term biotechnology was not even coined until that time and biomedical engineers did not yet exist. Now, over seventy years later, and having caught up with Vienna and Berlin of the 1920s and 30s, such people are not considered as wondrous.[95]

*Jewish physics* can best and most justly be characterized by recalling the activity of one who is probably its most prominent representative, the pureblood Jew, Albert Einstein. His relativity theory was supposed to transform all of physics, but when faced with it did not have a leg to stand on. In contrast to the intractable and solicitous desire for truth in the *Aryan* scientist, the *Jew* lacks to a striking degree any comprehension for truth.
—Philip Lenard, 1905 Nobel Prize winner in physics. In his 1936 book, *German Physics,* Lehmann's Verlag, Munich.

*Figure 76*
Erwin Finlay Freundlich.

Bebek, 48 Cevdet Pasha Caddesi

31st March, 1935.

W. F. Vaughan-Scott Esq.,
P.O. Box 1023
Istanbul.

Dear Mr. Vaughan-Scott,

As I told you yesterday, the purchase of the Telescope has come into a critical phase.

Till Monday, the 25th, I had the impression that everything was going straight. During your holiday I was asked by the Doyen of the Law Faculty to give him certain data concerning the contract, which I readily gave him. But the whole question was delayed partly by the longer absence of the Rector, who was in Geneva, then by the "Bayram" holidays, and then by a short illness of the Rector himself. So I was not able to see him before last Monday, when I asked him if the contract were finished to be signed. He answered that the whole question had taken a new direction, that the Government had forbidden to purchase the Telescope from England, and that he had taken up negotiations with the Representative of the House Zeiss in Gena, without having informed me about this new state.

I confess that I was so surprised that I did not know what to answer. In the afternoon the Representative of Zeiss telephoned and told me that he had been at the Rector and that they had almost come to an agreement, only the difference of

*Figure 77*
Some of the problems encountered by E. Finlay Freundlich in procuring Turkey's first telescopic instrument.

. 2 .

about LTqs. 500 remaining. In regard to this he wished to have certain information, which I refused to give. The next day, Tuesday, I was asked to see the General Secretary at 3 o'clock in the afternoon and I took the opportunity, before the Representative of Zeiss had entered the room, to explain to him that I was deeply alarmed about this state of the affair. According to my views, the British firm had received the "Adjudication", but he denied this, saying once more that the Conseil des Ministres had given strict order that the purchase be done in Germany on account of the fact that England refuses to buy goods from Turkey. I did not see any possibility to influence the matter, and simply assisted silently while he bargained with the Representative of Zeiss. I only pointed out that the tender of Zeiss, formerly presented, was for the moment of no use, on account of the fact that the construction of the Pillars of the Telescope had already begun according to the English designs, so that Zeiss would have to adapt their Telescope to the existing Pillars.

I ignore if they have come to a definite agreement since.

Sincerely yours,

E. F. Freundlich

*Figure 78*
Continues from previous page

YALE UNIVERSITY OBSERVATORY
NEW HAVEN, CONNECTICUT

May 23, 1934

Dr. E. Freundlich
University of Istanbul Observatory
Cevdet Pasa Caddesi 48
Istanbul-Bebek, Turkey

Dear Freundlich:

Some time ago we received from you a request for the Transactions of the Yale Observatory. We have sent you copies of all the volumes so far printed (see the last page of Volume 10) as well as a copy of the Bright Star Catalogue, which is not included among the Transactions. We have also entered the Observatory on our distributing list. These were sent through the Smithsonian Institution, and I presume may have reached you by now.

I learn from Comrie, who sent me a copy of his letter to you dated May 12, that you are looking for star catalogues and other books with which to build up your library. Elkin's collection must contain a great many books that you would like; for example, a complete set of the Astronomische Nachrichten (with the exception of two comparatively recent volumes and one number of an earlier volume), a complete set of the Jahresbericht, the Vierteljahrsschrift der Astronomischen Gesellschaft, volumes 1 - 65, the Astronomical Journal, volumes 7 - 42, the Monthly Notices of the Royal Astronomical Society, volumes 27 - 92, and a fairly large number of miscellaneous books. If you are interested in these, we shall make up a more complete list of them. Mrs. Elkin would prefer to sell the sets, but she would be glad to take a moderate sum for them if they are to go to an Observatory that is likely to use them. The miscellaneous books I am sure she would be glad to include gratis. In any case, the favorable exchange caused by the low international value of the dollar would enable you to secure these books at exceptional prices.

I have been very much interested to hear of your recent movements, and I should be glad to have a word from you telling me how things are going with your new observatory. Your American friends and colleagues will follow your progress with great interest and with their best wishes for your success.

Sincerely yours,

F Schlesinger

Frank Schlesinger

CS

*Figure 79*
Yale's astronomers' contributions of publications for the Istanbul observatory library.

*Figure 80*
Wolfgang Gleisberg, 1970.

*Figure 81*
Chemistry Professor Fritz Arndt, courtesy Dr. Lale Burk, Chemistry Department, Smith College.

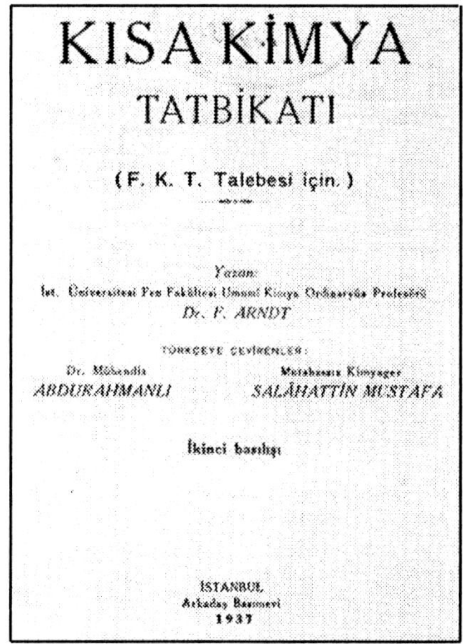

KISA KİMYA

TATBİKATI

(F. K. T. Talebesi için.)

Yazan:

[illegible]

Dr. F. ARNDT

TÜRKÇEYE ÇEVİRENLER:

Dr. Mühendis ABDURAHMANLI

Mütehassıs Kimyager SALÂHATTİN MUSTAFA

İkinci basılışı

İSTANBUL

Arkadaş Basımevi

1937

*Figures 82 and 83*

Some examples of the tangible and long-lasting contributions that Fritz Arndt made to science education in Turkey

Fen Fakültesi Neşriyatından:

KISA KİMYA

TATBİKATI

(P. C. N. Talebesi için.)

MÜELLİFİ:

[illegible]

Dr F. ARNDT

TÜRKÇEYE ÇEVİRENLER:

Dr. Mühendis Apturrahmanlı

[illegible] Salâhattin Mustafa

İstanbul

ARKADAŞ MATBAASI

1934

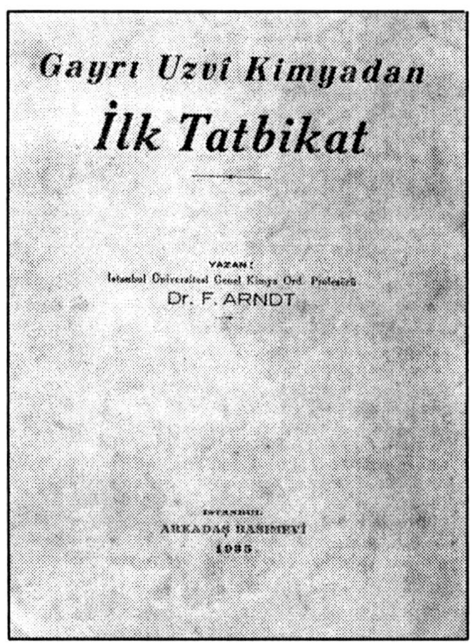

Gayrı Uzvî Kimyadan

İlk Tatbikat

YAZAN:

İstanbul Üniversitesi Genel Kimya Ord. Profesörü

Dr. F. ARNDT

İSTANBUL

ARKADAŞ BASIMEVİ

1933

*Figures 84 and 85*
Continued

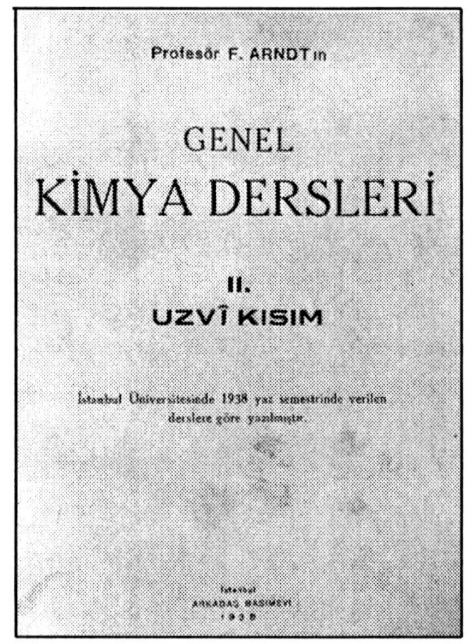

Profesör F. ARNDT'ın

GENEL

KİMYA DERSLERİ

II.

UZVÎ KISIM

İstanbul Üniversitesinde 1938 yaz semestrinde verilen derslere göre yazılmıştır.

İstanbul

ARKADAŞ BASIMEVİ

1939

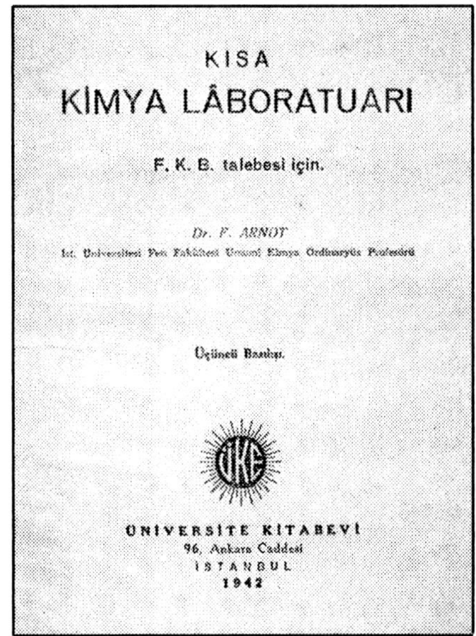

KISA

KİMYA LÂBORATUARI

F. K. B. talebesi için.

Dr. F. ARNOT

İst. Üniversitesi Fen Fakültesi Umumî Kimya Ordinaryüs Profesörü

Üçüncü Basılışı.

ÜNİVERSİTE KİTABEVİ

96, Ankara Caddesi

İSTANBUL

1942

*Figures 86 and 87*
Continued

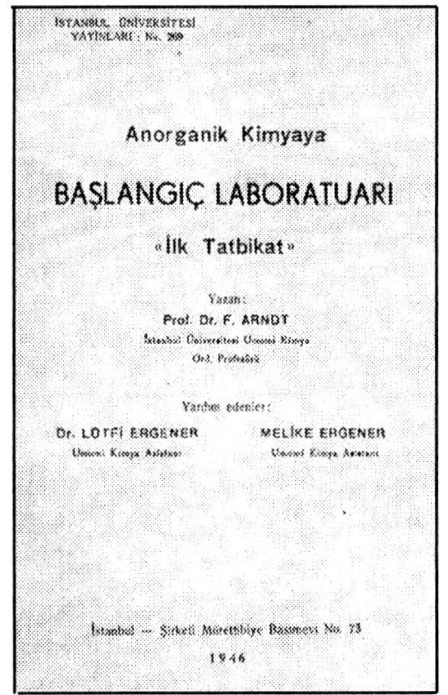

İSTANBUL ÜNİVERSİTESİ
YAYINLARI : No. 269

Anorganik Kimyaya

BAŞLANGIÇ LABORATUARI

«İlk Tatbikat»

Yazan:

Prof. Dr. F. ARNDT

İstanbul Üniversitesi Umumî Kimya

Ord. Profesörü

Yardım edenler:

| Dr. LÜTFİ ERGENER | MELİKE ERGENER |
|---|---|
| Umumî Kimya Asistanı | Umumî Kimya Asistanı |

İstanbul — Şirketi Mürettibiye Basımevi No. 73

1946

*Figure 88*
Professor Fritz Arndt and some of his Turkish graduate students.

*Figure 89*
Chemistry Professor Arndt and more of his former Turkish graduate students.

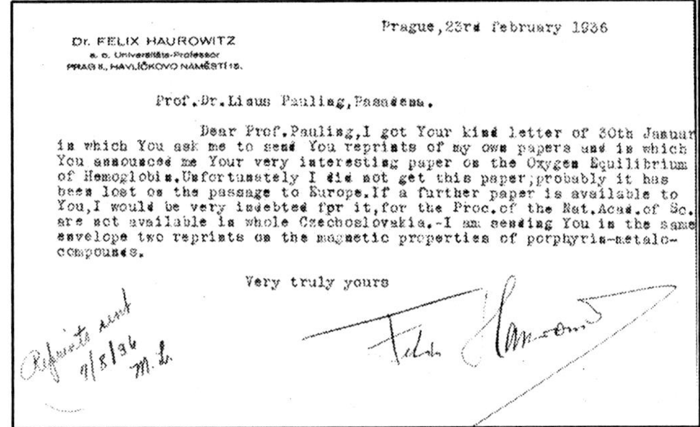

Dr. FELIX HAUROWITZ
a. o. Universitäts-Professor
PRAG II., HAVLÍČKOVO NÁMĚSTÍ 15.

Prague, 23rd February 1936

Prof. Dr. Linus Pauling, Pasadena.

Dear Prof. Pauling, I got Your kind letter of 30th Januar in which You ask me to send You reprints of my own papers and in which You announced me Your very interesting paper on the Oxygen Equilibrium of Hemoglobin. Unfortunately I did not get this paper; probably it has been lost on the passage to Europe. If a further paper is available to You, I would be very indebted fpr it, for the Proc. of the Nat. Acad. of Sc. are not available in whole Czechoslovakia. - I am sending You in the same envelope two reprints on the magnetic properties of porphyrin-metalo-compounds.

Very truly yours

Felix Haurowitz

Reprints sent 9/8/36 M. L.

*Figure 90*
Letter from Felix Haurowitz to Linus Pauling.
Their professional correspondence preceded Pauling's Nobel award by two decades.

Prof. Dr. Felix Haurowitz

BİOKİMYA

1 9 4 3

*Figure 91*
Haurowitz biochemistry textbook, 1943.

*Figure 92*
Dr Felix Haurowitz with his Turkish laboratory coworkers. Circa 1940s.

*Figure 93*
Ernst W. Caspari.

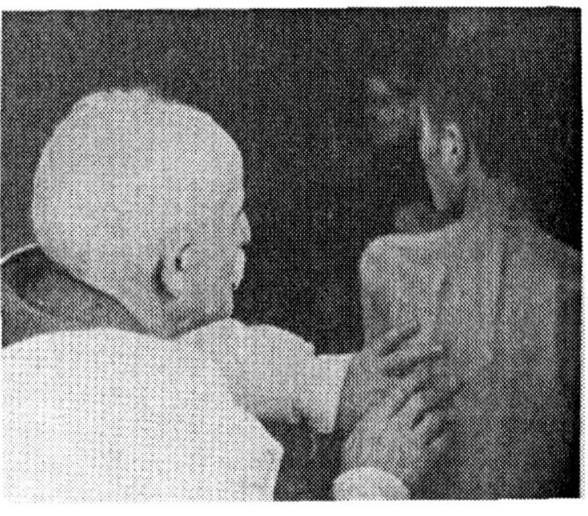

*Figure 93a*
Caspari's father in the Lodz ghetto.

*Figure 94*
Werner Lipschitz.

*Figre 95*
*Textbook of Biomedical Chemistry*,
Lipschitz, 1937.

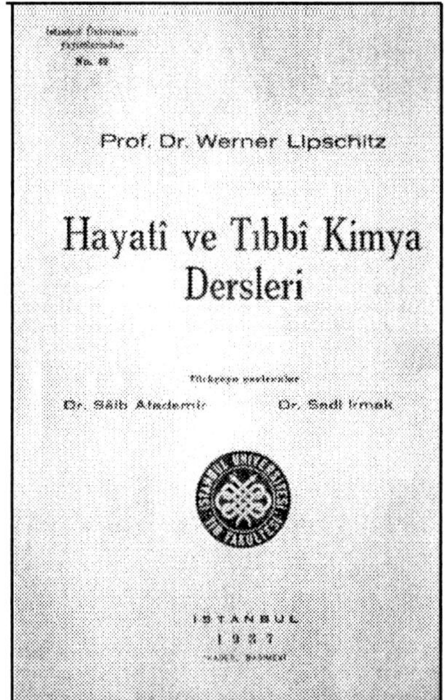

Prof. Dr. Werner Lipschitz

Hayatî ve Tıbbî Kimya Dersleri

Dr. Sâib Atademir Dr. Sadi Irmak

ISTANBUL
1937

*Figure 96*
Winterstein Physiology Text, 1943.

*Figure 97*
Winterstein Animal Physiology Text, 1946.

Haurowitz
Nisan yağmuru değil, Şubat dolusu!..

*Figure 98*
A cartoon of Winterstein, Haurowitz, and other textbook authors. 1945 Student New Year's spoof. Istanbul University Medical School.

*Figure 99*
Reiningers, Walter, Margaret, daughter Eva Ruth.

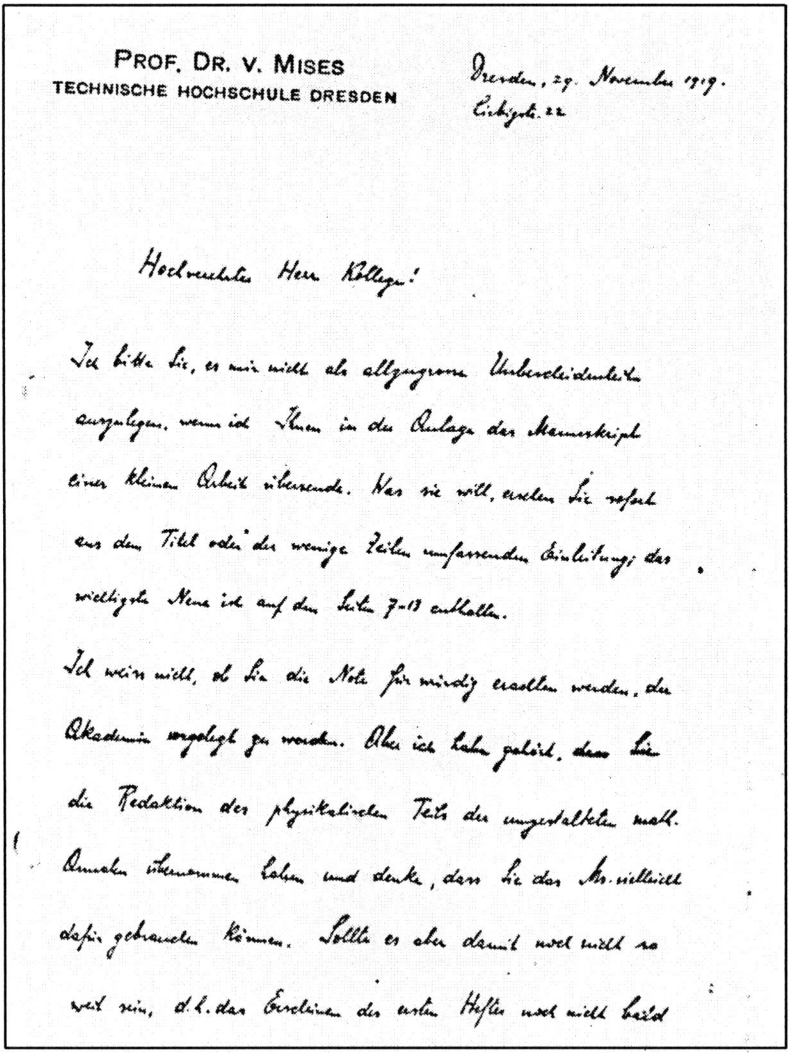

PROF. DR. V. MISES
TECHNISCHE HOCHSCHULE DRESDEN

Dresden, 29. November 1919.
Liebigstr. 22

Hochverehrter Herr Kollege!

Ich bitte Sie, es mir nicht als allzugrosse Unbescheidenheit auszulegen, wenn ich Ihnen in der Anlage das Manuskript einer kleinen Arbeit übersende. Was sie will, ersehen Sie sofort aus dem Titel oder der wenige Zeilen umfassenden Einleitung; das wichtigste Neue ist auf den Seiten 7–13 enthalten.

Ich weiss nicht, ob Sie die Note für würdig erachten werden, der Akademie vorgelegt zu werden. Aber ich habe gehört, dass Sie die Redaktion des physikalischen Teils der umgestalteten math. Annalen übernommen haben und denke, dass Sie das Ms. vielleicht dafür gebrauchen können. Sollte es aber damit noch nicht so weit sein, d.h. das Erscheinen der ersten Hefte noch nicht bald

*Figure 100*
Letter from von Mises to Albert Einstein, December 10 1919 (continues next page).

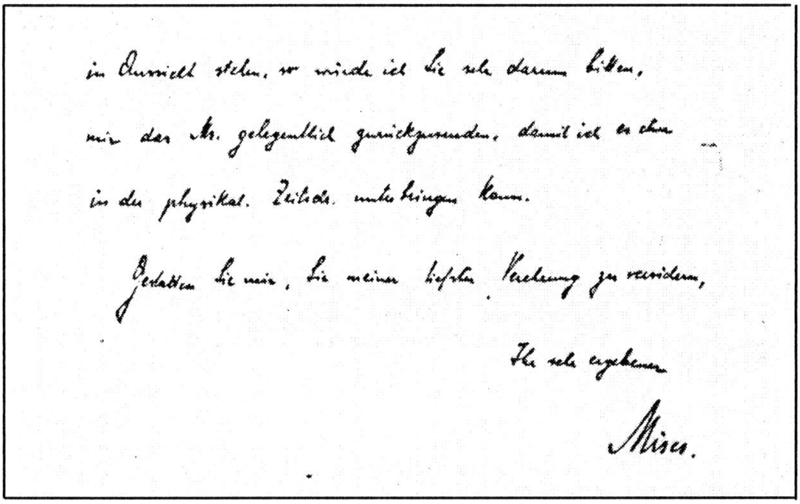

in Aussicht stellen, so würde ich Sie sehr darum bitten,
mir das Ms. gelegentlich zurückzusenden, damit ich es eben
in der physikal. Zeitschr. unterbringen kann.

Gestatten Sie mir, Sie meiner tiefsten Verehrung zu versichern,

Ihr sehr ergebener

Mises.

*Figure 101*
Letter, continued from previous page.

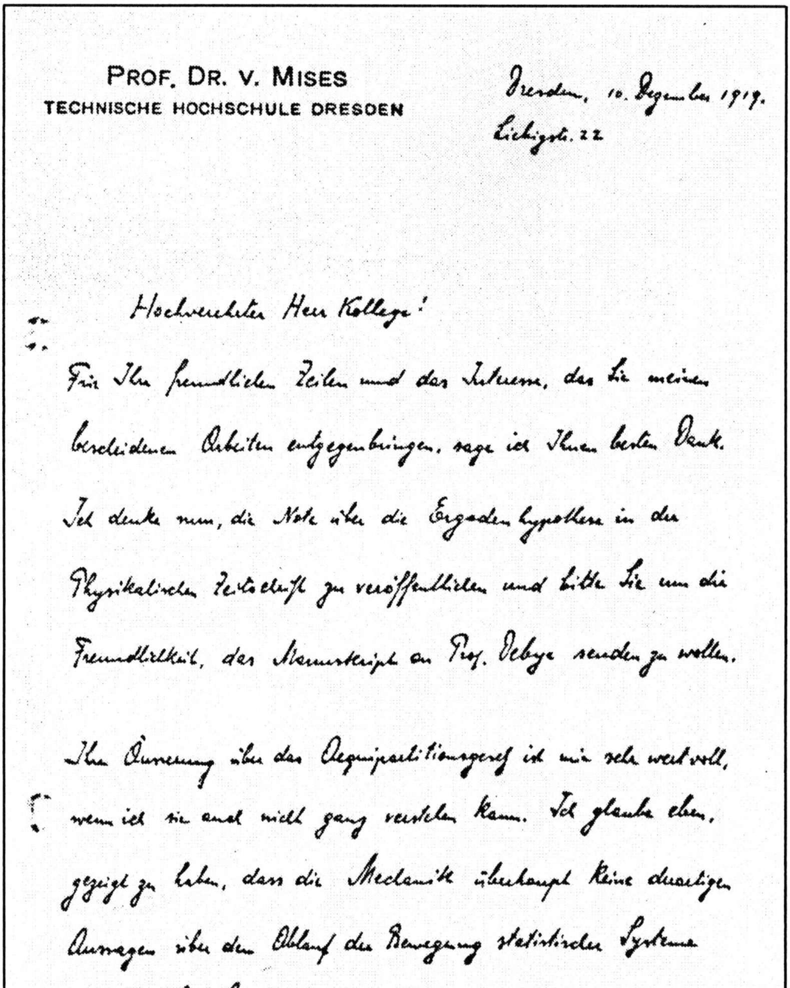

PROF. DR. V. MISES
TECHNISCHE HOCHSCHULE DRESDEN

Dresden, 10. Dezember 1919.
Liebigstr. 22

Hochverehrter Herr Kollege!

Für Ihre freundlichen Zeilen und das Interesse, das Sie meinen bescheidenen Arbeiten entgegenbringen, sage ich Ihnen besten Dank. Ich denke nun, die Note über die Ergodenhypothese in der Physikalischen Zeitschrift zu veröffentlichen und bitte Sie um die Freundlichkeit, das Manuskript an Prof. Debye senden zu wollen.

Ihre Äusserung über das Äquipartitionsgesetz ist mir sehr wertvoll, wenn ich sie auch nicht ganz verstehen kann. Ich glaube eben, gezeigt zu haben, dass die Mechanik überhaupt keine derartigen Aussagen über den Ablauf der Bewegung statistischer Systeme gestattet. Die Aussagen, die möglich sind (mit erdrückender Wahrscheinlichkeit ist zu erwarten, dass .....), fliessen nicht aus der

*Figure 102*
Letter from von Mises to Albert Einstein, November 29, 1919 (continues next page).

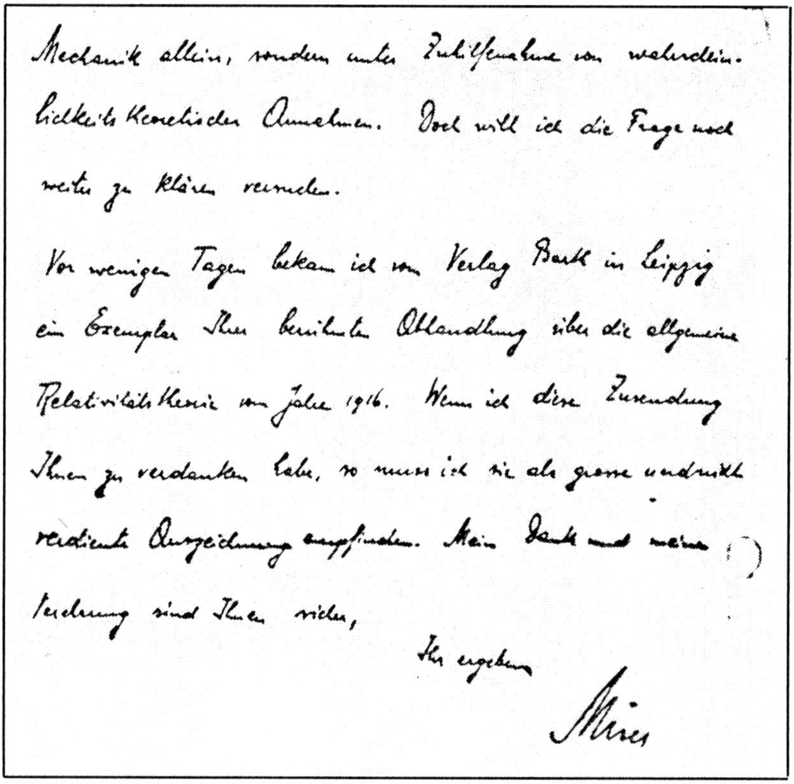

Mechanik allein, sondern unter Zuhilfenahme von wahrscheinlichkeitstheoretischen Annahmen. Doch will ich die Frage noch weiter zu klären versuchen.

Vor wenigen Tagen bekam ich vom Verlag Barth in Leipzig ein Exemplar Ihrer berühmten Abhandlung über die allgemeine Relativitätstheorie vom Jahre 1916. Wenn ich diese Zusendung Ihnen zu verdanken habe, so muss ich sie als grosse und unverdiente Auszeichnung empfinden. Mein Dank und meine Verehrung sind Ihnen sicher,

Ihr ergebener

Mises

*Figure 103*
Letter continued.

*Figures 104 and 105*
Richard von Mises.

*Figures 106 and 107*
Hilda Geiringer.

- 3 -

32. Mechanik isotroper Körper im plastischen Zustand, in collab.with H.Geiringer,
64 pages, Ergebnisse d.exakten Naturwissenschaften 13 (1934), p.310.

33. Ein neues Verfahren zur Bemessung auf Biegung beanspruchter Holzstaebe,
Schweizerische Bauzeitung, 104 ( 1934), p.201.

34. Der Einfluss der Verformung auf die Fliessbedingung zaehplastischer Körper,
ZS angew.Math.u.Mech. 15 (1935), p.76.

35. Über die Reziprozitaet von Masse u.Steifigkeit in der Schwingungslehre,
Revue de la Faculté des Sciences İstanbul 1 (1936), p.I/37.

36. Beitraege zum Mutationsproblem, in collaboration with A.Heilbronn,
Revue de la Faculté des Sciences İstanbul, 1 (1936), p.III/37.

37. Elastic Stability of Plane Frameworks,
Journal of the Aeronautical Sciences 3 (1936), p.388.

38. The Buckling of an Elastically Encastred Strut,
Journal of the Royal Aeronautical Society 40 (1936), p.833.

39. Tersimî Hendese ( İstanbul lectures on descriptive geometry ) vol.1. , 80 pages,
İstanbul 1937.

40. Die Knicksicherheit ebener Rahmentragwerke,
Revue de la Faculté des Sciences İstanbul 3 (1937), p.1.

41. Mécanique des solides isotropes au delà du domaine élastique, 66 pages,
Mémorial des Sciences Mathématiques, Fasc.87, Paris 1937.

42. Ebene elastische Spannungszustaende mit konstanter Hauptschubspannung,
Revue Math.de l'Union Interbalkanique 2 (1938), p.45.

43. Über Systeme von Kurvenkongruenzen,
Bull.Math.de la Soc.Roumaine des Sciences 40 (1938), p.187.

44. On Hencky-Prandtl Lines,
Revue de la Faculté des Sciences İstanbul 4 (1939), p.22.

45. On isotropic materials with continuous transition from elastic to plastic state,
Proc.5th Internat.Congress Appl.Mechanics, Cambridge 1939, p.234.

*Figure 108*
Page 3 of "Scientific Publications of Prof. Dr. Ing. Willy Prager, Istanbul." June 28 1939.

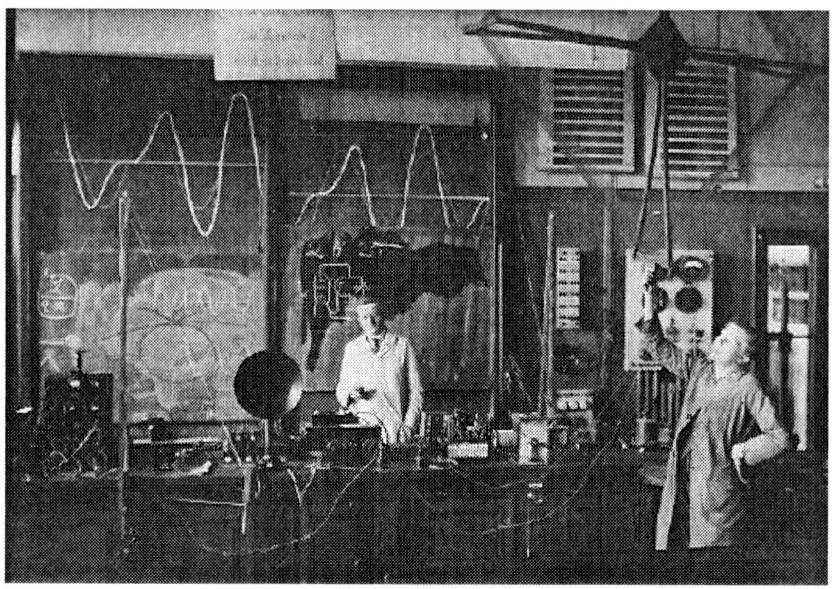

*Figure 109*
Von Hippel and assistant giving a lecture-demonstration in Jena (1927).
Courtesy of the Von Hippel family.

*Figure 110*
Von Hippel's laboratory servant at Istanbul University.
Courtesy of the Von Hippel family.

*Figure 111*
Hans Reichenbach.

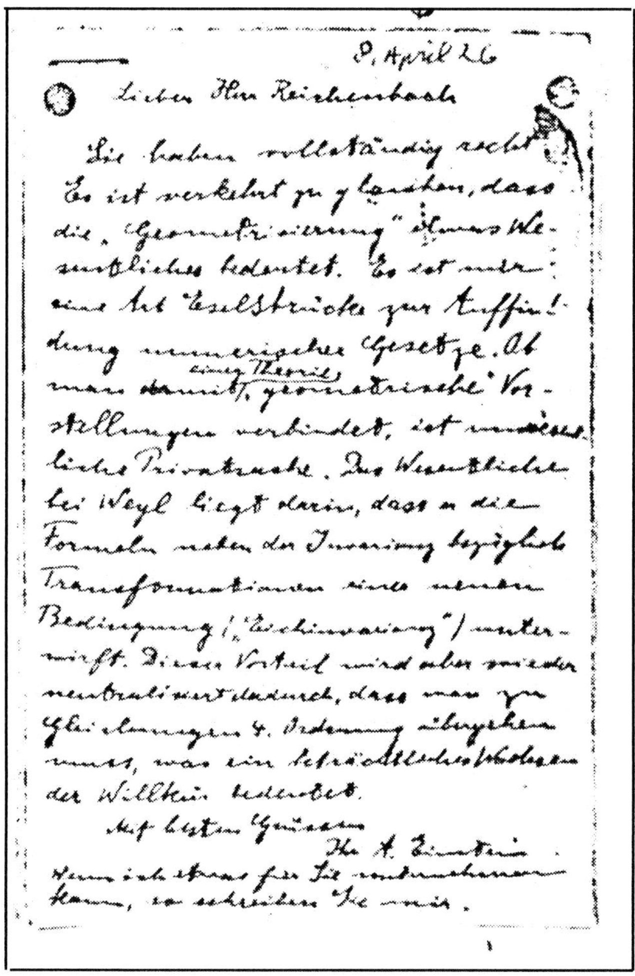

8. April 26

Lieber Herr Reichenbach

Sie haben vollständig recht. Es ist verkehrt zu glauben, dass die „Geometrisierung" etwas Wesentliches bedeutet. Es ist nur eine Art "Eselsbrücke zur Auffindung numerischer Gesetze. Ob man mit einer Theorie „geometrische" Vorstellungen verbindet, ist unwesentliche Privatsache. Das Wesentliche bei Weyl liegt darin, dass er die Formeln neben der Invarianz bezüglich Transformationen einer neuen Bedingung („Eichinvarianz") unterwirft. Dieser Vorteil wird aber wieder neutralisiert dadurch, dass man zu Gleichungen 4. Ordnung übergehen muss, was ein beträchtliches Wachsen der Willkür bedeutet.

Mit besten Grüssen
Ihr A. Einstein.

Wenn ich etwas für Sie unternehmen kann, so schreiben Sie mir.

*Figure 112*
A handwritten note from Albert Einstein to Hans Reichenbach April 8 1926.

# 9
# Problems They Encountered

## Adjustments to Local Conditions

It is a bit of an understatement to say that it is not easy for professionals in full flight during the course of their career to relocate themselves and their families and resume their work without their proper tools, equipment, and supplies, into a culture and land entirely unfamiliar to them (and a rather hostile place at that) when they are unable to speak with those around them (with all the benefits speech has to offer humans). But when one considers that the alternative was certain death—well, there is no choice.

These were men and women who had very high expectations of themselves; they were used to taking on and overcoming challenges, and they had come to a land where extraordinary things were expected of them. They could foresee making great contributions and beneficial social reforms.

After satisfying the need for shelter and safety came learning the new language. The German émigrés were contract-bound to lecture and publish in Turkish sooner than later. How to cross this Bosphorus? By inventing new types of boats and bridges.

Publish or perish is not a new doctrine in the ranks of academe. But, in this respect, these men and women were self-actuated. They wanted their colleagues young and old to know about the products of their creative minds, to provide a record for posterity. To some extent, like academics everywhere and during all times, they not only sought peers' recognition but also feedback. However, these souls were prohibited from publishing in Axis-power-controlled professional journals and only with difficulty could they reach American- or Allied-power journals. And even if they did succeed publishing in the latter, they often had no access to seeing that work in print until years later.

The émigrés, of course, had the option to publish in Turkish journals. Their "German" colleagues were eager to consult and to "form circles for discussion" as they had in the old Germany. Even if they succeeded in getting a paper into a western journal the authors were required to provide a Turkish language version of that article. It was obvious to all, however, that no one read Turkish journals outside of Turkey.[1]

Turkish is unlike any western European language. It comes closest to Hungarian and Finnish. Though there were a few native Hungarians among the émigrés, there were no Finns. Latinization of the Turkish alphabet helped in learning the language and setting up a vocabulary for a field of study, but few of the émigrés achieved sufficient mastery of the language to deliver a scientific lecture. Some did take to the language. Some tried and were booed by the students for their attempts. Students preferred the use of translators to poor Turkish.

Even in the best of circumstances, there is always something lost in translations. In matters of university teaching, it would have helped for the translators to know the subject matter. Those who knew the subject were unskilled in one of the languages, or perhaps imprecise; those fluent in both languages often knew little of what was being discussed. As many Germans found out to their distress or even peril, there were those among the translators who had other agenda.

There is no question that many Turkish professors resented the émigrés. Not surprisingly, those who had been dismissed as part of the *üniversite reformu* were bitter. Equally resentful were those who retained their jobs but were paid less than a quarter of the newcomers' salaries. In addition, the intrusive newcomers could not only bring assistants with them from Germany but also were given Turkish assistants, something that their Turkish counterparts had not had at any time. To add more fuel to the fire, more often than not, the Turkish professors were individuals who, in fact, had the credentials for the choice positions offered to the guest professors. Is it any wonder than that they, too, had little liking for their nominal superiors and often ignored or sabotaged their activities and instructions?

No doubt the *Dar-ül Fünun* had many competent and dedicated faculty members, but "there were also those who showed up at work only to collect their modest paychecks. Like all the fossilized elements at institutions, they were expected to put up a resistance to the reform project and the foreign intruders."[2] In medicine, Turkish professors as well as private practice physicians did not want competition from world-renowned German experts who were building and running the University clinics. Turkey had a very antiquated medical infrastructure—but those *who claimed* to be men of medicine out in the agrarian society still did not want to lose their living. This reform hit directly in their pocketbooks at a time when money was scarce for all. The émigré professors and their mandate were being constantly undermined by those elbowed aside and their allies. That is certain.

Professor Albert Malche had anticipated such problems might occur, so he wrote to Lauder W. Jones at the European office of the Rockefeller Foundation, on October 16 1933,[3] "Dare I suggest that you make a trip.... Your visit would be a great encouragement for the foreign professors, and it would be a highly appreciated mark of interest, I am sure, for the Ministry." Later, the Rockefeller Foundation was made aware of the various problems by reports it was receiving from its own representatives in the field. *"There is a strong anti-German feeling among the Turks."*[4]

Additionally, the Third Reich was keeping its watchful eye on those it had let out of the web. And Christian nationalists were also among the loose-knit groups undermining the émigrés in their work as were the anti-Semitic circles with direct ties to the Third Reich, the old-guard professionals the émigrés replaced, those not replaced but attempting to preserve vested interests, junior Turkish-native academics wanting to take over, Turkish colleagues who were getting paid much less for their work, and students with super-sensitivity to any perceived slights to national pride.[5] Not surprisingly, of course, academics were involved in the usual and customary gamesmanship that is played to this day in most societies' universities, including and especially those in the US.

There is also no doubt that the loose-knit alliance of several disparate subcultures frustrated the modernization of Turkish universities.[6] No doubt, great things were done. How much more could have been done? In the main, however, the émigrés enjoyed ministerial support[7] for achieving their professional aspirations. This in turn fueled their individual enthusiasms and *esprit de corps*[8] for the task at hand and challenges ahead. Yet in at least one documented case, the intrigues shortened tenure, that of Professor Arthur von Hippel in Turkey, resulting in a missed opportunity for Turkey of monumental proportions indeed. Based on his work before coming to Turkey, and, while there, von Hippel became the father of what we now know as *nanotechnology*, a development that is still, in the 21st century, reshaping all industries worldwide.

Von Hippel offered a thought of survival for the exiled Germans by thinking of it all as a wonderful test or experiment for psychologists. Reflecting on his relatively short experience as an Istanbul University Professor, he described the situation as follows:

> There were twenty five to thirty professors with their families—mostly refugees selected by Professor Schwarz and his advisors in Zurich—who formed the nucleus of a modern university. The old

> Turkish faculty had been dismissed, but was still a powerful adversary with connections in Parliament. Therefore we newcomers, with the shock of exile in our bones, found ourselves surrounded by intrigues in a strange culture. Any success or mishap affected us all. This was a severe testing ground for human qualities. It would have been an exciting experiment for a psychologist.[9]

The youngest of the émigrés, von Hippel provided very vivid accounts of his personal and professional experiences in Turkey. Over half a century after the fact, they were told mostly in a humorous vein. For instance, von Hippel related, "Checking in at the University [on first arrival] we found that the President could only speak French and Turkish, and the Minister of Education—normally residing in the new capitol, Ankara, in Asia Minor—spoke only English and Turkish. My American-English sufficed for the latter, but my horrible school French did not for the former. Somehow we managed, with the help of Professor Schwarz."[10]

Nevertheless at the time, many circumstances and incidents were indeed serious, some tragic, some funny to western eyes and some to eastern eyes. Von Hippel also discussed some of the early interactions between members of the "Academic Community in Exile" and their Turkish hosts. Among these are different ways that displaced Turkish academics tried to sabotage the newcomers both in their work and in person.

In addition to the plot against ophthalmologist Igersheimer, von Hippel recites another, potentially dangerous incident which took place immediately after Professor Kantorowicz had made a new set of shining teeth for the Shah of Iran:

> Our exhausted colleague [Kantotowicz] had just sunk into a well-deserved sleep when the soldska [soldiers] appeared again and took him back to the palace. His predecessor [a displaced Turkish dental professor] had told the Gazi that he made the teeth and that Kantorowicz had begged him for help because *he* had never been a professor of dentistry in Germany. A furious exchange of telegrams arose until the University of Frankfurt testified that Kantorowicz had been a full Professor of Dentistry there [and] in excellent standing.[11]

In his own case, von Hippel tells the following story: "[T]he son of a millionaire," his assistant coveted becoming the newly established laboratory's director. To speed things along, he somehow allegedly influenced the translator to jump on any opportunity to mistranslate von Hippel's lecture comment so as to incite nationalistic passions among the students.

It worked on the first try. "To my consternation, the students, extremely nationalistic, jumped up and looked like they wanted to murder me. The whole university was shut down by a student strike." This episode culminated in a Ministerial inquiry. My colleagues trembled and mostly deserted me."[12]

Though not intended as such by von Hippel, the above account of his Turkish assistant serves as a counterpoint in outcome to the beggar at the eye clinic's shouting "he will make you blind" experienced by his fellow émigré, ophthalmology Professor Igersheimer. While Igersheimer and Kantorowicz survived the ensuing ministerial investigations, in von Hippel's case of false translation, the outcome was quite different. His five-year university contract was reduced to one year.[13] Fortunately, von Hippel was able to obtain a visa to the United States and secure a position at MIT where he stayed and prospered till retirement. The fact that his father-in-law, James Franck, a Nobel laureate in physics, was already well positioned in America's academic world may have helped in obtaining the MIT post and hence, the visa.

There were academic pressures and political dangers. There were intrigues (palace and conference room) and petty tricks. There were informers in the palace walls. None of this was helped by the émigrés' impoverishment in the beginning, as they had fled throughout the war and as the known order of the world was ending. The émigrés also had to face harsher realities. One of these was the economy. The Turkish universities were strapped for money. This was especially true once the war started. In a letter dated March 4 1941, dealing mostly with scientific matters, to an editor-in-chief of a major scientific journal, Professor Haurowitz complains about not being able to get copies of journals published in Holland, not even the issues which include his articles. "Turkey has no money and will not permit buying foreign publications." Then there were more significant concerns such as the anti-Jewish riots that erupted in Eastern Thrace on June 24 1934 and continued for almost a month before being suppressed by Turkish government action in mid-July.[14]

As told by economist Fritz Neumark in his memoirs,[15] the German legation kept ratcheting up the pressure on the émigrés as years went by.

> [During] the first five to six years, the only connection most of us had with the [German] Consulate was limited to the procedure for passport renewal. Although no problems were faced in such procedures for a long time, later things were getting to be touchy for many of us. This became evident from the questionnaire attached to the document sent to us dated May 30 1938 on the orders of the German Ministry. In this questionnaire, besides the

starting date of our contracts with the Turkish government, we were being asked to provide information on whether we or our spouses were "Aryans" or Jewish and whether there were "non-Aryans" among our relatives.

The pressures thus started then went on to increase until the stamping of German passports belonging to Jews as defined according to national-socialist standards by big red letters of "*J*" began. This stamping was only the first step in even heavier oppressions. One day I learnt through a non-official source that I had been expelled from German citizenship with my wife and children without any reason being cited. An acquaintance in Switzerland saw this item in the German official newspaper No. 161, dated July 12 1940 that he read by chance. In this notice of the German Interior Ministry, it was also stated that "all my assets were confiscated." In fact, since I did not have any assets, what was meant was a small amount of money in a German bank belonging to my wife. The ejection of all "non-Aryan" Germans from citizenship happened a short time after this event. I am still unable to learn why such a special treatment was accorded to me. Anyway, many people like us were left without passports, not a desirable situation since war had started. Of course, to this was added the sadness that I and my wife felt on being officially thrown out of a country we still considered as our homeland. Here, I would like to stress the fact that the Turkish government caused no hardships to us during the time we had no passports; on the contrary, it helped us to go through this period with tolerance.

In many respects, Turkey was a century behind the Germany that the scientists had fled. Such was demonstrably the case in the interior of the country in Ankara. R. A. Lambert, visited both Istanbul and Ankara for the Rockefeller Foundation to report on conditions circa 1934. Lambert's diaries provide a vivid picture:[16]

The two-day journey [by train] through Syria and Turkey recall vivily my experiences in 1919-20. In spite of absence of fezzes and veils, the peasants and villagers seen along the way look much the same. In the cold rain in the Cilician Plain I observe a goodly number of barefoot men and boys, and ragged clothes are not rare. The people on the high snow-covered central plateau are better clad. The poor roads in Turkey are a contrast to the fine metaled highways of Palestine and Syria. Oil lamps are seen in R.R. stations whereas every Judean village now has light and power from the harnessed Jordan.

> [In Istanbul] there are still the sturdy hamals [porters] carrying incredible burdens. In 1920, I photographed one with a with a bale of cotton (500 pounds) on his back, and a colleague reported seeing another carrying a piano). But the city has lost much of its color. The picturesque dress of orthodox Jews, Albanian peasants, and others is no longer seen. And I have no doubt...and other foreign residents say, that Turkey has undergone a far greater change spiritually—using the term in broadest sense—that material changes here in Istanbul would indicate.[17]

However, Lambert's diaries include more than just observations on the changes in the sights and sounds of post-independence Turkish culture. Lambert took time out to keenly observe and to discuss with the relevant players all aspects of the émigrés' work. His February 17 1934 Istanbul diary entry speaks for itself:

> To transform the old Gov't offices into laboratories presented a problem, but the result is not bad. Light and space at least are ample. None of the departments is ready for teaching, - not to mention research. In anatomy, however, we see 4 large dissecting rooms 40 tables each with a cadaver ready for dissection. I am told that for each body there will be 10 students, so that 400 may work at the same time. (There are 200+ students per class). Shephard [Director of the American Hospital of Istanbul and Lambert's old friend] and I suggest that 4 students to a cadaver would be a better number, but the professor thinks we should not expect here American standards. There are German heads for all depts....except experimental. physiology, physiology, parasitology, and pharmaco-dynamics. It is noteworthy that in particularly every dept. the professor and staff are on the job busy getting things in order, and that nearly everybody looks hopeful and talks optimistically.[18]

On the last day of his stay in Turkey, Lambert's diary makes the observation that "it is too early to judge the Turkish effort. Within a year, possibly in six months, one may be able to say whether the German professors can become adjusted and can work here as they did in Germany. Schwarz, I am sure, recognizes the uncertainty, though he talks confidently. He says much now depends on the personality of the newcomers—that the Turks will meet them halfway but won't come all the way. Emphasizes the fact that the Gov't has been most liberal in all salary arrangements and has done everything possible to provide promptly adequate working conditions. Schwarz would like another RF visitor to come late next summer or fall—and see the difference."[19]

## Surveillance of Émigrés by Foreign Governments

The Rockefeller Foundation was not alone in reporting to its headquarters on the émigré professors' circumstances in Turkey. Both the German and the American embassies are known to have done it, and there is no doubt that the Soviet regime also kept a close eye on the situation. In one specific example, John Van Antwerp MacMurray, United States Ambassador to Turkey, on July 14 1936, signed a cover letter to "The Honorable Secretary of State." Transmitted with the cover letter was the "Memorandum Regarding German-Jewish Professors in the University of Istanbul," authored by S. Walter Washington, the embassy's Second Secretary. As is shown on the archival copy of the letter, upon receipt at State, a copy (significantly) marked "Confidential" was forwarded to the US Office (now it is Department) of Education on August 6 1936. Accurate or not in some of its anecdotes, this official document offers an interesting view of the situation circa 1936 while offering good reading. It is reproduced here in its entirety. (Fig. 113).[20]

> During the academic year that has just come to an end there were 35 German-Jewish professors in the University of Istanbul, 14 of whom belonged to the Faculty of Medicine. A complete list of them is attached to this report. Most of them came to Turkey in 1933 (See despatches [*sic*] No. 26 of November 19, 1933, and No. 34 of November 16, 1933), when the Turks decided to profit from the troubles of Jews in Germany by inviting some of the leading scientists and scholars of that race to come to this country. Some of them signed contracts for a period of three years, and some for periods of ten years, with the privilege of canceling after five years.
>
> The authorities at Ankara have attempted to give the German professors every possible facility for carrying on their work. Enormous sums have been spent on equipment for laboratories and hospitals. One now sees in Turkey hospitals equal in equipment to any in the world. In addition, more or less adequate appropriations have been made for operating these physical plants. It is understood that strong advocates and protectors of the professors exist in high circles in Ankara, and that any complaints which are made against them fall on deaf ears in the Capital.

Considerable friction, however, has existed in Istanbul. This was no doubt inevitable when a large group of foreigners of such note was introduced into an institution already established and staffed largely with citizens of the country. On the one hand, the Turkish manner of thought and conduct has not led to the cooperation and efficiency to which German professors are accustomed on the part of their associates and subordinates; and, on the other hand, it is natural for the Turkish professors to feel that good positions and high salaries, which could have been enjoyed by themselves, have been given to outsiders. The medical professors are supported in their dislike of the Germans by the entire medical fraternity of Istanbul. Although the German professors are prohibited from engaging directly in private practice, any resident of Istanbul may go to the clinics operated by them and receive free of charge treatment of a standard so much higher than that provided by the local doctors that the latter find that their patients are decreasing in number. Moreover, patients who are willing to pay high fees have no difficulty in finding Turkish doctors who will agree to summon German professors in consultation, which is a permissible means of circumventing the rules prohibiting private practice. As a consequence of these conditions, frequent appeals have been made to the nationalistic spirit of the people in order to stir up opposition to the "foreign influence," and the newspapers have not always appeared to be friendly to the Germans.

Some discussion has been heard in Istanbul regarding the desirability, or non-desirability, of the Germanization of the University which these professors are bringing about. In view, however, of the obvious importance of the question, it is surprising that more consideration has not been given to it. The writer has heard one young Turkish professor in the Faculty of Medicine argue that French culture has in the past dominated Turkish education and is more suitable to the country than German, and that the best method of improving Turkish educational standards is to send Turkish students abroad to prepare them to be teachers, rather than to bring foreign professors to Turkey. The disinterestedness of these statements was brought into question, however, when it appeared that the young man had himself just returned from studying in France. It is true that the French have been influential in the medical faculty of the University of Istanbul, but during the war the Germans gained a greater control over the remainder of the University. There are now one Frenchman in the Faculty of Medicine, one in that of Science, and one in that of Law. Their influence is powerless as against that of the 35 Germans, who will undoubtedly become a very important factor in increasing German influence in Turkey, outside the University as well as inside. In spite of the fact that all of these men are in this country because of their dissatisfaction with conditions at home, their culture is German and some of them were in fact leaders in German scientific and scholastic thought during the post-war period. *Their disagreement with the political regime in their home country has in no way changed their fundamental thought processes, and they show many evidences of their allegiance to the German nation, if not to the present Government. Among them may be found names famous in Germany a few years ago. Mention may be made of Dr. Erich Frank (internal medicine), Dr. Wilhelm Liepmann (gynecology), Dr. Rudolph Nissen (surgery), Dr. Joseph Igersheimer (ophthalmology), Dr. Finlay Freundlich (astronomy), Dr. Hans Reichenbach (philosophy), and Dr. Leo Spitzer (Romance languages).* The last-mentioned, having terminated his three-year contract, is leaving Turkey to take a position in Johns Hopkins University at Baltimore, but it is understood that he will be replaced here by another who is coming from Germany.

A great source of trouble for the Germans is language. Although interpreters were to be provided for three years, all of the contracts contained clauses obligating the German professors to learn Turkish and to be prepared to lecture in that language after the termination of this period. During the three years which have just come to an end, some of the professors have picked up a smattering of Turkish, some do not easily learn languages or are too old to do so, and all have found that they have been kept too busy to devote much time to language study. Turkish students do not generally understand German; but both those who do, and those who do not, often find that the subject matter of the lectures is made clearer when the professor speaks in German and has his remarks translated into Turkish by an expert interpreter than when he speaks Turkish badly. One professor has said that when he tried to speak Turkish to the students they stamped and yelled until he changed back into German. On the other hand, it would obviously be advantageous if all the professors could lecture in the native language of the students, and the fact that most of them are not prepared to fulfill this clause in their contract is a vulnerable spot of which their critics have not failed to take advantage. It remains to be seen what will happen when the fourth school year begins in the Autumn.

The question which has perhaps caused the greatest amount

of discussion and hard feeling is that of laboratory assistants and operating-room nurses and attendants. Among the professors who have the greatest prestige in Germany and other countries are those in the Faculty of Medicine whose work is in clinics. The Turkish Government has supplied them with excellent equipment, but they are men who expect to have also expert assistant personnel. The professor of surgery, for instance, is accustomed to walk into the operating room in his hospital in Germany and to find everything prepared for him to perform his operation, and then to be able to leave, after the essential task is done, with the confident knowledge that the last touches will be given to the patient by well-trained hands. In the University of Istanbul Hospital, however, he finds that the authorities expect Turks to assist him so that they may learn. One of the world's leading surgeons becomes in effect not only a teacher of surgery but also a teacher of every branch of hospital work from nursing upwards. He and several of his colleagues whose specialties involve principally work in clinics have protested against these conditions, and have demanded that some personnel, such as operating-room nurses, be brought from Germany. The Turkish authorities have generally resisted these demands, though in a few instances they have acceded to them.

Complaints are made by some of the Germans that even the young Turkish assistants who are actually doctors do not always cooperate to a degree which one should expect. One of the most famous professors recounts how he was called one evening to perform a most delicate operation. After he had got his patient on the operating table, he was washing his hands and preparing himself for the operation when he noticed that all his assistants were absent from the room. Upon looking out of the door he found them all in the corridor trying to see who could send the wheeled stretcher the greatest distance with one push. On another occasion, when he had finished his operation, he told the seven assistants who had been watching him that one of them could perform some of the last steps, all of them being fully capable of the task. After an interval he looked into the room to see how they were getting on and was surprised to find the patient lying alone and no one else in sight. Upon investigating, he found the seven assistants in the lounge room telling each other stories. When he reprimanded them for leaving the patient in a very uncomfortable state and not carrying out his orders, they replied that nothing had been done because he had not designated which one was to do it.

In the Faculty of Law, and in that of Letters, a slightly different difficulty has arisen. Some of the German professors are apparently in such demand by the students that their courses are crowded and there is a tendency to require from them more and more hours of lectures. The consequence has been for them to recommend that assistant professors and instructors be brought from Germany to relieve them of some of the burden. The Turks reply that their own fellows can do this work.

Dr. Leo Spitzer, Professor of Romance Languages, who has terminated his contract and is going to Johns Hopkins University, took advantage of his departure to make a public statement of his views on this matter. The local Press burst forth in indignation, an action which did not help matter.

The professors say that they are pleased with the reaction of the students, that they find them to be interested and to cause little difficulty. Troubles arise mainly with assistants and with the administration. With regard to the latter, the difficulties arise because of the bureaucratic nature of the Turkish Government. In spite of the Government's desire in principle to take advantage of the presence of the Germans to raise the educational standards in the University, and its willingness to purchase the most elaborate apparatus for laboratories, hospitals, et cetera, yet the enormous amount of "red tape" involved in carrying out these intentions causes much difficulty to the professors.

Despite the prominence given to the difficulties of some, it is believed that a majority of the Germans— those whose work is not primarily clinical— are quite satisfied with their positions here. Both in the Medical Faculty and in the other departments are found many who feel thankful that they have jobs which pay them quite well. It is perhaps unfortunate that the most famous, and those who are in the best position to obtain positions in other countries, happen to be the ones whose work requires clinics and for whom the Turkish Government has gone to the trouble of supplying a fully equipped hospital. These men because of their prestige and independence, have not hesitated to criticize what they have not liked; and the disputes which have consequently followed have placed their more satisfied colleagues in a false light.

The general opinion prevails that, under the Presidency of Atatürk, the German professors will be allowed to stay as long as they wish. Some of the more famous and the more dissatisfied may succeed, as has Dr. Spitzer, in finding positions to their liking elsewhere, when their present contracts have terminated. The majority, however, will probably adapt themselves to the local conditions. They will have their troubles, no doubt, but their value to the University of Istanbul is so obvious that it appears unlikely that they will be ousted, at least so long as the country is under its present control. SWW:mej (emphasis added).

Secretary of State Cordell Hull was also sent a document assessing the situation in Istanbul. It was also penned on July 14 1936 and the author was again J. V. A. MacMurray, America's ambassador to Istanbul. Annotated as CONFIDENTIAL, the memorandum "Nazi Activities in Turkey" was copied to "Berlin, Kaunas, and Riga." Presumably, this missive was directed to U.S. embassies respectively in Germany, Lithuania and Latvia. Because this document seems to have escaped the scholars' notice and because it reads so well while telling us precisely what was known to the State Department at the time, it too is reproduced here in its entirety.

Sir:

I have the honor to transmit the following information, as of possible interest to the Department, regarding the activities of the German Nazi Party organization in Turkey.

The German Colony in Turkey is estimated at roughly 1,000 grown persons, according to a statement which the German Consul General recently made to a number of my staff. Of this number, information obtained from the Press and from other sources is that only slightly more than 500 were present on the German vessel which on March 29th last sailed from Istanbul to the Black Sea, where they took part in the German plebiscite, this in spite of the fact that free transportation to Istanbul was provided for those who reside in the interior. The Press added that 9 votes were cast against Herr Hitler on this occasion, and an anti-Nazi source is the authority for the report that 50 percent of the votes cast were blank. Whether that report is true is of course questionable; but it seems to be the general opinion that a large number of the Germans of Istanbul, including some of the most prominent in business, are not in entire sympathy with the Nazi cause, though most of the non-sympathizers have identified themselves with Nazi organizations for reasons known only to themselves and perhaps to the local Nazi leaders.

Whatever may be the number of sincere believers in the Nazi principles, there is no doubt that the Party Chiefs completely dominate the Colony, and it is understood that, apart from the German-Jews (perhaps a hundred in number) who have left their country for political reasons and have settled temporarily in Istanbul, 99 percent of the Germans in Turkey have officially adhered to the Nazi Party or to other Nazi organizations. The most conspicuous among the exiled Jews are the 55 professors in the University of Istanbul, some of whom were formerly leaders in their professions in Germany. The sentiments most frequently heard by these scholars and scientists, however, are not those of revenge against the regime that is responsible for their exile, but of dissatisfaction at being in any country other than Germany whose customs and habits are theirs and where their forbears have lived for generations. It is also significant to note that, of the two managers of the local branch of the Deutsche Bank, one is a prominent Nazi but the other is a non-German Jew who the Nazi manager insists must be retained if the bank is to function. Consular officers in Istanbul have remarked that this Jewish manager is often present at social functions given by the German Consul General for his colleagues.

In Turkey, the vocal and active opposition to the Nazis springs from the local Colony of Levantine Jews. They occupy positions of prominence and influence in the retail trade and in the banking profession and are said to make every effort to injure the Nazis, especially by trying to kill German trade. They do not appear to be well organized, however, and as they do not control the wholesale and the importing business, or the large purchases made abroad by the Turkish government itself, their efforts to boycott German goods have not been successful; and Germany's importance in Turkish foreign commerce has gradually increased until it is now estimated that over fifty percent of Turkey's imports come from that country.

Germany's strong political position in Turkey for many decades, and the importance which she has recently acquired in Turkey's foreign trade, are undoubtedly responsible for the fact that Nazi activities in this country have been confined strictly to the German Colony and every effort has been made to present a united German front to the Turks. It may be noted, however, by any foreign resident of Istanbul that the German Colony lives more to itself than it did several years ago, and that its members seem to have their time well occupied with Colony activities. The principal German Club, the Teutonia, used to have many members of non-German nationality, but all of the latter have now resigned, and the club has become the center of Nazi activities. Likewise, the Ausflugsverein, an organization which promotes excursions and picnics, formerly had many non-Germans associated with it; whereas it has now become a purely German organization in which nature study has become subordinated to such practices as carrying many kilos of sand and gravel in their packs for long distances so as to harden the members. The only organization which the Germans share with others is the German High School which had for many years had such an excellent standing in all the diverse national groups which make up the population of Istanbul that it has apparently not yet been thought wise to destroy its value in promoting German culture among all peoples in this part of the world. Incidentally over 30 percent of the students in the German High School are followers of the Jewish faith.

Within the German colony, strict discipline is said to be exercised over the life of the members. Any recalcitrance is punished, the greatest penalty apparently being to place the name of the guilty one on a sort of black list, which involves loss of citizenship rights, passport, et cetera, and of one's job, if the Nazi chiefs can arrange it.

The most powerful Nazi organization in Turkey is said to be a local branch of the GESTAPO, headed by the German Consul General, Dr. Axel Toepke. This officer was from 1931 to 1934 German Consul General at Memel, where he is reported to have made himself *persona non grata* to the Lithuanian Government and was considered with apparently good reason to have been directly responsible for the anti-Lithuanian propaganda which culminated in the notorious Memel Nazi Trials. The intelligence service of the GESTAPO is said to be conducted both among refractory Germans who are expected to adhere to the Nazi organizations, and among the political exiles, emigrated Jews, et cetera. The organization has furthermore been known to collect funds under threats from local German firms, and also to make reports to the Turkish Government for the obvious purpose of causing difficulties to recalcitrant Germans.

The leader who is considered the most powerful in local Nazi circles is a Saxon by the name of Uhlig. He is said to have been formerly a superintendent of a concentration camp, and to have been sent here by the Government at Berlin for the purpose of organizing Nazi activities in the Colony. He heads an organization which is devoted to the military training of the men of the Colony. Exercises are regularly conducted by him, in the grounds of the Teutonia Club and also in the German Embassy building in Istanbul, which are said to be exactly in line with the exercises of the German Army; and the rough handling to which some of the less militaristic have been subjected has probably contributed toward the general fear and dislike with which Herr Uhlig is regarded.

Another important member of the Nazi organization is a Herr Sechser, President of the *Arbeitsfront*. He is a former mechanic, specializing in motor cylinder installations, and who has been awarded the degree of "Engineer" by his Party. All members of the Colony must join his organization, which procures jobs for members, supports destitute Nazis, sees that persons on the black list lose jobs and income if this can be arranged, and collects fees from all members.

The *Sturm Abteilung* and the *Sturm Staffel* are reported to have branch organizations in Istanbul. Other organizations to which the members of the German Colony are encouraged to devote their time are the *Hitlerjugend*, the *Jungvolk*, the *Bund Deutscher Mauris*, the *Nazi Lehrerbund*, the *Bund der Auslandsdeutschen*, the *Arbeitdienst*, the *Sportverein*, the *Turnverein*, and *Allemania*. The last mentioned, which was formerly a club of professionals and workmen whose members were absorbed by the *Teutonia* but are charged a smaller membership fee than the better-paid members of the latter club, is now a welfare organization for Nazis.

In summary it may be said that, although the German Colony in Turkey contains many elements who are believed not to be sympathetic with Nazi principles, yet the Party has succeeded in obtaining the adherence of practically all Germans who are here, keeps their time occupied with a number of organizations and clubs, and subjects them to strict discipline by means similar to those understood to be employed in Germany. These activities, however, seem to be confined completely to the Colony, there being no evidence that German internal politics are allowed to interfere with the country's relations with Turkey.[21]

Respectfully yours,
J. V. A. MacMurray (emphasis added)

So the U.S. government was well aware of the situation on the ground in Turkey. The émigré professors did not escape notice and being reported on. Nor did the U.S. embassy wait until 1936 to report on the émigrés. As indicated, Robert B. Skinner, MacMurray's predecessor in the U.S. Embassy, sent a memorandum dated November 16 1933 to the Secretary of State. Immediately under the Embassy letterhead and above the date, one can clearly see the entry "Subject: Expulsion of the Jews from Germany."

Sir:

> In connection with my despatch [*sic*] No. 26 of November 10, 1933, in regard to the difficulty of the Jews in Germany and the engagement of German Jews in this country, I now enclose as of possible interest in this connection a list of the names of foreign professors appointed to the University of Istanbul, *all of them, I imagine, being of the Jewish race, as indeed the names themselves sufficiently indicate.* (emphasis added).[22]

Thus, overlooking his "Jewish race" expression, within months of Germany's Nazi takeover, Ambassador Skinner, out of Istanbul, Turkey, considered it a duty to alert his superiors at the U.S. Department of State about the plight of Germany's Jews.[23]

The fact that President Roosevelt appointed Cordell Hull as Secretary of State on March 4 1933, i.e., eight months prior to the start of the above correspondence, and the fact that Hull ran the Department until 1944, cannot and should not be overlooked. There is no doubt that similar "Despatches" were coming in from other embassies as well. Therefore, it is difficult to rationalize Franklin D. Roosevelt's policy on the basis of "not knowing what was happening." Roosevelt formulated no significant and sustained response. The knowledge was there, but the will to act was not. In many other respects, FDR was a great president, but, in these matters, history justifies a mighty harsh judgment indeed.

Turkey's unquestioned leader and the émigrés' champion, passed away in late 1938. In his last political testament, Atatürk did call on his countrymen "to prepare as much as possible, and then what will be will be: to stay on the side of England, whose victory over the long run is certain."[24] Nevertheless, undeterred, German embassy and consular officials in Turkey were cranking up activities to win public sympathies for Germany and against the Allies, and they had many ready and willing helpers among native Turks. Theirs was the typical carrots-and-threats strategy. They showered Turkey with various incentives to become pro-Axis or at least to remain neutral. Nazi invasion always loomed as a threat and it was not at all clear whether Turkey could rely on the Soviets to come to its side.

On the night of August 21 1939, the Soviet news agency *TASS* announced that Germany's foreign minister, Joachim von Ribbentrop, was going to meet his Soviet counterpart, Vyachelsav Molotov. The trip's purpose was to sign a non-aggression pact with the USSR. The die for the invasion of Poland was cast. Russia was entering into a partnership with Hitler. They each were grabbing territories that did not belong to them, and, in the midst of all this, America declared neutrality on September

5 1939. In no time, Poland was occupied and divided. France, its ally of record, simply stood by.

To add insult to injury, on April 12 1939, Germany's infamous Propaganda Minister *Joseph Goebbels* visited Turkey to bolster local Nazis' activities. In the words of veteran foreign correspondents Douglas Frantz and Catherine Collins: Turkey was a prize that could not be ignored.... The Germans wanted the country as a foothold against the Soviets and a base from which to launch attacks on the Middle East.[25] Can you imagine being one of the German-Jewish émigrés and along comes Joseph Goebbels? Evil incarnate, carrots, diamonds, and threats. His visit was followed by the May 19 1939 *Ikdam* (then Istanbul's major newspaper) editorial which advocated prohibition of the use of non-Turkish languages in public places. If enacted, such prohibition would have been a major blow to the émigré professors' very ability to teach in Turkey. The drive to nationalization of the Turkish economy, especially after 1939, reflected itself in an increasingly strict employment policy to the detriment of foreigners. "For aliens including the '*Reichdeutschen*' (experts and workers on official secondments to Turkey within the framework of bilateral agreements) residency depended on having valid employment contracts, so a contract's expiration would normally lead to the employee being asked to leave the country."[26] There is sufficient evidence from archival sources, suggesting that starting in 1939 Istanbul University's top administration through its various acts began to send signals that at least some of the émigré professors might be overstaying their welcome. In short, 1939 brought the German émigré community many additional reasons for concern and fear.

The German legation made a number of flagrant attempts to both use and intimidate the émigré communities in Istanbul and in Ankara. In one ploy, the German Consul in Istanbul requested that pathologist Philipp Schwarz and Surgeon Rudolf Nissen appear at the consulate "as representatives of the Jews" to discuss passports and other issues. Schwarz is known to have replied, "I will come if you take down the Nazi flag," and so they did. The meeting took place and all passports were extended,[27] for a while at least.

The émigrés had cause and reason to suspect some of their own colleagues as well. Among the Nazi informers in Turkey were several Jews. Some later claimed they were blackmailed by the German embassy which knew about family ties they had in Germany. The others were given the right price for services rendered.[28]

As it turns out, "Information about the identity of emigrants *and at the same time about the network of informers which had been built up by the National Socialist Regime in order to keep the emigrant-scene under surveillance in Turkey*" can be found in the so-called "Scurla Report."[29] It is thanks to a coincidence that the German historian *Hans Detlef Grothusen*, whilst carrying out his investigations as curator of an exhibition about German-Turkish relations (on the occasion of the Centenary of the Birth of Atatürk 1981), came across "the report by *Dr. Herbert Scurla* amongst the piles of embassy records from 1924-1938. In May 1939, in possession of a wealth of Gestapo material and under orders from The Reich Ministry for Science, Education and National Education, he [Scurla] undertook a trip to Turkey. The purpose of the trip was to inspect the activities of the German university lecturers in Turkey, *a few of whom had been officially sent there and were loyal to the regime*, the majority, however, were made up of political refugees, who from the Turkish standpoint were given preference in obtaining employment when they applied for a position."[30] (emphasis added)

Following is an entry in Scurla's report regarding *Dr. Josef Dobretsberger*:

> *Dr. Dobretsberger, born in 1903, who used to lecture at Graz University, occupies the Professorial Chair for Political Economy in Istanbul. Dobretsberger was an Austrian minister in Schuschnig's Cabinet. Permission to change his residence to Istanbul in 1938 was only given after serious misgivings had been put aside. After leading personalities/public figures and Dobretsberger's colleagues had intervened and he personally has stressed repetitively, both orally and in writing, that his stay abroad was to be seen as a possibility to show his loyalty to The Third Reich. Dobretsberger has been placed in temporary retirement and has been given a pension. Even though there has not been any previous show of hostility against the State he immediately joins an emigrant group in Istanbul and avoids the strongly suggested connection to Professor Bodendorf. His wife's behavior must be seen as extremely hostile towards Germany. He has not appeared in the General Consulate again since his first meeting with Mr. Winter—the counselor to the Legation. The withdrawal of his original permission to transfer his place of abode seems to be urgently required.*[31] (emphasis added).

The entry for ophthalmologist Josef Igersheimer states:

> Igersheimer was living in Turkey and keeping a politically low profile. In 1938, he signed a contract with Istanbul University for an additional five years.[32]

For dentistry professor *Alfred Kantorowicz*, [Scurla] states:

> He was previously an active Communist.... Now, he is one of the most influential members of the refugee clique and one of our most disgusting opponents. His expulsion from citizenship has to be accelerated.

For hygiene (public health) professor *Dr. Julius Hirsch,* it reads:

> Since he is Communism-oriented, he declares everywhere his hatred towards the Third Reich. He must be expelled from citizenship.

In the case of economics professor *Fritz Neumark,* it simply reads:

> Since 1933, the *National Economics Board* belongs to Dr. Fritz Neumark, born in 1900, who is not from Aryan race. His wife is from the Aryan race. Neumark was formerly a professor in the Frankfurt University.

Is this a Nazi's way of saying that a Jew is running the Turkish economy? Then there is this entry:

> Professor Phillip Gross, last employed as head of department at the University of Vienna and has been on sabbatical leave from there since December 1936, has occupied, since then, the Professorial Chair for Chemical Technology—to run until 1942. Gross and his wife are non-Aryans. It remains to be proven—from Vienna—if there are any necessary steps to be taken against him.

Scurla also looked through librarian *Pfannenstiel's* personnel file. On April 14 1938, the ministry in Berlin reported in an outraged tone to its counterpart in Baden that Pfannenstiel was in Ankara and demanded to know who had given him the extraordinary permission to leave the country. The ministry of Baden, in a clever move, pointed out that Pfannenstiel did not have to ask for permission, as he was no longer a civil servant of Baden.[33] While in Turkey, Pfannenstiel continued to be carefully observed by the Gestapo. This is proven by the fact that he, as well as numerous other scientists, was thoroughly interviewed by Scurla during his visit to Ankara in May 1939.

In time, on Scurla's recommendation, Germany revoked the German citizenship of many of the émigrés. As much as Turkey liked what these disenfranchised souls were doing for the nation, that country was very reluctant to grant them citizenship for fear of Germany's retributions. This made émigrés *Haymatloz,*[34] or legally stateless. Consequently several of them, including Fritz Neumark, contacted *Dr. Edvard Beneš*, sitting President of the Czechoslovakian London-based government-in-exile. Their pleas were honored and those who made such requests were granted Czech citizenships.[35]

University of North Carolina Distinguished Quantum Physics Professor Emeritus *Eugen Merzbacher* recalls very vividly the process[36] and the effects of being made stateless:

> The issue of revocation of German citizenship is discussed in the book *Haymatloz*.[37] This includes a photo of a document from the archives of the German Embassy in Ankara, certifying the expatriation (Ausbürgerung) of my mother, Lilli (Sara) Merzbacher. Fritz Neumark's temporary travel documents, issued by the University of Istanbul, is also depicted.
>
> For reasons that were not clear to us at the time, my family (Siegfried and Lilli Merzbacher, and children, Eugen and Dorothea) were notified earlier than almost anyone else among the émigrés in Turkey of the revocation of their citizenship, in September 1940. Out of the blue, my father received a letter demanding that he present himself at the Embassy, with all our passports. We realized that this action could jeopardize our continuing existence in Turkey, at a time when it would be very difficult to migrate elsewhere, especially without passports. My father must have consulted his Turkish employers and received some assurance that they would try to protect him. In any case, although he was a gentle and non-confrontational person, he declared adamantly that he would not dream of setting foot in the German Embassy. My mother took the same position. So, I, who was then a brash 19-year-old university student, home on summer vacation, said that I had no qualms about going to the Embassy to hand over the passports to avoid difficulties from the Turkish side. We agreed that I should let go of the passports only if the Embassy would provide us with an official letter, confirming the transaction and certifying our "Ausbürgerung," or de-naturalization. I went to the Embassy and was received by a consular official named Böcking. He said: "Where are the passports?" and I told him that I had them with me, but I would deliver them only in return for an official receipt. He said: "Excuse me" and went next door to his secretary, who typed out the appropriate letter, to be signed by Herr Böcking. I have an official notarized Turkish translation of this letter in my possession.

Even though the loss of German citizenship brought some obvious perils with it, my family was rather proud of being singled out and of having been "individually de-naturalized," as it was called, rather than as part of a group action, as was done later in the War for many of the émigrés. Somehow, it seemed a badge of distinction. So, from then on we were "stateless." My parents never found out why they were treated selectively, but my sister and I learned some of the background in 2000 from the historians who set up the exhibition Haymatloz in Berlin. With typical German thoroughness, the Embassy and the German Foreign Office has preserved the relevant documents through the entire War and its aftermath, and we received copies from the archives in Bonn, which then was still the capital of the Bundesrepublik. Apparently, the Nazis based their decision on my parents' known political affiliations during the Weimar Republic. For a few years shortly after World War I, my father had been a member of the Reichsbanner, an activist arm of the SPD, the Social Democrats, and perhaps he marched in some demonstrations for the socialists. By the 1930s, his political orientation had shifted toward the center, and he voted for the German Democratic Party, rather than the SPD. My equally non-combative mother remained true to the SPD, but neither of them would ever have anything to do with the Communists. The Nazi document, supporting the revocation of our citizenship, nevertheless suggests that they have Communist leanings, and in particular singles out my mother as having a potentially nefarious political influence on my father. All of this would be funny, in retrospect, if it were not so absurd. None of us ever applied for return of our German citizenship. My sister is a UK subject, and my parents and I became proud naturalized U.S. citizens in the nineteen fifties.

Being deprived of a passport, even an invalid one, proved in the end to be a nuisance. When I wanted to leave Turkey to get a Ph.D. in theoretical physics in the West after the War, my first preference was England, because I knew that Cambridge was a leader in my field, and we had many relatives in Britain. Admission to Cambridge was extremely difficult to achieve at that time (because of the flood of returning veterans), but getting an entrance visa to the U.K. was even harder, if you did not have a valid travel document—even if it might have been decorated with a swastika! By contrast, the Americans were much more accommodating. As soon as I had the necessary affidavit of support, and admission to graduate school, the U.S. Consul, a Mr. Powhatan Baker, issued me what was called an "affidavit in lieu of passport," beautifully ornamented with a genuine red ribbon. In this, he stamped my immigration visa, and off I went. Although the Turkish authorities were sometimes capricious and arbitrary, and not always consistent, in their treatment of the émigrés, on balance our family owed them considerable gratitude for providing us a much-needed shelter during the difficult years before and during the War.[38] (Fig.114).[39]

The Scurla Report referred to the scientists who came to Turkey under the *Notgemeinschaft* umbrella as a "mob of immigrants" before noting that "German enemies exist in great numbers among them, especially in the Faculties of medicine and philosophy but also in law and public administration" and Professor Schwarz is referred to as "a non-Aryan element." In general, Istanbul University was described as having "turned Jewish."[40]

Scurla also notes that "since Istanbul University is the only institution which can contribute to the present scientific environment in Turkey and it is mostly under the influence of the emigrants, Germany should take strong measures to weaken this influence. Of these, the first should be firm action to revoke citizenship of those emigrants who are against Germany's interests and employed in Istanbul."[41]

Although Scurla recommended that the first expulsions should be made for non-Aryans; the first one who lost his citizenship was Professor Kessler, who was of Aryan origin but whose daughters have deserted him and returned to Nazi Germany. At one point, Scurla concludes that "it should be commonly agreed that the climate for German cultural-political activities at Istanbul University is not very favorable in the long term."[42]

## The Case of Friedrich Christiansen-Weniger

*Friedrich Christiansen-Weniger*, an agricultural expert in Ankara since 1932, that is before the Nazis took over the Reichstag, has a most interesting entry in the Scurla report.[43] It states that he was "Aryan, but *was told in 1936 that his further services in the German Reich were not wanted.* [No reason was given.] *His children are attending the Embassy School and are members of the Hitler Youth* and *the Embassy made efforts to rehabilitate him* . . . Embassy, Local Group, and academic teachers will support a rehabilitation of Christiansen-Weniger in the Reich, in a report to be expected soon, as they are of the firm conviction that the reports presented came about on the basis of inadmissible attribution of responsibility [to C-W] for events which Prof. Oldenburg is responsible for.... According to (in the sense of because of) representations of several gentlemen, in particular *Prof. Gleisberg*, Christiansen-Weniger, one of the closest colleagues of Prof. Oldenburg, has been removed from the area of the College of Agriculture and isolated from the German colony as well as German scientists in Ankara *by Prof. Falke by means of most unpleasant machinations*." (emphasis added)

The report goes on to say: Both the Embassy and also the local group of University Lecturers have emphatically supported Christiansen-Weniger, as he is not only the most influential German expert in the Turkish Ministry of Agriculture, but *has also proved himself to be outstanding both on the cultural-political level and as a man, and has also at all times shown a loyal attitude to the Third Reich*. (emphasis added)

The *Haymatloz* list[44] shows the Christiansen-Wenigers' two sons who were both with them in Ankara throughout Friedrich's stay there. The elder of the two was born in 1930 and the younger in 1932. By 1939, it is plausible that one or both were recruited into some locally operated organization for ethnic German youth such as the *Hitler Jugend*, especially if they attended the embassy school.

This entry by Scurla in his report to headquarters is particularly interesting because several of the second generation émigrés remember Christiansen-Weniger as an upstanding citizen, a fine human being, and an integral member of the émigrés' community. Thus a number of questions do arise. Was Christiansen-Weniger politically at odds with his young children? Did he use them for his own political gains and/or to advance his career? Many other Aryan Germans in Ankara and Istanbul turned down the opportunity of their kids joining the *Hitler Jugent* [youth]. This was certainly the case with the Reuter family. Did Christiansen-Weniger use his kids as cover for what he was really thinking or doing? What is it that he was telling the Embassy staff during their "efforts to rehabilitate him?" Was he living a double life and fooling his fellow émigrés? Did Christiansen-Weniger cheat Herr Scurla?

The Christiansen-Wenigers left Turkey in 1940. Their departure occurred shortly after the Scurla report was filed. Of all places, they went to occupied Poland. For a number of years, Professor Christiansen-Weniger worked as an expert at the *Pulawy* Agricultural Institute, operated under the auspices of *Generalgouvernement*, the Nazi administrative apparatus in its "Eastern Territories." This much is certain. Starting in 1939, Germany's embassy in Ankara applied much pressure on Aryan Germans to return to the Homeland. Those of military age who did not return were expatriated—banished. Friedrich Christiansen, however, was in his forties and his boys were nine and seven respectively. Moreover, hundreds of Aryan Germans ignored all these pressures and stayed on in Turkey rather than returning to serve the Nazis.

There is a current consensus among the second generation of émigrés that after his return to "Germany" from Turkey, Christiansen-Weniger was in contact with the *Kreisau* circle of Nazi opponents. To be sure, the Christiansen-Wenigers maintained good friendships with many of their former non-Aryan colleagues in Ankara over a period of decades. This, however, does not negate the fact that Christiansen-Weniger could never have landed and stayed on his "Polish" job unless he was back in the Reich's good graces and "his further services in the German [Third] Reich were...[again] wanted."

Also, according to understandings currently held by several who knew him in Turkey, "there [in western Poland] he protected his Polish collaborators and had contacts with the *Kreisau Circle*, especially Moltke."[45] Are all these understandings based on documented facts or on spins created by Friedrich (Fritz) Christiansen-Weniger himself? After the war, many Nazis, their sympathizers, their paid informers, and their quislings tried to reinvent themselves. Many became quite proficient at it. As may have been expected even as far back as the war's end, there will never be factual evidence to support Christiansen-Weniger's connectivity with the *Kreisau Circle* plotters.

Did Christiansen-Weniger go to *Pulawy* so as to be close to *Warthegau*,[46] the annexed—as opposed to merely occupied—part of Poland because he was in love with the *Trakehnen* horses being bred over there? Or did he go there to be closer to the *Kreisau Circle*? The elder son died in the war. Every answer opens several additional questions. One thing is certain, in 1952, Christiansen-Weniger returned to Ankara as Agriculture Attaché to the German Embassy.

However, even this fact must be considered in light of another fact. The existence of the Scurla Report was not uncovered until the 1980s, long after the diplomatic appointment had run its course. After retiring from his Attaché job, Christiansen-Weniger returned to Germany in 1962. His research is without doubt world-class. It is still being cited by agricultural scientists. Many of his publications reflect the work he did in Turkey as for example:

Christiansen-Weniger, F. 1970. *Ackerbauformen im Mittelmeerraum und Nahen Osten, dargestellt am Beispiel der Türkei.* DLG-Verlag, Frankfurt/Main.

Christiansen-Weniger, F. 1962. Vordringliche Probleme der türkischen Landwirtschaft. *Zeitschrift f. Kulturaustausch,* Jg. 12, Heft 2-3.

Gassner G., Christiansen-Weniger F., 1942. Dendroklimatologische Untersuchungen über die Jahresringentwicklungen der Kiefern in Anatolien. [Dendroclimatological investigations of the year ring developments of the Pine in Anatolien]. *Nova Acta Leopoldina,* Bd. 12, 80, 137 [in German].

"I met him in about 1970 at his retirement home near Kiel [said Klaus Eckstein]. He had been instrumental in setting up a branch of the *Atlantic College* in Germany, and he also informed me that he had, during the war, been an active member of the *Kreisauer Kreis* [civilian resistance circle]."[47]

Many decades later, one question begs to be asked. Is the Christiansen-Weniger affair an isolated situation or the tip of an iceberg? Scurla provides some responsive indications. His reports on the various individuals, as shown above, at times cite others who provided information to the Embassy staff. Among these are Prof. Walther Gleisberg,[48] Prof. Gustav Oldenburg, Prof. Friedrich Falke,[49] Dr. Friede,[50] and Dr. Baade. Moreover, archives of the State of Israel contain at least one report circa 1941 claiming that "among the Nazi agents there were a number of Jews."[51]

Christiansen-Weniger, is, to say the least, a bit of an enigma. As an agro-botanical scientist, in 1964, he published a somewhat compassionate paper titled "The social situation of the Turkish farmer 1923-1963"[52] in the learned journal *Sociologus* [Zeitschrift für Empirische Ethnosoziologie und Ethnopsychologie, or the *Journal for Empirical Social Anthropology*].

## The Case of Hubert Metzig, a Far Less-complicated Issue

In the case of *Hubert Metzig,* the Scurla ("Scurrilous") Report matches the recollections of the émigrés. Metzig, a linguist, was a resident in Turkey between 1937 and 1948. In 1943, he published an article in a Turkish newspaper favoring the Allies. As a result, he was fired from a German embassy job, and became a politically persecuted person. However, Scurla and the émigrés agreed that he was a psychopath. He had been fired from Germany's Propaganda Ministry because of shady money dealings and authoring a complimentary book on the New Turkey. The book, however, helped him obtain employment as a Lecturer in German at University of Ankara's department of History and Languages.

While in Ankara, he lived constantly in debt, and concluded his stay there by cheating the IRRC [International Red Cross]. Given return tickets to Europe for himself and for his family, he sold those for his family, and left alone. Later, he was spotted intermittently in both East and West Germany and claiming that he was a victim of various conspiracies.

**And Consider the Case of Hans Willbrandt**

At times, Scurla's reports laid out plans on how to handle and develop individuals who might be of future use to the Third Reich. Such was the case with *Hans Willbrandt*:

> "... the expert, acting at the Turkish Ministry for Economics, Dr. Willbrandt, is mentioned (for the Chair of General and Applied Economics), *whose personality is not* known in the Reich Ministry of Education and the Reich Ministry for Nutrition, as *he was merely active as unofficial assistant* at the Institute for Agricultural Market Research up to the end of June, 1933 and after the dissolution of the same became for a time joint owner of the "Land Advice" [consulting firm] and has been acting in Turkey as "expert" since the 1st December, 1934. According to information by the Gestapo, there is nothing personally or criminally to his detriment. Although he has until now *shown himself in Turkey to be fairly indifferent towards the German case,* it will nevertheless have to be considered, whether Willbrandt, who is beyond doubt outstandingly familiar with Turkish circumstances, should not be considered for taking on the Chair. Professor Spöttel thoroughly supported this. The Local Group Leader, Dr. Friede, intends to form a conclusive judgment on Willbrandt. He does not consider it impossible that Willbrandt, who is strongly opposed to Baade, and has presumably been forced into isolation on the grounds of *former relationships to Geheimrat Falke can* be *drawn closer into the German colony again.* (emphases added).

Now the word *Geheimrat* has several possible translations and interpretations. Before nobility was abolished in Germany circa 1919, some esteemed professors were given *Geheimrat* as an honorific title. Its closest British equivalent might be *Privy Counsellor.* It has no equivalent in America. A literal translation however shows it as a *secret advisor* or worse yet, *secret service agent*. In fact the *Geheimen Staatspolizei* or the German State Secret Police did have active agents[53] in Istanbul. If indeed Falke was old enough to have been bestowed such a title, would an NSDAP[54] ideologue the likes of Scurla have used it in reporting to his Nazi party superiors?

Variations (shortened versions like "Geheim." or "Geh.") of the term are used by Scurla several times in discussing or reporting on Falke. Why is it that the intrepid Nazi, Dr. Herbert Scurla, singles this one professor out for such respect when Scurla was so utterly disrespectful of others with equal or greater stature? In any case, it's the same Professor Falke who was involved in the "most unpleasant machinations" concerning

Christiansen-Weniger. So, was Herr Doktor Falke recognized by Scurla as an esteemed professor, a member of old Germany's titled nobility, or because he was an informer, possibly a "Nazi goon" or *all* of these?

As for Christiansen-Weniger, he may have been a traitor, a little innocuous Nazi, trying to be unnoticed, but knew some important people; he probably had a Nazi honor or two, had done some Nazi rough stuff, and in the turbulent post war years gets a position as Agriculture attaché for a reward. In short, the perfect undercover guy. Or, a veritable chameleon.

Physicist Eugen Merzbacher recalls that:

> One institution in Istanbul where there was professional contact between "our" group of émigrés and the official German colony of Nazis and collaborators (and perhaps even double agents) was the German Archeological Institute [currently the Goethe Institute]. Our Orientalist friends, such as Hans Güterbock, knew all the members of the Institute and often interacted with them at digs of antiquities in Anatolia. Some of us did not approve of these professional contacts. One interesting character who bridged these communities was a staunch German anti-Nazi nationalist named von der Osten (don't remember his first name) who had been wounded in or shortly after the First World War. He was a hundred percent Aryan and a fighter in the turmoil of the early post-WWI era, I believe. Was it the so-called Ostbund? I am not sure. His academic credentials were soft, but he had worked his way up to academic respectability and a professorship by learning the archeological ropes at important digs and expeditions in the Mid East. An interesting man whom we all trusted.... There were other such free spirits, sometimes adventurers, who chose emigration from the fatherland, even though they had no "Jewish blood" nor were they politically left wing. My family was always hospitable to such people, as they drifted through Ankara.[55]

## Apathy of America's Jewish Establishment

From 1933 through World War II, events and attitudes outside of Turkey must have deeply affected the émigrés' lives both directly and indirectly, just as they did everyones'.

On January 26 1934 Astronomer E. Finlay Freundlich,[56] wrote (in German) a lengthy letter to Henry Morgenthau. Both the letter and the response make it quite clear that Freundlich knew his addressee personally. The correspondence however does not make it clear whether it involved the elder Morgenthau, who under Woodrow Wilson was "American Ambassador to Constantinople" from 1913 to 1916, or his son Henry, Jr., a close friend of Franklin D. Roosevelt.

When Roosevelt became governor of New York in 1929, he appointed Morgenthau, Jr. as the state conservation commissioner and as chairman of his Agricultural Advisory Committee. And when Roosevelt became president, he appointed Morgenthau, Jr. as his Secretary of the Treasury. Both father and son were influential Democrats, members of the party "of workers, of the poor, of the weak, and the victimized." Whether father or son, each was an American Jew in a position of influence and Freundlich was trying to sensitize him to the plight of Jews in Germany. Here are some quotes from the Freundlich letter. They speak for themselves:

> I have endeavored over the whole of last year to save the Potsdam Institute, which, as you know, was founded and constructed by me, from catastrophe. And I would have been able to see it through, but precisely because of this, *a situation was created which endangered those of my colleagues who stood by me*. I therefore decided quickly to abandon my position in Potsdam and accepted the call to Constantinople.
>
> *What is happening in Germany is so humiliating, filthy, and untrue* that I could simply no longer bear living in such an atmosphere in good health. *I didn't think it possible that a nation of people, that possessed in so many regards such fine capabilities, has let itself become the souteneur* [Fr. lit. procurer, with a completely negative connotation] *of a historical development that the German public will hardly ever be able to atone for.*
>
> Bosch, the director of the I. G. in Germany, and one of the main founders of my Potsdam Institute, has in fact announced his concurrence with these plans. But the shortsightedness of the simply deranged Prussian Ministry of Culture's servant-girl gossip has made it impossible to get closer to this problem [i.e., building an institute for astronomical research]. This, although for once the Foreign Office and the appropriate posts in the Reich administration were actually ready to be reasonable. But the fact that I am non-Aryan and that a few of my jealous and shoddy colleagues are working towards my denunciation are enough to endanger a plan that could be vitally important for the future of German astronomy.
>
> I'd like more and more, when I carry out my plans, to make everything completely independent of Germany.
>
> *Because in such a time as this, where a few insane fools seek to con-*

> *fine the vision of the people through their national parochialism, the few truly civilized human beings should seek to hold high the banner of culture and science.* (emphasis added).

Morgenthau's brief response also speaks for itself. Unfortunately, it reflects the prevailing attitude among many of America's Jewish establishment at the time. What some have called a "banality of indifference" until it was much too late was complete apathy to the situation in Germany (Fig. 115).

This letter was not signed by Henry Morgenthau, Jr. Its signature does not match the "official" signature as it appears on U.S. currency for that era.[57] Although it may have been signed by a secretary, other evidence suggests the letter was written by the elder Morgenthau. Moreover, the Henry Morgenthau, Jr. Diaries for 1921-1941[58] do not seem to mention astronomer Freundlich.

Although much has been written about senior Morgenthau's deep and long lasting concern for the Armenians' plight during both WWI and Turkey's subsequent War of Independence, which did not end until in 1923, no record can be found[59] of either Morgenthau becoming active on behalf of their fellow Jews in Europe until the 1940s.

Regardless of which of the two Morgenthaus wrote that letter, the familial mindset behind it is best explained by Henry the III[rd]. In his book, *Mostly Morgenthaus,*[60] the very first sentence of the introduction reads:, "Early in life I sensed my parents' malaise in their Jewishness, which they mocked good-humoredly while remaining fiercely alert to attack from outsiders."

In the next paragraph he writes, "[Being Jewish] was a kind of birth defect that could not be eradicated but with proper treatment could be overcome, if not in this generation then probably in the next. The cure was achieved through the vigorous lifelong exercise of one's Americanism."

With the rest of the introduction, the author describes how coming to terms with his family's Jewish heritage-—and why they were so quick to assimilate into "American culture"—was one of the driving forces behind the writing of his book. Morgenthau III writes that "... by the time I came into the world [in 1917] all significant vestiges of ethnicity in my family had been thoroughly camouflaged, and the Morgenthaus had assumed protective coloration to blend in with Protestant America."[61]

In this regard, the Morgenthaus were not unlike many second and third generation families of European Jewish descent. This was especially pronounced among the more elite German Jewry in America. However, their position of prominence in the U.S. government lends their attitudes of malaise a particular poignancy throughout the 1930s and 40s. Stephen

S. Wise, the most prominent leader of the American Jewish community during the 1930s and 1940s, was judged as "cautious and ineffective" in his response to news of the Holocaust, by scholars at a conference held in the Library of Congress.[62]

Finally, and much too late, most of the established Jewish communities in America (ultimately even Roosevelt's own Secretary of the Treasury Henry Morgenthau, Jr.) were moved to act in behalf of fellow Jews being mass-exterminated in their ancestral lands. Word had begun to come of the dreaded killing grounds. In the words of his own son, Morgenthau III, who at the time was serving in Patton's Third Army in Europe:

> During the final years of the war, the plight of European Jews had been brought home to him [Morgenthau, Jr.] by three ardent *Christian subordinates.* He became uncompromisingly aggressive in his outrage. Like most Jews who wielded New Deal power and had ready access to the president, *my father had cautiously avoided Jewish issues.* His fundamental change of heart , *which emerged in 1943,* must have sprung from something hidden deep within his conscience. From that point on, *he maintained his lonely stance, enlisting few cohorts and many detractors.*[63] (emphasis added).

Even as late as 1943 there were Jews in position of influence in America who sought to keep a "low profile" on Jewry-affecting issues and worse, who tried to keep others from rocking the boat.[64] They were not alone. They were aided and abetted by America's media especially those owned by Randolph Hearst and surprisingly by the venerable *New York Times.*

Northeastern University Professor Laurel Leff discusses the *New York Times'* coverage of the Holocaust in her Cambridge University Press book, *Buried by the Times: The Holocaust and America's Most Important Newspaper.* Professor Leff describes how the *Times* consistently placed news about the Holocaust in less prominent places of the newspaper and downplayed the Jewish identity of Hitler's victims.

> One can be internationally minded without being indifferent to one's kinsmen.
> —Albert Einstein, Letter to Paul Epstein, October 5, 1919.

## Concern by American Academics for Their German Colleagues

In contrast, three weeks prior to the above Morgenthau letter, a distinguished American astronomer, Harlow Shapley, Director of the Harvard

College astronomical observatory and a non-Jew, responded quite differently to a similar plea (Fig. 116 and 117).

Shapley's response was not atypical of *individuals* in America's academic community as opposed to America's Jewish establishment. According to Laura Fermi:

> The early news of dismissals in Germany caused a great stir in academic circles. Many universities recognized at once their double opportunity: they could come out strongly for academic freedom and at the same time enlarge their staffs with the most eminent men from Europe. At a very brisk pace, university heads began consulting each other, exchanged copies of letters from Europe with requests or suggestions, and knocked on the doors of wealthy individuals and foundations to find ways of financing their hopes.[65]

Unfortunately, the potential or waiting supply of German academics far exceeded the ability of America's universities to absorb them. Jewish academics had to face the additional problem of latent, and sometimes overt, anti-Semitism that was widely spread within our very own elite institutions of higher learning.[66] As indicated, the few Jewish émigré women seeking academic employment faced yet another bigotry problem in this country that they had not previously encountered in German speaking Europe nor in Turkey—gender!

## Developments in Turkey

Starting in 1925, the Turkish government sent on the average 120 of its citizens annually to study in Germany, France, Belgium, Switzerland, and England.[67] In the late 1930s, many of them were back in Turkey with advanced degree in hand and looking for employment. By February 3 1941, library scientist *Walter Gottschalk* and pharmacy professor *Paul Pulewka,* among others, were let go[68] and Istanbul university froze all hiring of non-Turks. Additionally, as indicated, on January 5 1939, Turkey which passed a law foreclosed all possibilities for family reunifications to the émigré community.[69]

By the middle of 1941, the German expansion, both by alliance and conquest, grasped all within fifty miles of Istanbul.

> We knew that they wanted to go to Russia and there were two ways to go to Russia, either through Eastern Europe or through Turkey. And when they were in the Balkans we didn't know which way they were going to choose. We were all…father was worried,

of course. Every night we were waiting for the Germans.... Ozden Toker, Daughter of Ismet Inonu, Second President of Turkey[70]

I'd look out the window at the Marmara and wonder whether they were coming that night. Martin Harwit[71]

So we were just, praying every day that they wouldn't invade. Peter Engelmann[72]

And I remember the night when it was told to my father that Germany was going to Russia through Europe. He started to laugh and he laughed for hours. He was so relieved, so happy. Ozden Toker[73]

### The *Struma* Affair

As if all the above was not sufficiently unnerving, on February 24 1942, the Romanian steamer *Struma* incident sent shock waves internationally and it was of special concern to the émigré community. After ten weeks at anchor in Istanbul with an irreparable engine, all diplomatic maneuvering had collapsed. With the English adamantly not allowing the refugees on board to debark and go to Palestine, the designated Jewish homeland which was under British rule as part of a League of Nations mandate, the Turkish coast guard towed the *Struma* out of territorial waters. Several hours later, the ship sank in the Black Sea.

Of the 769 men women and children on board who were seeking refuge from Nazi-dominated Romania, only one survived. Contemporary records and recent studies conclude that the ship was torpedoed by a Russian submarine. However, to this day it is not clear as to who gave the order or why, nor can we know. It may well be that it was an on-the-spot decision by the submarine's commander. Not knowing who or what was on board but recognizing the ship to be Romanian, an enemy nation, it may well have been a case of the wrong decision made for the right reasons.

At the time, Turkey was very suspicious of Soviet intentions, had no confidence in England, was keenly aware of America's still prevalent isolationism, and was deathly afraid of the Nazis. The *Struma* tragedy set off a public debate in Turkey as it did in Palestine and the West. Some of it was ugly. It was "an extremely bitter moment in Turkey's search for a decent policy concerning its position in the war, the degree and character of neutrality, and the limits of its good will toward the refugees."[74]

To this day, when asked about Turkey's role vis-à-vis the Jews in

World War II, of those who know anything at all about the issue, most will respond citing the *Struma* incident. The *Struma* incident is about as much as the people teaching Holocaust history in America know about Turkey's role during that period.[75] Surprisingly, as of March 26 2006 when a paper based on this book was presented by this author at the 6$^{th}$ Annual Conference of the Israeli Society for the History and Philosophy of Science, no one was aware of this bit of history with the exception of a German historian in the audience. Those who cite the Struma incident are generally misinformed, placing the entire blame on Turkey. Generally forgotten is the fact that between September 1939 and the *Struma* incident in 1942, fifteen refugee ships from Europe went to Palestine via Turkey as part of the illegal immigration. The transit was resumed in 1944.[76]

To many of the émigré professors, it was yet another alarming reason to consider packing again. Only a handful found a way to exercise the option of emigrating to the West. They, too, were caught between a rock and a hard place as can be noted from a letter[77] dated October 21 1940 from Alvin Johnson, Director of the New School of Social Research responding to Classics Professor C. Bradford Welles at Yale. Knowing that his home institution would not even contemplate the matter because of its overt anti-Semitic hiring practice, Welles intervened in behalf of Andreas B. Schwarz for a possible job offer at the *New School* (New York). Among other reasons why the School would not consider Schwarz at that time was the following:

> As we understand it, that group in Constantinople is pretty organic. The Turks are not sure that these German professors love Turkey as they should. For anyone to leave before his contract expires is said to weaken the position of the rest.[78]

Apparently this position was strongly encouraged by the Rockefeller "Foundation financing the scholars" being brought to the New School according to another letter from Alvin Johnson.[79]

A statistical compilation of émigré departures (as percentage of total), for each year starting in 1933 and running through 1960 shows two peaks, ten years apart. These were 1938 and 1948.[80] The first peak was no doubt due to the fact that the 5-year contracts had run their course and some were not renewed. The second peak, obviously, involved those whose contracts were twice renewed but not renewed the third time and or opening of options resulting from the war's end.

However, between those two dates Atatürk died, Turkish nationalism was rising, the German embassy was exerting Nazi influences in overt and covert pressures, many Turkish nationals had been trained abroad as well as by the émigrés in Turkey, and the economic conditions were going from bad to worse. Salaries that were very high in 1933 were eroded by "inflation during the war years without compensatory wage adjustments" and there were no pension plans whatsoever according to Kathrin Meier-Rust's book.[81] She, too, recognized the fact that "although the Germans were committed to learning Turkish, most did not and had to rely on interpreters, resulting in a certain isolation from Turkish students and professors and Turkish culture in general."

All of these factors interacted with the fact that, topside, university administrators were not renewing contracts and, as indicated through various administrative acts, making it known that the welcome mat was no longer out. There are many documented examples of such practices. Case in point, prior to expiration of his contract in May 1941, Viennese radiologist *Georg Fuchs* informed his superiors that he was going to go to Palestine. The university was contractually bound to reimburse Dr. Fuchs for repatriation costs to any destination of his choosing. However, on grounds that he did not report for duty *during the last two days remaining in his contract*, his repatriation travel expenses were forever denied.[82]

The émigrés' problems, it seemed, were never going to end.

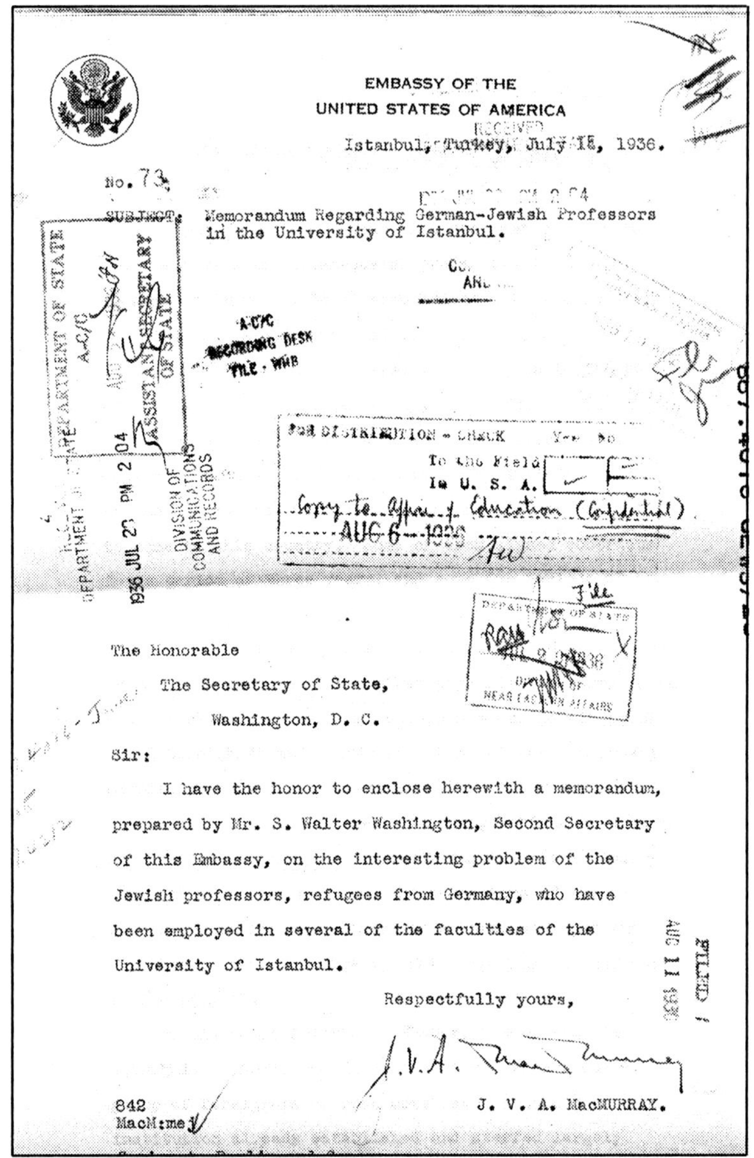
EMBASSY OF THE
UNITED STATES OF AMERICA

Istanbul, Turkey, July 15, 1936.

No. 73

SUBJECT: Memorandum Regarding German-Jewish Professors in the University of Istanbul.

The Honorable
The Secretary of State,
Washington, D. C.

Sir:

I have the honor to enclose herewith a memorandum, prepared by Mr. S. Walter Washington, Second Secretary of this Embassy, on the interesting problem of the Jewish professors, refugees from Germany, who have been employed in several of the faculties of the University of Istanbul.

Respectfully yours,

J. V. A. MacMURRAY.

842
MacM:me

*Figure 113*
Memorandum regarding German-Jewish Professors in the University of Istanbul.

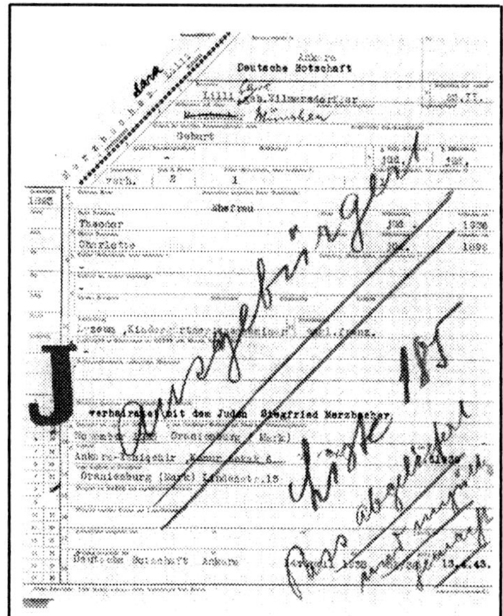
Deutsche Botschaft

Lilli

verheiratet mit dem Juden Siegfried Merzbacher

Deutsche Botschaft Ankara

*Figure 114*
Lilli Merzbacher's denaturalization notice. The German Embassy in Ankara has thus declared a person stateless.

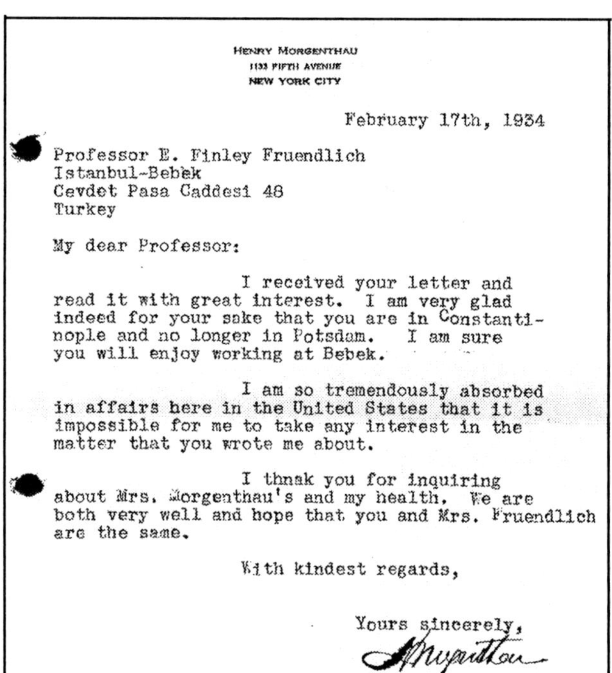
HENRY MORGENTHAU
1133 FIFTH AVENUE
NEW YORK CITY

February 17th, 1934

Professor E. Finley Fruendlich
Istanbul-Bebek
Cevdet Pasa Caddesi 48
Turkey

My dear Professor:

I received your letter and read it with great interest. I am very glad indeed for your sake that you are in Constantinople and no longer in Potsdam. I am sure you will enjoy working at Bebek.

I am so tremendously absorbed in affairs here in the United States that it is impossible for me to take any interest in the matter that you wrote me about.

I thnak you for inquiring about Mrs. Morgenthau's and my health. We are both very well and hope that you and Mrs. Fruendlich are the same.

With kindest regards,

Yours sincerely,

H Morgenthau

*Figure 115*
Henry Morgenthau's letter to Fruendlich.

HARVARD COLLEGE OBSERVATORY
CAMBRIDGE, MASSACHUSETTS

25 January 1934

Professor E. F. Freundlich, Director
University Observatory
Istanbul, Turkey

Dear Professor Freundlich:

I am directing to have your Observatory put on our mailing list to receive all the Harvard Observatory publications, as issued. I am also directing to have sent to you by way of the International Exchange the Henry Draper Catalogue and a considerable quantity of other moderately recent publications of the Harvard Observatory. We are not in a position at the present time, because of the expense of handling, to send you a more complete shipment of Harvard Observatory publications. Moreover, many of the earlier volumes are out of print. If, however, there are some special needs for you or your associates, of which you will write us, we will try to send them directly.

Needless to say, I am very glad to know that you have settled down in an agreeable community and are looking forward to further active work in astronomy. I hope that the administration duties in your new place will not long delay you in getting started on astronomical research. I hope the site you are in is suitable for astronomical work.

I wonder if there is any possibility that other German exiles can find a refuge with you. We hear that Dr. Wildt of Göttingen is desirous of leaving Germany; and also Dr. Beer.

The statement you send concerning the official German salute is almost unbelievable. There is to be an informal meeting of eastern American astronomers at New Haven in a week or so and I plan to discuss the documents that you have sent. At that time we are also going to consider some problems of scientific German exiles.

*Figure 116*
Shapley's letter to Freundlich.

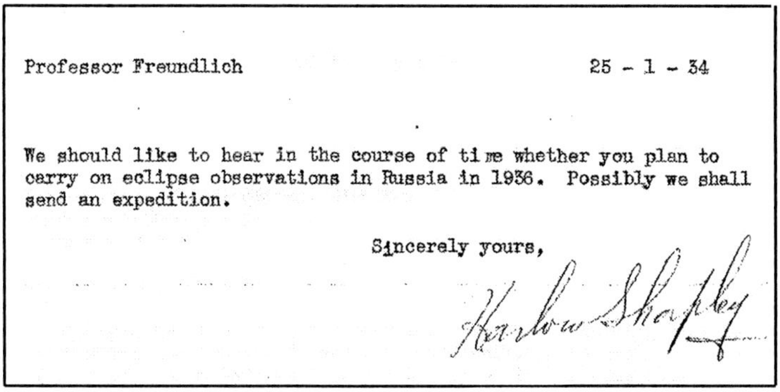

Professor Freundlich 25 - 1 - 34

We should like to hear in the course of time whether you plan to carry on eclipse observations in Russia in 1936. Possibly we shall send an expedition.

Sincerely yours,

Harlow Shapley

*Figure 117*
Letter, continued

# 10
# Turbulence Due to WWII

## Nazi Armies on Turkey's Doorsteps

It appeared that the Nazi momentum was unstoppable in December of 1939, three months after the outbreak of the war. The situation grew more bleak by the day. "Turkey's representative to Egypt told Chaim Weizmann [who later became the first President of the State of Israel] that his [Turkey's] country's leaders believed they would be attacked within three months. Both Russia and Germany were exerting heavy pressure on Turkey, and both were promising it the entire Middle East, including all the Arab countries it had controlled in the past, if only the Turks would join them."[1] Turkey was under great stress; it reacted with some negative results as well as with many positive surprises. On May 8 1939, a new German-Turkish trade agreement was signed in Ankara. Among other things, Germany was to continue to receive strategically needed chromium from Turkey.[2] Without this metallurgical input from Turkey, all German armaments production would have come to a screeching halt.

On March 4 1941, physiology professor *Hans Winterstein* wrote to a Dr. Beecher at the Massachusetts General Hospital: "In reality we must every minute be prepared for the outbreak of war and in this case, of course, nobody can know what will happen. On account of this, it would give me great comfort to be aware [that] somewhere else [there is a] possibility of existence and to know somebody to whom to apply in case of need."[3]

By April 1 1941, Greece had collapsed, German Armies in Bulgaria were within a five-hour car ride to Istanbul proper, and Britain was not doing very well in North Africa. All that plus the graphic images of the Luftwaffe's most recent municipal deconstruction, such as the destruction of Belgrade, gave Turkey and its entire émigré community cause for concern. They were clearly knowledgeable at all times of the Nazi/Soviet shifting tides. Churchill's moral support was not very satisfying. There were signs of an awakening among opposition factions in Turkey. Some were pro-Nazi. Some factions had good connections with, and influence in Turkey's banking circles having commercial ties to Germany.

Among these were the large landowner families and the newly rich construction contractors and industrialist oligarchs who, for the obvious pecuniary reasons, feared Soviets much more then they did the fascists. After all, they figured, the Friedrich Krupp and the I. G. Farben family dynasties thrived in Germany by feeding the Wermacht with all it needed from footgear to Panzers and from pencils to explosives. In the Soviet Union, on the other hand, such oligarchic dynasties had literally been exterminated after the Bolshevik revolution in 1918.

Anonymous posters bearing the message that Turkey should not place any trust in England were everywhere and they screeched loud and clear

> It is a lie that England is weak and does not have adequate forces and ammunition to help the countries tied to it in mutual assistance pacts. England has an army of three million stationed in the British Isles and huge amount of ammunition, but it is concerned for itself only and deceives those who depend on it. It sent a small army to Greece for appearance only, and it will not help Turkey in anything. Woe to the nation that pins its hopes on England.[4]

The posters were put up in large cities and small towns. They could not be missed.

All the German/Jewish intellectuals' worries and qualms about problems of language, teaching, equipment, and classrooms were dwarfed by the closing of the Istanbul University on April 19 1941. When the full-blown war broke out, the German embassy at Ankara summoned home all men who held valid German passports. In May, the Turkish army started serious preparations for an expected invasion. Several defense zones covered all of Anatolia, the bulk of Turkey on its Asian side. One of these zones along the Azerbaijani and Armenian borders faced the Russians. Much of that border is mountainous. Allied intelligence had learned that Germany was training some of its troops for mountain combat. As Greece had already fallen without much mountain combat, the Allies reasoned the natural destination for such troops to be Turkey. This evaluation was made known to the Turks. Consequently, Turkish civilians of all ages were being trained for guerilla warfare and some to fight in the mountains.

Moreover, Kathrin Meier-Rust, in her *Alexander Rüstow: Geschichtsdeutung und liberales Engagement* book,[5] observes that:

> The successful Nazi troop advances in the Balkans during the early spring of 1941 and the invasion of Turkey were possibilities

to be reckoned with, that German Jewish exiles in Turkey were threatened with possible deportation to Germany. This led Turkish authorities to consider a kind of preventive deportation of the German Jews to the interior of Anatolia. "Rüstow in his capacity as the representative of the Rescue and Relief Committee succeeded in averting this deportation at least for the Germans belonging to the staff of the University."[6]

The German embassy's summons to report for military service included some "half-" and "quarter-" Jews. Moreover, it could not be avoided. Based on an oral history she took from a friend at her husband's University of Chicago, Hans Güterbock, Mrs. Laura Fermi—the wife of the Nobel laureate - recounts that "one day Hittitologist Hans Güterbock was driving home in Ankara and found his street blocked by a German Embassy car parked with its doors sprawled open. He was summoned. At the embassy, however, he was told that university teachers were excused from military service because they were doing an important job of culture propaganda."[7] However, this state of affairs fueled distrust among the émigré community. According to Kathrin Meier-Rust, "friendly relationships among the group of German emigrants thrown together by chance did not always prove to be simple. The non-Jewish emigrants Rüstow and Röpke were viewed with suspicion by many of their fellow emigrants."[8]

## Failed Attempts to Solve Turkey's Economic Problems and Its Ethnic Paranoia

Turkey was facing many internal problems during the 1930s and 40s, some that threatened its very existence, and, no doubt, émigrés as well as Turks kept watchful eyes on the events that unfolded. Severe pressures on its economy caused by heavy military expenditures, hindrance to agricultural production due to partial mobilization of its army reserves, and shortages of raw materials, all combined to cause Turkey to pass two laws in 1942. These were intended for the wealthy, however, their application had a disproportionate effect on Turkey's minorities.

One law was called *Varlık Vergisi* or the Wealth Tax; the other was the *Land Reform Tax*. Under circumstances that existed at the time, imposition of such levies could have been considered to be a reasonable way of taxing those with an ability to pay. However, the design and administration of these laws was neither fair nor just. There were only two groups affected by the law with that kind of ability to pay: these were the large landowners who were getting wealthier from price increases on agricultural products, and Istanbul's merchants who took advantage of the high value of Turkey's exports and severe shortages of imported but essential goods.

The landholders were predominantly Turkish Moslems and the Istanbul merchants were Greeks, Armenians, and Jews. Large landowners were taxed no more than *5% of their properties' valuation, while corporations—the merchants—were taxed up to 232% of net profits in 1941.*[9] The exact percentage to be applied to a given business was left to the discretion of special panels. Payment was required within fifteen days. Failure to pay within a month carried a severe penalty: deportation to forced labor camps. The law was implemented by special Commissions comprised of businessmen, state employees, and chamber of commerce officials. The Commissions had the responsibility for deciding individual cases of tax assessment. These had to be decided based on the following classifications:

| | | |
|---|---|---|
| **E** | = | Ecnebi (Foreign nationals) |
| **GM** | = | Gayrimuslim (Non-Muslim) |
| **D** | = | Donme (Sabateans) |
| **M** | = | Müslüman (Muslim) |

Many of the taxed claimed that decisions rendered were completely arbitrary. To make things worse, appeals were roundly rejected. The press, led by the then pro-Axis *Cumhuriyet* and *Tasvir-i Efkar*, praised these measures and published names of delinquents. Almost exclusively, the names were Greek, Armenian, and Jewish. These two "laws," and others as well, whipped up public passions. At times, it seemed rather crude racism. One needs only look at some of the political cartoons that prevailed in the print media to see their vile anti-Semitic messages.[10] By January 20 1943, all those having failed to pay the Wealth Tax were rounded up and sent to a forced labor camp in *Aşkale,* East Anatolia (eastern Turkey).[11]

For many of the émigrés, the wealth tax was directed at the minorities, fellow Jews. Even though the émigrés were not religious, and some did not even identify with their roots, to the Nazis, and the Turkish nationalists they were "Jews." The émigrés knew that and they felt that Turkish nationalism may sooner or later engulf them as well, perhaps not as individuals per say but as part of a "group." All along, there were people in Turkey who opposed the persecution of minorities. They felt that despotic or even semi-despotic regimes could not be allowed to exist in the world that would emerge after Nazism's destruction. However, few influential voices in Turkey can be found on record as publicly opposing the Wealth Tax Act until it was cancelled in response to external pressures.[12]

Turks, these people were convinced, must follow progressive policies and reverse the character that the country had assumed under *Ismet Inönü*, Turkey's second president, and particularly under prime-minister[13] Sükrü Saraçoglu,[14] a necessary pre-condition for Turkey's proper place among the post-war family of nations. Fortuitously, on December 2 1943, the Ankara government had a change of heart and decided to pardon and free those Turks who were sent to forced labor for failure to pay the Wealth Tax. That happened roughly at the same time that Ankara's government summarily reversed its decision to expel Jews bearing other nations' valid passports.

It is interesting to note that Laurence Steinhardt, United States Ambassador to Turkey, did "whatever [he] properly could to lighten the burden of the Jewish minority in Turkey under the 'varlik vergisi'" according to a letter[15] he wrote on December 22 1943 to George V. Allen, at the Division of Near Eastern Affairs, Department of State. On the very same day, writing to Charles [Haim] Barlas, at the Jewish Agency for Palestine office in the Pera Palace Hotel, Istanbul, Steinhardt states

> With the exception of the high Turkish officials with whom I have discussed the subject on innumerable occasions, yourself and a few other informed representatives of various Jewish agencies, probably no one else is aware of the strenuous and persistent unofficial efforts that I have made not only in aiding Jewish refugees but in easing the lot of the minorities under the tax on fortunes.[16]

According to the Turkish Daily News, a 1999 award-winning Turkish movie, *Salkim Hanimin Taneleri* (Mrs. Salkim's Diamonds), "shows that a large community in Turkey is ready to share its country's 'dirty laundry' with the world, and join the long list of nations and communities who are trying to apologize for a past they are not proud of."[17]

The movie is based on a popular novel by *Yilmaz Karakoyunlu*, a former ANAP (Motherland Party) parliamentary deputy. The movie is set in the latter part of World War II (1942-4). Turkey was watching Germany, which had not yet suffered its first major defeat, and much of the Turkish public believed Germany to be invincible and ready to take command of the world. Turkey established "village institutes"[18] and began to prepare for the Nazi's fascist "New Order." Greece had already fallen and sections of the ruling Turkish elite were showing distinct sympathy towards the ideals of Nazi Germany. The title of the film refers to the wealth tax which "was to serve another purpose than simply to restore the Treasury's depleted resources: it was also to further the aim of 'Turkifying' the nation that began in the thirties."[19]

Significantly, a year before the *Varlık Vergisi* affair, in May of 1941, all non-Muslim men aged between twenty and forty were conscripted into the armed forces. However, they were not given any military training. Placed in labor battalions, they were assigned to road construction projects. These Turkish citizens were released in July 1942, and, four months later, received a second blow—the wealth tax, the *Varlık Vergisi*.[20]

## Attempted Turkification of Istanbul

Making the city of Istanbul less cosmopolitan by reducing its minority populations was driven by Turkey's fears of Soviet intentions to internationalize the Bosphorus straits with the assistance of Istanbul's minorities. These intentions were fully backed by Britain's elite. Additionally, according to Turkish historian *Rifat Bali:*

> ...the memory of the War of Independence never faded from the minds of the Republican elite, in whose eyes non-Muslims were "strangers whose loyalty was suspect" and were not founding members of the Turkish nation since they had not fought in the National War of Independence. The relationship between the Republican elites and the-non Muslim citizens was somehow a love-and-hate affair, as on one hand they put pressure on them for their Turkification but on the other hand they really did not want to embrace them as loyal citizens with full rights.

This negative legacy of the past resurfaced later in the atmosphere of World War II and recreated in the minds of the RPP's [Republican People's Party] intelligentsia the trauma of the years of Armistice and War of Independence. As a result, the Capital Tax levy promulgated in 1942, which rightfully intended to tax profits earned from speculations and black market operations, was implemented in a totally discriminatory manner against citizens of Jewish and Christian faiths and those of Dönme[21] origin. The discriminatory implementation of the levy was an unforgettable example of *de facto* discrimination against non-Muslims during the post Atatürk years of the *Single Party* period. It was, at the same time, testimony of the complete failure of Istanbul's Turkification policies.[22] There are those who claim that oppressing minorities was a contravention of the way of life espoused in Atatürk's vision for Turkey, yet the Turkification policies were initiated by its sitting Prime Minister Sükrü Saraçoglu himself soon after assuming office in 1942.[23]

In this atmosphere, the earlier arrival of "prominent Jewish refugees from Nazism had been bitterly opposed by Istanbul's German community which for the most part supported the efforts of Nazi ambassadors to undermine Turkish faith in Jewish abilities and displayed gratitude for their contributions. At times, they allied with Christian nationalist groups in efforts to drive the Jews out once and for all."[24]

Despite Berlin's pressure, the government of Turkey refused German demands to turn over the Jewish refugees marked for internment in death camps.[25] Additionally, having Romania and Bulgaria under effective German control, and the Nazis within five hours of Istanbul by land or by sea, was a bit of reality that Turkey and the émigrés had to face on a daily basis.[26]

### Turkey and Wartime Rescue Efforts

Marshall *Henri Phillippe Pètain,* the French super-general who delivered over half of France to the Nazis instead of defending her as he was obliged to do, publicly proclaimed on October 30 1940 that Jews were responsible for his country's collapse, not he, and urged his countrymen to collaborate with the Germans.[27] Neutral Turkey was greatly dependent on the Allied Powers and especially on England for a number of reasons. Romania had joined the Axis on November 23 1940, Slovakia a day later. Hungary entered the war on Germany's side April 12 1941 and Bulgaria, a German surrogate, invaded Greek Western Thrace on April 19. Yugoslavia joined the Axis on March 25. The Germans invaded Athens on April 27, and, on the same day, occupied the Greek islands, a stone's throw from the Turkish coast. A pro-Nazi coup had installed *Rashid Ali* as head of state in Iraq on April 1 1941 to the South, and the unpredictable Soviets, looking down from across Turkey's entire North, gobbled up Lithuania, Latvia, and Estonia, in June of 1940. The only good news for Turkey during this stage came in late fall of 1941. With the Crimean peninsula in German hands, the world recognized that Germany had decided to move onto Russia's Caspian Sea oil reserves via the north Caucasus route rather then via Turkey. This provided a bit of respite for all in Turkey, including the émigrés.

However, during this period, the Nazis were drawing up their "Final Solution" for liquidating the inmates of their ghettos and concentration camps. Understandably, the few who were ready and willing to rescue Jews from the Balkans and other parts of Europe viewed Turkey as a bridge to Palestine and to their safety. England, however, as if it did not have more important matters to worry about at the time with British cities being leveled from the air, tried very hard to prevent Jewish refugees from entering Palestine.

Throughout the 1930s and the war, the British Colonial Office applied much pressure on Turkey not to permit any passage through the Bosphorus nor its landmass of Jewish refugees trying to escape certain extermination. There were some in its Foreign Office who actually contemplated using the Royal Navy to sink some of those old decrepit boats that brought refugees down the Danube and through the Bosphorus.[28] England's official reasoning was that it did not want to enrage the Arabs. This is confirmed in a letter by Laurence Steinhardt, America's Ambassador to Turkey:[29]

> There is the problem of visas, none too much enthusiasm on the part of the British for a large number of Jewish refugees in Palestine as they have their eyes on the Arab world.

The situation was further complicated by the fact that the Arab countries in the immediate area were very much pro-Nazi, including those controlled by Vichy France such as Syria and most of North Africa. Thus, the numbers of refugees passing through Turkey had to be valued against the background of this political scenario within and outside of Turkey. Their number, however, is a matter of historical dispute.

Relying on the Central Zionist Archives where the files of the Jewish Agency and other institutions of this kind are kept, historian Tuvia Friling authoritatively states that, for geopolitical reasons following the *Struma* tragedy, Turkey's policy stopped "all activity, which from September 1939 to the beginning of 1942 had involved fifteen ships and over 12,000 refugees who left Europe as part of the illegal immigration to Palestine via Turkey.[30] The *Struma*, although not the only reason for this, effectively brought illegal immigration activities to a halt for the next two years, 1942 and 1943. They were not resumed until 1944."[31] However, Leni Yahil in her book, *The Holocaust—the Fate of European Jewry 1932-1945*, points out that "the boats that [did manage] to sail from Romania in 1942 were few, small, and chartered privately."[32] Historian Rifat Bali[33] claims 15, 000 to be the total number of Jewish refugees that passed through Turkey. Other sources claim this number to be closer to 20,000.[34]

Significantly, while Pètain's Vichy government announced on June 13 1941 that 12,000 Jews were sent to concentration camps for opposing French cooperation with Germany's Nazis,[35] in 1941 alone, 4,400 Jewish escapees from Nazism were known to have passed through Turkey on their way to Palestine according to historian Y. Slutsky.[36] However, based on her Ph.D. dissertation, Illegal immigration to Palestine during the Second World War 1939-1942, Dalia Ofer wrote that "according to the most optimistic of the reliable estimates, 10,000 people were rescued via Istanbul."[37] She recognizes however that: "There are those who claim that

20,000 were rescued, but this is undoubtedly an exaggeration."[38] To this one should add the fact that via the official channels alone during the war, 16,474 Jewish refugees managed to find their way to Palestine through Turkey.[39] The highest estimate of the total number is offered by historian Stanford Shaw who claims that 100,000 passed through Turkey "by the end of the war."[40]

The fact that the *Yishuv*, the Jewish community in Palestine,[41] had several operatives working in Turkey for a number of years prior to and throughout World War II is well documented. Documented also is the fact that all but about four worked in secret as their work was not sanctioned by the Turkish government.[42] The lion's share of their activities involved having Jewish refugees from Europe pass through Turkey to Palestine—a contravention of British government policy. However, according to Friling, an Israeli historian:

> ...in February 1941, these contacts bore fruit. The Turks promulgated the "Law Regulating the Passage through Turkey for Jewish Immigrants Oppressed in their Countries of Origin." The order was publicized in the Turkish press and over Radio Ankara, and Turkish consuls were instructed to issue transit visas to refugees who would come in groups and continue on their way to Palestine. The British embassy and representatives of the Jewish Agency also received official notification of the Turkish government's decision.[43]

Not so well documented is the fact that the Yishuv's workings did not go unnoticed by either the Jewish or the Nazi German communities in Istanbul. Even less-documented is the fact that these activities made a few members of the Jewish-German community in Turkey somewhat nervous. Such a response would have been only natural. All along, the Yishuv was doing all it could to get Turkey allied with England or at least to keep it neutral. Its leaders, Ben Gurion and Chaim Weizmann, were both following up on Atatürk's personal request to intercede in Turkey's quest for loans among the West's financial community. The Yishuv's leadership was not at all certain on which side Turkey would ultimately come down. "The Molotov-Ribbentrop Agreement would have a lasting impact on Turkey's policies, and it was difficult to assume that Turkey would ally itself with an enemy of Russia. When it decides or is forced to abandon its neutrality, 'we cannot not know on which side it will fight. Its position is a great unknown,'" Ben Gurion averred.[44]

Throughout much of the war, for various political, sentimental,[45] commercial, and even ideological reasons, Turkey openly maintained relations with the Nazis. She continued to sell strategic materials to Nazi Germany in spite of persistent pressure by the Allies to stop doing so. It was not until April 20 1944 that Turkey finally agreed to stop shipping the chromium required to produce Germany munitions, and, in August 1944, she severed diplomatic relations with Germany altogether. However, in between those two milestone dates a significant and largely unknown event did in fact take place. At 5:30 a.m. on July 6 1944, the "222 Transport," a train carrying 233 Jews, arrived in Istanbul from Germany's *Bergen Belsen* concentration camp on their way to Palestine. At about the same time, 114 ethnic Germans who had lived in Palestine were to be exchanged for the Jews going to Palestine. Not having a rail link between Asia and Europe, even for the "Orient Express," each group on their respective shores of the waterway was put on board of a white passenger steamer, the kind that still ferry people across the Bosphorus. After giving their passengers a beautiful tour by circling the waterway in opposite directions, each ferry delivered its passengers to continue on their journey by rail.[46]

Although this was not the first train transporting Jews from the occupied countries through Turkey and on to freedom in Palestine, it was the last. At all times, the record shows the Turks behaved very warmly to those in such transits. Elisheva Aurbach, who arrived in Palestine on the "222" and has seen the State of Israel emerge, offers the following reminiscences:

> Dear Arnold,
>
> I was very impressed after reading your book prospectus about the impact on present science and culture in Turkish higher education. And I feel a bit ashamed. How can I help you and add from my little experience? (I hope my English will be good enough to explain everything to you.)
>
> It is more than sixty years ago and I was a young girl after the terrible time in Bergen-Belsen and losing so many of my family (my parents died in Sobibor). I was chosen the only one of my family for this transport and as you could read in Oppenheimer's book,[47] nobody knows who made up the exchange list.
>
> My memory of Turkey is only the best. They were the first ones who treated us "humanely." We arrived by train to Istanbul into a world we had forgotten existed. There were also curiosities. In the train station, we had to go to the bathroom and did not know how to behave: no closet, naught but a hole in the ground. There was much hilarity until we understood the use of it.
>
> The boat ride on the Bosphorus in the most beautiful weather was something we won't forget. Everyone received a food packet

with delicious things, fruits we had not seen for years. We had no contact with Turkish people, we only saw them again after arriving on the opposite side of the Bosphorus where a train waited for us with English soldiers. Everyone was nice to us, no shouting, no pushing. We were suddenly human beings. I regret so much I can't give you more information. Please if you have questions, ask me, send me an e-mail and I try to answer you as good as possible.
With all the best wishes,
Yours, Elisheva.

Helmuth Mainz, an older member of the "222 Transport" group, recalled the following:

At 3:00 p.m., we find ourselves in Sophia [Bulgaria] which has been largely destroyed by [Allied] air raids. We do not stay long. After that, we go steeply into the mountains with three locomotives.

The following morning, we stop at the Turkish frontier, Svilingrad. We remain there until 2:00 p.m. and go for little walks. The Turkish government has sent us two fully stocked dining cars. So for breakfast we get real coffee, as much as we want, and fried eggs and bacon;[48] everything, of course, free of charge. We enjoy all that is on offer, the children are delighted. Some of our passengers cannot get enough of it. It is very hot...and we are pleased when we finally continue our journey.[49]

Another bit of dimly lit, largely unknown history is the fact that beginning March 15 1943 and continuing until May 23 1944, Turkish Consulates-General in Paris and Brussels arranged for no fewer then eight groups, averaging roughly fifty-three persons each, of former Turkish Jews to be returned to Turkey and to freedom by rail.[50] Moreover, throughout the war the "Taurus Express," the Turkish train, was used for transferring European Jews from Turkey's northern and western borders to its eastern border and on to Palestine.[51]

This was accomplished in spite of the problem that "transportation facilities here [in Turkey] on the single-track railway are...extremely limited by hammed in capacity," as noted by Ambassador Steinhardt.[52] Additionally, an estimated 1,000 others were transported by sea to Turkey in small boats out of southern France.[53] Here, too, Ambassador Steinhardt provided some insights as to the problems encountered:[54]

> [A]ll sorts of complications in trying to find a boat, prohibitive and extortionate prices, and illegal traffic in refugees which infuriates the Turks and last but not least when we have worked our way through all of these difficulties, refusal by the Germans to give safe conduct [passage] to such boats as we were able to lay our hands on.

Then there is the little known story of *Selahattin Ülkümen,* the Turkish consul-general on the Nazi occupied Greek island of Rhodes. In late July of 1944, the Germans began deporting the island's Jewish population. According to *Yad Vashem,*[55] Jerusalem's Holocaust Martyrs' and Heroes' Remembrance Authority, Ülkümen managed to save approximately 50 of its 1700 Jews, "13 of them Turkish citizens, the rest having some Turkish connection. In protecting those who were not Turkish citizens, he clearly acted on his own initiative." To wit, *Albert Franko,* already on a train to Auschwitz out of Piraeus in mainland Greece, "was taken off the train thanks to the intervention of Ülkümen, who was informed that Franko's wife was a Turkish citizen."

*Matilda Toriel,* a Turkish citizen living in Rhodes and married to an Italian citizen, recollected that on July 18 1944, all Jews were ordered to report the next day to Gestapo headquarters. "As she prepared to enter the building, Ülkümen approached her and told her not to go in." Even though she had never seen him before "he told her to wait until he had managed to release her husband." Ülkümen requested that the Germans release all Turkish citizens and their families. Moreover, he added twenty-five to thirty people to the fifteen on his original list of Turkish citizens. When the Gestapo demanded to see the papers of all, Ülkümen insisted that "according to Turkish law, spouses of Turkish citizens were considered to be citizens themselves, and demanded their release."[56]

No such law existed. "Ülkümen had simply fabricated it in order to save the Jews. In the end, all those on Ülkümen's list were released."[57] The rest of the Jews on the island, some 1,700 souls, ended up in Auschwitz. Years later, *Yad Vashem* honored Ülkümen with its *Righteous of the Nations* award.

Perhaps with the exception of the Ülkümen affair, none of these events went unnoticed by the émigré community. In fact, they feared that both the legal and the illicit *Yishuv* activities in Turkey might reflect on them and affect them negatively. Like their established German Jewish contemporaries in the US, anything that might cast aspersions on or threaten their own social status made the émigrés very nervous. Which brings us to the issue of the other Jewish refugees attempting to get through Turkey and on to Palestine. Only one of the émigrés, pediatrician *Albert Eckstein,* is known to come to the aid of these souls. In that lies much significance as well. No one else wanted to get involved; they all felt extremely unnerved by these happenings and right there in Istanbul. They felt threatened. They wanted to be the darlings of the Turkish upper crust but they were outsiders and not accepted. Just like Henry Morgenthau[58] Senior and Junior and just like many others. In prewar America the illegal (Jewish) refugee issue and the conflicts it caused inside Turkey rubbed off on them [American Jewry] or so they felt.

The émigrés must have been just as aware as was Ambassador Steinhardt that:

> While publicly avowing their desire to be helpful, the Turks are none too keen to assist in this humanitarian work. They do not regard the individual concerned as Jews but as Bulgarians, Rumanians [*sic*], etc., and they have a perfect spy complex.[59]

Some of the émigrés' fears were relieved on February 23 1945 when Turkey declared war on both Germany and Japan. Smart move on Turkey's part! Several weeks later, on May 7, the Germans surrendered unconditionally to the Allies and the War in Europe came to an end. On June 26 of the same year, Turkey was admitted to join the United Nations.

## Turkish Nationalism, Shortage of Funds, an Abrupt and Sad Parting for Many

Professor *İlber Ortaylı*, Director of Istanbul's *Topkapı Sarayi* Museum, a popular writer of newpaper articles and a TV personality in Turkey, provides this assessment of the emigres' situation:[60]

> Now on one hand, our university was very generous towards these men, assigned them departments in the Law and Medical Schools and bore with their whims. On the other hand, it was very cruel. The entourage of Fuat Köprülü, a noted professor of history in the 1930s and minister of Foreign Affairs during the 1950s, acted in a part-nationalist, part-jealous manner against these people. For example, Turkologist Tietze was not given the opportunity to teach at the university in his field. Instead he became a German language teacher in the Faculty of Forestry. The same was true for Turkologist Anhegger. Therefore we could not fully benefit from these men. Then there was the Faculty of *Languages, History, and Geography*, in Ankara; it was much bigger compared to İstanbul

> and they were kinder. For example, there was Ruben, the famous specialist on India. He returned to East Germany after the war, did not go back to the West. Then of course, there was Landsberger, the Assyriologist. There was Güterbock, the famous Hittitologist. There was Wolfram Eberhard, famous Sinologist. He wrote a history of China for the Historical Institute. He was the specialist on China and Central Asia for the Historical Institute.
>
> There they educated generations: That is, they tried to educate specialists in cuneiform or wedgewriting, archeology, and Chinese history. The Faculty was very conducive to this, a beautiful building designed by Bruno Taut and one of the richest library collections was housed there. Oriental manuscripts, for example, texts of *İsmail Sahip Efendi.*
>
> A generation was educated there. But something terrible also happened. The War ended, the Cold War started ,and with it, the tale of communism. Sad to say that two deputies of the Republican People's Party were among those who raided the Faculty. The first order of business was jealousy in this environment. The emigres were expelled. The people who founded the Faculty were hassled. America was ready to gather everyone anyway; they all went there. I met Landsberger in America.[61]

Sure enough, Frances Güterbock vividly remembers the fact that her husband Hans and eight others including colleagues *Eberhardt, Ruben,* and *Landsberger*, had their contracts terminated on only three months' notice.[62] "That caught us totally unprepared![63]" For a foreigner not to have a legal job was cause for expulsion from Turkey. Thus, each of the eight families had to scurry not just for a job but for a job in a country that would accept them. It certainly removed from Turkey not just one individual but a whole team of world-renowned scholars. Ultimately most [Ruben went to Chile and then to East Germany] came to the United States and prospered in their fields.

# 11
# Attempts to Emigrate to the United States

During the 1920s, 1930s, and through the 1940s, Americans were well aware of the anti-Semitism that was so prevalent in this country. Its existence, however, is not remembered today. Nor is it widely recognized that "Franklin Roosevelt's indifference to the systematic annihilation of European Jewry emerges as the worst failure of his administration."[1] In the eyes of some, December 7 1941 might be a good competitor for that ignominious accolade. For example, many well-educated, intelligent adults are shocked to hear that, in 1936, Albert Einstein[2] stated "that they did not want to hire Jews at Princeton [University]." This blanket exclusion continued as well at Harvard, Yale, and Brown of the Ivy League, some of their Seven Sisters, and many others, well into the late 1940s.

According to the *American Jewish Year Book,* Overt anti-Jewish prejudice within [America's] academy seemingly was at a high point in the 1920s and 1930s.... *Important private universities* had quotas limiting the number of Jewish undergraduates until the end of World War II. *Relatively few Jews were able to secure employment on the faculty of these schools.*[3]

It has been established that Turkey had done everything possible, at least initially, to welcome German, subsequently Austrian, and, in turn, German-speaking Czech professors needed to modernize her higher education and society as a whole. Despite its war-shattered economy, Turkey gave these émigrés excellent salaries and undertook many overhead expenses associated with creating the proper working environment for them. Importantly, it did so without heed to the individuals' religious heritage, or that of their spouses. The same cannot be said of America in general.[4]

To contrast the cultural preferences and prejudices of Germany, Turkey, and the United States, during the first half of the 20th century, throws into relief the tangible and intangible impacts, both positive and detrimental, to the people, of these three types of societies. These contrasts were evident at national and institutional levels, as well as in individual transactions. To this day, we see and feel the effects of such raw prejudices in individual and group behavior.

## Anti-Semitism in Hiring Professors at America's Universities

For purposes of its country's development, Turkey's government actively invited Germany and Austria's luminary [Jewish] professors, while the government of the United States did not. The welcome mat for fleeing Jewish musicians elevated America's classical orchestras to international pre-eminence.[5] Yet as indicated some of the elite East Coast universities[6] outright discriminated, turned a blind eye,[7] or worse played footsies with German universities that had already been Nazified.[8] According to historian Stephen H. Norwood, Harvard University President James Bryant Conant's insistence on treating Nazi academics as part of the "learned world,' *and his reluctance to offer faculty positions to prominent Jewish refugee scholars,* was shaped in part by his own anti-Semitic prejudices."[9]

When the DuPont Corporation sought his advice about hiring a German-Jewish scientist who had fled the Nazis, President Conant recommended against offering him a job because he was "very definitely of the Jewish type—very heavy." The scientist they rejected, Max Bergmann,[9] was described by the *New York Times* as "one of the leading organic chemists in the world."[10] And as late as 1945, Ernest E. Hopkins, President of Dartmouth College unabashedly declared, "Dartmouth is a Christian college founded for the Christianization of its students."[11]

The fact is, that no matter what statistical or quantitative measure one might use, the results will uniformly show that, prior to 1933, the premiere German universities such as Heidelberg, Breslau, Frankfurt, Munich, Göttingen, Königsberg, and even the University of Prague, Czechoslovakia, each employed more Jewish professors than did Harvard, Yale, Brown, and Princeton combined at the time and for over a decade beyond. The proof is easy. These American Ivy League schools had each kept their faculty *Judenfrei.*

To be sure, the Ivy League did not apply the Nazi definitions as to who was Jewish.[12] Richard von Mises was hired by Harvard even though he was born Jewish. Von Mises converted to Catholicism. Non-convert distinguished mathematician Hilda Geiringer (later Mrs. Richard von Mises) was hired by Harvard[13] but only to organize her late husband's archives. She was never offered a professorship. Brown University had Geiringer give many lectures, but never as a professor. The case of William Prager being given a professorial appointment by Brown in 1941 is murky in this regard. The infamous Scurla in his 1939 report to Berlin[14] lists him as "Nichtarier" (non-Aryan); he must have had at least three Jewish grandparents to "merit" this description. However, the *Actives-Museum Liste* indicates that he was a *Jude* (in italics) which was intended to mean "as judged by Nazi standards." A non-italicized "Jude" would have meant that he was a Jew by religion.[15]

So it is an open question as to whether Brown was non-discriminatory in hiring him or was Prager, like von Mises, a convert, or perhaps baptized. Part of the answer can be found in a typed "CURRICULUM VITAE" that Prager himself attached[16] to a letter from "Istanbul-Bebek, Insirah Sokagi 38,"dated "28.6.39" and addressed to Prof. Dr. *H. Weyl* at the *Institute for Advanced Studies* in Princeton. Under the heading Personal Data, Prager says, "Born in 23-5-03 in Karlsruhe (Germany) as Rumanian subject, became German by naturalization (1916), *of Protestant Confession...*" Next, in writing by hand, is the asterisked word "Aryan" At the bottom of the page, also hand-written, is "*Dismissed because one grandparent Jewish." The bottom line is that as far as Brown University was concerned, William Prager was not Jewish.

Thus, in 1941 Brown's Graduate School Dean *Roland G. D. Richardson,* who recognized Prager as a major prize and wanted him to direct the school's newly established program in Advanced Instruction and Research in Mechanics, a highly mathematical discipline, pushed to bring Prager to Providence. However, this was not easy to do. The State Department was not issuing visas at that point in time to people having relatives in Germany. Brown University with enough clout managed to have that bureaucratic rule circumvented for the Pragers. Then there was the issue of the travel route to be taken.

A German citizen of military age, Prager could not travel through Nazi-held countries. The saga of William Prager coming to the United States was best described by Martha Mitchell.[17] Apparently, the Prager's planned itinerary of Odessa a Black Sea seaport, through the Soviet Union, to Japan and on to San Francisco had to be cancelled when Germany invaded Russia. Austrian-born and Gottingen-educated historian of mathematics, Otto Neugebauer, who had arrived at Brown a year or two before, received the following telegram from Istanbul on the seriousness of the situation.

> US Visa Cancelled / Cabled Details Dean / Furniture Sold / Position Resigned / Situation Here Expected Deteriorate Soon / Impossible Stay for Czechoslovakians / Implore Help / Willy.

Interestingly, the "History of the Applied Mathematics Department" at Brown University tells us much about the university's tenacity and influence in securing Prager's coming to Providence:

> [T]hrough *the good offices of the British Foreign Secretary and the American State Department,* his passage to America was arranged. His journey was not without difficulty, however. He was turned back on his first route by the Japanese, his second attempt was frustrated by fighting in Irak [sic] and Syria, his third attempt came to grief in Iran, and his successful fourth attempt used one of the last commercial planes out of Basra and the next to the last boat out of Bombay." "In spite of the *best efforts of two governments,* his trip from Istanbul to Providence took more than six months and was completed only a few weeks before our entry into the war.[18]

Ultimately, Prager, his wife, and son, Stephen, who was twelve years old, "traveled by train to Baghdad, by plane to Karachi, India, and by ship on the *President Monroe* from Bombay around Capetown to New York, a forty-day journey which brought them to the United States in November 1941."[19]

"The applied mathematics program which thus got under way has been a valuable contribution to the nation at war and has thus repaid the Brown's very expensive effort"[20] of getting Prager to these shores. Based on his own graduate education in the engineering sciences and on subsequent readings, there is no doubt in this writer's mind that Brown University, and the Turkish government before it, did the right thing in the case of *William Prager.* However, *The Jews of Rhode Island,*[21] tells us that it was as late as *"1946"* when "Israel Kapstein bec[ame] the *first Jewish professor to gain tenure at Brown University.*[22]" (emphasis added) So, like Harvard in the case of Richard Von Mises, Brown did not consider Prager to be Jewish.

It is worth mentioning here that, in 1934, the Berlin house of *Springer Verlag* published a book on the *plasticity mechanics of isotropic bodies,* the mathematical theory of permanent deformation then mostly applied to metals, by *Hilda Geiringer* and *William Prager.* There is no question that Geiringer was one of the founders of the field of applied mechanics, a theoretical engineering science, and lectured in Prager's department at Brown University. In a letter dated May 21 1942, seeking a modest subvention from the Rockefeller Foundation to the meager pay given her at Bryn Mawr, Hermann Weyl one of the founders of the *Institute of Advanced Studies* in Princeton and a tireless advocate for the refugee scholars, wrote. "Mrs. Geiringer has been invited to lecture at the newly established School of Applied Mechanics at Brown University during this summer."[23]

In fact, her contributions to that 1942 Summer Program were discussed a year later in the prestigious *American Journal of Physics.*[24] Even though she kept being re-invited to give lectures at Brown, Geiringer was never offered a faculty-rank Brown University appointment. Was it because Geiringer never renounced her Jewish roots or is it because she was female, or both? The answer might lie in the university's archives. However, *Dr. Ruth Simmons*, Brown University's 18th president, personally has placed such archives out of reach to this author.[25] Times have really changed at Brown and elsewhere in America since the 1930s and 1940s: Dr. Simmons is Afro-American and a female.

As indicated in an earlier chapter, the *Ava Helen and Linus Pauling Papers* archive at Oregon State University includes correspondence between twice-Nobel laureate *Linus Pauling* and biochemist *Felix Haurowitz* as well as between Pauling and others regarding Haurowitz's search for employment in the States.[26] On September 3 1936 when Haurowitz was still in Prague, Pauling thanked Haurowitz for his letter regarding work with hemoglobin and enclosed a paper by a Dr. Mirsky and himself on the structure of proteins. While still in Turkey, Haurowitz applied for a position at Harvard, giving Pauling's name as a reference.

On September 25 1941, George Chase, "the Dean of the University," wrote to Pauling in behalf of Harvard's "President Conant,[27] "it would be helpful if you would send us your estimate of Professor Haurowitz's standing and whether you have any suggestions about possibilities in this country."[28] To which, on October 12 1941, Pauling replied, "I have been greatly interested in his work for a number of years. *In my opinion, he is one of the leading men in the world in the field of the chemistry of proteins.* His researches are characterized by imagination and good execution. His work on hemoglobin and on problems of immunology has been especially successful. I do not know at present of any opening for Professor Haurowitz in this country."[29]

Harvard did not make an offer. Although he had had his son baptized at birth, Haurowitz himself never converted. Harvard, however, observes an eighty-year restriction on access to personnel records,[30] Later, in 1949, Pauling was instrumental in placing Haurowitz at the University of Indiana.

Yale broke no barriers, either.[31] Daniel Brook, writing in *Black Issues in Higher Education* and the-renamed *Diverse Issues in Higher Education,* noted that "it was not until 1946 that the philosophy department tenured the college's first Jew, *Paul Weiss.*" Things changed in New Haven as well: "by 1970, one out of every six Yale college professors was Jewish. When the shock waves of the 1960s finally shook Yale's gothic ivory towers, anti-Jewish hiring discrimination became a thing of the past."[32]

Because the anti-Semitism practiced at America's universities in hiring was well known to the émigrés in faraway Turkey, one does not have to be an expert in psychoanalysis based on snips of handwriting to reach the conclusion that one of them, a world-class scholar, was under great duress and in mixed emotions back in 1939 when he was responding to the questions of "Religious Preference" for himself and his spouse while filling out a job application form for an Assistant Professorship at an east-coast American college. This particular individual was born Jewish. However, according to his son, throughout adult life he considered himself quite cosmopolitan, agnostic, and assimilated, first in his native Germany, and last in the United States, his adopted country. One does bring his "baggage" with him.

### Sexism and Age Discrimination in Hiring Professors at America's Universities

Fast forwarding to 1942 and moving to the United States during wartime, the days when "Rosie the Riveter" posters soliciting women to enter the workforce abounded so ships could be floated and aircraft sent aloft, American universities shied away from hiring mathematicians who were women, or men who were beyond an age limit that would be considered absurd by today's standards. As a case in point, Queens College was barely five years old and growing rapidly as part of the budding New York City university system. Seeing a possible opportunity to place one or two outstanding mathematicians, one of whom was Hilda Geiringer, the other being Max Dehn, who was not one of the émigrés in Turkey, Hermann Weyl wrote from the *Institute* at Princeton to Queens College mathematics professor, T. F. Cope, "In view of the growing shortage of well-qualified teachers of mathematics at the university level—probably soon to be aggravated by various naval and air-force training courses—I should like to draw your attention to the good services which could be rendered by European refugee mathematicians of high rank."

After describing Geiringer's and Dehn's qualifications, and noting the fact that both had already had over a year's teaching experience at American colleges, Weyl felt a need to add that "there is no doubt whatsoever of the political reliability of either of them." However, he continued, "Professor Dehn, a mathematician of great merit, one of the fathers of modern topology, *is probably too old for permanent employment.*" Still hopeful that the above notice which he felt obliged to include might not have been needed after all, Weyl added: "Dehn is a vigorous man in excellent health (still able to go for a four-day hike on the Olympic Peninsula, as he did last summer, carrying all provisions on his back)."

To further reinforce his recommendation of Dehn, Weyl noted: "He is an inspiring teacher, and could teach all branches of mathematics, including history and philosophy of mathematics." Weyl also pointed out that "Mrs. Geiringer is of that type of applied mathematician who could be of great service in the present emergency." Before sending his above letter to Queens College, Herman Weyl had already posted identical pleas to a Professor Harold Hotteling at Columbia University on February 12, to Professor Griffith C. Evans at the University of California, Berkeley, on February 26, and to Professor Tibor Rado at Ohio State University on March 21.[33] In all likelihood, Weyl was aware before approaching them that these particular institutions employed Jewish faculty members. So, anti-Semitism was not an issue.

The bottom line, however, is that there is no record of Queens College nor the other more established universities ever hiring either Geiringer or Dehn. Both finished their careers at America's lesser-known institutions of higher learning, Geiringer at Wheaton College, and Dehn at Black Mountain College, a college that had no accredited degrees, taught mainly creative arts, and no longer exists.[34]

## Gentlemen's Agreements at Public Universities

Although America's public universities did not have exclusionary faculty hiring practices written into their Charters, *de facto* a number of them had so-called "gentlemen's agreements" to do so; none would hire Jews through the 1940s and some not even into the 1950s. This legacy was statistically validated by a national survey conducted by the Carnegie Commission on Higher Education in 1969. The survey involved 60,000 faculty respondents and showed that Jews in the upper-age brackets were significantly low on America's university campuses e.g., 3.8% Jews vs. 79.0% Protestant and 13.7% Catholic.[35] These data *a-posteriori* document the historical, pervasive, and indisputable, impact of those "Gentlemen's Agreements."

## Émigré Options

All attempts to liberalize the U. S. quota system of immigration failed, even during the emergencies of the war and period of the Holocaust. Evidence is lacking as to whether or not any of the émigrés during the course of the war had the option of going to the States or the United Kingdom, given the restrictive US immigration numbers and Britain's practice of interning similarly situated individuals as "enemy aliens."[36] Moreover, university job opportunities were limited by the fact that America was coming out of an economic depression. So even if the émigrés could have obtained visas, it is known that some chose the certainty of an academic position in Turkey within their expertise against the distinct possibility of being unemployed or underemployed in the West.

As documented earlier, Rudolf Nissen switched his itinerary while en route to the United States upon receipt of a telegram with a job offer in Turkey. Albert Einstein on the other hand, allegedly was taking the Turkish option until he received a firm job offer at the last minute[37] from the Princeton Institute for Advanced Studies.[38]

## Albert Einstein Received Many Pleas for Help

In a letter dated July 11 1933, Albert Einstein was approached for help by his friend, Professor *Dr. Wilhelm Liepmann*. In a handwritten letter from Barcelona, his residence after his first escape from the Nazis, Liepmann asks Einstein to keep him in mind in case he gets word of a position for a gynecologist with a specialty in cancer control plus qualifications as surgeon and scientist. Apparently getting such a position in Spain had been difficult for Liepmann because of rules governing medical employment.

Einstein was also approached by his old colleague Hans Reichenbach[39] on April 12 1936:

> Dear Herr Einstein,
>
> You've heard nothing from me for a long time. In the meantime, however, Rudolf Kayser has written me that he has spoken to you about me and my plans.
>
> You know, that I have always wanted come to the U.S.A. As long as I was in Germany my efforts in this direction failed. Then came the Hitler mess, and I was happy to get the offer from Istanbul. This thing seemed at the time very promising to me: a professorship and the possibility of independently building the philosophy curriculum from the ground up. Unfortunately the two and a half years that I've been here have been a great disappointment to me. It's true that my position here is very independent; I am the only philosopher here. But the organization of the university is such that the natural sciences are quite cut off from philosophy. My chair is part of the Faculty of Letters; my students are exclusively students of the literature department without any background in mathematics or physics, and so I feel altogether out of place here. That due to the lack of other teaching staff I must also lecture on the history of philosophy is not really so bad; but that I am not in the least able to bring to the fore my

own philosophical ideas that I championed for such a long time in Germany pains me greatly.

Well, last year I received an invitation to spend a year at New York University. I would have gladly accepted, in the hope of then finding something further over there. But the government here refused me the requested leave of absence and also didn't offer me the possibility of getting out of my contract. My contract here runs for at least three years, and so at that time I had to stay here if I didn't want to be in breach of contract. This renunciation was very difficult for me.

In the meantime, my friend Carnap in Prague received an invitation to present guest lectures at the University of Chicago. He lectured there successfully, and, as I now hear, then received a call to Chicago as well as to Princeton University. If Carnap should decide for Princeton, I would likely receive the call to Chicago, as our mutual friend Morris wrote me from there. Morris, however, also wrote that Carnap is leaning more towards Chicago. In this case, the appointment at Princeton would be open. Therefore, I am already writing to you now because the mails take such a long time. By the time this letter reaches you, Carnap will probably already have made his decision and then the appointment in Princeton will immediately be up for discussion.

I would be very thankful if you—that is in the case Carnap rejects Princeton—would speak on my behalf. I suspect that the actual problem lies with Mr. Weyl. Over ten years ago, Mr. Weyl had spoken out very negatively about my papers on relativity theory; I then responded to him briefly in a paper. I suspect that Mr. Weyl's opposition persists to this day, and for that reason, I would be very grateful to you, if you could step in on my behalf.

I still want to add, that this year the government here is no longer able to detain me, since my three years will be up on October 1, 1936, and I can give notice on this date. At this end, therefore, there are no difficulties. Perhaps I may further note that I speak English well.

I would be grateful from the bottom of my heart, if you could help me to come to Princeton! The Hitler mess has—as in so many other cases—also destroyed my work in Germany. It is my hope to reconstruct it in America.

With affectionate greetings to you and your family, I am

Yours,

Hans Reichenbach

On May 2 1936, responding to Hans Reichenbach's inquiry about employment possibilities at Princeton University, Albert Einstein[40] cites personal experience of philosopher Rudolf Carnap, a mutual friend from their *Vienna* and *Berlin Circle* days: "Carnap told me the other day he was told explicitly *that they did not want to hire Jews at Princeton."* The Einstein letter goes on to say: "Thus even here not everything is gold, and who knows how it will be here tomorrow. Maybe the 'barbarians,' after all, are the better people."[41] (Fig. 118). The information contained in this letter was apparently circulated among the émigrés in Turkey. Astronomer E. Finlay Freundlich mentions this in his own letter to Einstein from Istanbul dated August 3 1936. In that letter, Freundlich tells Einstein that even though they have not communicated "for a while, [he] decided to get in touch because he believes that in times of such crisis in loyalty as the world is experiencing, likeminded people should keep in touch."

In a letter to Albert Einstein[42] postmarked 1938, Wanda Gottschalk writes:

> Most esteemed Herr Professor:
>
> The difficult times have given me the courage to approach you with a question.
>
> In 1935 my husband, the archivist and librarian Dr. Walther Gottschalk, born January 29, 1891, in Aachen, had to relinquish his position at the State Library in Berlin, because we are Jews. As people who deeply experience their Judaism and affirm it, who are Jews not because they have to be but because they want to be, we have until now found the strength to be bear our lot uprightly and with firm trust in God. But what makes my heart bleed and brings me to write to you today, is the thought that here such a capable Jew as my husband, like one paralyzed and forced into idleness, should let his young life pass by, whereas with a university or library appointment he could once again productively employ all his powers in the fields of science or librarianship.
>
> My husband became well known as a scholar through his book, "The Older Arab Concept of the Vow," and demonstrated his capabilities as a librarian in his "Hand Catalog of the Oriental Department of the State Librarian in Berlin."
>
> Because of my husband's almost unreal modesty, he would never on his own approach an academic institution with a request. Unbeknownst to him, therefore, I entreat you, esteemed Herr Professor, to be so kind as to bring it about that my husband might be invited by some university or library in Eretz [Palestine]

or there [the U.S.], so that he might once again find a position suited to his immense knowledge.

If this should not be at all be possible for you, most honored Professor, could you then advise me as to where I could turn with the same request?

With inexpressible thanks and the greeting of Zion,
Frau Wanda Gottschalk

P.S. Because of the circumstances in Germany I am requesting you to most kindly send your much appreciated response to: Frau Helene Horn, Sittard, Julianapleiu, Holland.

## New York's New School for Social Research a Counter Example to the Ivy League

> One of the most prominent collecting points was the New School for Social Research, which, in 1933, established a 'university in exile' with a faculty made up of expatriates. *These arrangements helped overcome immigration barriers erected by the United States.* In particular, for those who did not qualify under severely constraining national quotas, having a job offer from the New School or another institution made it possible to secure otherwise unattainable visas.[43] (emphasis added) *Journal of Economic Literature.*

The *New School for Social Research* in New York City was very instrumental in bringing a number of German intellectuals to the United States and to safety. Within the *Grenander Department of Special Collections & Archives* in Albany, New York, one can find a cache of correspondence documenting the indefatigable efforts of Alvin Johnson to save as many German intellectuals as possible. He worked at securing employment positions, financial assistance, and visas. If he has not been nominated for sainthood until now, it is not too late. Johnson tailored his strategies to the individuals he was approaching.

Writing to Columbia University chemistry professor Victor K. LaMer on September 10 1940, Johnson found it necessary to make the point that his "objective is not merely humanitarian." He went on to stress that, yes, "we have many first-rate scholars of our own, but not so many that it would not be worthwhile for us to enlist first-rate scholars thrown overboard by a totalitarian Europe." Johnson added "... even in your own magnificent field of chemistry I understand from my son, Alden J. Deyrup, who was a student of yours, that there is still room in this country for additional first-class men."[44]

Nor, did Johnson take a "no" answer without response. Based on a report from its "officers in the natural sciences," the Rockefeller Foundation decided not to offer subvention grants to some of the employment contracts. The very next day, Johnson wrote: "I have your note of October first [1940] informing me that you are not prepared to recommend grants for Philip Gross and Alexander Weinstein." Johnson told the Foundation that "we have been accumulating material on Philip Gross expecting to submit it to you. From the testimonials, he would appear to be a good man, though not of the very first rank. The field in which he is working—Chemistry of Solutions—is an important one, and in this he appears to be outstanding." Johnson goes on to politely request a confidential statement of the grounds for the negative decision because the material in his hands "does not justify a condemnation."

After comparing their respective recommendation letters additional correspondence between Johnson and the Foundation's *Thomas B. Appleget* brings to the fore that "we [The Foundation] as well as you asked [*Dean Joel H.*] *Hildebrand* of [Berkeley] California for his opinion of Gross. Our letter from Hildebrand contains a statement which did not appear in yours. To us Hildebrand wrote, 'I believe he is a good scientist but *hardly one of the outstanding ones who should be salvaged at all costs for the benefit of society*.'"[45] (emphasis added)

As indicated, the New School worked very closely with many private donors, organizations, and foundations to secure monies. It also worked closely with the State Department to secure visas. Often it created positions for individuals within its own faculty whose normal professional orientation might not quite fit into the School's "Social Research" mission. Such was the case of Dentistry Professor Alfred Kantorowicz. After being yanked out of a German concentration camp, he was well situated in Turkey. However, the Nazi army's arrival at Turkey's door made him once again seek employment elsewhere in, and a visa to, the USA. Several newly arrived and established American scientists actively lobbied in behalf of Kantorowicz's coming to the United States.

Among these was newly arrived Hans Reichenbach[46] who wrote to the Emergency Rescue Committee in New York City: "…we are certain that after the invasion of Turkey and his capture by the Nazis, Kantorowicz would once more be imprisoned by them and if not more harshly dealt with. Being 60 years old, it is highly improbable that he could survive another ordeal in a concentration camp." Reichenbach goes on to point out that Kantorowicz's daughter is married to an American citizen, biologist H.J. Muller. In this case, the lobbying almost succeeded. By Western Union Cablegram dated May 2 1941, Alvin S. Johnson notified Kantorowicz of a job offer as Associate Professor of Public Heath. On May 7, Kantorowicz cabled back an acceptance.[47] (Fig. 119)

Getting transit visas was another matter and, by October 23, Kantorowicz had to send a letter (Fig. 120). It speaks for itself

One month and three days after Germany invaded the Soviet Union, an August 25 1941 letter[48] from Alvin Johnson discusses the "great difficulties in securing transit visas through Turkey, Iraq, Iran, and British India." He then points out that the cost from Istanbul to New York via Bombay "would be at least $2500 per person."

On January 20 1942, outside of Berlin, the Wannsee Conference formalized "The Final Solution," i.e., the annihilation of all Jews within the Reich's reach. By June 1942, the gas ovens at Auschwitz became operational. By July, both Turkey's external conditions and the sociopolitical climate inside Turkey became ever more grave. This time, no smaller a personage then the American pioneer in functional psychology, and leading representative of the progressive movement in U.S. education during the first half of the 20th century John Dewey himself came to bat for Kantorowicz (Fig. 121).

Although not as precarious a situation that Jews in Nazi lands were in, even full-blooded Aryans situated in the relative safety of Turkey were frightened. A lady by the name of Ursula Bodlaender, the younger sister of émigré engineer, *Hans Bodlaender*, managed to reach the United States much earlier than her brother. In a letter dated October 23 1940, she pleaded the case of sinologist *Wolfram Eberhard* to the *New School's* administration In her letter, she states that: "Being a German [Eberhard was Aryan], his position in Turkey is at present very unsafe on account of the war and the conditions there." She goes on to point out that "even though he doesn't want and cannot return to Germany, *he is considered an enemy alien*,"[49] by the Turks, that is. In 1948, Eberhard finally received both a job at UCLA and a visa.

Decades before America enacted legislation forbidding age discrimination, *The New School* practiced age discrimination as a matter of policy. The matter of physicist Harry Dember is a case in point. Princeton Institute of Higher Studies Professor Hermann Weil, in a letter dated April 28 1941, tells Alvin Johnson: "I have just had a visit from Professor Winchester of Rutgers University who showed me a cable from Professor Harry Dember, Istanbul, Aksaray, who claims to be in extreme danger and cries for help." On the very next day, Johnson sends his reply: "I am very sorry to say that I cannot include Professor Harry Dember in my present project." After discussing the New School's financial predicament, Johnson adds: Professor Dember *is far beyond the age limit* of the scholars for whom this project was established.... I regret, therefore, that there is nothing I can do for him."[50]

## The Undaunted Department of State

A non-Jew by any standard, David S. Wyman prefaced his book, *The Abandonment of Jews: America and the Holocaust 1941-1945*, by saying that the "American State Department and the British Foreign Office had no intention of rescuing large number of European Jews. On the contrary, they continually feared that Germany or other Axis nations might release tens of thousands of Jews into Allied hands," "a situation the two great powers did not want to face."[51]

And the Department's bureaucrats became quite proficient at inventing hurdles instead of issuing visas; Franklin Delano Roosevelt "declined to question the State Department's arbitrary shutdown of refugee immigration to the United States, even when pressed by seven Jews in Congress."[52] An August 25 1941 letter[53] from Alvin Johnson to a Captain Charles B. Welles of the U.S. Army regarding Romance scholar *Andreas B. Schwarz* brings to light an interesting "Catch-22" that the U. S. State Department constructed:

> At the present time, it is nearly impossible for anyone in Istanbul to get visas and passage to America. *Our own State Department has made the granting of visas complicated and difficult since they do not want to bring over anyone who leaves near-relatives in territory under German control.* (emphasis added)

As if denying visas to people who had "near-relatives under Nazi rule" was not enough of a barrier to saving people from possible demise, the State Department created many other obstacles. Once again, according to Alvin Johnson's correspondence[54] (circa December 20 1940) regarding a request by Harvard's Dr. Otto Krayer to bring pharmacology professor Paul Pulewka to the USA from Ankara: "The fact that he [Pulewka] held an *administrative* job for several years eliminates the possibility of a teacher's non-quota visa." And, in a letter to Professor Hermann Muller dated July 15 1941, after the Nazis had already occupied Greece and were a stone's throw from Istanbul, Johnson notes that "on July 1st the State Department instituted new regulations for visa applicants. *All applications made under the old regulations and not yet acted upon, automatically lose validity*. It becomes necessary to make new applications based on the new regulations." (emphasis added.)

Saving foreign lives was obviously not a priority for the Department of State. In fact, because of State bureaucratic practices, "only 21,000 refugees were allowed to enter the United States during the three and one half years the nation was at war with Germany. That amounted to 10 percent of the number who could have been legally admitted under the immigration quotas [on the books] during that period."[55]

There were, however, exceptions even at State when the right people or organizations intervened. October 30 1939, the Chief of its Visa Division, A.M. Warren himself, followed up to a Miss Marjorie Schauffler of the *American Friends Service Committee* [56] who intervened on behalf of a mother and her child stranded in Lisbon because they could no longer enter England. Warren wrote: "With reference to your personal call at the Department on October 11, 1939, you are informed that a report has now been received from the American Consular Officer in charge at Lisbon, Portugal, in which it is stated the Hilda Polaczek Geiringer and her minor daughter, Magda, were granted immigration visas on October 23 and were leaving by clipper on October 28."[57]

## Visa In-hand, but No Job Prospects. A Job In-hand, but No Visa

A fine example of a visa in-hand but no job prospects—a copy of a letter postmarked "Istanbul" and dated May 28 1943 from biochemist Haurowitz to Professor Max Bergmann at the Rockefeller Institute for Medical Research in NYC reads: "the authorities in Washington have granted me and my family the visa. Friends and relations in America ask me to come as soon as possible. But all these people have no idea about the possibilities [job opportunities] in our branch. I suppose that you are informed about the fate of the German professors who have emigrated to the United States. Have they found satisfying appointments? And do you think that I could find something."[58]

In his response dated July 8 1943 on *Institute* letterhead, Bergmann offered: "As a rule, every scientist from abroad, even if he is famous the world over and is a Nobel Laureate, has to start here on a small scale, that is, with a small salary and one or two collaborators, and it depends on his achievement in his new position whether he makes progress. In general, it takes several months or one-half year for the newly-arrived scientist to find a job and nobody gets a job offered to him before he has immigrated. [It] is not certain whether you would find a job to your liking at once or not until after some time. During the last 10 years, everybody could be sure of finding a job. Now, under war conditions, it is almost impossible to predict anything."[59]

At last, the tides of war were beginning to run out. Having reached the war's first major turning point by breaking the *Wermacht's* siege of Stalingrad, the Red Army went on the counter-offensive in Russia. In the last three weeks of Stalingrad fighting (January 1943), 90,000 German troops died of cold and starvation, 100,000 were killed in battle, and hundreds of thousands of Germans, Hungarians, and Romanians were hauled off to Russia's POW camps. Among the German prisoners of war was General *Friedrich von Paulus,* who had been promoted by Hitler to the rank of Field Marshall in the last days of battle because no German Marshall had yet surrendered.[60] In July 1943, Russians overran the Germans tanks in the battle of Kursk, the Allies landed in Sicily, and Mussolini was deposed.

While this was happening, biochemist *Felix Haurowitz* stayed on in Turkey until he had a job waiting for him in the United States; he himself was in Turkey until 1949. Nevertheless, by 1947, his family immigrated to the U. S. so that their son and daughter could receive an American education. "While the daughter Alice was a freshman and taking steps to major in chemistry, the wife, Gina, and high school son, Martin, had become established with relatives in New York City."[61] Professor Haurowitz financially supported them from his Istanbul University earnings.

Few years earlier library scientist *Walter Gottschalk* found himself in the reverse situation from Haurowitz: he had received a job offer but could not get a visa. Writing on December 17 1939 from his refuge in Belgium, Gottschalk thanks *Albert Einstein* for all that he had done and tells Einstein that: "From the certain sanctuary that my Belgian relations have provided me with such indescribable hospitality, I have been able on my own to pursue my [professional] advancement to the point that I have been offered a professorship in Arabic language and culture at the Hebrew Union College in Cincinnati and a librarian's post at the University of Istanbul. Since the American Consul in Antwerp has, for reasons of formalities, made difficulties with our visas, I'll probably have to decide on Turkey."[62]

Mathematician Hilda Geiringer's case introduced a third variation on the theme: she was a woman. As far back as 1933, esteemed American mathematician *Richard Courant* wrote that "her scientific development has made her one of the rare productive and generally recognized representatives of applied mathematics in Germany. Under normal circumstances Mrs. Geiringer would certainly have all the chances of a brilliant career in Germany" Additionally, on March 29, 1939, Richard von Mises a few months before assuming a professorship at Harvard, wrote from Istanbul to mathematician Oswald Veblen at Princeton: "By an experience of [many] long years I have known Mrs. Geiringer as an extraordinarily good teacher of high pedagogical faculties. About her valuable scientific work you are informed by the joined co-authored papers."[63]

At that point in time, in desperation, Geiringer was willing to undertake an unpaid position at Bryn Mawr College in Pennsylvania[64] after having been told that monies were unavailable. "My contract with the Turkish government expires in the fall of this year" she wrote to fellow mathematician Oswald Veblen on March 29 1939. "...As the general political situation is insecure I am almost sure that it will not be renewed."

She then asked Veblen "to address some lines to the Bryn Mawr College in favour of [her] case." Esther Simpson, Assistant Secretary, of the *Society for the Protection of Science and Learning* of London, England, also wrote to Veblen pleading Geiringer's case. By saying "*we doubt very much whether a non-quota visa will be given to her for an unpaid appointment, and we know how difficult it is to obtain a paid position without being on the spot,*" [65] Esther Simpson described yet another saga variant faced by many of the émigrés at the time; i.e., one can't get into the United States unless there is a job waiting.

And then there was the case of dentistry professor Alfred Kantorowicz.[66] Got the visa, got the job—and got the bureaucracy involved. When he had a visa to the United States in the late 1930s, he had no job awaiting him. So he wouldn't come. Then he was offered a position at the New School for two years, which was fully paid for by his daughter and her husband. However "while he was trying to obtain transit visas through Middle East countries," his non-quota U.S. visa had expired. His daughter, Dorothea Muller, in a letter dated April 21 1942 feared that "by the time the visa will be granted my father's Czechoslovak passport will expire."

On August 4 1941, she was concerned that the visa would not be granted because "Dr. Kantorowicz's wife has a brother, sister, and mother in Germany." The New School held the position for Kantorowicz, many people and organizations including the *American Friends Service Committee* were very actively pursuing his getting a new visa and securing monies to pay for the passage. But lightning struck. Arrangements were made for Dr. and Mrs. Kantorowicz to come to the States via Russia and onboard "the American Liner President Taft leaving Kobe, Japan in September." However, a few days prior to Kantorowicz's leaving Turkey, there was news that "the ship has been requisitioned by the Navy." Delays continued, went on into 1944. In the meantime, the tides of war in Europe had somewhat relieved pressures on Turkey, the University of Istanbul renewed his contract, and Kantorowicz decided to stay. On May 4 1944, the New School fully refunded to the Mullers the $ 4,000 that was to be Kantorowicz's salary over the two-year contract.

### Financial Woes at America's Private Universities

Hilda Geiringer's saga could well be a book worth writing. Yes, after being stranded in Lisbon,[67] because "no further holders of German passports [were] allowed to enter England,"[68] On September 25 1939, she finally made it to these shores. But she was never offered the kind of job in America that she enjoyed both in Germany and in Turkey. There is absolutely no doubt that America was decades behind those countries in terms of providing women equal access to professional opportunities. However, with the help of many well-established and well-intentioned individuals, Geiringer was finally placed at a college run by women and for women, Bryn Mawr. It was not a permanent position and it was hardly well paid. Bryn Mawr was in financial distress.

Along these lines, Oswald Veblen minced no words in his letter of April 18 1940 to a Dr. Wilbur K. Thomas at the *Oberlaender Trust* in Philadelphia. "As you doubtless know better than I do, *Bryn Mawr is hard up for funds*, and they are therefore trying to get some temporary support for Mrs. Geiringer." In another attempt to raise money to create Hilda Geiringer's meager salary, Bryn Mawr University's president Marion Park approached the German émigré mathematicians who held good positions in American universities. She received a reply from Hermann Weyl on March 10 1941, saying sadly, "almost every one of us has to carry heavy personal obligations towards close relatives or friends whom he is trying to help to safety from concentration camps and Nazi persecution in Germany, France, Czechoslovakia, Norway, etc., or to whose sustenance he contributes."

Unlike Harvard, Brown, and Yale, the University of Chicago was much more open to absorbing intellectuals who were dismissed from German universities and could be of use to Chicago, be they Jewish or not. The case of Astronomer *Hans Rosenberg* is a good case in point. As shown in the letter from *Otto Struve*, Director of the Yerkes Observatory in Wisconsin, to Chicago's president, R. M. Hutchins, it was Struve who took the initiative in relocating a colleague in distress (Fig, 122 and 123).

On July 8, Hutchins acknowledged receipt and told Struve, "[W]e are now at work on the matter of bringing over a few German scholars; I shall be glad to include Dr. Rosenberg's name." Hutchins did not let any grass grow under his feet. He and his staff started phoning members of the Chicago Jewish community to secure funding. On July 12, he followed up a conversation he had with a *Frank A. Sulzberger* by forwarding a copy of the above letter from Struve (Fig. 124).

The response came just as swiftly (Fig. 125 and 126).

In rapid order, a package of what is known in academic circles as "soft money" was put together from Jewish and non-Jewish sources so as to be able to offer a one-year appointment to Rosenberg. No one wanted the word to get out to the Nazis and thus jeopardize the project, so *Dr. Ejnar Hertzsprung*, apparently a Dane but working as assistant director of the Leiden Observatory in as yet unoccupied Holland, was used as the messenger. The next letter speaks for itself (Fig. 127 and 128).

Again there was no time wasted (Fig. 129).

Others in the astronomy community pitched in with an offer to help, using a great deal of caution.

The University of Chicago "President's Papers" Archives[69] include much more correspondence pertaining to the Rosenberg case. These involve others in the astronomy world such as *Elis Stromgren,* Director of the Kopenhagen Observatory, who went out of his way to go to Hamburg after a Congress in Göttingen to meet with and assess Rosenberg's intentions. "He thinks his job may not last. He also would like his children out of danger. Jewish children have no future here," Stromgren quotes Rosenberg. The letter goes on to discuss terms and conditions raised by Rosenberg for his move to Chicago. The conditions discussed included customs duties Rosenberg will have to pay for his furniture, art, and the astronomic instruments that are in use at the Kiel observatory but which he personally owns.[70]

The correspondence also shows a previously unrecognized fact that Rosenberg was indeed married and had children and therefore the salary had to be upped to $ 4,000. Consequently, Chicago's administration had to go back out to the community hat-in-hand. On December 22 1933, Rosenberg himself wrote a letter to Struve. The letter says in part:

"I received from Professor Stromgren, Kopenhagen, and Professor Hertzsprung, Leiden, letter about your offer to provide me with a guest professorship at Yerkes Observatory. Since it is hard to discuss this matter from Kiel [Germany], I traveled to Kopenhagen to answer you."

The bottom line to this saga is that the appointment was made. In a lengthy letter from the Kopenhagen Observatory, Rosenberg accepted the offer made to him. However, in 1938 Rosenberg left Chicago to join the astronomy department at the University of Istanbul. The reasons for his doing this are not clear. Did Chicago run out of soft money? Did Rosenberg seek greener pastures? Was Rosenberg dissatisfied with his salary from Chicago because of knowledge that back in 1932, the *Institute for Advanced Studies* had offered Einstein and others salaries in the order of $15,000?[71] Most likely is the fact that Chicago had given him only a two-year contract and could not get outside money to renew it.

In 1940, Rosenberg died while in Istanbul.

Granted that Hans Rosenberg was not one of the exiled professors who was saved for us by the Turks. Nevertheless, the documentation that was made available of the processes involved to save him serves as a counterpoint to the position taken by other prestigious American universities. It also shows that even the University of Chicago was not ready to use "hard monies" from its own endowment and/or tuition income to recruit these high-value assets from the unfortunate and dire circumstances which they found themselves in. The correspondence leaves no doubt that Chicago wanted Rosenberg because it *needed* him to fill a specific void. Chicago had made a trade-off between "an eminent man but the requirements for the laboratory space and expenses [needed] make it inadvisable for us to consider him. Dr. Rosenberg, on the contrary will drop into place where he will find all the requirements for his work ready to hand."[72] "Would your committee consider that same grant of $4,000 for two years for Dr. H. Rosenberg who would be extremely useful to us?"[73]

Chicago apparently did not want to assume any overhead costs for employing highly qualified German Jewish individuals, no matter how good and needed they may have been. Nor was Chicago ready to be haven to any more. According to a letter of November 21 1933, to Dr. Warren Weaver of the Rockefeller foundation, "should we be able to invite Dr. Rosenberg, he would be our fifth German and possibly all that we should undertake to absorb for the present." This letter also gives us a hint as to why: "We find it very difficult to raise money for such purposes among the Jewish donors of Chicago. They were approached by the New York agencies and contributed rather liberally there and are disinclined to repeat."[74]

The Rosenberg/Chicago scenario was replicated on the east coast as well. It appears that in 1939, through his colleague Harvard Professor Harlow Shapely, another much more eminent astronomer than Rosenberg, E. Finlay Freundlich, was negotiating an academic position at Tufts College (Boston)[75] and simultaneously a "Research Associateship" at the Harvard Observatory (Cambridge). Significantly, there was not even a question or hope of a Harvard academic appointment: Be that as it may, even Tufts was ready to offer only a non-tenure track "lecturer" position on a two-year contract under the condition that the salary money came from elsewhere.

So a package was put together with $800 secured from the Rockefeller Foundation. "The Emergency Committee for Displaced Foreign Scholars has voted to contribute twelve hundred and fifty dollars. *Mr. Henry Morgenthau Senior* of New York City (emphasis added) pledged to contribute six hundred dollars...to permit us to bring to America a distinguished academic exile," states a letter from Tuft's College President, Leonard Carmichael dated February 14 1939.

The letter goes on to say, "I wish that at this time it were possible for me to promise that Tufts College would take over the payment of Professor Freundlich's salary at the conclusion of the [two-year] period mentioned above ... At the moment, I am reluctant to ask the Trustees to make an absolute guarantee of a commitment so far in advance because the income from our total endowment ... is being sharply restricted by current investment rates. If the [Rockefeller] Foundation finds it possible to assist in this matter, however, I can assure you that we shall be extremely grateful." In other words, the hat was still in the hand.

These "negotiations" were cut short by a March 13 1939 letter that Harlow Shapely wrote to Frank Hanson at the Rockefeller Foundation. "Dr. Erwin Finlay Freundlich...has now accepted a chair of mathematics and astronomy in St Andrews University. Again let me thank you for your interest and kindness in making the grant that would have been necessary in order to rescue Dr. Freundlich from Germany and Prague." Like St Andrews, many of America's public universities, UCLA (University of California at Los Angeles) among them, were neither shy to hire Jews nor financially "constrained," e.g., no outside "soft" money, no invitation, and no hiring.

In fairness to all of America's private, and to a much lesser extent, public, universities, a comment by Oswald Veblen made to Hilda Geiringer in a May 4 1939 letter[76] is instructive:

> All American colleges which depend upon income from endowments are suffering from the effects of the falling rate of interest. This is obliging them to curtail their expenses in all directions, and of course makes it hard for them to undertake any new commitments.

## A Bad Decision

Karl Strupp came to Turkey as part of the original 1933 *Notgemeinschaft* contingent but left in 1935 for France. Starting in late 1937, several people pleaded to bring him to USA. Who he was and who spoke for him is best described by the next set of three exhibits.[77] (Fig. 130, 131, 132).

The response to these pleas is shown next (Fig. 133).

Though he ultimately received an appointment at Columbia University, Karl Strupp never did make it to the United States. He died on February 28 1940 in Chattou near Paris.[78]

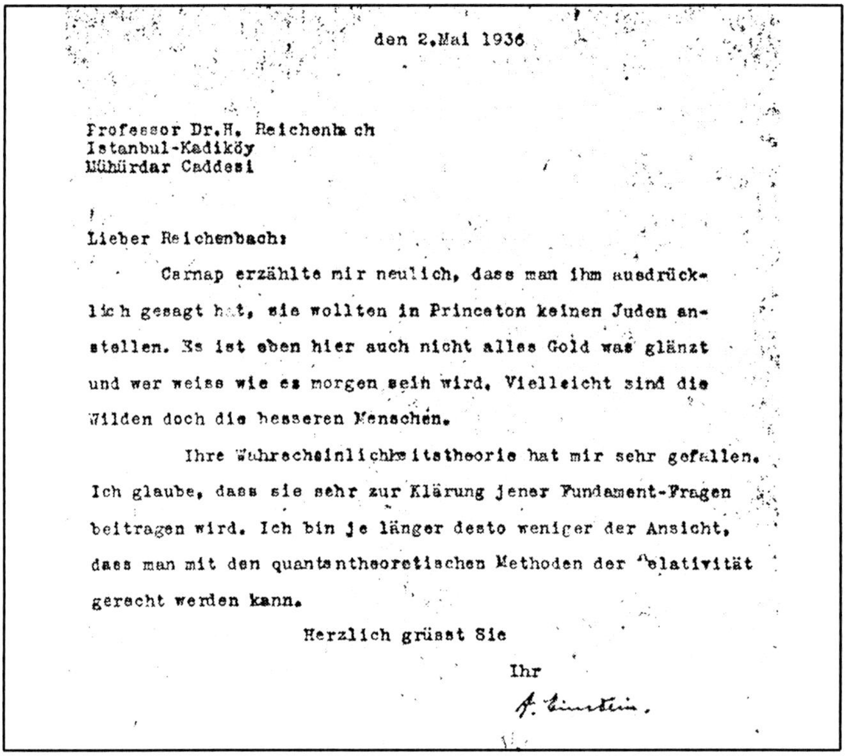

den 2.Mai 1936

Professor Dr.H. Reichenbach
Istanbul-Kadiköy
Mühürdar Caddesi

Lieber Reichenbach:

Carnap erzählte mir neulich, dass man ihm ausdrücklich gesagt hat, sie wollten in Princeton keinen Juden anstellen. Es ist eben hier auch nicht alles Gold was glänzt und wer weiss wie es morgen sein wird. Vielleicht sind die Wilden doch die besseren Menschen.

Ihre Wahrscheinlichkeitstheorie hat mir sehr gefallen. Ich glaube, dass sie sehr zur Klärung jener Fundament-Fragen beitragen wird. Ich bin je länger desto weniger der Ansicht, dass man mit den quantentheoretischen Methoden der Relativität gerecht werden kann.

Herzlich grüsst Sie

Ihr

A. Einstein.

*Figure 118*
Einstein letter to Reichenbach about anti-Semitic hiring practices at Princeton University, May 2 1936.

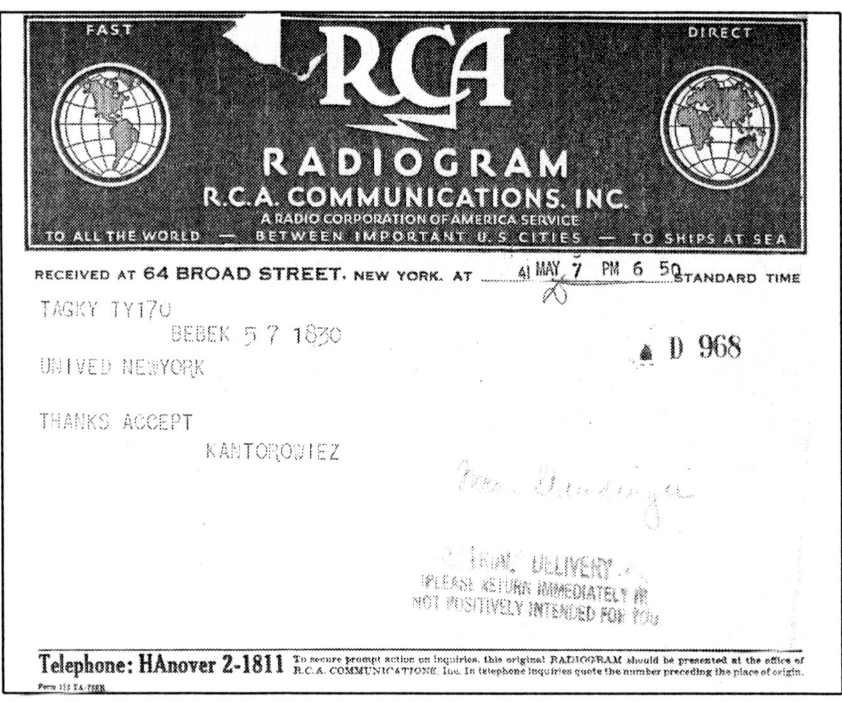

FAST DIRECT

RCA

RADIOGRAM

R.C.A. COMMUNICATIONS, INC.

A RADIO CORPORATION OF AMERICA SERVICE

TO ALL THE WORLD — BETWEEN IMPORTANT U.S. CITIES — TO SHIPS AT SEA

RECEIVED AT 64 BROAD STREET, NEW YORK, AT 41 MAY 7 PM 6 50 STANDARD TIME

TAGKY TY170

BEBEK 5 7 1830

D 968

UNIVED NEWYORK

THANKS ACCEPT

KANTOROWIEZ

DELIVERY

PLEASE RETURN IMMEDIATELY IF NOT POSITIVELY INTENDED FOR YOU

Telephone: HAnover 2-1811 To secure prompt action on inquiries, this original RADIOGRAM should be presented at the office of R.C.A. COMMUNICATIONS, Inc. In telephone inquiries quote the number preceding the place of origin.

*Figure 119*

Kantorowicz announces acceptance of position offered

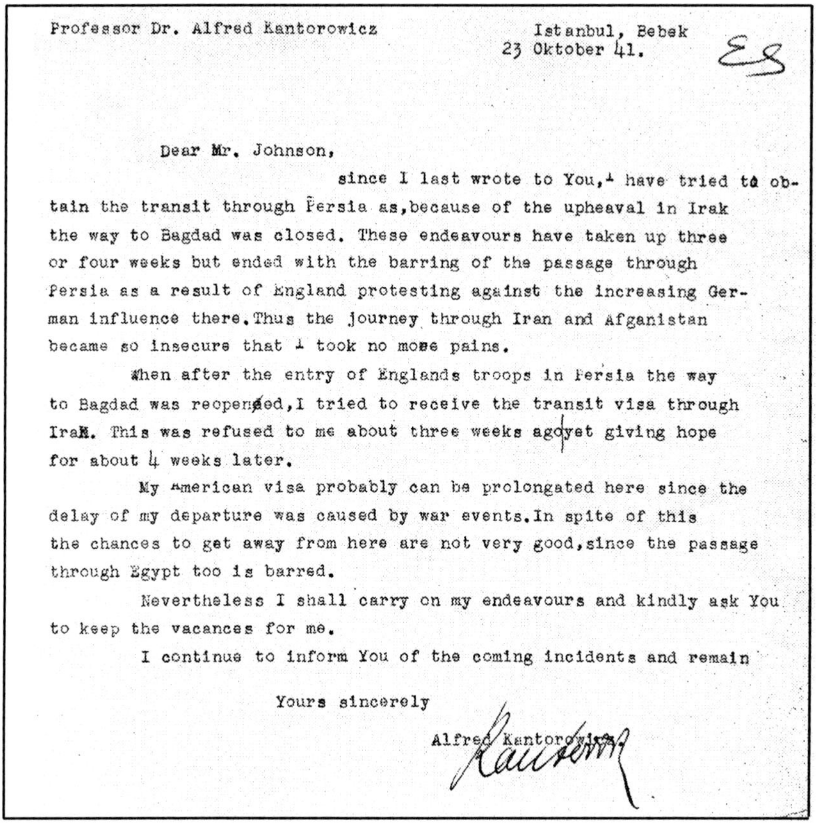

Professor Dr. Alfred Kantorowicz

Istanbul, Bebek
23 Oktober 41.

Dear Mr. Johnson,

since I last wrote to You, I have tried to obtain the transit through Persia as, because of the upheaval in Irak the way to Bagdad was closed. These endeavours have taken up three or four weeks but ended with the barring of the passage through Persia as a result of England protesting against the increasing German influence there. Thus the journey through Iran and Afganistan became so insecure that I took no more pains.

When after the entry of Englands troops in Persia the way to Bagdad was reopened, I tried to receive the transit visa through Irak. This was refused to me about three weeks ago, yet giving hope for about 4 weeks later.

My American visa probably can be prolongated here since the delay of my departure was caused by war events. In spite of this the chances to get away from here are not very good, since the passage through Egypt too is barred.

Nevertheless I shall carry on my endeavours and kindly ask You to keep the vacances for me.

I continue to inform You of the coming incidents and remain

Yours sincerely

Alfred Kantorowicz

*Figure 120*
Kantorowicz's letter of 23 October, 1941

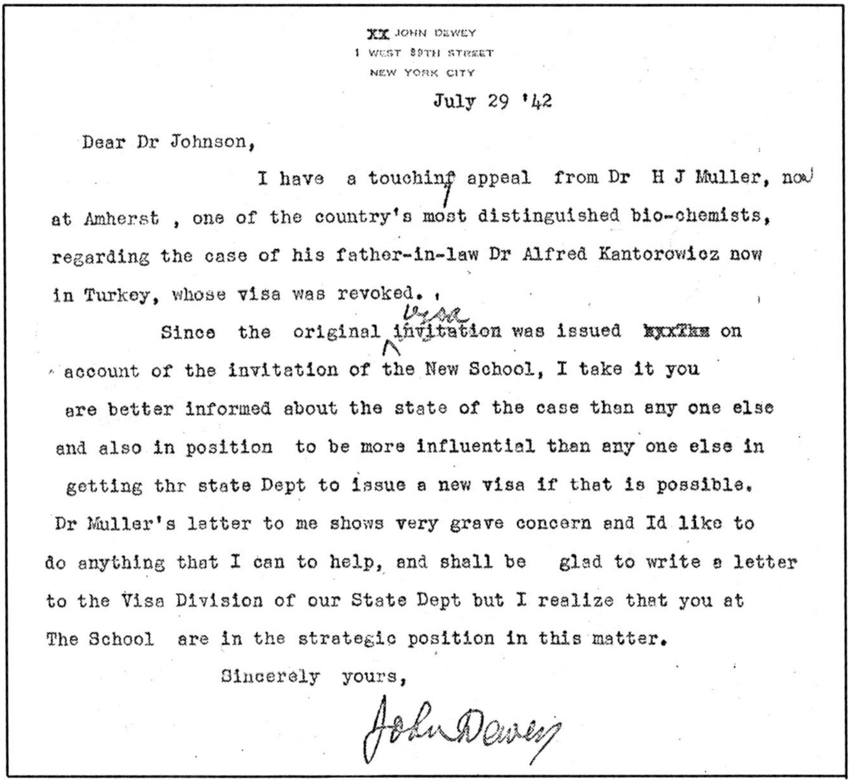

XX JOHN DEWEY
1 WEST 89TH STREET
NEW YORK CITY

July 29 '42

Dear Dr Johnson,

I have a touching appeal from Dr H J Muller, now at Amherst , one of the country's most distinguished bio-chemists, regarding the case of his father-in-law Dr Alfred Kantorowicz now in Turkey, whose visa was revoked.

Since the original visa invitation was issued on account of the invitation of the New School, I take it you are better informed about the state of the case than any one else and also in position to be more influential than any one else in getting thr state Dept to issue a new visa if that is possible. Dr Muller's letter to me shows very grave concern and Id like to do anything that I can to help, and shall be glad to write a letter to the Visa Division of our State Dept but I realize that you at The School are in the strategic position in this matter.

Sincerely yours,

John Dewey

*Figure 121*
John Dewey's letter of support for Kantorowicz.

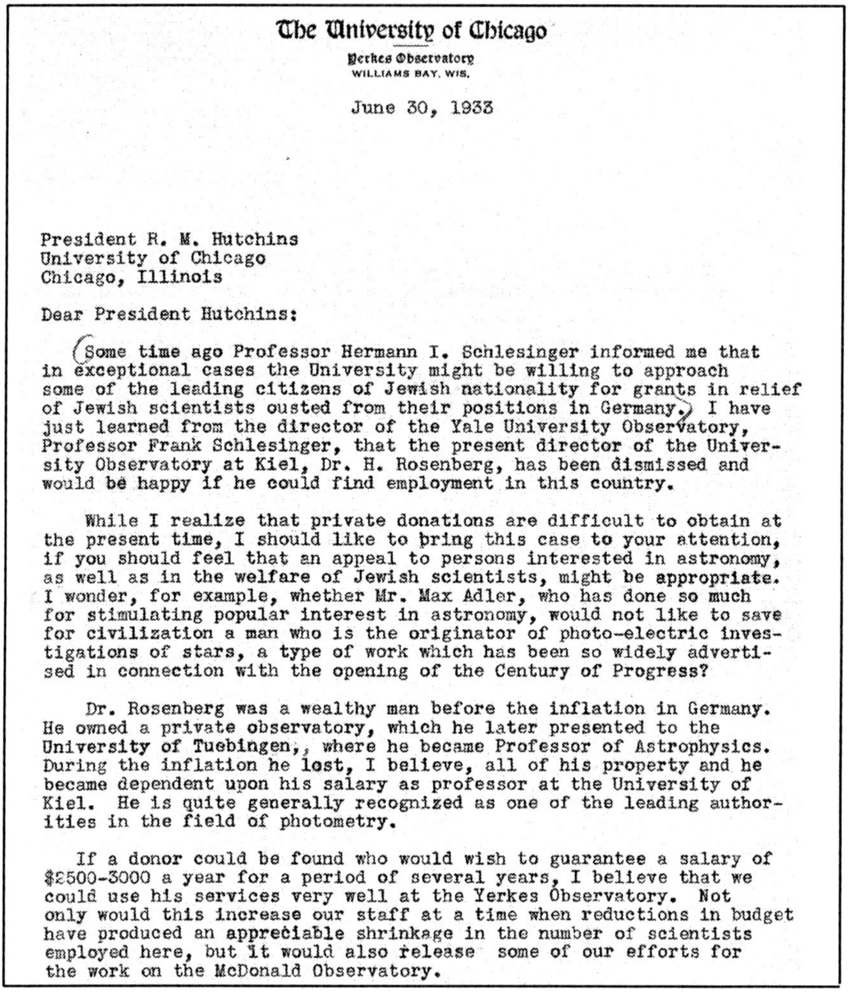

The University of Chicago
Yerkes Observatory
WILLIAMS BAY, WIS.

June 30, 1933

President R. M. Hutchins
University of Chicago
Chicago, Illinois

Dear President Hutchins:

Some time ago Professor Hermann I. Schlesinger informed me that in exceptional cases the University might be willing to approach some of the leading citizens of Jewish nationality for grants in relief of Jewish scientists ousted from their positions in Germany. I have just learned from the director of the Yale University Observatory, Professor Frank Schlesinger, that the present director of the University Observatory at Kiel, Dr. H. Rosenberg, has been dismissed and would be happy if he could find employment in this country.

While I realize that private donations are difficult to obtain at the present time, I should like to bring this case to your attention, if you should feel that an appeal to persons interested in astronomy, as well as in the welfare of Jewish scientists, might be appropriate. I wonder, for example, whether Mr. Max Adler, who has done so much for stimulating popular interest in astronomy, would not like to save for civilization a man who is the originator of photo-electric investigations of stars, a type of work which has been so widely advertised in connection with the opening of the Century of Progress?

Dr. Rosenberg was a wealthy man before the inflation in Germany. He owned a private observatory, which he later presented to the University of Tuebingen, where he became Professor of Astrophysics. During the inflation he lost, I believe, all of his property and he became dependent upon his salary as professor at the University of Kiel. He is quite generally recognized as one of the leading authorities in the field of photometry.

If a donor could be found who would wish to guarantee a salary of $2500-3000 a year for a period of several years, I believe that we could use his services very well at the Yerkes Observatory. Not only would this increase our staff at a time when reductions in budget have produced an appreciable shrinkage in the number of scientists employed here, but it would also release some of our efforts for the work on the McDonald Observatory.

*Figure 122*
Letter to University of Chicago President in support of astronomer Hans Rosenberg.

(2)

President R. M. Hutchins.

Dr. Rosenberg is about 54 years of age. I am of the impression that he is not married, but this may be erroneous as I have met him only once at his observatory in Kiel.

Very truly yours,

Otto Struve

OS:GE

Otto Struve, Director

*Figure 123*
Letter continued.

THE UNIVERSITY OF CHICAGO

DATE July 12, 1933

TO Mr. Hutchins DEPARTMENT

FROM Mr. Stifler DEPARTMENT

IN RE: Dr. H. Rosenberg

I saw Mr. Frank Sulzberger today about the case of Dr. Rosenberg, the Jewish director of the Observatory at Kiel. Mr. Sulzberger guarantees $1,000 of the salary suggested by Dr. Struve ($2,500-3,000). He further says that he will consult Mr. Max Adler and others and cooperate with us in securing the full amount. He was very cordial. I am sending him, at his request, all the data in our possession about Dr. Rosenberg.

cc to Mr. H. H. Swift
Mr. Otto Struve

*Figure 124*
Memo to President Hutchins regarding H. Rosenberg's salary subvention.

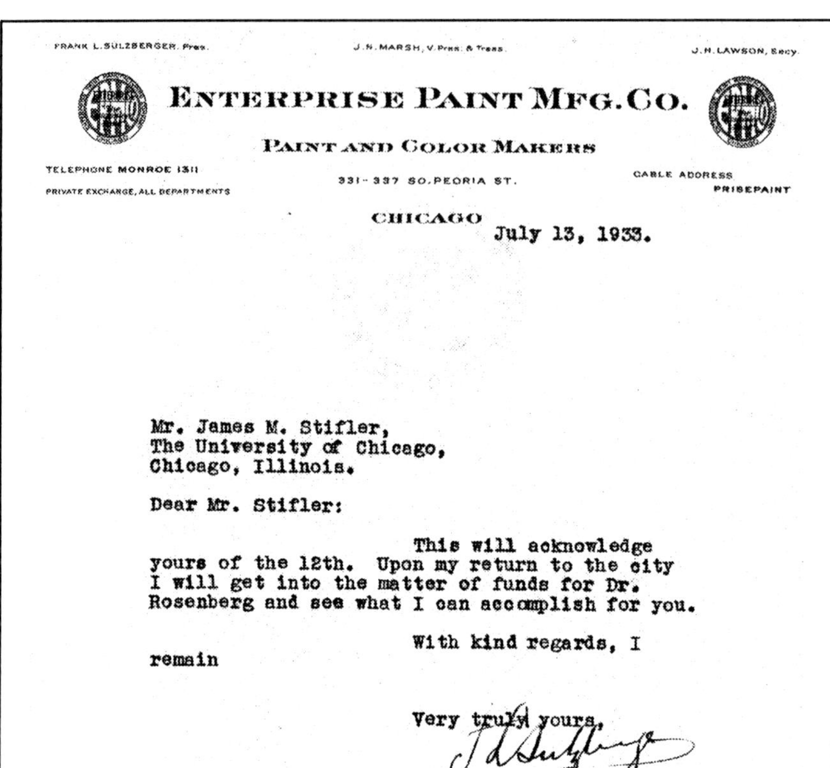

FRANK L. SULZBERGER, Pres. J. S. MARSH, V. Pres. & Treas. J. H. LAWSON, Secy.

ENTERPRISE PAINT MFG. CO.

PAINT AND COLOR MAKERS

TELEPHONE MONROE 1311
PRIVATE EXCHANGE, ALL DEPARTMENTS

331-337 SO. PEORIA ST.

CABLE ADDRESS
PRISEPAINT

CHICAGO

July 13, 1933.

Mr. James M. Stifler,
The University of Chicago,
Chicago, Illinois.

Dear Mr. Stifler:

This will acknowledge yours of the 12th. Upon my return to the city I will get into the matter of funds for Dr. Rosenberg and see what I can accomplish for you.

With kind regards, I remain

Very truly yours,

FLS:IC

*Figure 125*
Salary subvention from Chicago's Jewish community.

Lo .sville, Ky.,
#1 Realty Biulding,
July 21, 1933.

Dr. Otto Struve, Director
Yerkes Observatory,
Williams Bay, Wis.

Dear Dr. Struve:

Since the receipt of your letter of the 13th in reference to Dr. Rosenberg of Kiel I am glad to inform you that I have gotten in touch with several responsible Jewish Leaders. Only today I learned from Dr. Morris Flexner, a nephew of Dr. Abraham Flexner, who is also a nephew of Dr. Simon Flexner, who has been connected with the Rockefeller Foundation, informed me that his Uncle, Dr. Abraham Flexner, told him that the Rockefeller Foundation will pay one-half the salary of any eminent scientist who may be a victim of the Hitler Regime and who will be accepted by a responsible American University. I am also informed that if you or Dr. Hutchins would write to Dr. Max Mason who is now at the head of the Rockefeller Foundation that that could be arranged.

From the correspondence you sent me I note that Mr. Frank Sulzberger guarantees $1000.00 of the salary which would mean that together with the guarantee of the Rockefeller Foundation would make a total of $2250.00 which would leave only the small amount of $250.00 to be raised. I have no doubt whatever that some Jewish Citizen in Chicago will gladly make up that difference. If you are not able to find such a person let me know and I have some contacts in Chicago, from whom I believe the remaining $250.00 could be raised.

I have written letters to other responsible places and if I hear more information that will be helpful in the case of Dr. Rosenberg I will gladly communicate with you.

With kindest regards to you and Mrs. Struve and in the hope of hearing favorable reports that Mr. Rosenberg can be brought to America, and expressing my joy in the possibility of his connection with the University of Chicago, my own Alma Mater, I beg to remain

Very sincerely yours,

Charles Strull

#1 Realty Bldg.

Louisville, Ky.

*Figure 126*
Salary subvention from Chicago's Jewish alumnae

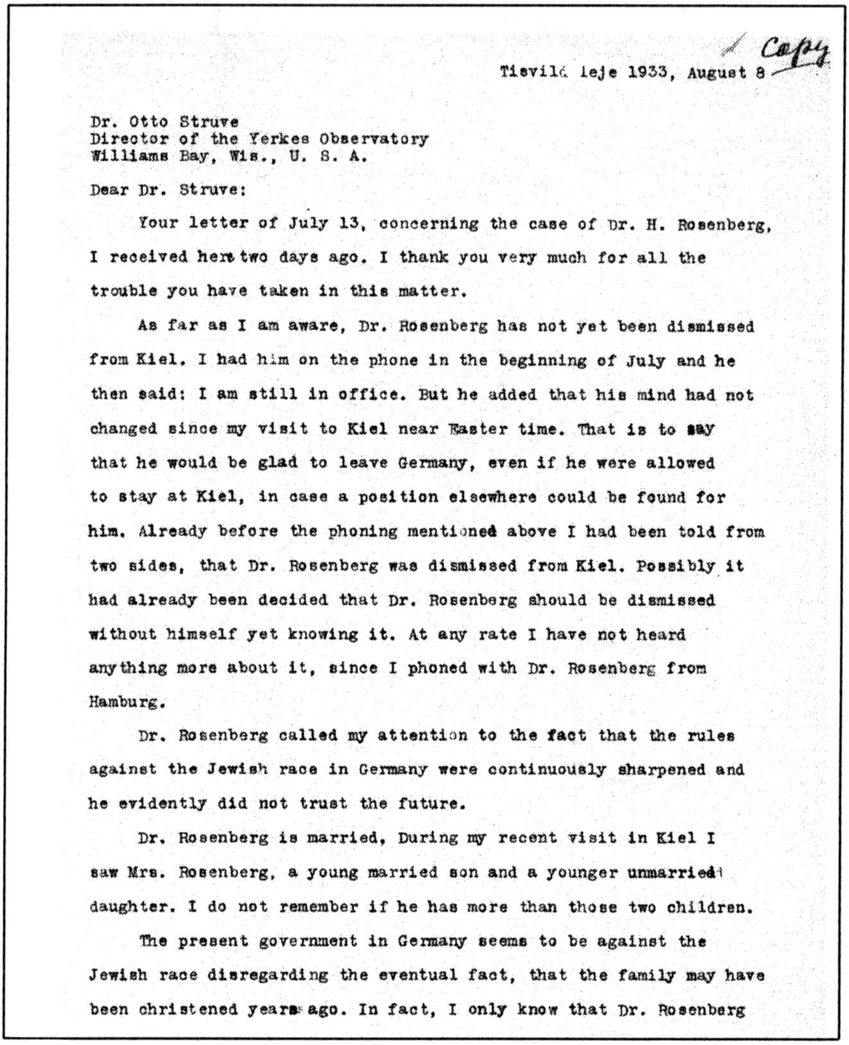

Copy

Tisvilde leje 1933, August 8

Dr. Otto Struve
Director of the Yerkes Observatory
Williams Bay, Wis., U. S. A.

Dear Dr. Struve:

Your letter of July 13, concerning the case of Dr. H. Rosenberg, I received here two days ago. I thank you very much for all the trouble you have taken in this matter.

As far as I am aware, Dr. Rosenberg has not yet been dismissed from Kiel. I had him on the phone in the beginning of July and he then said: I am still in office. But he added that his mind had not changed since my visit to Kiel near Easter time. That is to say that he would be glad to leave Germany, even if he were allowed to stay at Kiel, in case a position elsewhere could be found for him. Already before the phoning mentioned above I had been told from two sides, that Dr. Rosenberg was dismissed from Kiel. Possibly it had already been decided that Dr. Rosenberg should be dismissed without himself yet knowing it. At any rate I have not heard anything more about it, since I phoned with Dr. Rosenberg from Hamburg.

Dr. Rosenberg called my attention to the fact that the rules against the Jewish race in Germany were continuously sharpened and he evidently did not trust the future.

Dr. Rosenberg is married. During my recent visit in Kiel I saw Mrs. Rosenberg, a young married son and a younger unmarried daughter. I do not remember if he has more than those two children.

The present government in Germany seems to be against the Jewish race disregarding the eventual fact, that the family may have been christened years ago. In fact, I only know that Dr. Rosenberg

*Figure 127*
Third party's go between Rosenberg in Germany and the University of Chicago.

-2-

is considered as being of Jewish race. If he is also of Jewish religion I do not know and have never been interested to know. But this point is probably of no importance as the aim is to help a man, who is or may be dismissed for other reasons than inability.

I expect to be back in Leiden on August 21, but I am avoiding Germany on my way from Denmark to Holland. I shall try to get in touch with Dr. Rosenberg from Leiden, but I have to be very careful in doing so.

Very sincerely yours,

Ejnar Hertzsprung

*Figure 128*
Letter continued

The University of Chicago
Yerkes Observatory
WILLIAMS BAY, WIS.

August 21, 1933

My dear Mr. Stifler:

I am enclosing a copy of a letter which I have just received from Professor Ejnar Hertzsprung, assistant director of the Leiden Observatory, Holland. I would suggest that we cable Dr. Hertzsrung as soon as we have something definite to offer.

Very truly yours,
Otto Struve
Otto Struve, Director

OS:GB
Mr. James M. Stifler
Committee on Development
University
Chicago, Illinois

*Figure 129*
Struve's cover letter to UC's Development Committee regarding Rosenberg.

GREEK ROYAL LEGATION

17, Rue Auguste Vacquerie,
Paris.

Tel: Passy 38-65.

27th November 1937.

My dear colleague,

I thank you for your letter of the 22nd November.

You embarass me considerably by asking me for a general criticism of your scientific work, for I cannot compress into a few lines all the good I think of it.

But as I have to be short, I will say that during the very many years, during which I have followed your remarkable scientific activity with the full attention which it can command, I have constantly admired your method and erudition and the spirit of your work. Not a single instance can I recall where there have been noticeable gaps of knowledge or signs of insufficient impartiality. I have always taken the liveliest interest in your writings, and I have drawn therefrom very often considerable advantage. I therefore have much pleasure in availing myself of this opportunity to re-affirm that you are among the contemporary scientists who have best served the cause of International Law.

Yours very sincerely,

(signed) POLITIS.

Greek Ambassador to France, former Greek Foreign Secretary
President of the Institut de Droit International,
President of the Board of The Hague Academy of International Public Laws, etc.

Professor Karl Strupp.

*Figure 130*
Letter of support for Karl Strupp from the Greek Ambassador to France.

L. S. ROWE
DIRECTOR GENERAL

PEDRO DE ALBA
ASSISTANT DIRECTOR

German Jurist

THE PAN AMERICAN UNION IS THE INTERNATIONAL ORGANIZATION MAINTAINED BY THE TWENTY-ONE AMERICAN REPUBLICS FOR THE DEVELOPMENT OF GOOD UNDERSTANDING, FRIENDLY INTERCOURSE, COMMERCE AND PEACE AMONG THEM; CONTROLLED BY A GOVERNING BOARD COMPOSED OF THE SECRETARY OF STATE OF THE UNITED STATES AND THE DIPLOMATIC REPRESENTATIVES IN WASHINGTON OF THE OTHER REPUBLICS; ADMINISTERED BY A DIRECTOR GENERAL AND ASSISTANT DIRECTOR, CHOSEN BY THIS BOARD AND ASSISTED BY A STAFF OF INTERNATIONAL EXPERTS, STATISTICIANS, EDITORS, COMPILERS, TRANSLATORS AND LIBRARIANS.

PAN AMERICAN UNION

WASHINGTON, D. C., U. S. A.

ARGENTINA, BOLIVIA, BRAZIL, CHILE, COLOMBIA, COSTA RICA, CUBA, DOMINICAN REPUBLIC, ECUADOR, EL SALVADOR, GUATEMALA, HAITI, HONDURAS, MEXICO, NICARAGUA, PANAMA, PARAGUAY, PERU, UNITED STATES, URUGUAY, VENEZUELA

April 24, 1939.

My dear Dr. Johnson:

I am writing to you with reference to Dr. Karl Strupp, one of the most eminent of German jurists who has made important contributions in the field of international law.

Dr. Strupp because of the anti-semitic legislation was deprived of his professorship at the University of Frankfort and is now living in Paris where he has been giving some lectures before the Law Faculty. He is thoroughly conversant with the English language, and I am writing to ask whether there would be any possibility of securing a professorship for him.

Thanking you in advance for consideration of the matter, I am,

Very sincerely yours,

L. S. Rowe
Director General

Dr. Alvin S. Johnson,
Yale University,
New Haven,
Connecticut.

*Figure 131*
Letter of support for Karl Strupp from the Director General of the Pan American Health Union.

TIME & LIFE BUILDING
ROCKEFELLER CENTER
NEW YORK

EDITORIAL OFFICES

October 13
1939

Dr. Alvin Johnson, Director
The New School for Social Research
66 West 12th Street
New York City

Dear Dr. Johnson:

I am writing to inquire whether you know of any opening in the New School or elsewhere for Dr. Karl Strupp a noted German authority on international law and author of several well-known collections. He is a refugee from Germany who had a temporary permit to live in Copenhagen, but now has been obliged to go to France where I understand he has been interned in some camp. He is virtually destitute and is very eager to get a teaching job.

Is it true that if an opening can be found for him here, Foundation funds will be available for his support? If you happen to know of any place I wish you would let me know.

Sincerely yours,

Raymond L Buell

Raymond Leslie Buell
Round Table Editor

*Figure 132*
Letter of support for Karl Strupp from *Fortune Magazine.*

October 16, 1939

Dear Mr. Buell:

I have your letter of October 13th. I regret to say that I do not know of any opening for Dr. Karl Strupp.

The general rule is that if some educational institution is willing to take an exiled scholar, with the expectation of retaining him permanently on its faculty, the Emergency Committee and the Rockefeller Foundation will supply funds for the first year and part of the second year. The catch here is that the institution that takes such a scholar assumes responsibility for him for the rest of his academic life. Most institutions now are very wary of assuming such obligations.

Sincerely,

Alvin Johnson

Mr. Raymond Leslie Buell
FORTUNE
Time and Life Building
Rockefeller Center
New York, N. Y.

*Figure 133*
Letter regarding "no jobs" for Karl Strupp.

# 12
# Correspondence[1]

One way—and perhaps the best—to tell the story of a people in distress is to read and quote preserved correspondence. Our émigrés were fortunate in this regard—their precious and rare words were often treasured by those who received them. Some left us their memoirs. Only a few remain who can provide oral histories. Surprisingly, we are fortunate enough to have available third-party accounts, archives, and, most importantly, memories. Some of the émigrés were conduits for the correspondence of others abroad. Others who were young at the time of these events but old enough to recall their experiences, good and bad, have offered their reminiscences. These essays appear in the chapter that follows. First, some of the actual correspondence that took place across physical continents and the more difficult to straddle, manmade barriers.

## Conduits for Communication

The émigré professors were themselves communication links between colleagues and relatives left behind in German-occupied lands and those in the free countries. Library scientist *Dr. Walter Gottschalk* remained in Belgium until early 1941 before escaping to Turkey. Prior to 1941, Albert Einstein used Gottschalk to funnel money to his relatives in Nazi Germany. In a letter dated January 18 1940, Einstein thanks Gottschalk for his December 27 letter acknowledging that $20 was forwarded to his cousin, Frau *Suzanne Koch*. Next, Einstein requests that an equivalent amount be delivered to Miss Lina Einstein whose address is given only as "Ulm a. Donau, Herbruckerstr." Presumably, that was sufficient.

Einstein goes on to say, "I am committed to regularly supporting my sister-in-law and her husband (Mr. and Mrs. *Ludwig Gumbertz* in Berlin). I have been supporting these people via a similar arrangement I have with you. This arrangement runs through June. Under present circumstances,

I consider it too dangerous to hand over money to these people ahead of time. If you could hold your money back until then, I would like very much to make the payments the way you have suggested starting July 1. The payments will be $20 monthly."[2]

Such arrangements were possible until Belgium surrendered to the Nazis on May 28 1940. In the months leading up to being invaded, Belgium was considered a neutral country. Money could flow through it.

Earlier correspondence shows that Dr. Prof. *Carl Oppenheimer* and his editorial office were long situated in Berlin. He moved to Holland in 1939 to escape the Nazis, or so he thought. The Germans entered Holland on May 10 1940. Less than three months later, writing on *Enzymologia* letterhead, Dr. Prof. Carl Oppenheimer, that Journal's editor in The Hague, Holland,[3] wrote to Felix Haurowitz on August 2 1940 about matters involving an upcoming Haurowitz publication in the journal. At the end, he stated, "I ask you to write to my son *Hans (Hannan) Oppenheimer* at the *Agricultural Research Station* in Rehovot, Palestine, and tell him that we are fine." On September 2 1940, Oppenheimer thanks Haurowitz for writing to his son and indicates "hopes that he will soon get an answer." He then asks that Haurowitz "write to his son again and tell him that his parents are doing fine."

In a December 22 1940 letter showing a Zeist (U) Wilhelminalaan 35, return address, Prof. Carl Oppenheimer relates:

> Lieber Herr [Dear Mr.] Haurowitz,
>
> We are doing fine health-wise and our rooms are warm enough, good Dutch landlord takes good care of us at the Pension [boarding house] and is very friendly. You are lucky you don't have to be involved in the war. I am worried about the future. We must bear our troubles and destiny with calm and nobility. Money troubles disrupted the publishing house because of the war.
>
> Please write to my son. I have not heard from him. Please tell him at this holiday time, I think of him often. Received indirect news of younger son—but not for a while.
>
> You wrote about a teaching position in Turkey. Is it still open? I am now ready to consider it. How much pay? What are the conditions? Please help....

On *April 14 1941*, Haurowitz transmits the message to Oppenheimer that his son Hannan in Palestine had not heard from his younger brother for over six months. On December 25 of the same year, *Frau H. Oppenheimer* informs Haurowitz of *her husband's death* and thanks him for all his help. In a letter dated January 12 1942, Haurowitz informs Dr. Hannan

Oppenheimer, in Rehovot, Palestine, that his father, a dear colleague, has passed away in Utrecht, Holland. Haurowitz concludes his letter with "finally there was a letter, intended for you and your brother, I am enclosing it to this letter, hoping that the censor will let it pass as *it is the last message from a father to his children*."

Another letter to Oppenheimer in Palestine, dated *April 25 1942*, says, "I am very sorry that I have to give you sad news again. ...In the meantime, your mother wrote me... *I fear, a last letter from her*. She asks me to tell to you and your brother that she will find the peace she expects. All will be over, when I get her letter." Her death is confirmed by a third party in Holland. The information is transmitted in a June 30 1942 letter.

On July 28, Winston Churchill and Franklin D. Roosevelt agreed to open up a second front in Europe. About one month later, on June 30, the Nazis finished overtaking the Crimean peninsula by capturing Sevastopol, a Russian naval seaport across the Black sea from Turkey. This move brought them within a single night's sea journey to Istanbul and half that to Turkey's northern provinces. Germany's allies, Romania and Bulgaria, provided additional departure points for any and all hostile potentialities.

Barely eight days earlier, the Nazi leaders had quietly met in Berlin with Reinhard Heydrich, "the hangman of Europe," in charge to discuss the fate of Jews in Germany and the occupied territories, or the "final solution."

During this most difficult period, at least one of the émigré professors intervened successfully on behalf of Jews left behind in occupied lands. According to the memoirs of the American Ambassador to Ankara, Laurence Steinhardt, his counterpart, German ambassador Franz von Pappen wrote:[4] "I learned through one of the German émigré professors that the Secretary of the Jewish Agency had asked for me to intervene in the matter of the threatened deportation to camps in Poland of 10,000 Jews living in Southern France. Most of them were former Turkish citizens of Levantine origin. I promised my help and discussed the matter with M. Menemencioglu."

The German émigré professor that von Pappen was referring to was none other than his children's pediatrician, *Albert Eckstein*. And *Numan Rifat Menemencioglu* was Turkey's sitting Minister of Foreign Affairs. A career diplomat, he was the grandson of Turkish patriot Namik Kemal, poet and man of letters, advocate of freedom, opponent of the Ottoman Sultan Abdülhamit. Kemal's writings and ideas greatly influenced the intellectuals of the time, including Atatürk. Namik Kemal died in Cyprus while exiled and imprisoned by Sultan Abdülhamit. With this kind of heritage, Menemencioglu was a man to be reckoned with. Ambassador von Pappen continued "There was no legal basis to warrant any official action on his part, but he authorized me to inform Hitler that the deportation of these former Turkish citizens would cause a sensation in Turkey and endanger friendly relations between the two countries. This demarche succeeded in quashing the whole affair."[5]

### Efforts Had Been Made Since 1933

While still at an address in Le Coq-sur-mer bei Ostende, Villa Savoyarde (Belgium), on March 25 1933, Albert Einstein wrote to mathematician Frl. [Miss] Dr. Hilda Geiringer. By then, Einstein had a job offered as the first, or at least one of the first two, academic appointees to the newly formed Institute for Higher Studies in Princeton, funded by Jewish money. Writing to his colleague in German, Einstein said:

> I am formulating a plan to try to establish a university for refugees, i.e., exiled German Jewish docents and students. You have already seen this idea in my letter to Mr. Heller. This plan would only work if sufficient numbers of prominent educators are willing to try to make this idea a reality. Since I am estranged from Germany, it would be difficult for me to make contact with the appropriate people. Would you and Herr [Richard von] Mises be interested in this proposition? If so, you have the opportunity to make contact with the appropriate people so that a prognosis for this plan could be made.
>
> The location of such an endeavor would in my opinion be best near an English [sic] University. I know plans are being made to find work for Jewish professors at universities outside of Germany, but I am afraid that younger docents and students would be victimized by this plan. It seems to me, that only through the above mentioned plan, that the treasure of culture and development possibilities which German Jews possess, could possibly be saved. If you find people who can seriously consider this idea, and would be good to look me up and meet with me. Though I myself don't have organizational abilities but I could, with my influence and connections facilitate bringing this project to fruition, especially the financing of it. Please discuss this plan only with trusted individuals and let me know frankly what you and those close to you think of this plan.[6]

Interestingly, as early as March 1933, concerned about directly contacting Hilda Geiringer with this information since she was still in Germany and under the Nazis, Einstein had sent this letter to a Vienna address. The go-between was Dr. Ernst Geiringer, Hilda's brother, who on a commercial letterhead as is shown below, replied to Einstein on May 2 1933 that the letter had arrived and that he had "carefully sent it to her. When I receive a reply from her, I will take the responsibility of sending it on to you. I would appreciate it if you would send all subsequent correspondence also to this address and not to Berlin."[7] (Fig. 134).

Drafted in Paris on October 16 1933, the "Memorandum[8] of Professor L. W. Jones" [(LWJ), Chief of the Rockefeller Foundation's European office], Re: Conversation with Professor P. H. Schwarz, Secretary of the *Notgemenschaft der Deutscher Wissenschaftler im Ausland,* Zurich, Switzerland," states, "Professor P. H. Schwarz came by appointment to Paris for a conference with LWJ and discussed the recent letter of October 6 1933."[9] :

> Schwarz raised the question [first raised in that letter] concerning the assistance of the RF to obtain the *release of Professor Alfred Kantorowicz now in a concentration camp in Germany,* appointed to Professorship in Istanbul. LWJ informed Schwarz that of the attitude which must be taken by the officers of the RF concerning negotiations of such character and said that the officers in Paris could not approach such a problem.
>
> Prof. Schwarz said that it was the intention of those concerned with the call of professors to Istanbul to select some 20 younger deposed scholars, who might act as assistants to the older group. Among this group of younger scientist are Kallman, Goldstein, and others, names which would probably fall into the second class of deposed scholars, according to our classification. Schwarz asked whether there would be any hope of approaching the RF for some support towards the salaries of a few of these younger men. He said that in the scheme already set up no provision had been made for the call of these younger assistants.
>
> LWJ said that the Paris office had no authority for action on cases of this kind, since the University of Istanbul was only in the initial stage and was not yet organized. LWJ added that the negotiations which the officers of the RF could carry out were expected to be with well-established institutions. LWJ said...that Schwarz could rest assured that some time in the future—no date set—one or more of the officers would find an occasion to visit Istanbul, in order to learn more definitely concerning the organization of the new University and its possible development.[10]

The Memorandum concludes by saying, "Professor Schwarz handed LWJ… a contract signed between the Ministry of Public Instruction with the deposed German scholar, Professor Alfred Kantorowicz, now in a concentration camp in Germany."[11]

The contract was dated October 7 1933 and the record shows that Kantorowicz was extricated from the Camp and with wife, two sons, and two daughters was brought to Istanbul in no small measure due to the efforts of Dr. Philipp Schwarz. Additionally, among other things in the letter mentioned in the memorandum, which, incidentally, was marked CONFIDENTIAL, Schwarz informed Jones "in strict confidence" that he had "been commissioned by the Turkish Minister of Hygiene to cooperate in the appointments for 5 positions in the newly built city hospital in Ankara, as well as 3 positions in the new Research Institute of Hygiene."

Of course, these positions were above and beyond the thirty professorial positions for the University of Istanbul which were mostly assigned by the time of that letter. Moreover, the "younger scientist, Kallman" who Dr. Jones referred to, was never invited to Turkey, but he did survive the war in the most incredulous of ways. According to his son and only child, Klaus, Dr. Hartmut Kallmann and the entire family, including Klaus's Jewish Grandparents and his Aryan mother who would not divorce, stayed in Berlin up to and through the entire war.

The elder Kallmann, who received his Ph.D. in 1921 under Nobel laureate Max Planck, "thought that the Hitler government could not last long. Around 1933, my father had just begun promising research to develop the field of neutron photography (his idea) which he did not want to interrupt. He also did not want to leave his two aged parents behind. These were some of the reasons why he accepted a contract with IG Farben [a major chemical enterprise in Germany] to continue this research.… As part of the contract, he had to transfer his patents (about 70) to IG Farben. The contract also stipulated that he had to work primarily in the field of his specialty and that all discoveries and inventions that seemed to have commercial applications, would become property of IG Farben and/or AEG (Allgemeine Elecrisitaets Gesselshaft) which worked together with IG. Because of the racial laws he could not become a regular employee; a monthly stipendium of (I believe) 750 marks was paid. This money, of course, was generated by the patents that were transferred to IG Farben."[12]

Sure enough, the Rockefeller Foundation sent an emissary to Istanbul during February 1934. The emissary's diary shows that on February 18, Schwarz did not miss the opportunity to once again solicit the Foundation's help in extricating additional scientists left behind.

Writing from his New Jersey home to gynecologist *W. Liepmann* in

Istanbul, Albert Einstein[13] says on November 6 1937, "In today's mail I received the news that Frau *Dr. Lisl Katzenstein-Sendlbeck* is in a precarious position. She is a physician and midwife and could be very useful as a nurse. She is also the niece of the preeminent surgeon Moritz Katzenstein. She has received an order to leave the Ukraine. Her sister wrote me this and mentions that you need Help. I beg of you if at all possible to help her get some work. I hear that Frau Katzenstein is a hard working and dependable person. This is best demonstrated by the fact that the most critical and demanding Professor Katzenstein used her as a co-worker for four years. I know you will find a most helpful assistant in her."

Unfortunately, personnel archives of University of Istanbul's medical school show no record for a *Dr. Lisl Katzenstein-Sendlbeck.*

Obviously as a response to a plea for help, Albert Einstein's letter of November 12 1938, to Frau Wanda Gottschalk in Holland says:

> I have turned to the former President of the [Hebrew] University of Jerusalem, Dr. Hugo Bergmann, who is a friend of mine, as I myself have no connection to help your husband. As soon as I hear from him, you will hear from me.

With the four-power conference resulting in the September 30, 1938 "Munich Agreement" giving the Czech Sudetenland to Germany, the handwriting regarding the future of the rest of Czechoslovakia was clearly on the wall. On October 5, German troops marched through Sudetenland. Physiologist Hans Winterstein, who by then was well established in Istanbul, wrote a letter on October 10 1938 to biochemist Felix Haurowitz who, in turn, was well established in Prague. "Are you at all interested in a teaching position in biochemistry at the University of Istanbul? If yes, please send a CV and a list of your publications. This is an unofficial request with no strings attached."

This inquiry was followed by over a dozen negotiation letters spanning a period of almost five months. On January 31 1939, Haurowitz wrote to Winterstein, "Thanks for all your efforts. Of course, I am a bit nervous about initiating anything at this end without official documentation to assure me that I will be permitted to enter Istanbul officially. But I am not that impatient because it is pretty quiet here and as far as I can judge it will remain quiet." However in the very same letter, Haurowitz goes on to say: "It is strange, though, that among my German gentile colleagues, the same denunciation and mean-spirited rage has manifested itself as was evident when the Nazis were victorious in Germany's Vienna and the Sudetenland." But the negotiations continued. In his memoirs,[14] Haurowitz does say:

> [T]he Sudeten part of Czechoslovakia was abandoned to Hitler—Germany. The German University in Prague became an independent University of the German Reich and was expected to continue accepting German students from the Sudeten. I received at that time the offer of the Chair of Biochemistry at the University of Istanbul, Turkey. I hesitated to abandon my laboratory and my student co-workers. However, when I was informed that I was temporarily deprived of my privilege to teach and to examine, I decided finally to visit Istanbul and to see whether I would be able to continue doing research there. Since I found favorable conditions there, I accepted the Turkish offer. A few weeks later [March 5 1939] Hitler's troops invaded Prague. With my wife and two children, we left two weeks after by train for Istanbul. Although most of our property was seized by the Gestapo, we were allowed to take along our furniture and my library.

Once established in Istanbul, Felix Haurowitz tried to bring his then still alive colleague Carl Oppenheimer from Holland, to Turkish safety. Unfortunately, the only commitment Haurowitz could squeeze out of the university administration was for a one-year contract. This offer was extended to Oppenheimer who, in a letter of September 2 1940, declined on the grounds of the shortness of the contract and the hopes that the war will soon be over at which time he would seriously consider the offer. Oppenheimer however recommended, a "Professor Neuberg who is in Jerusalem and who has no family and no work to consider in such a move." He also mentions that the other professors who are still in Germany cannot be contacted and those in the United States would not leave. As for himself, he said he is "66 years old and still can work three more good years and would love to be considered for a more permanent position." Sadly, Carl Oppenheimer did not live through the end of the year that followed.

A letter dated August 5 1940 from St Andrews University speaks for itself:

> Dear Mr. Einstein,
>
> I am delighted in taking this opportunity to write you. I hope that after a long hiatus we can find a common bond between us. I have been for one year at the old Scottish University of St Andrews and I have erected a third observatory here.
>
> The building is just about to be finished. I hope that I finally can rest in the home of my mother and work here again. Last summer I spent several months in America and on several occasions I was a guest of Mr. Morgenthau; regrettably I wasn't able to visit

with you. I only heard from Philip Frank, whom I met in Harvard that you are doing well.

Now let's talk about the reason for this letter.

I was informed by a (female) friend at Harvard that Dr. Herbert Levy and his wife (who are currently still in Berlin) that there is a certain hope, to rescue Dr. Levy out of the Hell of Berlin. And, if I was informed correctly, your help was enlisted in supporting this distant relative of your former son-in-law.

I have promised my acquaintance here, to write to you and ask you as a personal favor to try everything possible to get Dr. Levy out of Germany. I would be very thankful, if you could provide a few words to let me know, how far this endeavor has progressed.

I hope to receive good news in this matter from you.

Sincerely,

E. F. Freundlich

### Attempts Had Been Made to Seek Outside Protection

On February 25 1934, barely six months after his arrival in Istanbul, astronomy professor Finlay Freundlich,[15] on his own initiative, contacted Sir Herbert Samuel, a London attorney, on behalf of "the 30 or so professors from various disciplines, mostly German Jews or half Jews who were invited by the government of Turkey to reform the university in Istanbul." In the rest of the two-page letter, he told the barrister in German all the good things the professors are doing for Turkey and then requested that Sir Samuel petition His Majesty's government to provide outside protection to this group of individuals and their families:

> We are rebuilding a modern university. After the denunciations I have suffered [in Potsdam, Germany] it was not hard to choose this beautiful city. We have however no protection from the German consulate here, because they are part of the rightlessness for Jews. Would it be possible to protect those professors who like it under the care of the British consulate? It is possible that the Turkish government would try to take advantage of our situation of statelessness.
>
> The question arises whether we could acquire English statehood [sic]. For me, I am half-English. I have a brother and two sisters living in England.

Unfortunately, the Home Office was not too forthcoming (Fig. 135). Britain was not about to offer protection to Freundlich and his colleagues in Istanbul.

## Interpersonal Communication

By mid-September 1936, totally frustrated with Turkish bureaucracy's throwing stumbling blocks in his efforts to procure a telescope and design and build the observatory, Freundlich decided to leave Turkey and restart the very same process in Prague. Following is his note of resignation from, of all things, the *Chamber Music Club*, organized and run by the German expatriate community in Istanbul:

> Istanbul, September 27, 1936
>
> Dear Dr. Ritter,
>
> Since I decided, several weeks ago, to leave the University of Istanbul, I think the Chamber Music Club should not count on me any more as a member. I wish therefore that you elect another member who would enjoy the meetings as much as I did. This Kuratorium [respite place] was one of my special pleasures. I wish the society the best and a long existence.
>
> With true Greetings,
> E. F. Freundlich

Before the war's end, Dr. Finlay Freundlich found his way to Scotland as guest professor of Astronomy at the University of St Andrews. Writing from St Andrews on August 5 1940, Freundlich tells Albert Einstein "It was good to hear from you again, in the two months since your last letter some of our common fears and only a few of our common hopes have come to pass." Among other things, Freundlich was referring to the fact that, after having already occupied the Channel Islands of Guernsey, Jersey, Big and Little Sark, all a part of the United Kingdom, Hitler proposed a peace pact with Britain on July 6.

The proposed pact was based on the partition of the world. Since Britain did not bite, on the nineteenth of the same month, Hitler told Britain "if the struggle continues it can only end in annihilation for one of us" and on July 23, the Czech government in exile was established in Britain under the leadership of Dr. Benes. Freundlich goes on: "It's been thirty years since we became acquainted and the theory of relativity was born. The integral summation of these years yields a very irrational proposition. Is the end result of yours and other's efforts necessarily such a world?"[16]

On March 29 1944, Freundlich resumed the correspondence. "Four years have passed since I last heard from you. That was shortly before the fall of France, which you had already foreseen. In the meantime virtually everything has been destroyed that made up our world 25 years ago." On a more hopeful note, Freundlich at St Andrews was "awaiting with longing the end of the war and the possibility of returning to Prague to resume the work begun five years ago of rebuilding the field of astronomy there."[17] Next, his thoughts turned to the problems of astronomy and the remainder of the letter reviewed developments in the study of the rotation of heavenly bodies.

Reversing time a bit, with Poland occupied and Czechoslovakia's Sudetenland in Germany's uncontested control, Felix Haurowitz wrote from Prague on January 22 1939, to his colleague Carl Oppenheimer in Berlin. The letter was mostly about scientific matters of common interest. However, at the very end, almost in passing, he mentioned, "I will have to leave Prague very soon. I will send you my new address as soon as I know what it is."

On November 26 1939, Oppenheimer, who is quite ill in addition to having been displaced to Holland, wrote about his editorial functions at the helm of *Enzymologia* that "it is the only joy in my professional life, since the war has put an end to all my plans and dreams."

And backtracking even further, while still in Istanbul, Freundlich received a number of letters from colleagues and friends left behind.[18] These are mostly in German. On December 29 1935, an Erick Nelson wrote Freundlich from Gudon, Italy:

> Of course you know how dreadfully difficult everything is these days, and it has certainly not improved in the meantime. The news one receives from home are mostly horribly depressing. My brother, who up until recently was doing fine with his practice because he was a combatant in WWI, will probably have to emigrate to America, since the practice has virtually stopped. And there's not the slightest promise of change.

The distinguished British astrophysicist Edward Arthur Milne wrote from Oxford, England, on February 7 1934 to Freundlich in Istanbul:

> I am very sorry that you have had such a painful and difficult year. I was afraid to write my sympathy when you were still in Germany, for fear letters would be opened in the post and possibly harm you. I am glad you found support from Rockefeller[19]—this is true, is it not? ...I do not think it would have been good your

coming to England. Schrödinger[20] is here, and some physicists from Leiptzig, also other literary people, but in no case with hopes of permanent [job] prospects.
P.S. I don't like the look of things in France at all."

On April 20 1936, a Professor Lanczos of Szekesfhervar, Hungary, mentioned hardships, personal illness, and also that of his wife, and of having had an extremely hard winter. No mention is made, however, of life under a government that started its anti-Semitic policies as far back as 1932. He also wrote of the possibility of being given a permanent mathematics position at Istanbul's (American) Robert College, but nothing is certain due to the economic crisis in Turkey. On July 14 1936, he followed up by saying. "Due to the general picture formed after receiving new information from Turkey, I do not believe anymore that the Turkish plan will succeed."

On July 3, 1936, 48-year-old Stefan Lux, a Jewish journalist from Prague, shot himself during a session of the *League of Nations* to protest the treatment of Jews in Germany.

In a letter dated October 8 1935 to a Dr. Hans Alexander on the staff of a Sanatorium in Agra, India, Freundlich wrote:

> Miss Lena Goldfield[21] has been suffering from pulmonary tuberculosis for years now… The climate here in Istanbul has proven to be extremely hazardous to her condition, so that regrettably she has been forced to give up her work here in order to undergo a more extensive course of treatment in a sanatorium. Professor Nissen is currently carrying out a Teilplastik surgery and as soon as she has recuperated she would like to undergo longer treatment, possibly in your sanatorium. Understandably enough, as a Jew she does not want to return to Germany, however well she has been accepted by Rothschild's Hospital in Nordrach up till now.
>
> On November 6 1936, Lena Goldfield wrote to her "loving uncle E., "Naturally I have read about the events in Prague. Kl [appears to be a cousin] was afraid it would happen, of course. And it is regrettable that these louts met with such approval. I read an interesting book about China that was written by an American woman who was raised by a Chinese family and who experienced the Communist government firsthand. When the students in China turned against the regime, a statesman ordered them to be dispersed by the fire department. That would have been a good example for those in Prague! I was overjoyed to hear that yet another Jewish professor was given the Nobel Prize![22]

And, on September 25 1936, she wrote a semi-coded message:

> Then Kl was in Heidelberg briefly, and since he was told when he arrived at Be's villa that no one was there, he went to Hochheim. Be's son is on his honeymoon; he married a German-American that he met during his stay in the US. His father has been very ill. He said to tell you that should you hear nothing further from him again you shouldn't think he has forgotten you. But he has had to be quite careful. He is with the air raid defense commission; the only ministry he has got anything to do with anymore is that of the Reichswehr, and he hopes to still be able to help there for the few years he has left to him, after he was unable to achieve anything in the other matter of business. Snoopery is terrible; a school-friend of Kl's almost lost his job because someone had "heard" that he'd associated with a Jewish family some eight years before!

The archives contain at least seven letters from Dr. Alexander to Freundlich regarding matters of health and accommodation at the Sanatorium.

Freundlich's newfound joys In Prague were short-lived for a number of reasons. One is obvious. Among the others, well, even before the Nazi's move into parts of Czechoslovakia, Freundlich received a beautifully handwritten note dated January 19 1937:

> My dear good uncle E.
>
> Thank you so much for your letter. I am pleased with your success. I am only sorry that I can not take part in it. I wish you with all my heart that things will work out just as well over there. I am terribly sorry that I have to prepare you for a new scare or new trouble but it will be surely the last time. I feel that I am, at the end of my rope and that is why I have decided to make an end of my life.
>
> I always was
> Yours,
> Lena Goldfield

Starting in 1933 and running through the war, events taking place in Germany were being communicated to the free world by, to, and via the émigrés in Turkey. On June 10, 1933, Richard von Mises wrote to the great Hungarian born aerodynamicist, Theodore von Kármán, who had emigrated to the United States and founded the Institute of Aeronautical Sciences in California, about a young German, Walter Tollmien, who was looking for a position:

> I have to advise you that the irrevocable prerequisite for any kind of employment or scholarship or suchlike is to make a statement on his word of honour that his four grandparents are Aryan and in particular are of non-Jewish descent. ...I believe that in a favourable case the prospects are not quite so bad as indeed a large part of all the previous candidates can be omitted under the present law.

Von Kármán forwarded the letter to Tollmien, writing on its back:[23] "Indeed a document of our time!"

A year later, the 1914 Nobel laureate, Max von Laue, an Aryan who stayed in Germany through the war, shared the following communications with Freundlich in a December 12 1934 letter: "Enclosed is a copy of the following letter from J. Stark." (The enclosure is shown in Fig. 136):

Signed off with a "Heil Hitler," Stark's August 21 1934 letter tells von Laue:

> You rejected my proclamation on the grounds that it was a political proclamation by intellectuals. This objection is false. In reality it was meant to show to the entire world the German people's great recognition of their great leader Adolf Hitler. Thus, you have refuted a public proclamation for Adolf Hitler, yet at the Wurtzburg Physics Congress, you were not embarrassed to make a declaration against the Nazi government and for the benefit of Albert Einstein, the traitor and criticizer of the Nazi regime and all this to the applause of all present Jews and Jew associates. I can not help but to express my deepest sorrow at the disparity between the two events.[24]

In other words, you are not toeing the party line. I am watching you. Beware! The response was quick (a week and a half later), short, to the point, and showed von Laue to be a *mensch,* a decent human being.[25] (Fig. 137).

> After the totally untrue recounting and perception on your part as described in your letter of August 21, I would appreciate not to receive any private communications from you in the future.
> With highest respect, [and with no Heil Hitler] Laue[26]

The fact that von Laue felt a need to share this communication at that time with his colleague Freundlich is truly significant. It certainly was a way of informing all his former colleagues who escaped the Nazified part of the world regarding Germany's prevailing climate in science. Von Laue knew that Freundlich was influential in scientific circles beyond those living in Turkey. He knew of Freundlich's former colleagues such as Einstein who managed to emigrate to the United States. He knew that a letter to Turkey with such information would be less likely to be censored than one to the U.S. or the UK. The fact that it was appended almost without comment is no less significant. Was it a means of buying self-insurance for future eventualities? Perhaps! Was it a way to preserving his own dignity? Perhaps! Was it a way of showing that not all German scientists remaining in Germany were bad Germans? Perhaps!

Also significant, it is obvious that Freundlich felt a need to keep this particular correspondence in his possession throughout his stay in Turkey, taking it with him on his re-emigration to Prague in 1937 and on his re-re-emigration to Scotland in 1939, although he himself was effectively on the run. Was this Freundlich's way of preserving hard factual information for future historians? Perhaps! Did he use it as a means of waking up people of influence to take action in the west? There is much evidence to suggest that he did. The fact that J [Johannes] Stark was also a recipient of the Nobel (1919) Prize in physics[27] was of major consequence in all of these considerations.

Like Freundlich and several others, philosopher Hans Reichenbach left Turkey before the War ended. The Albert Einstein archives at Princeton and Hebrew Universities contain an exchange of correspondence with Reichenbach. In letters to Reichenbach dated August 14 1940 and again on the August 22, soon after Reichenbach's arrival at UCLA from Turkey, Einstein, writing from Knollwood, Saranac Lake, New York, quotes his statement in behalf of Bertrand Russell [BR] who, like Reichenbach, was a mathematician, logician, and philosopher, among other things, and who had just been refused a position at the City College of New York for his political views. Einstein concludes his letter by saying "…we see here, that there is no protection against *Engerzigkeit* [meanspiritedness] and *Philistertum* [Philistine thinking] in any government."

Thus they noted that no society is fully immune from political intolerance and injustice although, in their native land, the concept was being extended by orders of magnitude (Fig, 138):[28]

> Great spirits have always found violent opposition from mediocrities. The latter can not understand it when a man does not thoughtlessly submit to hereditary prejudices, but honestly and courageously uses his thoughts in clear form. I confidently hope that in the BR [Bertrand Russell] affair it will become manifest that at least those of us who carry the responsibility know how to appreciate fully rational strength of character.[29]

In the week that all resistance had collapsed and the last of Warsaw ghetto's Jews had been killed, a letter dated May 28 1943 from Prof. Dr. Felix Haurowitz in Istanbul to professor Max Bergmann at the Rockefeller Institute for Medical Research in New York City reads: "I hear nothing about my cousin Leopold Pollak. I know only that he has been deported by the Germans. About ten of my near relatives have been deported; three of them died surely and I am not sure, how many of the others died. I am glad, that my brothers are safely in England and America and that my own parents died before, so that no nearest relatives remained there."
Throughout the war, American ambassadors to Turkey have played behind-the-scenes roles in helping to extract as many people as possible from Nazi control. As late as February 9 1944, Ambassador Steinhardt, writing to Haim Barlas, states:

> As I explained to you yesterday, while the Vichy Government has as yet given no commitment, there is every evidence that the intervention of the Turkish authorities has caused the Vichy authorities to at least postpone if not altogether abandon their apparent intention to exile these unfortunates to almost certain death by turning them over to the Nazi authorities.[30]

## Émigrés' Aversion to Making Risky Decisions

But it is also fair to speculate that the émigrés in Turkey as a group were what economists call "risk-averse." Dermatologist Berta Ottenstein was different. She left a secure job as a professor of medicine and head of the Skin Clinic in Istanbul for the United States with no job prospect in hand. She never did find one.

There is an exchange of correspondence (in German) during April 1946 between Haurowitz and Ottenstein, then living in Brookline, Massachusetts. In that letter, Haurowitz inquired regarding job opportunities in his profession at United States universities. She was very pessimistic but did suggest that there may be a position at the University of Utah and urged him to come. From several letters, it is clear that Haurowitz was unwilling to give up a secure position allowing him to transfer some of his salary to the United States for the support of his family until such time that he had secured a position in America.

In other correspondence to Ottenstein, as well as to others, he pointed out that although he was satisfied with his work in Turkey, his children had no future there. In a letter dated March 6 1946 to his colleague E. Finlay Freundlich in Scotland, Haurowitz was more specific:

> It was the only right thing to be done for the children, [sending them to the United States] who had visited [attended] here the English High Schools. There is the question, whether I should follow them. For the moment I prefer to wait, until travelling [*sic*] possibilities to Prague or to the United States will improve. Our fees here have been increased rather considerably and I have the right to transfer 1/5 of my income to USA, so that it is not quite easy to leave this post without having any security about a future appointment.

On 5 September 1948, Haurowitz informed Frau Dr. Berta Ottenstein that during July 1948, he had settled in at Indiana University and his family had joined him in Bloomington. Soon thereafter, Haurowitz began to help others in their attempts to secure jobs at American universities. In a letter dated January 20 1950, to Turkoligst Andreas Tietze, who was still in Istanbul, Haurowitz explains that Professor Stith Thomson, the Director of the Folklore Program and Dean of the Graduate School at Indiana University, was a good friend:

> He is very interested in Asian languages, but I don't think a permanent position is possible since [Sinologist Wolfram] Eberhardt at one time sought one and was not successful. Thomson thinks highly of Eberhardt and to my knowledge was instrumental in helping him get a position at Berkeley.
>
> Professor Voeglin is head of our Anthropology Department and by chance I also know him well. He understands a bit of Turkish and is very interested in all things Turkish. He also tried to bring Eberhardt here. If what you want is not a permanent position like Eberhardt required write then to him directly. Tell him whether you want to stay here or return to Turkey. I was going to show Dean Thomas your letter but I can't because you refer to Voegelin in a somewhat negative way.

### Attempts to Emigrate to the UK

Finlay Freundlich, who had lived in the UK on various occasions, was attempting to re-emigrate to Britain, two years after asking Barrister Samuels to intervene with the Home Office in behalf of all thirty of his colleagues in Istanbul. This time he wrote from Prague where he had mistakenly resettled, asking for himself and his family. The Home Office was just as unforthcoming as before (Fig. 139).

By the end of January, Freundlich recognized his mistake and was in communication with the UK-based *Academic Assistance Council* to intervene on his and a colleague's behalf (Fig. 140).

After Atatürk's passing, many in the émigré community feared that their safe haven would cease to exist. Among the fearful was Hilda Geiringer, von Mises' assistant, colleague, and collaborator. She was concerned that she might not find it easy to obtain a visa to the United States. In desperation, she wrote to von Mises from Istanbul: "Is there no way to marry *pro cura*? Here an emigrant who has a resident's permit has married his 'bride' and she was then allowed to come to him straight from Vienna."

Her fears of not receiving an entrance permit were thankfully unfounded. With her daughter, she went to Bryn Mawr College where she was appointed to a lecturer position.[31] Her trials and tribulations in coming to the States and in finding any kind of a university position whatsoever was well documented.

Sometime in 1941, ophthalmologist Joseph Igersheimer had asked his superior, Leonard Carmichael, President of Tufts University, to intervene with the State Department in matters of his son Walter's visa application. At the time, Walter was being interned as an "enemy alien" by the British in Canada. On October 21 1941, Carmichael wrote a Mr. A.M. Warren, Chief of Visa Division, Department of State:

> Dr. Joseph Igersheimer is a member of the staff of the Tufts College Medical School. He is a distinguished medical scientist and has done important work in the field of ophthalmology. Dr. Igersheimer came to America as a scientist called to deliver some significant lectures, and he has remained here because of political disturbances which developed in his absence. Dr. Igersheimer is a respected and distinguished member of the Medical School of Tufts College.

In an undated, handwritten letter, Igersheimer thanked Carmichael for the kindness extended in that regard and on December 31 1941, Carmichael wrote, "I certainly hope that my letter to the State Department may prove helpful in effecting your son's entrance into this country."[32] It was April 7 1943 when Walter first reached the US even though the Canadian government released him from custody on January 22 1942 by declaring him a "Friendly Alien" after all. Walter was forced by the State Department's inaction to spend the interim period in Cuba.[33]

Recognizing Britain's knee-jerk reaction to its recent (wartime) German émigrés, Alvin Johnson, writing to Columbia University chemistry professor Victor K. LaMer on September 10 1940, points out that a "great many refugee scholars accepted the hospitality of England." He goes on to say, "I do not know of one who did not wish to take part in the defense of England in whatever capacity the Government might determine." He concluded by lamenting that: "Wisely or unwisely, it [Britain] has treated them as enemy aliens, interning them as if they are eager to fight for Germany."[34]

## Post-war Communications

In letters (February 27 1946 and March 6 1946) exchanged between astronomer Freundlich, settled in Scotland, and Felix Haurowitz, still in Istanbul, one finds sad deliberations on the prospects of both returning to their native Prague and their former positions at its University. Part of the discussion centered on the potential election outcome involving Jan Masaryk and what impact that might have on their return.

History tells us that on March 10 1948, Masaryk died under questionable circumstances. By registered mail from Kadiköy, Istanbul, on July 4 1948, Turkey's library system designer and Einstein's friend Walter Gottschalk wished Haurowitz all the best in his new Bloomington, Indiana, surroundings and hoped that he already was reunited with his family. He concluded the letter by asking that Haurowitz "send two *CARE packages* to two close friends who are starving in Allied-occupied Germany."

Haurowitz and Linus Pauling maintained their cordial and personal relationship for many postwar years. Both were greatly concerned for the world's future. Responding to an invitation, Pauling wrote on January 27 1958: "Your letter arrived at a bad time...I am feeling pessimistic about the world as a whole. I do hope that I shall be able to visit Bloomington again before too long, to take part in your colloquium and to talk with you about the interesting work that you and your colleagues are carrying on; but I can't plan to do so at any time in the future." During this time, Pauling was very much preoccupied with the future, to wit:

> As international tension and competition between the U.S. and the Soviet Union accelerated, he [Pauling] also riveted public attention on the buildup and proliferation of nuclear weaponry—preparations for thermonuclear warfare that he believed would destroy most of the planet's living creatures. He addressed both issues in his popular book *No More War*! (1958). He maintained that patient, reasoned negotiation and diplomacy, using the objectivity and procedures of the scientific method, would settle disputes in a more lasting, rational, and far more humane way

than war. He asked scientists to become peacemakers. In this most intense phase of the Cold War, Linus Pauling's name was often in the news—as when he circulated a petition against atmospheric nuclear testing and the excessive buildup of nuclear arsenals. The petition was presented in early 1958 to the United Nations after being signed by some 9,000—eventually more that 11,000-scientists worldwide. The U.S. government's opposing position was defended—sometimes vituperatively—by most of the press and by various scientists, such as physicist Edward Teller, many of whom were federal employees.[35]

## Correspondence With Junior Colleagues

Examples of communications which began during the war and continued for nearly 20 years follow. A letter of August 21 1944 from Haurowitz to *Lahut Uzman*,[36] one of his former students in Turkey and a Turkish native, reads: "Thank you for your letter of June 24. I am very glad that you had the possibility to find a laboratory, in which you can continue scientific work. Tyrocidine and gramicidine are surely very interesting substances and I hope you will be successful in elucidating at least a part of their mysterious effect. ...A short time ago I published a small paper on Denaturation, Enzymatic Hydrolysis and Serological Specificity of proteins in *Istanbul Seririyati*, Vol. 26, June. Your experiments on the tryptic digestion of inactivated serum are described there. Your father had the intention to send you several copies. I hope he has done it. I enclose, at any rate, one of the copies to this letter. Another paper containing your experiments will be published in the near future."

On November 15 1944, using *Harvard Medical School* letterhead, Lahut Uzman wrote to Haurowitz, who was still in Istanbul: "I have just received your very kind letter of August 21 and the reprint of your paper on denaturation. Needless to say, sir, I am very grateful for your having included my very modest experiments." This, of course, started a productive collegial collaboration with much correspondence.

On March 11 1954 on *US Army Medical Service Graduate School* (Walter Reed Medical Center) letterhead, now Captain, Medical Corps, Lahut Uzman wrote: "I am enclosing a reprint of a recent publication of mine hoping that you may be interested in data on nucleic acids in the human."

On October 24 1960, Lahut Uzman, Assistant Professor of Neurology, Harvard Medical School, wrote, "Your very kind letter of October 13th in response to the reprint of my chapter in 'Metal-Binding in Medicine' leads me to assure you that my small tribute to you is one of claiming privilege on my part. In the confusion that has reigned in the role of copper in Wilson's disease it is unfortunate that due credit is not fully given to your very sound pioneering work on this subject." Other correspondence indicates that Haurowitz did this work while still in Prague, i.e., before 1939.

And, on July 7 1962, Uzman wrote, "The enclosed newspaper clipping contains news which may please you. With the whole world to choose from, the ad hoc committee chose me to be the first recipient of the *Bronson Crothers Professorship of Neurology* at Harvard. To be so elevated to the highest possible academic rank was surprising and flattering, especially since the faculty was fully aware of my physical handicap and limited life expectancy. You see, my dear Professor, for the past five years, I have been suffering from Hodgkin's disease and have been kept alive in the last two years by heavy X-ray treatments. Since the new chair also automatically makes me Neurologist-in-Chief, Children's Hospital and the Brighton Hospital, it was a very flattering mark of confidence that all these added responsibilities were placed on my shoulders. Needless to say, I am very happy that fate has allowed me to realize my wildest dreams so soon.

I hope your health continues to be well. You must be a grandfather many times by now. Please convey my best wishes to Frau Haurowitz."

So, American science and medicine started reaping benefits of at least one émigré professor trained Turkish national. All this started taking place while America was still in WWII. And, Uzman's contributions to American military medicine continued through the Korean war.

There is a treasure trove of correspondence spanning the early 30s well into the 50s between Hugo Braun and Felix Haurowitz. By April 24 1950, Braun, one of the few who returned to Germany and settled in at the *Munchen Hygienisches Institut,* wrote (in German): "The Turks were extremely gracious in saying good bye to me."

According to this letter, on their return trip to the "Heimat" (homeland) he and "Mrs. Braun could not stop to see their son and daughter because of financial considerations." Other letters mention that the "daughter suffered a leg wound as a soldier," while the "son—a medical doctor—served in a hospital."

Plowing through the correspondence, it becomes clear that both had served in Israel's 1948 War of Independence. By fast-forwarding to some 1961 correspondence, we learn that Braun's daughter, Irmgard, a Ph.D., worked in semiconductor research, was married to an Israeli mechanical engineer whose last name is Hegmon, and had just been offered a job at Pennsylvania State University.

There is much correspondence having to do with arrangements to have Haurowitz share American scientific journals with Braun as these were unavailable in war torn Germany. Also, Braun, as did Gottschalk, pleaded to have the Haurowitz family send *CARE packages* to the widow of a colleague who remained in Germany through the war.

In a letter dated April 28 1950, Haurowitz stated: "I never regretted the nine years I spent in Turkey, and I feel that the Turks conducted themselves toward us much better than some of the European professors [among us] toward the Turks." Moreover, on July 3 1954, Braun writes, "I think it is very nice of you to have your former Turkish coworker [Mutahar Yenson] working with you. Please do extend to him my heartfelt greetings and wishes. He was very decent to me while I was still in Turkey."

On April 3 1963, *Faruk L. Ozer*, M.D., staff member of the Hematology Research Laboratory, *University of Texas Medical Branch in Galveston*, wrote Dr. Haurowitz at the Department Biochemistry, University of Indiana: "As a former student of yours in Istanbul, I am taking the liberty of writing this letter concerning a phenomenon which we find difficult to explain." He then goes on to describe the unexplainable finding in "a human serum."

This started a renewed relationship among colleagues expanding science in America.

Evidently, Haurowitz's inability to locate in the United States for many years and his exile in Turkey battered his self-image. Alfred Frohlich, an old colleague who had situated at the May Institute for Medical Research of the *Jewish Hospital in Cincinnati*, wrote Haurowitz a short note on December 30 1946. "Hope your visit to the US will convince you how respected and honored you are here. It will only be a short time until you are reunited with your wife and children. I hope so." (Fig. 141).

In his own words to Hugo Braun,[37] on November 19 1950, as if having to reconfirm his worth to himself Haurowitz writes: "My colleagues in the U. S. seem to value my work because the New York Academy of Medicine, which had a two-day symposium about antibodies, asked me to be the honored speaker. They even paid for my traveling and hotel expenses."

On December 16 1953, Prof. Dr. H. Braun responded to Haurowitz: "Just received your letter and am happy that you took my suggestion to let me submit your name to the "Kuratorium" (curatorship) of the Paul-Ehrlich-Siftung (Trust). Please send a current CV."

On March 10 1960, *Michael Sela* wrote: "First of all please accept, though belatedly, my heartiest congratulations on the occasion of the *Ehrlich Award* and medal, stressing once again your contribution to science in general." This was indeed a most eloquent way of reminding us that this great scientist, among others, was saved for all of us by a 1939 invitation from the Republic of Turkey.

**Settling in to Normalcy**

*Leo Spitzer*, Professor of Romance Languages, apparently had a job offer from Johns Hopkins University back in 1934 but came to the USA in 1936. The delay was because of his contractual obligations to the University of Istanbul. Once at Hopkins, he tried to negotiate extra compensation for some extra teaching that he did at the university. An excerpt from that handwritten letter dated April 23 1937 and addressed to geographer "Dr. Isaiah Bowman," the university's president (1935 through 1948), provides insight into some of the relocation problems he, for one, encountered:

> When I came here I knew very heavy sacrifices would be necessary; my salary would be diminished by one third; the shipping of my library would be at my expense (1200$); I would have to buy new furniture and the adjustment of my family to a new country would cost much. But the quite unique kindness with which the university waited for me two years gave me the hope that those difficulties would be overcome in a satisfactory way.[38] (emphasis added).

During the mid-1950s, correspondence between Haurowitz and Braun indicates that each was settling down in his new surroundings, doing research, being invited to give lectures, and traveling to conferences. Haurowitz arranged to have medical journals sent to Germany still recovering from war's devastation. And, though they each lament the fact that they are too busy, they agree that "it is better to have too much work than too little."

In a letter dated February 11 1955, Haurowitz tells his friend Braun that "there is nothing new to report. We had our daughter Liese and husband here for Christmas. He was discharged from the Army and they both are resuming studies at Wisconsin. During their military service on the west coast, they often saw the Sgalitzers[39] and report that they are doing fine." The letter goes on to say that they saw the Army drafted son, Martin, two weeks ago and ends with best regards to their mutual friends (from Turkey), Marchionini and Goldschmidt.

In an exchange of letters on November 11 1955 and May 17 1956, Braun and Haurowitz both express concerns for their dear ones in light of "the unrest in Israel and Argentina." On September 20 1956, Haurowitz wrote to Braun, "You asked me about Frau Ottenstein in your last letter. I found out from [ophthalmologist] Igersheimer that she went swimming with girlfriends. While her friends swam out to sea, she stayed back in the shallow waters. She was observed to suddenly keel over and fall into the water. Before any one could help her, she was dead. It was not suicide, because she had just found out that the German government would agree to provide her a pension, and she would no longer have to worry about money."

He then changes the subject and informs Braun about his daughter Liese having had a baby and that he cannot get used to being a grandfather. On October 9 1957, Haurowitz told Braun that the German government agreed to reinstate his pension albeit small, and that he participated in a symposium at St Andrews University. While there, he visited with astronomy professor Freundlich and his wife. Freundlich had decided to retire and move to Wiesbaden, Germany, where the climate is more agreeable.

By 1960, Braun found his way to visit Israel and Turkey. On February 10, all he could say about the trip was that "it was quite tiring but nice. The Turks were very decent to me, both the faculty and my former co-workers." There was no mention of Braun's son, and daughter, who had gone to Palestine from Turkey, fought to establish the State of Israel, and apparently were still there during his visit.

On the positive side, by August 6 1962, Felix Haurowitz informed his then very ill friend, Hugo Brown, of the fact that his son, Martin, whom Braun knew "as a little boy," was doing a post-doc in astrophysics at Cornell and was offered an Assistant Professorship there which he had accepted.

Two old friends! Two old colleagues! Two fathers! Two human beings sharing traumatic experiences over an extended period! Two different levels of interest in their respective progeny's successes and well-being! Wars do have a way....

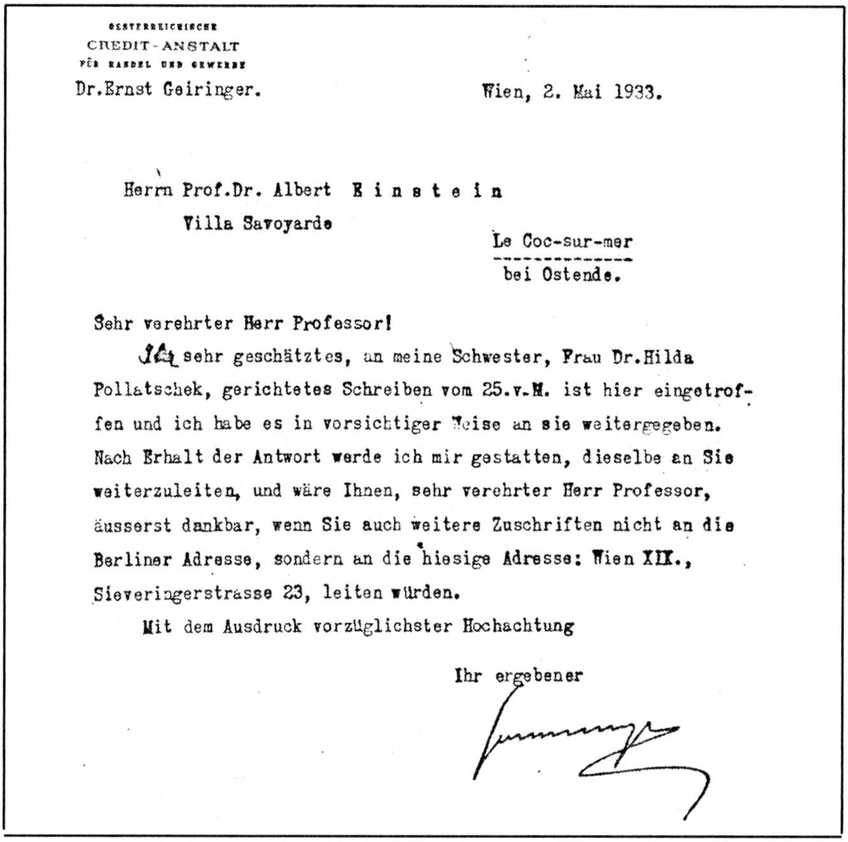

OESTERREICHISCHE
CREDIT-ANSTALT
FÜR HANDEL UND GEWERBE

Dr.Ernst Geiringer. Wien, 2. Mai 1933.

Herrn Prof.Dr. Albert Einstein
Villa Savoyarde
Le Coc-sur-mer
bei Ostende.

Sehr verehrter Herr Professor!

Ihr sehr geschätztes, an meine Schwester, Frau Dr.Hilda Pollatschek, gerichtetes Schreiben vom 25.v.M. ist hier eingetroffen und ich habe es in vorsichtiger Weise an sie weitergegeben. Nach Erhalt der Antwort werde ich mir gestatten, dieselbe an Sie weiterzuleiten, und wäre Ihnen, sehr verehrter Herr Professor, äusserst dankbar, wenn Sie auch weitere Zuschriften nicht an die Berliner Adresse, sondern an die hiesige Adresse: Wien XIX., Sieveringerstrasse 23, leiten würden.

Mit dem Ausdruck vorzüglichster Hochachtung

Ihr ergebener

Geiringer

*Figure 134*
Ernst Geiringer's letter to Einstein, May 2 1933.

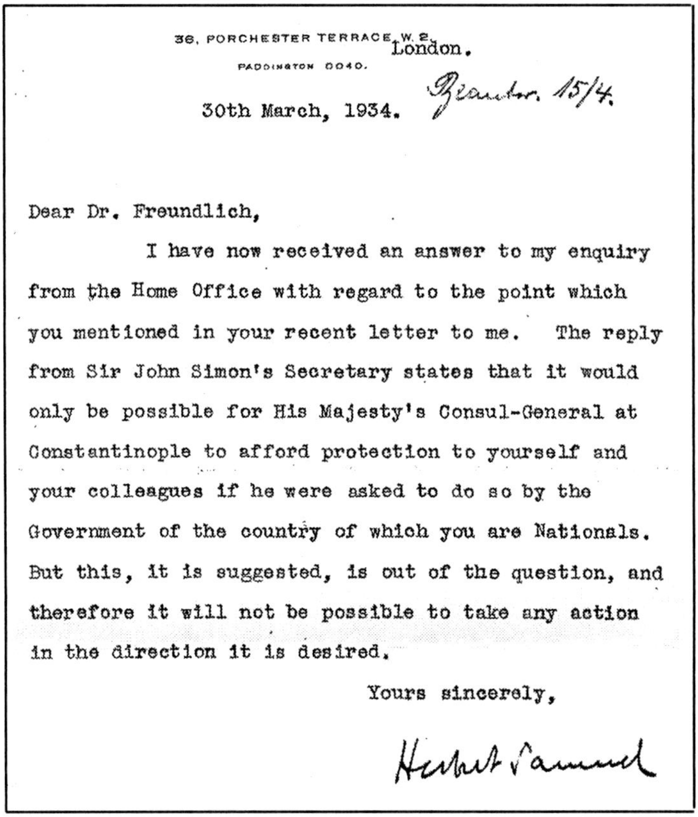

36, PORCHESTER TERRACE, W. 2.
London.
PADDINGTON 0040.

30th March, 1934.

Dear Dr. Freundlich,

I have now received an answer to my enquiry from the Home Office with regard to the point which you mentioned in your recent letter to me. The reply from Sir John Simon's Secretary states that it would only be possible for His Majesty's Consul-General at Constantinople to afford protection to yourself and your colleagues if he were asked to do so by the Government of the country of which you are Nationals. But this, it is suggested, is out of the question, and therefore it will not be possible to take any action in the direction it is desired.

Yours sincerely,

Herbert Samuel

*Figure 135*
A letter to Freundlich from Barrister Samuels.

Abschrift

J.Stark

Berlin-Charlottenburg, den 21.8.34.
Warchstr.25.

Sehr geehrter Herr v.Laue!

Sie haben die von mir angeregte Kundgebung mit der Unterstellung abgelehnt, es sei eine politische Kundgebung von Gelehrten. Diese Unterstellung ist falsch. Sie sollte in Wirklichkeit ein Teil des großen nationalen Bekenntnisses des deutschen Volkes zu seinem Führer Adolf Hitler vor aller Welt sein. Jetzt haben Sie eine öffentliche Kundgebung für Adolf Hitler abgelehnt, dagegen haben Sie auf der Würzburger Physikertagung sich nicht gescheut, zugunsten von Albert Einstein, dieses Landesverräters und Beschimpfers der nationalsozialistischen Regierung, unter dem Beifall der anwesenden Juden und Juden-Genossen eine öffentliche Kundgebung zu veranstalten, die sich letzten Endes gegen die nationalsozialistische Regierung richtete. Ich kann nicht umhin, Ihnen über dieses unterschiedliche Verhalten mein stärkstes Bedauern auszudrücken.

Heil Hitler!

(gez.) Stark

*Figure 136*
August 21 1934 letter to physicist Max von Laue from his professional "colleague" and fellow Nobel laureate, Johannes Stark.

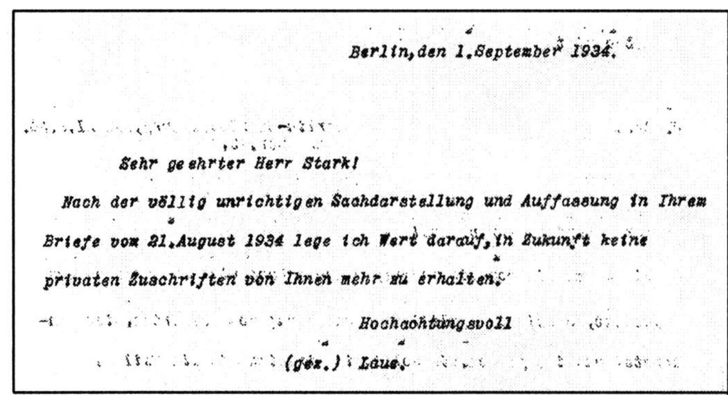

Berlin, den 1.September 1934.

Sehr geehrter Herr Stark!

Nach der völlig unrichtigen Sachdarstellung und Auffassung in Ihrem Briefe vom 21.August 1934 lege ich Wert darauf, in Zukunft keine privaten Zuschriften von Ihnen mehr zu erhalten.

Hochachtungsvoll

(gez.) Laue.

*Figure 137*
September 1 1934, reply letter from Max von Laue to Johannes Stark

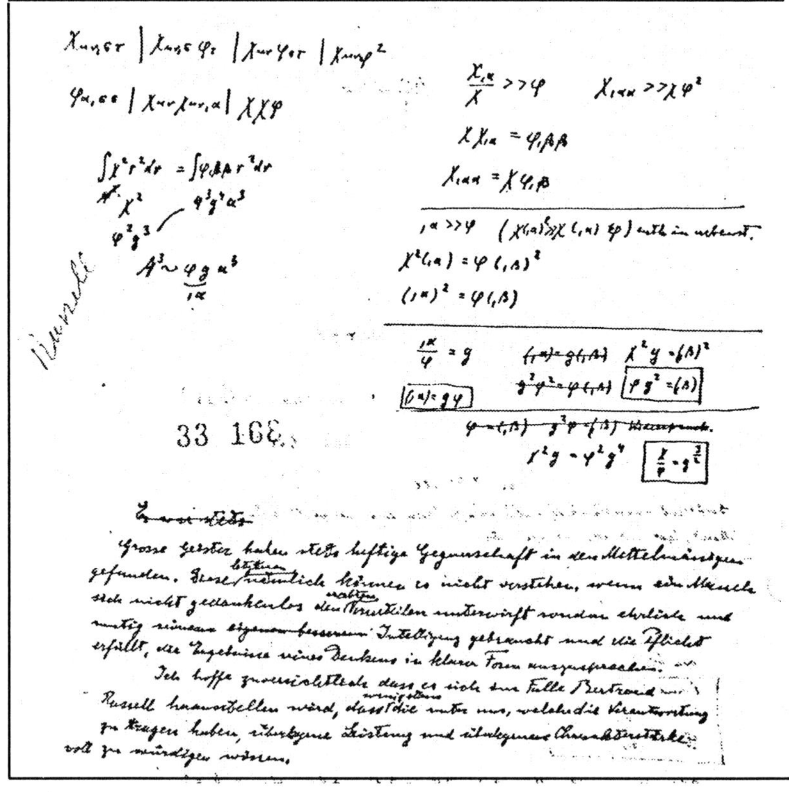

33 166

*Figure 138*
Draft of Einstein's famous "Great Spirits" quotation.

**Home Office,**
**Whitehall,**
**S.W.1.**

26th February, 1936.

Dear Sir Herbert Samuel.

You wrote to me yesterday with regard to the possibility of Professor E. Finlay Freundlich becoming naturalised. I am afraid that it is not permissible to make any exception in the case of distinguished persons in the matter of the statutory requirements as to residence, so that as long as conditions remain as at present, it will not be possible for Professor Freundlich to qualify for naturalisation.

Yours sincerely
Russell Scott

The Right Honourable
Sir Herbert Samuel, G.C.B., G.B.E.

*Figure 139*
Response from the Home Office to Barrister Samuels regarding Finlay Freundlich's attempt to re-emigrate to Britain.

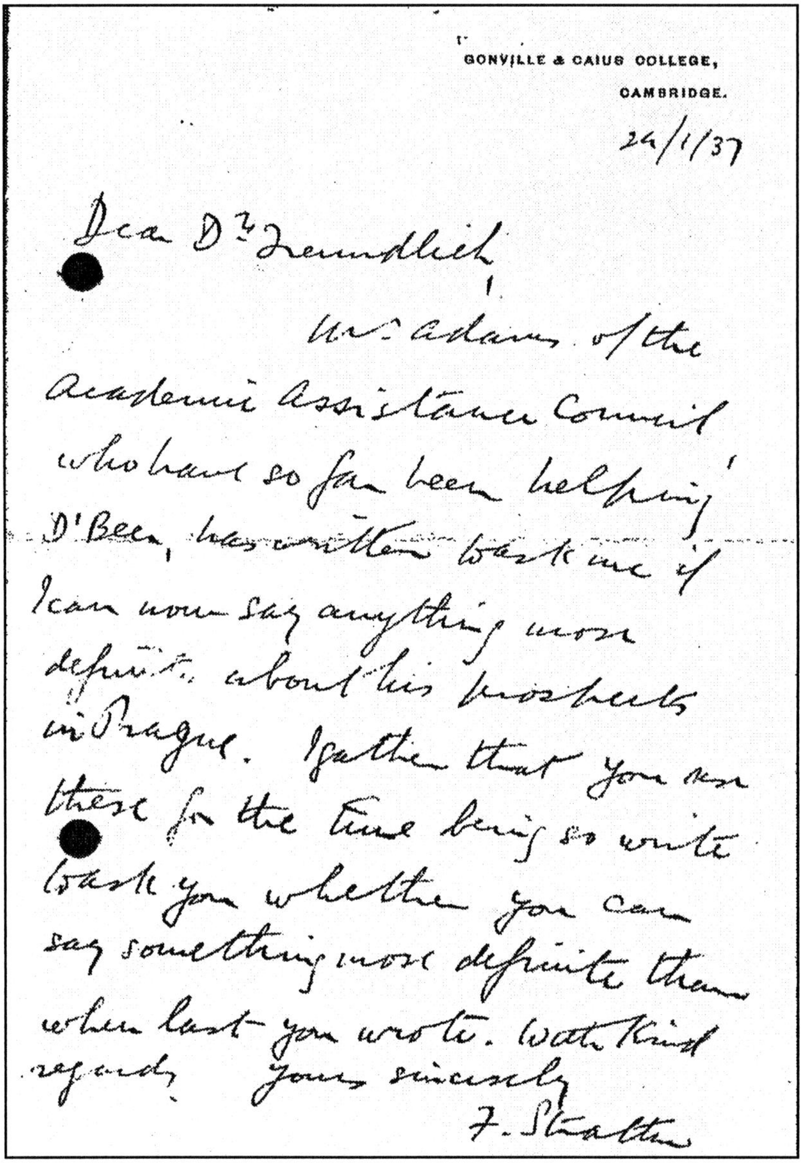

GONVILLE & CAIUS COLLEGE,
CAMBRIDGE.

24/1/37

Dear Dr Freundlich,

Mr Adams of the Academic Assistance Council who have so far been helping Dr Beer, has written to ask me if I can now say anything more definite about his prospects in Prague. I gather that you are there for the time being so write to ask you whether you can say something more definite than when last you wrote. With kind regards

Yours sincerely
F. Stratton

*Figure 140*
A January 24 1937 communication to Freundlich in Prague from the UK-based Academic Assistance Council.

*Figure 141*
Felix Haurowitz: A great man and a battered self-esteem.

# 13 Memoirs and Then Some

This chapter of additional memoirs and oral histories is included so that the reader may sense, and perhaps take away with greater understanding, a more resounding emotional impact of the experiences that befell these men, women, and children.

> We used to listen to the BBC news from London. It was mainly the war that we talked about—Hitler running over country after country. Compared to what people in Europe had to suffer, Turkey was a wonderful place—there's no question.[1]

## First-Generation Recalls

***From the memoirs of Arthur von Hippel,[2] father of what we now know as nanotechnology:***

> [O]ur personal lives became strongly affected by the fact that Daggie [Arthur's wife] was Jewish. Old "friends" suddenly appeared shortsighted and could not recognize us anymore. When I walked in the streets, people crossed over to the other side. Our father had to certify his "Aryan origin." Our East-Prussian uncle, Walther von Hippel, Chief-Officer of that Province and the family historian, who had been especially agitated by my marriage to Daggie, was thrown into jail by the Nazi Gauleiter [Party Governor] Koch, whom he had previously dismissed as incompetent. Our father defended Walther before the German Supreme Court and got him freed, but the Nazis simply put him back into jail. Uncle Walther wrote me a letter of apology and then committed suicide.
>
> My encounter with two professors of theology was in a lighter vein. One was a lovely man living not far from my father's house,

the other an ardent Nazi passing by. The former, cleaning up his vegetable garden, called over to the latter, "Dear colleague, today I have acted in your style: I have rooted out the entire Family Löwenzahn." (Löwenzahn is the German term for the dandelion and is also a Jewish name.)

In the spring of 1933, a Hitler edict banned Jewish students from the universities and Jewish professors were subsequently dismissed (Born, Courant, etc.). Opa Franck was exempted since he had received the Iron Cross, First Class, for heroism during World War I.[3] Obviously, he did not want this preference. We therefore sat down with him and some friends to formulate a statement of resignation. The friends included Kurt Hahn, the director of the progressive youth-movement school, Salem, at the Bodensee (founded by Prince Max von Baden, who subsequently emigrated to England and became the educator of young Philip Mountbatten, now Prince Philip of England.)

In the early morning hours, we telephoned the declaration to the "Göttinger Zeitung" [Göttingen News]. Opa's wonderfully dignified statement of April 1933 came as a bombshell to the Nazis and the University faculty who had made peace with them. A counter-declaration condemning the statement appeared in the "Göttinger Tageblatt" [Göttingen Daily] on April 24, signed by forty-odd professors and lecturers. Since the Nazis had already tapped our telephone lines, we were also individually attacked in the main Nazi-newspaper, the "Völkischer Beobachter [People's Observer]." I was so angry that I went to the Nazi-headquarters in Göttingen—ironically located on the "Jüdenstrasse [Jew Street]"—and tried to challenge its leader to a duel. They kept me waiting endlessly for him and nothing came of this childish gesture.

Unfortunately, the consequences for the "Göttinger Zeitung" were more serious. The paper was suppressed and ceased publication while the "Tageblatt" flourishes to this day.[4]

After Professor Franck's resignation, we young Assistant Professors took over: Hertha Sponer, Cario, Heinrich Kuhn (married to Professor Nohl's daughter Mariele), Werner Kroebel, and I. When I went to Professor Pohl to tell him that he was the only full Professor of Physics left and had to assume leadership, he went to bed. We young people therefore acted alone, brought the remaining Ph.D. students through the final stages and prepared to close down. One of these students, Gert Rathenau, later had a very distinguished and adventurous career and is still my close friend. Another one, Meyer-Leibnitz, became an outstanding

German scientist. Professor Franck's declaration was re-published in England, and Professor Lindeman of Oxford came over to help. Lindeman offered to take me back to Oxford, but we felt that Heini Kuhn, the only one of us with a Jewish background, was more endangered. Heini and Mariele therefore went on to Oxford and distinguished careers.

Soon thereafter, Professor Schwarz in Zurich succeeded in arranging with the Turkish dictator, the Ghazi Mustafa Kemal, that a new European-type university should be founded in Istanbul (formerly Constantinople) and about thirty European professors be hired to staff it. I was one of the "lucky ones" selected and went to Zurich to receive a German contract as "Professor of Electrophysics," my proper field, and a French contract as "Professor of Electro-Technique"— a designation which led to my later downfall. I arranged to take Dr. Rathenau as my Assistant, and Walter Rieger, the master mechanic of Professor Stern in Hamburg, as my master machinist, and prepared to leave. My friends in industry were greatly upset by my going into exile and gathered surplus equipment in their laboratories to help me get started.

The Curator of the University of Göttingen kindly tried to persuade me to swear the oath of allegiance to Hitler. I refused. As a former officer, I was under the jurisdiction of the German War Department and had to obtain permission to leave. Telephoning the officer in charge in Berlin, I was mistakenly greeted with warmth as a volunteer for the new order, but was then coolly dismissed when I explained that I had a Jewish wife and no intention to divorce her. A similarly chilly reception occurred at the town offices where I got rid of my responsibility for the Johannis Church tower and received my exit visa. Now I was ready for my trip to Istanbul via ship from Italy.

Daggie remained with Opa and the two young boys (Peter not yet two-and-a-half, Arndt about one year old) until everything in Turkey could be prepared for their arrival. The preceding account may sound unduly heroic but my actions were nothing of the kind. I felt only duty-bound and adventurous. The real hero of the occasion was Daggie, saddled with two little children and an unrealistic husband. In our last night together at Göttingen, a tremendous display of shooting stars occurred. We watched in awe in the backyard with our friends, the Beyers, and took it as an omen of things to come.

[On arrival in Istanbul] our first order of business...was to find suitable quarters for our families. We succeeded gloriously.

> Taking a steamer up the Bosphorus, we discovered a newly built apartment house located directly on the Bosphorus in Bebek about twelve miles above Istanbul and reachable by tramway or steamer from Galata. We were able to rent the five apartments. Professor Heilbronn and I took the top floor; the botanist, Brauner, and the mathematician, Prager, the middle floor; and the astronomer, Freundlich, the apartment next to the landlord on the ground floor. Each apartment had a large balcony with a wonderful view across the Bosphorus to Asia Minor. As the building was not yet completed, we needed temporary quarters for some weeks—but our families were now able to come [to Turkey from Germany].[5]

***An extract from the autobiography of Felix Haurowitz, written in October 1975 on request from the Home Secretary, National Academy of Sciences of the United States, upon Haurowitz's being elected to the Academy's membership:***[6]

> My wife, myself, and our children remember the life in Istanbul as a very happy time. Istanbul is in our view the most beautiful city of the world, certainly more beautiful than Naples, San Francisco, and Rio de Janeiro, all of which I have seen. It has not only the geographical beauties of all these but also the beauties of the ancient Roman aqueduct, the Roman and Byzantine city walls and monuments and the overwhelming beauties of the great mosques. The Turkish government expected the foreign professors to modernize the antiquated didactic methods of the Ottoman Empire.
>
> The first two years, a docent of physiology or pathology translated my lecture during the class. At the end of the second year, I was able to lecture in Turkish which made teaching and particularly examining much easier. I took over from my predecessor an excellent technical assistant, Miss Paula Schwerin, with whom I published a series of papers. However, I found also a group of hard working enthusiastic Turkish co-workers. Most of them are now professors in Istanbul or at universities in other Turkish cities. Even at present (1975), that is 27 years after having left Turkey in 1948, I am still in contact with my old co-workers. They expressed to me their feelings by asking the Senate of the University in Istanbul to confer on me the honorary degree of a doctor of medicine. This very rare title was bestowed on me in 1973.
>
> The yearly budget of the Department of Biological and Medical Chemistry in the University of Istanbul was approximately $2,000. Very little could be bought with this modest budget, particularly

during World War II, which began a few months after my arrival in Istanbul. We worked almost exclusively on problems of immunochemistry....

Much of my time in Istanbul was devoted to teaching elementary physiological chemistry to medical students. We had classes containing from 400 to more than 1,000 students per semester. The laboratory course had to be given in 5 or 10 parallel courses. A Turkish textbook of biochemistry that I wrote was published in several editions.

Turkey had at that time approximately 25 million inhabitants and only one medical school in Istanbul. Most of the physicians stayed in the large cities. Very few of them, after having lived in Istanbul as students, were willing to return to the villages on the mainland of Anatolia with their loam huts, their lack of cultural institutions and their isolation. To secure medical help for these large parts of the country, the government awarded scholarships to the best premedical students. These scholarships covered not only dormitory space, full board, and textbooks, but also clothing, stationery, and even satisfactory pocket money.

The students, after receiving the M.D. degree, were sent to those places in Anatolia which needed them most urgently, and had to serve there as many years as they had been supported by the government. They were allowed to have private practices, and some of them, used their income to return to the government the sums which they had received over the years. They were then free to move to any other place in Turkey. Many of them returned to the few large cities, Istanbul, Ankara, and Izmir (Smyrna).

Nevertheless, the governmental Scholarships with the obligations to work in small towns improved considerably the health service in Anatolia. I wonder whether some similar system might not improve the health service in the small towns of the United States that have great difficulties in attracting practitioners.

Although our family loved Istanbul, we knew that there would be no future for our children. They reached college age, and, in 1946, my wife and the two children moved to the United States, taking with them most of our furniture. They traveled by means of an American Liberty ship. Their passage took almost a month. I stayed in Istanbul since my contract with the university would last two more years. However, I visited my family during the summer vacation in 1947. At that time, my daughter was a student at Indiana University. She had applied to different schools, but had been accepted in Bloomington first.

Owing to the large number of students who at that time returned from the military service, my daughter did not find a room in a dormitory but was accepted as a paying guest in the house of Professor Harry G. Day who turned out to be Professor of Biochemistry. When he heard that I would visit my family in 1947, he invited me to come to Bloomington and to present there a talk. After the lecture, there was a reception at which I met Professor J. H. Muller, a geneticist and Nobel laureate whose wife happened to be the daughter of one of my colleagues in the medical school in Istanbul.

The next day, I was asked whether I would accept an appointment as professor of Chemistry at Indiana University and teach biochemistry. I told my colleagues that I would be glad to accept such an appointment but that I had to return to Istanbul for another year and that I had been invited by the Medical School in Basel, Switzerland, to accept appointment for the chair of Biochemistry. I had promised my Swiss colleagues that I would visit them after returning from the United States and wanted to postpone my decision to a date after my visit to Basel.

The formal offer of Indiana University arrived while I was on my way from the U.S. to Basel. Once there, I was told that the medical faculty had proposed me *primo et unico loco*, that is, as the only candidate, but that they would have to fight for their decision because the cantonal government in Basel would prefer a Swiss citizen. This fight might take more than a year. Under these circumstances, I accepted the appointment in Bloomington. I moved there in July 1948. The University provided us with a small, prefabricated house. In 1950, we moved into an old two-story house with a large back yard. We still live in it.

My family was accepted in Bloomington with deeply moving cordiality, not only by my colleagues but also by the officers of the University, by neighbors, and by almost everyone with whom we had to deal in our daily life. I do not know whether Hoosier hospitality is exceptionally high or whether it merely reflects average American hospitality. It made our "assimilation" to American life very easy. In the Department, I had to take over the teaching of introductory biochemistry. The students who took this course were chemistry juniors, and seniors, pre-med students, and also juniors, or seniors, in zoology, botany, and microbiology.

***From the memoirs[7] of economist Dr. Fritz Neumark, His First Impressions:***

> We were almost totally ignorant about the country we came to. We only knew that the sultanate and the caliphate were abolished, and, after the many wars it participated in and lost, the Ottoman Empire was transformed into a Republic led by Kemal Pasha during its Independence War. When I first saw the unrivaled beauty of Istanbul, on arriving by boat from Genoa on a misty autumn morning, I never thought that many of us would spend ten, even twenty years, in this city. Similar to many others who stayed on in my country and who were not Nazi, I thought that Hitlerism was a nightmare that would last two or three years at the worst, considering the fact that the first Hitler cabinet also included powerful conservative circles. This misjudgment was strengthened by the Rohm coup in 1934.[8]

***From the memoirs[9] of economist Dr. Fritz Neumark on issues of children and aetheism:***

> [Hans Reichenbach] was a scholar of intelligence, great culture, and humor. I could easily benefit from his ideas since we lived in the same house in Kadıköy. Although great differences of opinion may have existed among them, our children had become close friends. (The Reichenbachs were partisans of the Montessori school whose approach we did not adopt.) Unbeknownst to us, our son had become an atheist under the influence of Reichenbach's son. Once when Matthias broke an arm and had to stay in the German Hospital [of Istanbul] for several days (he was around ten at the time), he whispered to us, "Do you think that the nurses here still believe in God?"

***From the memoirs[10] of Dr. Erna Eckstein-Schlossmann, a collaborator with her husband, Dr. Albert Eckstein, on many of the data-collecting trips to the hinterlands of Anatolia:***

> April 1938, Vienna
>
> Şakir Kesebir's[11] five-year-old daughter, Tülin, was taken ill in Vienna. First pneumonia, then emphysema. Şakir Bey's[12] wife had gone there to visit their sons. She called from Vienna and said that the child's condition was very bad and that she could die. In the

meantime, Şakir Bey, who had already gone to Vienna, requests Schummi[13] to go to Vienna at once. Hitler had entered Austria only a few weeks before. I objected violently. At the end, Atatürk intervened and promised that Schummi would not take one step in Vienna unaccompanied. An attaché from the embassy would be with him at all times. He first went to Budapest on the train. There he was met by the First Attaché of the embassy who would accompany him in Vienna and they went to Vienna together. In the station, the girl's uncle met them and said, "You are too late. When I left the hospital, Tülin was taking her last breath."

Schummi said: "I am here now. I want to see the child," and went to the hospital. Schummi noticed that the child's face was purple and swollen and diagnosed the case as cardiac tamponade. He immediately proposed operating. The child was taken to the operating theatre. As Professor Denk, the surgeon, sees the child, he says: 'I do not operate on corpses."

When Schummi insists on an immediate operation, the thorax and the pericardium are opened, the infection cleaned, and the child's breathing eased. Schummi stayed in Vienna for three weeks. Schummi came back from Vienna in a depressed state. He had seen the unimaginable oppression of the Nazis. He had not taken one step different from those of his Turkish Shadow for these three weeks.

Schummi understood why the doctors were not able to pose a correct diagnosis. Their minds were elsewhere. A few weeks later, Mrs. Kesebir came back to Ankara with a Jewish doctor, a Social Democrat nurse and a girl whose Jewish fiancée was missing. All the things one could achieve with a diplomatic passport. Schummi was named by the family as the "second father." He was accepted as a member of the very large Kesebir family.

`In 1938, Schummi and I started on a three-month tour of 12 regions of Anatolia. Mrs. Kesebir took Minna[14] and the three children to her house in Çiftehavuzlar.[15] Their neighbors were the prime minister and the "sugar king"[16] of Turkey.

### *Son leaving for UK:*

In 1939, Herbert left for school in England. We were not going to see each other for several years. We wrote to each other every week. During the war, these letters used to come through South Africa and later, via Cairo. They took three months to arrive. During all these years, only one letter was lost. In 1940, we registered

Peter in Robert College [private secondary school] in Istanbul. It was debatable whether this was a good decision or not. He was taken in by the Kosswig family with great affection and accepted as the older brother (Fig. 142).

***Dr. Albert Eckstein's interactions with the diplomatic corps as told by his wife:***

At the request of the Turkish government, Schummi used to treat the children of not only allied embassies, but also those of the German Embassy. Mrs. von Pappen[17] used to come to the hospital herself with her grandchildren. Of course, they were examined not in the polyclinics but at Schummi's office. One day, when she came with one of the children, Schummi wanted the ENT specialist also to see the child. He sent them to ENT by assigning a male orderly to accompany them. After the examination, Mrs. von Pappen returned and thanked Schummi before leaving the hospital.

After a short time, the hospital director came to see Schummi and complained that he had treated Mrs. von Pappen badly. He said that Schummi himself should have accompanied her to the ENT. Schummi should have led her to the door himself as he did with other diplomats. He said that he is going to report this to the ministry. Schummi's reaction was very strong and it almost came to exchanging blows. Schummi at once called on his friend Selim Sarper, the minister of foreign affairs at the time. Sarper assured Schummi that he was completely in his rights. He (Sarper) calmed him down and presented Schummi his own worry beads.

A short time after the attempt on his life, von Pappen was complaining of earache, although he had not been wounded. He called Schummi and asked whether he could examine him. Schummi told him he better come to the hospital so that an ENT specialist could see him. Schummi informed the hospital director that von Pappen is coming. The hospital director met von Pappen at the door and conducted him to his room. Von Pappen said he would like to see Schummi.

Von Pappen greeted Schummi with open arms and said clearly so that everyone would understand: "I must express my happiness at meeting you and I thank you for all you have done for my family." He requested Schummi to accompany him to the ENT department. At the end, it turned out that both his eardrums had been perforated.

One day when the Germans were leaving Turkey, he was called to examine Commercial Attache Maitzig's child. The child had a high fever. Maitzig was head of the Nazis in Turkey and his office was headquarters for German spies. When Schummi was leaving the house, Maitzig said: "I thank you for your help. Perhaps I can do something for you in Germany. If you have any relatives over there."

Schummi's answer was: "At this time, all of them are dead. All!"

Maitzig, in an embarrassed manner, asked Schummi what he should pay for the examination. Eckstein retorted, "Your money is too filthy for me," and he turned his back and left.

***Kesebir's house on Ziya Gökalp Street, 1944:***

They got up from the dinner table. Eckstein was thinking about how he would approach the subject. His absent state of mind had caught Şakir Kesebir's attention. They had known each other for years. He knew Eckstein would be on top of things even in very difficult moments. They sat in the armchairs. Kesebir said the first words. Although they mostly talked about the weather, in general, during the war years, the first words were about the last news from the German fronts.

When the maid brought their coffees, they were on the subject of the most important event of the last days, the freezing of all relations between Germany and Turkey by the Turkish Parliament in August 1944. Things had gotten to be very difficult for many Germans. Several of us, e.g., us and the Eberts, had Czechoslovakian passports given by the English government (the Czechoslovak government in exile). The rest had the letter "J" marked in their passports. The women were named "Sara," the men had "?" marks. Those whose German citizenships were taken away had no problems.

But it was different for half-Aryans and those who had deserted Germany for political reasons. Following the government's decision, all Germans considered to be of the Aryan race and holding German passports were rounded up in their places of residence and sent to *Yozgat, Çorum,* and *Kırşehir.* Jewish Germans or Germans with no nationality were not touched. Those residing in Ankara were sent to Kırşehir. News were received that these Germans in holding camps, exiled for the second time, were having a hard time. A group was formed including Reuter, Landsberger, and Mrs. Eckstein.

Eckstein took a deep breath. It was evident that the subject bothered him from the way he was sitting in the armchair. "You know about the Germans sent to *Kırşehir*. We heard that their conditions are very bad. Although they carry German passports, a great majority of them have taken refuge in Turkey, escaping from Hitler. We who reside in Ankara have been collecting an amount of money each month and sending it to them with Eugene Merzbacher. We also organized a small library there. Of course, you know that this is against the orders of the Turkish government. On his last trip, the police in *Kırşehir* arrested our friend and confiscated everything on him including the money. Now we have collected some money again. But we do not know how to get this amount to them. I undertand you are asking for help from me on this matter. I do not know whether you stopped by in *Kırşehir* during your travels in Anatolia. However, you are aware that you should get official permission. If you wish, we will go to *Kırşehir* together with Mrs. Eckstein. The governor there, Bekir Sami Baran Bey, will help you on this matter."[18]

***On December 28 1944 in Ankara, Prof. Eckstein recalls discussions regarding Turkish plans to repatriate German passport holders:***

He [Şakir Kesebir] presented an important document to the USA Ambassador Laurence Steinhardt on the German exiles and their repatriation to Germany. He separated them into three age groups.

The losses of those over 60 being especially great due to death, sickness, and unsuitability for employment, they will support relocation with enormous difficulty. Most of them are completely destroyed by past deficiencies and hardships.

The émigrés between the ages of 40-60 have lived through the whole tragedy, the birth and the consequences of National Socialism, themselves and in their relatives. The disappointments about the Hitler Germany and sorrows are specially marked in this group, because their memories of old Germany are still alive and an integral part of their traditions and culture. Those who have found a second home in the allied or neutral countries and thus had the chance to survive, do not have the wish to go back to their old country, almost not at all. The terror of the concentration camps built to eradicate their families and friends in an organized manner will not be forgotten by themselves and, I hope, by the whole world.

Those between the ages of 25-40 will not be too willing to return to Germany either: the Nürnberg laws, the defilement of the temples, personal insults, bad treatment, family members in the concentration camps, and, finally, their escape to foreign countries which would protect them are the important markers of their childhood and later development.

Finally those under 25 are above all the children of the émigrés and their thoughts are similar to those of their parents. Since they have been accepted by the countries they emigrated to as orphans of sorts, for them, all bridges with Germany are broken.

I think most of these émigré scientists will accept the invitations to be received from German Universities and go back to their countries. The invitations do not have to be from the same universities from which they were thrown out by the Hitler regime. However, they have to be for posts with responsibilities matching the ones from which they were expelled and the conditions should be in accordance with these responsibilities.

***Ord. Prof. Dr. Abdülkadir Noyan writes about post-war relief to colleagues in Germany:***

News [soon after the war's end] was coming that the professors in the Faculties of Medicine in Germany were suffering from food shortages. On the proposal of Prof. Dr. Marchionini, it was agreed on principle to send help to these professors.

Each professor promised to donate a certain amount from his salary. A commission was set up with Prof. Dr. Marchionini, Prof. Dr. İrfan Titiz, and Prof. Dr. Nafiz Uzluk. The decisions made were as follows: A package of 5 kilogram of foodstuffs to be sent to each faculty experiencing shortages. Packages to contain foods such as rice, hazelnuts, noodles, raisins, figs. Letters of thanks came from the deans of the German Faculties who received these packages. However, we learned that the packages sent to academics in Berlin under Russian rule were opened and sometimes a part, other times the whole of the contents, were lost. Recipients in the British and American zones received the gifts regularly. These gifts were paid for by the professors for several months. Later, assistant professors (doçents) also participated in this charitable endavor.[19]

***Professor Fritz Neumark's recollections shed some more light on the émigrés' lifestyle:***

During the years [Ernst] Reuter was shuttling back and forth between the new capital and the old one, when he came to Istanbul where he was working as advisor to the marine transport administration, in order to avoid an uncomfortable hotel life which was also expensive, he stayed in a room reserved for him at my relatives. This dwelling, where Alexander Rüstow also had an apartment flat, was, at most, 50 meters away from our house. This closeness naturally facilitated the give-and-take of opinions, and, of course, arranging skat parties, a sort of card game, where Dr. Julius Stern, former educational advisor to the German School, was the third person.

And if today my friends among the members of the Scientific Councils of the Federal Finance or Economics Ministries concur that I have a certain courage, even recklessness, at the skat parties we play to release stress after meetings, I owe this to Reuter who was very bold in card games and who stated often that this quality of his should not be overlooked.

Mrs. Hanna Reuter also came often to stay with us in Istanbul, especially during the hot summer months. The wonderful opportunity to swim that the sea and the Bosphorus offered was certainly lacking in Ankara. Besides, the younger son of Reuter, Edzard (who used to be called Edzi then; now member of the Executive Board of Daimler–Benz, Co.) and our son, Mathias, had become close friends and used to visit each other during vacations.[20]

***These passages from Neumark memoirs also shed light on the émigrés' relationship to at least some of the other members of the German community:***

People we could describe as "non-refugees" were also working in Turkey during the critical years. However, this fact alone does not prove that they held the same opinions as the Nazis. Moreover, if these people had relatives in Germany about which they worried, they had to keep silent. The refugees either had no relations with them or very loose ones. This stance should of course be met with understanding. In fact, among them there were individuals who had the courage to keep silent or keep a low profile when required on subjects such as racial discrimination.

To give an example, I remember the young couple of Hans and

Elisabeth (Lilo) Grosskettler, with whom my wife and I formed a lively friendship during the first years. One day, Hans Grosskettler, the representative of a large German industrial firm, told me in an embarrassed but frank manner that according to the directions or "orders" of the German Consulate, they should not be seen in the company of "non-Aryans" such as ourselves in society. He asked us to consider his request of terminating our meetings outside and restricting our home visits with understanding. Since we knew each other well enough to know the real opinions of this charming couple, we restricted our meetings without being hurt but never completely ceased them.

I do not find justified the distinction which is sometimes made between the "forced refugees" and the "voluntary" ones. Of course, it is true that the socialists and the regime's opponents labeled the forced refugees as "incorrigible" politically, and, even more, the Jews did not have any choice. They had to leave Nazi Germany to escape death. However, seeking refuge by those who had no problems with respect to politics is an indication of their lofty moral qualities. Since they had ethical political ideals and a strong conscience, they also had no alternative but to seek asylum, although they could have gone along with the Nazi regime. Thus their reasons for seeking asylum were in fact treated as secondary and did not form an obstacle between the friendly relations of the two groups most of the time.[21]

***Newspaper correspondent Erol Guney, born in Odessa Russia, raised and educated in Turkey, contributed the following from Tel Aviv, Israel, where he now lives*:**

From 1934 to 1938, I studied philosophy, French, and English literature at the newly established University of Istanbul, and it was an exhilarating and unforgettable experience.

My fellow students and I were in love with European culture, but we knew it only from books. While at this university we were in daily contact with Professors like *Hans Reichenbach, Leo Spitzer, Erich Auerbach, Herbert Diekmann,* and quite a few others who were the embodiment of this culture. Moreover, they were not distant, they were eager to help us, to enlighten us, to justify the hopes of Atatürk in the role this university could play in the "westernization" of Turkey. They were certainly grateful to the Turkish Republic for giving them the possibility to work in their profession—just as they were no more welcome in their own country—and so they showed their gratitude by being even more devoted to their work.

Most of the students responded in kind. We came regularly to the lectures, listened attentively, asked numerous questions sometimes off the subject. Indeed, we were curious to know what these scholars, the first we encountered of that caliber, thought about the problems that preoccupied us in these troubled prewar years.

We also knew, or we felt, that our luck would not last for long and that American universities would offer them better and more stable conditions as well as more opportunities for their families—so we wanted to make the most and the best of the time they stayed with us. Indeed, we were right to do so. I had the luck to finish my studies with most of the professors with whom I started, but Leo Spitzer went to the States in 1936. Fortunately for me, Erich Auerbach, the future author of *Mimesis*, replaced him. In philosophy, Reichenbach remained until I finished my studies. Diekmann, who became one of the world's authorities on *Diderot*, was a relatively young man at the time and I became quite close to him. For a long time, he personified for me the perfect type of European intellectual, not a German, a French, or British, but a "real" European, much before Europe started on its long and difficult period toward unity. Auerbach had quite an influence on my literary taste and my career. One day, he told me, "I know that you want to be a teacher, and you certainly can do it, but I think that you would better succeed in journalism. Think about it." I did, and in the end, due to circumstances, I became a journalist and don't regret it. I know that other students were also influenced by the German professors in their studies and careers. In many cases the relations between professors and students became quite close though still very respectful. In Turkish culture, respect for the teacher as well as gratitude towards him is very strong, or at least it was in my time, but that did not prevent a certain familiarity. There were parties involving professors and students as well as common outings in the vicinity of Istanbul. Hans Reichenbach was a philosopher of a kind we had not known. He was a scientist, a friend of Einstein, whose theories he explained masterfully. He was also an enemy of philosophical terms which sound good but have no clear meaning. He killed my interest in metaphysical trends (as he did with some other students), but I must admit that most of the other Reichenbach students in Istanbul and I did not have the scientific background necessary to fully comprehend all of his teachings. Nevertheless, what we did understand was sufficient, I think, to avoid being swept away by the false ideologies prevailing at that time. Atatürk had a vision of Turkey as being part of western civilization and there is no doubt that Reichenbach, Auerbach, and all the German professors, each in his field, contributed greatly to bringing Turkey closer to the realization of Atatürk's dream. A long way still remains, and resistance to the admission of Turkey to the European Union is pronounced, but the first steps have been taken, starting with Atatürk's reforms, the bold move of closing the *Dar-ül Fünun*, and Turkey's golden age spurred by having the German professors. At the time, my fellow students used to say, "We must thank Hitler. Without him, most of these professors would have never come to Turkey."

Another bold move made by Atatürk's successor, Ismet Inönü, also contributed to advancing Turkey on the path of westernization. It was the decision by the State to take on the translation of the world's classical literature—in particular Greek classics. The "Modern World" started in Europe with the Renaissance and the Renaissance started with translations of Greek authors from antiquity. So renaissance in Turkey, thought President Inönü and Minister of Education Hasan Ali Yücel, must also start with translations of great authors from ancient Greece and continue to the great works of the western world while not ignoring those of the East and the Far East. The aim was to insure that the Turkish reader would have access to the "classics." It was therefore decided at a Congress involving many of Turkey's outstanding intellectuals to create within the Ministry of Education a bureau for the translation of the most important works of the world's literature. The Congress had indeed come to the conclusion that since the 19th century, such translations were neither systematic nor faithful in Turkey.

Too many books of doubtful value had been translated, while books of great value were not, either because they would not attract many readers or because they were too difficult to translate. Some of the great books therefore had been abridged, and long chapters judged tedious were simply redacted. The Congress deemed essential for the Turkish people to have at their disposal the great works of the human spirit in translations that which would belie the famous saying: "A translation is like a woman: if she is faithful she is not beautiful and if she is beautiful she is not faithful." That was the directive given by the Congress to the new Bureau. One can say that although, on the whole, it succeeded in making the translations "faithful," it did not succeed in making them all "beautiful." For that the translator would not only need to know the work's original language well, but he or she must be a talented writer in one's own language. Nevertheless, the Bureau published quite a few faithful and beautiful translations, and, by doing that, it established a "model," a standard which after a number of years all respectable editors had to follow. So, by the 1960s and 70s, there was little need for the State to perform the task. Today, however, one can say that a Turk who does not have a command of one or more of the great foreign languages in order to enjoy a book in the original can nevertheless be considered "cultivated." This is so because not only have the great works been translated, but all contemporary "bestsellers" quickly follow suit by being translated into Turkish.

Starting in 1939, the Bureau started publishing the *Tercume* (Translation) *Review.* The *Tercume Review* published by the *Tercume Burosu* (Bureau) was an important bridge between Turkey and the west. President Inönü and Hasan Ali Yücel attached great importance to it. Wherever they went, one of the first questions asked was "Did you read the Tercume?" This was the case even during the difficult and dangerous years of WWII. This had an important and influential circulation. The Review published extracts from the classics not yet translated into Turkish and poems, often with the original text on the opposite page, as an example of what a good translation ought to be. It also published articles about the art of translation and reviews of books translated and published by commercial houses. The review also published special volumes on Greek literature signifying to the Turkish public the important fact that much of that was developed on Turkish soil. For example, the present city of Mugla was the ancient Millet where philosophy was born.

The six and a half years I worked in the *Tercume Burosu* (Bureau) as General Secretary and translator of some 20 books have been the happiest years of my life. I felt that I was working for the culture of Turkey and culture in general. My great joy was in seeing young peasants who had been studying in the "Village Institutes" reading classics with eagerness, even more than the youth from the cities. The Village Institutes closed, but the Review continued till the middle 60s, and several good issues were published. By the 1960s, many private publications took the place of the Review and the State was no longer needed in this effort.

***And now, without comment, some extracts from the memoirs of Germany's Ambassador to Ankara, Franz von Pappen:***[22]

> The Nazi campaign against the Jews caused me further difficulties. Hitler ordered me to withdraw passports from all German émigrés in Turkey and deprive them of German citizenship. I resisted this order and informed Ribbentrop that the majority of the émigrés had left Germany with the full permission of the government and many of them had taken up posts in Turkish universities and other institutions. They had remained loyal to Germany, even though they found the Nazi government unacceptable. I could not see my way to carry out his instructions and told him that the Turkish Government would consider such a step inexplicable. Not a single émigré was molested in any way.
>
> I came in for renewed criticism from the party, which demanded a boycott of all Jewish firms in Turkey. I pointed out that such a restriction had no validity in a neutral country, and to underline the point I made most of own purchases in Jewish shops.
>
> I mention these incidents only to demonstrate that it was possible, even in the final stages of the regime of terror in Germany, for a person in my position to exercise normal instincts and refuse to obey such unprincipled orders.

## Second Generation's Memoirs and Oral Histories

***Miriam Schmidt, now residing in Hod Hasharon, Israel, is a daughter of ENT specialist Dr. Karl Hellmann. She shared the following recollections***[23]***:***

> I shall try to give you some of my memories, and whatever I know for sure of my father.
>
> I was eight years old when we arrived in Istanbul, and I was fifteen and a half when we left for Palestine, so naturally my recollections are those of a child and a youngster. I remember Istanbul as a great place to be in, especially through the years of the war. Naturally, my parents were very worried about the news of the war and what was happening in Germany, especially as my mother had her parents and her sister, brother-in–law, and nieces in Munich, and the brother of my father was still in Wuerzburg.
>
> There also was a short time after the Germans had occupied Greece that we had packed backpacks under our beds, in case the

Germans came to Istanbul and we would have to flee to Anatolia. Fortunately, this did not happen. My father managed to bring his brother, Bruno Hellmann, who was already in the Buchenwald concentration camp, to Istanbul[24] and my mother's parents from Munich before the start of the war.

Bruno Hellmann managed later to go the United States, my grandmother died in Istanbul, and my eighty-year-old grandfather, Dr. Felix Herzfelder, a well-known lawyer, came with us to Palestine in 1943. The sister of my mother, her husband, and her two daughters, were all killed by the Nazis, but that is a different story. My mother's brother, Dr. Franz Herzfelder, managed to survive in France.

In spite of all these worries, we as a family led a good life in Istanbul. We had a big circle of friends, mostly of the same origin as we were, but also many Americans who worked at the American colleges [more like prep schools] (one for boys, one for girls). My sisters studied in that college, and I had private lessons for the first two years, some of them given by Mrs. Heilbronn, the wife of Professor Heilbronn, a specialist in genetics. We were never hungry in spite of the war and some food restrictions, mainly of bread, which is eaten in huge quantities by the Turks.

We were never rich, but there was enough money for having a vacation all together every summer on the Uludağ and once we made a cruise on the Black Sea for ten days. We all loved the surroundings, the Bosphorus was right in front of our house; we could just jump in and have a lovely swim, naturally without any lifeguard or any restrictions. We knew enough Turkish to get along on the street and in the shops. We loved to watch the fishermen collecting their fish out of the nets, and everybody was very friendly.

My father was an extremely silent man who kept all his worries and anxieties to himself. He worked very hard, left early in the morning, and came home quite late, after a full day of seeing patients and doing surgery in the ear, nose, and throat ward, of which he was the head and which he had to organize and modernize. He sometimes used to tell about the patients coming from far, from Anatolia, maybe on horse or donkey, with serious diseases. He was a very good physician and a very gentle man, and his patients adored him. We also know some Jewish Turkish physicians working in Israel who had been his students and apparently respected him greatly.

There are a few facts about my father which might be important. When the negotiations with the University of Istanbul started, my father was asked if he would prefer to have some private practice, and work only halftime at the University, giving him the opportunity to earn more money. My father declined immediately, explaining that he was interested in the academic work including research, etc. When signing the contract with the University he had to promise to give his lectures in Turkish after 5 years of teaching. This he managed to do.

After having been in Istanbul for 7 years, his contract would have been prolonged for only one more year. That was when he decided to go to Palestine. He received certificates for immigration to Palestine from the British Consul, who had been his patient, for himself and our family, my mother, one of my sisters (my oldest sister had married Prof. Hans Güterbock and stayed in Ankara), my grandfather, and myself.

In then Palestine, he opened a private practice in Haifa and also got a few beds for surgery in one of the hospitals in Haifa. Unfortunately, he got ill with Parkinson's disease and had to stop surgery, but he continued his private practice as long as possible, until he could not continue because of the disease. He died in 1959 at the age of 67.

You have asked me about Dr. Kurt Steinitz, whom we have known very well. He was a wonderful man, was a medical doctor, and had a doctorate in Chemistry. He built the first artificial kidney in Israel. Unfortunately he died very early. His wife, Elisabeth Steinitz, 96, is living not far from us and we are great friends. I told her about you and she told me to give you her phone number. She is a little hard of hearing, but has perfect memory. Her sister, Erica Bruck, a physician, lives in the United States, and she was in Istanbul as well, and has written her memoirs from Istanbul. I have not seen them.

Miriam's older sister, Frances (Hellmann) Güterbock, offered the following oral history25:

What was it like to leave Germany for Turkey? I can tell you that it was so very sad. Even though I had been baptized, anyone with Jewish blood was "tainted." Although both my parents were Jewish, as were their parents, we never celebrated any Jewish holidays. Against my father's wishes, my mother had all of her three daughters baptized, though not in Wuerzburg where we lived so as not to offend my grandparents and others. My younger sister, Miriam, celebrated her first Passover Seder with the Freundlich family who lived in the same apartment building just below us in Istanbul. And I think that they were the only family in that entire community of German émigrés who observed any Jewish holidays whatsoever! By then I was approaching my twenties, but was totally clueless as to the meaning of Passover.

While in Germany, I had some very close friends in the Sophienschuler Gymnasium [high school] that I attended and they were not Jewish. One teacher, Mary Brater, a believer in Jesus as the Redeemer, took me to her summer camp in 1936. I thought she was very courageous because this was dangerous for her to do, especially because she was a relative of Rudolph Hess [Hitler's deputy] and that was known by everyone. Though it was forbidden for them to see me, some of my school friends and I spent the last night together talking and playing the records that were our favorites.

We, my mother and two sisters and I, left for Turkey by train from Munich. I was seventeen years old. Father was already there, having left a few months before. My father, Dr. Hellmann, had been trying to leave Germany since 1933. He registered with Philipp Schwarz's organization in Switzerland and hoped to find something that way. Finally, in 1936, the ear, nose, and throat specialist who was already in Turkey wanted to leave. He hated it and wanted to return to Austria, even though he was Jewish. The position opened up, and it was offered via Schwarz, and my father accepted it.

Coming of age in Turkey was so different from what it would have been in Germany had things been normal. We lived in Istanbul, in Bebek. I attended an all-girls' school, the American Girls College, as a day student. I lived at home and took the streetcar to classes.

We had almost no connection with Turks! Which was strange. There were Turkish girls in our school from extremely wealthy families in contrast with poor Greek girls who were there on scholarship. Also, some Armenian girls were in school. We, the German girls, were treated as untouchables. We were considered by many of the others to be so high up on a social and cultural level...given our backgrounds, that many were envious and had little to do with us. There were four or five of us professors' children who stayed together, partly because we were isolated. I had German and Armenian friends. No Greeks or Turks as friends.

Dating? As far as our German community was concerned, German or German/Jewish boyfriends were acceptable but Turkish boyfriends were frowned upon. The only German girl who had a Turkish boyfriend for a while was my friend Agnes the daughter of German [botany] professor Alfred Heilbronn.

I graduated with honors when I was twenty. What did I do? I married Hans Güterbock. September 2 1940. Hans was working in Ankara so I moved there, of course. It was a difficult transition. Going from cosmopolitan Istanbul, family and friends, to rural Ankara where I knew mainly Hans. I was the youngest faculty wife and it caused a bit of a stir since I had married the only eligible bachelor in the Ankara German community. I am sure they thought me silly and I probably was. I moved into Hans' place which was small although it did have a large living room where Hans had set up his work area—large desk and books. There was also a kitchen, two bedrooms, and a bathroom. This apartment was on the ground floor of a private home and I had use of the little garden out back.

I admit to having been a bit spoiled. In Istanbul, we had maids for cleaning and laundry, so I had to learn everything about keeping a home when I married. In Ankara, I did have a maid for doing the laundry and some cleaning. She worked on the average six hours a day for me. She had to wash everything in the bathtub using heated water from the kitchen. I learned to shop for produce at the weekly open market. One of the group of porters, all having large woven baskets who were always available, carried my groceries up to the apartment which stood on a hillside.

We lived in Ankara for eight years. I never really learned much Turkish until I lived there. Both of my sons, Walter and Tom, were born there. I gave birth to a daughter, but she died soon after.

Yes, I had heard about the Christiansen-Wenigers from Hans. They [had] lived in a house just across the way from ours. Before we married, Hans had been ill and Mrs. Christiansen had been very kind to him, looking out for him. She did not approve of what her husband was doing—spying on the German community. And she did not like the fact that he was away from home so much. They moved away before I arrived in Ankara, but Hans told me about them.

In 1944, when the Turkish government severed diplomatic relations with Germany, all those still having valid German passports, Nazis and anti-Nazis alike, were interned in three remote villages. Professors Landsberger and Eckstein and our family maintained contact with those in *Yozgat*. The internees were not allowed to send or receive letters but packages were allowed. So we sent them knitting wool and chocolates. We wrapped money inside the wool.

I remember that a Mr. von Aulock was interned in *Yozgat*. He was definitely "a Junker" from that class of society,[26] but he was never a Nazi. He used to be an officer in Deutsche Bank's Istanbul branch. He had a big house on the European side of the Bosphorus. Because he was a collector of archeological artifacts, he used to consult my husband on occasion.

After being interned at *Yozgat*, he became the benefactor of the anti-Nazi Germans there. He helped many people with money. He ordered fancy foods to be delivered from the outside. He arranged a city council where all could attend. His wife stayed in Istanbul, as she was Hungarian and not involved. He became famous because he had a real bathroom installed. He must have had access to his Fund. I do not know what happened to him.

While we were in Ankara, a Professor Jacobsen [Thorkild] from the Oriental Institute in Chicago came to visit but in reality to check Hans out. He was world famous and we were hoping for an invitation. Before that could happen, Hans and eight others...I only remember Eberhardt, Ruben, and Landsberger...had their contracts terminated with only a three-month's notice. That caught us totally unprepared. This was in 1948, and I was in the last stages of my pregnancy with Tom.

Axel Person, a professor that Hans knew in Uppsala, Sweden, learned of our situation and quickly arranged for Hans to become a lecturer at his university for eleven months. He also arranged for a university-provided apartment. He even arranged for a free sea voyage to Sweden on the ship called "Sameland" that was bringing grapes from Turkey and Greece to Sweden. When we arrived in Uppsala we were guests at his house for about three weeks until we settled in the apartment provided for us.

The offer from Chicago came through while we were in Sweden. While Hans's American colleagues at Uppsala were amazed that the offer included a tenured appointment, they also recognized the low salary. It was made clear to him that we will have difficulty living in Chicago on a $450 a month income. Because we were stateless, the Swedes got the proper documents for us to immigrate to the United States.

There was no proper housing for us when we arrived in Chicago so we moved into a community of prefabs sometimes referred to as the Maternity Row [in juxtaposition to Fraternity Row] along with veterans who were in graduate school studying under the

G.I. Bill. Nearly everyone was married and there were many who had children the same age as mine so it was really a nice group.

We lived there for one year and then moved to an apartment in the Hyde Park area. Hans prospered as a world class academic and our two sons received a good education. Tom is a sociology professor at the University of Virginia and Walter is a veterinarian in Michigan. I returned to Turkey several times when Hans went for excavations.

***Dr. Alice (Haurowitz) Sievert offered some views on women's duties and contributions:***

I wondered whether any part of your book addresses the contributions of the intrepid spouses of the various professors, without whom these gentlemen would have had a much more difficult time carrying out their work. I distinctly recall that from the beginning, my father had assistants who spoke German plus translators for his lectures. My mother had no telephone, but had a German cookbook, a Turkish-French Dictionary, and household help that was almost illiterate and spoke only Turkish. Yet, she found an apartment, hired help, kept us fed by shopping at the weekly outdoor markets from where a *hamal* [porter] carried the groceries up four flights of stairs, and, after that, she had to wash each lettuce leaf with soap and water to make sure that we did not catch typhoid fever from vegetables often fertilized with human and animal manure. And that was only part of it....

***Klaus Eckstein, from Cambridge England shared the following recollection of his childhood:***

....the part played by my father in helping a large number of Jewish children escape to Palestine—we were often visited by a somewhat mysterious little man, Herr [Hayim] Barlas[27], who was the representative of the Jewish Agency in Turkey. One day, he mentioned a transport of Jewish children from, I think, Sweden, whom the Turks would not let travel through, and asked my father to try to intervene. Father was friendly with the then Foreign Minister, Refik Saydam (also a medic), and he asked him for help.

Apparently, these children were not allowed to travel through Turkey, as the Turks had promised the British to stem the flood of illegal immigrants. The British were approached and gave their exceptional blessing to the transport to go through Turkey—I was too small then to take part, but apparently when the train passed through Ankara,[28] there were large crowds of refugees giving them fruit and sweets. My parents were then invited to Palestine in, I think, 1944, to meet these children, who had settled by then.[29]

***Klaus claimed that over the years he had tried to corroborate this recollection but failed in doing so. As it turns out, deep in the multilingual memoirs (Hebrew, English, Turkish, French, and German), Hayim Barlas provided the following (in Hebrew).[30]***

...During the war, quite a few Jewish and half–Jewish physicians lived in Ankara. These émigrés had received professional permits from Atatürk, the founder of the Turkish Republic who permitted entry of 50 well-known physicians who, upon the ascendance of the Nazis, were expelled from universities and "ejected" from science chairs by virtue of being "'racial" Jews. One of these was Prof. Eckstein who was well connected with leaders of the government as well as with the ambassadors of the United States, Great Britain, Switzerland etc., and was their "house doctor." Recommended by Prof. Eckstein, an assimilated Jew with a Christian wife, who was removed from Judaism until the Nürnberg Laws brought her closer to his people, I was given an appointment with U.S. Ambassador Steinhardt. That took place on May 5 1942. He received me cordially, telling me that he has already heard of me from his colleague the British Ambassador.

I briefed him on the circumstances back home and in the Diaspora and about my objectives as the representative of the Jewish Agency in Eretz, Israel, on the information we received indirectly from immigrants and refugees who reached Turkey miraculously, on conditions in Poland, in Romania, etc. When I asked for his help in negotiating with the Turkish authorities, he remarked that his position required great delicacy and that any action that could be viewed as solidarity with our aims could damage more than help since "*...it must be made clear that he is not the Ambassador of Jews but of the United States in a neutral country.*"[31] (emphasis added).

The above is independently supported by the "Minutes of the Conversation at the British embassy in Ankara on June 18 1942. Present were Mr. Morgan, British Minister, and Mr. Barlas, Jewish Agency."[32]

These minutes show that "Mr. Morgan" was told that "the Turkish Foreign Ministry (Mr. Akalcin) declared that the Turkish government will be prepared to reconsider favourably the question"..."of transit by land via Turkey for 270 children from Romania and Hungary." The rest of the minutes state that the children should be sent in groups of 50 to 60 and specify other logistical aspects of the transit.

**Klaus's claim is also augmented by the 1975 memoirs authored by his mother, Dr. Erna Eckstein-Schlossmann:**

> The Warburg Financial Institution had made possible the passage of many Jewish children from Germany to Denmark in 1935 and also had supported them financially. When the war started, it was understood that there was a chance of transferring these children to Sweden. However, financial support was not available at that time. The Soviet Union had given permission to these children to go to Palestine going through its territory, but the [Turkish] government did not consent to passage through its territory.
>
> Schummi [Dr. Eckstein] went to speak with the former Minister of Health, Dr. Refik Saydam, who was then the Prime Minister. Saydam told him that there was pressure from the British government not to grant visas to the Jews going to Palestine. However, Refik Saydam personally guaranteed the release of these visas. We gathered all our acquaintances and met the children at the train station. We gave them sweets, candies, and fruit. We met the majority of these children during our visit to Palestine in 1944.[33]

***The epilogue to this story comes from Rob Weiss, an organizer of some of the down-the-Danube refugee flotilla, and Israel's War of Independence veteran, living in Boynton Beach, Florida:***

> Dear Mr. Reisman,
>
> I'm very familiar with the work of Mr. Barlas. The Children's group of *madrich* [group leader in Hebrew] Joshko Indig was in contact with him from 1941 until 1945. With his help, ninety Jewish refugees and Austrian and German children (names and dates I have) left Belgrade, Yugoslavia on Thursday March 27 1941. The group traveled down the Danube to the Black Sea and then through the Bosphorus to Palestine.
>
> Chaim Barlas was active. His address was Pera Palas Istanbul and he spoke German fluently. All the children arrived in Palestine safely and entered Kibbutzim to continue their education. Some of them entered the Jewish brigade [sometimes known as the Palestine Brigade of the British army] and one of them paid the ultimate price.[34]
>
> Schaliach [emissary in Hebrew] Chaim Barlas left Istanbul for

> Palestine shortly after September 1945. We were in constant contact with him starting February 1941.[35]

The story of Jews being saved by having Turkey allow them the rights to passage cannot be closed without mentioning Monsignor Angelo Roncalli. Monsignor Roncalli was the Apostolic Delegate or Papal representative to Greece and Turkey during World War II.[36] He later became to be known as Pope John XXIII. There is now a great deal of evidence, more of which is still emerging, that Msgr. Roncalli played a pivotal role in saving the lives of thousands of Jews while serving in Istanbul as the apostolic delegate. In fact, it is now known that Chaim Barlas worked closely with Msgr. Roncalli.[37] "And, with the help of Bulgaria's King Boris, a reluctant Axis ally, Msgr. Roncalli used the Red Cross to save thousands of Slovakian Jews who had been deported to Bulgaria prior to extermination."[38]

And, to all this, one might add the name of Nazi Reichstag's chief representative in Turkey, the German Ambassador Franz von Pappen, a devout Catholic. In the end, Roncalli wrote to the Nuremberg tribunal sitting in judgment of major war criminals at the conclusion of WWII, that von Pappen "...gave me the chance to save the lives of 24,000 Jews." Von Pappen was the only high-ranking Nazi who was acquitted of all charges.

Interesting as this little known bit of history may be to pursue, we shall return to the main topic of this book.

***Peter A. Eckstein, M.D., also writing from Cambridge, UK, added the following to the very extensive memoir written by his brother Klaus and which appeared in a previous chapter:***

> My brother, Klaus Eckstein, has provided information already. I doubt if I can add a great deal to his as I left home aged thirteen years to attend a school in Istanbul and saw my parents [who lived in Ankara] only during holidays.
>
> My mother[39] was a determined lady—she lived to be 102 years old. She considered herself in charge of the émigré families in Ankara and held funds for those in need, was sort of "mother confessor" to very many people and was an active person in the social life of the émigrés as well as the diplomatic corps. She told me repeatedly how grateful she was to Hitler for forcing her to leave Düsseldorf. She felt that she would never had such a role as she played in Ankara.
>
> My father was an exceptional physician. Although he had specialized in pediatrics, his medical knowledge extended to the adult population as well and he was physician to the whole

diplomatic corps in Ankara, Allied as well as Axis diplomats. He was once asked by one of the leading Nazi members whose children and family he had treated if there was anything that he, the Nazi, could do for my father in Germany, to which my father replied that it was too late for any intervention.[40]

***Physicist Eugen Merzbacher recalls a 1936 visit to a Germany left behind:***[41]

Incredibly, in retrospect, my parents had gone back to Germany in the summer of 1936 for one last visit to see my aging grandfather. Rightly, as it turned out, it was regarded "safe" for us Jews to spend that summer vacation in Germany because of the protection afforded us by the Olympic Games. My parents took advantage of the visit to their home country to salvage a little more of their personal assets that they had left behind in their emigration in 1935, although the remainder of their belongings was confiscated shortly thereafter by the Nazis.

***Memoir of Dr. Alice (Haurowitz) Sievers as a youngster in Turkey and coming of age in America:***

On arrival in Istanbul, the only Turkish phrase my brother and I knew was *Türkçe bilmem*, i.e., "I don't know Turkish." We also knew little English and so Prof. Hirsch's daughter Julima tutored us to help us stay on track at the English High Schools. My classmates were mostly the daughters of expatriates and diplomats. There was a separate academic track for my Turkish fellow students since these had to complete Turkish elementary school before enrolling in a foreign school. Regrettably, that prevented me from becoming close friends with Turkish girls and I also never achieved great fluency in Turkish. Since we lived in Nişantaş, I had only occasional contact with the children of émigré professors, most of whom lived in Bebek and went to Robert College.

Our British school curriculum was impacted by wartime staffing problems. For instance, no science was taught until Mrs. Brauner (wife of Prof. Brauner) came to teach it in my senior year. My father had filled this void by slipping interesting scientific odds and ends into family conversations and had sparked my later interest in chemistry. Upon graduation, I took the University of London Matriculation Exam, which I passed with honors. This was useful later on, when I applied for acceptance at colleges.

Summers were a time to enjoy swimming. We alternated between the Floria beaches, various bathing piers, and the rocks on the shores of the Princes Islands. Much of Turkey was off-limits to foreigners during the war, and so all of our family vacations were spent on Uludağ, the mountain which rose above Bursa. We explored the mountains with other families and also with some of Father's Turkish co-workers who wanted to experience the novelty of mountain hiking. We stayed at the primitive lodge, which had a huge sleeping room filled with double-decker bunks, served three basic daily meals, and provided cold-water taps in the main hallway for washing. So we bathed in mountain streams and on our way back to Istanbul, we stopped off at a h*amam* in Bursa, where there were hot springs.

In Istanbul, we often spent Sundays taking long walks or getting together with friends at each others' homes. My parents' friends included personnel from the Czech Consulate, and the families of expatriate businessmen and fellow professors. As children, we particularly enjoyed visiting Dr. and Mrs. Fritz Arndt, whose home lay directly on the Bosphorus. We swam from their pier, ate Mrs. Arndt's great cookies, and sat in the garden to listen to discussions of academic topics, the war situation, and how to cope with the inflation which outpaced University salary increases.

My parents dealt with inflation by finding a very nice English lodger, who became a good friend. They also sold off their crystal and much of my father's large collection of orchestral and other music scores. My parents, fortunately, were able to bring all their possessions, except for money and most valuables, because we left Prague before the Nazi bureaucracy had become entrenched.

Although my parents interacted socially with Turkish colleagues, we were invited along only once. The occasion was a wonderful multi-course Turkish banquet served under an arbor in the garden of Prof. and Mrs. Mazhar Uzman. Tuba, their eldest daughter, was my schoolmate, though several years ahead of me. I believe that her younger siblings also attended my brother's and my schools.

Another memorable occasion was a formal dinner at our home for my father's Turkish colleagues. To make the event a success, Mother's Hungarian friend helped out by wearing a maid's uniform to serve the meal, replacing our very inexpert household help.

I also recall the visit to my parents of the Nobel-Prize winner,

Prof. Albert Szent-Györgyi who had come from German-occupied Hungary with his wife to visit Turkey, give a lecture, and "to breathe in some fresh air."

Because Turkey was a neutral country, my parents could correspond both with people living under German occupation and those in rest of the world. I only recently learned that my father kept family members in Prague in touch with others who had escaped to Britain, Palestine, or the United States. My grandmother had been prevented by the Nazis from joining us in Turkey and had later been deported to Terezin [Theresienstadt concentration camp in Bohemia and Moravia]. She could not write to us from there, and so my mother sent food packages to her by registered mail, with a return receipt requiring the recipient signature. We never knew if Grandmother was allowed to keep the food, but the signed receipts were proof that she was still alive. I still remember the sad day when a return receipt came back with a forged signature and we knew that we would never see Grandmother again.

As Axis armies invaded the Balkans, Greece, and Africa, my parents feared an invasion of Turkey and prepared to escape via Anatolia to Allied-occupied territory. They deposited a trunk of our possessions with friends in Ankara and then, during that summer, we moved to a Pension on the Anatolian side of the Marmara Sea. My parents believed that the Bosphorus might slow a German advance and give us a head start in crossing Anatolia, on foot if necessary. I thought that the Pension was wonderful. It lay right on the Marmara Sea and we could swim all day long. On the down side, my father had a much longer commute to work by tram and ferry.

After the war, my parents wanted my brother and me to continue our education in the United States. We could have had a very good education in Turkey, but foreigners could not obtain work permits. Since Father wished to honor his Turkish contract and had not yet found a situation in the U.S., my mother brought us children to the United States as soon as we could obtain passage. In New York, we stayed with Mother's relatives until they found us an apartment. I enrolled in high school, took the New York State Regents Examination, and applied to colleges recommended by Father's colleagues. One of these was Indiana University in Bloomington, Indiana, where I was admitted and given a full-tuition scholarship.

Since the University could not provide housing, because

veterans returning from WWII had priority, my parents were relieved to learn that Thea Muller, the daughter of our family friend Dr. Kantorowicz, Professor of Dentistry at the University of Istanbul, lived In Bloomington. (Her husband, Herman J. Muller was Professor of Genetics and shortly thereafter he was awarded the Nobel Prize), [1946 in Medicine].

Thea Muller introduced me to the family of Professor Harry G. Day, a biochemist. He and Mrs. Day accepted me as a lodger and treated me as a daughter from then on. They invited my mother to visit, and Dr. Day learned from her that Father was also a biochemist and was seeking a position in the United States. After reviewing my father's publications, Dr. Day arranged for him to lecture at Indiana University in the summer of 1947. Shortly thereafter, Father was asked to join the chemistry faculty and accepted the position, to start in 1948.

I was an adult before I understood the impact my quiet father had had on his Turkish co-workers and students. I recall one episode that illustrates this. In 1958, I was at a small hospital in Lake Forest, Illinois, delivering our son, and somehow my maiden name must have appeared on my admission record. The next day, two young Turkish doctors came to my room, asked if I was related to their former professor, and expressed their great admiration for him! That this admiration must have been shared by many of his Turkish colleagues and coworkers became evident when in 1973 he was awarded an Honorary Doctorate at the University of Istanbul.

*Alice Sievert also recalled her first educational experience in the States:*

I was rather busy on arrival in New York City, since my nearest school was Julia Richman High School (a magnet school) which gave me no opportunity to get bored. Squeezing one year's full load of senior courses, including three honors courses into a two-and-a-half month period, while also completing twelve college applications kept me rather busy and I did not pay much attention to anything else. It was a marathon not even matched in graduate school.[42]

*Memoir of her younger brother, Dr. Martin (Haurowitz) Harwit, who became Director of the National (US) Air and Space Museum in 1987 and resigned in May 1995 under fire from Congress, the news media, and*

***veterans groups for his handling of plans to display the Enola Gay, the B-29 bomber that dropped the first atomic bomb on Japan in 1945[43]:***

When we arrived in Istanbul, my parents wanted my sister and me to learn English and enrolled us in schools run by the British Council. The English High School for Boys taught all classes, science, mathematics, history, and literature in English, in the mornings. By law, every school child was to have half a day of lessons in Turkish. So we had history, literature, and geography lessons in Turkish in the afternoons, and we also had French classes then. The Turkish and English history lessons did not always agree.

The school had about 120 pupils. At one time, we counted thirty-two different nationalities, Greeks, Poles, Americans, Chinese, Egyptians, Germans, Maltese, British, Georgians, French—almost any country you could think of. The Turkish boys, of course, were in the majority, but probably accounted for not much more than half the pupils. My best friend, Andrew Lorant, a Hungarian only a few months older than I, whose family lived two floors below us in the same four-flat apartment building was Catholic. We always walked to and from school together from age eight to fourteen, were in all the same classes, played on the same soccer and cricket teams at school, and were known as "the inseparables."

Two other boys our age with whom we spent a lot of time were Rudy Grűnberg, whose family was Jewish, and his close friend Mahmut Hilmi, who I assume was Mohammedan; his father was the Egyptian consul in Istanbul. When Hilmi (we all knew each other in school by our surnames) had what probably was his tenth birthday, the four of us spent the afternoon outside his parents' apartment building in *Nişantaş*, taking turns running behind his new bicycle, clutching its seat to keep it erect until Hilmi got the hang of it and ended the afternoon a proficient bike rider.

Given the makeup of the boys, religion never was mentioned in school. In Prague, my sister and I had attended an evangelical grade school, where we had classes both in German and Czech. My parents had me baptized a Protestant at birth and, for some time after we moved to Turkey, they had us both take Bible lessons from an English priest. Father wanted us to be familiar with Christianity.

Aside from this, as far as I can recall, religion was never mentioned at home. True, we always had a Christmas tree, both in Prague and later in Istanbul, exchanged presents, and sang traditional Christmas carols led by Mother, who had a good voice and liked to sing; Father, who was a gifted pianist, accompanied her. But Christmas, for us, was more of an annual occasion to enjoy being together than a religious event. As long as my parents were both alive, we regularly continued to get together for Christmas in Bloomington, Indiana, where my parents settled after coming to the U.S.

I don't ever remember my father using a Yiddish or Hebrew word or phrase and, to the best of my recollections, none of the other professors we visited from time to time, or their wives or children did either. So it may not be surprising that I was totally taken aback, one day when I was about fourteen, when Father pointed out that he and Mother were Jewish. Since I was Protestant, I had assumed my parents must be, too.

My father was the most honest and ethical person I have known. I never knew him to tell me anything that I could not totally trust. He also was deeply agnostic. He had been painfully aware of anti-Semitism long before Hitler. He always said that he would not change his religion because people would think he was doing it for personal gain. But he wanted to keep his children from having to suffer anti-Semitism. Hence my baptism. Aside from this, however, his beliefs were agnostic.

A few years ago, when Secretary of State Madelaine [*sic*] Albright, who had also been born in Czechoslovakia, found out to her surprise that her family had been Jewish, nobody in America believed her. I did; it had happened to me. For Americans, it seems difficult to understand. But, for many Europeans, who had witnessed anti-Semitism for many decades, integration seemed a way to break these mutual hatreds. Religion seemed best when ignored.

I have inherited my father's agnosticism. Too many evils have been perpetrated in the name of a superior God, too many wars fought for a superior religion, too many people killed in the name of a superior faith. For me, religion is the source of most evils, even today.

For my mother, the move to Istanbul was liberating. In Prague, the family was supposed to live an elegant life. As a faculty member, my father's salary was low by the standards of his and Mother's textile-factory-owning families, but he would have preferred for the family to live on his salary. My grandparents, however, may have somehow contributed to keep up the larger family's lifestyle. My sister and I had a governess; there was a cook and also a maid. Mother did little except to get together with this staff each morning to decide on the meals they should prepare and the day's schedule to be followed.

All this changed in Istanbul. We did have a Turkish live-in maid. She probably was indispensable, since bargaining for every head of lettuce you bought on the market was an endless sport that a foreigner could not win. The maid, who knew the cost that each item should have, could help my mother at every turn in such matters. But Mother now also learned to cook, and became very good at it. To her, it was wonderful to be allowed to do things herself, and she made sure that we children also learned rudimentary practical matters. She taught me to cook simple meals, to sew on buttons, and to darn socks, which was important in wartime where nothing got thrown out.

Mother used to say she didn't want me to have to marry the first girl who came along, just because I did not know how to manage these chores myself. Later, when I went to college and graduate school in the United States and had very little money, these small skills came in more than handy, particularly when I joined cooking co-ops to save on the cost of meals.

After we came to the United States, my mother had no help at all at home, not even an occasional cleaning lady, whom other professors' wives often had. Mother said she was far more pleased to have the house to herself, with no intrigues, nobody else to have to depend on. It was one of the features of life in the United States she loved most. After the War, I believe, Father would have been quite happy to have had an academic position in Europe, where he was far better known than in the U.S. and where he had been honored by various academies. But, after Mother arrived, she took to the U.S., and said she would never go back. She wanted the whole family—all four of us— to settle in the States, and persuaded Father to grant her that wish. She wanted to be as far away as possible from Europe and the many wars it had suffered. And then, nobody in Czechoslovakia, in her family or in Father's, was left after the war. They had all emigrated or died—a few of old age, but most in the concentration camps, including her mother and brother, her two closest relatives. Her father had died of cancer in the late 1920s.

The moves from Prague to Istanbul, and then to the U.S. profoundly changed our family. We became much closer without the intervention of servants, and also became more self-reliant.

For me, perhaps the most remarkable aspect of our stay in Turkey was the incredibly dedicated interest that the foreign professors in Istanbul had for the children among them—not just their own, but all of us. Even when we were small they would talk with us.

Visiting the Arndt's at their place on the Bosphorus in Kadiköy always was a treat. Prof. Arndt would recite rhymes from the German caricaturist and satirist Wilhelm Busch that he seemed to know in endless numbers. And later we would sit and listen as the adults talked about the war, the daily problems it raised, adjusting to life in Turkey, and other problems, while Mrs. Arndt served a red currant jelly she had cooked, on which she poured a cover of milk. It gave us children a feeling of being part of these adults' community. I believe the adults, in turn, thought of us in the same way. For them, we may have represented the future for which they had made sacrifices by leaving their homelands.

It is that spirit of community that I remember most fondly when I think back on our lives in Turkey. Among these academics, as I think about it, the War had brought out the very best. Some of the strength of these men and women, I like to believe, may have rubbed off on many of us children, who were too young at the time to recognize how singular this group had been.

***The following is not great poetry in either language. However, it represents an artifact reflecting the atmosphere of the two German "colonies" in Ankara during the late 30s. It was written by Friedel (Elfriede) Gassner, an Aryan whose parents returned to Germany near the beginning of the war and by Marianne Laqueur, a non-Jew, whose father, August, was a physiotherapy professor at the University of Ankara and could not return. It was provided by Ms. Laqueur from a senior citizen's home in Wiesbaden, just before her passing in April 2006***:

Today we both are here, Emigrant and Nazi
Today we bring you cheer, Emigrant and Nazi.
Joy for some is pain for others
differences, we call that,
we shall explain the "how" and "what"
Emigrant and semigrant now in Ankara abide
And they think they are the guarantors of the German "Geist"
Nazi's on the other side, showing "modesty" is right
Not only Geist is still alive, but race, and the masses must abide.
'33 the blackest year when with scorn and mockery,
We were thrown from out of there, we were chased from where we were born

From all honors we were shorn, without pity and no less, lack of bread and our distress
To Turkish Ankara we came and found our circle just the same
In 1936 we began to thrive, we were industrious and "wunderbar,"
Our own might took us far, as might and deed, without the need from afar
Of help, we thrived on our own in Ankara.
Culture came with us from home
We treasure and keep it
One day a month it pays to free
It's lecture talk, it's culture's fee.
9:30 Saturday the hour you see hundreds stream,
To the handsome Colony house and to Embassy green,
It is a must, it is some fun, and you are there to share with some
German news and food in one, an only pot is shared by all
"Volksgemeinschaft" this they call.
Although interests keep us going, sometimes is the time too long, we
And all are sharp of knowing what keeps our neighbor strong.
Who sleeps with whom must not be hidden and where and why and when
Is it at home in a hotel or in the neighbor's den?
It is with us as it's all over, we know each other much too well,
But it proves to be much wiser, this your interest soon to quell.
Keep your sight on politics and enjoy your "Hausmusik."
A fool remains who does not long for wine and women and their song.
Emigrants and Semigrants, Nazis who are not our league,
They bring only "Heil" and "Sieg", this why "Gute Nacht" we chose
For, since they came: what we call close,
As our way out: Good Night we chose.
Verse No. 2 is recited as refrain between verses:
Emigfants and Semigrants
Now in Ankara abide
And they think they are guarantors
Of the German "Geist."

Translated by Frances Gutterbock April 3, 2006.

***Businessman Matthias Neumark recalls the education that was good enough for him to be admitted to the Harvard Business School. Economics professor Fritz Neumark's son, Matthias, was born in 1927:***[44]

Initially, I was tutored at home by an expatriate German teacher, and, in 1936, I was enrolled in the German School in Istanbul. This involved a commute from Asia to Europe on a daily basis aboard a commuter ferry. By 1938, this school had become infested with new teachers committed to Nazi doctrine, and, in late 1938 (after Kristallnacht), I was withdrawn from this school by my parents, as were several other children of German refugees. This was followed by an immersion course in English, which led to enrollment in the English high school in Istanbul. After graduation in 1943, I attended Robert College, an American liberal arts and engineering college, receiving the B.A. in 1947.[45]

***Engineer Peter Engelmann is the son of one of the group of German professionals invited to help in the non-academic aspects of the Reformu. He was married to Erica, one of the Hellmann sisters:***

I am a civil engineer. I graduated from an American [Robert] college [in Istanbul] in 1944, went on to study in this country ( U.S.A.), got a master's degree in '47, and worked in New York City for seventeen years for consulting firms doing industrial and transportation design. I came to Washington (D.C.) in 1964 and settled in the area after a year of working for the government on transportation issues. I joined the World Bank and was with them for twenty years as an engineer in mostly transportation and urban development. I retired in 1984 and formed a little company that did pre-investment advice, which is what I did at the World Bank mostly. In 1999, I retired from that company and settled in Charlottesville.

I was born the only son of a family of Berliners in Berlin, Germany, in 1924, right at the end of the tremendous inflation they had at the end of World War I. Both my parents were born in Berlin. My father was a banker and an accountant later and Mother was a kindergarten teacher. They married in 1923. My father had a Jewish background; actually both my parents were Lutheran Christians. They got married in a church in Berlin and we were Lutherans until I got confirmed in a Lutheran church. But, my father, because of his Jewish background, lost his job with a German bank in 1933.

We left Germany in 1936 when I was twelve and just about getting interested in religion. We went to Turkey because my father received a contract with the help of the Turkish government. He went to Istanbul as finance advisor to the Turkish steamship and harbor administration. I attended the German school in Istanbul at first because my parents felt that we would go back eventually. I had religion classes as part of the curriculum and I was confirmed in the German Lutheran Church. I thought of myself as Jewish only in the sense that I shared the history, and I knew, of course, why my father lost his job and why we had to leave Germany. I had some problems in the public school system in Germany before we went to Turkey.

Between 1933 and 1936, they sort of began changing the school system to be totally party-dominated and everything was Nazi-ish in Germany. Because we still felt this would blow over, I attended Istanbul's German school until November 1938 (Kristallnacht, Night of the Broken Glass) when we heard what had happened in Germany with all the smashing of the Jewish stores.

At that time, I started private lessons to enter the British high school. I have very specific memories which I am currently refreshing because I am trying to write my memoirs and looking at old photo albums of my class in the German high school in Berlin. There was this nice little boy who was my best friend. I walked home with him every day from school. Because his father was divorced, he normally stayed with me for supper and we did homework together. He was a very close friend.

One day I was walking home from school and he was walking ahead of me. I called him and he didn't turn around. Then when we got to the next intersection he stopped and said, "Peter, I heard you call me, but you know we'll always be friends, but my troop leader from the Hitler Youth lives in that apartment house over there and I just can't be seen walking with you anymore." And that was the end of it. At the time, I was ten or eleven and it was a pretty shocking experience.

Of course, my father was the kind of person who liked to tell me about the background of why he had lost his job…and what Hitler stood for. He was very much for the Pan-European movement which then was considered subversive because Hitler thought any uniting of Europe should be under German general supervision and domination.

My father had a good nose for things, and he saw the handwriting on the wall when others had their heads in the sand. He didn't have any property to lose and as a salaried employee he had to go where there was a job to be had. We were going to go to Colombia, Latin America, but the contract from Turkey came through earlier.

We emigrated first-class. We left with our furniture and our clothing. My father took the Orient Express to Istanbul ahead of us. My mother and I visited some relatives in Italy and we stopped by in Venice where we boarded a beautiful first-class cabin. The ship cruised from Trieste to Venice, Brindisi to Piraeus, Istanbul, and back.

That was my first trip on an ocean liner and my father, being with the steam ship and harbor administration in Istanbul, arranged with the Captain to have a bunch of roses placed in our cabin. It was a beautiful trip. During its four-hour stopover in Piraeus, my mother grabbed a cab and we drove up to the Acropolis. We walked up and took some photographs. Istanbul, upon our arrival, impressed us as one of the most beautiful cities in the world and we had a very good nine years there.

At first we settled in Pera, the modern part of Istanbul. Our apartment was within walking distance of Istanbul's German school and of the Lutheran church where I was confirmed.

I was extremely religious as a kid of thirteen going to confirmation class would be. We had this wonderful preacher, minister who looked like Jesus Christ in person and I admired him a great deal.

One day in September of 1939, he, this favorite minister of mine, gave a prayer from the pulpit for the victory of the German troops in Poland and for God's guidance to the Führer. That is when my religious empire collapsed. That was pretty much the end of my church attendance until going to the Unitarian church in this country when we expected our first child.

Actually, I consider myself a war profiteer in the sense that I really had a great time during the war. I didn't see a shot fired in anger, I was not drafted until after I came to this country, and I didn't have any part in the war except the shortages. However, we took part in the war of nerves. For a long time, we worried about the Germans taking Turkey the way they took Greece, Bulgaria, and Romania. They decided to go to Stalingrad via Russia rather than go through Turkey and that was our great fortune in the war years.

But in Turkey in 1936, it was very peaceful. There were few cars; there was no traffic congestion.

I took English lessons to enter the British High School, which I failed in, but then I took a full year of private classes in English, math and physics at home, and passed the entrance exam to freshman college, Robert College, Istanbul, which is on one of the most beautiful hills overlooking the Bosphorus. That waterway separates Europe from Asia and it is the narrows between the Blacks

Sea and the Marmara Sea. Robert College was right on top of a hill overlooking that fantastic seaway, and looking at the Asian side, which, at that time, was basically hills, agricultural land, and a few lovely old homes along the shores. The college, which was originally Methodist, but was non-religious at the time I got there, had an engineering school and I was fortunate enough to get a B.S. in Civil Engineering in Turkey in 1944.

Instruction was all in English except for Turkish language and Turkish history, which we took in Turkish. The instructors were American, and in the Engineering school, fortunately, most of them were MIT graduates, so I received the background to enter MIT's graduate program when I came to the United States, in 1945.

During the five years I attended Robert College, we lived in Bebek, a German émigré community on the European shore of the Bosphorus. There were two apartment houses known as the Professors' houses. We moved in one and the Hellmans lived in the other. The Hellman family was sort of the center of the émigré grouping with three lovely daughters, Frances, Erica, and Miriam.

Erica and I got to liking each other after a while. In 1942, the year she graduated from her college, we got engaged. It wasn't formal, of course. I had no income. She did get a little silver ring from me, but that was a secret. Her parents were never Zionist but were Jewish. When her father's five-year contract was over, they had to move. With no income, because medical doctors could not practice in Turkey unless they were citizens, he had no way to make a living. At that time, Israel [Palestine] was in need of doctors, so in 1943, the Hellmans left for Israel.

Erica and I corresponded for the next four years. It was wartime, the mail was slow, and it had to go through all kinds of censors. Palestine was under British control then so the mail had to go through more convoluted ways through Syria to Turkey.

When we were dating, we did things like swimming, hiking, or visiting each other in our homes. We would take a bus to Bursa, which was a lovely town with mountainous terrain and only two or three hours from Istanbul.

When Erica left with her family in 1943, there was nothing we could do. We weren't officially engaged. We didn't know how the war would go, Stalingrad had just happened, the invasion hadn't happened. It was a strange and very difficult time until things swung the other way.

Having been accepted by MIT and with an immigration visa in hand, I left Turkey on V E Day, May 8 1945. It was the first thing I heard on the radio when I boarded this little Liberty ship which had been carrying weapons to Odessa. I got a ticket because I had a visa. There were about four or five Turkish students on board with me, but the ship was basically a freighter. It loaded tobacco from Izmir for the way back to Norfolk to mix with Virginia's tobacco here. I got on board in Izmir and had one of the most wonderful trips ever. This was victory in Europe. The war in the Pacific was still on.

I was traveling alone. My parents hadn't gotten visas yet. I arrived in Norfolk, Virginia, kissed the soil, took the train to New York, was met there by a friend, went to visit my Aunt in Northampton, Massachusetts, and started at MIT in July. I lived in the dorm and just had time to finish one term when Uncle Sam caught up with me. I had gone to the Immigration and Naturalization office like every immigrant should after I established residence. They were nice to me, had me sign the right paper, and told me to walk down the block to the draft board and register there as well. It took six months, just the time of the first semester, to draft me. I was a G. I. This was November of 1945.

I was sent to Aberdeen, Maryland, for basic training. My next assignment was to go Germany to guard the peace. That was difficult. I was a G. I. I became a citizen in less than six months. They took a truckload of us from Aberdeen to the Baltimore Court house where the judge waived the waiting period and tests and made us citizens.

Because I was probably the only G. I. who didn't know how to drive a car, I did personnel administration in Germany. I was the only German speaker in the unit, so I was put in charge of civilian personnel. My first meetings with Germans had complications because we had to treat them nicely—they were citizens not prisoners.

Upon return in 1947, with an honorable discharge and the G. I. Bill to pay for my second term at MIT, I received my MS in Civil Engineering. I tried to get to Israel after graduating from MIT but was not allowed in by the British. Instead, Erica arrived on August 8 1947, and we were married on August 15. My parents came to New York before my Army discharge. They were living in New York. My father found a job, but, for them, it was much more difficult to adjust. They were struggling, but they made it.

***Berlin's Verein Aktives Museum created a wonderful exhibit of artifacts and stories dealing with the émigrés in Turkey. They also published a glossy soft-cover book describing that exhibition. Following are Dr. Eugen Merzbacher's comments on the "Haymatloz Exhibition" as they appeared in German, in the May 2000 or #43 edition of the Mitgliederrundbrief (Membership Newsletter):***

> I want to thank you and your colleagues in Berlin for the cordial reception. The opening of the exhibition was a great success, and I am very glad that I decided in the last minute to undertake the trip. Now that I have had time to read the catalogue with the attention it deserves, I have noted a number of interesting details that had escaped me on my altogether too brief visit to Berlin. I am especially impressed by the impartiality and objectivity which you and your historian friends have brought to this project, as exemplified by your refusal to whitewash in the articles the often ambiguous attitude of the Turkish authorities during the war
>
> It is, fortunately, a human tendency to superimpose in retrospect, after the passage of some decades, a rosy glow over the events of the past. For example, I find that I tend to forget the financial hardships experienced by my parents and most other émigrés during the final years in Turkey. Most of what was left of the old family jewels that they had been able to carry with them in their baggage when they left Germany in 1935 was sold in the bazaars of Ankara and Istanbul, in order to enable me to pursue my studies of physics. In the end, I arrived in the US with twenty dollars in my pocket.
>
> Notwithstanding the rather different experiences of other immigrants, it is an interesting commentary on America's willingness to welcome newcomers without prejudice that my parents were able to gain a foothold when they emigrated yet again to a new country in 1948. My father was sixty-five years old at that time. The West German Republic also was helpful in granting my parents in the 1950s a modest restitution payment, even though our family had resided in the Eastern zone (Oranienburg).
>
> When all is said and done, I will never forget that for many years Turkey was generous enough to harbor us and provide us with a second "Haymat." The exhibition and the catalogue document this ambivalence honestly.
>
> When Turkey finally severed diplomatic relations with Germany and searched for additional chits from the Allies, it designated Çorum, Kirşehir, and Yozgat, each a small town,

as sites to intern German nationals living in the country. These were not Soviet-style gulags nor Nazi-type concentration camps or ghettoes. They were closer to the internment camps to which the Japanese-Americans were sent. Anyone bearing a German passport without a "J" stamp identifying the carrier to be a Jew was sent to one of these towns.

The majority of those confined in Kirşehir were from Ankara, although some came from Istanbul as well, including a group of Roman Catholic nuns. Ironically, among the detainees were the Nazi sympathizers and those who loathed them. Ernst Reuter, the informal but acclaimed and acknowledged leader of the anti-Nazi German community who a few years prior had escaped from a Nazi concentration camp, was among the interned. This time it was along with his entire family. University of North Carolina physics professor Eugen Merzbacher, recalled that as a young man and a student at the Istanbul University, he was often dispatched to bring food and other necessities to the good German detainees.[46] Contents for these parcels were paid for by German émigrés who were not incarcerated.

In other words, they were paid for by holders of the "J" stamped passports, the Jews.[47] The leader of this aid effort, according to Merzbacher, "was my friend Benno Landsberger, a distinguished Assyriologist who had contact with Americans and some international aid organizations as well. I worked for quite a while as his private secretary."

One more remark: If you have the opportunity to contact Robert Anhegger, please give him my best regards. He was a close friend of Kurt and Elisabeth Steinitz, in whose home I rented a room for three years during my student days in Istanbul, and before they moved on to Palestine (now Israel).

***Civil Engineer Peter Engelmann of Charlotte Virginia provided the essay titled a "Detour to Yozgat":***

It was mid-summer 1944, I was twenty years old, had just finished school, and had received a BS in Civil Engineering from the American college (Robert College) in peaceful Turkey, while the rest of Europe was largely devastated and still at war. Germany was withdrawing from Russia and France, but bitter fighting was still going on outside its borders and, of course, in the Pacific. Turkey had broken diplomatic relations with Germany in late 1944, I believe, and an exchange of German and Turkish nationals was being discussed, our greatest fear....

All the German embassy staff and other Germans in Turkey who wanted to be returned to Germany were confined to the beautiful grounds of the German embassy in Tarabya, a suburb on the European side of the Bosphorus, while an exchange by rail with the Turkish embassy staff from Berlin was being planned. I am not sure that exchange ever took place as rail connections between Turkey and Germany were soon broken by Allied advances.

Germans who did not want to be returned to Germany however, were asked to request permission to remain in Turkey, in writing. The request form one had to sign for this purpose included a clause stating that the applicant was ready to reside anywhere in Turkey where the government wanted. We had come to Turkey in 1936. My father, who had lost his German citizenship for being "fully" Jewish, did not have to sign the form and was permitted to continue working as a CPA (certified public accountant) in Istanbul and travel freely within Turkey.

My mother, (an "Aryan"), and I, (a "half-Jew"), however, were still carried by Turkish authorities as Germans, since we had not officially lost our citizenship. In the spring of 1944, we were notified that we might have to relocate at a day's notice and to have a small suitcase packed and ready.

One sunny day in July 1944, while I was enjoying my post-graduate vacation at home, I was visited by a young man in a business suit, wearing a red tie. He identified himself as a member of the Police and said that I had to leave the next day for *Yozgat,* a small town in central Turkey, to reside there, as provided in said form. Since I had expected this (rumors moved fast those days in Turkey), I agreed. The next morning he reappeared and accompanied me to Haydarpaşa the railroad station on the Asian side of the Bosphorus, where trains to Ankara and points south left from Istanbul. No word about my mother, who stayed behind with my father, in our apartment in Istanbul.

At the railroad station, the platform was full of German-speaking people, most of whom did not know one another. Each was accompanied by a young Turkish gentleman in a neat business suit, with a red tie.

At one point, the young gentlemen asked their "German" charges to board the passenger train that had pulled up, added that buses would take us to *Yozgat* at some point beyond Ankara, and said good-bye.

There was something strange and dream-like about that trip. Here I was on a train, my love, Erika, somewhere in Palestine, my parents at home in Istanbul, heading for a place I did not know, with German-speaking people I had never met during eight years I had lived in Turkey. But at least there was no sign of military activity and, we were heading south, the right direction!

Somewhere, after we had passed Ankara, the train stopped and there were buses. The trip continued for an hour or two by bus, through the rather barren hills of Anatolia, until we pulled into to a small town nestled in a valley. It had narrow, stone-paved streets, neat-looking tile-roofed houses, and a large mosque in the center.

We were told this was *Yozgat*, that several houses had been reserved for us, that we could move about freely within the town, shop and walk anywhere we liked day and night within city limits, and that we could send and receive cables at the post office and receive packages, but no mail. And we were left on our own.

There was no welcoming committee to my knowledge, but somehow we were made welcome. I joined a group of twenty or thirty people in a large, unfurnished house. There were electric lights, bathrooms (*a la turka*)[48], and lots of rooms, no telephone, no radio, no known address, no guards. It was getting dark, someone had brought some food (bread, goat cheese, and olives), some water, and some wine. We settled into the spacious rooms, each with our little suitcase or knapsack, on the floor. Our first night in *Yozgat*.

The next day, we declared war on bedbugs. Houses of wooden construction, even though uninhabited for some time, can have their secret inhabitants which come out at night. Our weapon (promptly named V-2 after the German rockets launched at the time on Britain), consisted of kerosene-soaked cotton which we stuffed into the cracks between floorboards. It didn't help much, but it let us sleep better.

At the end of the second day, I received a cable from my father, saying that my mother was coming to *Yozgat* the next day. That night I drank a bit too much wine with my new friends, a group of other "mixed-bloods" like me, Czechs, two Austrian musicians who had played in the Park Hotel Dining Room in Istanbul and, on occasion, livened up our evenings with violin and accordion.

When my mother arrived, we promptly rented a neat four-room house on a side street not far from the center (nothing was far in *Yozgat*). We went about buying a small stove, some beds, and a table and chairs, all available at small stores in town.

Within a week, we were quite comfortable, with a small

*kelim* (rug) on the wall and a candlestick on the table. My mother and I had one of the upstairs rooms, the other was taken by a sculptor named Ferdinand Gross, a wonderful person! The two downstairs rooms were taken by one lady each: a German-Jewish economist, who had been at Istanbul University and was engaged to a Turk who came to visit occasionally, and the Czech lady, who was Ferdinand's friend. So, by the Victorian standards of the time, everything was nice and proper.

After a week or two, I got my first engineering job with local contractors who were building the County Administration Building, *Yozgat's* only reinforced concrete structure. They were glad to have a graduate engineer, needing somebody to count the reinforcing bars that were put into the wooden forms before concrete was poured. So I did construction supervision, learning how the real world uses engineering drawings, all through September and most of November. When it started to snow, they had to stop pouring concrete.

Then came Christmas. My mother started baking Christmas cookies on our stove and Ferdinand started to model clay figures for a crèche: Mary, Joseph, and the baby, plus animals. This was for the Christmas Eve service by Austrian nuns who had been on our train and were preparing for the Seasons' festivities. Incredibly, here, among largely [part-] Jewish immigrants in the middle of Anatolia, at the height of World War II, without communication to anywhere, there was a Christmas service in a schoolroom somewhere with candles, créche, music, and singing.

My father came to visit us, just in time to be there for Christmas Eve. We all found it strangely unreal. A few days later, he left for Ankara and convinced officials there that it made no sense to let the head of the family travel where he pleased, but keep his wife and son in *Yozgat*. So we were allowed to return to our Istanbul apartment early in January 1945.

On our return, there was a letter from the United States with the news that my immigration visa had been approved. I boarded an American ship, sailing for the United States on May 8 1945: V-E Day.

### *Oral history of a Çorum detainee:*

Engineer Hans, who prefers that his last name not be mentioned, was seventeen when his Aryan father and Jewish mother were rounded up by the Turkish police and sent to *Çorum*, 242 kilometers from Ankara and one of the three detention centers Turkey created for German passport holders. His family had come to Turkey before 1933. Hans's father worked as an accountant for one of the German companies and, unlike most of the émigré professors' children, Hans attended Turkish public schools. *Çorum* had no high school whatsoever so Hans was tutored by two of the older internees who, as he says, had nothing else to do while in camp. "They did it out of sheer boredom."

The family was interned for the full term and they lived on monetary support provided by "the Americans." Although there were some two hundred German internees in *Çorum,* Hans had contact with only five other non-Turkish families. Many of the other Germans who were interned were no doubt Nazi sympathizers, but in camp they all kept a low profile at being so if for no other reasons that, by then, the fortunes of war were no longer on their side. Hans described most of Turkey's Germans as *Mitlaufer* namely as those resigned to whatever political winds might be blowing at any one time.

At war's end, the family went back to Istanbul and lived in *Moda,* which, over time, became an upscale section of Istanbul on the Asian side. Hans became reacquainted with his old friend Matthias Neumark and they stayed in touch even after Matt left for his Harvard MBA studies and Hans, who lost some time due to the internment, pursued a Civil Engineering degree at Istanbul Technical University.[49] Hans came to the United States and pursued a career in civil engineering along the East Coast. He had no problem whatsoever being allowed to take, taking, and passing, the stringent examinations to become a licensed civil engineer in the State of New York.

***Berlin Astronomer Gerhard Ruben's contributed memoirs of being interned in Kırşehir:***

Summer 1945 we spent again on the hills overlooking Ankara, as foreigners were not allowed to leave the city because of the war. On August 28, my father was informed that on the next day our family would be transported to *Kırşehir,* one of the three places in Anatolia used for confinement. As my father was professor at the University of Ankara he tried to contact his minister, but in the ministry they professed to be unable to help him. Why he, the only Ankara university professor, was chosen to be interned, nobody could explain. Thus, everything we just had in the hills (including beds and mosquito nets) was bundled, and, on the next forenoon, we were sitting in a bus with several other internees and were driven southward.

It was an endless drive through the dry steppe. The only event was the crossing of the Kızıl Irmak on an aged bridge with a high arch, built by the Selçuk many centuries ago. My father told us that this river formerly was the frontier between the Persian Medes and the Greek Lydians. In the evening, we reached Kırşehir and were greeted by other internees who had arrived some days earlier. The first night we spent with one of these families, as far as I can remember, the Baades.

On the next day, we had to look for a lodging. We could afford only a small flat on the upper floor of a simple house in the *Kayaşeyhi*-lane behind the New Bath. We lived there until the end of the confinement, Christmas 1945. As almost all houses, ours too was built from clay and had a flat roof. Downstairs lived a man with his wife, who did the heating of the Bath. We had two rooms with a kind of hallway between them, leading to the "dry" closet and the downward staircase. Washing was a problem because there existed neither fresh water nor a sewage system. Water had to be brought every day from a well.

Rarely did we have electric current because the capacity of the power station was too low and besides the station was generally out of order. In the evenings, we had only an oil lamp which was so feeble you couldn't read for long. In winter, one room was heated. One of the internees had devised a small stove, which the local blacksmith was able to build from sheet steel in the necessary numbers for the confined. In this stove, we burnt soft coal, which smelled abominably.

For my mother it was difficult to provide food for us and ensure cleanliness. The range of products on offer was very limited. The most important food was *bulgur*, a coarsely ground low-quality wheat bread. Because of the war, wheat was deficient. Meat and vegetables were expensive. Meat was scarce and often tough and only from sheep. In summer, there were some fruits and vegetables, but the quality was mostly rather low. There was no cheese. Milk was available only in late spring and the beginning of summer, because in the dry season there was simply not enough forage.

As internees, we got from the government a small monthly allowance, as much as the Anatolian peasants got after a devastating earthquake. As far as I remember it was about 25 TL per capita. But, among the emigrants in Ankara there existed, at least since the beginning of the war, a fund for mutual support. In turn, one of the emigrants remaining in Ankara [Eugen Merzbacher] travelled to *Kırşehir* with a secret money belt and supplied us with medicaments, edibles, and possibly letters. Besides, that was the only way to get books!

From the point of hygiene, conditions were very bad. There were many flies and mosquitoes and other insects. In summer, we had often diarrhoea [sic] although everything was washed thoroughly. Drinking water had to be fetched from certain well-known "good sources." Other water came from so-called "black sources" or even from the water ditches which ran along many streets and served for general cleaning purpose and for watering of the gardens. The only really hygienic institution was the Turkish bath, which we visited regularly. There was a hospital, but the internees looked at it with severe skepticism. But there was a cultured man and capable physician, Dr. Süreyya.

Most of the internees in Kırşehir, reportedly about 170 Germans and Austrians, we did not know. Some of them were emigrants; others lived already for dozens of years in Turkey. The reason for the confinement of the emigrants was generally unknown. Among the emigrants we *were* well acquainted with included the families of Eduard Zuckmeyer (musician), Ina Gottfried (lecturer), Fritz Baade (economist), and Hubert Kleinsorge (geologist). After us, many "Reichsdeutsche," as we called them, arrived, who had refused to obey when the German government ordered them all to return to the Reich. Among them were former staff members of the German consulates, schools, and banks. My parents avoided contact with them. There were few links between the two groups of confined because of a certain mutual distrust. We were, however, acquainted with Hans von Aulock, a director of the German Orient-Bank.

The internees were not allowed to work, to posses a radio, to get letters, or to subscribe to a newspaper. To make life somewhat bearable, a chorus was organised with Eduard Zuckmeyer as choirmaster, which achieved considerable success. For the young internees, lessons were organised if a suitable teacher was available. Thus the Catholic Father Frindt, an Austrian who had been interned together with some nuns, gave lessons to my brother.

I had lessons in mathematics by Kurt Laqueur and in French by Eleonore Grünholz, a young Austrian émigré. Kırşehir is a protracted oasis surrounded by hills, dry steppe, and dessert. But within the oasis, one could take beautiful walking-tours. On other occasions, we looked for pieces of the attractive travertine to be found near the hot spring to grind and polish. Books were very scarce. I got two books from Ankara which I tried to understand: "Mathematics for the Millions" by Lancelot Hogben and "Popular Astronomy" by Newcomb and Engelman.

My father was an orientalist, more precisely, an Indologist, (study of India) and, as he could do nothing else, he explored Kırşehir in its evolution during the centuries. He had no library at his disposition and therefore his main source of information, besides some official documents, were the inhabitants of the city and its surroundings. He interviewed many of them as he spoke Turkish fluently.

While in Germany, he had worked for a time as a farmer and, therefore, he got in touch even with the Anatolian peasants. Among his more conspicuous partners were Esad Ağa, a representative of the old Ottoman aristocracy; Mehmet Ağa a former dervish, now a master saddler writing poetry; a witch, who professed to soothsay; and Ali, the head of a gang of robbers who controlled the surrounding area. There was even a historian, Cevat Hakkı, who had published many papers, and there were a poet and a mystic. The results of these discourses my father summarized in a manuscript, describing in detail the town, its structure and inhabitants, its past and present, and even its outlook.[50]

There were many traces of antiquity, e.g., potsherds and pieces of glass and parts of marble statues or columns, and the peasants sometimes brought old coins they had found while ploughing. Finds from the time of the Greeks were rather rare, among them parts of Greek inscriptions, but Roman remains were more abundant. Nothing was left from antique buildings. The thermal spring near the centre of the town had been certainly in use already in antiquity. Testimonials from the time of the Selçuks and later the Mengüç, the cultural high time of the town, were abundant.

At that time, Ahi Evran, the founder of the order of the Ahis, Hacı Bektaş Veli, founder of the mystic order of the Bektaşi, and the poet and philosopher, Aşık Paşa, lived in Kırşehir. Mosques and tombs of this time were well worth seeing. In the Cacabey Mosque, originally a *madrassa,* there was even a well from this time, which was used to observe the stars.

But my father was also interested in developments in recent time, the transition from the Turkey of the Ottomans to a modern nation as Atatürk intended. From the development of India, he knew that such changes do present problems. Twenty years after Atatürk's reforms, agriculture as well as handicraft were still extremely backward. For instance, the most important tool in agriculture was still the old oriental wooden hook-plough, updated by a small iron tip. Modern iron ploughs, which the government tried to introduce, were hardly accepted.

The peasants mistrusted the modernization, possibly just because it was initiated by the government. Besides they did not have horses strong enough for the heavy appliance. Productivity was correspondingly low. Characteristically, a considerable fraction of payments was accomplished by barter, even with craftsmen.

A serious problem was the general attitude towards productivity, differing considerably from the attitude in western Europe. As an example, at the end of the war the country ran short of wheat. Thereupon, American specialists advised the government to raise the price of wheat to stimulate its cultivation and thus to close the gap. The government followed their advice, but, as a result, the supply grew even less.

When the peasants noticed that they would get more money for their crop, they resolved to grow less wheat, as their need of money had not risen! This was actually an attitude of the Anatolian peasants and citizens towards property, prevalent probably not only in Asia, which may have hampered modernization of the economy seriously. At the same time the overwhelming majority of the people, about 90%, were extremely poor and barely earned the minimum subsistence although about 95% owned land. And living conditions of the peasants were even worse.

This reluctance towards innovations was rather pronounced among craftsmen, as well. For example, emigrants from Bulgaria brought a four-wheel carriage to Anatolia. The local cartwright built on their request this type of carriage for them. But for the locals he continued to build only the old cumbersome two-wheel carriages with massive wooden wheels. But there were people with initiative as well. The carpenter, İbrahim, built a water mill of European type with a perpendicular water wheel and with productivity about three times the productivity of the old Anatolian types with a horizontal water wheel. But nobody followed his example.

A very profitable cotton-weaving mill was installed by Ziya, and fabrication of garments was being carried out in home-work. This mill remained an exception, too. Some of the innovations were, by the way, stimulated by military service, where the conscripts came in contact with new technologies.

However, changes caused by Atatürk's reforms were not to be overlooked. Secularisation was pronounced, albeit religious elements and superstition frequently were noticeable. Only old women wore the black head scarves and covered their mouth when a man appeared. Merely as nurses, secretaries or as teachers a few women could work. On the market, one sole woman had a stand. But after attending the girls-institute in Ankara, a young woman opened, with great success, a training workshop for dressmakers for girls, something absolutely new!

The coeducation in schools affected the behaviour of the young generation. But although monogamy had been introduced by law, several of the well-to-do men had, in reality, more than one wife, but that might prove to be very expensive, as one of them admitted. The society in *Kırşehi*r was full of contradictions, but it was on the move.

***Elizabeth [Reichenbach] Austin commented:***

Hi, Arnold.

I have been reading your chapters with interest. They bring back so much of the past. All those names I remember, all those people we used to know.... I think your focusing on Turkey's role in helping so many of the refugee intellectuals to survive is a great idea. As you point out, little is known about the contribution Turkey made to intellectual achievement in the past century, and little is known about how these „cream of the crop" professors transformed Turkey's higher education. So the appearance of your book is very timely. A few comments on the text follow.

Something I don't think you know is that among my father's achievements in Istanbul was being instrumental in organizing skiing trips every winter for professors' families and for graduate students at the University to Uludağ, the Asia Minor "Mt. Olympus" near Bursa. We would take the boat to Mudanya and from there would go by bus to Bursa, and then, the next day, we would be driven up to the snow line and then proceed the rest of the way on horseback or on skis to the hotel on the high ridge.

We would stay at the hotel for a week and it was great fun. Skiing during the day—we even had, later on, a couple of expert skiers from Austria to teach the beginners —and at night partying, singing, masquerades and general hilarity. This is where we really mingled with the Turkish students and gave them a taste of winter sports. Conditions at the hotel were primitive, the toilets (Turkish-style toilets) froze regularly, and dinners consisted mostly of beans and mutton, but all this only added to the fun.

Nowadays, I understand, there is an aerial tram up the mountain and it has been developed for tourism. This was foreshadowed in a song composed for one of our parties by Dr. Ullmann that ended with the lines "Uludağninfunikuleri." [Uludağ funicular] We thought at the time that the idea was hilarious. Happy memories. This is one of the best.

***Art historian Dr. Elizabeth S. Ettinghausen, daughter of Austrian radiologist Max Sgalitzer, offered the following recollection of her voyage to the United States:***

When in the fall of 1943, my father, my mother and I, the youngest of their three children, left Turkey, we went by train and a motor coach from Istanbul, via short stops in Aleppo and Haifa, to Cairo, which we enjoyed exploring. Three days later we took the train to Alexandria, where—thanks to my father's good relationship with both the British and US authorities—we boarded, as the sole passengers, a U.S. Liberty ship, which, in a convoy of approximately sixty Liberty and Victory ships, all freighters, was to sail to New York.

While we were still docked far out in the harbor, I took a swim, but upon returning to the ship, some sailors told me that I was lucky not to have encountered a shark; I could never tell, whether they meant it in earnest or just tried to scare me.

The captain, a very nice and accommodating middle-aged man, was very happy to now have a doctor—my father—on board, who from then on was busy taking care of the whole crew.

While proceeding westward on board ship, we occasionally saw surveillance planes overhead.

Once the captain spotted a mine nearby. Lucky for us, he managed to avoid it. We stopped in Gibraltar harbor and were one of two ships nearest the shore. While our boat was fortunate enough not to be attacked by enemy underwater swimmers depositing depth charges, our sister ship next to us was not so lucky. The detonation shook our ship, but created a gaping hole in the other ship's underside. The damage was repaired. Once, an alarm brought us all to designated stations on shipboard for a while. I feared that this was "for real." Luckily, it turned out to be only practice.

We were at sea for one month before reaching the harbor of New York. What a magnificent sight it was and what a sense of relief to have reached our destination—the United States. However, because the war was still raging, security was tight. Since no messages could be sent from aboard ship while at sea, nobody knew of our arrival, and only upon landing could the ship's captain telephone my sister in Cambridge, MA informing her of our arrival. At my father's behest, she notified a friend of his, Mr. McMurray, the former US Ambassador to Turkey.

Though detention on Ellis Island for a routine processing could not be avoided, thanks to Ambassador Murray's intervention, after three days my parents and I entered New York City as free persons.

### *Detainees in Other Places:*

Peter Engelmann was a bit more fortunate in that he did not have to stay interned for the full term (until the end of the war), as did others. He was also fortunate to have found a job, to have found it almost on arrival, to find work that was in a manner of speaking within his profession, and be paid a relatively decent wage.

Others did not fare so well. They were interned until the end of the war in Europe, they had children of various ages to feed, and they had no income whatsoever. For the professors or "good" Germans like the Ernst Reuter family, their Jewish colleagues on the outside helped out as we were told by Eugen Merzbacher. The Austrian nuns were provided for by Monsignor Angelo Roncalli and the church in Istanbul. Many of the really "bad" Germans had their Turkish counterparts sending packages. And, after a while, all were provided for by the International Committee of the Red Cross (ICRC).

However in those days Turkey was not the only country to incarcerate good Germans along with bad Germans. In his memoir, Walter W. Igersheimer,[51] tells that after escaping from Nazi Germany and separated from his parents who were in Turkey, he was completing his medical studies in Britain when he was caught in the panic which led to internment of 60,000 German citizens living there. The "Germans" were placed behind barbed wire and treated as enemies.

Young Igersheimer found himself and many other Jewish refugees from Germany on a prison ship to Canada. On that voyage and heading for the same destination were a few hundred POW Nazi paratroopers. There he found "grossly unsanitary living conditions, cruel and abusive treatment by internment camp officials, and the withholding of medical treatment." [52]

Sadly, much of this experience was known to the father, Igersheimer senior, in Boston. Ultimately, it must have been gratifying for him to see his son Walter finish his medical education at Tufts in short order and with full university subvention after the Brits released him from their Canadian internment camp and a stay in Cuba awaiting a US visa. No less gratifying for the father was to see his son do post-graduate studies at Yale and be invited to join its faculty as Professor of Psychiatry and become a pioneer of group therapy.[53]

### *Psychiatrist Walter Igersheimer's reminiscences of life in Turkey:*[54]

My time in Turkey was very limited as I was sent off to study in the UK. When I was seventeen years old, I spent one summer vacation (three months) in Istanbul in 1934 and another nine months in 1935. I also briefly visited with my father in Romania under the protection of the country's chief of police who had been one of my dad's patients in Turkey.

My father was a fastidious person, especially about his personal appearance. His clothes, hair, and nails had to be just so. It was a time when children were to be seen but not heard. The family would have dinner together (where the children did not speak) and then Dad would go into his study for the evening. Mother on the other hand was more socially minded. Since my sister and I liked to dance, she gave a party for the Istanbul professors' children.

We all had a wonderful time until Dr. Adler (psychiatrist by profession but working in the pathology lab) attempted to demonstrate his ability to hypnotize. He was successful at putting Lotte Braun under but could not bring her out of it. Needless to say, this incident caused an uproar and it took several days for Lotte "to come around" to herself. I remember that we teenage boys liked to swim and play really just to have a good time.

I was happy to be reunited with Richard Honig who was my best friend from the time I was six years old. We did do a lot of swimming together around Istanbul. He received a good enough secondary school education there in order to be able to continue for a Ph.D. in physics from MIT. Once again, we were reunited in the USA after I was released from the Canadian internment camp.

The Kessler family lived in the same building as my parents. Their daughter, Gerhilde, seemed very nice. She was a student at Istanbul's German High School. There she fell in love with one of her teachers who happened to be a Nazi. Gerhilde then joined the Hitler Youth and became a passionate Nazi herself. She took her younger sister back to Germany with her when she left with the teacher, whom she apparently married. Her mother was quite ill, and she, too, left.[55]

## A Reflection on the Memoirs

The remainder of the interview with Dr. Igersheimer provided additional anecdotes of the good times experienced with other émigré teenagers during his visits to Istanbul. This interview corroborated inputs received by the author from others. It leaves no doubt that the émigrés' younger offspring really enjoyed their years in Turkey and all received an excellent education while there. For some, like Elizabeth (Reichenbach) Austin, education in Turkey was mostly at the elementary school level. For many like Martin (Haurowitz) Harwit, it ended at High School. A few obtained their undergraduate degrees as did Matt Neumark at Robert College and Eugen Merzbacher at Istanbul University.

All who made the attempt had no problem being directly admitted to America's most selective colleges and universities such as Oberlin, Harvard, Yale, and MIT. Their terminal degrees are all from the most prestigious universities, to wit Alice (Haurowitz) Sievert, University of Wisconsin, and Stephen Prager, Cornell.

> It was a wonderful life, in many ways, for a young boy growing up...because of the outdoors and the lovely climate and the sea, and everything that went with it. —*Martin Harwit*[56]

> I could not imagine having spent a better childhood anywhere else. —*Matthias Neumark*[57]

The more adult second generation members however do reflect the prevalence of wartime anxieties. To wit:

> It was a strange period: nobody trusted anybody outside their own friends. —*Marianne Laqueur*[58]

While sociologists and psychologists can certainly offer more detailed and multifaceted explanations, the duress the émigrés encountered suffices in explaining the unusually high rate of divorces and cross-marriages in their midst, as well as a high incidence of suicides among family members.

Among the divorced who were professionally most notable are Reichenbach, Geiringer, Arndt, Belling, Winterstein, Isaak, Kantorowicz, Anhegger, Hirsch, Rüstow, Reuter, Isaak, Praetorius, and Taut, whose wife never joined him in Turkey, while Kessler's wife left him and returned to Nazi Germany with both of their daughters.

To quote from Herbert Hoover's speech at the 1944 Republican National Convention: "Older men declare war. But it is youth that must fight and die. And it is youth that inherits the tribulations, the sorrow and the triumphs that are the aftermath of war."

*Figure 142*
Klaus and Peter Eckstein, 1940.

# 14
# Momentum Lost, Opportunities Foregone—Turkey's Policies and Practices

**L'Université ouvre le 5 Novembre**

Dans toutes les facultés de l'Université, les cours commenceront le 5 novembre prochain. Grâce aux mesures prises en temps utile, toutes les modifications et les réparations entreprises dans le bâtiment abritant l'Université, seront achevées d'ici là.

La nouvelle Université turque entrera en activité dans des conditions tout à fait nouvelles.

La faculté des lettres a été complètement transférée à l'hôtel Zeyneb Hanem. La Faculté de Droit est sur le point d'occuper les locaux de la Faculté des lettres. La construction du laboratoire destiné à la faculté de médecine dans l'édifice de Békir Agha Benlugu, sera achevée bientôt, de même que la modification des locaux transformés en laboratoires dans les hôpitaux de Djerrah Pacha, Hasséki et Gouréba et destinés à cette dernière faculté.

*Figure 143*
*The Time of the Émigrés. Le Journal d'Orient,* October 30, 1933.

University Opens Fifth of November:

> Courses will start on November 5 in all Faculties of the University. Thanks to necessary measures taken in a timely fashion, all alterations and repairs undertaken in the building housing the University will be completed by then.
>
> The new *Turkish University* will start its activities under completely new conditions.
>
> The Faculty of Letters has been entirely transferred to the *Zeynep Hanım Konağı*. The Faculty of Law will soon occupy the locale of the Faculty of Letters. The construction of the laboratory in the *Bekir Ağa Binası* intended for the use of the Faculty of Medicine will be soon completed. The same is true for alterations of the areas transformed into laboratories at the Hospitals of *Cerrah Paşa, Haseki* and *Gureba* for the same faculty. *Le Journal d'Orient* October 30 1933. Courtesy The Rockefeller Foundation Archives.

Swiss Professor Albert Malche, the man whose government-commissioned report laid out the blue print for the modernization of Turkey's entire educational system, commented on October 16 1933 about Turkey's past and the potential for its future. "At a distance one might be skeptical: *this great and noble country has so many reforms in its past which have come to almost nothing. There are opportunities for giving the country an intellectual and scientific elite* trained on the spot and which will be acquainted with the national resources and needs. I myself had doubts in the beginning. *I am convinced today* that we are assisting *a prodigious effort of oriental renaissance whose consequences will go very far.*"[1] (emphasis added).

To this historical commentary one can add a 2005 statement offered to the entire world in a website maintained by the government of the Republic of Turkey, to wit:

> "Because of its geographical location, the mainland of Anatolia has always found favour throughout history, and is the birthplace of many great civilizations."[2] Anatolia has for centuries been prominent as a center of commerce because of its land connections to three continents and the seas that surround it on three sides. Turkish territory is "located at a point where the three continents making up the old world, Asia, Africa, and Europe, are closest to each other, and straddle the point where Europe and Asia meet."[3]

Turkey is a land that should have thrived and become wealthy. Why, then, is Turkey today not more advanced scientifically, technologically, economically, and politically vis à vis other nations? There are no simple answers to that question. There are however several uncontestable facts worthy of consideration. In 1933, *de facto,* all of Turkey had but two universities. One of these was technical, and both were in Istanbul. Today, the Turkish system of higher education is countrywide and sports no fewer than seventy-two public and private universities, over forty percent of the professors are women,[4] and there has never been a glass ceiling for Turkish women in academic administration. Annually, over 1.7 million youngsters sit for the national university admission examination and the best of these get the widest choices for acceptance.

## Technology and Development

Industrialization and technology are known to be major driving forces for the economic growth of nations. Without this change from labor-by-hand to mass and automated production, nothing happens. Consequently, an efficient, institutionalized system for transferring technology should lead to efficient uses of resources. "Indeed, industrialization has been treated as a synonym for economic and socio-cultural development by many scholars, planning authorities, technologists, and politicians in developing countries."[5]

Based on the same logic that earned Prescott the Nobel Prize in 2004, Stephen L. Parente and Edward C. Prescott add to the above that the "key reason for the disparity in the standard of living among countries worldwide is impediments to adopting technology."[6]

Republican Turkey has inherited a long technology-transfer tradition. Over the centuries, the Ottoman Sultans were relatively open to importing and adopting various technologies and innovations from abroad so long as these served their military and, to a lesser degree, administrative interests. Some of these interests, like telegraphy (the system went on line in 1865) and railroads (The Ottoman Railway *Smyrna-Aydın* connection opened in 1866), had dual purposes; others, like technical education, slowly diffused to the civilian sector.

While there is no doubt that gunpowder and firearms did not originate in the Ottoman Empire, there is controversy regarding the immediate source, timing, and route of arrival. But both were happily accepted by the Turks, as everywhere else. The "*Kitab al-furusiyya bi rasm al-jihad*" by al-Hasan al Rammah, who died in 1294, contains the first description in Arabic of the purification and crystallization of saltpeter as well as seventy formulas for different varieties of gunpowder. Significantly, saltpeter was known as 'Chinese snow' in Arabic and as 'Chinese salt' in Persian.... The Ottomans apparently had acquired firearms by 1444 (Mehmed II), from whatever source, because they deployed cannon against Constantinople in that year."[7] The traditional Ottoman opposition to such innovations based on religious grounds was largely muted since Muslim law holds that innovations useful to winning a war are justifiable.[8] "Firearms did come to the Maghrib (the fertile coastal plain of North Africa) from Spain and to Turkey from the Balkans."[9]

The printing press was a different story. The first to be brought in around 1492 AD during the early years of the Spanish Inquisition was only capable of printing with the Hebrew alphabet. No one felt a need to convert it to printing in Arabic. The masses were illiterate and the Ottomans' agenda did not include changing the *status quo*. The *madrasa*-educated scribes were a highly esteemed profession, therefore not supportive of such mechanization. It was not easy to become fully literate while Turkish was written in the Arabic alphabet.

Two centuries or so later, a press designed by a Hungarian engineer to handle the Arabic alphabet did not meet with success either. The Ottomans simply did not lay the foundation nor import the prerequisites for the Age of Enlightenment to have taken hold so far to the East. Clearly, all of the Ottoman technology transfer that did take place was unidirectional from abroad, and it was strictly "undertaken in response to unrelenting pressure and compulsion imposed by the world outside their borders."[10]

While Western Europe focused on religions, conflict, and the persecution of religious minorities (roughly spanning the 15$^{th}$ (1492) through the 17$^{th}$ centuries), the sultans presided over a relatively tolerant regime. This facilitated enough science and technology transfer to keep the Ottomans competitive until the European Age of Enlightenment (17$^{th}$ and 18$^{th}$ centuries) tipped that balance. As science flourished in the West, any attempts to transfer the changes, information, and results, were failing in the increasingly insular Ottoman Empire, which was now becoming less tolerant.

In the 18th century, there were continuing attempts to import technology for building factories but these consistently failed. The Empire fell further and further behind, hence the appropriateness of the name "Young Turks" used for the officers and men led by Atatürk himself who put an end to Ottoman rule and established a Republic.

The Young Turks were just that, young, educated in western ways, and wanting what they saw all around them in the lands to the west. There was much ground to be regained, much progress to be made. They recognized that the empire had failed to implement the scientific and industrial reforms necessary for indigenously driven modernization. Compared to western European countries, the empire lost much ground in such development. It is undoubtedly fair to say that the Ottomans managed the empire in a manner that left it technology-dependent on the world outside.

## Republican Turkey's Development Strategies

From the very beginning, Turkey's republican government's primary agenda item was economic and social development. Economic development to them meant industrialization, pure and simple. Industrialization in turn meant heavy manufacturing. Unfortunately, the Young Turks inherited a poor agrarian country with no one in the private sector ready, willing, or able to set up large manufacturing plants. Therefore, such industrialization could only be done by creating State-owned and State-controlled enterprises. To accomplish this, Ankara introduced Soviet-style five-year plans.[11] In fact, the Soviet Union was the role model for the Republic's founders in many ways.

In 1932, Prime Minister Ismet Inönü visited Russia as well as Italy while seeking support for Turkey's technological and financial requirements. Subsequently, a group of Russian engineers and economists prepared a national investment report for Turkey. However, to get other opinions, Ankara also invited American and Italian experts. Based on reports from these panels, the Council of Ministers approved a state-controlled investment program in 1934.[12] This was the starting year of Turkey's first five-year plan.

However, even prior to implementation of its planned economy program during 1928 Ankara's government and the Ford Motor Company signed a twenty-five-year joint-venture contract to assemble automobiles for export to the Balkans, the Soviet Union, Iran, and the Middle East. This would constitute a major infusion of technology new to Turkey and create many jobs. Blue-collar jobs they may have been, but the pay was better then the alternative employments that were available.

Unfortunately, the global economic crises of the 1930s cut demand for automobiles in the targeted markets, ending Ford's production in the Tophane district of Istanbul and necessitating the closing of the plant.[13] Ford's outcome notwithstanding, the experience had set the pattern that called for Turkey to transfer much-needed technology from abroad via direct foreign investments, joint ventures, licensing, and build-operate-transfer arrangements. Turkey's early factories and industrial enterprises were built by foreign companies who brought their own people to train Turks on how to manage and operate these enterprises.

The Turkish five-year plans also included creation of a State-owned steel industry. "Based on a 1936 agreement between the Turkish and English governments the H. A. Brassert Company started construction [of the Karabuk Iron and Steel Factory] on April 3 1937. Construction was finished in three years."[14] The Turkish government policy of negotiated [with foreign companies and consortia] major infrastructure projects such as power plants and even toll-road contracts to design, install, operate the plant, and retain any earnings generated for an agreed upon period of years at which time the plant or facility would be transferred to Turkish ownership continues to the present.[15] As is the obvious flaw in such a *modus operandi,* the State continues the long tradition of being technology-dependent, albeit foreign companies that are awarded such contracts these days often use Turkish subcontractors to do some of the work. The policy/practice, however, does not encourage development of indigenous creativity.

Parallel to creating major state-owned enterprises, Turkey has been encouraging its private sector to do the same. However, here, too, until the late 1990s, Turkey's industrialization policy focused on large-scale manufacturing plants for wealth creation, job creation, and for import substitution. Once again, this involved acquiring, on a turnkey basis and mostly through joint ventures, very large-scale manufacture and marketing of products, as well as after-sale services such as in telecommunications where service is the product.[16] Unfortunately, Turkey's private sector had only a handful of entrepreneurs capable of creating such businesses. These were the emerging oligarchs who had been parlaying on previous successes in contracting to the Republic's government mostly in construction, one in pharmaceuticals.

Significantly, this mode of acquiring technology from abroad by the private sector tended to further centralize that sector in the hands of what Parente and Prescott call the "insiders."[17] To this day, the Turkish private manufacturing, mass retailing (e.g., supermarket chains), and mass service (as in telecommunications and banking) are all combined and dominated by the family-owned conglomerates. No doubt this policy also created jobs, but, once again mostly at the blue-collar level. The policy did reduce imports of medium-tech products while expanding exports of the same class of products. However, it did not create much demand for the scientists and engineers educated in Turkey's fine universities all of which still bear the "German" professors' legacy.

These policies and practices of importing technology and know-how have had, and continue to have, another deleterious outcome. They encourage a brain-drain that continues to bleed Turkey of some of its best and most-educated. Combined, these policies and practices result in Turkey's failure to produce an upward spiral for diffusion of indigenous technical innovations into start-up firms created by individual entrepreneurs and having no connection to the "establishment."[18]

Turkey has always felt a need for having strong armed forces. Its military infrastructure during the post-WWII and the "Cold War" period was brought up to snuff by being a partner in the North Atlantic Treaty Organization (NATO). The military technology and know-how, as in decades or even centuries prior, was acquired from the outside, fully crated. Most of the materiel was obtained from Turkey's NATO partners gratis. Turkey's "good fortune" in this respect was a disguised misfortune as it too was an impediment to indigenous development. With such largesse on the part of America, the UK, and other western arms-producing countries, Turkey had no incentive whatsoever to develop an indigenous armaments industry doing its own R&D which would have created employment for university graduates, especially those in sciences and in engineering.

Following WWII, Turkey's universities were further modernized this time on the American model, however, Turkey, until the late 1990s, did nothing at all to encourage technology-based startup companies nor did she show interest in any SMEs (the very important Small and Medium size Enterprises).

As indicated in an endnote to an earlier chapter, Stephen L. Parente and Edward C. Prescott used the words "ideas," "knowledge," and "technologies" interchangeably in their Nobel-winning rationale.[19] Keeping this in mind, they also suggest a somewhat applicable rationale for the differences in economic development between Turkey, and, in relevant aspects, similarly situated countries.

> Our view is that differences in international incomes are the consequences of differences in the knowledge individual societies apply to the production of goods and services. These differences do not arise because of some fundamental difference in the stock of usable knowledge from which a society can draw. Rather, these differences are the primary result of country specific policies that result in constraints on work practices and on the application of better production methods at the firm level.[20]

Beyond a doubt, modern Turkey is several decades ahead of western countries, particularly the United States, in terms of percentages of women working as physicians, (26%), engineers (27%), architects (33 %), lawyers (30%), and university professors (42%).[21] This is also true at the senior level administration of universities, government agencies, and management of private sector companies. Mustafa Kemal Atatürk would have been proud of this outcome. Gender equality in the workplace was part of his vision back in the 1920s and 1930s.

However, when comparing Turkey with similarly situated countries, it appears that starting 1938, Turkey lost much of its developmental momentum despite the émigrés' legacy.

## Turkey's Development *Strategies* as Compared to Similarly Situated Countries

There is much to be learned by comparing the developmental strategies and their results in three rather disparate countries, Turkey, Israel, and India.[22] While India became independent one year ahead of Israel in 1947, all three gained independence in the 20$^{th}$ century. At the time of their sovereignty, all three were quite undeveloped. Initially, all three considered economic development solely in terms of large state-owned enterprise industrialization based on imported technologies.

Like Turkey did in the 1930s, India's first Prime Minister, Jawahar Lal Nehru, advocated a planned economy with adoption of the Soviet-type Five-Year Planning system.[23] The focus of India's First Five-Year Plan (1951-56), however, was on basic amenities and basic infrastructure.

To a greater or lesser degree, in the late 1970s, all three countries began to shed their socialist, or at least statist (or *etatist)*, roots. However, in recent years, India's technologic development has reached what the economists call the "take-off stage." Yet Turkey is nowhere near as far along.

Unlike Turkey, India started its technological development by reverse-engineering both Soviet and western technology. Some had rightfully referred to this policy as "reinventing the wheel." India's engineers literally disassembled the equipment received, analyzed all aspects and recreated the design drawings. India then incrementally improved upon the equipment, adapted it to local or similar conditions, and produced it for import substitution and for export. This was done at state-owned enterprises and by a small group of established oligarchs such as the Tata and Birla Groups, among others.

Currently India is no longer technology-dependent on others in many spheres of manufacturing and agriculture. Moreover, during the last decade or so, India has instituted policies and practices that encouraged and supported research and development in information technologies. Consequently and significantly unlike Turkey, India's government helped to create many small business enterprises. Many of these SMEs have grown to become worldwide destinations for outsourcing of technology-involved work, not to mention customer service calls, cheap manufacture of goods, and the like.

Geographically closer, the lands comprising both Turkey and Israel for centuries were part of the Ottoman Empire. Some of the empire's heritage can be sensed to this very day in both countries. They gained their statehood exactly 25 years apart. At their founding, the economies of all three countries relied first and foremost on agriculture. By 1948 each country had roughly the same number of institutions of higher learning to draw upon for knowledge and knowledgeable talent. At the time, Israel already had three such institutions: the *Hebrew University of Jerusalem*, a full-fledged research-based university founded in 1925, the *Technion*[24] in Haifa, a research-based technical university founded in 1924, and the Weizmann *Institute for Science* in Rehovot, a research institution founded in 1934.[25] By 1947, India, too, had a fair foundation for science and technology. The *Indian Institute of Science at Bangalore* was established in 1909 and the *Indian Statistical Institute* in 1931. Before that, the *Presidency College* had been established in 1817, and the University of Calcutta in 1857.

Additionally, many other research institutions had been founded during India's colonial times: for example, the Indian Council of Medical Research (1911), the Indian Council of Agricultural Research (1929), the Council of Indian Scientific and Industrial Research (1942), and the Indian Standards Institution (1947). Turkey, of course, had the Ankara and Istanbul universities as well as the Istanbul Technical University. Thus, by 1948, the three countries had an adequate number of functioning western-type institutions/universities to draw upon for *ideas, innovations, technology,* and *knowledge.*

Whereas Turkey based its development predominantly on applying "existing ideas[26] to the production of goods and services," Israel did the same, but, additionally, Israel created "much usable knowledge[27] from which a society can draw." As a matter of public policy, Israel has efficiently transferred agricultural innovations from its universities and other public sector laboratories directly to its private sector. All along, the same was true in its construction sector and at all times the Israeli universities' based innovations were provided as a free good. The same has also been true in its high-tech sectors since the 1980s, though no longer on a gratis basis. The Israelis began running with the ball. They liked the benefits of change and were not constrained by any religious prohibition against it.

Additionally, Israelis, like the Turks, have always faced compulsory military service. Unlike in the Turkish military, the Israel Defense Forces (IDF) perform much of their own research and development. Some of this R&D was and is dictated by the top echelons, but much rises from the bottom. Innovations and ideas are encouraged at all levels, down to what is referred to in America as the "buck private."

> The army gets hold of everybody at age 18, and if they have a glimmer of potential, it [the State] catalyses their transformation

> to engineers or scientists. The technically minded are given [some find on their own] projects to develop and run, and are allowed to keep intellectual property that they develop, which results in many spinouts."[28]

Even if an innovation is highly classified, if in some modified format it has commercial potential, the individual innovators can take it with them upon discharge from the military. If they choose to commercialize their concept, in Israel they find no shortage of support infrastructures to help new entrepreneurs bring the idea or product to market.

On the other hand, Turkey has none of this heritage. India first entered the field in the late 1980s while Turkey didn't start creating the necessary institutions for such transfers until the late 1990s. Thus, in Turkey the required public and private infrastructure is only now gaining some significance. Because of this tardiness to act on such issues, Turkey has bypassed agriculture in this regard and, to a lesser degree, its construction sector. Although now focused on high-tech, the number of high-tech (liberally defined) ventures in Turkey that have matured sufficiently to be listed on any stock exchange can be counted on the fingers of one hand.[29] Israel, on the other hand, has dozens of (unquestionably) high-tech ventures listed on several stock exchanges worldwide.

Unlike in Israel, a Turkish innovator cum enterpreneur has very few options for venture capital other than personal or family sources. Of the small venture capital pool, most is offered, on paper at least, by banks. Lending institutions however tend to be beauracratic and risk-averse. Moreover, Turkish banks individually and collectively have experienced several crises during the last three decades of the 20th century,[30] and the industry's turbulence persisted well into the 21st century. Said turbulence certainly cannot be blamed on the banks having put too much of their monies into the riskiness of new technology-based ventures. The record shows that credits to all SMEs in Turkey, including the restaurants and garment manufacturers, account for no more than "3 to 4 percent of of the total bank credits given to private sector firms."[31]

In Israel, on the other hand, venture capital comes from a diversity of sources. Among these are domestic as well as foreign (venture capitalists) private individuals, large and small firms and corporations, NGOs, government, the trade union, and agricultural associations. Success has fed on success so that a number of American pension funds have made part of their investment portfolios availble as these were considered good risks with high profit potential. Israeli banks play a secondary role, if at all, in financing new ventures.

These differences between the two countries are in part due to the fact that Israel, on a per-capita basis, has been investing in its higher education significantly more than Turkey. In terms of investment in its R&D, Israel has by far outstripped Turkey in total outlays.[32] Prior to its statehood, Israel implemented an infrastructure to efficiently transfer innovations from its laboratories to the private sector with an emphasis on new ventures or start-ups by individual entrepreneurs, many of whom indeed owe their innovative and marketable high-tech ideas to service in the military.[33] Although formally in place, such infrastructure in Turkey has yet to bear fruit. Dilek Çetindamar Professor of Management at Istanbul's Sabanci University provides some of the reasons why:

> Turkey is the 13th most *bureaucratic country in the world.*" Some specifics: "An entrepreneur needs [no fewer than] *172 signatures from various government agencies in order to receive approval* to invest." Once these are all in hand, "the time needed to get permission to construct a plant can take *up to two years.*" "The total cost of the setting up procedure is around 4 percent of the total capitalization of the firm." And, overall, "in Turkey an entrepreneur spends [no less than] *20 percent of his or her time on bureaucratic issues;* this rate is 8 percent in the EU.[34]

Another significant difference in terms of technological development between these countries is that soon after gaining statehood, in its government procurements of technologic products from foreign suppliers, Israel required some form of reciprocity. We call that counter-trade. It is a modern variation of the ancient barter system. The policy started with requiring the foreign suppliers to *counter-purchase* some percentage of the contract's value of Israeli products for resale outside of Israel as part of the deal. It escalated to *co-production* and ultimately to *co-R&D* (research and development). Thus, Israel further created a demand for its own engineers and scientists while creating an export market.

To this day, in the words of Parente and Prescott, Turkey restricts "the set of technologies that the individual production units can use."[35] This restriction affects "total factor productivity at the aggregate level" and exists on "account of monopoly rights that industry insiders with vested interests tied to current production processes have."[36] Furthermore, "with the government's protection, these insiders impose[d] restrictions on work practices and provide[d] strong barriers to the adoption of better technologies."[37] To be sure, all three countries were guilty of these policies during their etatist, or socialist years. Since the eighties, however, Israel has discarded such practices with a vengeance. Turkey on the other hand, transferred the practices from large state-owned enterprises to its oligarchal conglomerates.

While making major contributions to Turkey's economic development, these conglomerates continue to make Turkey technology dependent by acquiring all their needs pretty much based on the 1928 Ford model.[38] Turkey, like many developing countries, managed to squander much of its indigenously developed talent through "country-specific policies that result in constraints on work practices and on the application of better production methods at the firm level."[39] Israel, on the other hand, engaged its indigenously educated cadres and, through immigration, imported much talent from abroad including some from Turkey.[40]

According to the World Bank:

> Knowledge,[41] and its application, is now acknowledged to be one of the key sources of growth in the global economy. The increasing importance of knowledge has created both challenges and opportunities for developing countries. In terms of challenges, it is clear that to be competitive internationally, countries must be able to participate effectively in the knowledge-driven supply chains and markets that now dominate the global economy. However, if properly adapted to circumstances and effectively addressed, the knowledge and information revolution presents significant opportunities for reducing poverty and promoting sustainable development.[42]

Turkey's agriculture was always free enterprise. In the days of the Ottomans, it was a feudal society with large landowners and peasants bound to their villages while working fields someone else owned along with, perhaps, a small parcel of their own. The landowners were predominantly members of old Moslem aristocratic families. The Republic did not introduce many changes in that regard. The large landowners had become prototypic of the urban oligarchs who developed after the founding of the republic, all but one having a Moslem heritage.[43]

Israel's agricultural sector, on the other hand, largely followed the socialist ideology. It was dominated by two types of communes—the *kibbutzim*[44] and the *moshavim*. In the *kibbutzim*, until very recently, there was no private ownership of anything not even the shirts, bicycles, or television sets, and all decision-making was done by committee. In the *moshavim*, each family owned and managed its own plot of land,[45] but all central services and major equipment were communal. All processing needs for raw agricultural products were also communal and organized on a regional basis. Agriculture prospered. Even with an exploding population due to mass in-migration of Jews,[46] Israel satisfied most, if not all, domestic needs while exporting an ever-increasing volume of out-of-season produce, fruit, flowers, and value-added processed foods.

As indicated during their formative decades, these countries' industrialization and banking involved state-owned enterprises. In the case of Israel, however, ownership in such enterprises was often shared with the *Histadrut*, the comprehensive umbrella trade union. Up to the 1970s, it is fair to say that the *Histadrut* and Israel's government were joined at the hip. This relationship was not merely in the political sphere but also in the circles of development. Together, they created and owned major industrial enterprises.

In agriculture, too, the *kibbutzim* enjoyed a special relationship with the government. Both government and donor agencies from abroad poured a great deal of money into Israel's agricultural development. This included agricultural research performed at its universities and several agriculture institutes. Such was hardly the case in Turkey. Even though an agricultural institute had been established in Ankara in the late 1920s, even though it involved some of the German expatriates, it is fair to say that, unlike Israel and, to a lesser extent, India, as a rule, Turkish universities had been detached from the multitude of Turkish farmers' ways of farming. Comparatively, such is the case to this very day.

## Turkey's Development *Results* as Compared to Similarly Situated Countries

Since independence, all three of these countries have had serious enemies on their borders. Hence, all three experienced major infusions of high-tech weaponry—a form of technology transfer. Israel used the technology transferred to great advantage in its own economic and social development,[47] India much less so, and Turkey hardly at all. Like many developing countries, Turkey over the years learned how to manufacture small weapons and munitions but acquired most of its more advanced weapons from abroad on a crated basis. Its military used the hardware until new technology made these weapons obsolete and the cycle of handed-out, updated replacement began again. So, the portion of GDP spent on its defense did not impact developments that would enhance the future value of Turkey's GDP.

Additionally, no matter how measured, how compared to western standards, including those in Israel and India, Turkey has provided very little money from either public or private sources for research at its universities or anywhere else. Combined with low pay levels in Turkey's universities this translates into low levels of academic research productivity and few innovations that can be transferred to the private sector. Without this, there is no culture of research and development followed by technology being transferred out. The development of this culture requires at least a generation or two. When Turkey accepted the scientists escaping from Nazism she got a tremendous boost, but this was not followed up with significant attempts to engage and keep the locally developed talent in subsequent generations.

The prestigious *World Economic Forum* (Geneva) and the *Institute for Management Development* (Lausanne) have jointly developed, and continue to periodically update, a competitiveness ranking for selected countries known as the "World Competitiveness Index" (WCI).[48] The Forum also periodically updates and publishes other macro-economic indicators comparing countries around the globe. Appendix 3 provides a number of these and other cross-national ratings as well as actual productivity data compiled from various public sources such as the World Bank (WB) and the International Money Fund (IMF). Individually, and in combinations, these are good indicators of Turkey's development status at any given point in time.

Turkey's model of technology transfer from abroad is the one typically invoked by developing countries. This model was very successful in developing Korea, Taiwan, and the other "Tiger" economies of Southeast Asia[49] and is now working miracles in mainland China. All of these countries, including Turkey, started their development process with an abundance of cheap labor. This was not the case with Israel. In countries bordering Israel, Turkey, and, more generally, the Middle East or North Africa, the model has been even less successful than in Turkey, even with their cheap-labor availability. This includes the petrol-blessed/based economies.

Moreover, it is safe to say that the former *French Orbit* countries of North Africa, Tunisia, and Morocco among others further suffer in their transfers of technology-based development because of dominant Francophone or Francophile cultural constraints. They have developed very few English or even German-speaking cadres. Consequently, they are dependent on technology that comes from, or through, France and, to a lesser degree, Belgium.[50] Turkey, on the other hand, is blessed with many of its educated elite having a good command of the English language. In all but one of Turkey's private universities, the language of instruction is English. At Galatasaray University, French is the language used. Moreover, some of the instruction at state universities is also given in English.

Beatty[51] suggested "two polar scenarios" for classifying a developing country's adoption and diffusion of foreign technology. Based on much documentation he classified 19$^{th}$ century Mexico as having fallen into his "foreign technology yielded *technological dependence*" scenario. By inference, he suggested that 19th century Japan fell into his "technology imports helped *to promote domestic technological capacity*" scenario.

Israel, to a large extent, and, in the information technology (IT) fields, India, fall squarely in the "technology imports *helped to promote domestic technological capacity*" category while Turkey, certainly up to the last decade and arguably to this day, is best described by "foreign technology *yielded technological dependence*." This classification is confirmed by a keynote speech delivered on November 8 2003 by Professor Kemal Namik Pak, "80 Years of the Republic of Turkey: Report on Science and Technology," at a workshop conducted by the *Austrian-Turkish Forum on Science.*

> Over the past two decades, there have been substantial developments in the Turkish S&T [Science and Technology] policies, along with those in the economy. Turkish economy rose to the upper echelons of (intermediate) technology producing counties, *after a long period of manufacturing under license. The Policy shift in the 1990s* has been from building a sound scientific infrastructure, to acquiring capabilities in science and technology, not only to achieve excellence in scientific and technological research, but also in converting scientific and technological findings into economical and/or social benefits. Hence, *the new S&T Policy of Turkey* aims at the establishment of a well-functioning National System of Innovation.

Starting by scrounging the world's scrap yards, Israel acquired foreign technology from many sources including the battlefield. Israel used the technology and learned from it and from, mostly in defense, field experience.[52] Additionally, its own universities and the public sector laboratories produced break-through innovations for domestic use, and for export, in a great diversity of technologies by a large number of the SMEs growing to significance in the global marketplace. Some were started by an individual with an idea for a marketable product such as drip irrigation created by individual farmers.

Israel is now an acknowledged high-tech industry leader in many sectors. These include defense, security, aerospace, biomedical, agricultural, IT (both hardware and software), chemicals, and pharmaceuticals, among others. Israel initiated its infrastructure for efficient and effective commercialization of university laboratory innovations back in the 1950s by launching the *YEDA*[53] organization at the Weizmann Institute of Science. On the other hand, the first technopark and business incubator in Turkey was established in 1985 by Istanbul Technical University and the Istanbul Chamber of Commerce.[54] The second one was created by the Middle East

Technical University (METU) in Ankara in 1991. So again, in the words of Prescott and Parente, there is a significant time lag in "country specific policies that result in constraints on work practices and on the application of better production methods [and innovations] at the firm level." In summary, Turkey's support of SMEs as a matter of public policy was not even considered until the 1990s[55] and has yet to prove its efficacy.

In India, its Prime Minister in 1984, Rajiv Gandhi, Indira Gandhi's son and Nehru's grandson, delineated his vision of taking India into the 21st century through a major emphasis on technological advancement, with a central role for the electronics industry including consumer electronics and software. This vision was implemented with vigor. Since then, India has forged international and multi-national strategic alliances in technological growth in a way that strengthened its being independent while pursuing the greater interdependence demanded by sophisticated and complex futuristic technology systems. India has sought to secure a special place in contract research through participation in the various international research value chains. She helped local firms build up their internal core technological capabilities in order to rapidly catch up with countries like as Israel.

Comparing these three countries, Turkey, Israel, and India, it was found[56] that they each practiced different models of institutionalizing technology transfer as a means to development. These are:

> (1) Acquire and use foreign technology from a limited number of suppliers—replace similarly—leading to manufacture under license or by joint ventures for import substitution and for export by a small group of established oligarchs. (Turkey)[57]
>
> (2) Reverse-engineer foreign technology; incrementally improve it, adopt it to local or similar conditions, and produce for import substitution and for export by state-owned enterprises and a small group of established oligarchs, ultimately leading to small and medium enterprises (SMEs) taking over in few niche technologies and growing to become worldwide suppliers. (India)[58]
>
> (3) Acquire foreign technology from whatever the source and by whatever the means, use it, learn from it and from the field—leading to production of breakthrough innovations for use and for export in a great diversity of technologies by a large number of SMEs growing to significance in the global marketplace (Israel)[59]

Moreover, in its development, China has invoked the first two of the above modes of institutionalizing technology transfer and, while it is moving into the third mode, it has finessed a fourth mode, that is to:

(4) Create a legal system and a business climate that fosters and condones the illegal appropriation of a product designed, manufactured, and marketed by a developed-country's firm but makes any attempt to remedy this wrong a practical impossibility.

Much as republican Turkey's founding fathers despised and rejected anything in the Ottoman tradition, the Republic inherited the above mode number (1) *modus operandi* from the Ottomans and by her own doing she has been held captive by it through the rest of the 20th century and well into the 21st. Because of this long tradition to acquire technology on a turnkey basis, the Indian model it appears was never considered by Turkey's public and private sectors. Some attributes of the Israeli model such as co-production are beginning to be invoked by the Turkish military at the time of this writing. However, the more recently developed Chinese model for technology transfer [mode number (4)] is precluded from Turkey's consideration by one of Atatürk's visions, a sincere desire to be part of Europe, and the various legal and ethical constraints implied thereby. It is also precluded by the commercial code and civil law placed on its books with the aid of the émigré professors back in the 1930s.

Scientific knowledge is commonly treated as a pure public good. Same is true for much of technological knowledge. Recent studies of physical science and technology, however, indicate that spillovers or diffusion of such knowledge is frequently localized, and that their most immediate impact is through face-to-face interaction between the knowledge creators and those who learn, extend, and apply the new knowledge.[60] Thus the very presence of the émigré scholars on Turkish soil and in Turkish classrooms and laboratories over an extended period of time can logically be claimed to have transferred and diffused much new and most current knowledge to a society thirsting for same. There is no question but that the sons and daughters of mother Turkey learned much from the German-speaking expatriates during the 1930s and 1940s. As the first generation of so-educated Turks is heading into the sunset, they are leaving behind their own legacy and Turkish institutions for generations to come.

In Turkey itself, the memories have lingered. In recent years, the subject has even become fashionable for media discussion. Starting at the turn of this century, some young German historians have been bringing this memory to the attention of their countrymen through seminars, exhibitions, and monographs.[61] The *Vereins Aktives* Museum in Berlin is especially active in this area. However, it is fair to say that the rest of the globe remains fairly ignorant of this bit of 20th-century history.

## The Ball Had Been Dropped a Few Times Too Many...the Momentum Was Lost

At several times and points along the way, Turkey lost the momentum started by the émigré professors in boosting its science and technology. Perhaps even more important is the fact that the momentum in social reforms initiated by Atatürk had run out of steam after 1938. As far back as 1943, Dr. Walter Livingston Wright, President of Istanbul's venerable (American) Robert College that he had served since 1935, noted in a memorandum to the United States State Department that Turkey's *Wealth Tax* widely considered as directed at the minorities was symptomatic of its political and social atmosphere. "It crystallized developments since the death of Atatürk and [was] a practical demonstration of a change in attitude of the government. Vigorous upbuilding of a young nation [he said then] is not now the aim of the official policy, rather it is the preservation of the class of officials with the human and natural resources which it can exploit."[62] A decade later, in the late 1950s, a Turkish social commentator had enough evidence to be able to say:

> In this country there are three layers of people differing from each other by civilization and education: the common people, the men educated in the *medreses*, [and] the men educated in [modern] secular schools. The first are still not freed from the effects of [old] Far Eastern civilization; the second are still living in an Eastern civilization; it is only the third group which has the benefits of western civilization. That means that one portion of our nation is living in an ancient, another in medieval, and a third in a modern age. How can the life of a nation be normal with such a threefold life? [63]

He then asked, "How can we be a real nation without unifying this threefold education?"[64] "The ultimate response which the nation made to this demand for concensus was, of course, to give one element—those with a modern secular education—increasing power over the rest."[65] Today, many of Turkey's elite are of the second generation having a modern education. They are now at the top of their careers and they can be found in all sectors of Turkish economy and society. Unfortunately, they have created social cliques. To say that the cliques have developed a system of patronage may be an overstatement. They do, however, promote their own. Who your parents were and those old school-boy ties, are unfortunately very much operative and real, albeit below the surface. They affect both hiring and promotions practices. This is true of the upper echelons in banking and industry as it is in private universities.[66] Although this is more or less true in every country, in Turkey per se it is contrary to the Ottomans' ways and to the republican fathers' visions.

Although egalitarianism is the official order of the day in universities, clannishness among their faculty and administration is visible on a daily basis. To be sure, clannishness is everywhere in the world, but what is surprising is the extent to which educated Turkish parents go to in order to make sure that their children, starting at preschool levels, go to the right "colleges" or private educational systems. Though rarely admitted by Turks, and generally denied, anecdotal evidence suggests that in great part this is motivated by building up alliances that will take them through life.

An educated Turkish native recently commented on this very issue. To wit, "although Turkey changed its government in 1923 and undertook major reforms, it did not change its people, who are steeped in tradition. Historically during the Ottoman Empire, educated Turks have been administrators, bureaucrats, and not business-minded nor particularly technically inclined. Also during the Ottoman years the majority of the population, which was agrarian, lacked a decent education. But all of this I believe is changing."[67]

Not so, said Professor Dilek Çetindamar, "but rather that 'university graduates' career plans involve working in large companies, since starting up a firm is considered a big risk. Therefore *no tradition of entrepreneurship exists*."[68] (emphasis added) When presented with this quote, the above Turkish educated native reacted: "Whether Turkey should deviate from being an agrarian society, and whether this is the best direction for its future can be questioned. In any case, *it will take a few generations of an educated people to shed the traditional ways which have kept Turkey behind*."[69] (emphasis added)

At the same time, reality shows us a large percentage of the Turkish population living in rural areas and in small towns still maintain a traditional Islamic patriarchal society. Therein lies another major problem because if but in part, according to some sociologists, notably Max Weber, "the scientific, rational mentality is incompatible with traditional, patrimonially organized society."[70] In some respects, Turkey is still in the same position it was in when Atatürk and his Young Turks took power in 1923. According to the IMF's Acting Director circa 2004:

> In 1955 Turkey's per capita income had been estimated to be roughly double that of Korea; by 1980, Turkey had fallen significantly behind the Asian tiger. Inflation had reached 100% in 1980. There were shortages in many sectors because of quantitative restrictions on imports and a shortage of foreign exchange.[71]

Paraphrasing the words of Parente and Prescott, "country specific policies that result[ed] in constraints on work practices and on the application of better production methods at the firm level." Returning to the IMF, "After years of false starts," a big shake-up in both policymaking and policy signaled a completely fresh approach. Starting in 1980, policy shifts were directed toward three main objectives:

> Economic stabilization, including a reduction in the rate of inflation.
>
> A deliberate shift away from import substitution to an export-oriented economy.
>
> A shift toward a more market-oriented economy."[72]

The financial liberalization policy beginning in the 1980s had a major impact on development by removing at least some of the country specific policies that impede development. It was an integral part of the "Thatcher revolution" process of privatization and ensuing globalization.[73] As a result of all three of the above shifts,[74] many multinational companies established wholly owned subsidiaries or joint ventures in several Turkish service as well as manufacturing sectors. Among these were: Citibank (1980), McDonalds (1986), Ford (1985), Toyota (1994), HSBC (2001), Ernst & Young (1983), and Motorola (1995).[75]

Backtracking in time and keeping in mind that the U. S. dollar lost a great deal of its purchasing power at the end of the 1920s, the Turkish Lira has been losing its value at an average ten-fold of the dollar's rate. Yet the émigré professors' salaries were kept at the 1933 amounts for many years. They were not indexed to inflation. Thus, many had to sell possessions they brought with them from their native lands. Following World War II, when Turkey was experiencing a major economic recession, many jobs had to be eliminated altogether. Universities were not sacrosanct; the library system was not immune.

On August 28 1948, the notable orientalist and architect of Turkey's libraries, Walter Gottschalk, sent a handwritten note from *Kadiköy*, Istanbul. It was addressed to his former colleague, Felix Haurowitz, who was just settling in at the University of Indiana. Among other news, Gottschalk mentioned that "we had to lay off a lot of people, half of the people here in Istanbul."[76]

At about the same time, many of the émigré professors were aging and beginning to worry about their retirement. Unfortunately, Turkey was not forthcoming in terms of pension guarantees. This was a major impetus for the final exodus of the "Germans."

Financial reasons played an important role for many of those who returned [to Germany and Austria]. This was because "it was not possible to reach an agreement for a retirement plan, good or bad, in spite of all the efforts of our Turkish colleagues. Those who did not have significant savings looked on their old age with trepidation."[77]

Moreover, during the first multi-party government in Turkey under the leadership of *Adnan Menderes* in the 1950s, the country reached great budget deficits that precipitated university faculty layoffs and resulted in one of the Army's coups. Those were but two of the *Üniversite Reformu's* several major setbacks. Then, during the 1980s, Turkey went through its own "McCarthy" period. Istanbul's Bilgi University Professor *İlber Ortaylı* recounts the results of one such setback:

> During the 1980 *coup d'etat* the universities were turned upside down with the accusation that they are turning out communists. Since the regime did not articulate a viable program, what they created was a monster. Our lives were blown apart. They wanted to get rid of some people but when it came to executing what they wished to do, they did not have any clear ideas. The 1980 regime thought that this would be done by some trusted professors. However, these trusted *hocas* also did not have any intellectual guidelines in their heads. These were pragmatic men, willing to implement things but it was not clear to them *why*. In fact, the biggest dilemma of *YÖK*, the Higher Education Council in 1980, was this. And it ended in disappointment. Even for those who started with good intentions, it ended in disappointment. Those who were involved with the implementation have found their place in history. No one can make a positive evaluation of their regressive reforms. Yet in 1933, such was not the case.[78]

If this were not sufficient, Ortaylı's response to the question "who were the politicians who assaulted the faculty?" was "*Behçet Kemal* and *Fahri Kurtuluş*. These deputies raided the office of the Rector in the *Languages, Histrory and Geography Faculty* building. This is a very important event in that time."[79] Professor *Dr. Aykut Kazancıgil,* translator of one of the most significant and well-documented sources on the subject of Atatürk's university reforms, the 1973 Widman book, added: "They seized *Şevket Aziz Kansu,* the rector at the time, and shook him up. Consequently, the Ministry of Education asked the professors of the İstanbul University for a report. What was asked of them was that they investigate the file in order to accuse a group of young teaching faculty with communism. *Reşit Galip* was not a communist. May God bless his soul. This is an outrage which was unheard of even during the reign of [Sultan] *Abdülhamit*."[80]

Unfortunately, the September 1980 military coup placed Turkey under martial law. It lasted three whole years. During this period hundreds of writers, journalists, and university faculty of varous ideological stripes were jailed. Others simply left the country.

As indicated in Chapter 6, throughout most of its history, republican Turkey has tried to maneuver among the scars of its turn-of-the-century wars; its national honor; memories of the Ottoman Empire; tortuous twists and turns in its economy; internal political oppositon, and the paralyzing fears of German invasion in the 1930s which did not cease until VE day. Turkey's conflict with Greece highlighted by Cyprus. Its fears of the Soviet Union, which lasted well into the 1980s, its ethnic strife with over 30,000 killed in conficts with the Kurdish population, and an Armenian diaspora pushing for recognition of its version of history in various forums worldwide were additional major issues to be dealt with.

And if that was not enough, being cradled in an arc of instability along its northeastern border spanning the ex-Soviet republic of Georgia with all the ethnic strife; the warring between Christian Armenia and Moslem Azerbaijan; a troublesome Iran; and war-wracked Iraq, being a modern and secular state when most of its population is traditional and Moslem; and fears of a large and threatening Islamic world which remain to this very day are a few other issues to deal with.

Additionally, until the start of the Cold War, both the United States and Britain were sending Turkey unclear and often conflictual messages on many strategic issues especially those involving the Jewish question. Though tangibly appreciated by the US, its participation in the Korean War resulted in many Turkish casualties but helped the Turkish economy for a few years. However, its indecisiveness—an unwillingness to say "no" flat out—to helping US troops transit Turkey on the way to the second Iraq war caused a rift in the relationship and another negative effect on its economy.

Even Nature was not always kind to Turkey. Many of its earthquakes were devastating. But the 800-pound grorilla in the room is the national self-image problem. Issues of ethnic lineage having an implict hierarchy often surface in conversation with westerners. As indicated Turkey is grappling with the duality of an educated, secular, and cosmopolitan class living in high-rent cities such as Istanbul and Ankara on the one hand, and a very poor rural substructure of arranged marriages, deeply rooted Islamic ways, and up to ninety-percent illiteracy among rural women.[81]

In quantitative terms, Turkey's entire educational system has made monumental progress during the course of some seven decades. Yet, this great success in making education available to all takers and at all levels and desired by millions has in fact evolved into a major impediment to

Turkey's development. A contradiction? Not at all! Turkey needs to do more to encourage creativity, the ability to synthesize information gained, individualism, entrepreneurship, curiosity, challenging of conventional widom or of authority, sense of adventure, ambition, and essay writing. Having said that, its annually administered national university entrance examination must be seriously reconsidered or dropped altogether. It cannot evaluate close to two million students in a single day without forcing Turkish elementary and secondary education into conformity to that which is measured by the State as "teaching effectiveness." Its designers must recognize the old adage "be careful what you measure, because what you measure you will get" in the long run.[82]

University graduates, especially in the sciences and technology should be encouraged to aspire to starting businesses, to becoming entrepreneurs, to becoming wealth creators, and to be doing that on their own instead of being quite satified as "hired hands," which, unfortunately, is the dominant case in Turkey. Innovations drive the economic engine—they help launch startup companies that are not condemned or destined to remain "Ma-and-Pa shops." They create jobs which are not limited to the blue-collar variety, and they create wealth and spinoffs to other commercial activitiy. This is not happening in today's Turkey because of a number of reasons—one being that its educational system at all levels does not foster it. Even, and perhaps especially, Turkey's private academies teach to enhance their students' performance on the University Entrance Examination which features questions that can and must be computer graded. Computers have yet to become capable of grading entrepreneurship or creativity, even in essay writing, among other such areas. So the schools concentrate on teaching facts, figures, and analytics. Synthesis and creativity are of secondary consideration, if at all.

Another reason is that government and the Turkish oligarchs in a position to do so have done so precious little to nurture emergence and growth of innovation based, technology-driven and independently owned SMEs. To be sure, the oligachic families do plow back significant amounts of their earnings into society's development. They have endowed schools, universities, and museums. They have not, however, created business incubators nor any other forms of supporting indigenous talent wanting to start innovation-based companies of their own. Understandably, it is not in their interest to do so.

Moreover, responses from more than 2000 firms to a 1998 survey conducted by Turkey's own *State Institute of Statistics* show that Turkish bureaucracy, lack of venture-capital availability, lack of government subsidies, lack of collaboration among universities, research organizations and private firms (especially the small companies), a miniscule number of patent or copyright holding by individuals, and a volatile economy *are widely perceived to discourage technology driven entrepreneurship in Turkey.*[83]

And what's more, quite differently than is the case in Israel, in Turkey, *"researchers do not show any interest in the problems of corporations, and similarly corporations do not trust researchers' capability in solving their problems."*[84] The above survey also shows that only " four (4) percent of [Turkish] innovative firms consider universities as a source of knowledge and technology, while only 2.7 percent of them see government research agencies as a source."[85] Such firms should be the greatest users of academia! Value judgments aside, Turkey's societal development has not exactly followed the innovation-driven economic development that has taken place in Israel and, more recently, in India's information technology sector.

And if all that was not enough, based on Turkey's cross-cultural and cross-national research into enrepreneurship Professor *Dilek Çetindamar* finds that, as of 2005, "Turkey underutilises youth and women entrepreneurial resources; entrepreneurs do not have the kinds of ties that might be helpful when they are first starting out; and entrepreneurs see as their main problems buraucracy and unstable state policies."[86]

It should be recalled that for a complexity of reasons, by using various bureaucratic means, many of the émigrés were "encouraged" to leave prematurely. These departures were detrimental to Turkey's more rapid and more consistent development. Within universities, the departures certainly opened up jobs for many of the by then highly educated Turkish natives. Beyond its universities, however, Turkey's inability to fully capitalize on the reforms made by the émigrés may be compared to an unattended rose garden. After Atatürk's death in 1938, the care was becoming more and more absent as time went on. Unattended some of Atatürk's visions entered into a naturally degrading process. The weeds took over. By 1943, the effects were so evident that Dr. Walter Livingston Wright, (outgoing President of Robert College) had the following to say in his July 14 (1943), Cairo-based exit interview,[87] "The fact is that Atatürk realized if Turkey was to remain independent it had to become Europeanized; it had to acquire not only the recognition but also the techniques of the Europeans. Atatürk was always running along that route. He put the fear of Allah into the administration right down to the lowest official."

Turkey, Wright wrote back in February 1943, is slipping backward into old and discredited ways." He detailed the above broad accusation in another part of his Memorandum. "The country is at the mercy of men with the limited vision of the hereditary bureaucrat who has little concern for the population except as a source of government income, who dislikes foreigners, and regards non-Moslem fellow citizens as a species of property fit only for exploitation. His animating force is not nationalism but personal advantage in terms of income." Later on, Wright introduced a more hopeful note: "but *I believe that the present drift will not continue long*."[88] (emphasis added)

Several decades later, it can be seen that a number of important aspects of the "vision" have indeed been maintained. To this day, Turkey remains a secular Republic. That is most significant from many a vantage point. The three modern universities established in Atatürk's lifetime have multiplied to over seventy two and, together, they produce more than 200,000 graduates annually. Turkey's urban centers are highly developed and the health status of its population is relatively good. Women's participation in the professions is higher than in most western countries. Turkey's industry is producing for import substitution and for export, and, as a member of NATO, Turkey is "independent" and fairly "Europeanized," especially so in its city centers.

## Now the Future Looks Bright

During the last decade of the previous century, Turkey's economy and, to a lesser extent, its society, have absorbed (as Atatürk had wished) many of "the techniques of the Europeans." Today, with its innovation centers, technology parks, regional economic development partnerships, and highly qualified workforce, Turkey appears to be well positioned again for economic takeoff. It is to be hoped that Turkey will turn its current challenges into opportunities and transform itself into a model of a contemporary secular State with a dominantly Moslem population that uses tolerance to its advantage, that properly develops and takes full advantage of its natural and vast human resources, and that serves as a catalyst in the resolution of one of the key conflicts of the globalizing world, while maintaining its unique ethnic and cultural heritage.

Dr. John Staudenmaier S.J., a historian of science and technology observed that:

> If past technological change is commonly discussed as if it were independent of any historical context, then the language used to speak of present technological issues will be radically impoverished. For this reason, I find the ahistorical nature of much popular technological analysis alarming. By the same token, I am concerned that so much general historical discourse pays so little attention to technology.[89]

There was a brief and shining moment in the early 1930s when Providence sent a group of the most active, intelligent, and dedicated people alive from Germany and Austria to Turkey to push and pull Turkey into modern times; to provide her students the tools they needed to continue on; as well as the inspiration to pass on not only knowledge but also the driving curiosity necessary for discoveries, change, and growth. The story of the exiles and the unselfish contribution of these German-Jewish émigrés is one of the least-known episodes of World War II in the non-Turkish, non-German, speaking countries.

It is time to change that, and tell their story in the English speaking world. It is time to acknowledge these heroes and heroines who tried so hard but, in some respects, were somewhat defeated in the end by apathy, by real problems Turkey faced, and by interests antagonistic to them.

This much we know—their students have never forgotten the teachers and to this day thank them and remember them with honor. Some of the memoirs in previous chapters attest to that.

# Concluding Remarks

> When one looks back to the time when the Axis pincers had reached Egypt and the Caucasus, one realizes better what anxieties must have harassed [the German émigrés in Turkey]. We are approaching the time when it will be the Nazi appointees in the German universities who will have reason for anxiety. Dr. Alvin Johnson,[90] May 4, 1944.

To get an idea of how the war affected various people at the time, one of the memoirs tells that on the south side of a relatively small sea, the émigré mothers' dilemmas had to do with how to deal with those "illiterate" and backward house servants "who spoke no German." But, north of the Black Sea, my own mother's problem often had to do with how far she could stretch one piece of dried bread and optimally share it with me. While we had to spend many a night, some moonlit, some rain-drenched, in fields and forests without cover over our heads, and often there would be strafing or bombing by the Luftwaffe, some of them begrudged the walk up four flights of stairs to their apartments. While we carried all our possessions through fields, meadows, forests, and over mountain ranges in an old potato sack, they were followed by a porter carrying their groceries from the market—different contexts and different forms of deprivation. Nevertheless, I was one of the lucky ones. I survived, and I am delighted that so did they.

As for Dr. Johnson's 1944 comment concerning "the Nazi appointees in the German universities who will have reason for anxiety," after having been de-Nazified with the help of some of the Turkey-saved luminaries who did return to the *heimat,* German universities recovered with America's largesse on the one side of the Berlin wall and Soviet largesse on the other. To be sure, over the intervening seven decades, Istanbul's "best German University in the world" has lost some of its sharper image. However, it is not very far behind the very best of Germany's current universities.

A member of the Turkish Parliament, Mr. *Onur Öymen*, said the following at the Seminar on "Culture as a Weapon, Academicians in Exile" in Berlin on July 19 2003:[91]

> A number of German professors had high reputations in their own countries and participated in major reform projects in Turkey besides their teaching activities. For example, *Andreas Schwarz* from Freiburg made an important contribution to the adoption of western laws in Turkey in 1930s. *Gustav Oelsner* from Hamburg, besides teaching architecture and city planning, played an important role in Turkey's city planning programs. *Paul Hindemith* was instrumental in building the Turkish State Conservatory in Ankara, *Carl Ebert* from Berlin founded the Turkish State Opera; and conductor *Ernst Praetorius* founded the President's Philharmonic Orchestra in Ankara. I cannot cite here the contributions of all the visiting professors, but I can tell you that all of them substantially contributed to the reform programs of the young Turkish Republic.

Over the years, Istanbul University's Academic Senate has voted to grant honorary doctorates to Fritz Neumark, Fritz Arndt, Richard von Mises, Kurt Kosswig, Felix Haurowitz, and Gustav Oelsner, among others.

What was recovered from the displaced assets of a once-humanist culture resulted in a significant contribution to the educational reforms of a new nation. At the same time, "Turkey placed a significant amount of German intellectual capital in escrow until it could be returned home safely and with interest."[92] For many of the émigrés, however, home was no longer the old *heimat.* It was America, and Israel.

While Turkey's main population and land are found in Anatolia with respect to geography and geopolitics, it is a country which has made considerable effort to approach the West, especially after the Kemalist revolution. However, it would be wrong to regard it as equal to the other western countries economically, socially and culturally. The country has special characteristics particular to itself which can only be grasped after repeated and long stays there.

> Leaving everything aside, the magically beautiful Bosphorus bridge opened on the 50th anniversary of the Republic may be regarded as a symbol that Turkey will connect Europe and Asia, East and West, today more than ever. Among those who feel this

in admiration and gratitude are German scientists, politicians and artists who looked for and found shelter along the Bosphorus during difficult times.[93]

# Epilogue

Professor *Albert Malche* began his October 16 1933 letter to *Lauder W. Jones* at the Rockefeller Foundation with, "Before departing for Turkey, may I bring to your kind attention, as did Professor [Philipp] Schwarz, the civilizing work which the Turkish Government has undertaken in reorganizing the University of Istanbul." Among the émigrés who served those developmental needs and who were thereby saved by the Turks from Nazi death camps and emerged from the Turkey-provided "Escrow" to contribute to America's by the war's end more mature and enlightened society were: Felix Haurowitz, and Hans Wilbrandt *University of Indiana*; Richard von Mises, *Harvard*; Hilda Geiringer (von Mises), *Bryn Mawr College*, the *National Research Council*, and *Brown University*; Hans Rosenberg, Benno Landsberger, and Hans Güterbock, *Chicago*; Werner Lipschitz, *Lederle Laboratories*; Joseph Igersheimer, *Tufts*; Philipp Schwarz, *Warren State Hospital*, PA; Hans Reichenbach, and Andreas Tietze, *UCLA*; Wolfram Eberhard, *UCLA* and *U. C. Berkeley*; Erich Auerbach, *Pennsylvania State University*, *Institute for Advanced Study at Princeton*, and *Yale*; Leo Spitzer, and Ruth Wilmans Lidz, *Johns Hopkins*; Alexander Rüstow, *Princeton*, *New School of Social research*, and *CUNY*; Hans Bremer, *University of Texas at Dallas*; Arthur von Hippel, *MIT*; Rudolf Nissen, *Brooklyn Jewish Hospital*, *The Nissen Center for the Treatment of Heartburn & Esophageal Disease*, Brooklyn, New York, and *Long Island College of Medicine*; Ernst Wolfgang Caspari, *Lafayette College*, *Wesleyan University*, the *University of Rochester*, and the *Genetics Society of North America* (president for many years) and member of the *Manhattan Project*; Werner Laqueur, *West Virginia*; William Prager, *Brown*; Alfred Kantorowicz, *University of Illinois at Chicago*, Kurt S. Lion, *MIT*[94]; Erich Uhlmann, *Chicago Radiological Society President* 1955-1956; Erika Bruck, *Children's Hospital of Buffalo*; Max Sgalitzer, *University of Colorado's Medical School in Denver*; Richard Honig, *DuBose Theological School, and the University of Georgia*; Carl Ebert, *UCLA* as well as *American theater and opera*; and, of course, Paul Hindemith, *Yale* and *worldwide music*.

Although none of the émigrés ever achieved Nobel laureate fame, a number of them had direct working relationships with those who did. As documented in this book. At a minimum, Hanz Reichenbach worked with Albert *Einstein*, Neils *Bohr*, Max *Planck*, Max *Born*, and Bertrand *Russell*; Felix Haurowitz with Linus *Pauling*; E. Finlay Freundlich with Albert *Einstein;* Max *von Laue* and Erwin *Schroedinger*; Richard von Mises with Neils *Bohr* and Albert *Einstein*; Benno Landsberger, and Hans Güterbock, were Enrico *Fermi's* colleagues and friends at the University of Chicago; Philipp Schwarz was instrumental in bringing James *Franck* and Max *Born* to Turkey as consultants; Wilhelm Liepmann corresponded with *Einstein*; and, of course, von Hippel was James *Franck's* son-in-law and he had worked with Neils *Bohr* in Denmark. Even Nobelist Enrico *Fermi*'s wife, Laura, a prolific writer of books on the history of science, discussed, or at least mentioned, no fewer than twelve of the émigrés by name in her *Illustrious Immigrants* book that had been published in 1968 by the prestigious University of Chicago Press.

For every émigré who could be listed as contributing to America's science and medicine, one could add their progeny, men and women who were raised, and at least partially educated, while in Turkey and who later came to western shores and made major contributions to America's science and culture. Among these are: Eugen Merzbacher, *North Carolina;* the von Hippel brothers, Eric, *MIT*, Peter, *Oregon*, and Frank, *Princeton*; Walter W. Igersheimer, *Yale*; Dankwart Rüstow, *Princeton* and *CUNY*; Walter Arndt, *Dartmouth*; Richard Honig, *RCA Laboratories*; Martin Harwit (Haurowitz), *Cornell*, as well as the *National Air and Space Museum;* his sister, Alice (Haurowitz) Sievert, *Abbott Laboratories*; Stephen Prager, *University of Minnesota;* Hans Wilbrandt, *Indiana University*; Clemens Auerbach, *Brookhaven National Laboratory;* Karl Zimmer and Thomas Laqueur, *UC Berkeley*; Hans Wolfgang Baade, *Texas*; George Sgalitzer, *U.S. Army Medical Corps*, and the list could go on.

Many of the émigrés ended up going to what was then Palestine. At least thirty-six individuals, including family members, are known to have gone there.[95] Among these was a group of seasoned health-care professionals. This group included Prof. Dr. Karl Hellmann, *ear, nose, and throat specialist;* Dr. Kurt Steinitz, *internal and laboratory medicine*; Dr. Werner Silberstein, *microbiologist;* Dr. Georg Fuchs, *radiologist*; Grete Lindenbaum, *radiological nurse*, Dr. Sara Gitla Lisier, *biochemist;* Caecilie Leuchtenberger, *cancer research;* Dr. Rudolf Leuchtenberger, *internal medicine*. There were others who returned to Germany, recouped their pension rights, served as Rectors, and helped to de-Nazify its universities.

Thus, Man's inhumanity to Man in one society brought about great developmental leaps in more humane settings. In this story, such was indeed the case.

# APPENDICES

# Appendix 1

## Contemporary Mission Statements of the Original Three Turkish Universities

### *Ankara University*

Ankara University was founded by Atatürk himself, for, in his own words, "those principles that describe a modern society, science, and enlightenment."[1]

The first and most impressive performance of the young Republic in the field of higher education was to establish the following higher education institutions: the School of Law, to train judiciary who were to realize the new order of law in the secular and democratic Republic (1925); the Institute of Technology for Agriculture, to lead the modernization of Turkish agriculture (1933); the School of Language, History, and Geography, to establish a bridge of language and culture between Turkey and the rest of the world and to conduct research on the rich culture of Anatolia (1935); and the School of Political Science, which had been training top-level public administrators under the name of Mektebi Mülkiye since 1859 and which was later moved to Ankara in 1936 upon the directive of Atatürk. We should also mention the schools of which the preparation stage was started by Atatürk which the establishment postponed until the beginning of 1940s due to World War II. Among those schools were Schools of Medicine and Science.

Ankara University comprising Faculty of Law (1925), Faculty of Language, History and Geography (1935), Faculty of Science (1943), and Faculty of Medicine (1945) was established officially in 1946. The University acquired the Faculties of Agriculture and Veterinary Medicine previously belonged to the Institute of Technology for Agriculture in 1948. The School of Divinity was founded in 1949, the Faculty of Political Sciences in 1950, the School of Pharmacy in 1960, the School of Dentistry in 1963 (became a faculty in 1977), Faculty of Educational Sciences in 1965, and the Faculty of Communication in 1965. Çankırı Faculty of Forestry and Health Education Faculties were opened to education in 1996.[2]

### *Istanbul Technical University*[3]

Istanbul Technical University's long and distinguished history began in 1773 when it was founded by Sultan Mustafa III.... Mustafa sought to modernize the army and the internal state machinery to bring his empire in line with the Powers of Western Europe. In 1845, the engineering function of the school was further widened with the addition of a program devoted to the training of architects. The scope and name of the school were extended and changed again in 1883 and, in 1909, the school became a public engineering school which was aimed at training civil engineers who could provide the infrastructure for the rapidly building country. By 1928, the institution had gained formal recognition as a university of engineering which provided education in both engineering and architecture. In 1944 (July 12), the name of the institution was changed to Istanbul Technical University and, in 1946, the institution became an autonomous university with architecture civil, mechanical, and electrical engineering.

With its 224-year long history, its modern teaching environment, and very strong teaching staff, Istanbul Technical University today is the personification of engineering and architectural education[4] in Turkey. And, just as Istanbul Technical University played a leading role in the modernization movement of the Ottoman Empire, it has also maintained its leadership position in the changes and innovations taking place in construction, industrialization, and technological realms during the modern days of the Turkish Republic.[5]

### *Istanbul University*

The foundation of Istanbul University, one of the oldest educational institutions not only of Turkey, but also of the world, was accomplished when Mehmet the Conqueror conquered Istanbul. Education began to be dispensed in theological schools (*madrasas* as they were then called) and, until the end of the 16th century, these schools were instrumental in educating the ruling cadres of the Ottoman society.

Through the educational reforms instigated by the founding of the Republic, the "madrasas" were abolished in 1924, and, as a first step in modernization, the Istanbul Dar-ül Fünun was established, comprising the fields of medicine, law, literature, theology, and science. The institution was renamed Istanbul University in accordance with Atatürk's university reform, and higher education was restructured in Turkey to meet the demands of contemporary conditions. *During these early years, Istanbul University welcomed foreign academics who were fleeing Germany and they became members of the teaching staff.* (emphasis added)

When the Turkish Republic was founded, Istanbul University was the only institution of higher education.[6] That is the reason why it is the provender for [feeder of] all the universities existing in Turkey today, and the academics educated here have initiated the establishment of the other institutions. Thus, Istanbul University has always been instrumental in the training and strengthening of our country's scientific cadres.

In addition to its scientific impact, Istanbul University has also been a leader in the movement towards enlightenment and modernization that began with the Republic by acting as a bridge between science and life. It is aware of its role in the perpetuation of Atatürk's principles and reforms and will persevere in this line in all issues pertaining to public life with no concessions from its decisive stand.

Istanbul University functions as a reflection of Turkey's history of science and independence. As was the case in its history, Istanbul University is still in the vanguard of scientific success. Our alumni figure in all strata of society and serve their country through the important positions they hold.[7]

# Appendix 2

**Lıst of the Émigré Professors and Their Disciplines**

ADLER, Kurt (Pathology)
ALSLEBEN Ernst Magnos (Internal Medicine).
ALTHAUSEN, Irmgard (Surgical Nursing)
ANHEGGER, Robert Friedrich Moritz (Turkology)
ANSTOCK, Heinz (Romance Studies)
ARNDT, Fritz (Chemistry)
AUERBACH, Erich, (Chemistry)
BAADE, Fritz (Consultant in Commerce)
BARTHOLD, Vasiliy Vladimiroviç (???)
BEAN, George Ewart
BELLİNG, Rudolph (Fine Arts)
BERGSTRÄSSER, Gotthelf
BERNHARD, Kurt (Engineer)
BODENDORF (Chemistry and Pharmacy)
BODENHEIMER,[1] Frederick Simon (Agricultural Entomology)
BODLAENDER, Hans (Engineering)
BOGATSCH, Ernst (Engineering)
BONATZ, Paul (Architect)
BOSCH, Clemens Emile (Numismology)
BOSSERT, Helmuth Theodor (Archeology)
BRAUN, Hugo (Bacteriology, Microbiology, and Epidemiology)
BRAUNER, Leo (Botany)
BREMER, Hans (Microbiology)
BREUSCH, Friedrich (Pathology, Chemistry)
BUCK, Eva (Philology)
BUEDING, Ernest (Pharmacology and Pathobiology)
BURKHART, Rosemarie (Romanticism)
CASPARI, Ernst (Biology, Genetics)

CHAPUT, (Geology and National Geography)
DEMBER, Alexis (Physics)
DEMBER, Harry (Physics)
DESSAUER, Friedrich, (Physics and Radiology)
DIECKMANN, Herbert (Romanisism)
DIECKMANN, Lieselotte (Greek and German Studies)
DOBRETSBERGER, Josef (*Political Economy)*
DOPPLER, Franz (Engineering)
DUDA, Herbert Walter
DUMÉZIL, Georges
EBERHARD, Wolfram (Sinology)
EBERT, Carl (Theater)
ECKSTEİN, Albert (Pediatrics, Venereal Diseases)
ECKSTEİN-SCHLOSSMAN, Erna (Medicine)
EİCHOLTZER, Herbert (Architecture)
ELSAESSER, Martin (Architecture)
ENGELBERG, Ernst (History)
FOUCHE Marcel (General Physics)
FRAENKEL, Lilly (Surgery)
FRANK, Alfred Erich (Internal Medicine)
FRIEDLÄNDER, Julius (Chemistry)
FREUNDLICH, Erwin Findlay (Astronomy)
FRICHE, Gerhard
FUCHS, George (Radiology)
FUCHS, Rudolf (Engineer)
FUCHS, Traugott (Romance Studies)
GABRIEL, Albert
GASSNER, Gustav (Botany, wood science)
GEİRİNGER, Hilda (von Mises) (Applied Mathematics)
GERNGROSS, Otto (Chemistry)
GIESE, Wilhelm Friedrich Carl
GLEISBERG, Wolfgang (Astronomy)
GOTTSCHALK, Walter (Librarianship)
GRANDT, (Geology and National Geography)
GROSS, Phillip (Chemical Technology)
GUTERBROCK, Hans (Archeology, Philology, History, and Hittitology)
GUTMANN, Walter (Music Director)
GUZWILLER, (Civil Law)
HATSCHEK, Gustav (Medicine)
HAUROWITZ, Felix (Biochemistry)
HECKMANN, Karl (Radiology)
HEILBRONN, Hans (Botany and Pharmacology)

HEILBRUNNER, Alfred (Botany)
HELLMANN, Karl (Otolaryngology)
HERSCH, Paul (Chemistry)
HERZOG, Reginald Oliver [Porges] (Industrial Chemistry)
HEYD, Kurt (Journalism)
HIRSCH, Ernst Edward (Commercial Law)
HIRSCH, Julius (Hygiene)
HİNDEMİTH, Paul (Music Composition)
HOFFMANN, Susanne (Ophthalmology)
HOLZMEISTER, Clemens (Architecture)
HONIG, Richard (Fundamental Law and its History)
HOROWITZ, W. (Radiology)
IGERSHEIMER, Josef (Ophthalmology and Venereal Diseases)
ISAAC, Alfred, (Economics)
KANTOROWICZ, Alfred (Dentistry)
KESSLER, Gerhard (Economics, Sociology, and Law)
KLEINSORGE, Hubert (Geology)
KOSSWIG, Curt (Marine Biology and Cancerology)
KRAEPELIN, Hans (Chemistry)
KRAINER, Leo (Musicology)
KRANZ, Walter (Classical Philology)
KRAUS, Fritz (Assyriology)
KLÄRE Krause (Medical Illustration)
LADEWIG, Peter (Pathology)
LANSBERGER, Benno (Assyriology)
LAQUEUR, August (Physical Therapy)
LAQUEUR, Kurt (Accountancy and Languages)
LAQUEUR, Werner (Pathology)
LEUCHTENBERGER, Rudolf (Internal Medicine)
LEVY, Leopold (Visual Arts)
LIEPMANN, Wilhelm (Gynecology and Obstetrics)
LINDENBAUM, Grete, (Nursing and Radiology)
LION, Kurt (Engineering)
LIPSCHITZ, Werner (Biochemistry and Pharmacology)
LISSNER, Helmuth (Biology)
LİSİER, Sura (Biochemistry)
LÖWE, Lotte (Chemistry)
LÖWENTHAL, Karl (Histology and Embryology)
MARCHAND, Hans (English)
MARCHİONİNİ, Alfred (Dermatology and Venereal Diseases)
MELCHIOR, EDUARD (Surgery)
MENDELSSOHN, Thomas (Physics)

MEYER, Max (ENT)
NEUMARK, Fritz (Economics and Law)
NEVİLLE, Andre (Zoology)
NISSEN, Rudolf (Surgery)
OBENDORFER, Siegfried (General Physiology)
OELSNER, Gustaf (Architecture)
OSTROROG, (Count) Léon Valerien
OTTENSTEIN, Berta (Dermatology)
PETERFI, Tibor (Biology)
PETERS, Wilhelm (Pharmacy)
PFANNENSTEL, Max (Geology and Librarianship)
POLLACZEK-GEIRINGER, Hilda (Applied Mathematics)
PRAGER, William (Applied Mathematics)
PREAETORİUS, Ernst (Conductor)
PULEWKA, Paul (Pharmacology and Toxicology )
REICHENBACH, Hans (Philosophy)
REIMANN, Friedrich (Internal Medicine)
REININGER, Margarethe (Radiology Nursing)
REININGER, Walter (Radiology Engineering)
REUTER, Ernst (Economics)
RITTER, Hellmut (Orientalist)
RİCCİ, Umberto (Economics)
ROHDE, Georg (Classical Philology)
ROSENBAUM, Harry (Physiology)
ROSENBERG, Hans (Astronomy)
ROYDS, Thomas (Astronomy)
RÖPKE, Wilhelm (Economics, Geography, National Economy, History of Economic Tendencies, and Law)
RUBEN, Walter (İndıa Expert)
RÜSTOW, Alexander (Economics, History of Economics, and Law)
SALOMON, Hans (Radiology)
SALOMON-CALVI, Peter (Geology)
SCHLENK Wilhelm (General Chemistry)
SCHNEE, Ludwig (Botany)
SCHNEIDER, Ernst (Botany)
SCHOCKEN, Wolfgang (Violinist)
SCHÖNFELD, Friedrich (Flutist)
*SCHÜCKİNG, Alfred (Mechanical Engineering)*
SCHÜTTE, Ludwig (Engineering)
SCHÜTTE-LİHOTZKY, Margarete (Architecture)
SCHWARTZ, Andreas B. (Roman Law)
SCHWARTZ, Philipp (Pathology, Anatomy)

SGALITZER, Max (Radiology)
SOLOMON-CALVİ, Wilhelm (Geology)
SPITZER, Leo (Romance Languages and Literature)
STEINITZ, Kurt (Chemistry)
STEPHAN, Walter (Plant Science)
STRUPP, Karl (International Law)
SÜSSHEIM, Karl (Orientology)
TAUT, Bruno (Architecture)
TIEDCKE, Sonja (Private Teacher)
TIETZE, Andreas (Turkology)
UHLMANN, Erich (Radiology)
VON ASTER, Ernst (Philosophy)
VON BÜLOW, Ester (Histology)
VON FRANCKENSTEIN, Heinrich Freiherr (Agronomy)
VON HIPPEL, Arthur R. (Physics)
VON MİSES, Richard (Applied Mathematics)
WAGNER, Martin (Architecture)
WEBER ???? (Astronomy)
WEINBERG, Toni (Microbiology)
WEINER, Karl (Language Teacher)
WEISS, Richard (Physical Chemistry)
WEISSGLASS, Carl (Radiology Engineering)
WILBRANDT, Hans (Agricultural Economics)
WILLMANNS, Ruth (Psychiatry)
WINKLER, Adolf (Violinist)
WINTER, Egon (Gynecology)
WINTERSTEIN, Hans (Experimental Physiology)
WOLF, Else (Nursing and Internal Medicine)
WOLODKEWİTSCH, Nikolaus (Radiology Engineering)
WOLTERECK, Richard (Biology)
WUNSCH, Walter (Oboist)
ZIELKE, Barbara (Archeology)
ZIMMER, Ernst (Geology)
ZIMMER, Karl-Ernst (Linguistics)
ZUCKMAYER, Eduard (Music)

# Appendix 3

## Quantitative Cross-country Comparisons

**Table 1: Turkey's Comparative Global Competitiveness Index and its components**

*Source: World Economic Forum (2004)*

**(Scale is 1 to 7), 2003**

| | India | Israel | Turkey |
|---|---|---|---|
| **Growth competitiveness index** | **3.90** | **5.02** | **3.65** |
| ***1. Macro-economic environment index*** | ***3.75*** | ***3.93*** | ***2.93*** |
| a. Macro-economic stability sub-index | 4.36 | 3.67 | 3.27 |
| b. Government waste sub-index | 3.56 | 4.17 | 2.47 |
| c. Credit rating sub-index | 3.74 | 4.22 | 2.71 |
| ***2. Public institutions index*** | ***4.26*** | ***5.82*** | ***4.07*** |
| a. Contracts and law sub-index | 4.65 | 5.39 | 4.03 |
| b. Corruption sub-index | 3.86 | 6.26 | 4.12 |
| ***3. Technology index*** | ***3.68*** | ***5.17*** | ***3.96*** |
| a. Innovation sub-index | 2.06 | 4.80 | 2.01 |
| b. Information & communication technology sub-index | 2.87 | 5.54 | 3.88 |
| c. Inbound Technology transfer sub-index | 5.31 | N/A | 4.72 |

*Figure 144*[1]

**Table 2: Comparative Development as of 2000**

| | **India** | **Israel** | **Turkey** |
|---|---|---|---|
| GDP (billion $) | 547.1 | 97.5 | 195.5 |
| *GDP/capita ($)* | *523* | *16,177* | *2,904* |
| GDP (billion $) – purchasing power parity | 2,808.8 | 115.0 | 434.9 |
| *GDP/capita ($) – purchasing power parity* | *2,686* | *19,079* | *6,462* |
| Trade/GDP ratio | 0.2381 | 0.9398 | 0.5258 |

Source: IMF, 2002[x]

*Figure 145*

When compared to geographically bordering countries, the following *World Bank Group* (2004) statistics speak for themselves:

***GDP per capita for 2002 (in 1995 constant dollars)***

| | |
|---|---|
| Israel | 16,676 |
| Turkey | 2,760 |
| Jordan | 1,660 |
| Egypt | 1,250 |
| Lebanon | 2,868 |
| Syria | 832 |

***Exports of goods and services for 2002 (in billions of 2002 US $)***

| | |
|---|---|
| Turkey | 54.6 |
| Israel | 38.6 |
| Jordan | 4.3 |
| Egypt | 14.5 |
| Lebanon | 2.4 |
| Syria | 7.6 |

***Exports of goods and services per capita for 2002 (in 2002 US $)***[3]

| | |
|---|---|
| Israel | 5,874.6 |
| Jordan | 828.1 |
| Lebanon | 540.2 |
| Syria | 449.5 |
| Egypt | 218.0 |
| West bank and Gaza | 129.3 |
| Turkey | 78.4 |

Comparing the *exports of goods and services per capita* with those of developed countries, we find for: Japan 3500; United States 3520; Korea 4003; Spain 4646; Italy 5531; France 6,512; UK 6823; and Germany 8,536. Thus, on a *per capita* basis, Israel's export of goods and services have surpassed that of Japan, the United States, Korea, Spain, and Italy, and are not significantly below that of France. In fact, when the 158 countries for which the *World Bank* has a complete set of data are ranked on the basis of *per-capita exports of goods and services,*[4] Israel, ranked 22nd, is only one removed from the 20th place held by France. Reisman (2005).

# Notes

## Introduction

[1] Rüstow (1979) <http://www.foreignaffairs.org/19790901faessay8208/dankwart-a-rustow/turkey-s-travails.html.> Viewed August 6 2005.

[2] Arguably, changing the alphabet comes in a close second. The totality of that policy however, presaged the notion that "barriers to riches" in developing counties can be overcome by creating a western knowledge-using society as discussed by Parente and Prescott (2000), and for which the 2004 Nobel Prize in Economics was awarded.

[3] The Bosphorus and the Dardanelles hold strategic importance.

[4] "Although the emigration of German scholars and writers to other European countries and particularly to the United States has been fairly extensively studied, the long-term sojourn of many noted academics, artists, and politicians in Turkey has received scant critical attention." Seyhan (2005).

[5] Samuelson (1988) 319

[6] Significantly: "It has nearly been forgotten that about sixty years ago the historical development went in exactly the opposite direction and that it was Turkey which accorded political asylum and work to Germans in a very generous way." Müller (1998).

[7] Based on a headcount from Haymatloz List (2000)

[8] Neumark (1980) 13

[9] Between 1928 and 1937, the Vienna Circle published ten books in a series named *Schriften zur wissenschaftlichen Weltauffassung* (Papers on scientific worldview), edited by Schlick and Frank. Among these works was *Logik der Forschung,* (Research logic) 1935, which was the first book published by K. R. Popper. Seven works were published in another series, called *Einheitswissenschaft* (Unified Science), edit by Carnap, Frank, Hahn, Neurath, Joergensen (after Hahn's death) and Morris (from 1938). In 1930 Carnap and Reichenbach undertook the editorship of the journal *Erkenntnis* (Cognition), which was published between 1930 and 1940 (from 1939, the editors were Neurath, Carnap, and Morris).

[10] <http://www.ejil.org/journal/Vol9/No2/art9-04.html>. Viewed September 12 2005.

[11] Ihsanoglu (2004)

[12] <http://www.itumuk.com/info/itu/ITUHistory.html>. Viewed July 28 2005.

[13] Other than some anecdotal information shown later, the author is unaware of any systematic study of the impact of this redesign/replacement on the large community of educators who taught outside the divinity aspects of the *madrasa* curricula. Short of that, it can only be assumed that, at minimum, their centuries-old status within the Ottoman society was significantly reduced by the new culture. Moreover, an entire generation of *madrasa*-trained administrators of public agencies, banks etc., was clearly impacted by the second order effect due to university trained cadres. These were just two of many socio-economic groupings dislocated in the aftermath of WWI in that part of the world. Many of these dislocations are still understudied and largely unknown. However, at the Dar-ül Fünun's medical school, "Refik Saydam, the Minister of Health at the time, took all those who were useful and sat with them in a meeting at the closed-down university building which he converted into the Nümune Hospital. The upshot was that he sent some to Afghanistan to establish a medical school there. And some he made into deputies. Others were settled into other jobs. That is, the healthy and employable ones among them were re-habilitated and rendered respectable once again. Kazancıgil et al. (2000).

[14] Istanbul Technical University's long and distinguished history began in 1773 when it was founded by Sultan Mustafa III as a military academy.... Mustafa sought to modernize the army and the internal state machinery to bring his empire in line with the Powers of western Europe. In 1845, the engineering function of the school was further widened with the addition of a program devoted to the training of architects. The scope and name of the school were extended and changed again in 1883 and, in 1909, the school became a public engineering school which was aimed at training civil engineers who could provide the infrastructure for the rapidly building country.

[15] Staudenmaier (1985)

[16] Tension between the secular state supported universities and the traditional culture persisted over decades. It is currently manifested in the symbolism of women's head scarves worn on campus—some students insist on making the point that is expressly forbidden. Also, over the years Islamic parties attempted to introduce legislation and or administrative actions in parliament exacerbating that tension.

[17] Neumark (1980) noted that three revolutions came together to make the 1933 "miracle" happen in Turkey: Russian in 1905, Turkish in 1923, and Nazi in 1933.

[18] Philip Schwarz, organizer of the *Notgemeinschaft* lost his sister and her entire family in Germany's gas chambers.

[19] For details, see Burk (2005) 240-41

[20] Müller (1998)

[21] Ibid.

[22] Fermi (1968) 67

[23] In 1492, after their conquest Spain Ferdinand and Isabella gave the Jews a choice: *conversion, death,* or *expulsion*. In that very same year, Sultan Bayazid II ordered the governors of all Ottoman provinces "*not to refuse the Jews entry or cause them difficulties, but to receive them cordially.*" Most accepted the refuge offered them

by Sultan Süleyman the Magnificent. <http://www.mersina.com/lib/Turkish jews/history/life.htm>. Viewed November 9 2005.

[24] Shaw (1993)

[25] Fischer-Appelt (2004)

[26] At that time, ordinarius professors brought in from foreign countries were paid 600 liras a month and professors received half that. During the same period, the prime minister's salary was 500 liras. Şarman, (2005) 154.

[27] During the prewar period, in addition to inviting those who needed a safe-haven from the Nazis, Turkey also invited German Jewish scholars who were comfortably settled elsewhere. The most notable, and perhaps one and only, was Frederick Simon (Shimon) Bodenheimer was brought in from the Hebrew University of Jerusalem.

[28] Widman (1981)

[29] Washington (1936)

[30] Parente and Prescott (2000) preface their book using the words "ideas" and "knowledge" (1, 2) as concepts but they conclude the book by using the word "technologies" instead, (133, 142, 143). Hence, these three words are used interchangeably within the context of their *Barriers to Riches* and hence in the reasoning for which the 2004 Nobel Prize in Economics was awarded. In this book, it is presumed that the émigrés brought with them each and all of the above concepts to Turkey.

[31] Meg Rich, Princeton University archivist. Personal communication. June 29 2005.

[32] From "....a contemporaneous source, the so-called 'Scurla-Report.'... Herbert Scurla, a senior [Nazi] executive officer, was sent to Turkey in 1939 by the Ministry of Science and Education to take stock of activities of German university professors there." Muller (1998), further provides documentation that the "German emigrants were observed very closely [by the Gestapo] in Turkey and pressure was put on appointments." The Scurla-Report was first published by Grothousen (1987).

[33] Shaw (1993)

[34] Friling (2002)

[35] A book was published in 1964 by the Princeton University Press titled *Political Modernization in Japan and Turkey.* The book represented work commissioned by the Social Science Research Council under a grant from the Ford Foundation. In a thirty- [30] page highly documented chapter discussing "Education in Turkey," which includes higher education from the days of the Ottomans through the 1950s, Frederick W. Frey, a Princeton PhD, Rhodes Scholar, the author by then of *Turkish Political Elite,* a professor at MIT and "member of the senior staff of its Center for International Studies" never mentions anything whatsoever about the role played by the German émigré professors in the evolution of Turkish higher education. Frey (1964). Nor is this major infusion of the best western knowledge into Turkish society mentioned anywhere else in this 500-page volume. Moreover, "[i]n May 1991, an international and interdisciplinary group of scholars convened at the *Wissenschaftskollegg* (Research collegiums) in Berlin to discuss the impact of forced emigration of German-speaking scholars and scientists after the Nazi takeover in 1933." Ash and Sollner, Ed. (1996). The result of that conference is the cited and ref-

erenced book. In its *Foreword,* Donald Fleming critically reflects on the established historical paradigm, e.g., "Germany had been intellectually punished for yielding to the Nazis and America and Britain intellectually rewarded for their political and civic virtues." Significantly, the book's (10-page, double-column, small-print) index has only one entry for Turkey. Page 10 mentions Turkey along with Palestine and Latin America in reference to studies documenting problems encountered by émigré academics. Strauss (1979) provides a compendium of "Archival Resources" and organizations that were set up worldwide to aid Jews persecuted by the Third Reich. While the book specifically addresses *The Emergency Committee in Aid of Displaced Foreign Scholars,* founded in 1933 in New York City, "It nowhere mentions the *Notgemeinschaft deutscher Wissenschaftler im Ausland* nor the work of Philipp Schwarz." "Turkey" does not appear in its 21-page detailed index. So, by 2005, there was still ample justification for saying, "Although the emigration of German scholars and writers to other European countries and particularly to the United States has been fairly extensively studied, the long-term sojourn of many noted academics, artists, and politicians in Turkey has received scant critical attention." Seyhan (2005). Hence, the above "dim-lit and largely unknown" claim.

[36] Staudenmaier, (1985)

[37] Neumark, F. (1980) 8-9

[38] Müller (1998)

[39] Strauss (1979)

[40] Document 867.4016 JEWS/5, National Archives and Records Administration, College Park, Maryland.

[41] Document 867.4016 JEWS/6, National Archives and Records Administration, College Park, Maryland.

[42] Adorno (1980)

**Chapter 1**

[1] Kazancigil (2000)

[2] Frey (1964)

[3] Chase (2003)

[4] <http://www.itumuk.com/info/itu/ITUHistory.html>. Viewed September 14 2005.

[5] Sisman (1992)

[6] The cradle of one of modern Turkey's premiere national soccer teams as well as alma mater for many of its current intellectuals and professionals.

[7] Bektas (2000)

[8] Frey (1964)

[9] On September 26 1933, Lorrin A. Shepard M.D. Director of the American Hospital of Istanbul wrote to R. A. Lambert at the Rockefeller Foundation European Office. "Ever since the republican revolution in Turkey progressive leaders of Turkish thought have become increasingly conscious that the University and the Medical School were behind times and inadequate. There has been a great deal of spoken and written criticism by Turks of the University and Medical School. During the past year, this culminated in a thorough investigation by the Turkish

Government carried out by Professor [Albert] Malche of Switzerland [formerly Director of Education of the Canton of Geneva]. The Government is now putting into effect Professor Malche's recommendations. [Among these was the need to develop a modern university center of first quality] *In order to have an effective reorganization however it was necessary to abolish the old University because according to law all the professors held office for life.* With the abolition of the University the old Arabic name "Dar-ül Fünun" has also been abolished. (emphasis added) Courtesy Rockefeller [Foundation] Archives Center.

[10] At the time, 1 USD = 1.8 TL. Hence, in absolute terms this consttuted a very attractive salary.

[11] Courtesy Rockefeller [Foundation] Archives Center

[12] Ibid.

[13] Ibid.

[14] Extracted from "Statement of Mr. Onur Öymen, *Member of Turkish Parliament,* at the Seminar on "Culture as a Weapon, Academicians in Exile" in Berlin on July 19 2003.

[15] Ibid.

[16] Courtesy Rockefeller [Foundation] Archives Center.

[17] Lahut went on to an illustrious career albeit short lived due to early death, as the first recipient of the Bronson Crothers Professorship of Neurology at Harvard.

[18] Merzbacher retired from the University of North Carolina as Distinguished Professor of Quantum Physics.

[19] Author's personal knowledge.

[20] Personal communication, December 4 2005.

[21] Akar and Can (2005)

[22] Ibid.

[23] Courtesy Rockefeller [Foundation] Archive Center. Schwarz's observation regarding the displaced Turkish clinicians' acceptance of the German émigrés was either premature or pure graciousness on his part.

[24] Müller (1998)

[25] Tracy B. Kittrege writing to someone with initials EED on October 13 1933, re: "New Turkish University in Stambul" Courtesy Rockefeller [Foundation] Archive Center.

[26] Courtesy Rockefeller [Foundation] Archive Center.

[27] Staudenmaier (1985)

[28] Arın Namal: Beiträge jüdischer Wissenschaftler zu den vorklinischen Fächer der Medizin bei der türkischen Universitätsreform von 1933. In: Albrecht Scholz, Caris-Petra Heidel (Ed.): *Emigrantenschicksale. Einfluss der jüdischen Emigranten auf Sozialpolitik und Wissenschaft in den Aufnahmeländern.* [Medizin und Judentum Band 7]. Frankfurt am Main 2004, 83-99.

[29] Philipp Schwarz, Notgemeinschaft, (Hrsg.u.eingel..v. Helge Peukert) Marburg (1995) 85.

[30] Gürgey (2005)

[31] Although Fritz Arndt (1885-1969) had been to Turkey before being expelled from Germany in 1934, he stayed in Turkey until 1955.

[32] Gürgey (2005)

[33] Ibid.

[34] Turkey's private universities are paying their faculty as much as four times what is paid their equivalents in state universities because of budgetary constraints in the public sector over many years. This created an unfortunate tension between the two systems. Moreover, because private universities can only absorb a limited number of faculty, the public budgetary constraints resulted in what anecdotal information suggests to be a brain-drain mostly involving male academics leaving the sector or going abroad. Currently 42% of Turkey's professors are women. <http://www.hurriyetim.com.tr/haber/0,,sid~436@nvid~485095,00.asp>

[35] <http://www.bilkent.edu.tr/>. Viewed August 6 2005.

[36] <http://ihsandogramaci.bilkent.edu.tr/>. Viewed June 9 2005.

[37] Private communication, November 25 2005.

## Chapter 2

[1] The organized Jewish community in Palestine. Its informal government is sometimes referred to as the Jewish Agency.

[2] After the 1938 *Anschluss*, there was no Austrian army per se. Austrians served in Germany's Wehrmacht and Gestapo units alongside Germans. Hungary and Romania were Allies of Germany.

[3] A fairly complete listing shown in the Appendix to this book indicates that there were at least 176. Granted, not all on this list were equally "*renowned.*" Also not all on this list were "*German scientists and artists.*" Many were Austrian, some were Czech, and at least one each was Italian and French. All, but one, Simon Bodenheimer who was brought in from the Hebrew Univerity of Jerusalem for reasons discussed later however, were in Turkey to escape Nazism at the Turkish government's invitation.

[4] <http://www.auswaertiges-amt.de/www/en/laenderinfos/laender/laender_ausgabe_html.> Viewed on October 7 2005.

## Chapter 3

[1] Lopez (2004)

[2] The Chamber of Architects of Turkey. Reisman et al. (2004)

[3] Schütte-Lihotzky (1999)

[4] <http://www.archinform.net/arch/2554.htm.> Viewed June 2 2005.

[5] Holzmeister (1999)

[6] Shaw (1993)

[7] Curl (1999) 857

[8] Ibid.

[9] Lane (1968)

[10] <http://www.reference.com/browse/wiki/Bruno_Taut>. Viewed July 30 2005.

[11] Ibid.

[12] <http://www.emmet.de/por_taut.htm>. Viewed October30 2005.

[13] Sean Kisby, Bruno Taut: *Architecture and Colour*, Welsh School of Architecture Year 3

[14] Ibid. <http://www.kisbee.co.uk/sarc/ext-sa/taut.htm> Viewed September 26 2005

[15] Curl (1999 p 857)

[16] Ibid.

[17] See "The Contribution of Foreigners to the Republic" by Kazancıgil et al. (2000)

[18] Dick Osseman. Personal URL <http://members.chello.nl/dosseman/>. Viewed June 3 2005. Reprinted with personal endorsement from photographer Dick Osseman.

## Chapter 4

[1] Benno Landsberger was among those who were given the title *Ordinarius Professor*.

[2] Güterbock, Nachruf 204

[3] <http://hometown.aol.com/rechcigl/myhomepage/philadelphia.html>. Viewed November 18 2005.

[4] Güterbock, Nachruf 204

[5] <http://ccwf.cc.utexas.edu/~davida/cc303/outline2.html>. Viewed August 4 2005.

[6] Erica Reiner, John A. Wilson Distinguished Service Professor of Assyriology, Emerita, Oriental Institute University of Chicago <http://www.aps-pub.com/proceedings/1463/305.pdf >. Viewed June 11 2005.

[7] Bertrand Lafont, CNRS, The Collections of the Louvre and the Istanbul Museum, Presented to the CDLI Avalon Meeting, October 2001. <http://cdli.ucla.edu/comm/reports/Oct/Lafont20020131.html>. Viewed October 8 2005.

[8] Shaw (1993) 354

[9] *Liste* der Emigrantinnen und Emigranten und NS-Verfolgten in der Türkei. Stand 25.7.2000: 1054 *Fettgedrucke.*

[10] Müller (1998) 302

[11] Ibid.

[12] Dr. Rudolf Juchhoff started work at Bonn University's library after receiving his PhD in 1921. He held many management positions and became a professor in Germany in 1949. He joined the Department of Library Science at Istanbul University in 1964. In addition to teaching courses, he also took part in the opening of Istanbul University Faculty of Letters' general library. He died in 1968. <http://www.istanbul.edu.tr/edebiyat/edebiyat/p3a82.htm> He appears to have been in Berlin during both World Wars. <http://www.istanbul.kutuphaneci.org.tr/bulten/2002/haziran.pdf>. Thus he was not one of the exiled professors. Viewed August 24 2005.

[13] Müller H. (1998) 298

[14] According to Ms. Mihittin Lugal of Istanbul, a Turkish librarian who worked in this library after Pfanistel, traces of his activities can be found to the present day. (Interview August 1995) Müller (1998) 300.

[15] Müller (1998) 301

[16] Ibid.

[17] Otuken (1957)

[18] Shaw (1993)

[19] After accepting Islam, Turks abandoned the Orkhon and Uighur alphabets, and began using the Arabic script. Vowels widely used in Turkish caused reading problems with the Arabic script. Attempts to solve the problem were made in 1878, and again in 1908. Different opinions were put forward. Some supported use of the Arabic script, others proposing that Arabic characters should be written separately with some special signs to read vowels, yet others proposed replacement of Arabic with the Latin script. No action took place until the founding of the republic when the alphabet problem was again discussed in 1923, at the Izmir Economic Congress. A paper proposing the adoption of the Latin alphabet was submitted and Congress agreed that it should be considered by the Ministry of National Education. In 1927, it was agreed that Latin symbols should be used in physics, chemistry and mathematics courses in the universities and academies. Contemporaneously stamps were issued bearing *Türkiye Postalari,* Turkish Post, written in Latin letters. In 1928, the Grand National Assembly passed a law promulgating use of international numerals. The new alphabet was adopted by law, on November 1, 1928. <http://www.turkishembassy.org/countryprofile/history.htm>

The current Turkish alphabet is composed of 29 letters. It has all the letters in the English alphabet, except "q", "w", and "x" it has the characters ç, ğ, ö, ş, and ü. <http://www.turkishlingua.com/alphabet.html>

<http://www.nationmaster.com/encyclopedia/Turkish-alphabet>. Viewed July 10 2005.

[20] Kazancıgil et al. (2000)

[21] Shaw (1991)

[22] <http://www.fu-berlin.de/info/fub/chronik/b-picts/1949-1960/rohde.html>. Viewed December 14 2005.

[23] Wellek (1991)

[24] Said (1983)

[25] Ibid.

[26] The author is grateful to Jean Hull Herman, Editor-in-Chief of *MÖBIUS, The Poetry Magazine* for sixteen years and author of two books, for pointing out that she was amazed to learn that Erich Auerbach was among those saved by the Turks for all, everywhere, who have sought, seek, and will seek, a well-rounded education. Now that she knows the conditions under which *Mimesis* was written, she will go back and re-read it. Personal communication, December 12 2005.

[27] Jaeckel (2004)

[28] Ibid

[29] Kazancıgil et al. (2000)

[30] Fermi (1968) 353

[31] Szyliowicz (1992)

[32] Seyhan (2005)

[33] It was awarded a "Class 'A' Wetland Diploma" by the European Council in 1976 and the certificate was renewed four times. In 1993, the lake was included in the list of wetlands covered by the well-known Ramsar Convention, which became

effective December 21 1976. The aim of the convention is to prevent the decline of wetland habitats globally and maintain their ecological functions and wild life. The signatory countries agree to include wetland conservation in national planning, to promote sound utilization of wetlands, to create wardened nature reserves, and to facilitate wetland-based research. Arcak et al, (undated). <http://www.toprak.org.tr/isd/isd_12.htm> Viewed September 2, 2004.

[34] <http://www.istanbul.edu.tr/fen/biyoloji/tarihce.htm>. Viewed September 25 2004.

[35] <http://www.istanbul.edu.tr/fen/biyoloji/m_zooloji_muz.htm.> and <http://www.cevrekoleji.k12.tr/heberler.htm.> Viewed September 27 2004.

[36] Justus Liebig *Genetisches Institut* Giessen University, Germany <http://www.ncbi.nlm.nih.gov/entrez/query.fcgi?cmd=Retrieve&db=PubMed&list_uids=1924175&dopt=Abstract>. Viewed July 20 2005.

[37] Villwock (2004) 8-9

[38] Ibid.

[39] At the time, a member of the Faculty of Fishery Sciences at the University of Istanbul.

[40] Kosswig served as chair of zoology as well as Director of the institute after returning from Turkey in 1955.

[41] Ibid.

[42] Neumark (1982) 69

[43] Gustav Gassner was mentor to Wilhelm Klauditz who founded the Braunschweig Institute for Wood Research known today as the WKI-Institute in 1946.

[44] Being the last legally elected rector, he regained that position after the war (1945/1946). He died in 1955.

[45] <http://www.vernetztes-gedaechtnis.de/thgassner.htm>. Viewed September 21 2004

[46] Kallman (2005)

[47] According to Kallman (2004), Curt Kosswig was not subject to any provision of the Civil Service laws of 1933. He told Kallman "many years ago…while living in Istanbul in 1943, I received a draft notice from the German army. Needless to say I disregarded it." Also, "Kosswig told me in 1968 that he left because he did not want anybody to dictate him who his friends were and with whom he could correspond. He said he left precipitously by air, one step ahead of the Gestapo. A similar reason is given in the article by Fischer-Appelt." Kallman (2005).

[48] Kazancıgil et al. (2000)

[49] < http://www.bgci.org.uk/botanic_gardens/TurkeyCukurovaUniversityBGCN25.html>. Viewed September 20 2004.

[50] Harpaz (1984) 10-11

[51] Harpaz (1984) 11

[52] <http://sci.ege.edu.tr/~zooloji/basoglu.html>. Viewed September 25 2004.

[53] <http://www.istanbul.edu.tr/english/socrates/faculty4.htm>. Viewed September 20 2004.

**Chapter 5**

[1] See Tully Potter, <http://www.arbiterrecords.com/notes/139notes.html> Viewed September 29 2005.

[2] Sadie (1996)

[3] Ibid.

[4] Ibid.

[5] Zeynep Özery, The Presidential Symphony Orchestra. <http://www.byegm.gov.tr/yayinlarimiz/NEWSPOT/1997/Nov/N7.htm>. Viewed October 8 2005.

[6] Ibid.

[7] Ibid.

[8] Ibid.

[9] <http://www.kulturturizm.gov.tr/portal/sanat_en.asp?belgeno=7895>. Viewed on October 10 2005.

[10] <http://www.byegm.gov.tr/REFERENCES/turkishmusic2001.htm>. Viewed on October 10 2005.

[11] *Opera in Turkey*. <html://www.turkishculture.org/performing_arts/opera.html>. Viewed on October 10 2005.

[12] Shaw (1993)

[13] Turkish Daily News. October 5 1996

[14] Neumark (1982) 84-85

[15] <http://www.amarquartet.ch/en/content/biografie.php>. Viewed September 29 2005.

[16] Merzbacher (2005). Personal communication August 15.

[17] Turkish internment of non-Jewish Germans during the waning days of WWII will be discussed later in the book.

[18] Merzbacher (2005). Personal communication August 15.

[19] Neumark (1982) 85

[20] <http://www.DanielPipes.org/subscribe.php>. Viewed December 23 2005. *Understanding the Ban in Iran on Western Music* by Daniel Pipes, *Middle East Quarterly*, December 16 2005.

[21] <http://www.DanielPipes.org/subscribe.php>. Viewed December 23, 2005. *You Need Beethoven to Modernize*, by Daniel Pipes, *Middle East Quarterly*, September 1998.

[22] <http://encyclopedia.thefreedictionary.com/Rudolf%20Belling>. Viewed February 16 2006.

[23] Ibid.

[24] Ibid.

[25] Ibid.

[26] The archive is managed by his daughter Elisabeth Weber-Belling (belling-archiv@web.de), <http://encyclopedia.thefreedictionary.com/Rudolf Belling>.

[27] <http://www.cnn.com/2001/WORLD/asiapcf/central/03/04/afghan.buddhas/>. Viewed December 26 2005.

[28] <http://www.dexigner.com/forum/index.php?showtopic=564> Viewed December 23, 2005.

[29] Reisman (2005) 343

[30] <http://www.haaretz.com/hasen/spages/386088.html>. Viewed December 15 2005.

[31] Lehmann-Haupt, H. (1973) xviii and <html://fcit.coedu.usf.edu/holocaust/resource/REVIEWS/Petropou.htm>. Viewed December 14 2005.

[32] Ibid.

## Chapter 6

[1] Inalcik, H. (1992)

[2] Frey (1968) 209

[3] Ibid.

[4] Inalcik, H. (1992). It should be noted that among all the modernization policies initiated by Atatürk, none was as important, and in fact, vital as the adoption of the Latin alphabet in 1928. This produced two important results. It effectively cut off ties with the written legacy of the past and made possible access to the accumulated works of the west.

[5] Üsdiken (2003) 87

[6] Neumark (1982) 52

[7] Neumark (1982) 77

[8] Ekim (2003) 20

[9] Ibid.

[10] Grothusen (1987) 43

[11] Zmirak (2002)

[12] Neumark (1982) 52

[13] Gregg (2001)

[14] Ebeling, R. M. (1999) Wilhelm Röpke: *A Centenary Appreciation*, Published in The Freeman: Ideas on Liberty, October. The Foundation for Economic Education. <http://www.fee.org/vnews.php?nid=4444>. Viewed August 18 2005.

[15] Attarian (2003). <http://www.findarticles.com/p/articles/mi_m0354/is_3_45/ai_n6140123> Viewed August 20 2005.

[16] On June 30 1934, Hitler killed Ernst Röhm, commander of the Storm Troops, on the false grounds that Röhm intended a coup d'état. http://www.jewishvirtuallibrary.org/jsource/Holocaust/knives.html>. Viewed February 17 2006.

[17] Neumark (1982) 52

[18] Gregg (2001)

[19] Wilhelm Röpke, *The Solution of the German Problem* (New York: G. P. Putnam's Sons, 1947), 59–60; and J. Kaufmann, *In Memoriam, Wilhelm Röpke: Humanistic Liberal, Nieuwe Rotterdamsche Courant*, February 19 1966.

[20] Zmirak <http://www.antiwar.com/article.php?articleid=1927>. Viewed August 20 2005.

[21] Ritenour (2004)

[22] Ibid.

[23] Zmirak (2002)

[24] <http://www.findarticles.com/p/articles/mi_m0354/is_3_45/ai_n6140123>. Viewed July 8 2005.

[25] Zmirak, <http://www.antiwar.com/article.php?articleid=1927>. Viewed August 20 2005.

[26] Reisman (2005) and Reisman et al. (2004)

[27] Leicester, J. (2005) *German Election Deepens Sense of Paralysis,* Associated Press, Paris.

[28] Neumark (1982) 53

[29] The full three-volume opus was published in German in 1950.

[30] Attarian (2003) <http://www.findarticles.com/p/articles/mi_m0354/is_3_45/ai_n6140123>. Viewed August 20 2005.

[31] In 1949, he returned to Germany and served twice as Rector of the University of Frankfurt.

[32] Seyhan (2005)

[33] Neumark (1982) 54

[34] Ibid.

[35] Rüstow, A. (1980)

[36] Walter E. Grinder and John Hagel III, Liberty & Power: Group Blog. Viewed October 1 2005.

[37] Meier-Rust (1993) 64

[38] Ibid.

[39] Ibid. 68, 70

[40] Ibid.

[41] Ibid.

[42] Neumark (1982) 61

[43] <http://www.museumonline.at/1999/schools/classic/istanbul/exilturkei_e.htm>. Viewed June 11 2005.

[44] Neumark (1982) 59-60

[45] Shaw (2001)

[46] Neumark (1982) 57

[47] Kazancıgil et al. (2000)

[48] Neumark (1982) 57

[49] Neumark (1982) 56

[50] Neumark (1982) 62

[51] Fritz Baade, ``Fighting Depression in Germany,'' in Emma S. Woytinsky, ed., *So Much Alive: The Life and Work of W.S. Woytinsky* (New York: Vanguard Press, 1961) 64.

[52] At the author's invitation, this section was contributed by Matthias Neumark of Charlottesville, Virginia, on June 21 2005.

[53] Neumark, Matthias. Personal communication, November 20 2005.

[54] Ibid.

[55] Shaw (1993) 354

[56] Neumark (1982) 58

[57] Neumark's son, Matthias, remembered knowing the entire Kessler family. Matthias recalled that Mrs. Kessler suffered from a serious illness and the fact that a daughter, after being so influenced by her Nazi teacher in Istanbul, went back to Germany. Apparently, she co-opted her mother and sister to do the same. For Professor Kessler, a strong anti–Nazi, this was a serious blow. Perhaps this explains the aloofness or detachment noticed by the students. Personal communication, June 21 2005.

[58] <http://www.istanbul.edu.tr/fen/astronomy/tanitim/tarihce/history.htm>.

Viewed August 22 2005.

[59] Shaw (1993) 355

[60] Neumark (1882) 63

[61] Courtesy The Grenander Department of Special Collections & Archives, University at Albany, New York

[62] Obtained from <http://www.onuroymen.com/docs/konusma37.doc> on September 10 2005.

[63] Üsdiken and Cetin (2001)

[64] Üsdiken (2004)

[65] <http://www.istanbul.edu.tr/fen/astronomy/tanitim/tarihce/history.htm>. Viewed October 20 2005.

**Chapter 7**

[1] Shaw (1991)

[2] Namal (2005)

[3] A *Diary* entry for Friday, February 16 1934 by Dr. R. A. Lambert states: "There is no doubt that the Turkish government is determined to make the Med. Fac. a first-class institution and that the authorities realize it will take more than five years to train Turks to succeed the German professors who have been brought in as heads of departments; it is expected that many of the five-year contracts will be renewed. The Turkish government, like that of [Soviet] Russia, is planning on a grand scale and wants quick results. Courtesy Rockefeller [Foundation] Archive Center."

[4] Public Health in today's parlance.

[5] Shaw (1993) 359

[6] Fermi(1968) 67

[7] Courtesy Rockefeller [Foundation] Archive Center.

[8] Ibid.

[9] Neumark (1982) 74

[10] Ibid.

[11] Bentwich (1953) 55

[12] Richter (1954)

[13] Widman (1999) 20

[14] Neumark (1980) 73

[15] Neumark (1980) 70-71

[16] Kazancıgil et al. (2000)

[17] This section is based on a forthcoming paper by A. Namal and A. Reisman, "A Tale of Three Medical Researchers Saved by Turkey from Nazism." They went on to impact healthcare delivery in Turkey, Israel, and the USA."

[18] Ibid.

[19] This section is based on an oral history provided by Elisabeth Steinitz, (Kurt Steinitz's widow), and recorded in Hod Hasharon, Israel, on August 10 2005 by Miriam Schmidt for the purposes of this book.

[20] <http://www.bbc.co.uk/dna/h2g2/alabaster/A647949 (2005)>. Viewed September 14 2005.

[21] The document bearing the photo is part of the employment application. The following information is shown" *Name*: Kurt; *Father's Name*: Franz (pediatric); *Family Name*: Steinitz; *Place and Date of Birth*: 1907, Breslau; *Nationality*: German; *Marital Status. If married, date of marriage*: Married, 09.02.1934. Istanbul University Rectorate Personnel Department, (Archive), Kurt Steinitz, File Nr. 4109/175.

[22] This section is based on a forthcoming paper by A. Namal and A. Reisman, "A Tale of Three Medical Researchers Saved by Turkey from Nazism." They went on to impact healthcare delivery in Turkey, Israel, and the USA."

[23] These are: 1. Devices for collection of skin puncture blood specimens—second edition (approved guideline). 2. Evacuated tubes for blood specimen collection—third edition (approved standard). 3. Percutaneous collection of arterial blood for laboratory analysis—2nd edition (approved standard). 4. Procedures for the collection of diagnostic blood specimens by skin puncture—3rd edition (approved standard). 5. Procedures for the collection of diagnostic blood specimens by venipuncture—third edition (approved standard). 6. Procedures for the handling and transport of diagnostic specimens and etiologic agents. Third edition.

[24] Volume 17 (12) December 1998, 1105-1113

[25] Personal communication, September 12 2005.

[26] Shaw (1991)

[27] This section is based on Akar et al. (2005)

[28] Akar (2003)

[29] Ibid.

[30] Ibid.

[31] Akar (2004), Ash (1996)

[32] Moll (1995) 1204-1207

[33] Albert Eckstein's Private File from Ankara Nümune Hospital. Official Private File (1935)

[34] Dr. Saydam did his residency at the Berlin Military Medical Faculty between 1910-1912.

[35] Philipp Schwarz's father-in-law was professor Tschulok, a scientist of natural sciences, who had taken refuge in Switzerland after the 1905 Russian revolution. He was a good friend of Albert Malche, professor of pedagogy who was called on to visit Turkey and prepare a report on university reform. At the time, persecution of German scientists had already begun in Germany. It seems Malche saw the double opportunity and got in touch with Schwarz. Neumark (1980) notes that three revolutions came together to make the 1933 "miracle" happen in Turkey: Russian in 1905, Turkish in 1923, and Nazi in 1933.

[36] Eckstein-Schlossman (1975)

[37] Eckstein (1937 and 1938)

[38] Following are the (per-100-women-based) results: <insert 0endmortality.tif>

[39] Eckstein (1938)

[40] Because it was written soon after his arrival, we presume that Dr. Eckstein wrote this report in German and it was translated into Turkish. He may well have said, "Some of the child deaths reported by women aged 40-44 may involve deaths of adult 'children' since these women were married around 14 years of age. Thus, some of their children would already be adult when the women were 40-44 years

old. So, these deaths should not be included in child mortality figures.

[41] Many fertility, infant, and child mortality estimates have been offered for those years. However, Eckstein's visits represented the first attempt to collect data from a large sampling. It is not clear what was meant by infants and children, i.e. which age groups. Also, an average for Turkey at that time, as is true now, is not to be taken too seriously. Eckstein did not visit eastern Anatolia, the real backwater. So even more than 50% infant mortality may have been true for the East while the lower figure of 33% given in Widman (1981) may be true for the wealthier parts of Anatolia.

[42] The population was decimated after many wars, forced dislocations, diseases, etc. So the government advocated population growth. This continued until the early 1960s when birth control was initiated by the government.

[43] Tekand (1998)

[44] Eckstein (1975)

[45] The first full-fledged private university in Turkey.

[46] Akar (2003)

[47] Ibid.

[48] According to Turkish pediatrics professor Nejat Akar, "I had seen the last case in 1978 when I was a very young pediatrician. We saw another case of noma but underlying a malignancy." Private communication, February 2005.

[49] Eckstein, A. (1949)

[50] "According to my observations, the average breastfeeding period extends over one year in Turkey against an average period of 4.1 months in Germany as reported by the Reich Health Office in 1940. This period even falls to 3.3 months in some provinces. The technique of feeding also shows basic differences. In western European and Anglo Saxon countries, infants are only fed at fixed times, on the average every 4 hours, i.e., 5 times in 24 hours. On the other hand, in Turkey, free feeding not restricted by time is in practice. This way, infants are fed whenever they need nourishment which means an average of 10-12 times in 24 hours during the first months. Thus, Turkish babies get more nourishment which would influence the increase of body weight. It is possible that this technique of feeding also improves the suckling capacity of mothers thus facilitating natural feeding by breast during the first year. It is evident that general care and particularly protecting babies from all diseases are very important for the development of breastfeeding infants.

The following considerations have to be kept in mind in establishing a norm for gain in body weight of infants:

Regular and correct weight measurements have to be taken for each child.

Infants should be fed under ideal conditions; i.e., with breast milk until the end of 5 months. After this, they should be given one meal of cereals and another meal of vegetables while the other meals should consist of mother's milk. The milk production of the mothers' breasts should be sufficient to nourish the infant." (Eckstein 1947b)

[51] Akar (2003) 88-89

[52] Eckstein Albert, Ord. Prof. Dr. Ankara Medical Faculty, Official private file, 1945-1949

[53] *Rapor über die Errichtung von Allgemeinen Kinderkrankenhauser in der Türkei.*

[54] Kiziltan (1949)

[55] Akar, N. (2003)

[56] **Life Goes On**

**Dr. Selahattin Tekand:** His assistant. For years, he treated thousands of children in İzmir and was actively working up to three years before death. He passed away on July 6, 1999.

**Prof. Dr. Sabiha (Cura) Özgür**: His assistant. After she left the Department of Pediatrics, Ankara Medical Faculty, she founded the Pediatric Health and Diseases Department at the Faculty of Medicine, Ege University. She served as its chief for many years. After training hundreds of pediatricians, she is presently retired and spends the summers in Çeşme.

**Prof. Dr. İhsan Doğramacı*:** His assistant. Founder of Hacettepe and Bilkent Universities. The first head of Yüksek Öğrenim Kurulu, The Higher Education Council of Turkey, and the only living co-signer of WHO's charter. Never retired.

**Dr.Neriman Olgur:** His assistant. First worked at the Keçiören Children's Home, then as assistant chief and chief at the Haydarpaşa Nümune Hospital, İstanbul. Retired at the present. Lives in Moda in İstanbul. Has a photo of the hoca on the console in her living room.

**Klaus Eckstein:** His son. Taught school in England. Presently retired. Comes to Turkey every few years. Worked as English consultant in the Ayşe Abla School in Ankara. Spends his vacations in Side. Has seven children, including three adopted ones.

**Dr. Herbert Eckstein:** His son. Pediatric urologist. Worked in Ankara as pediatric surgeon during the founding years of Hacettepe Hospital, between April, 1958 - December, 1960 and contributed to the establishment of that department. His particular field of interest concerned stones of the urinary system. He passed away in 1987. In 1995, a memorial conference was held in his name in İstanbul and a scientific book published in memoriam.

**Dr. Peter Eckstein:** His son. Spent his career as a General Practioner. Lives in England . 74 years old. Retired.

**Dr. Erna Schlossmann Ekstein:** His wife. Came back to Turkey in 1956 at the invitation of Prof. Dr. İhsan Doğramacı. Worked during the establishment of the Hacettepe Children's Hospital. Returned to Germany in the beginning of 1960s. Settled in Cambridge, England in 1964. Visited Turkey in 1994. Passed away in March 1998 at the age of 104.

**Noma:** Noma is no longer seen.

**The Children's Hospital in his dream:** The foundation stone was laid by Dr. Bahtiyar Demirağ in Cebeci in 1952. It was completed in 1963.

**Prof. Dr. Bahtiyar Demirağ:** Became the chief of Pediatrics in the Faculty of Medicine, Ankara University in 1950. He was instrumental in the transformation of this hospital into an institution. He trained great numbers of pediatricians. Died in Ankara in 1981.

**Prof. Dr. Şükrü Cin:** His patient. He remembers Eckstein's examinations as being more affectionate than those of the other pediatricians in Ankara. He was chief of the Pediatrics Department at Ankara University for the years 1989-2004. He is retired now.

**10 lira banknote:** Taken out of circulation on April 1 1950.

[57] Albert's nickname used by the family and friends.

[58] Ekstein (1975). Unpublished memoirs of Dr. Erna Schlossmann Ekstein.

[59] Personal communication with Miriam (Hellmann) Schmidt. April 5, 2006.

[60] Namal (2005)

[61] This section is based on *Joseph Igersheimer, ophthalmologist and visionary: his contributions in exile and beyond* by Arin Namal and Arnold Reisman

[62] Sloane (1969)

[63] Igersheimer's son, Walter, personal communication, August 21 2005.

[64] Courtesy University of Istanbul Archives, personnel records.

[65] Hoffmann, being Jewish, was thus saved from the Nazis. She came as a single woman but left Turkey married to émigré physiology professor Hans Winterstein. In 1956, they returned to West Germany. In a two-page letter handwritten in French to the Istanbul University Rector in which Igersheimer pleads reconsideration of the university's decision not to renew his former assistant's (Miss Susanne Hoffmann), contract. The letter was dated May 29 1940 and written in Boston. As a good measure via a telegram, he announced to the Rector that the letter had been sent. (<insert 8telgraf.tif>

[66] (anonymous): Haberler. Tıp Dünyası. 1934 (VII) 3: 2412.

[67] Nissen (1969) 212

[68] Neumark (1982) 102-3

[69] Neumark (1982) 70-1

[70] See Tıp Yolunda Yılbaşı Dergisi 1935, 16.

[71] Eugen von Hippel (1841-1916) was professor of ophthalmology in Königsberg and a pioneer in the field of corneal grafting. His son, Arthur von Hippel, was one of the émigré professors in Turkey. He re-emigrated to the USA, joined the MIT faculty, and is considered the Father of Nanotechnology.

[72] Bengisu (1988) 330-1

[73] Since trachoma was very common in countries east of Turkey, Turkey was also seriously affected by the problem. In 1923 after its founding, the Republic of Turkey started to fight this illness. A trachoma hospital was established in the eastern Anatolian city of Malatya where trachoma was most prevalent. See Fight against Trachoma Association President Dr. *Nuri Fehmi's* radio conference text. İstanbul Seririyatı 1935 (XVII) 3:15-17. 1281 (28.4%) of the 4508 blindness cases diagnosed in 110,995 patients that had been referred to the University Eye Clinic between the years of 1934 and 1943 were due to cornea thicknesses. See Bengisu, op.cit., 94.

[74] Bengisu (1988) 93

[75] Frantz and Collins (2003 p 115)

[76] Courtesy University of Istanbul Archives, personnel records.

[77] Ibid.

[78] See *Türk Oftalmoloji Gazetesi* 1936 (II) 1: 3-9. *Türk Oftalmoloji Gazetesi* 1936 (II) 3: 117-129. *Türk Oftalmoloji Gazetesi* 1937 (II) 5: 245-253. *Türk Tabii ve Fiziki İlimler Cemiyeti Arşivi 1938*/1939, 7: 16-23. *Türk Oftalmoloji Gazetesi* 1938 (II)2: 536-542. *Türk Oftalmoloji Gazetesi* 1939 (III) I: 1-7. *Türk Oftalmoloji Gazetesi* 1939 (III) 4: 203-210. and *Tıp Fakültesi Mecmuası* 1939, 9: 1085-1111 among others.

[79] İstanbul University Rectorate Personnel Department File Nr: 4109/111. From the Minister of Education to the President of İstanbul University, May 12, 1939. This was on the eve of Germany's invasion of Poland. Turkey though neutral had

good relations with Germany. The émigré community in Turkey was understandably concerned for their own safety in Turkey. The region Igersheimer wanted to work in is closest to Palestine. Were Turkish government members concerned that he might bolt? Perhaps.

[80] Istanbul University Rectorate Personnel Department File No: 4109/111. From Igersheimer to the Rector of Istanbul University, April 27 1939.

[81] Von Hippel (2003)

[82] Ibid.

[83] Schwarz (2003) 86

[84] Ernst E.Hirsch, *Anılarım. Kayzer Dönemi, Weimar Cumhuriyeti, Atatürk Ülkesi.* Translated by Fatma Suphi, Ankara (1997), 213. Ernst E Hirsch: Aus des Kaiserszeiten durch die Weimarer Republik in das Land Atatürks. Eine unzeitgemaesse Autobiographie. München, 1982.

[85] In spite of Igersheimer's esteem in Ankara's upper echelons and the public at large, more likely because of it, the totality of evidence indicates that his bosses in Istanbul, the Dean and the Rector considered Igersheimer to be "unmanageable." Making a superstar's life difficult by an academic mediocrity in a position of administrative power is unfortunately not limited to the University of Istanbul.

[86] Dekolman is the Turkish version of the French word "décollement," meaning coming unglued, coming unstuck. It also means detachment. Referring to retina detachment (décollement de la retine), dekolman is used in ophthalmology. The title is therefore a play on words. It refers to the operation in question and the ridiculous position the doctors put themselves in.

[87] Sabahattin Ali: Sırça Köþk. YKY Publishing, Istanbul (2004), 70-77.

[88] Hillebrecht (2000) 33-4

[89] Igersheimer and Darragh (2005)

[90] Igersheimer's son, Walter, personal communication, August 21 2005.

[91]<http://dl.tufts.edu/view_text.jsp?urn=tufts:central:dca:UA069:UA069.005.DO.00001&chapter=D00020>. Viewed March 1 2006

[92] In Oto-Nöro-Oftalmoloji, 1953, (VIII) 2: 31-38.

[93] Personal communication, August 11 2005.

[94] Sloane (1969) 174-175

[95] Ibid.

[96] Liebermann-Meffert and Rossetti (1996)

[97] <http://www.arss.org/eng/history.htm>. Viewed October 15 2005.

[98] <http://ats.ctsnetjournals.org/cgi/content/abstract/69/2/651>. Viewed September 25 2005.

[99] Neumark (1982) 52-76

[100] See Reza Shah with Kemal Atatürk on his official visit to Turkey in 1934 <http://www.iranian.com/DariusKadivar/2003/April/Tehran43/>. Viewed January 15 2006.

[101] Von Hippel (76) <http://vonhippel.mrs.org/vonhippel/life/AvHMemoirs9.pdf >. Viewed October 7 2005.

[102] Courtesy Rockefeller [Foundation ] Archives Center. Kantorowicz was first a prisoner of the Nazis at Borgermoor. Langhoff (1935) 184-186. Additional evidence shows that the Rockefeller Foundation claimed to be unable to interfere directly in the matter of extraditing Kantorowicz from the concentration camp.

[103] The carbon copy of this letter does not show the date of the letter which

was addressed to the Emergency Rescue Committee in New York City requesting a "non-quota immigration visa for Professor Alfred Kantorowicz.... Director of the Dental College at the University of Istanbul." In greatest likelihood, it was sent early in 1940 because of the return address used by Reichenbach. Courtesy The Grenander Department of Special Collections &Archives, University at Albany, New York.

[104] <http://www.ncbi.nlm.nih.gov/entrez/query.fcgi?cmd=Retrieve&db=PubMed&list_uids=8258568&dopt=Abstract>

[105] Loevy and Kowitz (1993) 263-269

[106] <http://litten.de/fulltext/kantoro.htm>, <http://www.istanbul.edu.tr/dishekimligi/>. Viewed October 25 2005.

[107] Loevy and Kowitz (1993) 268

[108] Neumark (1982) 70

## Chapter 8

[1] See the review of Ekmeleddin Ihsanoglu (ed.), *Osmanli Astronomi Leitaturu Tarihi* by Ziauddin Sardar in *Nature* **394** (1998) 634. Also, for a good overview, see the chapter "Introduction of Western Science to the Ottoman World: A Case Study of Modern Astronomy (1660-1860)" by Ekmeleddin Ihsanoglu, 67-120, in Ekmeleddin Ihsanoglu (ed.), (1992) *Transfer of Modern Science and Technology to the Muslim World,* The Research Centre for Islamic History, Art and Culture, (IRCICA)

[2] Obituary in *The Times* <http://www.aam314.vzz.net/Freundlich.html>. Viewed September 30 2005.

[3] Much of the section on Freundlich is based on *J J O'Connor* and *E F Robertson* <http://www-groups.dcs.st-and.ac.uk/~history/Mathematicians/Freundlich.html>. Viewed September 30 2005.

[4] According to astrophysicist Martin Harwit, the current view seems to be that "instrumentation available to Freundlich at the time was too crude to provide definitive results and that nowadays one could probably not find any astronomer who would credit Freundlich with validating Einstein's theories. Arthur Stanley Eddington, whose expedition in 1919 to observe the deflection of light from a distant star at the time of a total solar eclipse validated the general relativistic deflection of light, is currently usually credited with confirming Einstein's ideas."

[5] <http://www-history.mcs.st-andrews.ac.uk/Mathematicians/Freundlich.html>. Viewed September 24 2005.

[6] Ibid.

[7] All Freundlich correspondence is courtesy of the Archives St Andrews University.

[8] <http://www-groups.dcs.st-and.ac.uk/~history/Mathematicians/Freundlich.html> Viewed September 30 2005.

[9] Merzbacher (2005). Personal communication, August 15.

[10] Personal communication, January 24 2006.

[11] <http://www.istanbul.edu.tr/fen/astronomy/tanitim/tarihce/history.htm>. Viewed September 30 2005.

[12] Gürgey (2005)

[13] Widman ( 1973)

[14] See Burk (2005) 235-257

[15] Burk (2003)

[16] Gürgey (2005)

[17] The full list of Arndt's Turkish texts can be found in Burk (2003). They were all described by Emre Dölen, "Ord. Prof. Dr. Fritz Arndt"ın Türkçe Yayınlanmış Yapıtları" in *Doğa ve Bilim*, 11, 68-76 (1982).

[18] The Turkish, Ottoman, German, and English dictionary (*Lügatçe*) of chemistry terms is included in the 1947 and 1953 editions of Arndt's *Denel Anorganik Kimya* (Experimental Inorganic Chemistry). Courtesy Dr. Lale Aka Burk.

[19] Gürgey (2005)

[20] Kazancıgil et al. (2000)

[21] ibid

[22] ibid

[23] <http://www.indiana.edu/~liblilly/lilly/mss/html/haurowit.html>. Viewed June 30 2005.

[24] <http://www.jbc.org/content/vol140/issue2/index.shtml>. Viewed October 15 2005.

[25] Putnam (1994)

[26] <http://www.indiana.edu/~liblilly/lilly/mss/html/haurowit.html>. Viewed July 22 2005.

[27] Aub (1964)

[28] These omissions are indeed significant in the context of this book's story.

[29] Hochmann (1964)

[30] Neumark (1982)

[31] Eicher (1987)

[32] <http://www.amphilsoc.org/library/mole/c/Caspari.htm>. Viewed October 18 2005.

[33] Ibid.

[34] Felicia Karo-Weingarten living in St. Paul Minnesota, who was in the Lodz Ghetto from its very beginning in early May 1940 until August 1944, remembers the German physician Caspari's fame. Because she was never treated by him and had never met him, she could not identify the photo. However, she did say that Jews from Germany were not deported to Auschwitz for extermination, instead they were sent to *Chelmno*. Personal communication, October 1 2005. The record shows that Jews from *Frankfurt am Main*, the city of residence from which Caspari's mother was originally deported to Lodz, were sent to *Chelmno* for immediate extermination in the following periods: Jan. 17-Jan. 30, 1942; Feb. 23-Apr. 3, 1942; May 5-May 16, 1942; Sept. 1-Sept. 12, 1942; and June 24-July 15, 1944. Krzysztof Gorczyca, Zdzisław Lorek, Kalendarium Chełmna, The list of places from which Jewish people were murdered in the Chelmno-on-Ner extermination center. A copy of the list can be found in the District Museum, Konin, Poland. Located approximately 50 miles west of Lodz, in the *Warthegau*, Poland, *Chelmno* was the first Nazi extermination camp. Felicia Karo was raised on *14 Magistraska Ul.* in Lodz, in the very same apartment building as this author. Seven years older, she remembers playing together with the author and his older sister in the building's courtyard. Unlike Felicia who lost her entire family, the Reismans eluded Lodz Ghetto's experiences (Reisman and Reisman (1982).

[35] Sütlüpınar and Ergun (2003) 269-277

[36] Paper presented at the VI Meeting of the Turkish Pharmacological History Society, 5-7 June, 2002 and subsequently published in *Eczacılık Tarihi Araştırmalar*, Editor: Prof. Dr. Afife Mat, Sunulan Bildiriler, Üniversite Yayın No: 4390, Eczacılık Fakültesi Yayın No: 80, ISBN 975-404-679-4, Istanbul, 2003.

[37] <http://www.istanbul.edu.tr/istanbultip/tr/akademik_birimler/temel/fizyoloji/>. Viewed June 18 2005.

[38] Kazancıgil et al. (2000).

[39] <http://www.physik.uni-frankfurt.de/paf/paf84.html , <http://www.istanbul.edu.tr/edebiyat/ edebiyat/MKanarIstanbulUniversitesi.doc>. Viewed October 4 2005.

[40] Namal (2003)

[41] Personal communication, November 21 2005.

[42] Courtesy of University of Istanbul, Faculty of Medicine, Personnel Records.

[43] Carl Weisglass. *Research on a Double-Valve-Rectification System. The Starting Process* in İstanbul Üniversitesi Fen Fakültesi Mecmuası / Revue de la Faculté des Sciences de l'Université d'Istanbul VIII (1943) 1, S.1-8; Carl Weisglass, *Research on the Lapping Period in a Double-Valve-Rectifying System with Metal Rectifier* in İstanbul Üniversitesi Fen Fakültesi Mecmuası VII (1942) 1/2, S. 45-57; Carl Weisglass, *Die Messung von Wechselströmen und -spannungen mit Hilfe von Gleichstrommessgeräten mit Trockengleichrichtung* in İstanbul Üniversitesi Fen Fakültesi Mecmuası V (1940) 1/2, S.18-34; and Carl Weisglass, *Research on a Double-Valve-Rectification System* in İstanbul Üniversitesi Fen Fakültesi Mecmuası V (1941) 3/4, S.240-255.

[44] Rainer Maria Rilke was born on December 4 1875 in Prague and is generally considered the the 20th century's greatest poet in the German language. His haunting images tend to focus on the problems of Christianity in an age of disbelief, solitude, and profound anxiety. Generally, he is considered among Modernist poets. However, his religious dilemmas may set him apart from some of his peers. <http://www.thecry.com/existentialism/rilke/>. Viewed February 18 2006.

[45] Anonymous (unknown). However, there is much evidence suggesting that Hilda Geiringer von Mises penned this document during the 1960s as part of her editing the von Mises' archives for Harvard. Information presented in the document and its organization, required not only good scientific knowledge of von Mises' many and disparate scientific interests but also a great deal familiarity of his personal life. The end of the document states: "The Richard von Mises Papers occupy 13 linear feet of shelf space and are stored in twenty one five-inch gray manuscript boxes and seven octavo-size four-inch green manuscript boxes. The collection was donated in three parts by Mrs. Hilda von Mises: part I, Boxes I-XIX, 1965; part 2, Boxes XX and XXI, February 1967; part 3, Boxes XXII - XXVIII, November 1967.

The document also notes "Von Mises' large collection of books and papers by and about the poet Rainer Maria Rilke was previously presented to Harvard University." Hence, these are archived and available to scholars.

[46] <http://www-gap.dcs.st-and.ac.uk/~history/Mathematicians/Mises.html>. Viewed June 4 2005.

[47] Von Mises Papers, HUG 4574,105, Box 2, Folder 1946-1948, Harvard University Archives

[48] Ibid.

[49] Anonymous (unknown)

[50] Ibid.

[51] Grinstein and Campbell (1987) 43

[52] O'Connor J. J. and Robertson (2001)

[53] O'Connor and E. F. Robertson (2005) <http://www-gap.dcs.st-and.ac.uk/~history/Mathematicians/Mises.html>. Viewed September 30 2005

[54] <http://www-history.mcs.st-andrews.ac.uk/Mathematicians/Veblen.html>. Viewed December 8 2005.

[55] Ibid.

[56] See Hilda Geiringer's "Work," Grinstein and Campbell (1987) 43.

[57] An archival document addressed to the Minister of Education, Ankara. "Your Excellency," courtesy the Freundlich Letters, St Andrews University, Scotland.

[58] O'Connor and Robertson (2005). <http://www-history.mcs.st-andrews.ac.uk/Mathematicians/Geiringer.html>. Viewed July18 2005.

[59] Ibid.

[60] See Hilda Geiringer's "Work," "Works about Hilda Geiringer" Grinstein and Campbell (1987) 44.

[61] Ibid. "Works about Hilda Geiringer" (46). Anonymous (undated). "History of the Applied Mathematics Department" 12 pages. Courtesy Brown University Archives. Found and supplied by Holly Snyder, University Archivist, Brown University, on January 1 2006. The text of the document provides indication that this document was created between 1942 and 1945. It too refers to these notes by saying: "Special lecture notes in mimeographed form were carried away by departing students and led to a spontaneous demand for additional copies from the Government and industrial laboratories. This demand became so heavy that it was necessary to place some of the notes on sale. To date, the lecture notes of 14 courses have been offered in this way, and 7500 copies have been sold."

The document goes on with the following judgment. "The value of so wide a distribution of special literature in the field of applied mathematics is intangible and not readily appraised. There can be little doubt, however, that its influence has been important and lasting.

[62] O'Connor and Robertson (2005). <http://www-history.mcs.st-andrews.ac.uk/Mathematicians/Geiringer.html>. Viewed September 14 2005.

[63] Oswald Veblen Papers, Container 31. Manuscripts Division, Library of Congress.

[64] Ibid.

[65] Ibid.

[66] Ibid.

[67] Von Mises Papers, HUG 4574,105, Box 2, Folder 1946-1948, Harvard University Archives.

[68] Grinstein and Campbell (1987) 43

[69] O'Connor and Robertson (2005)

[70] National Academis Press, Memorial Tributes, 233. <http://books.nap.edu>. Viewed October 5 2005.

[71] <http://www-groups.dcs.st-and.ac.uk/~history/Mathematicians/Prager.

tml>. Viewed October 19 2005

[72] Veblen Papers, Container 32. Manuscripts Division, Library of Congress.

[73] Drucker, D.C. (1984) Memorial Tributes, *National Academy of Engineering*, Volume 2 (233,234)

[74] Ibid.

[75] This term was not known at the time. It is a breakthrough technology at this very time.

[76] <http://vonhippel.mrs.org/>. Viewed October 1 2005.

[77] Dresselhaus (2004) 76-77

[78] Ibid.

[79] <http://nanoatlas.ifs.hr/arthur_von_hippel.html>. Viewed October 1 2005.

[80] Although not a very nice way of referring to laboratory help in today's politically acceptable parlance, the term Servant was actually used by von Hippel in his memoirs. The man was the son of a poor family and did not have proper clothing for work, so von Hippel bought him the white lab coat. The man wore it with pride.

[81] <http://vonhippel.mrs.org/vonhippel/life/AvHMemoirs9.pdf> Viewed on October 7, 2005.

[82] Von Hippel (73) <http://vonhippel.mrs.org/vonhippel/life/AvHMemoirs9.pdf> Viewed on October 7 2005.

[83] Von Hippel (71)

[84] Von Hippel (79)

[85] Reproduced by permission on behalf of the Family Trust, from Eric von Hippel. Private e-mail communications, June 24 2005.

[86] Ibid.

[87] Ibid.

[88] <http://nanoatlas.ifs.hr/arthur_von_hippel.html>. Viewed on October 7 2005.

[89] <http://www.lionprecision.com/corp/corp-history.html>. Viewed on October 7 2005.

[90] Merzbacher (2005). Personal communication, August 14 2005.

[91] Courtesy the Freundlich Letters, St Andrews University, Scotland.

[92] <http://www.iep.utm.edu/>. Viewed July 29 2005.

[93] The land was part of the *Rancho San Vicente y Santa Monica,* a Spanish land-grant ranch sold off in pieces to Anglos after Mexico's defeat in the Mexican-American War. It was an agricultural district (soybeans and avocados) at the time of its annexation by Los Angeles in 1916.

[94] Reprinted with permission from Mia (widow) Reichenbach. Telephone conversation, August 11 2005.

[95] To wit undergraduate engineering at UCLA was first fully available as a four-year program in 1953. Following is a direct quote from <http://www.ee.ucla.edu/about/history.htm> as viewed on January 27 2006.

"Dean Boelter was an innovator with highly original ideas about undergraduate engineering education. He felt that the conventional departmentalization of a College of Engineering leads to walls being created between departments that prevent interdisciplinary activities. Since he also felt that the future of engineering was interdisciplinary, he decided that the College of Engineering at UCLA would have a single department and that UCLA would offer undesignated B.S., M.S., and Ph.D. degrees. Further, the first three years leading to the B.S. would be completely unified, with the junior year consisting of seven core courses that covered dynamics, fluid mechanics, thermodynamics, strength of materials, electric circuits and machines, applied mathematics, and professional ethics. A two-year sequence of interdisciplinary laboratories would span the junior and senior years."

## Chapter 9

[1] Fermi (1968) (68)

[2] The *Dar-ül Fünun* was abolished on July 31 1933 and the Istanbul University was established in its place on August 1 1933. A small fraction of the original *Dar-ül Fünun* teachers were rehired.

[3] Courtesy Rockefeller [Foundation] Archives Center.

[4] Internal Rockefeller Foundation correspondence, October 23 1933. From Daniel P. O'Brien, MD Assistant Director, Medical Sciences to his boss Alan Gregg MD, Director in New York.

[5] With negativisms toward perceived capitalist and (western) colonialist influences fueled by, at the minimum, a youthful adulation of the communist ideology. These particular negativisms persist to this very day among some graduate students as was indeed experienced by this book's author during many lectures, seminars, and over beers (1999-2003) at both public and private universities in Turkey.

[6] In an effort to stymie any resistance, the architects of the university reform prepared a law that ordered the closure of the *Dar-ül Fünun* on July 31 1933 and the establishment of the new university on August 1 1933.

[7] The constant attention paid these émigrés by the highest echelons of Turkish government combined with bad news emanating from their homelands and shortages of supplies and equipment, created what appears in retrospect as a new setting for the "Hawthorne effect"—an ever-enhanced productivity at the highest intellectual levels of "hired labor." There is no doubt that the émigrés were aware of happenings in their homelands.

[8] Some of the social interactions in this tight-knit expatriate community are described by von Hippel. <http://vonhippel.mrs.org/vonhippel/life/AvHMemoirs9.pdf>. Viewed October 7 2005.

[9] <http://vonhippel.mrs.org/vonhippel/life/AvHMemoirs9.pdf>. Viewed October 5 2005.

[10] Von Hippel (73) <http://vonhippel.mrs.org/vonhippel/life/AvHMemoirs9.pdf> Viewed on October 7 2005.

[11] Von Hippel (76-77) <http://vonhippel.mrs.org/vonhippel/life/AvHMemoirs9.pdf> Viewed on October 7 2005.

[12] <http://vonhippel.mrs.org/vonhippel/life/AvHMemoirs9.pdf >. Viewed September 25 2005.

[13] Ibid.

[14] Shaw (1993) 379

[15] Neumark (1982) 123

[16] R.A. Lambert's diary entry for February 15 and 16 1934. Courtesy Rockefeller [Foundation] Archive Center.

[17] Lambert's Diary. Compliments of Rockefeller [Foundation] Archive Center.

[18] Compliments of Rockefeller [Foundation] Archive Center.

[19] Ibid.

[20] National Archives document 867.4016 JEWS/20

[21] National Archives document 867.00 Nazi/1

[22] National Archives document 867.4016 JEWS/6. This quote provides an unintended message of historical significance. The use of the "Jewish race" on the part of an educated American who obviously meant nothing pejorative about it. In other cotemporaneous correspondence as that involving R. M. Hutchins then President of the University of Chicago, one finds usage of "the Jewish nation" in referring to Jewish Americans. Use of such expressions in business correspondence leaves little doubt that circa the 1930s, America's own establishment has not come to terms with what to call their fellow (ethnic) Americans.

[23] National Archives document 867.4016 JEWS/5

[24] Friling (2002) 322

[25] Frantz and Collins(2003) 122

[26] Erichsen (2000)

[27] Kazancıgil et al. (2000)

[28] May 5 1941 report on his visit to Turkey, by *Yishuv* representative Eliahu Epstein. Friling (2002) 328.

[29] Grothusen (1987). A chronology of Herbert Scurla's rise in, and activities for, the Nazi hierarchy under the various pseudonyms he used is given in Simon (2004). Entries numbered 0500-0511, for the year 1939 show his activities during two trips to Turkey.

[30] <http://www.museumonline.at/1999/schools/classic/istanbul/exilturkei_e.htm>. Viewed October 22 2005.

[31] Ibid.

[32] Sabine Hillebrecht (Hrsg.), *Haymatloz-Exil in der Türkei* 1933-1945, Berlin (2000) 33-34.

[33] Müller (1998)

[34] Turkish spelling for the German word *heimatlos*.

[35] Matthias Neumark, personal communication June 18 2005.

[36] Eugen Merzbacher, personal communication July 1 2005.

[37] Haymatloz (2000) 149-155

[38] Personal communication October 25, 2005.

[39] With permission from Eugen Merzbacher August 26 2005.

[40] Grothusen (1987) 125

[41] Ibid.

[42] Grothusen (1987) 116

[43] Grothusen (1987)

[44] Haymatloz List (2000)

[45] Helmuth von Moltke born in Kreisau, Germany, in 1907 became an international lawyer with many friends in Britain and the United States. Opposed to Hitler, in 1933, he began making contacts with anti-Nazi resistance. He was detained by the Gestapo in January 1944 after it was discovered that he was warning conspirators that they were about to be arrested. After the July Plot, Moltke was charged with treason and executed at Ploetzensee Prison on January 23 1945. <http://www.

spartacus.schoolnet.co.uk/GERmoltke.htm>. Viewed October 25 2005. Moltke apparently used his expertise in international law to help rescue many German and Danish Jews.

[46]"The *Warthegau* (Wartheland), territory established by the Germans in October 1939 in the greatest part of Poland—that which was incorporated into the Reich; the Warthegau existed until it was liberated in January 1945. It was the largest administrative unit in the Reich, covering a total of 16,966 square miles. At the beginning of World War II, 4,922,000 people lived in the area, including 385,000 Jews and 325,000 Germans. The *Warthegau* was run by Arthur Greiser, who intended to *turn the region into a model of racial purity.* He divided the population into superior persons, the [Aryan] Germans—and the inferior persons, including Poles, Jews, and Gypsies. Within weeks, the superior group had taken all the high posts in the business, political, and economic administration of the region and received many privileges. Members of the "inferior group" were badly persecuted. More than 70,000 Poles were murdered and others were sent to forced labor and Concentration Camps. The Germans also persecuted Poles by restricting their movement, expelling many, giving them the most meager of food rations, welfare, and health services, and preventing certain couples from getting married. *The Germans confiscated 95.5 percent of Polish* property, closed down their schools, and forbid Poles from developing their cultural and social lives. Even using the Polish language was restricted. *As soon as the Warthegau was established, the Germans began instituting anti-Jewish measures. Jews were forced to wear Jewish badges, sent to labor camps, and were forbidden to use public transportation. Jewish property was confiscated, and Jews were banned from cultural, educational, and political activities. Some Jews were also murdered. From early 1940 to late 1941, the Jews were herded into 173 ghettos and forced labor camps. Many died of starvation, overwork, and unsanitary conditions; several thousand were murdered. Beginning in December 1941, most of the Jews were exterminated.* During the last few months of the war, the Germans slowed the rate of extermination so that the remaining Jews could be exploited for their work abilities. Altogether, 380,000 *Warthegau* Jews were killed, and only 5,000 survived. In addition, hundreds of Gypsies living in the *Warthegau* were also murdered." (emphasis added)
<http://www1.yadvashem.org/odot_pdf/Microsoft%20Word%20-%206496.pdf>. Viewed October 25 2005.

*Chelmno*, the first Nazi extermination camp and the site of biologist Ernst Caspari mother's most likely final destination, was in the *Warthegau.*

[47] Personal communication, August 20 2005.

[48] Prof. Walther Gleisberg, not to be confused with astronomer Wolfgang Gleissberg, was Rector at the College of Agriculture and Veterinary Medicine in Ankara. Gleisberg was Aryan, Gleissberg was not.

[49] Falke was Founding Dean of the School for Agriculture & Veterinary Medicine in Ankara. However it appears that his academic approach did not conform with Turkish objectives. He was considered to be too abstract or theoretical and not sufficiently pragmatic. It also appears from the Scurla report that he was dismissed from the adminstrative position.

[50] Scurla refers to Dr. Friede as *Ortsgruppenleiter,* i.e., involved in the local *NSDAP* Party activities.

[51] "Report of Eliahu Epstein on his visit to Turkey, May 5, 1941." Friling (2002) 328

[52] Christiansen-Weniger (1964)

[53] Grothusen (1987) 80

[54] National *Socialist* German *Workers'* Party. (emphasis added)

[55] Personal communication, August 26 2005.

[56] All correspondence involving Freundlich has been made available by the St Andrews University Archives in Scotland.

[57] <http://www.uspapermoney.info/sign>. Viewed September 25 2005.

[58] Blum (1959-1965) contains excerpts of Henry Morgenthau, Jr.'s diaries from 1928-1941.

[59] If indeed there is a record to the contrary, it has eluded this writer.

[60] Morgenthau (1999) *xiii*

[61] Ibid.

[62] News Release, June 9 2004, "Stephen Wise Was Cautious and Ineffective During Holocaust, Say Scholars at Library of Congress Panel." The David S. Wyman Institute for Holocaust Studies.

[63] Ibid. xix

[64] Ibid. At the end of the war in Europe American Jews became united as never before. This included the Morgenthaus as well. Henry the III'd tells that: "Out of office, my father was a natural choice to lead the American effort on behalf of the remnants of world Jewry and the anticipated establishment of the State of Israel."

[65] Fermi (1968) 72

[66] A copy of a 1936 letter from Albert Einstein documents this assertion in Chapter 12.

[67] Şarman (2005)

[68] According to February 3 1941 letter addressed to Felix Haurowitz. It is not clear from the archival copy who the writer was. However, the author was a scientist, probably a chemist, and all indications are that he was writing from Ankara. It would be a good guess that the letter came from biochemist Otto Gerngross who at the time was working at the Higher Institute of Agriculture in Ankara. Courtesy The Lilly Library, Indiana University, Bloomington, Indiana.

[69] Hillebrecht, S. (2000) 33-34

[70] "Desperate Hours" Documentary film, Shenandoah Films. P O Box 1339. Hedgesville,WV 25427. USA. <http://www.shenandoahfilm.com/>. Viewed October 21 2005.

[71] Ibid.

[72] Ibid.

[73] Ibid.

[74] Friling (2002) 335-337

[75] This assertion is made based on the author's (unabashedly unscientific) sampling of individuals known to him.

[76] Friling (2002) 339

[77] All quotes from correspondence involving Alvin Johnson and/or the New School are courtesy of The American Council for Émigrés in the Professions M.E. Grenader Department of Special Collections and Archives, University at Albany Libraries.

[78] Ibid.

[79] Letter dated August 21 1941, to Captain Welles, U.S. Army. Courtesy The Grenander Department of Special Collections & Archives, University at Albany, New York.

[80] Haymatloz (2000) 111

[81] Meier-Rust (1993)

[82] Amal (2000)

**Chapter 10**

[1] Friling (2002) 323

[2] Four days later, as a means of keeping all options open, a Turkish-English joint declaration of friendship and mutual assistance in case of aggression or war in the Mediterranean area was also signed in Ankara.

[3] Courtesy The Grenander Department of Special Collections &Archives, University at Albany, New York.

[4] Friling (2002) 327, 328

[5] Meier-Rust (1993) 71. Meier-Rust claims that this effort "occupied his [Rüstow's] time almost exclusively for several weeks."

[6] Ibid.

[7] Fermi (1968) 67. The Fermis knew the Güterbocks personally. Both husbands were with the University of Chicago for a number of years.

[8] Meier-Rust (1993) 65

[9] Bali (2005) 325

[10] Bali (2005) cover page, 181-188, 234-252

[11] Document No. 867.512/2-243, dated February 2 1943, Records of the Department of State Relating to Internal Affairs of Turkey, 1930-1944. NARA RG 59. Also, Bali (2005) 306

[12] Among these were several editorials appearing in the New York Times, Bali (2005) 343-354, and behind-the-scenes maneuverings as claimed by US Ambassador Steinhardt.

[13] He served as prime minister from 1942 until 1946.

[14] Saraçoglu served as prime minister of the Turkish republic from 1942 to 1946.

[15] Laurence Steinhardt Papers, Library of Congress, Container 82. item 57.

[16] Laurence Steinhardt Papers, Library of Congress, Container 82. item 59

[17] <http://www.turkfilm.net/arc46.html>, <http://www.imdb.com/title/tt0156038/> Viewed January 15 , 2006 and <http://www.turkishdailynews.com/past_probe/12_12_99/Dom2.htm>. Viewed January 15 2006.

[18] The "Village Institutes" were established by Hasan-Ali Yucel, Minister of Enlightenment, to train promising boys from the rural areas as village teachers.

[19] <http://www.turkfilm.net/arc46.html> and <http://www.imdb.com/title/tt0156038/>. Viewed January 15 2006 and <http://www.turkishdailynews.com/past_probe/12_12_99/Dom2.htm>. There is some evidence that the *Varlık* trauma is still very much part of public opinion views regarding minorities in Turkey. Bali (2005) 133-180 offers a critical analysis of the reason for the transformation of the novel's Jewish characters into Armenians in the movie and of the public and intellectuals' reaction to the movie.

[20] Bali (2005) 45-46

[21] Donmeh (*dönme*) is a Turkish word for a religious convert. It refers to a group of Jews of the Near East who followed Sabbatai Zevi (also called Shabbatai Zvi) and converted to Islam in 1666. Zevi's conversion is generally understood to have been forced. Many *dönme* hoseholds kept their Jewish faith secret much like the Marranos did in Mexico. Bali (2005)

[22] Rifat N. Bali. "Politics of Turkification. During the Single Party Period." unpublished paper submitted in the conference "Turkey: Towards Post-Nationalism?" Basel University, Dept of Islamic Studies, Basel 14-16 October 2004.

[23] "Educated persons and merchants took exception to the policy and some said: 'We have barely restored the prestige we lost during the Ottoman regime, and here we are about to lose it again.'" Friling (2002). To this very day, issues of national prestige are of unusually great concern to Turkish citizens.

[24] Shaw (1991)

[25] Krecker (1964), Neumark (1980), and Shaw (1991)

[26] There is now much documentary evidence to support the notion that all along Archbishop Roncalli (later known as Pope John XXIII), as Vatican Nuncio in Istanbul, worked behind the scenes to support the *Yishuv's* overt and covert activities of saving Jews from the Nazis and transporting them through Turkey. His support lasted even during the course of the war. Of course, at the time the émigrés had no way of knowing about this source of support in behalf of Jews. Hence, mention of this is relegated to a footnote in this book. It certainly is not a footnote to history. Many references documenting this fact have been compiled and are available through the Raoul Wallenberg Foundation. <http://www.raoul-wallenberg.org.ar/english/roncalliinformesintesis.htm>

[27] Shaw (1993) 400

[28] Frantz and Collins (2003) 123

[29] Laurence Steinhardt Papers, Library of Congress, Container 82. Letter dated April 1 1944, from Ambassador Laurence Steinhardt to William Rosenblatt, 80 Broad Street, New York City.

[30] Friling (2002) 338

[31] Ibid.

[32] Yahil (1990) 626

[33] Personal communication, December 1 2005.

[34] Frantz and Collins (2004) 114. Additionally, an inquiry to one of the most authoritative Holocaust archives brought the following response. "It is quite difficult to estimate precisely that number and we at Yad Vashem are not less dependent on the works of researchers like Stanford Shaw, Rifat Bali or Franz and Collins. However, the number 100,000 seems highly improbable and the reality must be closer to numbers like 15,000-20,000." Personal communication, Shaul Ferrero, November 29 2005. An inquiry to the US Holocaust Memorial Museum in Washington DC resulted in the following response: There is no "official" museum statistic on this matter, although the museum website's *Holocaust Encyclopedia* gives the figure of 16,000 Jewish refugees (legal and "illegal") who passed through Turkey to Palestine during the course of the war. There are no reliable statistics on those refugees passing through Turkey on their way to countries other than Palestine. The *Holocaust Encyclopedia* statistic is based on Dalia Ofer's

book, *Escaping the Holocaust*, New York: Oxford University Press (1990) 320 and the exact figure she gives is 16,474. Dina Porat, in her book *The Blue and White Stars of David* (Cambridge, Mass: Harvard University Press, 1990) on page 106 gives the figure 15,000. While no statistics are ever sacrosanct, especially those which include "illegals," Ofer is the foremost expert on the subject and there is no reason to seriously doubt her statistic on this particular matter. Severin Hochberg, historian, USHMM. Personal communication, November 29 2005.

[35] Shaw (1993) 406

[36] Slutsky (1972) 171

[37] Ofer (1977) 437

[38] Ibid.

[39] Slutsky (1972) pg 171

[40] Shaw (1993 p 266)

[41] At times commingled with the *Jewish Agency for Palestine*, the officially recognized body, entity, or organization, officially recognized by both Turkey and Britain to represent the *Yishuv*.

[42] Friling (2001) 267. Also see Frantz and Collins (2003) and Rubin (1992).

[43] Friling (2001) 332

[44] Friling (2001) 323

[45] Turkey and Germany were allies in WWI.

[46] Oppenheim (1996) 152-153

[47] Oppenheim (1996)

[48] The circumstances at the time or memory of happenings many years ago may explain the author's confusion of bacon with perhaps *sucuk* (Turkish sausage) or *pastırma* (something like pastrami) neither of which are pork products.

[49] Helmuth Mainz, Appendix 2 in Oppenheimer (1996) 181.

[50] Shaw (1993) 417-420

[51] Friling (2005) 148, 256

[52] Laurence Steinhardt Papers, Library of Congress, Container 82. Letter dated April 1, 1944, from Ambassador Laurence Steinhardt to William Rosenblatt, 80 Broad Street, New York City.

[53] Ibid. 199

[54] Laurence Steinhardt Papers, Library of Congress, Container 82. Letter dated April 1 1944 from Ambassador Laurence Steinhardt to William Rosenblatt, 80 Broad Street, New York City.

[55] Yad Vashem (2004) Turkey.

[56] Ibid.

[57] http://www.byegm.gov.tr/YAYINLARIMIZ/newspot/2003/july-aug/n6.htm Viewed February 3 2006.

[58] Morgenthau (1999)

[59] Ibid.

[60] Kazancıgil et al. (2000)

[61] Ibid.

[62] In comparison, American universities are duty-bound to give a full year's notice in terminating tenure track professors.

[63] Interview by Arnold and Ellen Reisman on September 24 2005. See chapter 13 for full interview.

**Chapter 11**

[1] Wyman, D. S. (1984) xi

[2] By a nine-page handwritten note on the stationery of the Charing Cross Hotel in Strand, London, UK, Oswald Veblen, who was then a chaired professor of Mathematics at Princeton University, tried to recruit Albert Einstein to the University as a Research Professor "free from the duty of teaching undergraduates" and with the sole duty to advance your science. (Oswald Veblen Papers, Library of Congress, Box 4.) Einstein did not bite. Later in 1932, after the formation of the Institute for Advanced Studies (an independent institution though located in Princeton) to which Veblen himself had moved, he was more successful in persuading Einstein to come.

[3] Lipset and Ladd, Jr. (1971) 90. Also, labor economist Selig "Perlman sought for posts frantically at *Cornell and Arkansas, but as a Jew he was rejected*." Benjamin Solberg "An intellectual afraid." *The Nation*, June 26 1929, 769-770. Seligman was given an appointment at the University of Wisconsin where his work reached international acclaim.

[4] Historians who specialize in the question of America's response to the Holocaust are urging the Franklin D. Roosevelt Museum, to correct a panel in its exhibit that claims there was nothing President Roosevelt could have done to save many more Jews from the Holocaust. "There are numerous steps that the Roosevelt administration could have taken to save lives, such as granting refugees temporary haven in America or in Allied-controlled regions; pressuring the British to open Palestine to refugees; ordering the bombing of the gas chambers at Auschwitz or the railways leading to them; and giving broader funding and power to the U.S. War Refugee Board." "Roosevelt Museum Distorts FDR's Record on the Holocaust; Historians Protest." July 7 2005. http://www.wymaninstitute.org/boston-cont.php>. Viewed October 25 2005.

[5] Toscanini was a vocal anti-Nazi, who made his views known in Europe until the last possible minute. NBC created an orchestra for him, and he broadcast concerts regularly to great acclaim. Many of the broadcasts are still regarded as great recordings. His chosen successor (Guido Cantelli) perished in a plane crash, and the orchestra was subsequently disbanded, but Toscanini's impact on the music scene is undeniable. Arthur Rubinstein born in Lodz, Poland, the same city as this author, escaped from Paris to Los Angeles in 1940. In August 1939, with the worsening situation in Europe, George Szell and his wife settled in New York. In 1946, he became Musical Director of Cleveland and a United States citizen. He elevated that orchestra to world-class status.

[6] Columbia, Johns Hopkins, and Cornell Universities did not have discriminatory hiring practices. However, for financial reasons during the 1930s, they were not hiring many faculty.

[7] The Princeton Institute for Advanced Studies was established with Jewish money. It was and it is a separate entity from Princeton University. One of the first professors hired in 1933 by the Institute was Albert Einstein. Alvin Johnson, who took over as director of the reorganized the *New School*, helped found the "University in Exile" to accommodate the newly displaced and exiled German scholars. The University in Exile, which was later to become the Graduate Faculty

for Political and Social Science of the *New School*, was a haven for many and, the New School after rededicating itself to scholarly research quickly became one of the more prominent schools of social science in the United States. The New School virtually transplanted the entire Kiel Institute of economists. <http://cepa.newschool.edu/het/schools/newsch.htm>. Viewed October 22 2005.

[8] In 1936, Harvard sent a representative to celebrations at the University of Heidelberg which, like all German universities at that time, had expelled all its Jewish professors and changed its curriculum to reflect Nazi ideology. Harvard also cultivated friendly ties with another Nazi German university, Göttingen. <http://www.wymaninstitute.org/bostoncont.php>. Viewed on October 27 2005.

[9] Max Bergmann, formerly director of the Kaiser-Wilhelm Institute for Leather Research, joined the Rockefeller Institute in 1933; he was one of many German scientists of the intellectual migration. A protégé of Emil Fischer, Bergmann had developed in Germany a leading center for protein chemistry, attracting students from around the world. His successful career continued in his new homeland, which he considered "the best country on the globe" (*Felix Haurowitz* file, July 8 1943). His research program, which focused on the action of proteolytic enzymes on synthetic peptides and on the problem of protein structure, aimed at explaining the biological specificity of proteins. As determinants of specificity, proteins were then generally regarded as the active hereditary material in the chromosomes; Bergmann's investigations were also intended to account for this genetic specificity. The Bergmann Papers—letters, reports, addresses, and lectures— are therefore important not only for the history of biochemistry, but also for the history of molecular genetics. The correspondence shows Bergmann to be a *central figure within the international network of protein chemists, and instrumental in helping other émigré biochemists in the 1930s.* (emphasis added) <http://www.amphilsoc.org/library/guides/kay/Primary.htm>. Viewed on October 27 2005.

[10] "Harvard's Nazi Ties" by Stephen H. Norwood, October 26 2005. The David S. Wyman Institute for Holocaust Studies. Viewed October 26, 2005. <http://www.wymaninstitute.org/articles/2004-11-harvard.php>. Viewed January 5 2006.

[11] Bloomgarden, L. (1960) 152. "Our Changing Elite Colleges" *Commentary*, February.

[12] It was not until "1971, when Jewish students accounted for twenty-five per cent of the enrollment, [that] Brown [Univeristy] appointed the first university-sponsored Jewish chaplain in the Ivy League. The appointment of Richard A. Marker as associate chaplain of the University and associate Hillel director was financed by Brown, National Hillel, and the Jewish Federation in Providence." Martha Mitchell (1993) **Jews.** *Encyclopedia Brunoniana*, 310-313. <http://www.brown.edu/Administration/News_Bureau/Databases/Encyclopedia/search>. Viewed October 25 2005

[13] It is interesting to note that Judah Monis had to become a Christian, and several times thereafter to declare the sincerity of his conversion, prior to receiving his appointment as instructor of Hebrew at Harvard, in the 1720s. *Jewish Virtual Library.* <http://www.jewishvirtuallibrary.org/jsource/biography/monis.html>. Viewed October 26, 2005. On the other hand, in response to a direct inquiry by a Jewish merchant in 1770, Brown University's Corporation expressed a willingness to appoint a Jew as professor of the Hebrew language. Bronson (1914 pp. 98-

100); Brown was the Baptist answer to Congregationalist Yale and Harvard; Presbyterian Princeton; and Episcopalian Penn and Columbia. <http://www.brown.edu/Administration/Admission/gettoknowus/ourhistory.html>. Viewed on October 24 2005.

[14] Grothusen (1987)

[15] Personal communication with Christiane Hoss, Historian, aktives-museum. October 19 2005.

[16] Veblen Papers, Container 32. Manuscripts Division, Library of Congress.

[17] Mitchell (1993) 445

[18] Anonymous (undated), "History of the Applied Mathematics Department" 12 pages. Courtesy Brown University Archives. Found and supplied by Holly Snyder, University Archivist, Brown University, on January 1 2006. The text of the document provides indication that this document was created between 1942 and 1945.

[19] Mitchell, (1993) 445

[20] Anonymous (undated), "History of the Applied Mathematics Department"

[21] Goodwin and Smith (2004) 234

[22] Kapstein's appointment was in Brown's Department of English.

[23] Oswald Veblen Papers, Manuscripts Division, Library of Congress, Box 31.

[24] Richardson, Dean R. G. D. (1943) 67-73

[25] On November 2 2005 President Simmons wrote the following email:

> Dear Mr. Reisman,
>
> Thank you for sharing your interest in research that touches on Brown's history. I regret that Brown does not have the resources to provide assistance to individuals outside the University with their research projects. Should you find yourself on the Brown University campus at any point, however, I encourage you to make arrangements to access Brown's public archives personally.
>
> My very best wishes to you.
>
> Sincerely,
>
> Ruth J. Simmons

A follow up query as to whether employment archives are part of "Brown's public archives" and, if not, would they be made available if I did "find [my]self on the Brown University campus" was never responded to.

[26] The totality of this correspondence represents the years: 1935-1936, 1943, 1945, 1947, 1951, 1957-1958, 1966, and 1974.

[27] According to "Administrators Lent Harvard's Prestige to Nazis, Historian Says" an article in the *Chronicle of Higher Education* by SCOTT MCLEMEE in the November 26 2004 issue:

> The administration of Harvard University welcomed officials of the German government to the university's campus during the 1930s. *It also sent representatives to attend festivities at German universities undergoing "Nazification," giving the regime a much-needed aura of legitimacy.* So the record shows, according to Stephen H. Norwood, a professor of history at the University of Oklahoma, who presented his findings at a conference at

Boston University. "I can give example after example after example" *of the Ivy League institution's "indifference to anti-Semitic violence in Germany at the time,"* said Mr. Norwood (emphasis added) <http://chronicle.com/weekly/v51/i14/14a01501.htm>. Viewed October 26 2005.

[28] Courtesy the *Ava Helen and Linus Pauling Papers* archive at Oregon State University

[29] Ibid.

[30] By letter of November 3 2005, Lawrence H. Summers, President of Harvard University, stated: "I appreciate your interest in Harvard's history and I am sorry that we cannot be of assistance to you. My colleague in the archives department stated our policy accurately with regard to releasing information."

[31] The counterexamples are Johns Hopkins University. "Hopkins' first Professor of Mathematics, James Joseph Sylvester, was Jewish. He was appointed to his position in February 1876. The University opened in October 1876. While Sylvester was the only Jewish faculty member of the original six professors, other Jewish persons were subsequently appointed and/or promoted to various faculty ranks." James Stimpert, Archivist (Arts and Sciences), Johns Hopkins University. Personal communication, October 24 2005.

The same is true of Duke University. "Samuel Mordecai, who was appointed dean of the Trinity Law School in 1905, was raised Jewish. Several of the early Medical Center faculty were Jewish, including Harold Amos, chair of the department of Medicine, 1929-1933." Tim Pyatt, Duke University Archivist. Personal communication, October 24 2005. "The first Jewish professor at Cornell was Dr. Felix Adler who taught from 1874 to 1876, even though there were very few Jewish professors in any colleges or universities in the 19th century. Although there were a number of Jewish instructors, Harry Caplan (taught Classics, 1919-1980) and Wallie Abraham Hurwitz (mathematics) were Cornell's first Jewish professors after Adler. Elaine Engst, Olin Library, Cornell University. Personal communication, October 24 2005.

[32] "A Tough Decision for Yale's Jewish Students—Brief Article." *Black Issues in Higher Education,* February 3 2000 by Daniel Brook <http://www.diverseeducation.com/>. Viewed December 6 2005.

[33] Oswald Veblen Papers, Manuscripts Division, Library of Congress, Box 31.

[34] <http://www-groups.dcs.st-and.ac.uk/~history/Mathematicians/Dehn.html>. Viewed October 22 2005.

[35] Lipset and Ladd, Jr. (1971) 92. However, following WWII, the floodgates on America's campuses were opened to Jewish students and professors alike. There were many reasons for this. One of these was the fact that the elite universities were on academic and financial decline. Irrespective, over the remainder of the 20th century "the Jews were the vanguard of a social movement that…transformed the American university system and the nature of the American elite." Brooks, D. (2005 p18) "Getting In: How three elite colleges protected the privileged." *New York Times.* November 6. Book Review Section.

[36] Igersheimer (2005)

[37] Shaw (1993)

[38] The Institute was and is a separate entity from the University.

[39] Albert Einstein Archives Princeton University, Document No. 20-107 1and 2

[40] Albert Einstein Archives Princeton University, Document No. 20-118

[41] Discrimination against Jews at America's East Coast private colleges and universities was not limited to faculty hiring. A small liberal arts women's school in Boston proudly announces on its website "that [John] Simmons created one of the only private colleges that *did not impose admission quotas on Jewish students during the first half of the 1900s.*" (Emphasis added) <http://www.simmons.edu/> Viewed October 7, 2005.

[42] Albert Einstein Archives Princeton University, Document No. 53-184. 1and 2.

[43] Scherer (2000) 616

[44] Courtesy The Grenander Department of Special Collections & Archives, University at Albany, New York.

[45] Ibid.

[46] The carbon copy does not show the date of the letter. In greatest likelihood, it was sent early in 1940 because of the return address used by Reichenbach. Courtesy The Grenander Department of Special Collections & Archives, University at Albany, NY

[47] Courtesy The Grenander Department of Special Collections & Archives, University at Albany, New York.

[48] Ibid.

[49] Ibid.

[50] Oswald Veblen Papers, Library of Congress, Box 30.

[51] Wyman, D.S. (1984) *ix, x*

[52] Wyman, D.S. (1984) 311. Ironically, "the era's most prominent symbol of humanitarianism turned away from one of history's most compelling moral challenges." Ibid. 313.

[53] Oswald Veblen Papers, Library of Congress, Box 30.

[54] Albert Einstein Archives, Princeton University. Unnumbered document.

[55] Wyman, D. S. (1984)

[56] The American Friends Service Committee (AFSC) was founded in 1917 by members of the Religious Society of Friends (Quakers) in the United States

[57] Oswald Veblen Papers, Library of Congress, Box 30.

[58] Courtesy The Lilly Library, Indiana University, Bloomington, Indiana.

[59] Ibid.

[60] Clifton (1999) 546

[61] Day (1994) 377

[62] Albert Einstein Archives, Princeton University, Document 55 204-1.

[63] Oswald Veblen Papers, Library of Congress, Box 30.

[64] In a May 23 1939 letter to Veblen, Geiringer states: "I wrote [to Bryn Mawr] that I am ready to work for one or two terms at the College without remuneration in order to find an opportunity of introducing myself and of getting in touch with competent persons.

[65] Oswald Veblen Papers, Library of Congress, Box 31.

[66] This paragraph is based on correspondence involving a series of letters. Courtesy The Grenander Department of Special Collections & Archives, University at Albany, NY.

[67] In a handwritten note dated December 7 1939, Hilda Geirneiger tells Profes-

sor Veblen, "I know quite well that it was you who decided that I was to be saved from this horrible situation in Portugal, and I shall never forget it." Ibid.

[68] Frantic letter by Oswald Veblen to Professor Anna Pell Wheeler, at Bryn Mawr College seeking a formal appointment to a faculty position for Geiringer "over the immigration hurdle." Oswald Veblen Papers, Library of Congress, Box 31

[69] Courtesy of the Special Collection Department, The University of Chicago Library.

[70] Letter Mr Stifler, dated September 7 1993.

[71] Minutes of Regular Meeting of the Insitute for Advanced Studies. October 10 1932.

Courtesy of the Princeton The Institute for Advanced Study.

[72] Courtesy of the Special Collection Department, The University of Chicago Library.

[73] Letter dated November 3 1933, to Stephen P. Duggan, Emergency Committee in Aid of Displaced German Scholars.

[74] Courtesy of the Special Collection Department, The University of Chicago Library.

[75] The very same institution that got ophthalmologist Igersheimer, an eminent scholar, by giving him no more than an Assistant Professorship.

[76] Oswald Veblen Papers, Manuscripts Division, Library of Congress, Box 31

[77] Courtesy The Grenander Department of Special Collections & Archives, University at Albany, New York.

[78] Professor Michael Stolleis, Direktor of the Max-Planck-*Institut für Europäische Rechtsgeschich.* Personal communication, November 24 2005.

**Chapter 12**

[1] Except as noted all of the correspondence involving Felix Haurowitz is Courtesy The Lilly Library, Indiana University, Bloomington, Indiana.

[2] Einstein archives Document 55 205, Princeton University's

[3] In a letter of January 5 1939, Oppenheimer stated: "Since my resettlement [from Berlin] in Holland, I found out from my publisher, that that you have found a new residence in Istanbul. Congratulations! ...Let me know how you are faring personally. Would love to hear from you. "

[4]Von Pappen (1953) 521-522. Library of Congress, Manuscripts Division.

[5] Ibid.

[6] Albert Einstein Archives Princeton University, Document No. 53 610

[7] Ibid.

[8] Courtesy Rockefeller [Foundation] Archive Center.

[9] Ibid.

[10] Ibid.

[11] Ibid.

[12] Personal communication, July 12 2005.

[13] Ibid. Document No. 53 612

[14] An extract from the Autobiography of Felix Haurowitz, written in October

1975, on request by the Home Secretary of the National Academy of Sciences of the United States, upon Haurowitz's being elected to the Academy's membership.

[15] Except as noted, all correspondence involving E. Finlay Feundlich is courtesy his archives at Special Collections, University of St Andrews Library, Scotland

[16] Albert Einstein Archives Princeton University, Document No. 11 185-1

[17] Ibid. Document No. 11 186-1-3

[18] Except as noted, all correspondence involving E. Finlay Feundlich is courtesy his archives at Special Collections, University of St Andrews Library, Scotland.

[19] This refers to the Rockefeller Foundation's funding of the acquisition of Turkey's first telescope.

[20] Erwin Schrödinger, winner of the 1933 Nobel Prize in Physics.

[21] A niece, according to the letter from Milne she was taken along to Istanbul by Freundlich, e.g., Milne wrote, "We were glad that Kate, Hanse, and *Goldfield* are with you safely." (emphasis added)

[22] The only 1936 Nobel recipient who was Jewish was Otto Loewi. He received it for discoveries relating to chemical transmission of nerve impulses.

[23] <http://www-gap.dcs.st-and.ac.uk/~history/Mathematicians/Mises.html>. Viewed October 25 2005.

[24] Courtesy St Andrews (Scotland) University archives.

[25] There is now much evidence that a group of German scientists conspired to sabotage Nazi efforts to create the atomic bomb. See Kramish (1986). The Nazi atomic bomb program began at least two years ahead of its counterpart in the US. In his footnote to chapter 11, Powers, (1993 p. 507) reprints the following statement which he attributes to Werner Heisenberg another Nobel laureate who stayed in Berlin through the war. "Dr. Hahn, *Dr. von Laue,* and I falsified the mathematics in order to avoid development of the atom bomb by German science." (emphasis added). If this statement is to be believed, then Max von Laue did much more than simply let the word out to Freundlich as to what was happening in German science. Additionally, Dr. Klaus Kallmann cited earlier provides the following recollection.

> One day in 1941 or 1942, I left with my father [physicist Hartmut Kallmann] in the morning around around 9 am to go to the subway station [in Berlin]. We were just about half way across the street, when my father suddenly said out of nowhere that there is a new explosive being developed from atom splitting. It is so powerful that something as small as a doughnut can destroy an entire city. 'They' are going to test it today at 12 noon at *Wuensdorf*. If it succeds, we shall hear it. But it will not go off, because the calculations are wrong. (*Wuensdorf* is located south of *Zossen* south of Berlin; a large German army training ground was located there.) Why should my father have told me that? He had never talked to me about nuclear bombs or atom splitting before. He must have been agitated and extremely worried that perhaps the calculations were *not* wrong. The impressions I gained at that very moment was that he had determined that the calculations were wrong and that he kept his mouth shut. This conversation was so frightening and startling to me that it is indelibly inscribed in my mind. Hence, I know the exact spot in the street

where the revelation took place. Nothing happened at noon time and eventually I thought it was all a misunderstanding, especially since after the war I always read that the Germans never did go far in their research on atomic bomb development. Personal Communication July 12, 2005.

[26] After the war, von Laue was arrested by the Allied Forces, briefly interned in England, and returned to Germany. In 1951, he became director of the prestigious Max Planck Institute for Research in Physical Chemistry. Max von Laue died in 1960. Stark, too, was arrested and released but spent the last years of his life in his private laboratory on his country estate, Eppenstatt, near Traunstein in Upper Bavaria, investigating the effect of light deflection in an unhomogeneous electric field. Stark died in1957.

[27] From 1933 until his retirement from that position in 1939, Stark was the elected President of the Physico-Technical Institute. At the same time, he was also President of the *Deutsche Forschungsgemeinschaft* German Association for Research. Starting 1933, he attempted to become the Führer of German physics through the *Deutsche Physik* or Aryan physics movement against the "Jewish physics" of Einstein et al. <http://www.absoluteastronomy.com/encyclopedia/j/jo/johannes_stark.htm>. Viewed September 20 2005.

[28] Princeton University archival document 33 168.

[29] Princeton University archival document 33 163.

[30] Laurence Steinhardt Papers, Library of Congress. Container 82, Item 17.

[31]<http://www-history.mcs.st-andrews.ac.uk/Mathematicians/Geiringer.html>. Viewed October 18 2005.

[32] Courtesy Digital Collections and Archives, Tisch Library, Tufts University.

[33] Igersheimer (2005) 189,204

[34] Courtesy The Grenander Department of Special Collections & Archives, University at Albany, NewYork.

[35] <http://lpi.oregonstate.edu/lpbio/lpbio2.html>. Viewed October 25 2005.

[36] Lahut was the son of Dr. Mazhar Osman, Turkey's first and historically most eminent neuropsychiatrist. To this very day, according to a personal correspondence from a Turkish friend: "Everyone has heard of Mashar Osman in Turkey, so much so that if a friend does something crazy, people will say 'Let me take you to Mashar Osman' to indicate that he is fit to see a psychiatrist. The term "Mashar Osmanlık" also widely used means again that somebody is due to see a psychiatrist. Lahut died at an early age.

[37] One of the few émigré professors who returned to Germany. By 1953, he was located at the *Hygienishes Institute* of the University of Munich.

[38] Records of the Office of the President. Record Group 02.001, series 1, file #54. Courtesy of Johns Hopkins University.

[39] As indicated, Max Sgalitzer was the eminent researcher in radiology who was able to bring to Turkey members of his engineering and nursing staff.

**Chapter 13**

[1] Dr. Martin (Haurowitz) Harwit, in "Desperate Hours" Documentary film, Shenandoah Films, P O Box 1339. Hedgesville,West Virginia 25427. USA. <http://www.shenandoahfilm.com/>. Viewed October 19 2005.

[2] Reproduced by permission, from Eric and Frank von Hippel on behalf of the Family Trust. Private e-mail communications, June 24 2005.

[3] Franck was in charge of an infantry company that was supposed to storm the French trenches. When zero hour came, he led the charge but no one followed. Fortunately, the French knew of the plans and had evacuated their first line of trenches. As a result, Franck was able to capture the French position single-handed.

[4] For another description of these events, see Chapter 2 in Beyerchen (1977).

[5] Von Hippel, 71 <http://vonhippel.mrs.org/vonhippel/life/AvHMemoirs 9.pdf>. Viewed on October 7 2005.

[6] Supplied with permission to print by Dr. Alice (Haurowitz) Sievert, Executrix of the Felix Haurowitz estate, September 2 2005.

[7] Neumark (1982) 42. Permission to print granted by Mathias Neumark, Charottsville, VA.

[8] An allegedly attempted coup by Germany's (SA) militia chief Ernst Rohm and followers. It was foiled by Hitler. Rohm and his followers were executed.

[9] Neumark (1982) 64. Permission to print granted by Mathias Neumark, Charottsvile, VA.

[10] Unpublished. Excerpts were obtained from Dr. Nejat Akar, Professor of Pediatrics, Ankara University who in tern obtained a full copy from Ecksteins' son Klaus living in Cambridge, UK. Through a personal communication, Klaus Eckstein granted permission to reprint portions of the memoirs in this text.

[11] Then minister of economics and agriculture

[12] Turkish culture uses the word "Bey" after the first name as a sign of respect for men. For women, "Hanım" is used.

[13] Affectionate nickname used by the family for Albert.

[14] According to Ecksteins' son, Klaus of Cambridge, U. K., "Minna had originally been a kitchen maid for my grandfather, Prof. Schlossmann (joint author of the "Handbuch der Kinderheilkunde, the first serious book on pediatrics). My grandfather was, inter alia, the Court Physician to His Majesty, the King of Saxony, and managed for Minna, then a young girl, to work in the Royal kitchens for a time and to learn the secrets of "noble" cookery. Later on, she became the cook in my grandfather's household, and shortly after my parents moved to Ankara, she came there to cook for us and also to look after the children. She returned to Germany (Dresden) in 1938, survived the war and died, I think, about 1960." Personal correspondence, January 3 2005.

[15] Then a resort area on the Asian side (coast) of Istanbul, now considered to be within Istanbul.

[16] She wants to point out that it was a posh area. The "sugar king" was someone who had become very rich by speculating in sugar imports.

[17] Franz von Pappen was German Reich's ambassador to Turkey (1939-44) after arranging the Anschluss (Nazification of Austria) as ambassador to Austria (1934-39). Von Pappen was the only accused war criminal that was found not guilty as charged at the Nurenberg Trials. <http://www.jewishvirtuallibrary.org/jsource/Holocaust/JudgePapen.html>

[18] Akar (2003) based on Eckstein-Schlossmann (1975).

[19] Noyan (1959)

[20] Neumark (1982) 77

[21] Neumark (1982) 67

[22] Von Pappen (1953) 521-522

[23] Personal communication, August 28 2005.

[24] When asked to elaborate on this claim, Elizabeth Schmidt offered the following:

> I have no idea how my father managed to take my uncle Bruno out of Buchenwald. He managed to bring him to Turkey based on a status of an employee of the university/government. Maybe he paid some "Bakshish" [bribes]. Later on, there was trouble, because the Turks would not let him stay and there was one incident when the police came and took him to the Bulgarian border. Again, my father intervened and managed to bring him back after some hours of suspense. Ultimately, and fortunately he managed to get into the USA. I think he received the affidavit from a relative of ours.... Uncle Bruno was a self-made man. He worked with wood in Germany. In the United States, he became the night manager of a hotel in New York and later moved to Miami, where again he was the manager of one of the hotels. There he married (the first time in his life) at the age of 65 a lovely woman, also from Germany, and they lived a very happy life. I visited them a few times. They had a tiny house on one of the islands in Miami Beach, and he grew orchids. They are both dead by now." Personal communication, August 20 2005.

The second part of the quote tells us that "Uncle Bruno" did not have the qualifications one would expect from someone who was officially invited by the Turkish government with "a status of an employee of the university/government." Hence, "*Bakshish*" was the operative word in his being invited to Turkey for official duties as "an employee of the university/government." Given the above as background and the fact that the salary paid the Prime Minister in those days was 500 Turkish Liras while the Ord. Professors received 600, it is not a long stretch of imagination that someone high up in Turkey's Foreign Office was instrumental in having the Germans open Buchenwald's gates and let Bruno Hellmann out. For a small consideration, of course!

[25] Interviewed by Arnold and Ellen Reisman on September 24 2005.

[26] The elites, or Junkers, were typically loyal to the Prussian crown and narrow minded in their political and social outlook. They had a vest interest in maintaining the status quo—in other words maintaining their advantage (civil, social, political and over others. Family background usually invested a highly autocratic, intensively conservative and monarchical outlook on life whereby the individual was a Prussian patriot, became part of the nobility and accepted its beliefs. <http://www.kdhs.org.uk/history/v2/as/as_unit2/elites_junkerclass.htm>. Viewed on October 7 2005.

[27] Hayim Barlas was the official representative of the *Yishuv* the Jewish Agency in Ankara. It was he who hosted the arrival in Istanbul of the "222 Transport" as well as many of the other refugee groups transiting Turkey by rail. According to Mirjam Bolle born in Holland and living in Jerusalem, one of the "222" passengers

it was he who "treated us to all the goodies Elisheva wrote you about." Personal communication, August 7 2005.

[28] Only one railroad line connecting Palestine and Turkey existed before 1942. It was built by the Ottomans and went through Damascus entering what is now Israel at the southern tip of the Sea of Galilee (Kinneret). The railroad then proceeded west through Afula and on to Haifa where it connected to a line going to Egypt. In 1942, the British built a seaside railroad tunnel just north of what is now Kibbutz Rosh Hanikra. This opened a link to Haifa via Beirut.

[29] Personal communication February 17 2005. Klaus may have been off by one year in his recollections, but the fact that the Ecksteins traveled to Palestine is confirmed in a Memorandum dated April 27 1943, addressed, "To the General Directorate of Security, Ankara" and stating, "Professor Dr. Eckstein has departed from our hospital today on leave of 21 days starting April 27 1943 until May 17 1943 to travel to Lebanon-Jerusalem. I respectfully submit this to your attention." Signed by the Chief Physician [presumably Cuptu Capci]. Akar and Can (2005)

[30] Barlas (1975) 126

[31] Lawrence Steinhardt was Jewish. His family migrated from Germany.

[32] Barlas (1975) 237-238

[33] Eckstein (1975)

[34] His tombstone at the Allied Military Cemetery in *Piangipane* near Ravenna, Italy reads:

Ernst (M) Wadel, born Vienna, Austria, 1-27-1925, Private # 38479 of the Palestine Regiment, killed 6th April 1945 on the Savo River crossing, Italy. Laid to rest with all military honors.

[35] Personal communication, September 9 2005.

[36] He served in that capacity from January 5 1935 to the middle of 1944. From 1925 to 1934, he served in Bulgaria in the same capacity.

[37] On September 7 2000, the Raoul Wallenberg Foundation in New York sent the following letter to The *Righteous Among The Nations* Department of *Yad Vashem,* Israel's State Holocaust Memorial Authority.

"We, at The International Raoul Wallenberg Foundation, as an organization whose aims are to enhance the solitary deeds of people like Raoul Wallenberg, respectfully ask you to consider to honor the name of Angelo Giuseppe Roncalli as a 'Righteous Among the Nations.'"

[1] We are gathering information and preparing documents from many sources, for example (a) Correspondence between *Chaim Barlas representative for the Jewish Agency for Palestine and Mgr. Roncalli Apostolic delegate in Istanbul,* as quoted in the book "Hatzaloh-1976" by Chaim Barlas, (b) "Pius XII and the third Reich" by Saul Friedlander, (c) "The Politics Of Genocide" by Randolph L. Braham, (d) the "Encyclopedia Judaica," S. V. Roncalli, and more which not only shows the tremendous efforts made by Angelo Giuseppe Roncalli but the underlying greatness of the man. (emphasis added)

[2] We are asking the Vatican to provide us with additional primary sources pertaining to Archbishop Roncalli's tenure as Nuncio in Istanbul and his co-operation with Nuncio Rota of Budapest and Raoul Wallenberg.

[3] This letter was read for the first time at the Permanent Observer Mission of the Holy See to the United Nations, on September 7 2000 in the presence of

Ambassadors, Rabbis, Clergy and his Excellency Vatican Secretary Of State Cardinal Angelo Sodano to whom this letter will be presented. We will start an international effort to get others to join us. We have recently spoken with Mr. Guy Von Dardel and Mrs. Nina Lagergren, Raoul Wallenberg's brother and sister, and as you may know Mrs. Nane Annan, the wife of Kofi Annan, the Secretary General of the United Nations, is Raoul Wallenberg's niece, and we all were inspired by the work of Angelo Roncalli, whose life we want to celebrate."

[38] D'Hippolito, J. (2004) Pope John XXIII and the Jews, *FrontPageMagazine.com*. August 20 2004. <http://www.frontpagemag.com/Articles/ReadArticle.asp?ID=14732>. Viewed August 20 2005.

[39] It is of some consequence in the context of this book that Dr. Erna Schlossmann-Eckstein was fully Aryan, even by the Nazi's litmus test.

[40] Personal communication (letter), August 4 2005.

[41] Merzbacher (2005), Personal communication, August 15.

[42] Personal correspondence, October 1 2005.

[43] See his 1996 book *An Exhibit Denied: Lobbying the History of Enola Gay*, Copernicus. New York.

[44] Personal communication, June 29 2005.

[45] After graduation, he decided to obtain an M.B.A. in the U.S. Advised by his father to do so, he applied to the Harvard Business School and to Wharton and was accepted by both. He graduated from Harvard in 1949. On balance, Matt Neumark and his cohorts fondly recall growing up in Turkey. All those contacted have done very well in the US. Most went on to receive a PhD, and became university professors. Among these are Walter Arndt, Eric, and Peter von Hippel. At least one, Frank von Hippel served the United States government. Through most of his career, he was an expert in nuclear non-proliferation. Some like Matt Neumark and Andrew Schwarz did not follow their fathers' footsteps and became business executives. After finishing their university education, two of the women devoted their lives to raising families. One of these was Elizabeth (Reichenbach) Austin.

[46] Personal communication, June 7 2005.

[47] Haymatloz (2000) 194

[48] Ceramic fixtures that are simply holes in the bathroom floor.

[49] Oral history provided to the author by phone on October 1 2005.

[50] Walter Ruben (Edit. Gerhard Ruben): Kırşehir, Eine altertümliche Kleinstadt Inneranatoliens. Arbeitsmaterialien zum Orient, Band 13, Ergon Verlag, Würzburg 2003.

[51] Son of émigré ophthalmologist, Joseph Igersheimer.

[52] Ingersheimer and Darragh (2005)

[53] Ingersheimer and Darragh (2005) xviii

[54] This section is based on a long-distance telephone interview by the author and Mrs. Reisman (August 20 2005). Dr. Walter Igersheimer is now blind, but his mind, recollections, and wit are as sharp as ever.

[55] The fact that this did take place and that the mother was taken to Germany by her daughter was independently confirmed by two other members of the second generation.

[56] Dr. Martin (Haurowitz) Harwit in "Desperate Hours" Documentary film, Shenandoah Films, PO Box 1339. Hedgesville, West Virginia 25427. USA. <http://www.shenandoahfilm.com/>. Viewed September 25 2005.

[57] Matthias Neumark in "Desperate Hours" Documentary film, Shenandoah Films, PO Box 1339. Hedgesville, West Virginia 25427. USA. <http://www.shenandoahfilm.com/>. Viewed September 25 2005.

[58] Marianne Laqueur, daughter of physiotherapist August Laqueur. Born in 1918, Laqueur is the oldest of the "second generation." Hence, her memories better reflect the adults' thinking. Personal e-mail communication from Wiesbaden, Germany, February 17 2006

**Chapter 14**

[1] Courtesy Rockefeller [Foundation] Archives Center.

[2] <http://www.turkishembassy.org/>. Viewed December 19 2005.

[3] Ibid.

[4] Reisman et al. (2004)

[5] Denizer (1997)

[6] Parente and Prescott (2002)

[7] Lewis (1982)

[8] Ibid.

[9] Chase (2003)

[10] Inalcik (1992

[11] GeoCities (2003)

[12] <http://www.geocities.com/ystezel/articles/tusiad.html>. Viewed August 25 2005.

[13] TURKISHTIME (2003)

[14] TDCI (2003)

[15] Francis (1987) 217

[16] Reisman (2005)

[17] Those well connected with the country's "establishment," e.g., the established oligarchs.

[18] Parente and Prescott (2002)

[19] See footnote 33.

[20] Parente, and Prescott (2002) 1-2

[21] Reisman et al. (2004) and Reisman 2005

[22] Gupta and Reisman (2005)

[23] Nehru, J. L. (1936/1972). *Introduction to M. R. Masani: Soviet Sidelights*, rpt. in Selected Works of Jawaharlal Nehru (New Delhi, 1972) 7: 128-29.

[24] 2004 Nobel Prize in Chemistry went to Professors Avram Hershko and Aaron Ciechanover of the Technion.

[25] The Ziff Institute was founded in 1934. In 1949, it was renamed as the Weizmann Institute of Science.

[26] See footnote 18 above.

[27] Ibid.

[28] The Secret of Israel's Success. *The Economist*, November 10, 2005. <http://www.economist.com/business/displayStory.cfm?story_id=5149411&tranMode=none>. Viewed December 28 2005.

[29] Reisman (2005). To erase any doubt the author queried several very knowledgeable and highly placed individuals in the Turkish academic and banking

communities -an unscientific search no doubt. This however identified only a handful of high-tech businesses that have matured enough to be listed on any stock exchange. One of these, Escort Computer, was founded in 1991 and, as of 2005, it aims. "To supply the customer with the latest technological innovations from around the world." Most of the other "high tech" companies registered/listed on the Istanbul Stock Exchange (ISE). are once again joint-ventures with companies in developed countries. They mainly offer manufacturing, installation, marketing, and service for technology developed abroad. Among the independents are Aselsan, which designs and services subsystems for the Turkish military, while 1-LBS-Logo Business Solutions, is the only Turkish software company listed on the ISE. There appear to be none on NASDAQ. Turkcell, "the leading provider of mobile communications services in Turkey,"is based mainly on technology licensed from abroad. Incidentally, this company is the only Turkish company listed on the New York Stock Exchange.

[30] Çetindamar (2003) 261

[31] Çetindamar (2003) 249

[32] Parente and Prescott (2002). Thus, Israelis "create[d] new ideas to increase their standard of living."

[33] As indicated, Parente and Prescott (2002) use the words *ideas, knowledge,* and *technology* interchangeably. They are not alone though their use is in the context of a nation's economic development. In the 1980s and 1990s, a huge literature was created dealing with "knowledge management." The subject became the basis for university graduate curricula worldwide and, of course, consulting companies jumped on the bandwagon. Yet many philosophers, Kant and Polanyi among them, would take issue with such commingling of these words as concepts. These philosophers would argue that knowledge unlike information or technology uniquely requires, or involves, the human brain. Irrespective of the above, this book presumes what is intuitive and is obvious. Movement of knowledgeable humans across sectors, disciplines, cultures, or countries, is tantamount to transferring any knowledge or technology they possess. This is especially important when such knowledge or technology is implemented in creating new products taken to market, thereby creating wealth. Also, Reisman (2005)

[34] Çetindamar (2003) 263

[35] Parente and Prescott (2002)

[36] Ibid.

[37] Ibid.

[38]Additionally, these days the conglomerates obtain technology via licensing arrangements.

[39] Ibid.

[40] For example, professor Israel Hanukoglu was born in Istanbul, Turkey. After an Istanbul based elementary and secondary education and a Ph.D. from the University of Wisconsin, he served as staff scientist at the prestigious Weizmann Institue for Science and later moved his Molecular Biology laboratory to the College of Judea and Samaria. With almost 70 publications in world-class biomedical journals, he is now department head in charge of training new cadres as well as in creating knowledge. From 1996 to 1999, he served as Science Adviser to the Prime Minister. After his civil service, he established Israel's premiere science

and technology directory Israel Science (2005) and remains as its editor. There are many other important scientists and doctors of Turkish Jewish origin in Israel. Additionally, there are many Turkish Jews in hi-tech business and Israel's defense forces. They maintain good relations with Turkish colleagues, have hosted Turkish scientists in various research laboratories, organized bi-national conferences, and coauthored and published scientific papers with colleagues from Turkey.

[41] See footnote 33.

[42] <http://www.worldbank.org/wbi/knowledgefordevelopment/>. Viewed October 25 2005.

[43] Üzeyir Garih, and Isak Alaton founded the *Alarco Holdings* conglomerate in the 1950s. They are both Turkish Jews.

[44] An "im" at the end of a word makes the word plural.

[45] According to law, only one son can inherit the farm in order to keep the farm intact.

[46] The large wave of immigrants from the Soviet Union did include many scientists and engineers bringing with them much useful knowledge and know-how. This did not happen until the late 1980s and it peaked in 1991. By this time, Israel was much more developed then was Turkey in the early 1930s. Arguably this migration of highly educated talent and the "German" émigré professors' infusion into Turkey are somewhat comparable in *scale, timeframe*, and perhaps *scope*, but certainly not in terms of *impact* on the host society. Without a doubt, the impact on Turkey was orders of magnitude qualitatively more significant.

[47] See Reisman, A. (2005).

[48] <http://www.weforum.org.gcp>. Viewed August 22 2005.

[49] Except perhaps in garment goods, Turkey pretty much bypassed the production of knockoffs phase.

[50] See Reisman and Saha (2005)

[51] Beatty (2004) 168

[52] Reisman (2005)

[53] Founded by Brigadier (Res) Eliahu Ben Hur, the author's engineering school classmate.

[54] <http://ekutup.dpt.gov.tr/bilim/yucelih/biltek.pdf>.

[55] "Turkish republican history has traditionally been marked by the indifference, not to say the overt distaste, of economic policy makers vis-à-vis such enterprises which do not resemble modern, large-scale production units long associated with the ideals of industrial development. In contrast to this traditional approach, Turkish politicians, especially since the beginning of the 1990s, have begun to emphasize the significance of SME development, not only in relation to the employment opportunities they provide, but also in relation to their contribution to industrial progress and export growth." Bugra, A. (2005) <http://www.boun.edu.tr/government/council.html>

[56] Gupta and Reisman, A. (2005)

[57] Reisman (2005)

[58] Gupta and Reisman, A. (2005)

[59] Reisman (2005)

[60] See Audretsch and Stephan (1996), Branstetter, (1996), and Jaffe and Trachtenberg (1998).

[61] See Haymatloz (2000)

[62] Document No. 867.512/2-243, dated February 2 1943, Records of the Department of State Relating to Internal Affairs of Turkey, 1930-1944. NARA RG 59. Also, Bali (2005) 306

[63] Gokalp (1959)

[64] Ibid.

[65] Frey (1968) 209

[66] In state universities, rectors are elected by the faculty for limited terms.

[67] Personal communication to the author.

[68] Çetindamar (2003) 248

[69] Personal communication to the author.

[70] Inalcik (1992)

[71] Krueger (2004)

[72] Krueger (2004)

[73] Balkan and Yeldan (1996) and Denizer (1997)

[74] At the same time Turkish manufacturers especially in the garment industry established plants in former Comintern countries e.g., Bulgaria and Rumania to circumvent trade quotas. Although the relationship between Russia and Turkey started in 1932 with Prime Minister Ismet Inönü's Moscow visit, it was mostly a one way proposition with technology flowing from Russia to Turkey. However, in 1990 many Turkish construction companies started to work in Russia building apartment complexes for Russian soldiers returning from East Germany. Nowadays, banking, telecommunication, glass, machine industries, textile, and consumer goods are some of the important investment areas for Turkish companies in Russia, the former Comintern countries, the Turkic republics, and other countries in the world. NTVMSNBC (2004).

[75] Reisman et al (2004)

[76] Courtesy Manuscripts Department, Lilly Library, Indiana University.

[77] Neumark (1982) 153

[78] Kazancıgil et al. (2000)

[79] Ibid.

[80] Ibid.

[81] Sullivan (2005) B7

[82] See Parker and Reisman, (2004)

[83] Çetindamar (2003) 250

[84] Ibid.

[85] Ibid. 249

[86] Çetindamar (2005)187

[87] Document No.43906, dated July 26 1943, Entry 16, Records of the Research and Analysis Branch. OSS, (Regular Series) 1941-1945.

[88] Records of the Department of State [US] relating to Internal Affairs of Turkey 1930-1944, document dated February 2 1943, no. 867.512/2-243, NARA RG59.

[89] Staudenmaier (1985)

[90] A letter to Dr. and Mrs. Muller returning the $4,000 that was to pay the two-year salary of Dr. Kanotorowicz. The Grenander Department of Special Collections & Archives, University at Albany, NY.

[91] Obtained from <http://www.onuroymen.com/docs/konusma37.doc> on September 10 2005.

[92] Seyhan (2005)

[93] Neumark (1982) 183

[94] While a professor at M.I.T. Kurt Lion wrote several books on instrumentation, including "Instrumentation in Scientific Research, Electrical Input Transducers" (1959). Participated with the National Science Foundation in developing a curriculum for electronic instrumentation; and in 1958 founded Lion Research, Inc. (later changed to Lion Precision). Though he passed away in the 1960s, the company is still very much in the high-tech instrumentation business. <http://www.lionprecision.com>. Viewed August 25 2005.

[95] Based on a headcount from Haymatloz List (2000)

## Appendix 1

[1] This "value-laden embrace" (Staudenmaier (1985)) of modern universities by Mustafa Atatürk, Turkey's most revered personage, initiated a "design stage" of the country's system of higher education by his "leadership" qualities and position, the institutionalization of the "enduring nature of government policy" and simultaneously the "enduring nature of cultural values."

[2] <http://www.ankara.edu.tr/english/>. Viewed October 25 2005.

[3] Turkish military academies the *Muhendishane-i Bahri-i Humayun* and the *Muhendishane-i Berri i Humayun* were merged to form the roots of what is today the Istanbul Technical University.

[4] Currently, it also includes basic sciences and management Faculties.

[5] <http://encyclopedia.thefreedictionary.com/Istanbul%20Technical%20University>. Viewed October 15 2005.

[6] With all due respect to this direct quote, it should be pointed out that, starting 1909, a civil engineering school did exist. It was transformed into Istanbul Technical; University.

[7] <http://www.istanbul.edu.tr/>. Viewed November 22 2005.

## Appendix 2

[1] Unlike the others, he was brought in from the Hebrew University of Jerusalem. Not a refugee from Nazism

## Appendix 3

[1] World Economic Forum (2004), Global Competitiveness Report, 2003-2004, and Gupta and Reisman (2005)

[2] IMF (2002). International Financial Statistics Yearbook. Washington DC

[3] Based on data supplied by *The World Bank Group*, (2004), Reisman (2005)

[4] These findings are pregnant with meaning: 20 countries fall below $100 worth of exports per capita and 73 or 46% fall below $500. Among the latter are; Philippines, Peru, Brazil, Pakistan and India as well as oil exporting Nigeria.

# References

Adelson, A. and Lapides, R. Eds. (1989). *Lodz Ghetto.* Viking, Penguin Books, New York. Adorno, T.W. (1980). Minima Moralia: Refexionen aus dem beschadigten Leben. In *Gesamelte Schriften,* ed. R. Tiederman, Vol 4 Suhrkamp, Frankfurt, Germany.

Akar, N. (2003). *Anadoluda bir Çocuk Doktoru. Ord. Prof. Dr. Albert Eckstein.* Genişletilmiş 2. Baskı, Ankara: Pelikan Yayınları.

Akar, N. (2004). Albert Eckstein: a pioneer in pediatrics in Turkey. *Turkish Journal of Pediatrics* ; 46:(4) 295-7.

Akar, N., Reisman, A., and Oral, A. (2005). *Modernizer of Turkey's Pediatrics: Albert Eckstein in exile.* Forthcoming in the *Journal of Medical Biography.* Downloadable from: http://ssrn.com/abstract=694403.

Akar, N. and Can, A. (2005). *Anadolu'da 15 yil / 15 years in Anatolia with Ord. Prof. Dr. Albert Eckstein,* Ankara University Press. Ankara Turkey.

Anonymous (unknown). *Richard von Mises Biographical Sketch.* Document HUG 4574.5. Harvard University Archives. Pusey Library, Cambridge.

Arcak, S., Haktanır, K., Kibar, M., and Dengiz, O. (undated). *Ecological Changes in Manyas Lake Related to Boron Pollution and WaterRegime,* Department of Soil Science, Faculty of Agriculture, University Of Ankara, Ankara, http://www.toprak.org.tr/isd/isd_12.htm.

Ash, M.G. and Sollner A. Ed. (1996). *Forced Migration and Scientific Change: Émigré German-Speaking Scientists and Scholars After 1933.* German Historical Institute, Washington DC, Cambridge University Press.

Attarian, J. (2003). The maturing of a humane economist. A review of *Wilhelm Ropke: Swiss Localist, Global Economist,* by John Zmirak, Wilmington: ISI Books, 2001. http://www.findarticles.com/p/articles/mi_m0354/is_3_45 Viewed December 21 2005.

Aub, F. (1964). In Memoriam Professor Dr. Hugo Braun. *Med Monatsschr.* Mar. 18:142-3. Audretsch, D.B. and Stephan, P. (1996). Company-Scientist Locational Links: The Case of Biotechnology. *American Economic Review.* 86(3) 641-52.

Bali, R. (2005). *The 'varlik vergi' affair: A study of its legacy.* Isis Press, Istanbul, Turkey.

Bali, R. (2004). Turkey: towards post-nationalism? Conference in Basel 14-16 October SGMOIK/SSMOCI. (Schweizerische Gesellschaft Mittlerer Osten und Islamische. Kulturen) and Basel University, Department of Islamic Studies, Europainstitut and Department of History.

Bali, R. (1999). *Cumhuriyet Yillarinda Turkiye Yahudileri: Bir Turklestirme Seruveni (1923-1945)* Iletisim Yayinlari, Istanbul, Turkey.

Barlas, H. (1975). *Hazalah bi-Ymei Sho'ah* (Rescue during the Holocaust) Tel Aviv.

Bektas, Y. (2000). The Sultan's Messenger: Cultural Constructions of Ottoman. Telegraphy, 1847-1880, *Technology and Culture*. 41(4) 669-96

Bentwich, N. (1953). *The Rescue and Achievement of Refugee Scholars: The Story of Displaced Scholars and Scientists, 1933-1952.* Martinus Nijhoff, The Hague.

Bengisu, N. (1988). Keratoplastide endikasyon.TürkTıpCemiyetiMecmuası19 47 (XIII)3: 90, 94. Halit Pazarlı, Oftalmoloji. In: E Kadri Unat (Ed.), Tıp Dallarında İlerlemelerin Tarihi, İstanbul.

Beyerchen, A. D. (1977). *Scientists Under Hitler,* Yale University Press, New Haven.

Blum, J. M. (1959-1965). *From the Morgenthau Diaries* edited by John Morton Blum. Houghton Mifflin, Boston.

*Bogaziçine siginanlar* (2005). (Bosphorus exiles). New Orleans, LA : International Turkish Video and Film Center, http://www.lib.duke.edu/ias/NewBooks/Mideast/May_2002.

BOUN.EDU (2005). http://www.boun.edu.tr/government/council.html.

Branstetter, L. (1996). Are Knowledge Spillovers International or International in Scope: Microeconomic Evidence from U.S. and Japan. *NBER Working Paper, 5800.*

Braun, (1907). *Uber den Nachweis der Antigene mittels der Komlementfixationsmetode.* Berliner klin. Wschr., 1907, Nr.48.

Bronson, W. (1914) *History of Brown University*, Brown University Press, Providence, RI.

Bürgel, K./ Riener, K (2005). *Wissenschaftsemigration im Nationalsozialismus II,* , ISBN 3-9807334-5-9.

Burk, L. A. (1994). "Fritz Arndt: A Leading German Chemist in a Changing Turkish State," *ACS 208th National Meeting Book of Abstracts.* Part I: History of Chemistry Division, #8.

Burk, L. A. (2000). "Fritz Arndt's Turkish Textbooks: The Scientist and Historical Change," *ACS 220th National Meeting Book of Abstracts.* Part I: History of Chemistry Division, #3.

Burk, L. A. (2003). "Fritz Arndt and His Chemistry Books in the Turkish Language," *Bulettin. History of Chemistry.* 28 (1), 42-53.

Burk, L. A. (2005). "An Open Door: German Refugee Professors in Turkey" in Peter I. Rose, ed., *The Dispossesed-An Anatomy of Exile,* University of Massachusetts Press, 235-57.

Çetindamar, D. (2003). *The Growth of Venture Capital: A Cross Cultural Comparison.* Praeger, Westport, Conn., London.

Çetindamar, D. (2005). Policy Issues for Turkish entrepreneurs. *International Journal of Entrepreneurship and Innovation Management.* 5 (3/4) 187-205

Chase, K. (2003). *Firearms: A Global History.* Cambridge University Press.

Christiansen-Weniger, F. (1964). Die soziale Lage des türkischen Bauern von 1923-1963. In: *Sociologus,* N.F. 14.

Clifton, D. ed. (1999). *Millenium: 20th Century Day by Day*. DK Publishing, NY.

Cremer, J. and Pryztulla, H. (no date). *Exil Türkei 1933 - 1945*, Lipp Verlag,

Cura, S. (1996). Private interview. July 1996, Çeşme Turkey.

Curl, J. S. *A Dictionary of Architecture*. Oxford University Press, Oxford, UK.

Day, G. H. (1994). *The Development of Chemistry at Indiana University, 1829-1991*. Biographical Memoirs V.64 National Academies Press. National Academy of Sciences Washington, DC.

Denizer, C. (1997). *The effect of financial liberalization, new bank entry on market structure and competition in Turkey*. Development Research Group, World Bank. http://www.mngt.waikato.ac.nz/research/ejrot/cmsconference/2003/abstracts/the-coldwar/usdiken.pdf .

Denny-Brown, D. (1963). Obituary: Luftu Lahut Uzman. *Transactions of the American Neurological Association*, New York, 1963, 88. 302-4.

Dresselhaus, M.S. (2004). Obituaries: Arthur Robert von Hippel, *Physics Today* (September) pp76-7.

Drucker, D.C. (1984). William Prager 1903-1980. Memorial Tributes: *National Academy of Engineering*, Volume 2. 233-234

Dzwillo, M. (2004 pgs 29-33). *Mitteilungen aus dem Hamburgischen Zoologischen Musem und Institut, 101. Band. Kosswig-Gedenksymposium*, Istanbul 26 und 27 October 2004. Hamburg.

Eckstein A. (1937). Eckstein A. *Köyde Hayat*[5], *ULUS*, 8-9 Sonteşrin.1937, Ankara, Turkey.

Eckstein, A. (1938b). *Anatolian Impressions*, Private notes.

Eckstein, A. (1938c). *Köylerdeki sıhhi şartlar, köylünün sıhhi vaziyeti hakkında bilhassa çocuklar nazari itibara almak üzere yapılan tetkikata ait mütalaa.*Anadolu Kliniği, 1-36, Kader Basımevi, İstanbul, Turkey.

Eckstein, A. (1938d). *Anatolische Dorfkinder. La Turquie Kemaliste.*

Eckstein, A. (1939). *Türkiye'de nüfus siyasetine ve içtimai hijyene ait meseleler ile bunların çocuk hekiminin vazifesi noktai nazarından tetkiki*. Birinci Türk Çocuk Hekimliği Kongresi. Ankara *Ekspres Basımevi, İstanbul*, Turkey.

Eckstein, A. (1947a). *Noma tedavisinde yenilikler*. Ankara Üniversitesi Tıp Fakültesi Mecmuası, 1: 87-94.

Eckstein, A. (1947b). *Türkiyede Çocuk Hastalıkları ve çocukların korunması problemleri*. Ankara Universitesi Tıp Fakültesi Yayını. No: 3, Ankara, Turkey.

Eckstein, A. (1949). *Çocukluk* Çağında *Sıtma. Ankara Üniversitesi Tıp Fakültesi Mecmuası*, 3 (1-2): 1-19. (Çeviri: D. Güzin Çelikmen).

Eckstein, A., Tekiner H., and Özlem, N. (1941). *Çocuk Neşvünema, tegaddi ve metabolizmasının fiziyoloji ve patolojisi*. Ankara : Sıhhat ve İçtimai Muavenet Vekaleti Neşriyatı.

Eckstein-Schlossmann, E. (1975). *Memories of Turkey*. Unpublished pages. 46 Typewritten pages, made available through Professor Nejat Akar, Department of Child Health and Diseases, Medical Faculty, Ankara University, Ankara, Turkey.

Eicher, E.M. (1987). Ernst W. Caspari: genticist, teacher, and mentor. *Molecular Genetics of Development*. 24, pgs. xv-xxix.

Ekim, N.A. (2003), *Kader Birliği, 1933 Sonrası Türkiye'ye Göç Eden Alman Bilim Adamları, Philipp Schwartz, Belge Yayınları*, (United Destiny, German Scientists who emigrated to Turkey after 1933) Translated by Nagehan Alçı, Ekim, Belge

Yayınları, Istanbul, Turkey.

Erichsen, R (2000). *Haymatloz - Exile in Turkey from 1933 to 1945: An exhibition of the Aktives Museum at the Akademie der Kunste in Berlin.* (January to June 2000).

Erichsen, R. (2000). *EJOS*, Volume III published by the Department of Arabic, Persian and Turkic Languages and Cultures, Faculty of Arts, Utrecht University.

Eyer, H. (1964). In Memoriam Hugo Braun. *Zentralbl Bakteriol* (Orig.) May; 192: 409-19.

Fermi, L. (1968). *Illustrious Immigrants.* University of Chicago Press, Chicago.

Feuer, L. S. (1982). The Stages in the Social History of Jewish Professors in American Colleges and Universities. *American Jewish History*, 71, pp. 432-65.

Findikoglu, Z.F. (1946). *Economics Education in Turkey and the Founding of the Faculty of Economics*, (Tr. From Turkish). I.U. Iktisat Facultesi.

Fischer-Appelt, P. (2004). Keynote address given by the President of the University of Hamburg. Proceedings of the Kosswig Memorial Symposium published by the Hamburg Zoological Museum and Institute

Frankel, M. (1999). *The Times of My Life and My Life with the Times*, Random House, NY.

Frantz, D. and Collins, C. (2003). *Death on the Black Sea: The Untold Story of the Struma and World War II's Holocaust at Sea*, Harper Collins Canada.

Frey, F. W. (1964). "Education in Turkey" in ed Ward, R.E.and D.A. Rüstow, *Political Modernization in Japan and Turkey.* Princeton University Press, Princeton, NJ 205-35.

Friling, T. (2002). Between Friendly and Hostile Neutrality: Turkey and the Jews during World War II. In Ed. Rozen, M. *The Last Ottoman Century and Beyond: The Jews of Turkey and the Balkans 1808-1945.* The Goldstein-Goren Diaspora Research Center. 309-423.

Friling, T. (2001). Studies in Russian and East European Jewish History and Culture. *Shvut* 10 (26). Research Center, Ben-Gurion University, Israel.

Friling, T. (2005). *Arrows in the dark,* Universtiy of Wisconsin Press. Madison WI.

Gill, C. (2005). *The Music of Heinrich Mannfred,* CD with annotations. Private printing, Cleveland Heights, OH.

Gokalp Z. (1959). *Turkish Nationalism and Western Civilization: Selected Essays of Zia Gokalp,* ed Berkes N. New York.

Goodwin, G.M. and Smith, E. ed. (2004). *The Jews of Rhode Island,* Brandeis University Press, Waltham, Massachusetts.

Gregg, S. (2001). A Humanist for Our Time A review of *Wilhelm Röpke: Swiss Localist, Global Economist,* ISI Books, by John Zmirak. The Acton Institute. http://www.acton.org/publicat/randl/review.php?id=417 Viewed August 18 (2005).

Grinstein, L.S. and Campbell, P.J. (1987) *Women of Mathematics,* Greenwood Press, Westport Conn.

Grothusen, K. D. (1987). *Der Scurla-Bericht. Bericht des Oberregierungsrates Dr. Herbert Scurla von der Auslandsabteilung des Reichserziehungsministeriums in Berlin uber seine Dienstreise nach Ankara und Istanbul von 11-25. Mai 1939: Die Tatigkeit deutscher Hochschullehrer an turkischen wissenschaftlichen Hochschulen.* Frankfurt,Germany.

Grothusen, K. D. (1987). *Der Scurla Bericht (die Tätgkeit deutscher Hochschullehrer in der Türkei, 1933–1939, )* Dagyeli Verlag, Frankfurt, Germany.

Gupta, V. and Reisman, A. (2005). *Comparative Institutional Technology Transfer in India, Turkey, and Israel: Historical Policies and Development Outcomes.* Working paper. Downloadable from: http://ssrn.com/abstract=711124.

Gürgey, I. (2005). TÜRKÇE AŞIĞI BİR BİLİM ADAMI, Ord. Prof. Dr. Fritz Arndt (A Man of Science in Love with Turkish): Ord. Prof. Dr. Fritz Arndt) *Forthcoming in: Çağdaş Türk Dili Dergisi* (Journal of Contemporary Turkish Language).

Harpaz, I.(1984). Frederick Simon Bodenheimer (1897-1959): Idealist, Scholar, Scientist. *Annual Review of Entomology*, 29: 1-23.

Haymatloz List (2000). *LISTE der Emigrantinnen und Emigranten und NS-Verfolgten in der Türkei,* Schriftenreihe des Vereins Aktives Museum, Berlin.

Haymatloz (2000). *Schriftenreihe des Vereins Aktives Museum,* Berlin. volume 8

Hillebrecht, S. (2000). *Haymatloz: Exil in der Türkei* 1933-1945, Berlin 33-4.

Hirsch, E.E. (1982). *Aus des Kaisers Zeiten durch die Weimarer Republik in das Land Atatürks. Eine unzeitgemäße Autobiographie.* J. Schweitzer, Munich.

Hohmann, G. (1964). In Memoriam Professor Dr. Hugo Braun. *Munch Med Wochenschr.* Jan 17(106) 130-1.

Holzmeister, C. (1999). *Autobiography.* http://www.museumonline.at/1999/schools/classic/istanbul/holzmbioe.htm.

http://en.wikipedia.org/wiki/Margarete_Sch%FCtte-Lihotzkyhttp://en.wikipedia.org/wiki/Margarete_Sch%FCtte-Lihotzky.

http://www.archinform.net/arch/2554.htm.

http://www.emmet.de/por_taut.htm.

http://www.greatbuildings.com/architects/Bruno_Taut.html.

http://www.isop.ucla.edu/cnes/people/article.asp?parentid=12112.

http://www.mersina.com/lib/Turkish jews/history/life.htm.

http://www.museumonline.at/1999/schools/classic/istanbul/exilturkei_e.htm.

http://www.mimarlarodasi.org.tr/index.cfm?Sayfa=Oda&Sub=dagilim.

http://www2.let.uu.nl/Solis/anpt/ejos/pdf/Erichsen1.pdf.

Igersheimer, J. (1988). Keratoplastik hakkında. *Türk Tıp Cemiyeti Mecmuası* (V)3 68-9. Naci Bengisu, Keratoplastide endikasyon.*Türk Tıp Cemiyeti Mecmuası* 1947 (XIII) 3: 90-4. Halit Pazarlı, Oftalmoloji. In: E Kadri Unat (Ed.), Tıp Dallarında İlerlemelerin Tarihi, İstanbul 330-31.

Igersheimer, W. (2005). Blatant Injustice The Story of a Jewish Refugee from Nazi Germany Imprisoned in Britain and Canada during World War II. McGill-Queen's University Press, Motreal.

Ihsanoglu, E. (1992). ed. *Transfer of Modern Science & Technology to the Muslim World,* IRCICA, Istanbul, Turkey.

Ihsanoglu, E. (2004). The Madrasas of the Ottoman Empire, *Publication 4055, Foundation for Science, Technology and Civilisation,* Manchester, UK. http://www.fstc.co.uk.

IIE (1983). *Tribute to the Pioneers of the Science of Business in Turkey.* Pp38-9 cited in Üsdiken, B. and Cetin, D. (2001).

Inalcik, H. (1992). "Some remarks on the Ottoman Turkey's modernization process" in E. Ihsanoglu. *Transfer of Modern Science & Technology to the Muslim World.* IRCICA, Istanbul, Turkey.

*Jaeckel, R (2004). Andreas Tietze: Remembered by a Former Student.* Personal Communication.

Jaffe, A. B. and Trachtenberg, M. (1998). International Knowledge Flows: Evidence from Patent Citations. *NBER Working Paper, 6507.*

Kallman, K. (2004). Personal communication.

Kallman, K. (2005). Personal communication.

Kazancıgil, A., Ortaylı, I, and Tanyeli, U. (2000). Türkiyenin Yabancıları, *Cogito,* Yapı Kredi Yayınları, Üç aylık düşünce dergisi, Sayı:23, Yaz, s.119-132..

Kiziltan, A. (1949). *Çocuk Hastaneleri.* İstanbul Teknik Üniversitesi, Mimarlık Fakültesi, II bina Kürsüsü Tezi, İstanbul Matbaacılık, TAO, 1951.

Klingenstein, S. (1991). *Jews in the American Academy 1900-1940: The Dynamics of Intellectual Assimilation.* Yale University Press, New Haven.

Kramish, A (1986). The Griffin: The Greatest Untold Espionage Story of World War II Houghton Mifflin.

Krecker, L. (1964). *Deutschland und die Turkei im Zweiten Weltkrieg,* Wolfgang Goethe University, Frankfurt.Lopez, B. A. Virtual Vienna, http://www.virtualvienna.net/columns/billie/margaretesl.html.

Lane, B.M. (1968). *Architecture and Politics in Germany, 1918-1945*: Harvard University Press, Cambridge, MA.

Langhoff, W. (1935). Rubber Truncheons E.P.Dutton, New York.

Leff, L. (2005). *Buried by the Times: The Holocaust and America's Most Important Newspaper* Cambridge: Cambridge University Press.

Lehmann-Haupt, H. (1973). *Art under a Dictatorship.* Octagon Press, New York.

Lewis, B. (1982). *The Muslim Discovery of Europe.* Weidenfeld and Nicolson, London.

Liebermann-Meffert, D., Rossetti M. (1996). The 100th birthday. *Chirurg.* 67(10):1053-9.

Lipset, S. M. and Ladd, E. C., Jr. (1971). Jewish Academics in the United States; Their Achievements, Culture and Politics. *American Jewish Year Book* 72: 89-128.

Loevy, H. T. and Kowitz A. A. (1993). Alfred Kantorowicz, pediatric dentistry innovator. *Journal of Dentistry for Children,* 60(4-5). July-October.

Lopez, B. A. (2004). http://www.virtualvienna.net/columns/billie/margaretesl.html.

Mayer, JB. (1951). *Gedenkschrift. Annales Paediatrici* 177;15

Meier-Rust, K. (1993). *Alexander Rüstow: Geschichtsdeutung und liberales Engagement.* Klett-Cotta, Stuttgart.

Metin, H. M. and A. Umit Berkman (no date). "'Türkiye'de Kamu Yönetimi Arastirma ve Eg itiminde Kavramsal Kuram ve Yöntem Sorunlari," ('Problems of Conceptual Theory and Methodology in Turkish Public Administration Research and Training'). *Amme Idaresi Dergisi* (Ankara) 12, no. 2 (June 1979): 3-18.

Mitchell, M. (1993). William Prager, *Encyclopedia Brunoniana,* The Brown University Library, Providence, R.I.

Moll, H. (1995). Emigrierte Deutsche Padiater: Albert Eckstein, Werner Solmitz. *Monatsschr Kinderheilkd,* 143: 1204-7.

Moller, H. (1984). *Exodus der Kultur: Schriftsteller, Wissenschafler, un Kunsler in der Emigration nach 1933,* Beck, Munich, Germany

Morgenthau, H. III (1999). *Mostly Morgenthaus: A Family History,* Ticknor & Fields, New York

Müller, H (1998). German Librarians in Exile in Turkey, 1933-1945. *Libraries &*

*Culture*, 33, (3) 294-305.

Namal, A. (2003). "Prof.Dr.Max Sgalitzer (1884-1974). Ein österreichischer Leiter des Radiologischen Institutsder Universität Istanbul," *Zeitgeschichte*, 1, 37-49.

Namal, A. (2005). http://www.stiftung-sozialgeschichte.de/sozgeschonline/Emigration_Tuerkei.htm.

Namal, A. (2005). *Zwischen Emigration aus NS-Deutschland und Ankunft in Palästina bzw. Israel: Jüdische Wissenschaftler an der Universität Istanbul*, Paper presented at: MEDIZIN UND JUDENTUM, 8. Medizinhistorisches Kolloquium, Dresden, September 7-8.

Namal, A. and Reisman, A. *Joseph Igersheimer, Ophthalmalogist and Visionary: His Contributions in Exile and Beyond*. Working paper, downloadable from: http://ssrn.com/abstract=764426. Forthcoming in the *Journal of Medical Biography*.

Neumark, F. (1980). *Zuflucht am Bosphorus*, Knecht, Frankfurt.

Neumark, F. (1982). *Boğaziçine Sığınanlar*, Translated by Şefik Alp Bahadır, Ercivan Matbaası, Istanbul.

Nissen, R.(1969). *Helle Blätter, dunkle Blätter. Erinnerungen eines Chirurgen*. Stuttgart.

Noyan, A. (1959). *Ankara Tıp Fakültesi Kuruluş Tarihçesi*. Ankara Üniversitesi Tıp Fakültesi Yayınlarından Sayı: 76. Ankara, Ajans Türk Matbaası.

NTVMSNBC (2004). http://www.ntvmsnbc.com/news/284564.asp?cp1=1

O'Connor, J. J., Robertson, E. F. (2001). http://www-history.mcs.st-andrews.ac.uk/Mathematicians/Mises.html

O'Connor, J. J. and Robertson, E. F. (2005). http://www-history.mcs.st-andrews.ac.uk/Mathematicians/Geiringer.html

Ofer, D. (1977). "The Jewish Agency Delegation in Istanbul (1943)" in: Gutman, Y. and Zoroff, E. (editors), *Rescue Attempts during the Holocaust*, Gefen Publishing, Jerusalem.

Official private file (1935). *Official private file of Ord. Prof. Dr. Albert Eckstein*, Ankara Nümune Hastanesi, 1935-1945.

Official private file (1945) *Official private file of Ord. Prof. Dr.Albert Eckstein*, Ankara Medical Faculty, 1945-1949.

Oppenheim, A. N. (1996). *The Chosen People: The story of the '222 transport' from Belgen Belsen to Palestine*. Vallentine Mitchell, London, Portland, OR.

Otuken, A. (1957). Prof. Helmutt Ritter in Istanbul Kutuphanelleri hakinda bit raporu, *Turk Kutuphaneler Derugi Bulteni* VI(1-2).

Parente, S.L. and Prescott, E.C. (2000). *Barriers to Riches*, The MIT Press, Cambridge, MA.

Parker, B. R. and Reisman, A. (2004) "Socio-economic considerations" Invited chapter in *Encyclopedia of Social Measurement* (Kimberly Kempf-Leonard, Ed.), Vol. 3 pp 547-57. Elsevier: San Diego.

Petropoulos, J. (1996) *Art as Politics in the Third Reich*. University of North Carolina Press, Chapel Hill and London.

Powers, T. (1993). *Heisenberg's War: The Secret History of the German Bomb*, Knopf, Germany ISBN 0394514114.

Putnam, F. W. (1994). FELIX HAUROWITZ March 1, 1896-December 2, 1987, *Biographical Memoirs National Academy of Sciences*, V.64.

Reisman, A. (2005), Comparative Technology Transfer: A tale of development in two neighboring countries, Israel and Turkey. *Comparative Technology Transfer and Society*, 3(3) Pgs. 322-70.

Reisman, A., Capar, I., and Aktaş, E. (2004). *"Turkey's Development: The Role of Technology Transfer."* Working paper. Downloadable from: http://ssrn.com/abstract=607841.

Reisman, A. and Cytraus, A, (2004). Institutionalized Technology Transfer in USA: A Historic Review, Downloadable from: http://ssrn.com/abstract=585364.

Reisman, A. (2004c). Israel's Economic Development: The Role of Institutionalized Technology Transfer. Downloadable from: http://ssrn.com/abstract=579883.

Reisman, A. and Capar, I. (2004*), The Nazis' Gifts to Turkish Higher Education and Inadvertently to Us All: Modernization of Turkish universities (1933-1945) and its impact on present science and culture.* Working paper. Downloadable from: http://ssrn.com/abstract=624525.

Reisman, A. and Reisman, E. (1982). *Welcome Tomorrow*, North Coast Publishing, Cleveland, OH.

Richardson, Dean R.G.D. (1943). Advanced instruction and research in mechanics" *American Journal of Physics*. 11 67-73

Reisman, A. and Saha, P.K., (2005*) Francophone Non-European countries: Common Attributes and National Development* Working paper. Downloadable from: http://ssrn.com/abstract=732924.

Richter, R. (1954). "Ankara'dan Bir Mektup," *Cilt Doktoru*, Yıl 5, Sayı 11, Kasım, 518.

Ritenour, S. (2004). *Biography of Wilhelm Ropke.* http://www.vonmises.org/content/roepke.asp.

Röder, W. and Strauss, H.A. (1980). *Biographisches Handbuch der deutschsprachigen Emigration nach 1933 Band I* (Politik, Wirtschaft, Öffentliches Leben). München u.a. S.699.

Rubin, B. (1992). *Istanbul Intrigues*. Pharos Books, New York.

Rüstow, A. (1980). *Freedom and Domination: A Historical Critique of Civilization* a truncated version of *Taking Bearings on the Present*, Princeton University Press, Princeton, NJ.

Sadie, S. (1996). *The Grove Concise Dictionary of Music*, Macmillan Press Ltd., London.

Saha, P. K. (1983). *Languages People Die For, Gamut*, Fall, 46-56.

Said, E. W. (1983). *The World, the Text and the Critic* Harvard Unversity Press, Cambridge.

Samuelson, P. (1988). The Passing of the Guard in Economics. *Eastern Economics Journal*. 14(4) pp. 319-29.

Sarman, K. (2005). *Türk Promethe'ler, Cumhuriyet'in Öğrencileri Avrupa'da (1925-1945)*. Türkiye İş Bankası Kültür Yayınları.

Scherer, F. M. (2000). The Emigration of German-Speaking Economists after 1933. *Journal of Economic Literature*. XXXVIII Sept. pgs 614-26.

Schütte-Lihotzky, M. (1999). *Erinnerungen aus dem Widerstand* (Memories from the Time of the Resistance) http://www.museumonline.at/1999/schools/classic/istanbul/lihotzky_e.htm.

Schwartz, P. (1995). *Notgemeinschaft Zur Emigration deutscher Wissenschaftlernach 1933 in die Turkei.* Metropolis-Verlag, Marburg, Germany.

Schwartz, P. (2003). *Kader Birliği, 1933 Sonrasi Türkiye'ye Göç Eden Alman Bilim Adamlari* (United Destiny, German Scientists who emigrated to Turkey after 1933), translated by Nagehan Alçi, Belge Yayınları, Istanbul, Turkey. Original in German: Philipp Schwartz, *Notgemeinschaft zur Emigration Deutscher Wissenschafter nach 1933 in die Türkei,* Metropolis Verlag, 1955.

Seyhan, A. (2005). German Academic Exiles in Istanbul: Translation as the *Bildung* of the Other," forthcoming in *Nation, Language, and the Ethics of Translation,* edited by Sandra Bermann and Michael Wood, Princeton University Press.

Seyhan, A. (2005). *German Academic Exiles in Istanbul.* brynmawr.edu/german/aseyhan/syllabi/essay.html

Shaw, S.J. (1991). *The Jews of the Ottoman Empire and the Turkish Republic* Macmillan Press, London.

Shaw, S.J. (1993). *Turkey and the Holocaust,* Macmillan Press, London

Simon, G. (2004). *Chronologie Herbert Scurla.* http://homepages.uni-tuebingen.de/gerd.simon/scurla.pdf .

Sisman, A.(1992). "The foundation of Galatasaray Mekteb-i Sultanisi and the first years of instruction (1868-1871)" in E.Ihsanoglu. *Transfer of Modern Science & Technology to the Muslim World.* IRCICA, Istanbul, Turkey.

Sloane, A. E. (1969) Biographical Sketch of Josef Igersheimer. *Survey of Ophthalmology.* 14 174-5.

Slutsky, Y. (1972). *History of the Hagana, vol. III: From Resistance to War.* Zionist Library, Tel Aviv.

Staudenmaier, J. M. (1985), *Technology's Storytellers.* Society for the history of technology and MIT Press, Cambridge, Massachusetts.

Strauss, H. A. (1979). *Jewish Immigrants of the Nazi Period in the USA: Volume1, Archival Resources.* K.G. Saur, New York, Munchen, London, Paris.

Sullivan, E. (2005). "Always at a crossroads: Turkey pivots between East and West, past and future." *Cleveland Plain Dealer,* October, 24,

Sütlüpınar, N. and Ergun, F. (2003). Pharmacological studies of Prof. Dr. Paul Pulewka in Turkey in *Studies in Turkish Pharmacological History,* Papers presented at the VI. Meeting of the History of Turkish Pharmacology in Istanbul, 5-7 June, 2002, edited by Prof. Dr. Afife Mat, Istanbul University Publication No: 4390, Pharmacology Faculty Publication No: 80, ISBN 975-404-679-4, Istanbul.Turkey.

Synnot, M. G. (1979). *The Half-Open Door: Discrimination and Admissions at Harvard, Yale, and Princeton, 1900-1970.* Greenwood Press, Westport, London.

Szyliowicz, J. S. (1992) 'Functionalist perspectives on technology: The case of the printing press in the Ottoman Empire" in Ihsanoglu, E. (1992) Ed. *Transfer of Modern Science & Technology to the Muslim World,* IRCICA, Istanbul, Turkey.

TDCI (2003). (http://www.tdci.gov.tr/html/tarihce.html).

Tekand, S. (1998). Private communication, İzmir.

TURKISHTIME (2003). (http://www.turkishtime.org/sector_4/160_en.asp).

Üsdiken, B. (2003) "Plurality in Institutional Environments and Educational Content: The Undergraduate Business Degree in Turkey" in Rolv Petter Amdam, Ragnhild Kvalshaugen and Eirinn Larsen (eds.) *Inside the Business Schools: The Content of European Business Education,* Oslo: Abstrakt, Liber, Copenhagen Business School Press, Chap. 4, pp. 87-109.

Üsdiken, B. (2004), *The Cold War and Management Exporting managerial 'knowledge' to the outpost: Penetration of 'human relations' into Turkey, 1950-1960.* http://www.mngt.waikato.ac.nz/research/ejrot/cmsconference/2003/abstracts/thecoldwar/usdiken.pdf.

Üsdiken, B. and Cetin, D. (2001). From Betriebwirtschaft to Human Relations: Turkish Management Literature before and after the Second World War. *Business History,* 43, (2), 99-124.

Villwock, W. (2004). *Mitteilungen aus dem Hamburgischen Zoologischen Musem und Institut, 101. Band. Kosswig-Gedenksymposium,* Istanbul 26 und 27 October. Hamburg, Germany.

Widman, H. (1973) *Exile und Bildungshilfe: Die Deutschsprachige Akademische Emigration in die Türkei nach 1933.* Bern: Lang Verlag, Trans. Atatürk Reformu. Ankara: 1988.

Von Hippel, A. (2003). http://vonhippel.mrs.org/.

Von Pappen, F. (1953). *Memoirs,* E. P. Dutton, New York. Translated by Brian Connell.

Washington, S. W.(1936). Report by the Second Secretary of the American Embassy. (Istanbul), "Memorandum regarding German-Jewish Professors in the University of Istanbul", enclosed in *J. V. A. MacMurray to Secretaty of State no. 73, 14 July 1936. Department of State Decimal File 867.4016 JEWS 20* at the National Archives, Washington, D. C.

Wellek, R. (1991) *A History of Modern Criticism 1970-1950,* Volume 7, Yale University Press, New Haven CN.

Widmann, H. (1999). *Atatürk ve Üniversite Reformu,* Turkish translation by Prof. Dr. Aykut Kazancıgil and Doc.Dr. Serpil Bozkurt, Kabalcı Yayınevi, Istanbul, Turkey.

Widmann, H. (1981). *Exil und Bildungshilfe: Die deuschshprahige academische Emigration in die Turkei nach 1933,* (Bern/Frankfurt, 1973). Istanbul ISBN 3 261 00731 I. Translated into Turkish as *Atatürk Üniversite Reformu, (Ataturk's Uuniversity Reform).* A. Kazancigil, S. Bozkurt. İstanbul Üniversitesi Cerrahpaşa Tıp Fakültesi Atatürk'ün Yüzüncü Doğum Yılını Kutlama Yayınları, Özel Seri 3, İstanbul.(Original Printing).

Wiedemann H. R. (1994). Albert Eckstein. *European Journal of Pediatrics* 153;303.

Wyman, D. S. (1984). *The Abandonment of Jews: America and the Holocaust 1941-1945,* Pantheon Books, New York.

Yahil, L. (1990). *The Holocaust - the Fate of European Jewry 1932-1945* Oxford, University Press. Oxford, UK.

Zmirak, J. (2002) *Wilhelm Röpke: Architect of Liberty,* Ludwig von Mises Institute, http://www.mises.org/story/866. Viewed August 18 2005.

# Index

Printed in the United States
66919LVS00004B/2

9 780977 790883